MATH Trailblazers®

A BALANCED MATHEMATICS PROGRAM INTEGRATING SCIENCE AND LANGUAGE ARTS

Teacher Implementation Guide

THIRD EDITION

KENDALL/HUNT PUBLISHING COMPANY
4050 Westmark Drive   Dubuque, Iowa 52002

A TIMS® Curriculum
University of Illinois at Chicago

Teacher
Implementation
Guide

Math Trailblazers®

A Balanced Mathematics Program Integrating Science and Language Arts

A TIMS® Curriculum from the University of Illinois at Chicago

---

Dedication

This book is dedicated to the children and teachers who let us see the magic in their classrooms and to our families who wholeheartedly supported us while we searched for ways to make it happen.

—The TIMS Project—

UIC The University of Illinois at Chicago

The original edition was based on work supported by the National Science Foundation under grant No. MDR 9050226 and the University of Illinois at Chicago. Any opinions, findings, and conclusions or recommendations expressed in this publication are those of the authors and do not necessarily reflect the views of the granting agencies.

GRADE 3

Acknowledgments

Teaching Integrated Mathematics and Science (TIMS) Project Directors

Philip Wagreich, Principal Investigator

Joan L. Bieler

Howard Goldberg (emeritus)

Catherine Randall Kelso

Director

Third Edition   Joan L. Bieler

Curriculum Developers

Third Edition   Lindy M. Chambers-Boucher   Philip Wagreich
                         Janet Simpson Beissinger

Contributors

Third Edition	Eileen Wynn Ball	Sandy Niemiera
	Jenny Bay-Williams	Christina Nugent
	Ava Chatterjee-Belisle	Janet M. Parsons
	Elizabeth Colligan	Leona Peters
	Marty Gartzman	Catherine Reed
	Carol Inzerillo	

Editorial and Production Staff

Third Edition	Kathleen R. Anderson	Christina Clemons
	Lindy M. Chambers-Boucher	Anne Roby

TIMS Professional Developers

	Barbara Crum	Cheryl Kneubuhler
	Catherine Ditto	Lisa Mackey
	Pamela Guyton	Linda Miceli

TIMS Director of Media Services

Henrique Cirne-Lima

TIMS Research Staff

	Stacy Brown	Catherine Ditto
	Reality Canty	Kathleen Pitvorec
	Alison Castro	Catherine Randall Kelso

TIMS Administrative Staff

	Eve Ali Boles	Enrique Puente
	Kathleen R. Anderson	Alice VanSlyke
	Nida Khan	

Director

Second Edition	Catherine Randall Kelso	

Curriculum Developers

Second Edition	Lindy M. Chambers-Boucher	Jennifer Mundt Leimberer
	Elizabeth Colligan	Georganne E. Marsh
	Marty Gartzman	Leona Peters
	Carol Inzerillo	Philip Wagreich
	Catherine Randall Kelso	

Editorial and Production Staff

Second Edition	Kathleen R. Anderson	Georganne E. Marsh
	Ai-Ai C. Cojuangco	Cosmina Menghes
	Andrada Costoiu	Anne Roby
	Erika Larsen	

Principal Investigators

First Edition	Philip Wagreich	Howard Goldberg

Senior Curriculum Developers

First Edition	Janet Simpson Beissinger	Carol Inzerillo
	Joan L. Bieler	Andy Isaacs
	Astrida Cirulis	Catherine Randall Kelso
	Marty Gartzman	Leona Peters
	Howard Goldberg	Philip Wagreich

Curriculum Developers

First Edition	Janice C. Banasiak	Jenny Knight
	Lynne Beauprez	Sandy Niemiera
	Andy Carter	Janice Ozima
	Lindy M. Chambers-Boucher	Polly Tangora
	Kathryn Chval	Paul Trafton
	Diane Czerwinski	

Illustrator

First Edition	Kris Dresen	

Editorial and Production Staff

First Edition	Glenda L. Genio-Terrado	Sarah Nelson
	Mini Joseph	Birute Petrauskas
	Lynette Morgenthaler	Anne Roby

Research Consultant

First Edition	Andy Isaacs	

Mathematics Education Consultant

First Edition	Paul Trafton	

National Advisory Committee

First Edition	Carl Berger	Mary Lindquist
	Tom Berger	Eugene Maier
	Hugh Burkhart	Lourdes Monteagudo
	Donald Chambers	Elizabeth Phillips
	Naomi Fisher	Thomas Post
	Glenda Lappan	

Preface

This third edition of *Math Trailblazers* is the product of about 20 years of concerted effort by the TIMS (Teaching Integrated Mathematics and Science) Project. The TIMS Project has its roots in the pioneering work of Howard Goldberg, Professor of Physics at the University of Illinois at Chicago (UIC) and a Carnegie Foundation Professor of the Year in 1995. Over the past two decades, the TIMS Project has worked with children, teachers, and administrators to improve the quality of mathematics and science curricula and instruction in the Chicago area and nationwide. In 1990, the TIMS Project was awarded a grant by the National Science Foundation to develop a new elementary mathematics curriculum to meet the needs of children who will be entering the world of work in the 21st century. After years of research and development, including pilot- and field-testing in hundreds of classrooms, the first edition of the curriculum was published as *Math Trailblazers* in 1997 and 1998.

The primary goal of *Math Trailblazers* has been to create an educational experience that results in children who are flexible mathematical thinkers, who see the connections between the mathematics they learn in school and the thinking they do in everyday life, and who enjoy mathematics. The curriculum is based on the premise that children can succeed in mathematics and that if more is expected of them, more will be achieved. The curriculum incorporates the best of traditional mathematics, while widening the horizons of students' mathematical thinking.

Since the initial publication of *Math Trailblazers*, the TIMS Project has continued its research and development work, studying how to implement the curriculum in the most effective ways. We have learned considerably more about the importance of teacher professional development and whole-school change. The dedication and insight of our teacher collaborators constantly encouraged us. Feedback from hundreds of teachers who tested early versions of *Math Trailblazers* and thousands of others who used the program over the past ten years significantly reshaped our view of the curriculum and inspires our continuing efforts to improve it.

The first edition of *Math Trailblazers* was grounded in mathematics education research literature as well as our own research and experience as curriculum and staff developers. It was also inspired by the 1989 publication of the National Council of Teachers of Mathematics *Curriculum and Evaluation Standards for School Mathematics*. In this edition we drew from advances in research over the decade as well as NCTM's updated vision for school mathematics, as embodied in the NCTM's *Principles and Standards for School Mathematics*.

New editions of *Math Trailblazers* have made the curriculum easier for teachers to use. The math facts program was realigned in the 2nd edition and in this edition assessment and review components of the curriculum are more clearly highlighted. This edition also features an improved format for the *Unit Resource Guide* as well as new content in the *Teacher Implementation Guide* aimed at teachers and administrators. This content was suggested and shaped by our experience as professional developers working with schools and districts across the country that implement *Math Trailblazers*. It includes **Building the *Math Trailblazers* Classroom,** strategies and tips gathered from classroom teachers; **Teaching the *Math Trailblazers* Student: Meeting Individual Needs,** integral structures and features of *Math Trailblazers* that make it accessible to all children, including sections on working with English Language Learners, Special Education students and gifted and talented students; **Language in the *Math Trailblazers* Classroom,** strategies to help students learn to effectively communicate in the math classroom; and an **Administrator Handbook,** strategies to successfully guide implementation of the curriculum.

This third edition of *Math Trailblazers* is one more step in the continuing evolution of the curriculum. The Project is now housed within UIC's Learning Sciences Research Institute, providing a permanent home for interdisciplinary collaboration between mathematicians, scientists, mathematics educators, learning scientists, and teachers as we continually work at providing the best possible mathematics curriculum. We hope that teaching *Math Trailblazers* will be an enjoyable and productive experience for you and your students.

Philip Wagreich
Professor, Department of Mathematics, Statistics, and Computer Science
Director Emeritus, TIMS Project
University of Illinois at Chicago

Joan L. Bieler and Catherine R. Kelso
Co-Directors, TIMS Project
University of Illinois at Chicago

Teacher Implementation Guide
Table of Contents

Grade 3 *Math Trailblazers*
Table of Contents

This Table of Contents includes page numbers for the teacher material in the *Unit Resource Guide* plus corresponding page numbers in the student books (*Student Guide* and *Adventure Book*).

Introduction

The Introduction outlines the *Teacher Implementation Guide's* various sections and explains how best to use them.

A teacher and a student explore equivalent fractions.

Introduction

What Is the *Teacher Implementation Guide?*

The *Teacher Implementation Guide* is the reference manual for *Math Trailblazers*®. It, combined with the *Grade 3 Facts Resource Guide* and the *Unit Resource Guide,* provides a comprehensive set of resources to assist in implementing the curriculum. The *Unit Resource Guide* is the teacher's working guide, providing information and instructions related to the planning and teaching of units and individual lessons—it is intended to be used on a day-to-day basis. The *Grade 3 Facts Resource Guide* is a compilation of the components of the third grade math facts program, including background material. The *Teacher Implementation Guide* supplements the *Unit Resource Guide* and the *Grade 3 Facts Resource Guide* by addressing larger issues related to the curriculum. Information in the *Teacher Implementation Guide* can be roughly categorized into three groups: general background about *Math Trailblazers;* specific information about the program; and deep background about important math and science concepts. The *Teacher Implementation Guide* is a valuable resource for long-range planning for math instruction, curriculum, related implementation issues, and staff development.

Brief descriptions of sections found in the *Teacher Implementation Guide* follow:

- **Foundations of *Math Trailblazers***
  The underlying philosophy of the program is described.

- **Components and Features Guide**
  Math Trailblazers is a multicomponent program. Grade 3 includes three books for students (the *Student Guide, Discovery Assignment Book,* and *Adventure Book*) and three volumes for teachers (the *Teacher Implementation Guide*, the *Grade 3 Facts Resource Guide,* and the *Unit Resource Guide*). A *Teacher Resource CD* is also available for teachers. The Components and Features Guide is a road map for understanding the purposes of the various components and where to find key information. Important features taken from actual student and teacher pages are illustrated.

- **Grade 3 Overview**
  The Overview is an extended table of contents for the Grade 3 curriculum. Pacing suggestions in unit outlines help you plan your instruction schedule. Unit summaries include a narrative description of each unit's content and a list of important math concepts covered. This provides a snapshot view of the curriculum for your grade.

- **Connections with the NCTM *Principles and Standards***
  Math Trailblazers was developed to reflect the goals and approaches outlined in the *Principles and Standards for School Mathematics* of the National Council of Teachers of Mathematics (NCTM). This section includes detailed information, about how the program aligns with the *Principles and Standards.*

- **Scope and Sequence**

  The Scope and Sequence is organized to correspond with the NCTM *Principles and Standards,* providing additional detailed information about *Math Trailblazers'* alignment with the *Standards.* The scope and sequence chart is divided into two sections—one for the unit lessons and one for the Daily Practice and Problems and the Home Practice.

- **Summary of Approaches to Math Facts and Whole-Number Operations**

  The *Math Trailblazers* program for presenting the math facts and whole-number operations is summarized in this section. Background information about our approach and expectations for the grades are outlined.

- **Daily Practice and Problems and Home Practice Guide**

  An essential component of *Math Trailblazers* is a carefully designed sequence of short problems in Grades 1–5, called the Daily Practice and Problems (DPP). In third through fifth grades, a component called Home Practice (HP) is introduced. This component provides additional practice with skills and concepts.

- **Assessment**

  Math Trailblazers includes a comprehensive program of student assessment. The philosophy and components of this program are described in the Assessment section *Teacher Implementation Guide.* Assessment materials from the curriculum illustrate key ideas. Specific suggestions for implementing the assessment program are included.

- **TIMS Tutors: Background Information for Teachers**

  This section includes a series of documents called TIMS Tutors which provide extensive information on topics in pedagogy, mathematics, and science. The tutors serve as a source of deep background information. Some tutors, such as the tutor on math facts, supply specific information needed by teachers to plan particular portions of the *Math Trailblazers* program. Other tutors, such as the tutor on mass, focus on math and science content. Still others, such as the tutor on portfolios, address teaching strategies.

- **Building the *Math Trailblazers* Classroom**

  This section contains strategies and tips gathered from classroom teachers. Topics include the organization of materials and classrooms, as well as student groupings to best implement *Math Trailblazers.*

- **Teaching the *Math Trailblazers* Student: Meeting Individual Needs**

  From its earliest days, the authors developed the *Math Trailblazers* curriculum on a foundation of equity. This means that all children in all classrooms have the right to access rigorous mathematics. This section describes the integral structures and features of *Math Trailblazers* that make it accessible to all children. It also contains a section for working with English Language Learners and Special Education students, as well as suggestions for working with gifted and talented students.

- **Language in the *Math Trailblazers* Classroom**

  Language plays an important role in the *Math Trailblazers* Classroom. Language is used to convey mathematical problems. For example, vignettes of everyday situations are often used as contexts for establishing and exploring mathematical content. Both written and spoken language are essential to communicate mathematical ideas, strategies, and solutions.

This section describes strategies to help students learn to effectively communicate in the math classroom, including tips on how to help students learn mathematical vocabulary in context.

- **Manipulatives List**

  A listing of the manipulatives required for program implementation is included in this section.

- **Literature List**

  Math Trailblazers uses commercially available trade books in many lessons. A listing of these trade books is included in this section.

- **Games List**

  Games are often used in *Math Trailblazers* to engage students in practicing basic arithmetic skills and other math concepts. Once introduced, these games can be used throughout the year for ongoing practice. A complete listing and description of the games for your grade are provided.

- **Software List**

  Math Trailblazers does not require the use of computers. We do, instead, suggest some software programs that can supplement the curriculum. A listing of these programs and some suggested uses for them are provided.

- **Suggestions for Working with Parents**

  When adopting a math program that is new and different, such as *Math Trailblazers*, it is important to keep parents informed and educated about the program. Some hints for working with parents regarding *Math Trailblazers* are outlined in this section. A brochure about the curriculum and a parent letter describing the math facts program are also provided. The documents are in both English and Spanish.

- **Glossary**

  Most *Math Trailblazers* lessons include mathematical terms relevant to the lesson. The glossary defines many of these terms and can also be used to locate key vocabulary in the lessons. Most definitions cite the locations of the term in the curriculum.

- **Index**

  The index is a list of major mathematical topics and their locations in the curriculum. The *Student Guide, Discovery Assignment Book, Adventure Book, Unit Resource Guide* and *Teacher Implementation Guide* are all referenced in this index.

How to Use the *Teacher Implementation Guide*

Use of this guide will differ depending upon your purpose. Suggestions for using it for different purposes are described here.

If you are a teacher considering whether to use *Math Trailblazers*:
The *Teacher Implementation Guide* provides useful information for adoption committees or individual teachers who are considering *Math Trailblazers*. General information about the program that will be most helpful for this group includes the Foundations, alignment with the NCTM *Principles and Standards,* Scope and Sequence, and the Overview. The Components and Features Guide will help reviewers understand the purposes of the different

student and teacher books. Other specific information, such as the Math Facts and Whole-Number Operations section and the Assessment section, may also be useful for potential users of the curriculum.

If you are a teacher who is about to use *Math Trailblazers* for the first time:

There is too much information in the *Teacher Implementation Guide* and the *Unit Resource Guide* for any teacher to digest all at once. To make effective use of the *Teacher Implementation Guide,* it is best to select portions to examine at different points in the curriculum implementation. Prior to using *Math Trailblazers,* glance at the Foundations section to get a sense of our overall philosophy. However, you will probably want to spend more time reviewing the sections that provide specific information about using the curriculum. This information will help you get started and plan for the year.

Carefully review the Components and Features Guide to see the big picture of the program's components and features. This information will eventually become second nature as you gain experience with the curriculum, but it will be helpful at first to see what is included in the program. We suggest you review the Overview to get a feel for what is covered over the year and can plan ahead. It will be easier to make instructional decisions if you know what is planned for later lessons. The Assessment section and the Daily Practice and Problems Guide are essential and should be read prior to beginning the curriculum. Among the TIMS Tutors, we suggest that you first review *Math Facts*. It outlines our philosophy and plan for introducing the math facts. The manipulatives and literature lists are useful tools if you are ordering manipulatives. The section on working with parents will also be useful to read prior to using the curriculum. Use the rest of the *Teacher Implementation Guide* as the need arises.

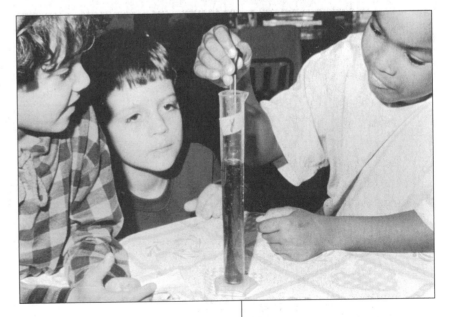

If you are a teacher who is already using *Math Trailblazers*:

During your first several years of using *Math Trailblazers,* you will likely refer to the *Teacher Implementation Guide* on an ongoing basis. You will find the TIMS Tutors particularly valuable in helping you better understand the content and approaches of key parts of the curriculum. There are numerous pointers in the *Unit Resource Guide* to individual tutors. The Scope and Sequence supplements the Overview in providing detailed information about when specific concepts are covered. Review the Games List and Software List periodically to help you in lesson planning. Any background information not found in the *Unit Resource Guide* is probably in the *Teacher Implementation Guide.*

If you are a school administrator in a school using *Math Trailblazers*:

The school administrator is the leader of the *Math Trailblazers* implementation. As the instructional leader, the school administrator works with the staff to establish, communicate, and support the goals of the mathematics program as the implementation unfolds. The *Administrator Handbook* section contains a description of the important components of a math implementation and explanations of strategies to successfully guide the implementation. It also contains blackline masters to use in presentations with staff and other audiences. Important sections from the *Teacher Implementation Guide* are also included.

If you are planning staff development sessions about *Math Trailblazers*:

Implementation of *Math Trailblazers* is most effective when accompanied by a comprehensive professional development program. An orientation to *Math Trailblazers* is made available to schools using *Math Trailblazers* through Kendall/Hunt Publishing. We recommend that schools continue their professional development throughout the lifetime of the implementation. The TIMS Project has developed presenters' guides for a variety of professional development sessions. These guides, called Teacher Enhancement Resource Modules (TERMs), contain a guide for presenters with explanatory text, discussion questions and answers, and blackline masters. Most TERMs include video that demonstrates the *Math Trailblazers* curriculum in action. Used together the 18 TERMs provide approximately 70 hours of staff development in both the content and pedagogy of *Math Trailblazers.* The TERMs are available through Kendall/Hunt Publishing.

For specific suggestions about planning local staff development related to *Math Trailblazers,* contact the Teaching Integrated Mathematics and Science (TIMS) Project at 800-454-TIMS or Kendall/Hunt Publishing Company at 800-542-6657. Information is also available on the *Math Trailblazers* Implementation Center website at *www.math.uic.edu/IMSE* and at *www.mathtrailblazers.com.*

Foundations of Math Trailblazers

The Foundations of *Math Trailblazers* describes the principles behind *Math Trailblazers* and discusses the curriculum's key features.

Students work together to solve problems.

Foundations of *Math Trailblazers*

Math Trailblazers is an elementary mathematics curriculum for schools that want their math programs to reflect the goals and ideas of the National Council of Teachers of Mathematics (NCTM) *Principles and Standards for School Mathematics.* With funding from the National Science Foundation (NSF) the TIMS (Teaching Integrated Mathematics and Science) Project at the University of Illinois at Chicago created a comprehensive program that embodies the *Principles and Standards.*

Math Trailblazers is based on the ideas that mathematics is best learned in real-world contexts that make sense to children; that all students deserve a richer and more challenging curriculum; and that a balanced and practical approach to learning mathematics is what students need and teachers want.

Features of *Math Trailblazers*
Alignment with Reform Recommendations

The *Principles and Standards,* which was released in 2000, is an update of three groundbreaking volumes published a decade earlier that collectively became known as the "NCTM *Standards.*" This publication was extended in 2006 with the release of the *Curriculum Focal Points for Prekindergarten through Grade 8 Mathematics: A Quest for Coherence,* which was "offered as a starting point in a dialogue on what is important at particular levels of instruction as an initial step toward a more coherent, focused curriculum in this country." (NCTM 2006, p. vii) However, in describing the relationship between the documents, the NCTM states that the *Principles and Standards* "remains the definitive reference on the development of mathematical content and processes across the grades." (NCTM 2006, p. 1)

The NCTM documents outline a vision for school mathematics that includes: a mathematically challenging curriculum that is coherent and covers a broad range of mathematical content; a strong focus on engaging students in mathematical problem solving; conceptually oriented instruction that stresses thinking, reasoning, and applying; appropriate uses of calculators and computers; and a strong commitment to promoting success in mathematics among all students—not merely those who traditionally have done well. Most states incorporated this vision for mathematics teaching and learning into their mathematics standards.

The first edition of *Math Trailblazers* took more than six years of work that included extensive pilot and field testing of the materials. After publication of the first edition, continued NSF support enabled the TIMS Project to develop implementation models and professional development materials that assisted teachers and schools as they adopted the program.

In developing the second edition of *Math Trailblazers,* we looked carefully at the NCTM *Principles and Standards* and reorganized portions of the *Math Trailblazers,* such as the math facts program, to keep *Math Trailblazers* closely aligned with the new NCTM recommendations. TIMS researchers also studied how the program impacted student achievement. The second edition of *Math Trailblazers* therefore represented more than twelve years of NSF-supported work related to the curriculum.

The third edition provides materials in an easier-to-use format, as well as new content for teachers and administrators. This content was suggested and shaped by other lessons learned from our years of professional development work with schools and districts across the country that implement *Math Trailblazers.*

The importance of a coherent, well-developed curriculum is clear in the *Principles and Standards,* which states:

A curriculum is more than a collection of activities: it must be coherent, focused on important mathematics, and well articulated across the grades. *A school mathematics curriculum is a strong determinant of what students have an opportunity to learn and what they do learn. In a coherent curriculum, mathematical ideas are linked to and build on one another so that students' understanding and knowledge deepens and their ability to apply mathematics expands. An effective mathematics curriculum focuses on important mathematics—mathematics that will prepare students for continued study and for solving problems in a variety of school, home, and work settings. A well-articulated curriculum challenges students to learn increasingly more sophisticated mathematical ideas as they continue their studies.* (NCTM, 2000, p. 14)

Math Trailblazers was developed with that goal in mind. It is a *Standards-*based curriculum in the truest sense—developed explicitly to reflect national standards for K–5 mathematics, and now revised to maintain close alignment with those standards as they have evolved.

More specific connections between *Math Trailblazers* and the NCTM *Principles and Standards* are discussed in Scope and Sequence & the NCTM *Principles and Standards* (Section 5).

High Expectations and Equity

The first principle in the *Principles and Standards* is the Equity Principle. It challenges a myth prevalent in the United States that only a few students are capable of rigorous mathematics. The Equity Principle states:

> *Excellence in mathematics education requires equity—high expectations and strong support for all students.* (NCTM, 2000, p. 12)

Accordingly, we introduce challenging content in every grade: computation, measurement, data collection, statistics, geometry, ratio, probability, graphing, algebraic concepts, estimation, mental arithmetic, and patterns and relationships.

Contexts for this demanding content begin with students' lives. Lessons are grounded in everyday situations, so abstractions build on experience. By presenting mathematics in rich contexts, the curriculum helps students make connections among real situations, words, pictures, data, graphs, and symbols. The curriculum also validates students' current understandings while new understandings develop. Students can solve problems in ways they understand while being encouraged to connect those ways to more abstract and powerful methods. Within the same lesson, some students may work directly with the manipulatives to solve the problems while other students may solve the same problems using graphs or symbols. The use of varied contexts and diverse representations of concepts allows children of varying abilities to access the mathematics.

Problem Solving

A fundamental principle of *Math Trailblazers* is that mathematics is best learned through actively solving real problems. Questions a student can answer immediately may be worthwhile exercises, but *problems,* by definition, are difficult, but not impossible.

The importance of problem solving is echoed in the NCTM *Principles and Standards,* which states:

> *Problem solving is the cornerstone of school mathematics. . . . The goal of school mathematics should be for all students to become increasingly able and willing to engage with and solve problems.*

> *Problem solving is also important because it can serve as a vehicle for learning new mathematical ideas and skills (Schroeder and Lester). A problem-centered approach to teaching mathematics uses interesting and well-selected problems to launch mathematical lessons and engage students. In this way, new ideas, techniques, and mathematical relationships emerge and become the focus of discussion.* (NCTM, 2000, p. 182)

As recommended by NCTM, problem solving in *Math Trailblazers* is not a distinct topic but permeates the entire program, providing a context for learning concepts and skills. Throughout the curriculum, students apply the mathematics they know and construct new mathematics as needed. Students' skills, procedures, and concepts emerge and develop as they solve complex problems.

Connections to Science and Language Arts

Real-world problems are naturally interdisciplinary, so any problem-solving curriculum should integrate topics that are traditionally separated. Accordingly, we have integrated mathematics with many disciplines, especially science and language arts.

Connections to Science
Math Trailblazers is a full mathematics program that incorporates many important scientific ideas. Traditionally, school science has focused on the results of science. Students learn about plate tectonics, the atomic theory of matter, the solar system, the environment, and so on. Knowing basic facts of science is seen as part of being educated, today more than ever. However, the facts of science,

important and interesting as they are, do not alone constitute a comprehensive and balanced science curriculum.

Science has two aspects: results and method. The results of scientific inquiry have enriched human life the world over. More marvelous than the results of science, however, is the method that established those results. Without the method, the results would never have been achieved. *Math Trailblazers* aims to teach students the method of science through scientific investigation of everyday phenomena. During these investigations, students learn both mathematics and science.

The method scientists use is powerful, flexible, and quantitative. The TIMS Project has organized this method in a way that is simple enough for elementary school children to use. Students use the TIMS Laboratory Method in a rich variety of mathematical investigations. In these investigations, students develop and apply important mathematical skills and concepts in meaningful situations. Their understanding of fundamental scientific concepts is also enhanced through the use of quantitative tools.

Investigations begin with discussions of experimental situations, variables, and procedures. Then students draw pictures that indicate the experimental procedures and identify key variables. Next students gather and organize data in data tables. Then they graph their data. By analyzing their data or studying their graphs, students are able to see patterns. These patterns show any relationships between the variables. Students can use the relationships to make predictions about future data. The last phase of the experiment is an in-depth analysis of the experimental results, structured as a series of exploratory questions. Some questions ask students to make predictions and then to verify them. Other questions probe students' understanding of underlying concepts and explore the role of controlled variables. As students advance through the curriculum, the questions progress from simple to complex, building eventually to problems that require proportional reasoning, multiple-step logic, and algebra.

The TIMS Laboratory Method initiates children into the authentic practice of science. Identifying variables, drawing pictures, measuring, organizing data in tables, graphing data, and looking for and using patterns are a major part of many scientists' work. This is a major goal of science: to discover and use relationships between variables—usually expressed in some mathematical form—in order to understand and make predictions about the world.

The science content in *Math Trailblazers* focuses on a small set of simple variables that are fundamental to both math and science: length, area, volume, mass, and time. Understanding these basic variables is an essential step to achieving scientific understanding of more complex concepts. Measurement is presented in meaningful, experimental situations.

Emphasizing the scientific method and fundamental science concepts helps students develop an understanding of how scientists and mathematicians think. These habits of mind will be important in all aspects of life in the 21st century. See the TIMS Tutor: *The TIMS Laboratory Method* for more discussion of these ideas.

Connections to Language Arts

Reading, writing, and talking belong in mathematics class, not only because real mathematicians and scientists read, write, and talk mathematics and science constantly, but also because these activities help students learn. The NCTM *Principles and Standards* emphasizes the importance of communication and discourse for students to achieve at higher levels.

In school mathematics, results should be accepted not merely because

someone in authority says so, but rather because persuasive arguments can be made for them. A result and a reason are often easier to remember than the result alone. By discussing the mathematics they are doing, students increase their understanding. They also extend their abilities to discuss mathematics and so to participate in a community of mathematicians. Talking or writing about mathematics is part of every lesson. Journal and discussion prompts are standard features in the teacher's guide for each lesson.

Reading is also built into this curriculum. Many lessons, especially in the primary grades, use trade books to launch or extend mathematical investigations. The curriculum also includes many original stories, called *Adventure Books,* that show applications of concepts or sketch episodes from the history of mathematics and science. Literature is used to portray mathematics as a human endeavor, so that students come to think of mathematicians and scientists as people like themselves. Mathematics embedded in a narrative structure is also easier to understand, remember, and discuss. And, of course, everyone loves a good story. In addition, students regularly write about their mathematical investigations, even in the early grades.

Collaborative Work

Scientists, mathematicians, and most others who solve complex problems in business and industry have always worked in groups. The reasons for this are simple: Most interesting problems are too difficult for one person. Explaining one's work to another person can help clarify one's thinking. Another person's perspective can suggest a new approach to a problem. Ideas that have been tested through public scrutiny are more trustworthy than private notions.

All these are reasons for collaborating in schools as well. But there are other reasons, too. Students can learn both by receiving and by giving explanations. The communication that goes with group work provides practice in verbal and symbolic communication skills. In group discussion, a basic assumption is that mathematics and science ought to make sense—something, unfortunately, that many students stop believing after only a few years of school. Social skills, especially cooperation and tolerance, increase, and the classroom community becomes more oriented towards learning and academic achievement.

Assessment

There are three major purposes for assessment. First, assessment helps teachers learn about students' thinking and knowledge: information that can then be used to guide instruction. Secondly, it communicates the goals of instruction to students and parents. Finally, it informs students and parents about progress toward these goals and suggests directions for further efforts.

Assessment in *Math Trailblazers* reflects the breadth and balance of the curriculum. Numerous opportunities for both formal and informal assessment of student learning are integrated into the program. Many assessment activities are incorporated into the daily lessons; others are included in formal assessment units. Assessment activities include a mix of short, medium-length, and extended activities. Some are hands-on investigations, others are paper-and-pencil tasks. In all cases, assessment activities further students' learning.

For a detailed discussion of assessment in *Math Trailblazers,* refer to Assessment (Section 8) and the TIMS Tutor: *Portfolios.*

More Time Studying Mathematics

One cannot reasonably expect to cover all the concepts in a traditional program, add many new topics, and utilize an approach that emphasizes problem solving, communication, reasoning, and connections in the same amount of time used to teach a traditional math curriculum. In developing *Math Trailblazers,* we have attempted to achieve some efficiencies, such as building review into new concepts and using effective strategies to teach math facts and procedures. However, there is no magic in *Math Trailblazers.* Implementing a comprehensive, reform mathematics curriculum will require a significant amount of time. **We assume that in Grades 1–5 one hour**

every day will be devoted to teaching mathematics. In Kindergarten, the class make-up and the activity will determine the length of the class.

In some schools, finding an hour per day for math instruction may require a restructuring of the daily school schedule. Please note, however, that because *Math Trailblazers* includes extensive connections with science and language arts, *some* time spent with *Math Trailblazers* can be incorporated within science or language arts time. Thus, it may be possible to allot the one hour per day of mathematics instruction by simply scheduling math and science instruction back to back or including literature connections and journal writing in language arts.

Hard work on the part of students and more time engaged in mathematical problem solving are important ingredients to success in mathematics— no matter what program you are using. Because students using *Math Trailblazers* are actively involved in applying mathematics in meaningful contexts, our experience is that students will be highly motivated to spend extra time studying mathematics.

Staff Development and Broad School Support: Essential Ingredients

Developing the curriculum and working with schools over the last 20 years has taught us that implementing a *Standards*-based mathematics program will progress more smoothly if it is accompanied by a solid support system for teachers. Ideally, this includes a professional development program that includes workshops on content and pedagogy, leadership development, in-school support, and the means to address a variety of concerns as they arise.

Overall implementation of *Math Trailblazers* will be much easier in a school that organizes support for the new program. Necessary tools such as manipulatives, overhead projectors, and transparency masters need to be provided in adequate quantities. Institutional considerations, such as classroom schedules that allot necessary time for instruction and provide time for teachers to meet and plan together, need to be implemented. In-classroom support from resource teachers is extremely helpful. Storage and check-out systems for shared manipulatives need to be in place. Ways to engender parental support for the program, including possible ways to involve some parents in providing classroom assistance to interested teachers during math time, should be developed.

Administrators need to maintain a long-term perspective recognizing that program implementation will take some time—and they need to communicate this clearly to teachers. In short, schools need to examine their current situations and make necessary modifications to develop a school environment that supports the kind of teaching and learning that characterizes *Math Trailblazers*.

A Balanced Approach

A reform mathematics program should take a balanced and moderate approach. *Math Trailblazers* is balanced in many different ways with whole-class instruction, small-group activities, and individual work. New mathematical content is included, but traditional topics are not neglected.

Children construct their own knowledge in rich problem-solving situations, but they are not expected to reinvent 5000 years of mathematics. Concepts, procedures, and facts are important, but are introduced thoughtfully to engender the positive attitudes, beliefs, and self-image that are also important in the long run. Hands-on activities of varied length and depth, as well as paper-and-pencil tasks, all have their place. The program's rich variety of assessment activities reflects this broad balance.

Either-or rhetoric has too often short-circuited real progress in education: problem solving vs. back-to-basics, conceptual understanding vs. procedural skill, paper-and-pencil computation vs. calculators. *Math Trailblazers* is based on the view that these are false dichotomies. Students must solve problems, but of course they need basic skills to do so. Both concepts and procedures are important, and neglecting one will undermine the other. There is a place in the curriculum both for paper-and-pencil algorithms and for calculators, and for mental arithmetic and estimation. The careful balance in *Math Trailblazers* allows teachers and schools to move forward with a reform mathematics curriculum while maintaining the strengths of their current teaching practices.

Research Foundations of *Math Trailblazers*

The first edition of *Math Trailblazers* was completed in 1997. The roots of the curriculum, however, date back to the late 1970s and the work of Howard Goldberg, a particle physicist at the University of Illinois at Chicago (UIC). Building on the work of Robert Karplus and others, Goldberg developed a framework for adapting the scientific method for elementary school children and applied that framework within a series of elementary laboratory investigations (Goldberg & Boulanger, 1981). Goldberg was joined in 1985 by UIC mathematician Philip Wagreich and, together with others, formed the Teaching Integrated Mathematics and Science Project (TIMS).

Thus, the motivation behind TIMS came from two sources, one with roots in science and one with roots in mathematics. The scientific impetus stemmed from the desire to teach science to children in a manner that reflects the practice of scientists. Modern science is fundamentally quantitative; therefore, quantitative investigations should have an important role in children's science education. The mathematical impetus was to find a way to make mathematics meaningful to children. Engaging children in quantitative investigations of common phenomena harnesses their curiosity in a way that builds on their understanding of the natural world, which, in turn, helps promote study of rigorous mathematics (Isaacs, Wagreich, & Gartzman, 1997).

Initially, TIMS focused primarily on the development and implementation of a series of quantitative, hands-on activities, the *TIMS Laboratory Investigations* (Goldberg, 1997). The laboratory investigations continue the tradition of Dewey (1910) and others in focusing on the method of science and on exploring a relatively small set of fundamental scientific concepts in depth. Several studies provided clear evidence that the *TIMS Laboratory Investigations* are effective in promoting students' development of mathematics and science concepts (Goldberg & Wagreich, 1990; Goldberg, 1993).

Based largely on the success with the supplemental *TIMS Laboratory Investigations,* the National Science Foundation (NSF) supported the TIMS Project to develop a comprehensive, elementary mathematics curriculum that would align with the National Council of Teachers of Mathematics (NCTM) *Curriculum and Evaluation Standards for School Mathematics* (NCTM, 1989). The first edition of *Math Trailblazers* is the result of this work. As part of the revision process for the second edition, the authors made changes so that the new edition aligns with the current NCTM recommendations as outlined in the *Principles and Standards for School Mathematics* (NCTM, 2000).

The third edition provides materials in an easier-to-use format, as well as new content for teachers and administrators. This content embodies the lessons learned from our TIMS Project's 20 years of professional development work with schools and districts that implement *Math Trailblazers.*

In developing each edition of *Math Trailblazers,* the authors drew upon research findings from a wide variety of sources, as well as from the broad experiences of the authoring group. In this section we highlight a portion of the research that helped guide the curriculum's development and other current research that validates the approaches used.

A Problem-Solving Curriculum

A distinguishing element of any *Standards*-based mathematics curriculum is that problem solving is used as a context for students to learn new concepts and skills. Throughout *Math Trailblazers,* students apply the mathematics they know and construct new mathematics as needed. Students' skills, procedures, and concepts emerge and develop as they solve problems. Students also practice skills and procedures as they apply them in diverse and increasingly challenging contexts. Problem-solving contexts can emerge from real-life investigations or from more mathematical situations. The problems serve as the motivation for purposeful use of mathematics.

Using problem solving as a cornerstone of the mathematics curriculum has been promoted by educators dating back to Dewey and has received considerable support from current mathematics education researchers. (See Hiebert et al., 1996; Schoenfeld, 1985 and 1994; National Research Council, 2001; and NCTM 1989 and 2000 for a discussion of problem solving in the curriculum.)

A curriculum that emphasizes solving problems can use many different contexts. In developing *Math Trailblazers,* the authors first identified the key mathematical concepts and skills to be developed and then selected problem-solving contexts to support student learning in these areas. Our earlier work and that of others (e.g., Cognition and Technology Group at Vanderbilt, 1997) had confirmed the value of using quantitative laboratory investigations for this purpose. Drawing from this work, eight to ten laboratory investigations were adapted and integrated into *Math Trailblazers* in each grade, beginning with first grade. These investigations are supplemented by many other contexts for problem solving.

Challenging Mathematics in All Grades for All Students

An assumption in the development of *Math Trailblazers* was that students can learn more challenging mathematics than is covered in traditional mathematics curricula. This has been underscored in international comparison studies (Heibert, 1999; McKnight et al., 1987; Stigler & Perry, 1988; Schmidt, McKnight, & Raizen, 1996; Stigler & Hiebert, 1997; Stevenson & Stigler, 1992) and in analyses of U.S. mathematics instruction (Flanders, 1987; Lindquist, 1989). Maintaining high expectations and providing access to rigorous mathematics for all students has proven effective regardless of the socioeconomic status and ethnicity of the students (National Research Council, 2001; Newmann, Bryk, & Nagaoka, 2001; Smith, Lee, & Newmann, 2001). Therefore, mathematical expectations in *Math Trailblazers* are high and grow steadily. Review of concepts and skills is carefully built into new and increasingly challenging problems as the program builds upon itself both within and across grades.

Balancing Concept and Skill Development

The importance of developing a strong conceptual foundation is emphasized in research that guided the development of all content strands in *Math Trailblazers*. Many educators have long recognized the importance of balancing conceptual and skill development. New conceptual understandings are built upon existing skills and concepts; these new understandings in turn support the further development of skills and concepts.

A wide body of research affirms that instructional programs that emphasize conceptual development can facilitate significant mathematics learning without sacrificing skill proficiency (see Hiebert, 1999). Research affirms that well-designed and implemented instructional programs can facilitate both conceptual understanding and procedural skill.

This research had a profound effect on development of *Math Trailblazers*. For example, such research helped define the curriculum's program for developing number sense and estimation skills (Sowder, 1992) and for learning math facts and whole-number operations (Carpenter, Carey, & Kouba, 1990; Carpenter, et al., 1999; Fuson, 1987, 1992; Fuson & Briars, 1990; Fuson et al., 1997; Isaacs & Carroll, 1999; Lampert, 1986a, 1986b; Thornton, 1978, 1990a, 1990b). Work with fractions and decimals was informed by research that stressed the need to develop conceptual understandings of fractions and decimals prior to introducing procedures with the four arithmetic operations (see Behr & Post, 1992; Ball, 1993; Cramer, Post, & del Mas, 2002; Lesh, Post, & Behr, 1987; Mack, 1990; Hoffer & Hoffer, 1992). Similar research findings on student understanding of geometric concepts shaped the development of lessons in geometry (see Burger & Shaughnessy, 1986; Crowley, 1987; Fuys, Geddes, & Tishler, 1988).

In direct response to research such as that cited here, every content strand within *Math Trailblazers* interweaves the promotion of conceptual understanding with distributed practice of skills and procedures.

Field Testing and Research on the Curriculum in Classrooms

NSF funding allowed sequential development of the program to be coupled with extensive field testing in schools. As a result, curriculum development became an iterative process involving considerable interaction between the developers and field-test teachers. Comments and suggestions from teachers were incorporated into revisions that were often retested in classrooms one or more times before final revisions were made. Field-test teachers met regularly with the program's authors, and classrooms were often visited as part of the development process. Teachers using the early versions in their classrooms addressed content, language, format, practical considerations, and other issues related to each lesson.

In addition to assessing feedback from field-test teachers, independent researchers and TIMS Project staff conducted preliminary studies that helped affirm the efficacy of the content placement and approaches in the early versions of the materials (Burghardt, 1994; Perry, Whiteaker, & Waddoups, 1996; Whiteaker, Waddoups, & Perry, 1994). These preliminary studies provided an additional means for the authors to monitor the effectiveness of the developing program.

Early studies of student achievement in *Math Trailblazers* classrooms in both urban and suburban schools have shown that students using the curriculum performed as well, and often better, on mandated standardized tests than students in those schools prior to implementation of *Math Trailblazers*. (Carter, et al., 2003; Putnam, 2003) "[The results] indicate that the balanced problem-solving approach found in *Math Trailblazers* has been successful in improving student learning and achievement in mathematics." (Carter, et al., 2003)

In developing the second edition, we benefited from the suggestions and comments of teachers throughout the country who were using the published *Math Trailblazers* materials. Input from teachers, for example, resulted in the major changes to the second edition's teacher guides. Teachers' feedback also directed us to modify or eliminate some lessons.

In third edition development, changes were made to the format and content for teachers and administrators based on surveys, focus groups, and feedback from teachers and administrators. The format of the third edition materials is easier for teachers to use. New content for teachers and administrators assists with implementation issues in the classroom, school, and district. This content embodies 20 years of professional development work by the TIMS Project with schools and districts that implement *Math Trailblazers*.

Extensive field testing during the program's development, current research and evaluation in schools, and our ongoing conversations with *Math Trailblazers* teachers have helped us develop a challenging, yet grade-level-appropriate program that reflects the needs and realities of teachers and students.

References

The following references are cited in the above document. Additional references to research literature are included in many *Unit Resource Guides* following the Background and in many sections of the *Teacher Implementation Guide* including the Assessment section and the TIMS Tutors.

Ball, D. "Halves, Pieces, and Twoths: Constructing and Using Representational Contexts in Teaching Fractions." In T. P. Carpenter, E. Fennema, and T.A. Romberg (Eds.), *Rational Numbers: An Integration of Research,* pp. 157–195. Lawrence Erlbaum Associates, Hillsdale, NJ, 1993.

Behr, M.J., and T.R. Post. "Teaching Rational Number and Decimal Concepts." In *Teaching Mathematics in Grades K–8: Research Based Methods.* Allyn and Bacon, Boston, 1992.

Burger, W., and J.M. Shaughnessy. "Characterizing the Van Hiele Levels of Development in Geometry." *Journal for Research in Mathematics Education,* 17, pp. 31–48, National Council of Teachers of Mathematics, Reston, VA, 1986.

Burghardt, B. Results of Some Summative Evaluation Studies: 1993–1994 Evaluation Report. (An unpublished report to the National Science Foundation.) 1994.

Carpenter, T.P., D. Carey, and V. Kouba. "A Problem-Solving Approach to the Operations." J.N. Payne, ed., *Mathematics for the Young Child.* National Council of Teachers of Mathematics, Reston, VA, 1990.

Carpenter, T.P., E. Fennema, M.L. Franke, L. Levi, and S.E. Empson. *Children's Mathematics: Cognitively Guided Instruction.* Heinemann, Westport, CT, 1999.

Carter, M.A., J.S. Beissinger, A. Cirulis, M. Gartzman, C.R. Kelso, and P. Wagreich. "Student Learning and Achievement with *Math Trailblazers.*" S.L. Senk and D.R. Thompson, eds., *Standards-Based School Mathematics Curricula: What Does the Research Say about Student Outcomes?* Lawrence Erlbaum Associates, Inc., Hillsdale, NJ, 2003.

Cognition and Technology Group at Vanderbilt. *The Jasper Project: Lessons in Curriculum, Instruction, Assessment, and Professional Development.* Erlbaum, Mahwah, NJ, 1997.

Cramer, K., T. Post, and R. del Mas. "Initial Fraction Learning by Fourth- and Fifth-Grade Students: A Comparison of the Effects of Using Commercial Curricula with the Effects of Using the Rational Number Project Curriculum." *Journal for Research in Mathematics Education,* 33(2), pp. 111–144.

Crowley, M.L. "The Van Hiele Model of Development of Geometric Thought." *Learning and Teaching Geometry, K–12, 1987 Yearbook.* Edited by Mary Montgomery Lindquist. National Council of Teachers of Mathematics, Reston, VA, 1987.

Curriculum and Evaluation Standards for School Mathematics. National Council of Teachers of Mathematics, Reston, VA, 1989.

Dewey, J. "Science as Subject-Matter and as Method." *Science,* 31(787), pp. 121–127, 1910.

Flanders, J. "How Much of the Content in Mathematics Textbooks Is New?" *The Arithmetic Teacher,* 35(1), pp. 18–23, 1987.

Fuson, K.C. "Teaching Addition, Subtraction, and Place-Value Concepts." L. Wirszup and R. Streit (eds.), *Proceedings of the UCSMP International Conference on Mathematics Education: Developments in School Mathematics Education Around the World: Applications-Oriented Curricula and Technology-Supported Learning for All Students.* National Council of Teachers of Mathematics, Reston, VA, 1987.

Fuson, K.C. "Research on Whole Number Addition and Subtraction." *Handbook of Research on Mathematics Teaching and Learning,* pp. 243–275, D.A. Grouws, ed. Macmillan Publishing Company, New York, 1992.

Fuson, K.C., and D.J. Briars. "Using a Base-Ten Blocks Learning/Teaching Approach for First- and Second-Grade Place-Value and Multidigit Addition and Subtraction." *Journal for Research in Mathematics Education,* 21, pp. 180–206, 1990.

Fuson, K.C., D. Wearne, J. Hiebert, H. Murray, P. Human, A. Olivier, T. Carpenter, and E. Fennema. "Children's Conceptual Structures for Multidigit Numbers and Methods of Multidigit Addition and Subtraction." *Journal for Research in Mathematics Education,* 28, pp. 130–162, 1997.

Fuys, D., D. Geddes, and R. Tishler. "The Van Hiele Model of Thinking in Geometry among Adolescents." *Journal for Research in Mathematics Education, Monograph Number 3.* National Council of Teachers of Mathematics, Reston, VA, 1988.

Goldberg, H. *A Four Year Achievement Study: The TIMS Program.* University of Illinois at Chicago Institute for Mathematics and Science Education, Chicago, IL, 1993.

Goldberg, H. *The TIMS Laboratory Investigations.* Kendall/Hunt, Dubuque, IA, 1997.

Goldberg, H.S., and F.D. Boulanger. "Science for Elementary School Teachers: A Quantitative Approach." *American Journal of Physics,* 19(2), pp. 120–124, 1981.

Goldberg, H., and P. Wagreich. "A Model Integrated Mathematics Science Program for the Elementary School." *International Journal of Educational Research,* 14(2), pp. 193–214, 1990.

Goldberg, H., and P. Wagreich. "Teaching Integrated Math and Science: A Curriculum and Staff Development Project for the Elementary School." *Issues in Mathematics Education: Mathematicians and Education Reform.* N. Fisher, H. Keynes, and P. Wagreich, eds., American Mathematical Society, Providence, RI, 1990.

Hiebert, J. "Relationships between Research and the NCTM Standards." *Journal for Research in Mathematics Education,* 30(1), pp. 3–19, 1999.

Hiebert, J., T.P. Carpenter, E. Fennema, K.C. Fuson, P. Human, H. Murray, A. Olivier, D. Wearne. "Problem Solving as a Basis for Reform in Curriculum and Instruction: The Case of Mathematics." *Educational Researcher,* 25(4), pp. 12–21, 1996.

Hoffer, A.R., and S.A.K. Hoffer. "Ratios and Proportional Thinking." In *Teaching Mathematics in Grades K–8: Research Based Methods.* Allyn and Bacon, Boston, 1992.

Isaacs, A.C., and W.M. Carroll. "Strategies for Basic-Facts Instruction." *Teaching Children Mathematics,* 5(9), pp. 508–515, 1999.

Isaacs, A.C., P. Wagreich, and M. Gartzman. The Quest for Integration: School Mathematics and Science. *American Journal of Education,* 106(1), pp. 179–206, 1997.

Lampert, M. "Knowing, Doing, and Teaching Multiplication." *Cognition and Instruction,* 3 (4), pp. 305–342, 1986a.

Lampert, M. "Teaching Multiplication." *Journal of Mathematical Behavior,* 5, pp. 241–280, 1986b.

Lesh, R., T. Post, and M. Behr. "Representations and Translations Among Representations in Mathematics Learning and Problem Solving." C. Janvier, ed., *Problems of Representation in the Teaching and Learning of Mathematics.* Lawrence Erlbaum Associates, Hillsdale, NJ, 1987.

Lindquist, M.M., ed. *Results from the Fourth Mathematics Assessment of the National Assessment of Educational Progress.* National Council of Teachers of Mathematics. Reston, VA, 1989.

Mack, N.K. "Learning Fractions with Understanding: Building on Informal Knowledge." *Journal for Research in Mathematics Education,* 21(1), National Council of Teachers of Mathematics, Reston, VA, January 1990.

McKnight, C.C., F.J. Crosswhite, J.A. Dossey, E. Kifer, J.O. Swafford, K.T. Travers, and T.J. Cooney, *The Underachieving Curriculum: Assessing U.S. School Mathematics from an International Perspective.* Stipes Publishing Company, Champaign, IL, 1987.

National Research Council. *Adding It Up: Helping Children Learn Mathematics.* J. Kilpatrick, J. Swafford, and B. Findell, eds. National Academy Press, Washington, DC, 2001.

Newmann, F.M., A.S. Bryk, and J.K. Nagaoka. *Authentic Intellectual Work and Standardized Tests: Conflict or Coexistence?* Consortium on Chicago School Research, Chicago, 2001.

Perry, M., M. Whiteaker, and G.L. Waddoups. "Students' Participation in a Reform Mathematics Classroom: Learning to Become Mathematicians." In K. Fuson (Chair), *Effects of Reform Mathematics Curricula on Children's Mathematical Understanding.* Symposia conducted at the annual meeting of the American Educational Research Association, New York, 1996.

Principles and Standards for School Mathematics. National Council of Teachers of Mathematics, Reston, VA, 2000.

Putnam, R.T. "Commentary on Four Elementary Mathematics Curricula." S.L. Senk and D.R. Thompson, eds., *Standards-Based School Mathematics Curricula: What Does the Research Say about Student Outcomes?* Lawrence Erlbaum Associates, Inc., Hillsdale, NJ, 2003.

Schmidt, W.H., C.C. McKnight, and S.A. Raizen. *A Splintered Vision: An Investigation of U.S. Science and Mathematics Education.* Kluwer, Norwell, MA, 1996.

Schoenfeld, A.H. *Mathematical Problem Solving.* Academic Press, Orlando, FL, 1985.

Schoenfeld, A.H. "What Do We Know about Mathematics Curricula?" *Journal of Mathematical Behavior,* 13(1), pp. 55–80, 1994.

Schroeder, T.L., and F.K. Lester, Jr. "Developing Understanding in Mathematics via Problem Solving." In *New Directions for Elementary School Mathematics,* 1989 Yearbook. National Council of Teachers of Mathematics, Reston, VA, 1989.

Smith, J.B., V.E. Lee, and F.M. Newmann. *Instruction and Achievement in Chicago Elementary Schools.* Consortium on Chicago School Research, Chicago, 2001.

Sowder, J. "Estimation and Number Sense." *Handbook of Research on Mathematics Teaching and Learning,* pp. 243–275, D.A. Grouws, ed., Macmillan Publishing Company, New York, 1992.

Stevenson, H.W., and J.W. Stigler. *The Learning Gap.* Simon & Schuster, New York, 1992.

Stigler, J.W., and J. Hiebert. "Understanding and Improving Classroom Mathematics Instruction: An Overview of the TIMSS Study." *Phi Delta Kappan,* 79(1), pp. 14–21.

Stigler, J.W., and M. Perry. "Mathematics Learning in Japanese, Chinese, and American Classrooms." G.B. Saxe and M. Gearhart, eds., *New Directions for Child Development, No. 41: Children's Mathematics.* Jossey Bass, San Francisco, CA, 1988.

Thornton, C.A. "Emphasizing Thinking Strategies in Basic Fact Instruction." *Journal for Research in Mathematics Education,* 9 (3), pp. 214–227, 1978.

Thornton, C.A. "Solution Strategies: Subtraction Number Facts." *Educational Studies in Mathematics,* 21 (1), pp. 241–263, 1990a.

Thornton, C.A. "Strategies for the Basic Facts." *Mathematics for the Young Child,* pp. 133–151, J.N. Payne, ed. National Council of Teachers of Mathematics, Reston, VA, 1990b.

Whiteaker, M., G.L. Waddoups, and M. Perry. "Implementing a New Mathematics Curriculum: Constructing Models for Success." Paper presented at annual meeting of the American Educational Research Association, New Orleans, 1994.

Components and Features Guide

The Components and Features Guide presents reduced-size curriculum pages and descriptive boxes that cover each element of *Math Trailblazers*.

Students use Activity, Lab, and Game Pages, which are provided in the student books.

Components & Features

Components of *Math Trailblazers*

The following pages offer a walk-through of the *Teacher Implementation Guide, Unit Resource Guide, Facts Resource Guide, Teacher Resource CD, Student Guide, Discovery Assignment Book,* and *Adventure Book.*

Teacher Materials

TEACHER IMPLEMENTATION GUIDE (TIG)

- reference guide for teachers, containing program philosophy, overview, and in-depth reference documents, including a section on assessment
- black and white, nonconsumable
- glossary, including locations of key vocabulary terms in the curriculum
- curriculum index with page references to key vocabulary terms

TEACHER RESOURCE CD

Teacher resource containing:

- Daily Practice and Problems (DPP) items
- Observational Assessment Record
- Individual Assessment Record Sheet
- Letters Home (English and Spanish)
- sections from the Facts Resource Guide
- Assessment, Transparency, and Blackline Masters
- Reproducibles
- Student and Teacher Rubrics

UNIT RESOURCE GUIDE (URG)

- comprehensive guide providing essential background information and materials for day-to-day planning, instruction, and assessment
- four-color, nonconsumable
- contains:
  Letters Home (English and Spanish)
  Unit Outlines
  Daily Practice and Problems
  Observational Assessment Record
  Lesson Guides
  Materials Lists
  Assessment Pages
  Transparency and
    Blackline Masters
  Answer Keys
  Glossary

FACTS RESOURCE GUIDE GRADES 2–5

- compilation of math facts materials for each grade
- black and white, nonconsumable
- contains:
  DPP and Home Practice
    math facts items
  Facts Quizzes
  Games
  Lessons focusing on
    Math Facts
  Math Facts Philosophy
  Flash Cards

Student Materials

STUDENT GUIDE (SG)

- core material for students
- four-color
- soft-cover, consumable: Grades 1, 2
- hard cover, nonconsumable: Grades 3, 4, 5
- glossary and index: Grades 1, 2
- Glossary/Index: Grades 3, 4, 5

DISCOVERY ASSIGNMENT BOOK (DAB) GRADES 3–5

- consumable student pages
- soft-cover, black and white
- double- and single-sided worksheets

ADVENTURE BOOK (AB)

- collections of illustrated stories focused on math and science concepts
- available in four-color Big Adventure Book and consumable black-and-white books in Grades 1, 2
- available in soft-cover, four-color, nonconsumable format in Grades 3, 4, 5

Administrator Materials

ADMINISTRATOR HANDBOOK

- Describes important components of a math implementation
- Strategies for administrators to successfully guide implementation
- Blackline Masters for presentations to staff, parents, or other audiences
- Important sections for administrators from *Teacher Implementation Guides*
- black and white, nonconsumable

Letter Home (Parent Letter)

The Letter Home is designed to be signed and sent by the teacher. It explains what students will study and how their families can help. Spanish versions of letters are also provided.

Carta al hogar
El área de diferentes figuras

Fecha: _____

Estimado miembro de familia:

El área es la cantidad de superficie necesaria para cubrir algo, como la cantidad de alfo saria para cubrir un piso, papel tapiz para cubrir una pared o piel para cubrir un cuerpo. unidad, su hijo/a explorará el área de superficies planas.

Hallaremos el área de figuras que tienen lados rectos, curvos o irregulares, como la que aquí. Para hallar el área de una figura irregular, los estudiantes calcan la figura en pape cuadrículas de un centímetro. Primero cuentan los cuadrados de un centímetro llenos d figura. Luego juntan las partes restantes (por ejemplo, mitades) en cuadrados completo permite hacer una buena estimación del área de la figura. La clase aplicará el conocimi el área en un experimento en el cuál se investigar qué marca de toallas de papel absorb cantidad de agua.

Mientras estudiamos el área en clase, usted puede ayudar a reforzar este concepto en casa haciendo las siguientes actividades.

- **Medir el área de la huella de la mano.** Haga que varios miembros de la familia calquen las huellas de sus manos en una hoja de papel y pídale a su hijo/a que compare el área de cada una cubriéndolas con monedas de un centavo o frijoles. Compare el área de las huellas de sus manos con el área de las huellas de sus pies. ¿Cuál es mayor?
- **Calcar figuras.** Ayude a su hijo/a a buscar distintas figuras en la casa, tales como un plato o la hoja de una planta. Calque las figuras en papel. Pídale a su hijo/a que compare el área de las diferentes figuras cubriéndolas con monedas de un centavo o frijoles.
- **Conceptos básicos.** Ayude a su hijo/a a estudiar las restas básicas de los grupos 7 y 8 usando tarjetas.

Gracias por tomarse el tiempo para practicar matemáticas con su hijo/a en casa. Esto ay hijo/a a relacionar las matemáticas con experiencias cotidianas.

Atentamente,

_____

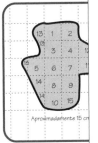

Contar el número de centíme cuadrados en una figura para el área.

Letter Home
Area of Different Shapes

Date: _____

Dear Family Member:

Area is the amount of surface needed to cover something—the amount of carpet to cover a floor, wallpaper to cover a wall, or skin to cover a body. In this next unit, your child will explore the area of flat surfaces.

We will find the area of shapes that have straight, curved, or irregular sides, such as the shape shown here. To find the area of an irregular shape, students trace the shape on centimeter grid paper. They first count the number of full centimeter squares inside the shape. Then they piece together the remaining parts (for example, halves) into full squares. This gives a good estimate of the shape's area. The class will apply its knowledge of area to an experiment that investigates which brand of paper towels absorbs the most water.

As we study area in our classroom, you can help reinforce the concept of area at home with the following activities.

- **Measure Your Handprint's Area.** Have different members of your family trace their handprints on a piece of paper and ask your child to compare the area of each by covering them with pennies or beans. Compare the area of your handprints with the area of your footprints. Which has more area?
- **Shape Tracings.** Help your child look for different shapes around the house, such as a plate or leaf. Trace the shapes on paper. Ask your child to compare the area of the different shapes by covering them with pennies or beans.
- **Math Facts.** Help your child study the subtraction facts in Groups 7 and 8 using flash cards.

Thank you for taking time to do math at home with your child. It helps your child connect mathematics to everyday experiences.

Sincerely,

_____

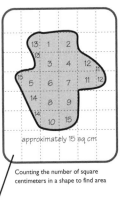

approximately 15 sq cm

Counting the number of square centimeters in a shape to find area

Components & Features

Art — Most letters include an illustration relating to the unit's activities.

Outline

The Outline indicates the number of lessons, what they are about, supplies you will need for them, how much time they will take, and other materials you may want to introduce. The Outline also includes helpful planning information such as a summary of the unit, Pacing Suggestions, Assessment Indicators, related trade books and software as well as ideas for differentiation.

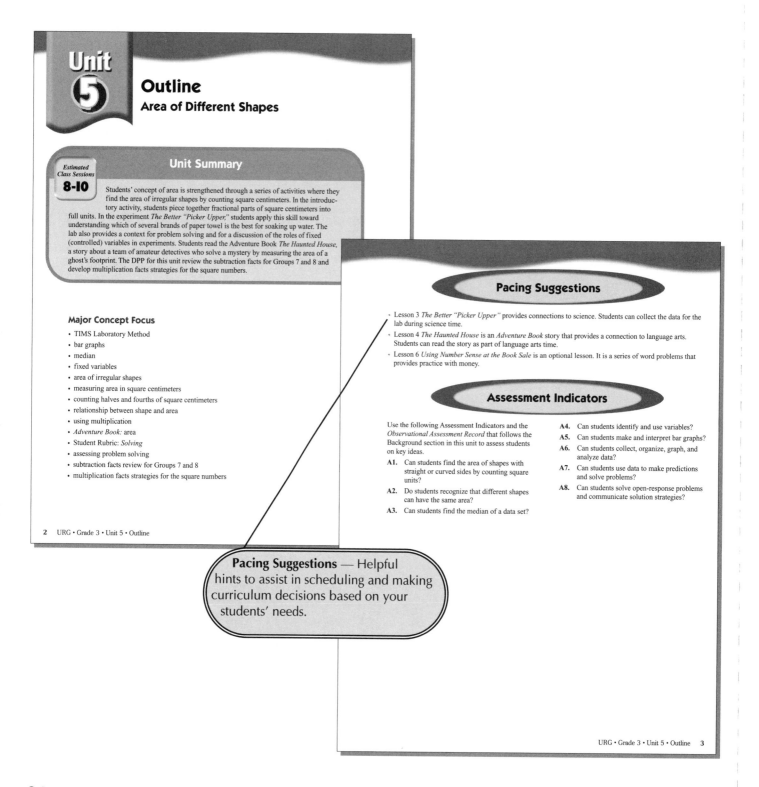

Unit 5

Outline
Area of Different Shapes

Estimated Class Sessions 8–10

Unit Summary

Students' concept of area is strengthened through a series of activities where they find the area of irregular shapes by counting square centimeters. In the introductory activity, students piece together fractional parts of square centimeters into full units. In the experiment *The Better "Picker Upper,"* students apply this skill toward understanding which of several brands of paper towel is the best for soaking up water. The lab also provides a context for problem solving and for a discussion of the roles of fixed (controlled) variables in experiments. Students read the Adventure Book *The Haunted House*, a story about a team of amateur detectives who solve a mystery by measuring the area of a ghost's footprint. The DPP for this unit review the subtraction facts for Groups 7 and 8 and develop multiplication facts strategies for the square numbers.

Major Concept Focus

- TIMS Laboratory Method
- bar graphs
- median
- fixed variables
- area of irregular shapes
- measuring area in square centimeters
- counting halves and fourths of square centimeters
- relationship between shape and area
- using multiplication
- *Adventure Book:* area
- Student Rubric: *Solving*
- assessing problem solving
- subtraction facts review for Groups 7 and 8
- multiplication facts strategies for the square numbers

2   URG • Grade 3 • Unit 5 • Outline

Pacing Suggestions

- Lesson 3 *The Better "Picker Upper"* provides connections to science. Students can collect the data for the lab during science time.
- Lesson 4 *The Haunted House* is an *Adventure Book* story that provides a connection to language arts. Students can read the story as part of language arts time.
- Lesson 6 *Using Number Sense at the Book Sale* is an optional lesson. It is a series of word problems that provides practice with money.

Assessment Indicators

Use the following Assessment Indicators and the *Observational Assessment Record* that follows the Background section in this unit to assess students on key ideas.

- **A1.** Can students find the area of shapes with straight or curved sides by counting square units?
- **A2.** Do students recognize that different shapes can have the same area?
- **A3.** Can students find the median of a data set?
- **A4.** Can students identify and use variables?
- **A5.** Can students make and interpret bar graphs?
- **A6.** Can students collect, organize, graph, and analyze data?
- **A7.** Can students use data to make predictions and solve problems?
- **A8.** Can students solve open-response problems and communicate solution strategies?

URG • Grade 3 • Unit 5 • Outline   3

Pacing Suggestions — Helpful hints to assist in scheduling and making curriculum decisions based on your students' needs.

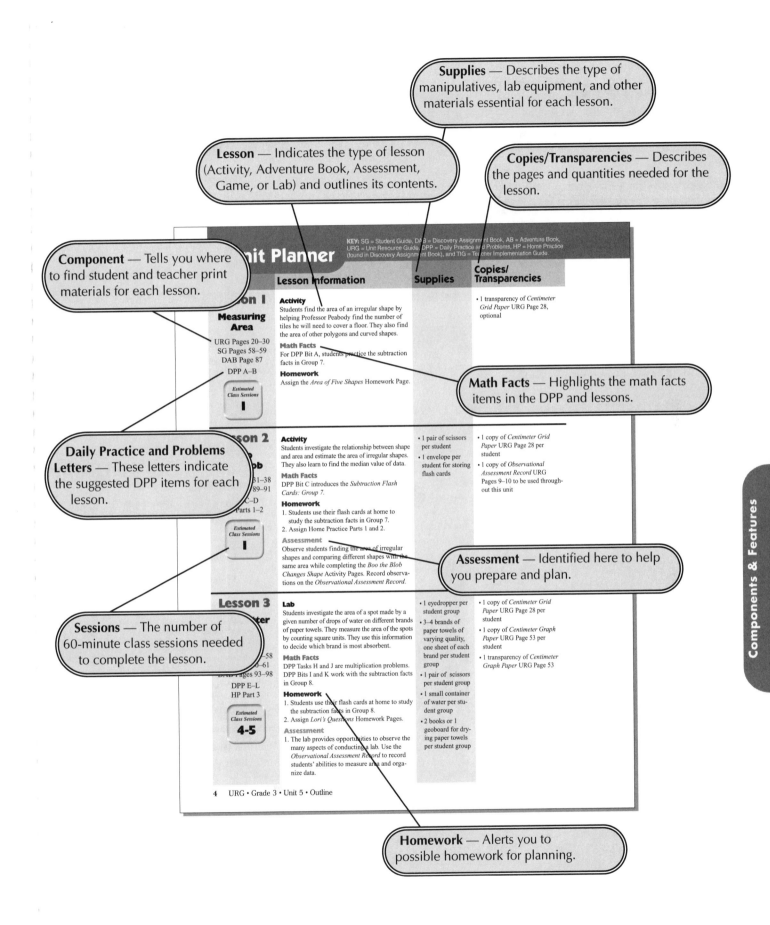

Supplies — Describes the type of manipulatives, lab equipment, and other materials essential for each lesson.

Lesson — Indicates the type of lesson (Activity, Adventure Book, Assessment, Game, or Lab) and outlines its contents.

Copies/Transparencies — Describes the pages and quantities needed for the lesson.

Component — Tells you where to find student and teacher print materials for each lesson.

Daily Practice and Problems Letters — These letters indicate the suggested DPP items for each lesson.

Sessions — The number of 60-minute class sessions needed to complete the lesson.

Math Facts — Highlights the math facts items in the DPP and lessons.

Assessment — Identified here to help you prepare and plan.

Homework — Alerts you to possible homework for planning.

KEY: SG = Student Guide, DAB = Discovery Assignment Book, AB = Adventure Book, URG = Unit Resource Guide, DPP = Daily Practice and Problems, HP = Home Practice (found in Discovery Assignment Book), and TIG = Teacher Implementation Guide.

Unit Planner

	Lesson Information	Supplies	Copies/Transparencies
Lesson 1 **Measuring Area** URG Pages 20–30 SG Pages 58–59 DAB Page 87 DPP A–B *Estimated Class Sessions* **1**	**Activity** Students find the area of an irregular shape by helping Professor Peabody find the number of tiles he will need to cover a floor. They also find the area of other polygons and curved shapes. **Math Facts** For DPP Bit A, students practice the subtraction facts in Group 7. **Homework** Assign the *Area of Five Shapes* Homework Page.		• 1 transparency of *Centimeter Grid Paper* URG Page 28, optional
Lesson 2 URG Pages 31–38 89–91 C–D Parts 1–2 *Estimated Class Sessions* **1**	**Activity** Students investigate the relationship between shape and area and estimate the area of irregular shapes. They also learn to find the median value of data. **Math Facts** DPP Bit C introduces the *Subtraction Flash Cards: Group 7*. **Homework** 1. Students use their flash cards at home to study the subtraction facts in Group 7. 2. Assign Home Practice Parts 1 and 2. **Assessment** Observe students finding the area of irregular shapes and comparing different shapes with the same area while completing the *Boo the Blob Changes Shape* Activity Pages. Record observations on the *Observational Assessment Record*.	• 1 pair of scissors per student • 1 envelope per student for storing flash cards	• 1 copy of *Centimeter Grid Paper* URG Page 28 per student • 1 copy of *Observational Assessment Record* URG Pages 9–10 to be used throughout this unit
Lesson 3 URG Pages 52–58 60–61 DAB Pages 93–98 DPP E–L HP Part 3 *Estimated Class Sessions* **4-5**	**Lab** Students investigate the area of a spot made by a given number of drops of water on different brands of paper towels. They measure the area of the spots by counting square units. They use this information to decide which brand is most absorbent. **Math Facts** DPP Tasks H and J are multiplication problems. DPP Bits I and K work with the subtraction facts in Group 8. **Homework** 1. Students use their flash cards at home to study the subtraction facts in Group 8. 2. Assign *Lori's Questions* Homework Pages. **Assessment** 1. The lab provides opportunities to observe the many aspects of conducting a lab. Use the *Observational Assessment Record* to record students' abilities to measure area and organize data.	• 1 eyedropper per student group • 3–4 brands of paper towels of varying quality, one sheet of each brand per student group • 1 pair of scissors per student group • 1 small container of water per student group • 2 books or 1 geoboard for drying paper towels per student group	• 1 copy of *Centimeter Grid Paper* URG Page 28 per student • 1 copy of *Centimeter Graph Paper* URG Page 53 per student • 1 transparency of *Centimeter Graph Paper* URG Page 53

4   URG • Grade 3 • Unit 5 • Outline

Components & Features

Connections — The material in *Math Trailblazers* lessons often can be related to books, magazine articles, and computer programs. When a Connection is recommended for use with a specific lesson, it is included in the Lesson Guide.

Preparing for Upcoming Lessons

Place eyedroppers in a learning center for students to explore prior to Lesson 3. You may want to introduce eyedroppers in a whole class setting.

You will need to purchase three different brands of paper towels for Lesson 3.

Connections

A current list of literature and software connections is available at *www.mathtrailblazers.com*. You can also find information on connections in the *Teacher Implementation Guide* Literature List and Software List sections.

Literature Connections
Suggested Titles

- Gabriel, Nat. *Sam's Sneaker Squares*. The Kane Press, New York, 2002.
- Murphy, Stuart J. *Room for Ripley*. HarperCollins Publishing, New York, 1999.

Software Connections

- *The Factory Deluxe* promotes spatial reasoning and practices finding area.
- *Graphers* is a data graphing tool appropriate for young students.
- *Kid Pix* allows students to create their own illustrations.
- *National Library of Virtual Manipulatives* website (http://matti.usu.edu) allows s[...] manipulatives including geoboards, base-ten pieces, the abacus, and many others[...]

Teaching All Math Trailblazers Students — Helps you plan lessons that challenge all your students.

6   URG • Grade 3 • Unit 5 • Outline

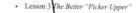

Teaching All Math Trailblazers Students

Math Trailblazers® lessons are designed for students with a wide range of abilities. The lessons are flexible and do not require significant adaptation for diverse learning styles or academic levels. However, when needed, lessons can be tailored to allow students to engage their abilities to the greatest extent possible while building knowledge and skills.

To assist you in meeting the needs of all students in your classroom, this section contains information about some of the features in the curriculum that allow all students access to mathematics. For additional information, see the Teaching the *Math Trailblazers* Student: Meeting Individual Needs section in the *Teacher Implementation Guide.*

Differentiation Opportunities in this Unit

Laboratory Experiments

Laboratory experiments enable students to solve problems using a variety of representations including pictures, tables, graphs, and symbols. Teachers can assign or adapt parts of the analysis according to the student's ability. The following lesson is a lab:

- Lesson 3 *The Better "Picker Upper"*

Journal Prompts

Journal prompts provide opportunities for students to explain and reflect on mathematical problems. They can help both students who need practice explaining their ideas and students who benefit from answering higher order questions. Students with various learning styles can express themselves using pictures, words, and sentences. Teachers can alter journal prompts to suit students' ability levels. The following lessons contain a journal prompt:

- Lesson 3 *The Better "Picker Upper"*
- Lesson [...]

DPP Challenges

DPP Challenges are items from the Daily Practice and Problems that usually take more than fifteen minutes to complete. These problems are more thought-provoking and can be used to stretch students' problem-solving skills. The following lessons have a DPP Challenge in them:

- DPP Challenge B from Lesson 1 *Measuring Area*
- DPP Challenge L from Lesson 3 *The Better "Picker Upper"*

Extensions

Use extensions to enrich lessons. Many extensions provide opportunities to further involve or challenge students of all abilities. Take a moment to review the extensions prior to beginning this unit. Some extensions may require additional preparation and planning. The following lessons contain extensions:

- Lesson 2 *Boo the Blob*
- Lesson 3 *The Better "Picker Upper"*
- Lesson 4 *The Haunted House*
- Lesson 6 *Using Number Sense [...]*

Differentiation Opportunities in this Unit — This section identifies the games, laboratory experiments, journal prompts, and extensions you can use to meet the varying needs of your students.

URG • Grade 3 • Unit 5 • Outline   7

Background

The Background explains what students will learn in the unit and places the material in the larger context of the *Math Trailblazers* curriculum.

Unit 5

Background
Area of Different Shapes

Area is the amount of surface needed to cover something—the amount of carpet to cover a floor, wallpaper to cover a wall, or skin to cover a body. Area is measured in square units, such as square inches or square meters. For example, ecologists measure the amount of rain forest destroyed each day in square miles. Neurobiologists measure the area of individual connections between nerve cells in square microns. (One square micron is $\frac{1}{100,000,000}$ of a square centimeter.)

In third grade, students find the area of flat surfaces. Building on the ideas they developed in first and second grades, they begin this unit by finding the area of shapes with straight sides. Then, they learn to measure the area of shapes with curved sides. The activities and experiment in this unit provide a context in which to develop a working definition of area by counting square units.

Students face a series of problems that cannot be solved by measuring length or width, but only by measuring area:

- How many tiles will it take to cover a floor?
- Can two or more different shapes have the same area?

- Can two amateur detectives identify a classmate by measuring the area of a footprint?
- How much material will it take to make a raincoat?

In the lab in Lesson 3 *The Better "Picker Upper,"* students decide which of several brands of paper towels is the most absorbent. The lab allows students to use their knowledge of area and the scientific process to explore many facets of a problem. They identify the variables in the experiment and collect, record, and graph data. Students identify the most absorbent towel by interpreting the graph and answering the questions posed in the lab.

Developing a conceptual understanding of area in the primary grades gives students information they need to solve problems similar to those in this unit. It also provides the framework for more advanced work with area in mathematics and science, such as finding the surface area of three-dimensional figures. For more information, refer to the TIMS Tutor: *The Concept of Area* in the *Teacher Implementation Guide.*

Components & Features

Observational Assessment Record

The *Observational Assessment Record* is a form used to record observations of students' progress.

Assessment Indicators — These are the Assessment Indicators listed in the Unit Outline. They highlight the skills and concepts you should look for as you observe students working on activities in the unit.

Additional lines are provided to help document students' progress with other content.

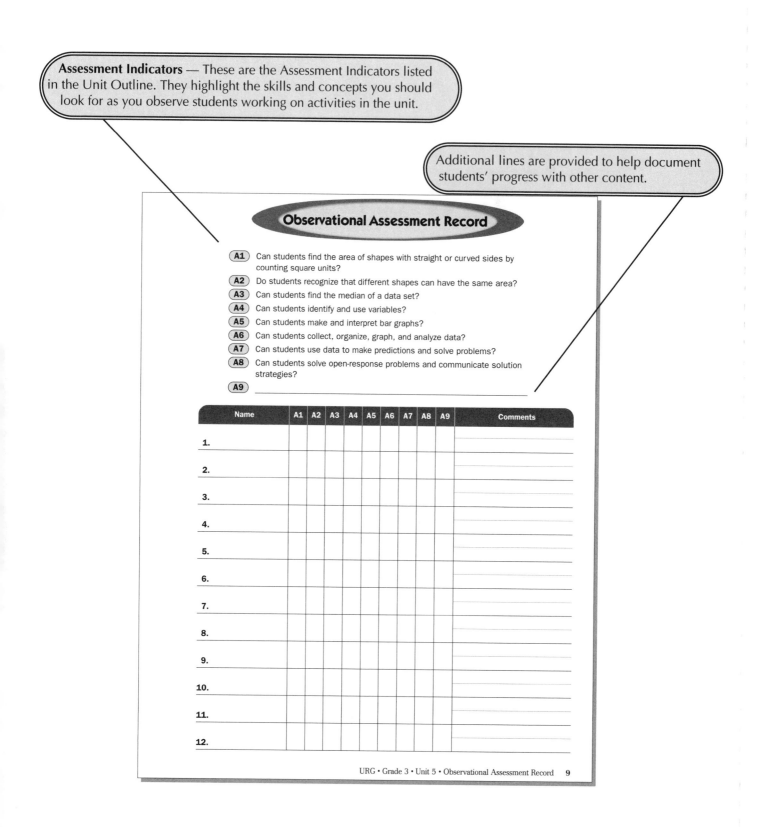

Observational Assessment Record

A1 Can students find the area of shapes with straight or curved sides by counting square units?

A2 Do students recognize that different shapes can have the same area?

A3 Can students find the median of a data set?

A4 Can students identify and use variables?

A5 Can students make and interpret bar graphs?

A6 Can students collect, organize, graph, and analyze data?

A7 Can students use data to make predictions and solve problems?

A8 Can students solve open-response problems and communicate solution strategies?

A9 _____

Name	A1	A2	A3	A4	A5	A6	A7	A8	A9	Comments
1.										
2.										
3.										
4.										
5.										
6.										
7.										
8.										
9.										
10.										
11.										
12.										

URG • Grade 3 • Unit 5 • Observational Assessment Record   9

Daily Practice and Problems

The Daily Practice and Problems (DPP) is a series of short exercises that provide continuing review of math concepts, skills, and facts. Each DPP set includes a Teacher's Guide, which provides specific information on the study and assessment of the math facts in the current unit.

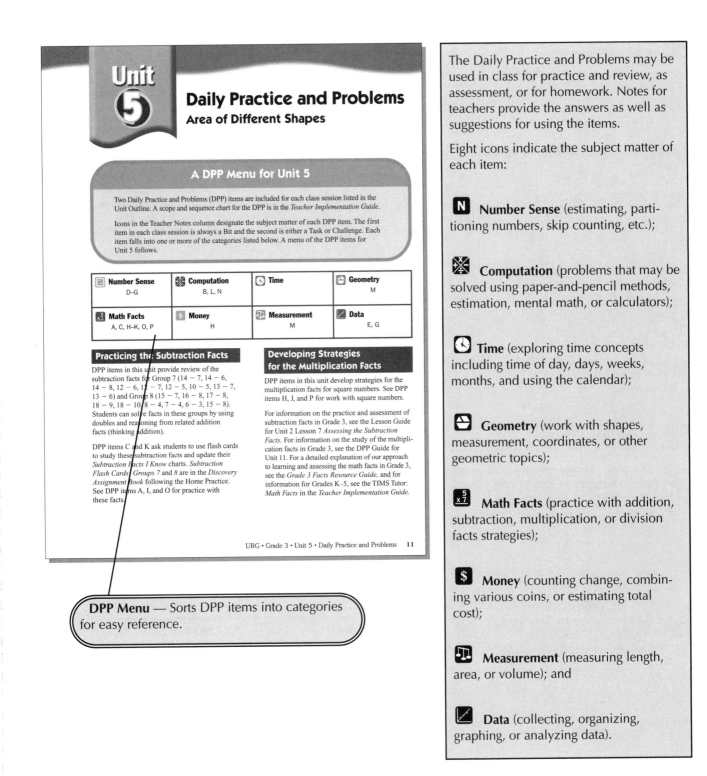

Unit 5
Daily Practice and Problems
Area of Different Shapes

A DPP Menu for Unit 5

Two Daily Practice and Problems (DPP) items are included for each class session listed in the Unit Outline. A scope and sequence chart for the DPP is in the *Teacher Implementation Guide*.

Icons in the Teacher Notes column designate the subject matter of each DPP item. The first item in each class session is always a Bit and the second is either a Task or Challenge. Each item falls into one or more of the categories listed below. A menu of the DPP items for Unit 5 follows.

Number Sense D–G	Computation B, L, N	Time	Geometry M
Math Facts A, C, H–K, O, P	Money H	Measurement M	Data E, G

Practicing the Subtraction Facts

DPP items in this unit provide review of the subtraction facts for Group 7 (14 − 7, 14 − 6, 14 − 8, 12 − 6, 12 − 7, 12 − 5, 10 − 5, 13 − 7, 13 − 6) and Group 8 (15 − 7, 16 − 8, 17 − 8, 18 − 9, 18 − 10, 8 − 4, 7 − 4, 6 − 3, 15 − 8). Students can solve facts in these groups by using doubles and reasoning from related addition facts (thinking addition).

DPP items C and K ask students to use flash cards to study these subtraction facts and update their *Subtraction Facts I Know* charts. *Subtraction Flash Cards Groups 7* and *8* are in the *Discovery Assignment Book* following the Home Practice. See DPP items A, I, and O for practice with these facts.

Developing Strategies for the Multiplication Facts

DPP items in this unit develop strategies for the multiplication facts for square numbers. See DPP items H, J, and P for work with square numbers.

For information on the practice and assessment of subtraction facts in Grade 3, see the Lesson Guide for Unit 2 Lesson 7 *Assessing the Subtraction Facts*. For information on the study of the multiplication facts in Grade 3, see the DPP Guide for Unit 11. For a detailed explanation of our approach to learning and assessing the math facts in Grade 3, see the *Grade 3 Facts Resource Guide*, and for information for Grades K–5, see the TIMS Tutor: *Math Facts* in the *Teacher Implementation Guide*.

URG • Grade 3 • Unit 5 • Daily Practice and Problems   11

DPP Menu — Sorts DPP items into categories for easy reference.

The Daily Practice and Problems may be used in class for practice and review, as assessment, or for homework. Notes for teachers provide the answers as well as suggestions for using the items.

Eight icons indicate the subject matter of each item:

N **Number Sense** (estimating, partitioning numbers, skip counting, etc.);

Computation (problems that may be solved using paper-and-pencil methods, estimation, mental math, or calculators);

Time (exploring time concepts including time of day, days, weeks, months, and using the calendar);

Geometry (work with shapes, measurement, coordinates, or other geometric topics);

$\frac{5}{\times 7}$ **Math Facts** (practice with addition, subtraction, multiplication, or division facts strategies);

$ Money (counting change, combining various coins, or estimating total cost);

Measurement (measuring length, area, or volume); and

Data (collecting, organizing, graphing, or analyzing data).

Components & Features

There are two Daily Practice and Problems items for each nonoptional class session noted in a Unit Outline. The first of these is always a TIMS Bit and the second is either a TIMS Task or a TIMS Challenge.

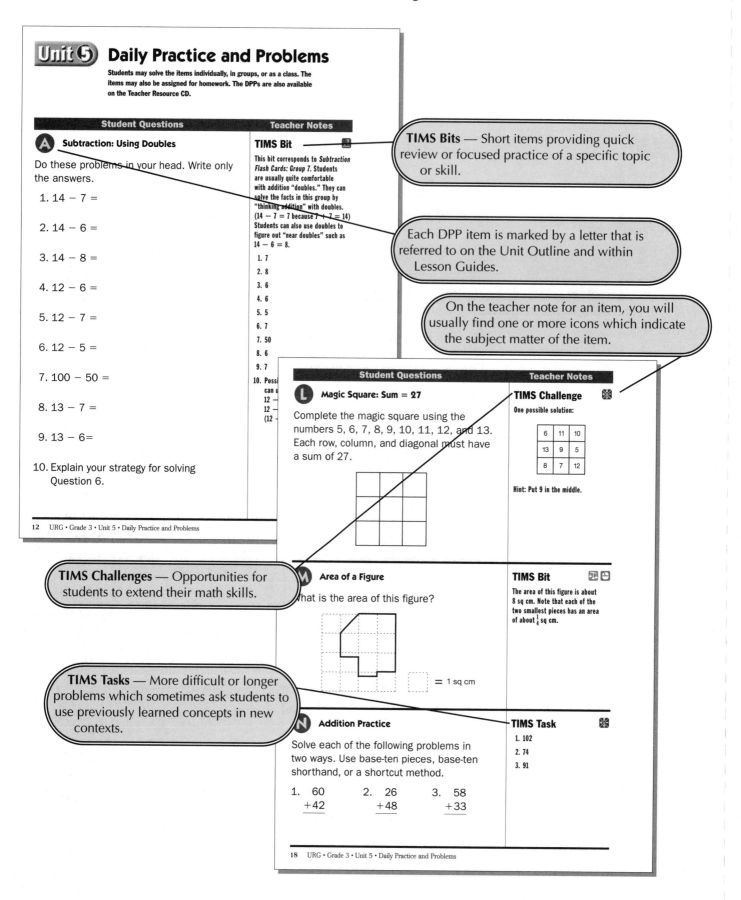

Unit 5 Daily Practice and Problems

Students may solve the items individually, in groups, or as a class. The items may also be assigned for homework. The DPPs are also available on the Teacher Resource CD.

Student Questions	Teacher Notes

A Subtraction: Using Doubles

Do these problems in your head. Write only the answers.

1. 14 − 7 =

2. 14 − 6 =

3. 14 − 8 =

4. 12 − 6 =

5. 12 − 7 =

6. 12 − 5 =

7. 100 − 50 =

8. 13 − 7 =

9. 13 − 6=

10. Explain your strategy for solving Question 6.

TIMS Bit

This bit corresponds to *Subtraction Flash Cards: Group 7*. Students are usually quite comfortable with addition "doubles." They can solve the facts in this group by "thinking addition" with doubles. (14 − 7 = 7 because 7 + 7 = 14) Students can also use doubles to figure out "near doubles" such as 14 − 6 = 8.

1. 7
2. 8
3. 6
4. 6
5. 5
6. 7
7. 50
8. 6
9. 7
10. Possi...
can u
12 −
12 −
(12 −

12   URG • Grade 3 • Unit 5 • Daily Practice and Problems

TIMS Bits — Short items providing quick review or focused practice of a specific topic or skill.

Each DPP item is marked by a letter that is referred to on the Unit Outline and within Lesson Guides.

On the teacher note for an item, you will usually find one or more icons which indicate the subject matter of the item.

Student Questions	Teacher Notes

L Magic Square: Sum = 27

Complete the magic square using the numbers 5, 6, 7, 8, 9, 10, 11, 12, and 13. Each row, column, and diagonal must have a sum of 27.

TIMS Challenge

One possible solution:

6	11	10
13	9	5
8	7	12

Hint: Put 9 in the middle.

TIMS Challenges — Opportunities for students to extend their math skills.

M Area of a Figure

What is the area of this figure?

= 1 sq cm

TIMS Bit

The area of this figure is about 8 sq cm. Note that each of the two smallest pieces has an area of about $\frac{1}{4}$ sq cm.

TIMS Tasks — More difficult or longer problems which sometimes ask students to use previously learned concepts in new contexts.

N Addition Practice

Solve each of the following problems in two ways. Use base-ten pieces, base-ten shorthand, or a shortcut method.

1.   60
   +42

2.   26
   +48

3.   58
   +33

TIMS Task

1. 102
2. 74
3. 91

18   URG • Grade 3 • Unit 5 • Daily Practice and Problems

Lesson Guide

The Lesson guide is a how-to manual explaining what you need for the lesson and what it involves.

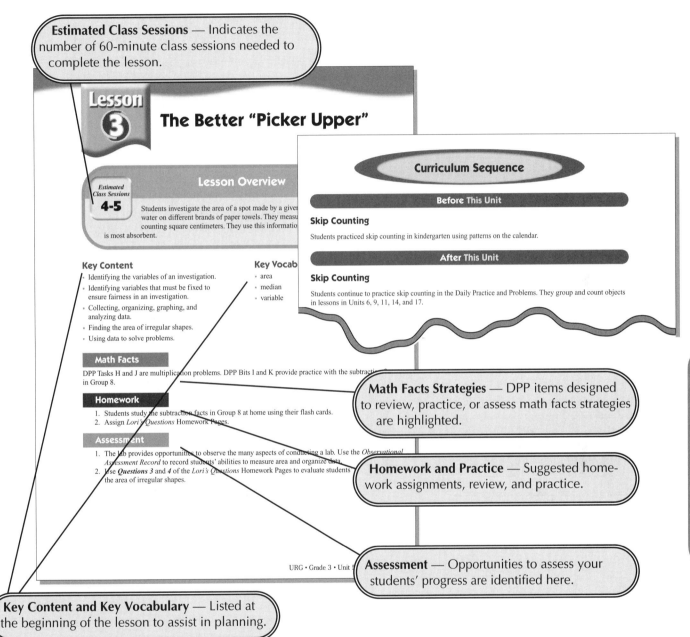

Estimated Class Sessions — Indicates the number of 60-minute class sessions needed to complete the lesson.

Lesson 3

The Better "Picker Upper"

Estimated Class Sessions
4-5

Lesson Overview

Students investigate the area of a spot made by a given water on different brands of paper towels. They measu counting square centimeters. They use this informatio is most absorbent.

Key Content
- Identifying the variables of an investigation.
- Identifying variables that must be fixed to ensure fairness in an investigation.
- Collecting, organizing, graphing, and analyzing data.
- Finding the area of irregular shapes.
- Using data to solve problems.

Key Vocab
- area
- median
- variable

Math Facts

DPP Tasks H and J are multiplication problems. DPP Bits I and K provide practice with the subtraction in Group 8.

Homework

1. Students study the subtraction facts in Group 8 at home using their flash cards.
2. Assign *Lori's Questions* Homework Pages.

Assessment

1. The lab provides opportunities to observe the many aspects of conducting a lab. Use the *Observational Assessment Record* to record students' abilities to measure area and organize data.
2. Use **Questions 3** and **4** of the *Lori's Questions* Homework Pages to evaluate students the area of irregular shapes.

URG • Grade 3 • Unit

Curriculum Sequence

Before This Unit

Skip Counting

Students practiced skip counting in kindergarten using patterns on the calendar.

After This Unit

Skip Counting

Students continue to practice skip counting in the Daily Practice and Problems. They group and count objects in lessons in Units 6, 9, 11, 14, and 17.

Math Facts Strategies — DPP items designed to review, practice, or assess math facts strategies are highlighted.

Homework and Practice — Suggested homework assignments, review, and practice.

Assessment — Opportunities to assess your students' progress are identified here.

Key Content and Key Vocabulary — Listed at the beginning of the lesson to assist in planning.

Components & Features

Materials List

Materials List — Everything you and students need for the lesson, including curriculum pages and manipulatives.

Supplies and Copies

Student	Teacher
Supplies for Each Student	**Supplies**
• 1 envelope for storing flash cards	• food coloring, optional
Supplies for Each Student Group	
• eyedropper	
• 3–4 brands of paper towels of varying quality, one sheet of each brand	
• scissors	
• small container of water	
• 2 books or 1 geoboard for drying paper towels	
Copies	**Copies/Transparencies**
• 1 copy of *Centimeter Grid Paper* per student (*Unit Resource Guide* Page 28)	• 1 transparency of *Centimeter Graph Paper* (*Unit Resource Guide* Page 53)
• 1 copy of *Centimeter Graph Paper* per student (*Unit Resource Guide* Page 53)	

All blackline masters including assessment, transparency, and DPP masters are also on the Teacher Resource CD.

Supplies — Indicates manipulatives and other supplies needed for the lesson.

Print Materials — Outlines all the copies and transparencies needed for the lesson and where to find them.

Student Books

The Better "Picker Upper" (*Student Guide* Pages 60–61)
Subtraction Flash Cards: Group 8 (*Discovery Assignment Book* Pages 85–86)
The Better "Picker Upper" (*Discovery Assignment Book* Pages 93–96)
Lori's Questions (*Discovery Assignment Book* Pages 97–98)

Student Books — Highlights which student books and pages are needed for the lesson.

Daily Practice and Problems and Home Practice

DPP items E–L (*Unit Resource Guide* Pages 14–18)
Home Practice Part 3 (*Discovery Assignment Book* Page 81)

Note: Classrooms whose pacing differs significantly from the suggested pacing of the units should use the Math Facts Calendar in Section 4 of the *Facts Resource Guide* to ensure students receive the complete math facts program.

Assessment Tools

Observational Assessment Record (*Unit Resource Guide* Pages 9–10)

URG • Grade 3 • Unit

Assessment Tools — Reminds you of opportunities to use the *Observational Assessment Record* and other Assessment tools.

DPP Items — To be completed as a warm-up or review.

Daily Practice and Problems

Suggestions for using the DPPs are on page 49.

E. Bit: Averaging Data (URG p. 14)

Julie did a study of candy color. Here is her data. Find the median number of candies for each color. The first one is done for you.

C Color	Sample 1	Sample 2	Sample 3	Median
red	3	5	4	4
brown	11	10	13	
orange	5	1	4	
green	5	4	5	

F. Task: More Comics (URG p. 15)

On an average day in the United States, 1096 copies of a certain comic book series are sold.

Show this number with base-ten pieces.

Show this number with base-ten shorthand.

G. Bit: Averaging (URG p. 15)

In an experiment, Franco measured the area of different types of leaves. Here is his data. Find the median area for each type of leaf.

T Type of Leaf	Trial 1	Trial 2	Trial 3	Median
Oak	48 sq cm	55 sq cm	50 sq cm	
Maple	86 sq cm	90 sq cm	84 sq cm	
Birch	10 sq cm	10 sq cm	12 sq cm	

H. Task: Kim's Savings (URG p. 16)

1. Kim earns $7 each week mowing lawns. She wants to buy jeans that cost $45. The tax will be $3. How long will she have to save to buy the jeans? Will she have to save longer than a month?
2. Leila earns $10 each week babysitting. How much money will she earn in 10 weeks?

I. Bit: Subtraction: Using Doubles (URG p. 16)

Do these problems in your head. Write only the answers.

1. $16 - 8 =$ 2. $17 - 8 =$
3. $15 - 8 =$ 4. $18 - 9 =$
5. $18 - 10 =$ 6. $15 - 7 =$
7. $8 - 4 =$ 8. $7 - 4 =$
9. $60 - 30 =$
10. Explain your strategy for solving Question 4.

J. Task: Story Solving (URG p. 17)

$8 \times 8 = ?$ Write a story and draw a picture about 8×8.

Write a number sentence on your picture.

K. Bit: Subtraction Flash Cards: Group 8 (URG p. 17)

1. With a partner, sort the flash cards into three stacks: Facts I Know Quickly, Facts I Know Using a Strategy, and Facts I Need to Learn.
2. Update your *Subtraction Facts I Know* chart. Circle the facts you answered quickly. Underline those you knew by using a strategy. Do nothing to those you still need to learn.

L. Challenge: Magic Square: Sum = 27 (URG p. 18)

Complete the magic square using the numbers 5, 6, 7, 8, 9, 10, 11, 12, and 13. Each row, column, and diagonal must have a sum of 27.

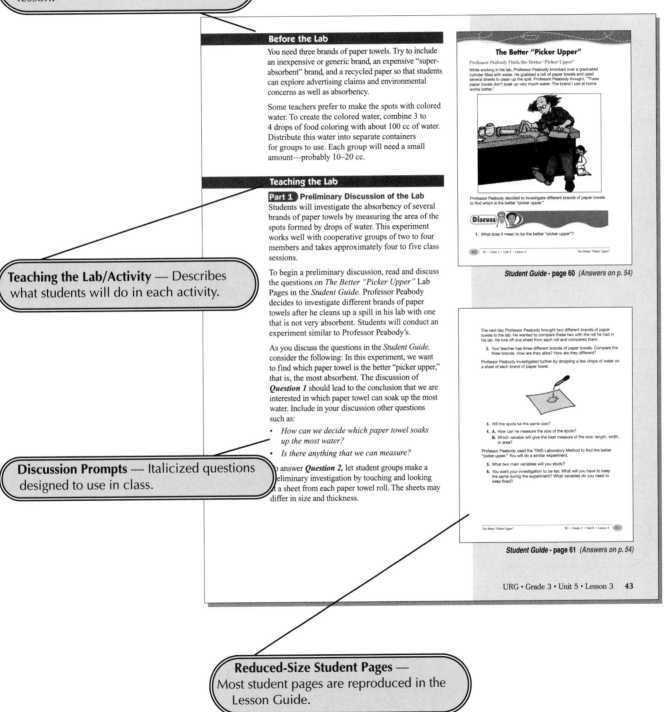

Before the Lab/Activity — Covers what you need to prepare ahead of time for the lesson.

Before the Lab

You need three brands of paper towels. Try to include an inexpensive or generic brand, an expensive "super-absorbent" brand, and a recycled paper so that students can explore advertising claims and environmental concerns as well as absorbency.

Some teachers prefer to make the spots with colored water. To create the colored water, combine 3 to 4 drops of food coloring with about 100 cc of water. Distribute this water into separate containers for groups to use. Each group will need a small amount—probably 10–20 cc.

Teaching the Lab

Part 1 Preliminary Discussion of the Lab
Students will investigate the absorbency of several brands of paper towels by measuring the area of the spots formed by drops of water. This experiment works well with cooperative groups of two to four members and takes approximately four to five class sessions.

To begin a preliminary discussion, read and discuss the questions on *The Better "Picker Upper"* Lab Pages in the *Student Guide.* Professor Peabody decides to investigate different brands of paper towels after he cleans up a spill in his lab with one that is not very absorbent. Students will conduct an experiment similar to Professor Peabody's.

As you discuss the questions in the *Student Guide,* consider the following: In this experiment, we want to find which paper towel is the better "picker upper," that is, the most absorbent. The discussion of *Question 1* should lead to the conclusion that we are interested in which paper towel can soak up the most water. Include in your discussion other questions such as:

*   *How can we decide which paper towel soaks up the most water?*

*   *Is there anything that we can measure?*

To answer *Question 2,* let student groups make a preliminary investigation by touching and looking at a sheet from each paper towel roll. The sheets may differ in size and thickness.

Teaching the Lab/Activity — Describes what students will do in each activity.

Discussion Prompts — Italicized questions designed to use in class.

The Better "Picker Upper"

Professor Peabody Finds the Better "Picker Upper"

While working in his lab, Professor Peabody knocked over a graduated cylinder filled with water. He grabbed a roll of paper towels and used several sheets to clean up the spill. Professor Peabody thought, "These paper towels don't soak up very much water. The brand I use at home works better."

Professor Peabody decided to investigate different brands of paper towels to find which is the better "picker upper."

Discuss

1. What does it mean to be the better "picker upper"?

Student Guide - page 60 (Answers on p. 54)

The next day Professor Peabody brought two different brands of paper towels to the lab. He wanted to compare these two with the roll he had in his lab. He tore off one sheet from each roll and compared them.

2. Your teacher has three different brands of paper towels. Compare the three brands. How are they alike? How are they different?

Professor Peabody investigated further by dropping a few drops of water on a sheet of each brand of paper towel.

3. Will the spots be the same size?
4. A. How can we measure the size of the spots?
    B. Which variable will give the best measure of the size: length, width, or area?

Professor Peabody used the TIMS Laboratory Method to find the better "picker upper." You will do a similar experiment.

5. What two main variables will you study?
6. You want your investigation to be fair. What will you have to keep the same during the experiment? What variables do you need to keep fixed?

Student Guide - page 61 (Answers on p. 54)

URG • Grade 3 • Unit 5 • Lesson 3   43

Reduced-Size Student Pages — Most student pages are reproduced in the Lesson Guide.

Components & Features

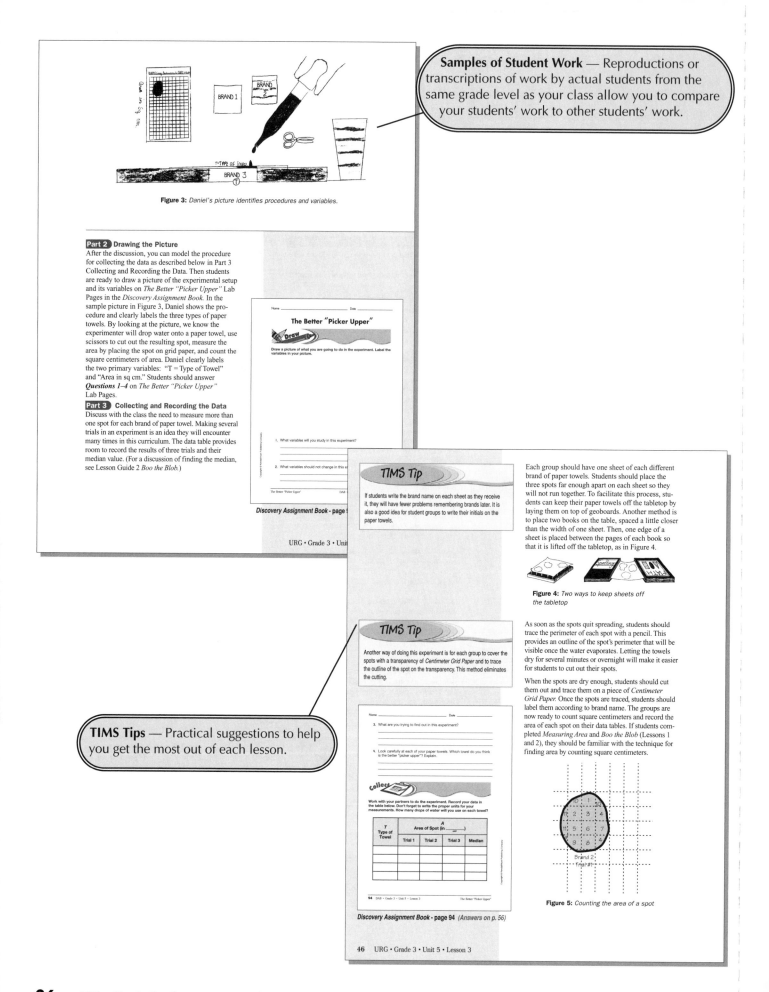

Figure 3: *Daniel's picture identifies procedures and variables.*

Samples of Student Work — Reproductions or transcriptions of work by actual students from the same grade level as your class allow you to compare your students' work to other students' work.

Part 2 Drawing the Picture

After the discussion, you can model the procedure for collecting the data as described below in Part 3 Collecting and Recording the Data. Then students are ready to draw a picture of the experimental setup and its variables on *The Better "Picker Upper"* Lab Pages in the *Discovery Assignment Book.* In the sample picture in Figure 3, Daniel shows the procedure and clearly labels the three types of paper towels. By looking at the picture, we know the experimenter will drop water onto a paper towel, use scissors to cut out the resulting spot, measure the area by placing the spot on grid paper, and count the square centimeters of area. Daniel clearly labels the two primary variables: "T = Type of Towel" and "Area in sq cm." Students should answer *Questions 1–4* on *The Better "Picker Upper"* Lab Pages.

Part 3 Collecting and Recording the Data

Discuss with the class the need to measure more than one spot for each brand of paper towel. Making several trials in an experiment is an idea they will encounter many times in this curriculum. The data table provides room to record the results of three trials and their median value. (For a discussion of finding the median, see Lesson Guide 2 *Boo the Blob.*)

Discovery Assignment Book - page 9

URG • Grade 3 • Unit

TIMS Tip

If students write the brand name on each sheet as they receive it, they will have fewer problems remembering brands later. It is also a good idea for student groups to write their initials on the paper towels.

TIMS Tip

Another way of doing this experiment is for each group to cover the spots with a transparency of *Centimeter Grid Paper* and to trace the outline of the spot on the transparency. This method eliminates the cutting.

TIMS Tips — Practical suggestions to help you get the most out of each lesson.

Discovery Assignment Book - page 94 (Answers on p. 56)

Each group should have one sheet of each different brand of paper towels. Students should place the three spots far enough apart on each sheet so they will not run together. To facilitate this process, students can keep their paper towels off the tabletop by laying them on top of geoboards. Another method is to place two books on the table, spaced a little closer than the width of one sheet. Then, one edge of a sheet is placed between the pages of each book so that it is lifted off the tabletop, as in Figure 4.

Figure 4: *Two ways to keep sheets off the tabletop*

As soon as the spots quit spreading, students should trace the perimeter of each spot with a pencil. This provides an outline of the spot's perimeter that will be visible once the water evaporates. Letting the towels dry for several minutes or overnight will make it easier for students to cut out their spots.

When the spots are dry enough, students should cut them out and trace them on a piece of *Centimeter Grid Paper.* Once the spots are traced, students should label them according to brand name. The groups are now ready to count square centimeters and record the area of each spot on their data tables. If students completed *Measuring Area* and *Boo the Blob* (Lessons 1 and 2), they should be familiar with the technique for finding area by counting square centimeters.

Figure 5: *Counting the area of a spot*

While students are gathering and recording data, check the results of each group. Although we expect a certain amount of error, the measured area of the three spots for each type of paper towel should be relatively close. In Daniel's data table shown in Figure 6, the results of the three trials for both Brand 1 and Brand 2 are as close to one another as we can expect.

However, the data for Brand 3 looks suspect: the area for the first trial is almost double the area found in the third trial. These differences provide an opportunity to discuss the possibility of making mistakes—perhaps Daniel did not trace or cut out one of the spots as carefully. This is also a good time to point out problems that can occur if the fixed variables are not actually held constant—perhaps the first spot contained too many drops. If possible, this group should perform a fourth trial and use this data to judge which trial contains the most error and replace it with the new trial.

T Type of Towel	A Area of Spot (in ___ sq cm)			
	Trial 1	Trial 2	Trial 3	Median
Brand 1	3 sq cm	2 sq cm	3 sq cm	3 sq cm
Brand 2	11 sq cm	13 sq cm	13 sq cm	13 sq cm
Brand 3	11 sq cm	8 sq cm	6 sq cm	8 sq cm

Figure 6: *Daniel's data table*

Part 4 Graphing the Data

This experiment is a good opportunity for the class to begin using *Centimeter Graph Paper* for drawing bar graphs. Since they will no longer have guidelines to use, you may need to model how to draw bars on this type of graph paper. Be sure students draw their bars on the lines and place the labels indicating the towel brands below the lines not the spaces, as in Figure 7. We use this convention so the transition from bar graphing to point graphing in Unit 7 will be easier.

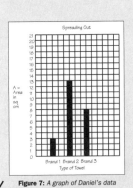

Figure 7: *A graph of Daniel's data*

Part 5 Exploring the Data

Questions 5–7 ask the students to read information directly from the graph. To answer *Questions 8* and *9*, on the other hand, most students will probably want to do some additional experimentation and may take an entire period to find their answers. It is a good idea for students to work on these questions in groups before discussing them with the class. Students often find many different ways to solve problems, and the groups may come up with several possibilities. Try to discuss the advantages and disadvantages of each method.

Let students experiment with the towels and eyedroppers as they develop their solutions. A typical student response to *Question 9* is given by Juanita below. Note that Juanita made use of the spots from her original investigation and multiplication.

Juanita's response: *I would take my middle test sample and on a new sheet I would trace as many circles as I could as close together as I could. Enough to fill the whole sheet. Then I would count how many circles I had and multiply that # by 3 drops to get my estimate.*

Question 10 continues with the ideas explored in *Question 9.* Two answers to this question are probable: (1) The towel with the tallest bar will soak up the most water, or (2) the towel with the shortest bar will soak up the most water. These opposing views can lead to a lively class discussion. Those students who defend the first position probably believe that "bigger is better." However, the discussion should result in the generalization that the towel with the shortest bar is the better "picker upper." On this towel, the three drops of water are concentrated in the smallest area, leaving more of the paper towel to soak up more water.

Journal Prompt

What is area?

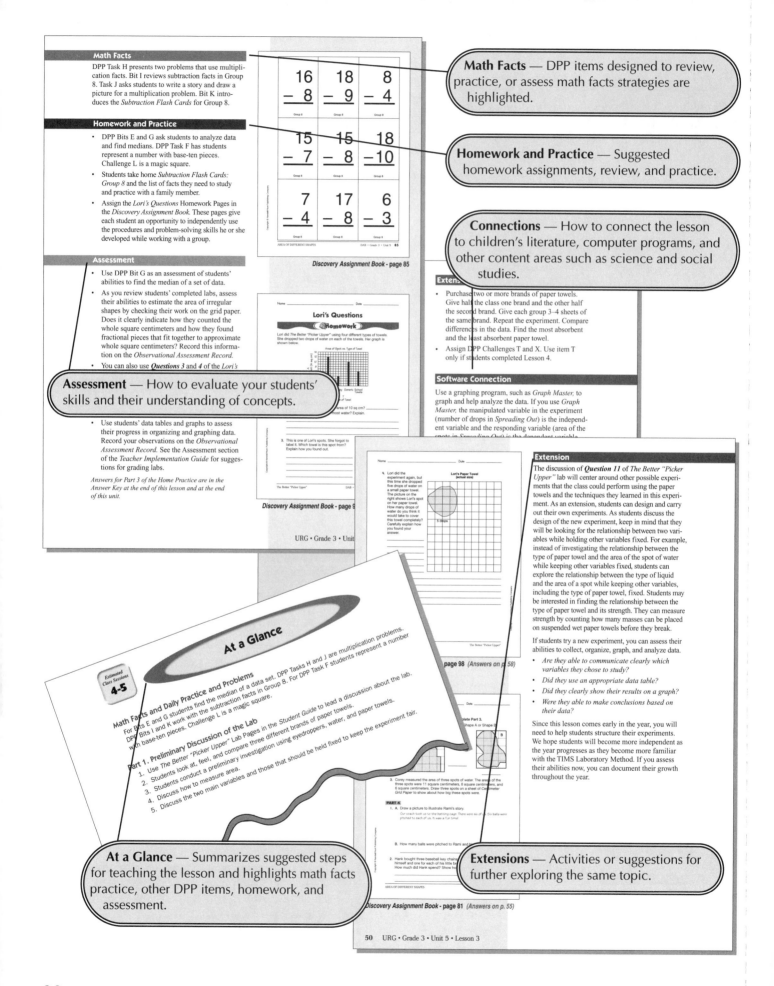

Math Facts

DPP Task H presents two problems that use multiplication facts. Bit I reviews subtraction facts in Group 8. Task J asks students to write a story and draw a picture for a multiplication problem. Bit K introduces the *Subtraction Flash Cards* for Group 8.

Homework and Practice

• DPP Bits E and G ask students to analyze data and find medians. DPP Task F has students represent a number with base-ten pieces. Challenge L is a magic square.

• Students take home *Subtraction Flash Cards: Group 8* and the list of facts they need to study and practice with a family member.

• Assign the *Lori's Questions* Homework Pages in the *Discovery Assignment Book*. These pages give each student an opportunity to independently use the procedures and problem-solving skills he or she developed while working with a group.

Assessment

• Use DPP Bit G as an assessment of students' abilities to find the median of a set of data.

• As you review students' completed labs, assess their abilities to estimate the area of irregular shapes by checking their work on the grid paper. Does it clearly indicate how they counted the whole square centimeters and how they found fractional pieces that fit together to approximate whole square centimeters? Record this information on the *Observational Assessment Record*.

• You can also use *Questions 3* and *4* of the *Lori's*

• Use students' data tables and graphs to assess their progress in organizing and graphing data. Record your observations on the *Observational Assessment Record*. See the Assessment section of the *Teacher Implementation Guide* for suggestions for grading labs.

Answers for Part 3 of the Home Practice are in the Answer Key at the end of this lesson and at the end of this unit.

Discovery Assignment Book - page 85

Discovery Assignment Book - page 9[]

URG • Grade 3 • Unit

Extension

• Purchase two or more brands of paper towels. Give half the class one brand and the other half the second brand. Give each group 3–4 sheets of the same brand. Repeat the experiment. Compare differences in the data. Find the most absorbent and the least absorbent paper towel.

• Assign DPP Challenges T and X. Use item T only if students completed Lesson 4.

Software Connection

Use a graphing program, such as *Graph Master*, to graph and help analyze the data. If you use *Graph Master*, the manipulated variable in the experiment (number of drops in *Spreading Out*) is the independent variable and the responding variable (area of the []

Extension

The discussion of *Question 11* of *The Better "Picker Upper"* lab will center around other possible experiments that the class could perform using the paper towels and the techniques they learned in this experiment. As an extension, students can design and carry out their own experiments. As students discuss the design of the new experiment, keep in mind that they will be looking for the relationship between two variables while holding other variables fixed. For example, instead of investigating the relationship between the type of paper towel and the area of the spot of water while keeping other variables fixed, students can explore the relationship between the type of liquid and the area of a spot while keeping other variables, including the type of paper towel, fixed. Students may be interested in finding the relationship between the type of paper towel and its strength. They can measure strength by counting how many masses can be placed on suspended wet paper towels before they break.

If students try a new experiment, you can assess their abilities to collect, organize, graph, and analyze data.

• *Are they able to communicate clearly which variables they chose to study?*
• *Did they use an appropriate data table?*
• *Did they clearly show their results on a graph?*
• *Were they able to make conclusions based on their data?*

Since this lesson comes early in the year, you will need to help students structure their experiments. We hope students will become more independent as the year progresses as they become more familiar with the TIMS Laboratory Method. If you assess their abilities now, you can document their growth throughout the year.

At a Glance

Estimated Class Sessions
4-5

Math Facts and Daily Practice and Problems
For Bits E and G students find the median of a data set. DPP Tasks H and J are multiplication problems. DPP Bits I and K work with the subtraction facts in Group 8. For DPP Task F students represent a number with base-ten pieces. Challenge L is a magic square.

Part 1. Preliminary Discussion of the Lab
1. Use *The Better "Picker Upper"* Lab Pages in the *Student Guide* to lead a discussion about the lab.
2. Students look at, feel, and compare three different brands of paper towels.
3. Students conduct a preliminary investigation using eyedroppers, water, and paper towels.
4. Discuss how to measure area.
5. Discuss the two main variables and those that should be held fixed to keep the experiment fair.

page 98 *(Answers on p. 58)*

Discovery Assignment Book - page 81 *(Answers on p. 55)*

50   URG • Grade 3 • Unit 5 • Lesson 3

Lesson Guide for the Adventure Book

The Lesson guide is a how-to manual explaining what you need for each lesson and what it involves.

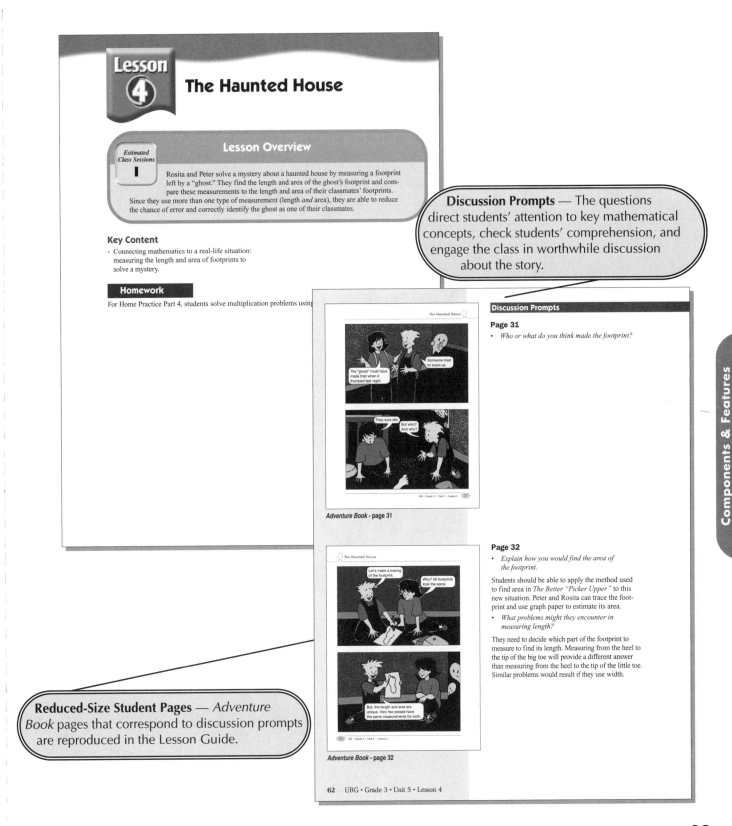

Discussion Prompts — The questions direct students' attention to key mathematical concepts, check students' comprehension, and engage the class in worthwhile discussion about the story.

Reduced-Size Student Pages — *Adventure Book* pages that correspond to discussion prompts are reproduced in the Lesson Guide.

Student Pages

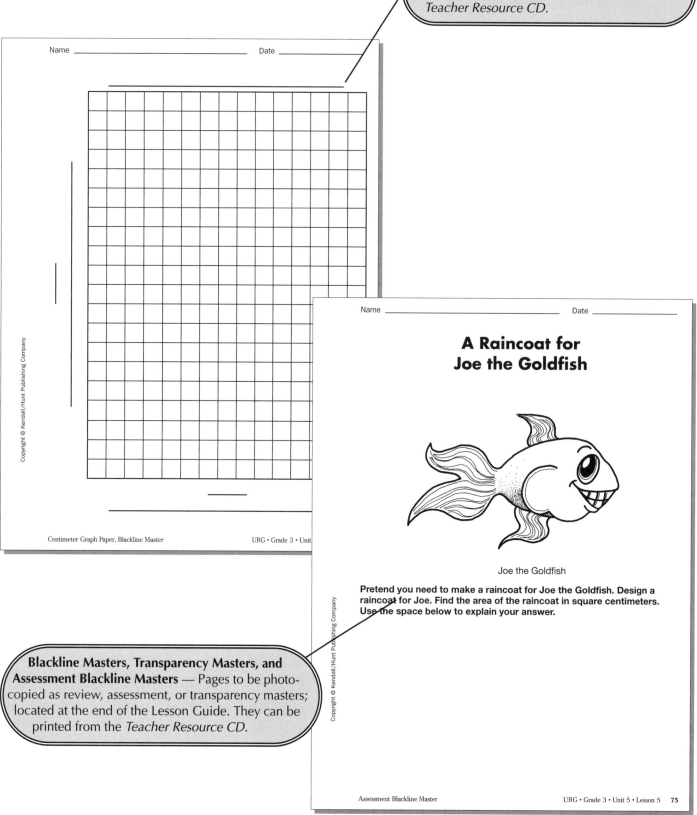

Name _____ Date _____

Copyright © Kendall/Hunt Publishing Company

Centimeter Graph Paper, Blackline Master   URG • Grade 3 • Unit

Name _____ Date _____

A Raincoat for Joe the Goldfish

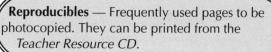

Joe the Goldfish

Pretend you need to make a raincoat for Joe the Goldfish. Design a raincoat for Joe. Find the area of the raincoat in square centimeters. Use the space below to explain your answer.

Copyright © Kendall/Hunt Publishing Company

Assessment Blackline Master   URG • Grade 3 • Unit 5 • Lesson 5   75

Answer Key

An Answer Key at the end of each lesson provides answers to questions in the *Student Guide, Discovery Assignment Book,* and *Unit Resource Guide* pages. Reduced pages showing the questions are provided beside the answers.

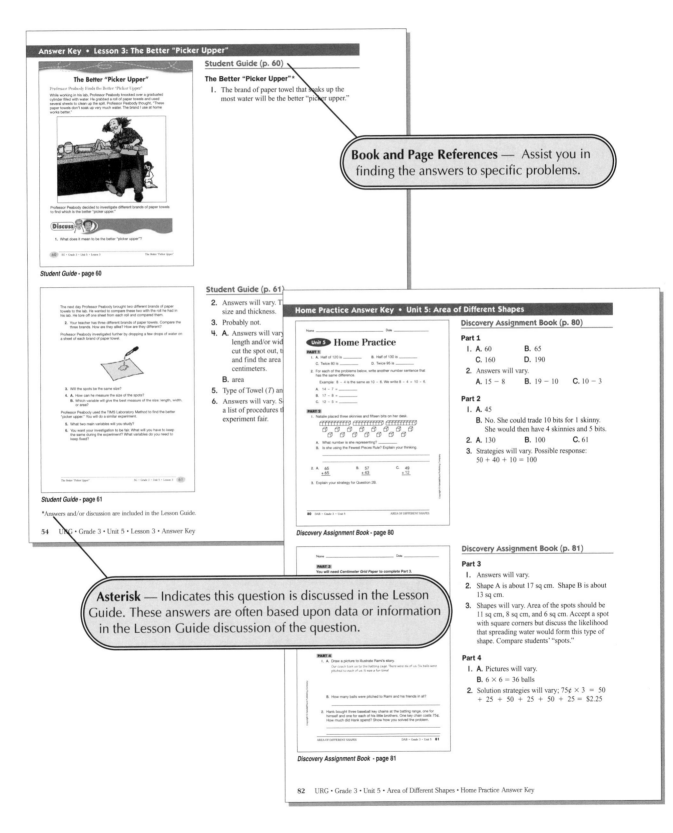

Book and Page References — Assist you in finding the answers to specific problems.

Asterisk — Indicates this question is discussed in the Lesson Guide. These answers are often based upon data or information in the Lesson Guide discussion of the question.

TEACHER IMPLEMENTATION GUIDE

The *Teacher Implementation Guide* is the reference manual for *Math Trailblazers*. Information in the *Teacher Implementation Guide* can be roughly categorized into three groups: general background about *Math Trailblazers*, specific information about the program, and deep background about important math and science concepts.

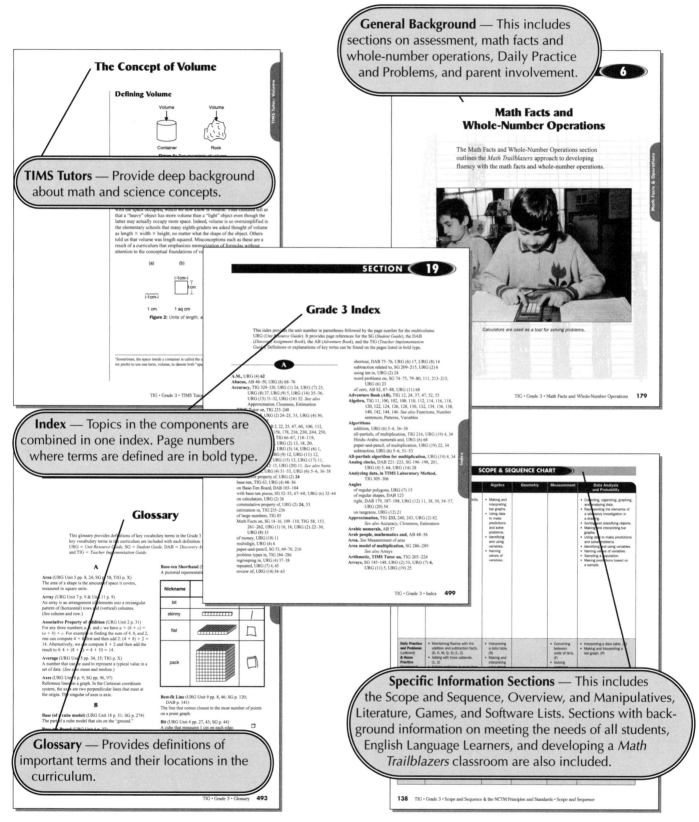

General Background — This includes sections on assessment, math facts and whole-number operations, Daily Practice and Problems, and parent involvement.

TIMS Tutors — Provide deep background about math and science concepts.

Index — Topics in the components are combined in one index. Page numbers where terms are defined are in bold type.

Glossary — Provides definitions of important terms and their locations in the curriculum.

Specific Information Sections — This includes the Scope and Sequence, Overview, and Manipulatives, Literature, Games, and Software Lists. Sections with background information on meeting the needs of all students, English Language Learners, and developing a *Math Trailblazers* classroom are also included.

FACTS RESOURCE GUIDE

The *Facts Resource Guide* provides a single location for all math facts material for the grade and an alternative schedule for classrooms that depart significantly from the suggested pacing of units. Almost all student materials in the *Facts Resource Guide* are also located in the *Student Guide, Discovery Assignment Book,* or *Unit Resource Guides.*

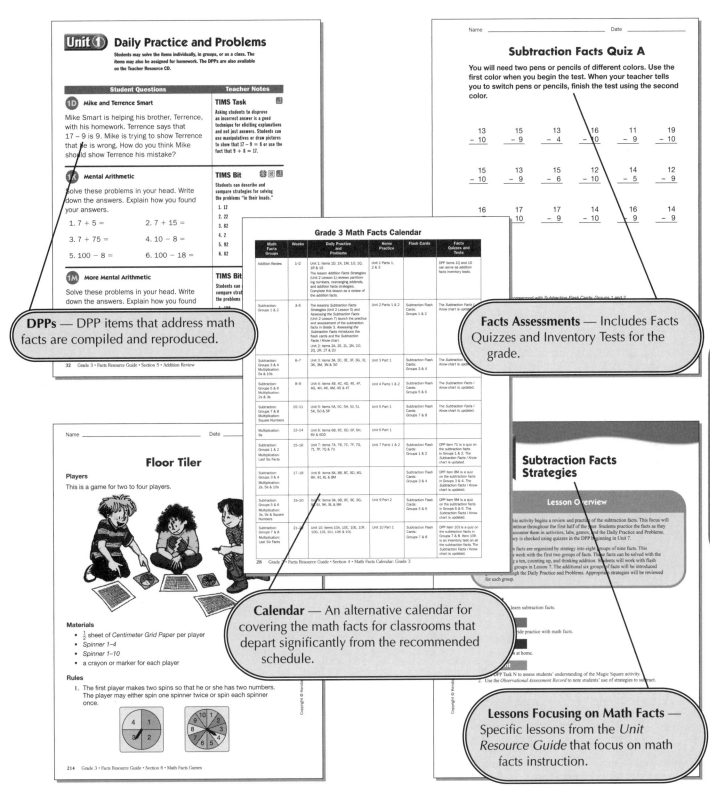

DPPs — DPP items that address math facts are compiled and reproduced.

Facts Assessments — Includes Facts Quizzes and Inventory Tests for the grade.

Calendar — An alternative calendar for covering the math facts for classrooms that depart significantly from the recommended schedule.

Lessons Focusing on Math Facts — Specific lessons from the *Unit Resource Guide* that focus on math facts instruction.

Components & Features

The *Teacher Resource CD* provides key items from other components of the curriculum. This CD includes: Letters Home (Spanish and English); Daily Practice and Problems (with and without teacher notes); *Observational Assessment Record* pages; *Individual Assessment Record Sheet;* all Blackline Masters and Transparency Masters; Teacher Rubrics and Student Rubrics; frequently used masters; and all the *Facts Resource Guide.*

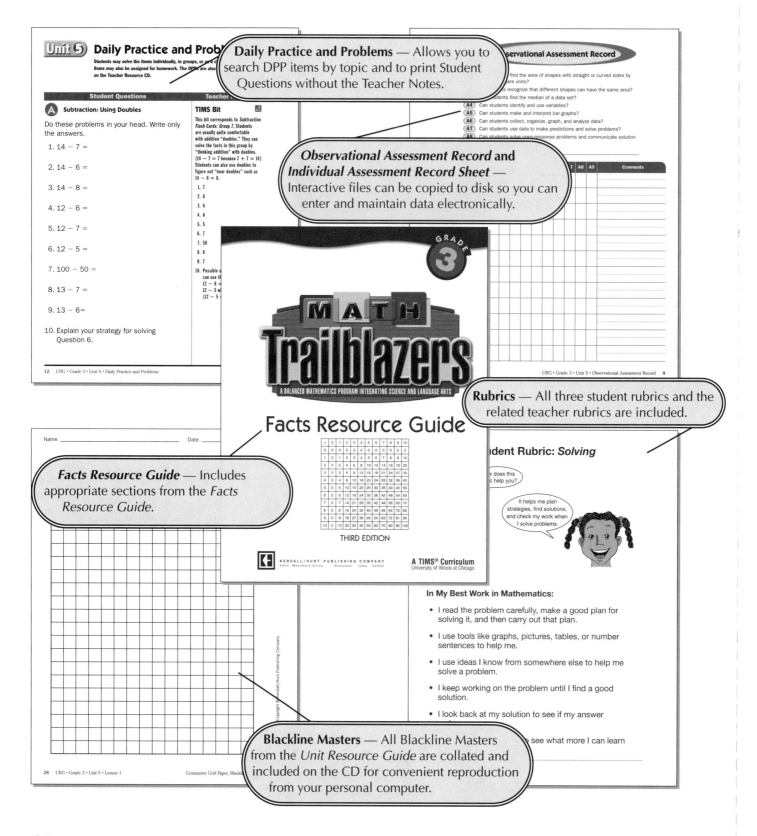

Daily Practice and Problems — Allows you to search DPP items by topic and to print Student Questions without the Teacher Notes.

Observational Assessment Record and Individual Assessment Record Sheet — Interactive files can be copied to disk so you can enter and maintain data electronically.

Facts Resource Guide — Includes appropriate sections from the *Facts Resource Guide.*

Rubrics — All three student rubrics and the related teacher rubrics are included.

Blackline Masters — All Blackline Masters from the *Unit Resource Guide* are collated and included on the CD for convenient reproduction from your personal computer.

The *Student Guide* contains most nonconsumable student materials, including activities, labs, and games.

Unit 5

Area of Different Shapes

	Student Guide	Discovery Assignment Book	Adventure Book	Unit Resource Guide*
Lesson 1				
Measuring Area	●	●		
Lesson 2				
Boo the Blob		●		
Lesson 3				
The Better "Picker Upper"	●	●		
Lesson 4				
The Haunted House			●	
Lesson 5				
Joe the Goldfish				●
Lesson 6				
Using Number Sense at the Book Sale	●			

Unit Resource Guide pages are from the teacher materials.

57

Unit Opener — A list of lesson numbers, names, and locations in the curriculum materials.

Components & Features

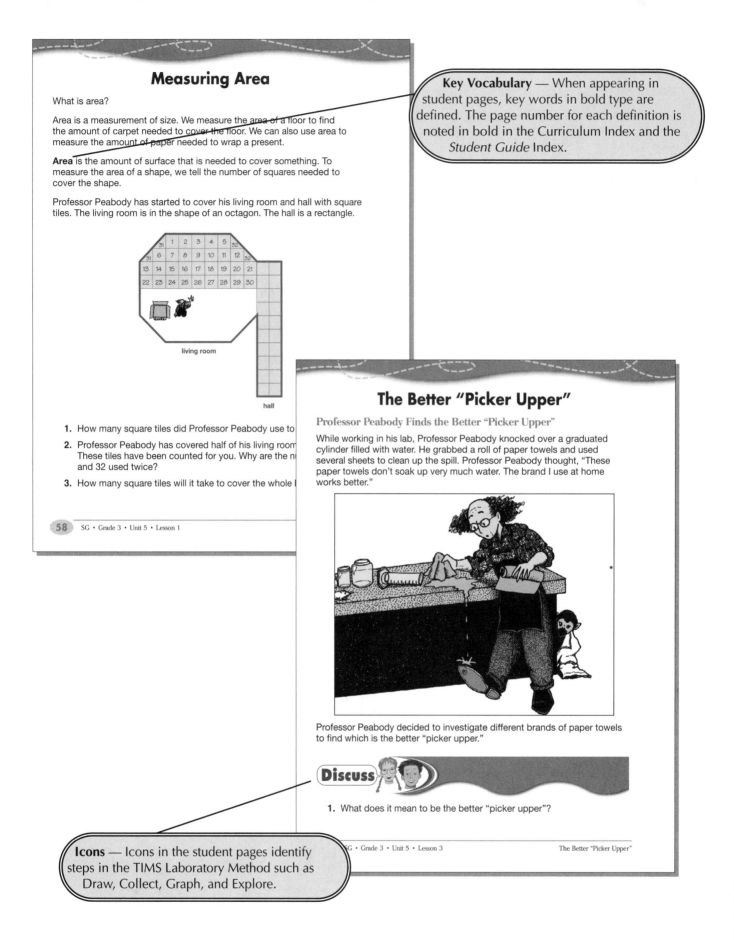

Measuring Area

What is area?

Area is a measurement of size. We measure the area of a floor to find the amount of carpet needed to cover the floor. We can also use area to measure the amount of paper needed to wrap a present.

Area is the amount of surface that is needed to cover something. To measure the area of a shape, we tell the number of squares needed to cover the shape.

Professor Peabody has started to cover his living room and hall with square tiles. The living room is in the shape of an octagon. The hall is a rectangle.

living room

hall

1. How many square tiles did Professor Peabody use to

2. Professor Peabody has covered half of his living roo These tiles have been counted for you. Why are the n and 32 used twice?

3. How many square tiles will it take to cover the whole

Key Vocabulary — When appearing in student pages, key words in bold type are defined. The page number for each definition is noted in bold in the Curriculum Index and the *Student Guide* Index.

The Better "Picker Upper"

Professor Peabody Finds the Better "Picker Upper"

While working in his lab, Professor Peabody knocked over a graduated cylinder filled with water. He grabbed a roll of paper towels and used several sheets to clean up the spill. Professor Peabody thought, "These paper towels don't soak up very much water. The brand I use at home works better."

Professor Peabody decided to investigate different brands of paper towels to find which is the better "picker upper."

Discuss

1. What does it mean to be the better "picker upper"?

Icons — Icons in the student pages identify steps in the TIMS Laboratory Method such as Draw, Collect, Graph, and Explore.

Price List

Title	Author	Price
Betsy-Tacy	Maud Hart Lovelace	20¢
Mr. Popper's Penguins	Richard and Florence Atwater	25¢
Ramón Makes a Trade	Barbara Ritchie	45¢
Superfudge	Judy Blume	50¢
Fudge-a-mania	Judy Blume	50¢
Charlie and the Chocolate Factory	Roald Dahl	75¢
James and the Giant Peach	Roald Dahl	75¢
Ramona Quimby, Age 8	Beverly Cleary	95¢
Ramona and Her Father	Beverly Cleary	95¢
Children of the Fire	Harriette Gillem Robinet	$1.00
Amazing Grace	Mary Hoffman	$1.50
Little House Books	Laura Ingalls Wilder	4 for $1.00

1. Pretend you are going to the book store with quarters.
   A. Do you need three or four quarters to buy *Ra____ Age 8?*
   B. How many quarters do you need to buy *Bets____*

2. Susie has $1.00. Can she buy *Ramón Makes a T____* Why or why not?

3. James has $1.00. Can he buy *Betsy-Tacy, Mr. P____ Fudge-a-mania?* Why or why not?

4. Tino has $1.25. Does he have enough money to ____ *Trade* and *Ramona and Her Father?* Why or why____

Using Number Sense at the Book Sale   SG • Grade____

Grade 3

Index

This index provides page references for the *Student Guide.* Definitions or explanations of key terms can be found on the pages listed in bold.

3-D objects, 266–272
  drawing, 268–271

Ⓐ

Addend, 15
Addition
  with base-ten pieces, 52–53, 67–68
  facts, 7, 14–22, 109–110
  paper-and-pencil, 53, 69–70, 209–210, 213–215
Addition and subtraction, review, 209–215
Area, 58–59, 66, 136, 163–166, 169, 171, 273, 275–276, 283
  of irregular shapes, 59, 59–61
  square centimeters, 59–61

Ⓑ

Bar graph, 3–6. *See also* Labs
  interpreting, 17, 32–33
  making, 17
  to a point graph, 83–84
Base, of a cube model, **274**
Base-Ten Board, 44
Base-ten pieces, 44–53
  addition with, 52–53, 66–68
  representing decimals, 218–221
  subtraction with, 71–72
Base-Ten Recording Sheet, 44
Base-ten shorthand, 44–53, 46–53, 67–68, 210
  representing decimals, 218–221
Best-fit line, 120

Ⓒ

Centimeters, square, 59–61
Clocks
  history of, 194–195
  telling time, 54–55, 196–198, 201
  water, 199–200
Congruent, 168, 253
Connecting cubes, building with, 104
Coordinates, 97–102, 105–108, 136
Cube, 270
  skeleton of, 271–272
Cube model problems, 276, 281
Cube models/plans, 273–284
Cubic centimeters, 236

Ⓓ

Data, patterns in, 83
Data collection and analysis, 85, 98, 111, 124, 172. *See also* Labs
Data table, 4, 9, 17–18, 126, 131. *See also* Labs
  predictions using, 137
Decimal fractions, 218–221, 219
Decimals
  and common fractions, 218–219
  representing with base-ten pieces, 218–221
  representing with base-ten shorthand, 218–221
Designs, from many cultures, 132–134
Digit cards, 7
Dissections (in geometry), 158–175
Division, 148, 152–154
  fact families, **153**
  problem solving, 295–297
  symbols for, 153
  using Mathhoppers, 88–94

Components & Features

DISCOVERY ASSIGNMENT BOOK

The *Discovery Assignment Book* contains consumable student materials for activities, labs, and homework.

Name and Date Lines — Since the *Discovery Assignment Book* is consumable, a name and date line has been provided.

The Home Practice is a series of problems that supplements homework assignments.

Each Home Practice is divided into several parts. Each part can be assigned separately.

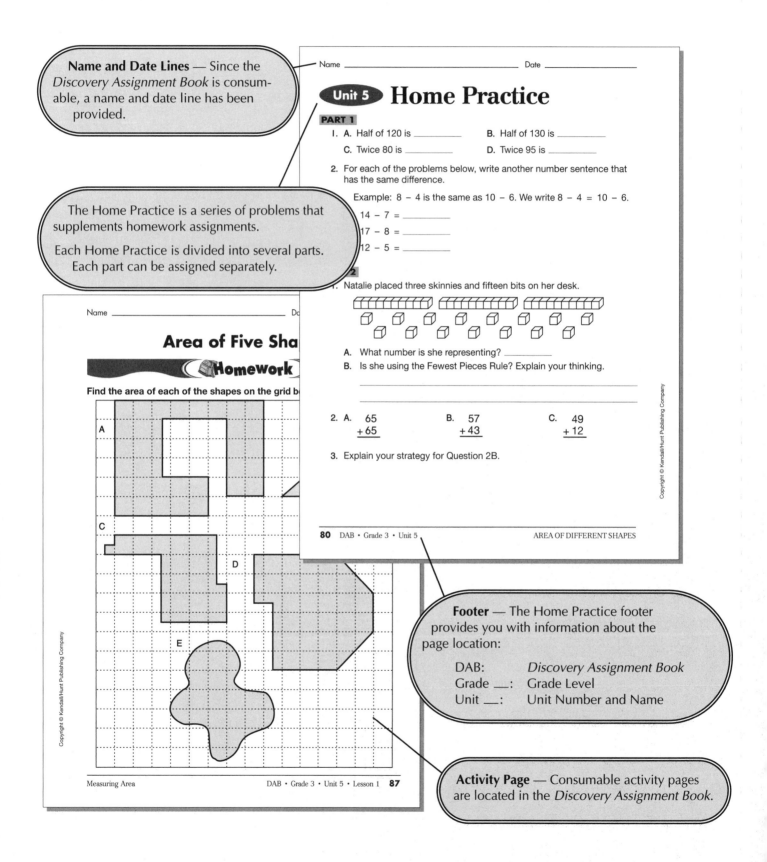

Name _____ Date _____

Unit 5 Home Practice

PART 1

1. A. Half of 120 is _____   B. Half of 130 is _____
   C. Twice 80 is _____   D. Twice 95 is _____

2. For each of the problems below, write another number sentence that has the same difference.

   Example: 8 − 4 is the same as 10 − 6. We write 8 − 4 = 10 − 6.

   14 − 7 = _____

   17 − 8 = _____

   12 − 5 = _____

2

1. Natalie placed three skinnies and fifteen bits on her desk.

   A. What number is she representing? _____
   B. Is she using the Fewest Pieces Rule? Explain your thinking.

   _____

   _____

2. A. 65   B. 57   C. 49
       + 65   + 43   + 12

3. Explain your strategy for Question 2B.

Copyright © Kendall/Hunt Publishing Company

80   DAB · Grade 3 · Unit 5   AREA OF DIFFERENT SHAPES

Name _____ Da

Area of Five Sha

Homework

Find the area of each of the shapes on the grid b

A

C

D

E

Copyright © Kendall/Hunt Publishing Company

Measuring Area   DAB · Grade 3 · Unit 5 · Lesson 1   **87**

Footer — The Home Practice footer provides you with information about the page location:

DAB: *Discovery Assignment Book*
Grade __: Grade Level
Unit __: Unit Number and Name

Activity Page — Consumable activity pages are located in the *Discovery Assignment Book*.

ADVENTURE BOOK

Illustrated stories that present mathematics and science concepts.

QUICK REFERENCE GUIDE

What I Want to Know	Where to Find It
What does this lesson cover?	*Unit Resource Guide*–Unit Outline *Unit Resource Guide*–Lesson Guide *Teacher Implementation Guide*–Overview
What are the "big ideas" in this lesson or the entire unit?	*Unit Resource Guide*–Unit Outline *Unit Resource Guide*–Lesson Guide–Key Content *Unit Resource Guide*–Unit Background *Teacher Implementation Guide*–Overview
What do I need to prepare for this lesson?	*Unit Resource Guide*–Unit Outline–Preparing for Upcoming Lessons *Unit Resource Guide*–Lesson Guide–Before the Activity *Unit Resource Guide*–Lesson Guide–Materials List
What manipulatives do I need for this lesson?	*Unit Resource Guide*–Unit Outline *Unit Resource Guide*–Lesson Guide–Materials List
What have students covered on this topic in previous grades or previous units?	*Unit Resource Guide*–Lesson Guide–Curriculum Sequence— Before This Unit *Teacher Implementation Guide*–Scope and Sequence *Teacher Implementation Guide*–Overview
What will students cover on this topic in later units?	*Unit Resource Guide*–Lesson Guide–Curriculum Sequence— After This Unit *Teacher Implementation Guide*–Scope and Sequence *Teacher Implementation Guide*–Overview
How do I teach this lesson?	*Unit Resource Guide*–Lesson Guide
Where is a quick summary of each lesson to help teach the lesson?	*Unit Resource Guide*–Lesson Guide–At a Glance
How long will it take to do this lesson (or the entire unit)?	*Unit Resource Guide*–Unit Outline–Estimated Class Sessions *Unit Resource Guide*–Lesson Guide *Teacher Implementation Guide*–Overview
How do I deal with potential trouble spots?	*Unit Resource Guide*–Lesson Guide–TIMS Tip *Unit Resource Guide*–Lesson Guide–Content Notes *Teacher Implementation Guide*–TIMS Tutors
How do I organize my class to do this lesson?	*Unit Resource Guide*–Lesson Guide
Where are the Blackline and Transparency Masters?	*Unit Resource Guide*–Letter Home *Unit Resource Guide*–Lesson Guide *Teacher Resource CD*
Where are Journal Prompts?	*Unit Resource Guide*–Lesson Guide
Where are the remediation activities?	*Unit Resource Guide*–Daily Practice and Problems *Unit Resource Guide*–Unit Outline–Optional Review Lessons *Facts Resource Guide*–Addition and Subtraction Math Facts Review section

What I Want to Know	Where to Find It
Where is the skill practice and review?	*Unit Resource Guide*–Daily Practice and Problems *Student Guide*–Homework sections *Discovery Assignment Book*–Home Practice *Facts Resource Guide*–Daily Practice and Problems, Home Practice, Addition and Subtraction Math Facts Review section *Teacher Resource CD*
Where are the enrichment activities?	*Unit Resource Guide*–Lesson Guide–Extensions *Unit Resource Guide*–Daily Practice and Problems–Challenges *Unit Resource Guide*–Optional Lessons
What information is available for parents?	*Teacher Implementation Guide*–Parents and *Math Trailblazers*–Parent Brochure; Information for Parents: Math Facts Philosophy (English and Spanish) *Unit Resource Guide*–Letter Home *Unit Resource Guide*–Unit 2–Information for Parents: Math Facts Philosophy
What should I assign as homework?	*Unit Resource Guide*–Lesson Guide–Homework and Practice, At a Glance *Discovery Assignment Book*–Home Practice
How do I assess students' progress?	*Unit Resource Guide*–Unit Background–Assessment Indicators *Unit Resource Guide*–Daily Practice and Problems–Facts Quizzes *Unit Resource Guide*–Observational Assessment Record *Unit Resource Guide*–Assessment Units *Unit Resource Guide*–Assessment Lessons *Unit Resource Guide*–Lesson Guide–Assessment Pages *Unit Resource Guide*–Lesson Guide–Assessment *Unit Resource Guide*–Lesson Guide–Journal Prompts *Teacher Implementation Guide*–Assessment section *Teacher Implementation Guide*–Assessment section–Individual Assessment Record Sheet *Teacher Resource CD*
Where do I find connections to literature, computer software, and other content areas such as social studies and science?	*Unit Resource Guide*–Unit Outline *Unit Resource Guide*–Lesson Guide–Connections *Teacher Implementation Guide*–Literature List *Teacher Implementation Guide*–Software List
How do I find background information about concepts underlying each activity?	*Unit Resource Guide*–Unit Background *Unit Resource Guide*–Lesson Guide–Content Notes *Teacher Implementation Guide*–TIMS Tutors
How does this activity or unit fit into the "big picture" for my grade?	*Teacher Implementation Guide*–Overview *Teacher Implementation Guide*–Scope and Sequence *Unit Resource Guide*–Unit Background *Unit Resource Guide*–Lesson Guide–Curriculum Sequence

Components & Features

What I Want to Know	Where to Find It
What will my students do this year?	*Teacher Implementation Guide*–Overview *Teacher Implementation Guide*–Scope and Sequence
What manipulatives do I need for the entire year?	*Teacher Implementation Guide*–Manipulatives List
Where is the scope and sequence?	*Teacher Implementation Guide*–Scope and Sequence
Does this curriculum match my district's objectives?	*Teacher Implementation Guide*–Scope and Sequence & the NCTM *Principles and Standards* *Teacher Implementation Guide*–Overview *Teacher Implementation Guide*–Assessment section–*Individual Assessment Record Sheet* *Unit Resource Guide*–Unit Background–Assessment Indicators
Where is the *Student Guide* Index?	*Student Guide*–Index
Where is the index for the curriculum?	*Teacher Implementation Guide*–Index

Overview

The Overview presents brief descriptions and lists of featured
concepts. It provides a quick reference to locate concepts
and activities.

Students solve a problem using money.

Overview

Overview

The overview reflects the scope, sequence, and tone of the third-grade curriculum. The fundamental assumption of all the units is that math concepts and skills are best acquired through active involvement in problem solving. Thus, problem-solving activities are pervasive. Mathematics content—measurement, graphing, computation, logical reasoning, fractions, data analysis, geometry, and estimation—is included within problems in each unit. The TIMS Laboratory Method, used in laboratory experiments throughout the curriculum, incorporates experiences with some of the important tools for investigation and experimentation: drawing a picture, measuring, collecting and organizing data, constructing a graph, and posing and answering questions about the data.

Units also include:

- Suggestions for journal writing;
- Recommended homework assignments for most lessons;
- Parent letters that discuss the important ideas within the unit and provide suggestions for home activities that support lessons in school;
- Assessment, both through formal instruments and through the informal observations that a discourse-rich curriculum makes possible.

Many units include *Adventure Book* stories and recommendations for using related trade books and children's literature. A recommended software list accompanies most units. Some of the units in the first semester include activities that review materials from second grade so students new to the curriculum will have the necessary skills and concepts for third grade.

Home Practice. The Home Practice in the *Discovery Assignment Book* consists of short problems that can be assigned as homework or assessment throughout the unit. The Home Practice includes skill practice and problems that are related to the current unit or previous units. Problems can be solved in many ways with a variety of tools including calculators, data tables and charts, graphs, manipulatives, and paper-and-pencil strategies.

Daily Practice and Problems. The Daily Practice and Problems (DPP) is a vital component of the curriculum and can be found at the beginning of each unit in the *Unit Resource Guide* and the *Teacher Resource CD*. These short exercises provide ongoing practice and review. Two DPP items are provided for each class session. TIMS Bits are short items that provide quick review of a topic or focused practice on a specific skill. TIMS Tasks and TIMS

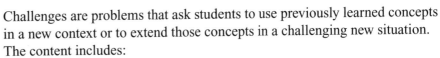

Challenges are problems that ask students to use previously learned concepts in a new context or to extend those concepts in a challenging new situation. The content includes:

- estimation
- computation
- number sense
- using data
- addition facts review
- subtraction and multiplication facts practice and assessment

- counting and numeration
- money
- geometry
- problem solving

- time
- logic
- measurement
- using graphs

Summaries, pacing suggestions, and outlines of the third-grade units follow.

Unit 1: Sampling and Classifying · 10 Sessions

Unit Summary

This unit introduces significant mathematics content and establishes a positive classroom atmosphere for the beginning of the school year. Activities are adaptable to a range of abilities. Working cooperatively in small groups and handling manipulatives appropriately are encouraged.

The first activity is an investigation of the number of letters in the first names of classmates. In the lab *First Names*, students apply basic techniques of data collection and analysis—organizing data in tables, making graphs, and discussing the meaning of results—in a familiar context. Students also solve problems involving addition and subtraction, practice mental computation while playing a game, and solve puzzles to develop logical reasoning skills.

In the unit's second lab, students create and study a population. In the lab *Kind of Bean,* students take a sample of a population of beans and make predictions using the TIMS Laboratory Method. The unit ends with the Adventure Book, *You Can't Do That,* a cautionary tale about group work and individual responsibility. The DPP for this unit reviews the addition facts.

Major Concept Focus

- TIMS Laboratory Method
- variables and values
- classification
- multiple solution strategies
- communicating problem-solving solutions
- Game: mental computation with addition
- word problems
- bar graphs
- sampling
- predicting
- logical reasoning
- addition facts review
- *Adventure Book:* working in groups

Pacing Suggestions

- The pacing schedule for the year assumes that mathematics instruction begins on the first day of school and that students receive 60 minutes of mathematics instruction each day. See the *Teacher Implementation Guide* for more information on Pacing. The first lesson is a data collection activity set in a context specifically designed to engage students on the first day of school.
- Take advantage of connections to science. Lesson 3 *Kind of Bean* is a laboratory investigation that uses science skills. Students can collect data for the lab during science time.
- It is not necessary to stop and make sure students have mastered each skill before moving on to Unit 2, since later units will review and extend the skills and concepts developed in Unit 1. Students will also review skills in the Daily Practice and Problems in each *Unit Resource Guide* and Home Practice in the *Discovery Assignment Book.*

The table below shows resources that provide information on the development of concepts and skills throughout the year.

Resources for Pacing	Location
Curriculum Sequence	In Most Lesson Guides
Unit Scope and Sequence	*Teacher Implementation Guide*
Daily Practice and Problems and Home Practice Scope and Sequence	*Teacher Implementation Guide*
Individual Assessment Record Sheet	*Teacher Implementation Guide*

Preparing for Upcoming Lessons

Three types of beans, such as black, pinto, and navy, are needed for Lesson 3.

Place connecting cubes in an accessible location so students can explore them before beginning Unit 2.

Unit Planner

KEY: SG = Student Guide, DAB = Discovery Assignment Book, AB = Adventure Book, URG = Unit Resource Guide, DPP = Daily Practice and Problems, HP = Home Practice (found in Discovery Assignment Book), and TIG = Teacher Implementation Guide.

	Lesson Information	Supplies	Copies/Transparencies
Lesson 1 **First Names** URG Pages 23–39 SG Pages 2–6 DAB Pages 5–8 DPP A–F *Estimated Class Sessions* **3**	**Lab** Students gather, organize, graph, and analyze data about the length of first names. **Math Facts** DPP Task D provides practice with math facts. **Homework** Students complete *Family Names Data Table* and *Family Names Graph* Homework Pages in the *Discovery Assignment Book.* **Assessment** Students complete the *Lisa's Class Graph* and *Careless Professor Peabody* Assessment Blackline Masters.	• 1 self-adhesive note per student	• 1 copy of *Lisa's Class Graph* URG Page 34 per student • 1 copy of *Careless Professor Peabody* URG Page 35 per student • 1 transparency of *First Names Data Table and Graph* DAB Page 5, optional
Lesson 2 **Turn Over** URG Pages 40–47 SG Page 7 DPP G–H HP Parts 1–2 *Estimated Class Sessions* **1**	**Game** Students practice mental computation with addition while playing a simple game. **Math Facts** Home Practice Parts 1 and 2 provide practice with math facts. **Homework** Assign Home Practice Parts 1 and 2.	• 10 index cards per student pair, optional • playing cards, optional	• 1 copy of *Digit Cards 0–9* URG Pages 45–46 copied back to back per student pair • 1 transparency of *Digit Cards 0–9* URG Page 45
Lesson 3 **Kind of Bean** URG Pages 48–63 SG Pages 8–10 DAB Pages 9–13 DPP I–N HP Parts 3–4 *Estimated Class Sessions* **3**	**Lab** A population is simulated with beans. Students take a sample and make predictions using the TIMS Laboratory Method. **Math Facts** DPP Bits K and M provide practice with math facts. **Homework** 1. Assign the *Toni's Candy Grab* Homework Page. 2. Assign Parts 3 and 4 of the Home Practice. **Assessment** 1. Students complete the *Who's Right?* Assessment Pages. 2. Use the *Observational Assessment Record* to note students' abilities to collect, organize, graph, and analyze data.	• collection of 3 types of beans per student pair • 1 small container such as margarine tub or yogurt cup per student pair • 1 teaspoon per student pair • 1 larger scoop or spoon per student pair, optional • large container of mixed beans • 3 kinds of beans such as 1 lb of black beans, 2 lbs of navy beans, and 4 lbs of pinto beans	• 1 copy of *Who's Right?* URG Pages 57–59 per student • 1 transparency of the *Kind of Bean* graph DAB Page 10 • 1 copy of *Observational Assessment Record* URG Pages 11–12 to be used throughout this unit

	Lesson Information	**Supplies**	**Copies/ Transparencies**
Lesson 4 **Line Math Puzzles** URG Pages 64–71 DAB Pages 15–19 DPP O–P *Estimated Class Sessions* **1**	**Activity** Students design and solve puzzles to develop logical reasoning skills and practice addition. **Math Facts** DPP Bit O provides math facts practice. **Homework** Assign the *Your Own Line Math Puzzle* Homework Page. **Assessment** Use DPP Task P as an assessment.	• scissors	• blank transparency, optional
Lesson 5 **You Can't Do That** URG Pages 72–78 AB Pages 1–11 DPP Q–R *Estimated Class Sessions* **1**	**Adventure Book** Students discuss the difference between cooperative learning and cheating. **Math Facts** Use DPP Bit Q to assess students' fluency with the addition facts. **Assessment** Use DPP Bit Q to assess students' fluency with the addition facts. Record the information on the *Observational Assessment Record.* For students who need more work with the addition facts, see the Addition and Subtraction Math Facts Review section in the *Grade 3 Facts Resource Guide.*		
Lesson 6 **A Sample of Problems** URG Pages 79–84 SG Page 11 DPP S–T *Estimated Class Sessions* **1**	**Activity** Students solve word problems involving addition and subtraction. The context of the problems is based on the first three lessons. **Math Facts** DPP Bit S is a quiz on the addition facts. **Assessment** 1. Use DPP Bit S to assess fluency with the addition facts. Record the information in the *Observational Assessment Record.* 2. Transfer appropriate documentation from the Unit 1 *Observational Assessment Record* to the students' *Individual Assessment Record Sheets.*		• 1 copy of *Individual Assessment Record Sheet* TIG Assessment section per student, previously copied for use throughout the year

Overview

Unit 2: Strategies: An Assessment Unit .... 12 Sessions

Unit Summary

This unit provides baseline measures about a broad range of students' mathematical understandings and competencies. The activities include opportunities for teachers to assess students' arithmetic skills, mathematical concepts, and abilities to solve problems and communicate solutions.

Students investigate patterns in addition and subtraction sentences for two of the activities. Portfolios of student work are organized during this unit. The information from the formal assessment instruments in this unit will complement samples of student work to provide a comprehensive and balanced picture of students' mathematical understandings near the beginning of the school year.

The unit also includes the Adventure Book, *Yü the Great,* which introduces students to magic squares. The DPP for this unit reviews the subtraction facts for Groups 1 and 2.

Major Concept Focus

- addition and subtraction facts practice
- subtraction facts review for Groups 1 and 2
- number sense
- *Adventure Book:* origin of magic squares
- magic squares
- collecting, organizing, and graphing data
- bar graphs
- interpreting graphs
- Student Rubric: *Knowing*
- communicating problem-solving solutions
- assessment of problem solving

Pacing Suggestions

Students' fluency with the addition and subtraction facts and their abilities to solve problems and communicate their reasoning will determine how quickly the class can proceed through this unit. The following recommendations will help you adapt the unit to your students' needs.

- In Lesson 5 *Subtraction Facts Strategies* and Lesson 7 *Assessing the Subtraction Facts,* students assess their fluency with the subtraction facts and begin a systematic review of facts they need to study. The subtraction facts are divided into eight groups of nine facts each. In this unit they review the subtraction facts in Groups 1 and 2. Work with the remaining groups of facts is distributed throughout the Daily Practice and Problems and Home Practice in each unit. All students should continue learning new concepts and skills while they are working on the facts.

- The math facts program is closely linked to the recommended schedule for teaching lessons. Therefore, classrooms that differ significantly from the suggested pacing will need to make accommodations to ensure that students receive a consistent program of math facts practice and assessment throughout the year. The *Grade 3 Facts Resource Guide* outlines a schedule for the study of the subtraction and multiplication facts in classrooms that move much more slowly through lessons than is recommended in the Lesson Guides. For more information, see the *Grade 3 Facts Resource Guide* and the TIMS Tutor: *Math Facts* in the *Teacher Implementation Guide.*

Unit Planner

	Lesson Information	Supplies	Copies/ Transparencies

Lesson 1

Addition Facts Strategies

URG Pages 28–38
SG Pages 14–15
DAB Pages 25–27
DPP A–D

Estimated Class Sessions
2

Activity
Students partition numbers, rearrange addends, and use strategies with addition facts.

Math Facts
DPP Bit A provides practice with math facts.

Homework
1. Assign the *Switch It!* Homework Page in the *Discovery Assignment Book*.
2. Assign the *Calculator Explorations* Homework Page.

Assessment
Students complete the *Calculator Challenges* Assessment Page.

Supplies:
- 40 connecting cubes per student pair
- 1 calculator per student pair

Copies/Transparencies:
- 1 copy of *Calculator Challenges* URG Page 36 per student
- 1 transparency of *Calculator Explorations* DAB Page 27, optional

Lesson 2

Spinning Sums

URG Pages 39–53
SG Pages 16–18
DAB Pages 29–31
DPP E–H
HP Parts 1–2

Estimated Class Sessions
2

Activity
Students spin two spinners to randomly generate addition sentences. They record these facts in a data table and graph the number of times they spin each sum.

Math Facts
DPP Bit E provides practice with math facts. Parts 1 and 2 of the Home Practice provide addition and subtraction practice.

Homework
Assign Home Practice Parts 1 and 2.

Assessment
Use the *Observational Assessment Record* to note students' abilities to use strategies to add quickly and accurately.

Supplies:
- 1 clear plastic spinner (or pencils with paper clips) per student group
- 1 blank transparency, optional

Copies/Transparencies:
- 1 copy of *Horizontal Bar Graph* URG Page 50 per student group
- 1 transparency of *Spinners 2–9* DAB Page 29
- 1 transparency of *Spinning Sums Data Table* DAB Page 31
- 1 transparency of *Horizontal Bar Graph* URG Page 50
- 1 copy of *Observational Assessment Record* URG Pages 15–16 to be used throughout this unit

Lesson 3

Yü the Great A Chinese Legend

URG Pages 54–63
AB Pages 12–25
DPP I–J
HP Part 3–4

Estimated Class Sessions
1

Adventure Book
This story introduces Lo-shu, a pattern on the back of a turtle, which was the first magic square.

Homework
Assign Parts 3 and 4 of the Home Practice in the *Discovery Assignment Book* for homework.

	Lesson Information	Supplies	Copies/Transparencies
Lesson 4 **Magic Squares** URG Pages 64–72 SG Pages 19–21 DAB Page 33 DPP K–L *Estimated Class Sessions* **1**	**Activity** Students solve magic squares to develop problem-solving and addition skills. **Math Facts** Task L is a line math puzzle. **Homework** Assign the homework in the *Student Guide*.	• scissors • calculators	• blank transparency • 1 transparency of *Digits* DAB Page 33
Lesson 5 **Subtraction Facts Strategies** URG Pages 73–80 SG Pages 22–27 DAB Page 35 DPP M–P *Estimated Class Sessions* **2**	**Activity** Students begin a review of subtraction facts through the use of strategies. **Math Facts** DPP items N and O provide practice with math facts. **Homework** Students play *Nine, Ten* at home. **Assessment** 1. Use DPP Task N to assess students' understanding of the Magic Square activity. 2. Use the *Observational Assessment Record* to note students' use of strategies to subtract.	• 2 clear spinners (or pencils and paper clips) per student pair and 2 for the teacher	• 1 transparency of *Spinners 11–18 and 9–10* DAB Page 35
Lesson 6 **Spinning Differences** URG Pages 81–92 DAB Page 29 DPP Q–T *Estimated Class Sessions* **2**	**Assessment Activity** In this assessment activity, students spin two spinners and randomly generate subtraction sentences to find the most common difference. **Math Facts** DPP items Q, R, and T provide practice with math facts. **Assessment** Use the *TIMS Multidimensional Rubric* to score the activity, focusing on the Knowing dimension.	• 2 clear spinners (or pencil-paper clip substitute) per student pair	• 1 copy of *Spinning Differences* URG Page 90 per student • 1 copy of *Spinning Differences Data Table* URG Page 91 per student • 1 copy of *Horizontal Bar Graph* URG Page 50 per student • 1 transparency or poster of Student Rubric: *Knowing* TIG, Assessment section • 1 copy of *TIMS Multidimensional Rubric* TIG, Assessment section • 1 transparency of *Spinners 2–9* DAB Page 29, optional

(Continued)

Overview

	Lesson Information	Supplies	Copies/ Transparencies

Lesson 7

Assessing the Subtraction Facts

URG Pages 93–104
DAB Pages 37–43
DPP U–V

Estimated Class Sessions
1

Assessment Activity
Students are introduced to the *Subtraction Flash Cards* and the *Subtraction Facts I Know* chart as a means of self-assessment.

Math Facts
DPP Bit U provides practice with addition facts.

Homework
Students take home the flash cards for Group 1 and Group 2 to practice the subtraction facts with a family member.

• 1 envelope for storing flash cards per student

• 1 copy of *Information for Parents: Grade 3 Math Facts Philosophy* URG Pages 13–14 per student

• 1 back-to-back copy of *Subtraction Flash Cards: Group 1* URG Pages 101–102 per student, optional

• 1 back-to-back copy of *Subtraction Flash Cards: Group 2* URG Pages 103–104 per student, optional

• 1 transparency of *Subtraction Facts I Know* DAB Page 43, optional

---

Lesson 8

Number Sense with Dollars and Cents

URG Pages 105–111
SG Pages 28–29
DPP W–X

Estimated Class Sessions
1

Activity
Students solve word problems from a list of items and prices.

Assessment
1. Use the *Observational Assessment Record* to document students' abilities to verbally communicate mathematical reasoning.
2. Transfer appropriate assessment documentation from the Unit 2 *Observational Assessment Record* to students' *Individual Assessment Record Sheets*.

• 1 copy of *Individual Assessment Record Sheet* TIG Assessment section per student, previously copied for use throughout the year

Unit 3: Exploring Multiplication .... 8 Sessions

Unit Summary

This is the first in a series of multiplication and division units distributed throughout the year. It begins a formal study of the concepts, applications, notation, and procedures involved in multiplying and dividing. Students solve problems about decorating T-shirts using the data on first names collected in Unit 1. Then they investigate things that come in 2s, 3s, 4s, etc., and use this information to solve problems such as finding the total number of wheels on five trucks. In another investigation, they use counters to divide numbers into groups in as many ways as possible.

Students write story problems to illustrate multiplication and division sentences. The ongoing activity, *Multiples on the Calendar,* introduces multiples and begins work with the multiplication facts. The DPP for this unit reviews the subtraction facts for Groups 3 and 4 and develops strategies for the multiplication facts for the fives and tens.

Major Concept Focus

- multiplication concepts
- multiplication as repeated addition
- partitioning
- multiplication facts strategies

- multiplication stories
- multiplication number sentences
- communicating problem-solving solutions

- investigating patterns
- subtraction facts review for Groups 3 and 4
- multiplication facts strategies for the 2s and 3s

Pacing Suggestions

This unit begins work with multiplication and division. Units that follow use the multiplication concepts developed in this unit to build additional skills and concepts. These skills and concepts are developed in a careful sequence as shown below. See the *Math Trailblazers Classroom* section in the *Teacher Implementation Guide* for more information on Pacing.

Unit 5:   Applying multiplication in a laboratory investigation (Lesson 3).

Unit 7:   Developing multiplication concepts including multiplication as repeated addition, multiplication on a number line, writing multiplication sentences, and representing multiplication using data tables and graphs.

Unit 8:   Using multiplication with map scales.

Unit 9:   Representing multiplication using data tables and graphs and solving multiplication problems involving mass.

Unit 10: Representing multiplication using data tables and graphs (Lesson 1) and solving problems involving multiplication (Lessons 1, 3, and 4).

Unit 11: Representing multiplication with arrays, building a multiplication table, developing strategies for multiplication facts, practicing multiplication facts using flash cards, and developing strategies for division through problem solving.

Unit 16: Solving multiplication and division problems involving volume (Lesson 2).

Unit 19: Developing strategies for multiplying one-digit by two-digit numbers and solving problems involving multiplication and division.

Unit 20: Representing multiplication using data tables and graphs, assessing the multiplication facts, and solving problems involving multiplication and division.

- Teach the units in the order in which they are written. Students will revisit important concepts and skills as they experience them in new contexts as the units progress. Units that do not contain significant multiplication content will include practice and review in the Daily Practice and Problems in the *Unit Resource Guide* and the Home Practice in the *Discovery Assignment Book.*
- Use the recommended session numbers for each lesson as a guide. It is not necessary to wait until students master each concept and skill as they will revisit them in later units and practice them in the Daily Practice and Problems and Home Practice throughout the year. Use the Assessment Indicators as a guide for the appropriate time to assess specific skills. The Assessment Indicators for all the units are listed on the *Individual Assessment Record Sheet* in the Assessment section of the *Teacher Implementation Guide.*
- Lesson 6 *More T-Shirt Problems* is a series of word problems that are appropriate for homework. The lesson is also suitable for a substitute teacher since preparation is minimal.

Preparing for Upcoming Lessons

Allow students to explore base-ten pieces in a learning center before beginning Unit 4.

Unit Planner

KEY: SG = Student Guide, DAB = Discovery Assignment Book, AB = Adventure Book, URG = Unit Resource Guide, DPP = Daily Practice and Problems, HP = Home Practice (found in Discovery Assignment Book), and TIG = Teacher Implementation Guide.

	Lesson Information	Supplies	Copies/Transparencies

Lesson 1

T-Shirt Factory Problems

URG Pages 22–29
SG Pages 32–33
DPP A–B

Estimated Class Sessions
1

Activity
Students use data from Unit 1 Lesson 1 *First Names* to solve problems about decorating T-shirts with their first names.

Math Facts
DPP Bit A provides practice with skip counting by ten.

Homework
Assign the following problem for homework: Your family is making T-shirts with their names on them. Draw pictures of all the T-shirts your family will need. If each letter costs 10 cents, how much will all the letters cost? Explain your solution.

Assessment
1. Assess students' abilities to solve problems and to work in groups by asking them to write a report of their group's strategies and solutions to Question 5 of the *T-Shirt Factory Problems.*
2. Use the *Observational Assessment Record* to document students' abilities to interpret bar graphs.

Supplies:
- connecting cubes or other counters
- calculators

Copies/Transparencies:
- 1 transparency of *T-Shirt Factory Problems* graph SG Page 32
- 1 copy of *Observational Assessment Record* URG Pages 11–12 to be used throughout this unit

Lesson 2

In Twos, Threes, and More

URG Pages 30–39
SG Pages 34–36
DAB Page 53
DPP C–F
HP Parts 1–2

Estimated Class Sessions
2

Activity
Students list items and then write multiplication problems about them.

Math Facts
DPP item C provides subtraction facts practice. Bit E reminds students to practice subtraction facts using the *Subtraction Flash Cards: Group 3.* Challenge F is a magic square problem.

Homework
1. Send home the *In Twos through Twelves* Activity Page. Families add new items to these lists.
2. Assign the Homework section in the *Student Guide.*
3. Collect one problem from each group and combine them into a class-generated homework assignment.
4. Assign Home Practice Part 1.
5. Students study the subtraction facts in Group 3 at home using their flash cards.

Assessment
1. Assess students' abilities to solve problems by asking them to solve a problem such as, *"How many corners are there on eight triangles?"* Note students' abilities to use words, pictures, or number sentences to show how they solved the problem.
2. Use Home Practice Part 2 as an assessment. Record students' abilities to solve problems involving multiplication on the *Observational Assessment Record.*

Supplies:
- 1 envelope for flash cards per student group
- several large index cards per student group, optional
- easel paper for making class lists
- tape for hanging class lists

	Lesson Information	**Supplies**	**Copies/ Transparencies**
Lesson 3 **Multiplication Stories** URG Pages 40–50 SG Pages 37–40 DPP G–J *Estimated Class Sessions* **2**	**Activity** Students illustrate multiplication problems with pictures and stories. **Math Facts** DPP Bit G provides practice with subtraction facts and develops mental math skills. Bit I reminds students to practice the subtraction facts in Group 4 using flash cards. **Homework** 1. Assign the homework problems in the *Student Guide.* 2. Students study the subtraction facts in Group 4 at home using their flash cards. **Assessment** Assess students' abilities to solve multiplication problems by asking them to write a story for a problem such as $8 \times \frac{1}{4}$, 10×9, or 20×3.	• connecting cubes or other counters • envelopes for flash cards • markers or crayons, optional	
Lesson 4 **Making Teams** URG Pages 51–58 DAB Pages 55–58 DPP K–L *Estimated Class Sessions* **1**	**Activity** Using counters as a model, students partition the students in a class into teams of equal size. Students write number sentences. **Math Facts** DPP Bit K develops multiplication math facts strategies. **Homework** Students complete *Groupings and Number Sentences for Ten* and the *Groupings and Number Sentences for Fifteen* Homework Pages in the *Discovery Assignment Book.*	• assortment of counters per student	• 1 transparency of *Class Teams Table* DAB Page 55
Lesson 5 **Multiples on the Calendar** URG Pages 59–65 DPP M–N HP Parts 3–4 *Estimated Class Sessions* **1**	**Activity** Students begin an ongoing activity translating calendar dates into number sentences that involve a product and a remainder. **Math Facts** DPP items M and N provide math facts practice. **Homework** Assign Home Practice Part 3. **Assessment** You can use Home Practice Part 4 as an assessment. Record students' abilities to create stories for multiplication sentences and write number sentences for multiplication situations on the *Observational Assessment Record.*	• beans or other counters, optional • large classroom calendar with space for writing number sentences	• 1 copy of *Calendar Multiplication* URG Page 64 per student

(Continued)

Overview

	Lesson Information	Supplies	Copies/Transparencies
Lesson 6 **More T-Shirt Problems** URG Pages 66–70 SG Page 41 DPP O–P *Estimated Class Sessions* **1**	**Activity** Students work on word problems involving multiplication and division. **Math Facts** DPP Bit O provides multiplication facts practice. **Assessment** 1. Use the *Observational Assessment Record* to record students' abilities to solve multiplication and division problems and explain their reasoning. 2. Transfer appropriate observations from the Unit 3 *Observational Assessment Record* to each student's *Individual Assessment Record Sheet*.	• calculators • connecting cubes or other counters	• 1 copy of *Individual Assessment Record Sheet* TIG Assessment section per student, previously copied for use throughout the year

Unit 4: Place Value Concepts . . . . 11–13 Sessions

Unit Summary

This unit extends students' work with place value to four-digit numbers and helps them build their understanding of our number system. The activities lay the conceptual groundwork for adding and subtracting four-digit numbers using paper-and-pencil procedures, which will be formally introduced in Unit 6. Base-ten pieces provide a concrete representation of the relationship between the different digits in our number system. They help students visualize how different digits in a number are used to represent different quantities. Students practice writing and telling time on analog and digital clocks. They continue to practice this skill in the Daily Practice and Problems and in future units. The DPP for this unit reviews the subtraction facts for Groups 5 and 6 and develops strategies for the multiplication facts for the twos and threes.

Major Concept Focus

- number sense
- partitioning numbers
- regrouping
- place value
- base-ten number system
- multidigit addition
- addition algorithms
- ordering large numbers
- telling time to five minutes
- Student Rubric: *Knowing*
- subtraction facts review for Groups 5 and 6
- multiplication facts strategies for the 2s and 3s

Pacing Suggestions

- Lesson 2 *The TIMS Candy Company* develops place value concepts using base-ten pieces. It takes three to five days to complete. Students' familiarity with base-ten pieces and place value concepts will govern how many sessions they need to complete the activities.
- Lesson 6 *Time for Problems* is a series of word problems that are appropriate to assign for homework. The lesson is also suitable for a substitute teacher since preparation is minimal.

Preparing for Upcoming Lessons

Place eyedroppers in a learning center for students to explore prior to beginning Unit 5. You may want to introduce eyedroppers in a whole-class setting. You will need to purchase three different brands of paper towels for Unit 5.

Unit Planner

	Lesson Information	Supplies	Copies/Transparencies
Lesson 1 **Breaking Numbers into Parts** URG Pages 23–38 DAB Pages 67–69 DPP A–D HP Parts 1–2 *Estimated Class Sessions* **2**	**Activity** Students partition two-digit numbers. They represent these groups with connecting cubes and discuss special groupings of tens and ones. **Math Facts** DPP Tasks B, C, and D develop strategies for the multiplication facts. **Homework** Assign Parts 1 and 2 of the Home Practice in the *Discovery Assignment Book*. **Assessment** Use the *Observational Assessment Record* to note students' abilities to partition and represent numbers using connecting cubes.	• 100 connecting cubes per student pair	• 3 copies of *Connecting Cubes Recording Sheet* URG Page 34 per student • 1 copy of *Base-Ten Board Part 1* URG Page 32 per student pair • 1 transparency of *Base-Ten Board Part 1* URG Page 32, optional • 1 transparency of *Connecting Cubes Recording Sheet* URG Page 34, optional • 1 copy of *Observational Assessment Record* URG Pages 11–12 to be used throughout this unit
Lesson 2 **The TIMS Candy Company** URG Pages 39–67 SG Pages 44–51 DAB Pages 71–74 DPP E–J *Estimated Class Sessions* **3-5**	**Activity** Students represent quantities with base-ten pieces. **Math Facts** DPP items E, F, G, and H provide practice with math facts. **Homework** 1. Assign *Questions 1–9* in the Homework section after Part 3. 2. Assign *Questions 10–12* in the Homework section after Part 4. 3. Students practice the subtraction facts in Group 5 using their flash cards. **Assessment** Students complete the *Are These the Fewest Possible?* and *Are They the Same?* Assessment Blackline Masters.	• 1 set of base-ten pieces (2 packs, 14 flats, 30 skinnies, and 50 bits) per student pair or group of 3 • 1 envelope per student for storing flash cards • tape, optional	• 1 copy of *Are These the Fewest Possible?* URG Page 56 per student • 1 copy of *Are They the Same?* URG Page 57 per student • 1 copy of *Base-Ten Board Part 1* and *Part 2* URG Pages 32–33 per student • 1 copy of *Base-Ten Recording Sheet* URG Page 58 per student or more as needed • 1 copy of *Base-Ten Pieces Masters* URG Pages 59–60 or more as needed, optional • 1 transparency of *Base-Ten Board Part 1* and *Part 2* URG Pages 32–33 • 1 transparency of *Base-Ten Recording Sheet* URG Page 58 • 1 transparency of *Base-Ten Pieces Masters* URG Pages 59–60, optional

	Lesson Information	Supplies	Copies/Transparencies
Lesson 3 **Base-Ten Addition** URG Pages 68–79 SG Pages 52–53 DAB Pages 75–76 DPP K–N HP Parts 3–4 *Estimated Class Sessions* **2**	**Activity** Students use base-ten pieces to model two-digit addition with regrouping. A standard addition algorithm is introduced. **Math Facts** DPP Bits K and M provide practice with the subtraction facts in Group 6. **Homework** 1. Assign Part 4 of the Home Practice. 2. Students practice the subtraction facts in Group 6 using their flash cards. **Assessment** 1. Students solve a problem and are assessed with the Student Rubric: *Knowing*. 2. Use Home Practice Part 3 as a quiz.	• 1 set of base-ten pieces per student pair or group of 3 • 1 envelope per student for storing flash cards	• 1 copy of *Base-Ten Board Part 1* and *Part 2* URG Pages 32–33 per student • 1 copy of *Base-Ten Recording Sheet* URG Page 58 per student or more as needed • 1 transparency of *Base-Ten Board Part 1* and *Part 2* URG Pages 32–33 • 1 transparency of *Base-Ten Recording Sheet* URG Page 58
Lesson 4 **Bubble Sort** URG Pages 80–83 DPP O–P *Estimated Class Sessions* **1**	**Activity** Students arrange numbers in order. **Assessment** Use the *Observational Assessment Record* to note students' abilities to compare and order large numbers.	• 1 sheet of paper or index card per student	
Lesson 5 **It's Time** URG Pages 84–95 SG Pages 54–55 DAB Page 77 DPP Q–T *Estimated Class Sessions* **2**	**Activity** Students practice telling time to the nearest five minutes. Students tell and write time on analog and digital clocks. **Math Facts** DPP items S and T provide practice with math facts. **Homework** Assign some or all of the Lesson 6 problems. **Assessment** Students complete the *Time* Assessment Page.	• 1 brass fastener per student • analog demonstration clock • 1 pair of scissors per student	• 1 copy of *Time* URG Page 93 per student

(Continued)

Overview

	Lesson Information	Supplies	Copies/Transparencies
Lesson 6 **Time for Problems** URG Pages 96–100 SG Page 56 DPP U–V *Estimated Class Sessions* **1**	**Activity** Students solve word problems about time. **Homework** Assign some or all of the *Time for Problems* as homework. **Assessment** 1. Use DPP Bit U as an assessment. 2. Use the *Observational Assessment Record* to note students' abilities to tell time to the nearest five minutes. 3. Transfer appropriate documentation from the Unit 4 *Observational Assessment Record* to students' *Individual Assessment Record Sheets*.	• students' analog clocks from Lesson 5	• 1 copy of *Individual Assessment Record Sheet* TIG Assessment section per student, previously copied for use throughout the year

Unit 5: Area of Different Shapes . . . . 8–10 Sessions

Unit Summary

Students' concept of area is strengthened through a series of activities where they find the area of irregular shapes by counting square centimeters. In the introductory activity, students piece together fractional parts of square centimeters into full units. In the experiment *The Better "Picker Upper,"* students apply this skill toward understanding which of several brands of paper towel is the best for soaking up water. The lab also provides a context for problem solving and for a discussion of the roles of fixed (controlled) variables in experiments. Students read the Adventure Book *The Haunted House,* a story about a team of amateur detectives who solve a mystery by measuring the area of a ghost's footprint. The DPP for this unit reviews the subtraction facts for Groups 7 and 8 and develops multiplication facts strategies for the square numbers.

Major Concept Focus

- TIMS Laboratory Method
- bar graphs
- median
- fixed variables
- area of irregular shapes
- measuring area in square centimeters
- counting halves and fourths of square centimeters
- relationship between shape and area
- using multiplication
- *Adventure Book:* area
- Student Rubric: *Solving*
- assessing problem solving
- subtraction facts review for Groups 7 and 8
- multiplication facts strategies for the square numbers

Pacing Suggestions

- Lesson 3 *The Better "Picker Upper"* provides connections to science. Students can collect the data for the lab during science time.
- Lesson 4 *The Haunted House* is an *Adventure Book* story that provides a connection to language arts. Students can read the story as part of language arts time.
- Lesson 6 *Using Number Sense at the Book Sale* is an optional lesson. It is a series of word problems that provides practice with money.

Preparing for Upcoming Lessons

Place eyedroppers in a learning center for students to explore prior to Lesson 3. You may want to introduce eyedroppers in a whole-class setting.

You will need to purchase three different brands of paper towels for Lesson 3.

Unit Planner

KEY: SG = Student Guide, DAB = Discovery Assignment Book, AB = Adventure Book, URG = Unit Resource Guide, DPP = Daily Practice and Problems, HP = Home Practice (found in Discovery Assignment Book), and TIG = Teacher Implementation Guide.

	Lesson Information	Supplies	Copies/Transparencies
Lesson 1 **Measuring Area** URG Pages 20–30 SG Pages 58–59 DAB Page 87 DPP A–B *Estimated Class Sessions* **1**	**Activity** Students find the area of an irregular shape by helping Professor Peabody find the number of tiles he will need to cover a floor. They also find the area of other polygons and curved shapes. **Math Facts** For DPP Bit A, students practice the subtraction facts in Group 7. **Homework** Assign the *Area of Five Shapes* Homework Page.		• 1 transparency of *Centimeter Grid Paper* URG Page 28, optional
Lesson 2 **Boo the Blob** URG Pages 31–38 DAB Pages 89–91 DPP C–D HP Parts 1–2 *Estimated Class Sessions* **1**	**Activity** Students investigate the relationship between shape and area and estimate the area of irregular shapes. They also learn to find the median value of data. **Math Facts** DPP Bit C introduces the *Subtraction Flash Cards: Group 7.* **Homework** 1. Students use their flash cards at home to study the subtraction facts in Group 7. 2. Assign Home Practice Parts 1 and 2. **Assessment** Observe students finding the area of irregular shapes and comparing different shapes with the same area while completing the *Boo the Blob Changes Shape* Activity Pages. Record observations on the *Observational Assessment Record.*	• 1 pair of scissors per student • 1 envelope per student for storing flash cards	• 1 copy of *Centimeter Grid Paper* URG Page 28 per student • 1 copy of *Observational Assessment Record* URG Pages 9–10 to be used throughout this unit
Lesson 3 **The Better "Picker Upper"** URG Pages 39–58 SG Pages 60–61 DAB Pages 93–98 DPP E–L HP Part 3 *Estimated Class Sessions* **4-5**	**Lab** Students investigate the area of a spot made by a given number of drops of water on different brands of paper towels. They measure the area of the spots by counting square units. They use this information to decide which brand is most absorbent. **Math Facts** DPP Tasks H and J are multiplication problems. DPP Bits I and K work with the subtraction facts in Group 8. **Homework** 1. Students use their flash cards at home to study the subtraction facts in Group 8. 2. Assign *Lori's Questions* Homework Pages. **Assessment** 1. The lab provides opportunities to observe the many aspects of conducting a lab. Use the *Observational Assessment Record* to record students' abilities to measure area and organize data.	• 1 eyedropper per student group • 3–4 brands of paper towels of varying quality, one sheet of each brand per student group • 1 pair of scissors per student group • 1 small container of water per student group • 2 books or 1 geoboard for drying paper towels per student group	• 1 copy of *Centimeter Grid Paper* URG Page 28 per student • 1 copy of *Centimeter Graph Paper* URG Page 53 per student • 1 transparency of *Centimeter Graph Paper* URG Page 53

	Lesson Information	Supplies	Copies/ Transparencies
	2. Use *Questions 3* and *4* of the *Lori's Questions* Homework Pages to evaluate students' abilities to find the area of irregular shapes.	• 1 envelope per student for storing flash cards • food coloring, optional	
Lesson 4 **The Haunted House** URG Pages 59–66 AB Pages 26–42 DPP M–N HP Part 4 *Estimated Class Sessions* **1**	**Adventure Book** Rosita and Peter solve a mystery about a haunted house by measuring the area and length of a "ghost's" footprints. **Homework** For Home Practice Part 4, students solve multiplication problems using square numbers.		
Lesson 5 **Joe the Goldfish** URG Pages 67–76 DPP O–P *Estimated Class Sessions* **1**	**Assessment Activity** Students work in pairs or groups to determine the amount of material it would take to make a raincoat for Joe the Goldfish. They design the coat and determine its area in square centimeters. Students are introduced to the Student Rubric: *Solving*. **Math Facts** DPP items O and P practice math facts. **Assessment** 1. Document students' abilities to solve open-response problems and communicate solution strategies using the *Observational Assessment Record*. 2. Use the Unit 5 *Observational Assessment Record* to update students' *Individual Assessment Record Sheets*.	• 1 pair of scissors per student group	• 1 copy of *A Raincoat for Joe the Goldfish* URG Page 75 per student • 1 copy of *Centimeter Grid Paper* URG Page 28 per student group • 1 transparency of *A Raincoat for Joe the Goldfish* URG Page 75, optional • 1 transparency of *Centimeter Grid Paper* URG Page 28, optional • 1 copy of *Individual Assessment Record Sheet* TIG Assessment section per student, previously copied for use throughout the year
Lesson 6 **Using Number Sense at the Book Sale** URG Pages 77–81 SG Pages 62–64 *Estimated Class Sessions* **1**	OPTIONAL LESSON **Optional Activity** Students solve word problems from a list of books and prices. **Homework** Assign some or all of the problems for homework.		

Overview

Unit 6: More Adding and Subtracting . . . . 16–18 Sessions

Unit Summary

Students' experiences with two-digit addition and subtraction, base-ten pieces, and a standard algorithm are extended to three- and four-digit numbers. Students continue developing their own strategies for adding and subtracting large numbers and they learn to use standard procedures. The emphasis is on solving problems involving addition and subtraction in context. The Adventure Book *Leonardo the Blockhead* looks at the historical and multicultural roots of the base-ten number system we use today. The DPP for this unit develops strategies for the multiplication facts for the nines.

Major Concept Focus

- number sense
- place value
- base-ten system
- multidigit subtraction
- subtraction algorithms
- rounding
- Game: multidigit addition and subtraction
- palindromes

- partitioning
- ordering large numbers
- multidigit addition
- addition algorithms
- computational estimation
- *Adventure Book:* addition and subtraction algorithms
- Student Rubric: *Knowing*
- communicating problem solving
- multiplication strategies for the 9s

Pacing Suggestions

This unit develops concepts, estimation, and paper-and-pencil skills for addition and subtraction. Use the recommended session numbers for each lesson as a guide. It is not necessary to stay on a topic until students master each skill, especially paper-and-pencil procedures, as students will revisit them in later units. Practice is distributed throughout the year in the Daily Practice and Problems and Home Practice.

Preparing for Upcoming Lessons

Place pattern blocks, rulers, and metersticks in a learning center for students to explore prior to beginning Unit 7.

Unit Planner

KEY: SG = Student Guide, DAB = Discovery Assignment Book, AB = Adventure Book, URG = Unit Resource Guide, DPP = Daily Practice and Problems, HP = Home Practice (found in Discovery Assignment Book), and TIG = Teacher Implementation Guide.

	Lesson Information	Supplies	Copies/ Transparencies
Lesson 1 **The 500 Hats** URG Pages 27–32 DPP A–B HP Part 1 *Estimated Class Sessions* **1**	**Activity** *The 500 Hats of Bartholomew Cubbins* provides a context for partitioning, adding, and subtracting two- and three-digit numbers. **Math Facts** DPP Task B provides practice with multiplication facts for the nines. **Homework** 1. Students can write other stories with addition and subtraction problems. 2. Assign Part 1 of the Home Practice. **Assessment** Use the *Observational Assessment Record* to note students' abilities to solve problems involving addition and subtraction using mental strategies.	• 1 set of base-ten pieces (2 packs, 14 flats, 30 skinnies, and 50 bits) per student pair or group of three • 1 calculator per student, optional • *The 500 Hats of Bartholomew Cubbins* by Dr. Seuss or another story that refers to numbers in the hundreds	• 1 copy of *Observational Assessment Record* URG Pages 13–14 to be used throughout this unit
Lesson 2 **The Coat of Many Bits** URG Pages 33–40 SG Page 66 DPP C–F *Estimated Class Sessions* **2-3**	**Activity** Students trace an outline of their coats or jackets onto a sheet of paper and measure the area covered by the outline. The data collected is used in several problem situations. **Math Facts** DPP items C, D, and F provide practice with math facts. **Homework** Students complete *Questions 5–7* on *The Coat of Many Bits* Activity Page.	• 1 student's coat (or jacket, sweater, or sweatshirt) per student group • 1 large sheet of paper at least 2 yards by 1 yard per student group • 1 set of base-ten pieces (14 flats, 30 skinnies, and 50 bits) per student pair or group of three • crayons • 1 index card per student group • tape • 1 pair of scissors per student group	
Lesson 3 **Adding with Base-Ten Pieces** URG Pages 41–60 SG Pages 67–70 DAB Pages 103–104 DPP G–L HP Part 2	**Activity** Students expand their understanding of addition and place value with larger numbers. **Math Facts** DPP Challenge H provides practice with multiplication facts. **Homework** 1. Assign *Questions 3–6* on the *Adding on the Base-Ten Board* Activity Pages in the *Discovery Assignment Book* after Part 1. 2. Assign the Homework section in the *Student Guide* after Part 2.	• 1 set of base-ten pieces (2 packs, 14 flats, 30 skinnies, and 50 bits) per student pair or group of three	• 1 copy of *Base-Ten Board* URG Pages 51–52 per student pair • 1 copy of *Base-Ten Recording Sheet* URG Page 53 per student • 1 transparency of *Base-Ten Board* URG Pages 51–52, optional • 1 transparency of *Base-Ten Recording Sheet* URG Page 53, optional

(Continued)

Overview

	Lesson Information	Supplies	Copies/ Transparencies
Estimated Class Sessions **3-4**	3. Assign Part 2 of the Home Practice for more practice with addition and subtraction. **Assessment** Use the *Observational Assessment Record* to note students' progress representing addition using base-ten pieces.		
Lesson 4 **Subtracting with Base-Ten Pieces** URG Pages 61–79 SG Pages 71–76 DAB Pages 105–108 DPP M–T **Estimated Class Sessions** **4**	**Activity** Students expand their understanding of subtraction and place value with larger numbers. **Homework** 1. Assign the Homework section of the *Subtracting on the Base-Ten Board* Activity Pages in the *Discovery Assignment Book* after Part 1. 2. Assign the Homework section in the *Student Guide* after Part 2. **Assessment** 1. Use **Questions 6–14** in the *Student Guide* to assess students' abilities to solve problems involving addition and subtraction. **Question 10** can be scored using the Knowing dimension of the *TIMS Multidimensional Rubric*. 2. Use the Homework section in the *Discovery Assignment Book* and the *Observational Assessment Record* to note students' progress subtracting using base-ten pieces and paper and pencil. 3. Use Task R as a short assessment.	• 1 set of base-ten pieces (2 packs, 14 flats, 30 skinnies, and 50 bits) per student pair or group of three	• 1 copy of *Base-Ten Board* URG Pages 51–52 per student pair • 1 copy of *Base-Ten Recording Sheet* URG Page 53 per student • 1 transparency of *Base-Ten Board* URG Pages 51–52, optional • 1 transparency of *Base-Ten Recording Sheet* URG Page 53, optional • 1 copy of *TIMS Multidimensional Rubric* TIG, Assessment section
Lesson 5 **Close Enough!** URG Pages 80–90 SG Pages 77–80 DPP U–Z **Estimated Class Sessions** **3**	**Activity** Students explore estimation strategies and round to the nearest ten and hundred. **Math Facts** DPP Task V provides practice with math facts. **Homework** Assign the Homework section in the *Student Guide*. **Assessment** Use the *Observational Assessment Record* to note students' abilities to estimate sums and differences using convenient numbers.	• 1 set of base-ten pieces (14 flats, 30 skinnies, and 50 bits) per student pair or group of three and 1 set for the teacher	• 2 copies of *Hundreds Template* URG Page 88 per student pair or more as needed • 2 transparencies of *Hundreds Template* URG Page 88 or more as needed

	Lesson Information	Supplies	Copies/Transparencies
Lesson 6 **Leonardo the Blockhead** URG Pages 91–100 AB Pages 43–58 DPP AA–BB *Estimated Class Sessions* **1**	**Adventure Book** This story is based upon the role of the great Italian mathematician Fibonacci in the introduction of the Hindu-Arabic numeration and associated algorithms into Europe. **Assessment** Use DPP Bit AA as an assessment of students' progress with subtraction.	• map of Europe, North Africa, and the Middle East, optional	
Lesson 7 **Palindromes** URG Pages 101–108 DPP CC–DD HP Parts 3–4 *Estimated Class Sessions* **1**	**Activity** Students practice addition with two-, three-, and four-digit numbers and discover number patterns as they explore palindromes. **Math Facts** Challenge DD provides practice with multiplication facts and computation. **Homework** Assign Parts 3 and 4 of the Home Practice. **Assessment** Use the *Observational Assessment Record* to note students' abilities to add using paper and pencil.	• 1 calculator per student • colored markers or crayons • 1 set of base-ten pieces per student pair or group of three	• 1 copy of *100 Chart* URG Page 107 per student • 1 transparency of *100 Chart* URG Page 107
Lesson 8 **Digits Game** URG Pages 109–116 DAB Page 109 DPP EE–FF *Estimated Class Sessions* **1**	**Game** Students attempt to make the largest or smallest answer to addition and subtraction problems by strategically placing the digits on a playing board. **Homework** Students can play the game at home with their families. **Assessment** 1. Use the *Observational Assessment Record* to note students' abilities to add and subtract with paper and pencil. 2. Transfer appropriate assessment documentation from the Unit 6 *Observational Assessment Record* to students' *Individual Assessment Record Sheets*.	• 10 index cards per student group, optional	• 1 copy of *Digit Cards 0–9* URG Pages 115–116 copied back to back per student group • 1 copy of *Individual Assessment Record Sheet* TIG Assessment section per student, previously copied for use throughout the year

Unit 7: Exploring Multiplication and Division . . . . 11–12 Sessions

Unit Summary

Students continue developing their conceptual understanding of multiplication and division use graphs to explore multiples. To do this, students collect and graph data. This is students' first experience making point graphs. Students work with a recipe for lemonade and use multiplication, division, and graphing to solve problems related to increasing quantities in the recipe.

Mathhoppers, imaginary creatures that jump specified numbers of units on a number line, help students explore multiplication and division concepts.

Students use the division symbol when they solve problems in the context of planning a birthday party. In the culminating activity, students investigate the multiplicative relationship between the number of sides of a regular figure and its perimeter. They measure a side and the perimeter of the figures, record and graph the data, and analyze the results using multiplication and division.

The DPP for this unit reviews and assesses the subtraction facts in Groups 1 and 2 and develops strategies for learning the last six multiplication facts (4×6, 4×7, 4×8, 6×7, 6×8, 7×8).

Major Concept Focus

- multiplication concepts
- multiplication as repeated addition
- multiplication sentences
- interpreting remainders
- point graphs
- measuring length in centimeters
- investigating patterns
- assessing problem solving
- subtraction facts review and assessment for Groups 1 and 2

- division concepts
- division as repeated subtraction
- division sentences
- graphing and analyzing data
- number lines
- perimeter of polygons
- communicating problem-solving solutions
- Student Rubric: *Telling*
- strategies for the last six multiplication facts

Unit Planner

	Lesson Information	Supplies	Copies/Transparencies
Lesson 1 **Lemonade Stand** URG Pages 26–45 SG Pages 82–85 DAB Pages 115–118 DPP A–D *Estimated Class Sessions* **2**	**Activity** Students use multiplication, division, and graphing to solve problems involving a recipe for lemonade. The activity introduces point graphs. **Math Facts** DPP items A, B, and C provide practice with math facts. **Homework** 1. Assign the *Mr. Green's Giant Gumball Jamboree* Homework Pages in the *Discovery Assignment Book.* 2. Students study the subtraction facts in Group 1 at home using their flash cards. **Assessment** Use *Mr. Green's Giant Gumball Jamboree* and the *Observational Assessment Record* to note students' abilities to make and interpret point graphs.	• 1 ruler per student • lemons, sugar, water, paper cups, and a pitcher to make and serve lemonade, optional	• 1 copy of *Two-column Data Table* URG Page 37 per student • 2 copies of *Centimeter Graph Paper* URG Page 38 per student • 1 copy of *Subtraction Flash Cards: Group 1* URG Pages 39–40, copied back to back per student, optional • 1 transparency of *Lemonade Stand Graph* URG Page 41 • 1 transparency of *What Went Wrong?* URG Page 42 • 1 copy of *Observational Assessment Record* URG Pages 13–14 to be used throughout this unit
Lesson 2 **Katie's Job** URG Pages 46–56 DPP E–F HP Parts 1–2 *Estimated Class Sessions* **1-2**	**Assessment Activity** Students work individually or in groups to solve problems using a graph and multiplication and division. They are introduced to the *Telling* rubric as a guide for their work. **Math Facts** Task F provides computation and facts practice. **Homework** Assign Parts 1 and 2 of the Home Practice. **Assessment** 1. Score student work using the Telling dimension of the *TIMS Multidimensional Rubric.* 2. Add the completed work to student portfolios.	• 1 calculator per student • 1 ruler per student	• 1 copy of *Katie's Job* URG Pages 53–54 per student • 1 transparency of *Katie's Job* URG Pages 53–54, optional • 1 copy of *TIMS Multidimensional Rubric* TIG, Assessment section • 1 transparency or poster of TIMS Student Rubric: *Telling* TIG, Assessment section, optional
Lesson 3 **Mathhoppers** URG Pages 57–69 SG Pages 86–89 DAB Pages 119–121 DPP G–J HP Part 3 *Estimated Class Sessions* **2**	**Activity** Mathhoppers are creatures that can jump a specified number of units on a number line. Students solve mathhopper problems that further their study of multiplication and division. They connect multiplication to repeated addition and division to repeated subtraction. **Math Facts** DPP items G and I provide practice with math facts. **Homework** 1. Assign the *Professor Peabody's Mathhoppers* Homework Page. 2. Assign Part 3 of the Home Practice. 3. Students study the subtraction facts in Group 2 at home using their flash cards.	• 1 meterstick or measuring tape (for use as a number line) per student group • 1 green pattern block or other marker (for use as a mathhopper) per student group • about 60 centimeter connecting cubes per student group and some for the teacher • 1 pair of scissors per student	• 1 copy of *Subtraction Flash Cards: Group 2* URG Pages 65–66, per student copied back to back, optional • 1 transparency of the first *Mathhoppers* Activity Page SG Page 86

(Continued)

Overview

	Lesson Information	Supplies	Copies/Transparencies
	Assessment Use the *Observational Assessment Record* to record students' abilities to represent multiplication and division using manipulatives, number lines, and words and to write number sentences for multiplication.	• 1 calculator per student • tape	
Lesson 4 **Birthday Party** URG Pages 70–77 SG Pages 90–92 DPP K–N *Estimated Class Sessions* **2**	**Activity** Using the context of a birthday party, students work on a variety of problems they can solve using division. The division symbol is introduced. **Homework** Assign the Homework section of the *Birthday Party* Activity Pages. **Assessment** Use journal entries to assess students' abilities to communicate their solution strategies and represent multiplication and division using manipulatives, number lines, and other tools.	• 30 or more counters per student pair • 1 calculator per student	
Lesson 5 **The Money Jar** URG Pages 78–88 SG Pages 93–94 DPP O–P *Estimated Class Sessions* **1**	**Activity** Students solve a series of problems in which they must decide how to divide money equally among the members of a family. They write division number sentences to show their solutions. **Math Facts** DPP Task P provides practice with division. **Homework** Assign the homework problems on *The Money Jar* Activity Pages. **Assessment** 1. Use DPP Task P to assess students' understanding of division. 2. Use the *Observational Assessment Record* to note students' abilities to represent division using manipulatives.	• play money: 60 pennies, 50 dimes, and 10 nickels per student • 1 calculator per student • scissors, optional	• 1 copy of *Money Masters* URG Pages 85–87 per student group to substitute for play money, optional
Lesson 6 **Walking around Shapes** URG Pages 89–102 DAB Pages 123–128 DPP Q–V HP Part 4 *Estimated Class Sessions* **3**	**Activity** Students investigate the relationship between the length of a side and the perimeter of regular polygons, using data tables and line graphs. They use the patterns they find to solve problems, working with multiples of 3, 4, 5, and 6. **Math Facts** DPP Bit Q practices math facts. Bit U is a quiz on subtraction facts. **Homework** 1. Assign the *Walking around Squares* Homework Pages. 2. Assign Part 4 of the Home Practice.	• 1 ruler per student	• 1 copy of *Subtraction Facts Quiz A* URG Page 25 per student • 1 copy of *Professor Peabody's Shapes Data* URG Page 98 per student • 3 copies of *Centimeter Graph Paper* URG Page 38 per student • 1 transparency of *Walking around Triangles* DAB Page 124 • 1 transparency of *Centimeter Graph Paper* URG Page 38

Lesson Information	**Supplies**	**Copies/ Transparencies**
Assessment 1. Students complete the *Professor Peabody's Shapes Data* Assessment Page. 2. DPP item U is a quiz on the subtraction facts in Groups 1 and 2. 3. Use the *Observational Assessment Record* to note students' abilities to find perimeter. 4. Transfer appropriate documentation from the Unit 7 *Observational Assessment Record* to students' *Individual Assessment Record Sheets*.		• 1 copy of *Individual Assessment Record Sheet* TIG Assessment section per student, previously copied for use throughout the year

Unit 8: Mapping and Coordinates . . . . 7–10 Sessions

Unit Summary

Students learn to locate objects using coordinates. A plastic figure, named Mr. Origin, is used to specify the origin and coordinate directions. For example, in the first lesson, students are given coordinates such as "four steps right" and "six steps front" and then, using Mr. Origin, they locate objects in the room.

They practice finding the distance between objects on a map using a scale by finding distances between familiar objects on a map of a student's desk. Then, to apply their knowledge, they build a miniature town using connecting cubes and make a coordinate map of the town on graph paper. Throughout these activities, students measure distances using units of measure from both the metric system and the customary system. An Adventure Book, *The Ghost Galleons,* tells about a family who uses coordinates to help them find sunken treasure. The DPP for this unit reviews and assesses the subtraction facts in Groups 3 and 4 and develops strategies for the multiplication facts for the twos, fives, and tens.

Major Concept Focus

- coordinates
- making and interpreting scale maps
- predicting length
- checking predictions
- measuring length in nonstandard units
- measuring length in centimeters and feet
- *Adventure Book:* using coordinates to find treasure
- Game: adding or subtracting to make 10
- subtraction facts review and assessment for Groups 3 and 4
- multiplication strategies for the 2s, 5s, and 10s

Pacing Suggestions

- Lesson 4 *The Ghost Galleons* is an *Adventure Book* story that connects mathematics and language arts. Students can read the story as part of language arts time.
- Lesson 6 *Tall Buildings* is an optional lesson. These problems can be assigned as homework throughout the unit or solved in class. Since the lesson requires little teacher preparation, it is appropriate to leave for a substitute teacher.

Preparing for Upcoming Lessons

Place two-pan balances, standard masses, and clay in a learning center for students to explore prior to beginning Unit 9.

Unit Planner

KEY: SG = Student Guide, DAB = Discovery Assignment Book, AB = Adventure Book, URG = Unit Resource Guide, DPP = Daily Practice and Problems, HP = Home Practice (found in Discovery Assignment Book), and TIG = Teacher Implementation Guide.

	Lesson Information	Supplies	Copies/Transparencies
Lesson 1 **Meet Mr. Origin** URG Pages 21–32 SG Pages 96–98 DPP A–B HP Parts 1–2 *Estimated Class Sessions* **1-2**	**Activity** Students are introduced to the idea of locating an object using the manipulative Mr. Origin. They measure the two coordinates of an object, first using footsteps and then rulers. **Math Facts** DPP Bit A and Task B provide practice with math facts. **Homework** Assign Home Practice Parts 1 and 2.	• 1 Mr. Origin per student group and 1 for the teacher • 2–3 rulers per student group • a "treasure" for a treasure hunt • 10 index cards • tape	• 1 copy of *Three-column Data Table* URG Page 31 per student
Lesson 2 **Sara's Desk** URG Pages 33–43 SG Pages 99–102 DPP C–D *Estimated Class Sessions* **1**	**Activity** Students use a scale map of an imaginary student's desktop to answer some questions about distances between objects on the desk and to re-create a similar configuration on their own desks. They play a game that uses coordinates. **Math Facts** For DPP Bit C students work with *Subtraction Flash Cards.* Task D provides practice with multiplication facts. **Homework** 1. Assign the Homework section after introducing the *Find the Panda* game in class. Each student will need a copy of the directions and two copies of the game board. 2. Students study the subtraction facts in Group 3 at home using their flash cards. **Assessment** Observe students' abilities to locate points using coordinates and to use a scale map. Record your observations on the *Observational Assessment Record.*	• 1 Mr. Origin per student group • 1 ruler per student • 1 calculator, pencil, book, and eraser per student to reproduce Sara's desk	• 3 copies of *Find the Panda Game Board* URG Page 40 per student • 1 copy of *Subtraction Flash Cards: Group 3* URG Pages 41–42 copied back to back per student, optional • 1 transparency of the first *Sara's Desk* Activity Page SG Page 99 • 1 transparency of *Find the Panda Game Board* URG Page 40, optional • 1 copy of *Observational Assessment Record* URG Pages 11–12 to be used throughout this unit
Lesson 3 **Mapping a Tiny TIMS Town** URG Pages 44–66 SG Pages 103–108 DAB Page 133 DPP E–J *Estimated Class Sessions* **3-4**	**Activity** Using centimeter connecting cubes, students build a tiny TIMS town on their desks. Placing Mr. Origin in one corner of their town, they record the coordinates of the buildings and draw a map using these coordinates. They use the map to predict distances. **Math Facts** DPP Bits G and I work with the subtraction facts in Group 4. **Homework** 1. Assign the Homework section in the *Student Guide.* 2. Students study the subtraction facts in Group 4 at home using their flash cards.	• 1 sheet of paper at least 33 cm by 33 cm (newsprint) per student group • 32 centimeter connecting cubes per student group • 1 pair of scissors per student group • 1 Mr. Origin per student group • glue or tape, optional	• 1 copy of *Tape Measures for TIMS Town* URG Page 56 per student group • 1 copy of *Maps* URG Pages 57–58 per student • 1 copy of *TIMS Town Tree Planting Club* URG Page 59 per student group, optional • 1 copy of *Centimeter Graph Paper* URG Page 60 per student • 1 copy of *Subtraction Flash Cards: Group 4* URG Pages 61–62 copied back to back per student, optional

(Continued)

Overview

	Lesson Information	**Supplies**	**Copies/ Transparencies**
	Assessment 1. Students complete the *Maps* Assessment Blackline Masters. 2. Record students' abilities to make and use scale maps on the *Observational Assessment Record*.	• green crayons or markers (for the extension) • 1 ruler per student	• 1 transparency of *Centimeter Graph Paper* URG Page 60
Lesson 4 **The Ghost Galleons** URG Pages 67–75 AB Pages 59–76 DPP K–L HP Parts 3–4 *Estimated Class Sessions* **1**	**Adventure Book** Two children are in the Caribbean searching for the wrecks of two Spanish galleons. Inspired by Mr. Origin, they decide to plot the location of the items they find on a grid with an origin. In doing this, they uncover an important clue to the location of the sunken ship and its treasure. **Math Facts** DPP Task L develops strategies for the multiplication facts for the fives and tens. **Homework** Home Practice Part 3 provides practice with addition and subtraction computation. Part 4 provides practice making and interpreting point graphs.		
Lesson 5 **Tens Game** URG Pages 76–84 SG Pages 109–110 DPP M–N *Estimated Class Sessions* **1**	**Game** Students play a card game in which they add or subtract card numbers to make ten. **Math Facts** DPP Bit M is a quiz on the subtraction facts in Groups 3 and 4. **Homework** Students can play the game at home with family members. **Assessment** 1. Use DPP Bit M to assess students' fluency with the subtraction facts in Groups 3 and 4. Note students' progress on the *Observational Assessment Record*. 2. DPP Task N can be used as a quiz on coordinates. 3. Transfer appropriate documentation from the Unit 8 *Observational Assessment Record* to students' *Individual Assessment Record Sheets*.		• 1 copy of *Subtraction Facts Quiz B* URG Page 20 per student • 2 copies of *Number Deck 0–11* and *Number Deck 12–23* URG Pages 81–84 copied back to back per student group • 1 copy of *Individual Assessment Record Sheet* TIG Assessment section per student, previously copied for use throughout the year
Lesson 6 **Tall Buildings** URG Pages 85–88 SG Page 111 *Estimated Class Sessions* **1**	OPTIONAL LESSON **Optional Activity** Students complete a series of word problems about tall buildings. **Homework** Assign some or all of the problems for homework.	• 1 calculator per student	

Unit 9: Using Patterns to Predict .... 7 Sessions

Unit Summary

Students use a two-pan balance and standard masses to find the mass of various objects. Then, in the lab *Mass vs. Number,* they investigate how to predict the total mass of a number of identical objects. For example, if one pencil has a mass of 11 grams, then multiplication or repeated addition yields 44 grams for the mass of 4 pencils. They see that such procedures give a good, though possibly inexact, prediction. For example, the measured mass of the 4 pencils might turn out to be 46 grams.

Students discuss the concept of experimental error, possible sources of experimental error, and explore ways to make predictions when the data contains experimental error. In particular, point graphs are used to make predictions when data points are close to a straight line. The unit provides a context for a variety of problem-solving situations involving multiplication and division. The DPP for this unit reviews and assesses the subtraction facts in Groups 5 and 6 and develops strategies for the multiplication facts for the threes, nines, and square numbers.

Major Concept Focus

- measuring mass in grams
- measurement error
- TIMS Laboratory Method
- predicting mass
- checking predictions
- using multiplication and division
- point graphs
- investigating patterns
- best-fit line
- variables and values
- fixed variables
- subtraction facts review and assessment for Groups 5 and 6
- multiplication strategies for the 3s, 9s, and square numbers

Pacing Suggestions

- Lesson 1 *Measuring Mass* and Lesson 2 *Mass vs. Number* provide connections to science. Students can measure mass and collect the data for the lab during science time.
- Lesson 3 *More Mass Problems* is a set of word problems. These problems can be distributed throughout the unit as homework.

Unit Planner

KEY: SG = Student Guide, DAB = Discovery Assignment Book, AB = Adventure Book, URG = Unit Resource Guide, DPP = Daily Practice and Problems, HP = Home Practice (found in Discovery Assignment Book), and TIG = Teacher Implementation Guide.

	Lesson Information	Supplies	Copies/Transparencies
Lesson 1 **Measuring Mass** URG Pages 20–38 SG Pages 114–118 DPP A–D HP Parts 1–2 *Estimated Class Sessions* **2**	**Activity** Students measure mass of small objects using a two-pan balance and standard metric masses. They compare their results and discuss why they may have gotten different answers for the mass of the same objects and whether these differences are reasonable. **Math Facts** DPP items A, B, and C provide practice with math facts. **Homework** 1. Students complete the Homework section on the *Measuring Mass* Activity Pages. 2. Assign Parts 1 and 2 of the Home Practice. 3. Students study the subtraction facts in Group 5 at home using their flash cards. **Assessment** 1. Students complete the *Balancing Masses* Assessment Pages. 2. Use the *Observational Assessment Record* to note students' abilities to measure mass in grams.	• 1 two-pan balance per student group • 1 set of standard masses (ten 1-gram, ten 5-gram, five 10-gram, and two 20-gram masses) per student group • 1 set of objects to measure per student group • 1 small piece of clay for leveling the balances per student group	• 1 copy of *Balancing Masses* URG Pages 30–31 per student • 1 copy of *Subtraction Flash Cards: Group 5* URG Pages 33–34 per student copied back-to-back, optional • 2 copies of *Two-column Data Table* URG Page 35 per student • 1 transparency of *Professor Peabody Travels to the Moon* URG Page 32, optional • 1 copy of *Observational Assessment Record* URG Pages 11–12 to be used throughout this unit
Lesson 2 **Mass vs. Number** URG Pages 39–59 SG Pages 119–123 DAB Pages 139–142 DPP E–L HP Parts 3–4 *Estimated Class Sessions* **4**	**Lab** Students investigate how the mass of identical objects is related to the number of objects. They make predictions using the patterns they find in their data. Students also explore reasons why measurements are not exact. **Math Facts** DPP items E and G provide practice with subtraction facts. Items I, J, K, and L provide practice with multiplication facts. **Homework** 1. Assign the Yolanda's Oat Bran Bars Homework section in the *Student Guide.* 2. Assign Parts 3 and 4 of the Home Practice. 3. Students study the subtraction facts in Group 6 at home using their flash cards. **Assessment** 1. Students complete the *Robin's Marbles* Assessment Page. 2. Use DPP Task J as assessment.	• 1 two-pan balance per student group • 1 set of standard masses (ten 1-gram, ten 5-gram, five 10-gram, and two 20-gram masses) per student group • 10–15 nearly identical objects per student group • 1 small piece of clay for leveling the balances per student group	• 1 copy of *Robin's Marbles* URG Page 52 per student • 1 copy of *Two-column Data Table* URG Page 35 per student • 3 copies of *Centimeter Graph Paper* URG Page 55 per student • 1 copy of *Subtraction Flash Cards: Group 6* URG Pages 53–54 per student copied back-to-back, optional

	Lesson Information	**Supplies**	**Copies/ Transparencies**
Lesson 3 **More Mass Problems** URG Pages 60–67 SG Pages 124–127 DPP M–N *Estimated Class Sessions* **I**	**Activity** Students complete a series of mass problems involving tables and graphs. **Math Facts** DPP Bit M is the *Subtraction Facts: Quiz C.* **Homework** Assign some or all of the problems for homework. **Assessment** 1. DPP Bit M assesses subtraction facts. 2. Use the *Observational Assessment Record* to document students' abilities to solve multiplication problems involving mass. 3. Transfer appropriate documentation from the Unit 9 *Observational Assessment Record* to students' *Individual Assessment Record Sheets.*	• 1 ruler per student	• 1 copy of *Subtraction Facts: Quiz C* URG Page 19 per student • 3 copies of *Centimeter Graph Paper* URG Page 55 per student • 1 copy of *Individual Assessment Record Sheet* TIG Assessment section per student, previously copied for use throughout the year

Overview

Unit 10: Numbers and Patterns: An Assessment Unit .... 6–8 Sessions

Unit Summary
The formal assessment activities in this unit, together with ongoing informal and formal assessment activities in the other units, help teachers monitor student progress. Paper-and-pencil problems and short tasks provide information about concepts and skills developed in Units 1–9. A review of student portfolios allows you to examine student progress since the beginning of the school year. Student work in designing and carrying out the lab, *Stencilrama,* enables you to assess many of the skills and concepts developed in preceding units. Students' abilities to communicate mathematical ideas are also assessed. The DPP for this unit first reviews and assesses the subtraction facts in Groups 7 and 8 and then assesses all the subtraction facts. DPP items also develop strategies for the last six multiplication facts (4×6, 4×7, 4×8, 6×7, 6×8, 7×8).

Major Concept Focus
- TIMS Laboratory Method
- measuring length in inches
- point graphs
- predicting
- checking predictions
- investigating patterns
- subtraction facts practice
- Game: subtraction facts
- money
- communicating problem-solving solutions
- assessing problem solving
- midyear test
- subtraction facts review and assessment for Groups 7 and 8
- assessment of all the subtraction facts
- strategies for the last six multiplication facts

Pacing Suggestions
- Lessons in this unit provide review, application, and assessment of concepts and skills in Units 1–9. Students' abilities with these skills and concepts will determine how quickly they can move through the unit.
- Lesson 4 *Word Problems for Review* is an optional lesson. You can distribute the problems in that lesson for homework throughout the unit or students can work on them together in class.

Unit Planner

KEY: SG = Student Guide, DAB = Discovery Assignment Book, AB = Adventure Book, URG = Unit Resource Guide, DPP = Daily Practice and Problems, HP = Home Practice (found in Discovery Assignment Book), and TIG = Teacher Implementation Guide.

	Lesson Information	**Supplies**	**Copies/ Transparencies**

Lesson 1

Stencilrama

URG Pages 22–44
SG Pages 130–134
DAB Pages 147–150

DPP A–F
HP Parts 1–2

Estimated Class Sessions

3

Assessment Lab
Students make borders by using a stencil. They investigate the relationship between the number of stencils and the length of the border by collecting and graphing data. Then students use the data to make predictions and solve problems involving multiplication.

Math Facts
DPP Bits A and E provide practice with the subtraction facts in Groups 7 and 8. DPP Bit C encourages students to practice the subtraction facts in Group 7 using the *Subtraction Flash Cards.* Task F develops strategies for the multiplication facts.

Homework
1. Assign Home Practice Parts 1 and 2.
2. Assign the word problems in Lesson 4.
3. Students study the subtraction facts in Groups 7 and 8 at home using the flash cards.

Assessment
1. Use the *Observational Assessment Record* to document students' abilities to measure length in inches and to collect, organize, graph, and analyze data.
2. Add this lab to students' portfolios.
3. Score *Questions* **5** and **6** using the *TIMS Multidimensional Rubric.*

Supplies:
- 1 3 × 5 inch index card per student group
- 1 pair of scissors per student group
- 1 ruler per student
- colored markers
- strips of paper approximately 36″ by 7″ or large paper grocery bags per student group
- 1 meterstick per student
- examples of designs from different cultures
- examples of stencils, optional

Copies/Transparencies:
- 1 copy of *Centimeter Graph Paper* URG Page 36 per student
- 1 copy of *Subtraction Flash Cards: Groups 7* and *8* URG Pages 37–40 per student, copied back-to-back, optional
- 1 copy of the *TIMS Multidimensional Rubric* TIG Assessment section
- 1 copy of the *Observational Assessment Record* URG Pages 9–10 to be used throughout this unit

Lesson 2

Problem Game

URG Pages 45–63
SG Page 135
DAB Pages 151–153

DPP G–H
HP Parts 3–4

Estimated Class Sessions

1

Game
Students review subtraction facts while playing a game.

Math Facts
DPP Bit G asks students to practice the subtraction facts in Group 8 using *Subtraction Flash Cards.*

Homework
1. Remind students to use their flash cards to study the subtraction facts.
2. Assign Home Practice Parts 3 and 4.

Supplies:
- 1 game token or centimeter connecting cube per student
- 1 clear plastic spinner or pencil with paper clip per student group

Copies/Transparencies:
- 1 copy of *Subtraction Flash Cards: Groups 1–8* URG Pages 37–40 and 51–62 per student, copied back-to-back

(Continued)

Overview

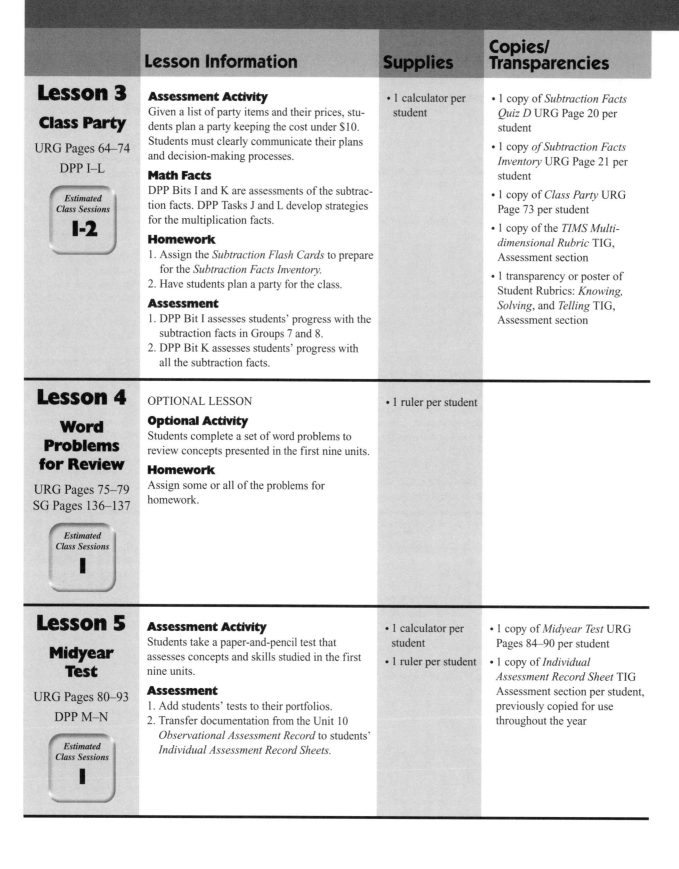

	Lesson Information	Supplies	Copies/ Transparencies
Lesson 3 **Class Party** URG Pages 64–74 DPP I–L *Estimated Class Sessions* **1-2**	**Assessment Activity** Given a list of party items and their prices, students plan a party keeping the cost under $10. Students must clearly communicate their plans and decision-making processes. **Math Facts** DPP Bits I and K are assessments of the subtraction facts. DPP Tasks J and L develop strategies for the multiplication facts. **Homework** 1. Assign the *Subtraction Flash Cards* to prepare for the *Subtraction Facts Inventory.* 2. Have students plan a party for the class. **Assessment** 1. DPP Bit I assesses students' progress with the subtraction facts in Groups 7 and 8. 2. DPP Bit K assesses students' progress with all the subtraction facts.	• 1 calculator per student	• 1 copy of *Subtraction Facts Quiz D* URG Page 20 per student • 1 copy *of Subtraction Facts Inventory* URG Page 21 per student • 1 copy of *Class Party* URG Page 73 per student • 1 copy of the *TIMS Multi-dimensional Rubric* TIG, Assessment section • 1 transparency or poster of Student Rubrics: *Knowing, Solving,* and *Telling* TIG, Assessment section
Lesson 4 **Word Problems for Review** URG Pages 75–79 SG Pages 136–137 *Estimated Class Sessions* **1**	OPTIONAL LESSON **Optional Activity** Students complete a set of word problems to review concepts presented in the first nine units. **Homework** Assign some or all of the problems for homework.	• 1 ruler per student	
Lesson 5 **Midyear Test** URG Pages 80–93 DPP M–N *Estimated Class Sessions* **1**	**Assessment Activity** Students take a paper-and-pencil test that assesses concepts and skills studied in the first nine units. **Assessment** 1. Add students' tests to their portfolios. 2. Transfer documentation from the Unit 10 *Observational Assessment Record* to students' *Individual Assessment Record Sheets.*	• 1 calculator per student • 1 ruler per student	• 1 copy of *Midyear Test* URG Pages 84–90 per student • 1 copy of *Individual Assessment Record Sheet* TIG Assessment section per student, previously copied for use throughout the year

Unit 11: Multiplication Patterns .... 10-11 Sessions

Unit Summary

The study of multiplication and division continues by solving problems about an amusement park called Lizardland. Students also look for patterns in the multiplication table and build rectangular arrays to develop strategies for learning the multiplication facts. They apply these patterns to the multiplication of multiples of 10 and 100. The Adventure Book *Cipher Force!* discusses addition, subtraction, multiplication, and division involving zero. Students learn to use *Triangle Flash Cards* to practice multiplication facts. This unit launches the systematic practice and assessment of the multiplication facts that continues in Units 12–20 in the DPP. The DPP for this unit provides practice with and assesses the multiplication facts for the 5s and 10s.

Major Concept Focus

- multiplication concepts
- division concepts
- multiplication sentences
- division sentences
- division and zero
- *Adventure Book:* zero and the four operations
- multiplication facts strategies
- multiplication facts practice
- multiplication tables
- array model of multiplication
- multiplying by multiples of ten
- turn-around facts
- factors
- square numbers
- prime numbers
- Game: products, factors, and rectangular arrays
- investigating patterns
- money
- communicating problem-solving solutions
- practice and assessment of the multiplication facts for the 5s and 10s

Pacing Suggestions

- In Lesson 4 *Completing the Table,* students assess their fluency with the multiplication facts for the fives and tens and begin a systematic review of those facts they need to study. Work with the remaining groups of facts is distributed throughout the Daily Practice and Problems and Home Practice in each unit. All students should continue learning new concepts and skills while working on the facts.
- Because the math facts program is closely linked to the recommended schedule for teaching lessons, classrooms that differ significantly from the suggested pacing will need to make accommodations to ensure that students receive a consistent program of math facts practice and assessment throughout the year. The *Grade 3 Facts Resource Guide* outlines a study schedule for the math facts for classrooms that move much more slowly through lessons than is recommended in the Lesson Guides. For more information, see the TIMS Tutor: *Math Facts* in the *Teacher Implementation Guide.*

Unit Planner

	Lesson Information	Supplies	Copies/ Transparencies
Lesson 1 **Lizardland Problems** URG Pages 26–33 SG Pages 140–144 DPP A–B *Estimated Class Sessions* **1**	**Activity** Students solve multiplication problems by using clues they find in a drawing of the Lizardland Amusement Park. They then write and solve their own multiplication problems about the drawing. **Math Facts** DPP Task B provides practice with multiplication facts. **Homework** Assign the homework on the *Lizardland Problems* Activity Pages. **Assessment** Use the *Observational Assessment Record* to note students' abilities to solve multiplication problems and explain their reasoning.	• 1 calculator per student	• Poster made by enlarging the Lizardland picture found on *Lizardland Problems* SG Pages 140–141, optional • 1 copy of *Observational Assessment Record* URG Pages 13–14 to be used throughout this unit
Lesson 2 **Handy Facts** URG Pages 34–43 DAB Pages 159–164 DPP C–D *Estimated Class Sessions* **1**	**Activity** Students generate the multiplication facts for 0, 1, 2, 3, 5, and 10; record them on a blank multiplication table; and look for patterns among the table entries. **Math Facts** DPP Bit C and Task D provide practice with multiplication facts. **Homework** Assign the *Nickels and Dimes* Homework Pages for homework. **Assessment** Use the *Observational Assessment Record* to note students' abilities to use patterns to learn the multiplication facts.	• counters, number lines, or *100 Charts,* optional	• 1 copy of the *100 Chart* URG Page 41 per student, optional • 1 transparency of *My Multiplication Table* DAB Page 159
Lesson 3 **Multiplication and Rectangles** URG Pages 44–56 SG Pages 145–148 DPP E–H *Estimated Class Sessions* **2**	**Activity** Students arrange square-inch tiles into rectangular arrays. They explore turn-around facts, prime numbers, and squares. They derive multiplication facts and record them on their multiplication tables. **Math Facts** DPP Bit E provides practice with multiplication by 0 and 1. Task F is multiplication fact practice. **Homework** Assign the Tile Problems Homework section on the *Multiplication and Rectangles* Activity Pages. **Assessment** *Questions 3–4* of the Homework section may be used for an assessment.	• 25 square-inch tiles of one color per student	• 2 copies of *Centimeter Grid Paper* URG Page 52 per student • 1 copy of *Three-column Data Table* URG Page 53 per student, optional • 1 copy of *Square-Inch Grid Paper* URG Page 54 per student • 1 copy of *My Multiplication Table* with the 0, 1, 2, 3, 5, and 10 columns completed, DAB Page 159 per student • 1 transparency of *Centimeter Grid Paper* URG Page 52 • 1 transparency of *My Multiplication Table* with the 0, 1, 2, 3, 5, and 10 columns completed, DAB Page 159

(Continued)

Overview

	Lesson Information	Supplies	Copies/Transparencies
Lesson 4 **Completing the Table** URG Pages 57–69 SG Pages 149–151 DAB Pages 165–169 DPP I–L HP Parts 1–2 *Estimated Class Sessions* **2**	**Activity** Students complete their multiplication tables by finding the remaining facts through skip counting or using a calculator. Symmetry in the table is discussed as well as patterns for multiples of nine. Students learn to use the *Triangle Flash Cards* to practice the multiplication facts. **Math Facts** DPP items J and L provide practice with multiplication facts. **Homework** 1. Assign the Homework section of the *Completing the Table* Activity Pages. 2. Students take home their lists of facts they need to study and the *Triangle Flash Cards* to practice the facts with a family member. 3. Assign Parts 1 and 2 of the Home Practice.	• 1 calculator per student, optional • 1 envelope for storing flash cards per student	• 2 *Small Multiplication Tables* (1 for class and 1 for home) URG Page 67 per student, optional • 1 copy of *My Multiplication Table* (completed in Lessons 2 and 3) DAB Page 159 per student • 1 transparency of *My Multiplication Table* (completed in Lessons 2 and 3) DAB Page 159 • 1 transparency of *Multiplication Table* URG Page 66
Lesson 5 **Floor Tiler** URG Pages 70–75 DAB Pages 171–173 DPP M–N *Estimated Class Sessions* **1**	**Game** After spinning two numbers, players use the product to color in rectangles on grid paper. Players take turns spinning and filling in their grids. **Math Facts** DPP Task N provides practice with multiplication facts. **Homework** Students play *Floor Tiler* at home. **Assessment** Use the *Observational Assessment Record* to note students' abilities to represent multiplication using rectangular arrays.	• 1 clear plastic spinner or pencil and paper clip per student pair • 1 crayon or marker per student	• 1 copy of *Centimeter Grid Paper* URG Page 52 per student • 1 transparency of *Centimeter Grid Paper* URG Page 52, optional • 1 transparency of *Spinners 1–4 and 1–10* DAB Page 173, optional
Lesson 6 **Division in Lizardland** URG Pages 76–84 SG Pages 152–154 DPP O–P HP Parts 3–4 *Estimated Class Sessions* **1**	**Activity** Students explore the relationship between multiplication and division through problems about the Lizardland Amusement Park. They discover that there is no turn-around rule for division, and they investigate division involving zero. **Math Facts** DPP items O and P provide practice with multiplication facts. **Homework** 1. Assign the Homework section of the *Division in Lizardland* Activity Pages. 2. Assign Parts 3 and 4 of the Home Practice. **Assessment** Use *Question 17* of the Homework section as an assessment.	• counters, optional	• 1 completed copy of *My Multiplication Table* DAB Page 159 per student • 1 classroom copy of Lizardland poster from Lesson 1, optional

	Lesson Information	Supplies	Copies/Transparencies

Lesson 7
Cipher Force!

URG Pages 85–93
AB Pages 77–94

DPP Q–R

Estimated Class Sessions

1

Adventure Book
A group of superheroes and their nine-year-old companion fight crime using addition, subtraction, multiplication, and division with zero.

Math Facts
DPP Bit Q provides practice with multiplication facts using mathhoppers. Task R examines products of 36.

Homework
Remind students to practice at home for the quiz on the multiplication facts using the *Triangle Flash Cards: 5s* and *10s*.

Assessment
1. To assess this lesson, students can write a response to one of the first three Journal Prompts.
2. Use DPP item R to assess students' abilities to write number sentences for multiplication situations.

Lesson 8
Multiples of Tens and Hundreds

URG Pages 94–100
SG Page 155
DAB Page 175

DPP S–T

Estimated Class Sessions

1-2

Activity
Using base-ten pieces, students investigate multiplication by multiples of 10 and 100.

Math Facts
DPP Bit S is the Quiz on 5s and 10s. Task T builds number sense and provides practice with math facts.

Homework
Assign the *Professor Peabody's Multiplication Tables* Homework Page in the *Discovery Assignment Book*.

Assessment
1. Use DPP Bit S and the *Observational Assessment Record* to note students' fluency with the multiplication facts for the fives and tens.
2. Transfer appropriate documentation from the Unit 11 *Observational Assessment Record* to students' *Individual Assessment Record Sheets*.

Supplies (Lesson 8):
- 1 calculator per student
- 1 set of base-ten pieces per student
- overhead base-ten pieces, optional

Copies/Transparencies (Lesson 8):
- 1 completed copy of *My Multiplication Table* DAB Page 159 per student
- 1 transparency of *Professor Peabody's Multiplication Tables* DAB Page 175
- 1 copy of *Individual Assessment Record Sheet* TIG Assessment section per student, previously copied for use throughout the year

Overview

Unit 12: Dissections .... 7–9 Sessions

Unit Summary

Students make, draw, measure, describe, and analyze plane geometric figures. Much of the work involves figures that can be made with small sets of constituent pieces; we say the figures are "dissected" into the pieces. In the first activity, students use Tangrams to solve puzzles and create shapes. In *Building with Triangles,* students build plane geometric shapes with triangles and then investigate congruence, transformations (turns and flips), area, perimeter, and symmetry. They study relationships between attributes of shapes (e.g., the number of sides and the number of corners). As culminating activities, students solve geometric puzzles and play a geometric game similar to tic-tac-toe. The DPP for this unit provides practice with and assesses the multiplication facts for the 2s and 3s.

Major Concept Focus

- multiple representations of shapes
- naming two-dimensional shapes
- spatial visualization skills
- analyzing shapes
- measuring area in square inches
- measuring perimeter in centimeters
- congruence
- sides
- corners (vertices)
- angles
- right angles
- flips
- turns
- line symmetry
- Game: geometric game requiring logical reasoning
- practice and assessment of the multiplication facts for the 2s and 3s

Pacing Suggestions

Lesson 6 *Focus on Word Problems* is an optional lesson. These problems can be solved in class or assigned as homework throughout the unit. Since the lesson requires little teacher preparation, it is appropriate for a substitute teacher.

Unit Planner

	Lesson Information	Supplies	Copies/Transparencies
Lesson 1 **Tangrams** URG Pages 21–38 SG Pages 158–165 DAB Page 185 DPP A–D HP Part 1 *Estimated Class Sessions* **2**	**Activity** Students explore tangram puzzles—those in which pieces are joined edge to edge. Students solve several puzzles, discuss why others are unsolvable, and design their own puzzles. **Math Facts** DPP Bit A introduces the *Triangle Flash Cards: 2s* and *3s*. Bit C provides practice with the twos. **Homework** 1. Assign Home Practice Part 1. 2. Have students share the puzzle they made on the *Making a Tangram Puzzle* Activity Page with a family member. 3. Assign some of the problems in the Puzzling Tangrams section of the *Tangrams* Activity Pages in the *Student Guide*. 4. Remind students to take home their *Triangle Flash Cards* to study with a family member. **Assessment** Use the Journal Prompt as an assessment.	• 1 set of tangram pieces per student • 1 envelope for storing tangram pieces per student • 1 envelope for storing flash cards per student • 1 ruler per student	• 1 copy of *Tangram Pieces Master* URG Page 32 per student pair, optional • 1 transparency of *Hints for Puzzling Tangrams* URG Page 33
Lesson 2 **Building with Triangles** URG Pages 39–56 SG Pages 166–169 DAB Pages 187–188 DPP E–F HP Part 2 *Estimated Class Sessions* **1-2**	**Activity** Students make shapes by putting two or three isosceles right triangles together edge to edge. They trace shapes on paper and measure, describe, and analyze them. **Homework** 1. Assign the Building with Three Triangles section for homework. 2. Assign Home Practice Part 2. **Assessment** 1. During the activity observe students' abilities to identify right angles, recognize congruent shapes, show lines of symmetry, and measure area and perimeter. Record your observations on the *Observational Assessment Record*. 2. Use the Journal Prompt to assess students' abilities to explain their reasoning.	• 1 pair of scissors per student • 1 centimeter ruler per student • 1 envelope for storing triangles per student group • markers or crayons • 3 small triangles from 2 tangram sets per student group • 1 square from a set of tangrams, optional per student group	• 1 copy of *Lines of Symmetry* URG Page 51 per student, optional • 1 or 2 copies of *Right Triangle Master* URG Page 52 on heavy paper, optional • 1 transparency of *When Are Shapes the Same?* URG Page 53 • 1 copy of *Observational Assessment Record* URG Pages 11–12 to be used throughout this unit
Lesson 3 **Building with Four Triangles** URG Pages 57–73 SG Pages 170–172 DPP G–J HP Part 3 *Estimated Class Sessions* **2**	**Activity** This activity extends the previous activity. Students investigate shapes they can make by putting together four isosceles right triangles edge to edge. **Math Facts** For item J, students illustrate multiplication number sentences. **Homework** 1. Assign some of Professor Peabody's Shape Riddles. 2. Assign Home Practice Part 3. **Assessment** Students complete the *Three Tans* Assessment Pages.	• 1 pair of scissors per student • 1 centimeter ruler per student • plain paper to sketch shapes • 1 envelope for storing cutout shapes per student group • 2 sets of trangrams per student group	• 1 copy of *Four Triangles Data Tables 1* and *2* URG Pages 65–66 per student group, optional • 1 copy of *Tangram Pieces Master* URG Page 32 per student group, optional • 1 copy of *Three Tans* URG Pages 67–68 per student • 1 transparency of *Four Triangles Data Tables 1* and *2* URG Pages 65–66 • 1 transparency of *Tangram Pieces Master* URG Page 32, colored and cut out or 2 sets of tangram pieces

(Continued)

Overview

	Lesson Information	Supplies	Copies/ Transparencies
Lesson 4 **Dissection Puzzles** URG Pages 74–83 SG Pages 173–175 DAB Page 189 DPP K–L HP Part 4 *Estimated Class Sessions* **1**	**Activity** Students solve puzzles that require dissecting figures in specific ways. In each puzzle, they put together a set of pieces edge to edge to make various shapes. **Math Facts** DPP Bit K provides practice with the multiplication facts for the threes. **Homework** 1. Puzzles may be assigned for homework. 2. Assign Home Practice Part 4. **Assessment** 1. Puzzle C provides an opportunity to observe students' abilities to analyze and describe two-dimensional shapes. Record your observations on the *Observational Assessment Record.* 2. Transfer information from the Unit 12 *Observational Assessment Record* to students' *Individual Assessment Record Sheets.*	• 1 pair of scissors per student • 1 set of tangram pieces per student, optional	• 1 copy of *Individual Assessment Record Sheet* TIG Assessment section per student, previously copied for use throughout the year
Lesson 5 **Hex** URG Pages 84–89 DAB Page 191 DPP M–N *Estimated Class Sessions* **1**	**Game** Students play a geometric game similar to tic-tac-toe or "boxes." Later, this game will be adapted to provide practice in estimation and mental computation. **Math Facts** DPP Bit M is a quiz on the twos and threes multiplication facts. **Homework** 1. Encourage students to play *Hex* with a family member. 2. Assign the word problems in Lesson 6 for homework. **Assessment** DPP Bit M is a quiz to assess the twos and threes multiplication facts.	• 25 of each of 2 kinds of beans or other small markers per student pair	• 1 transparency of *4-by-4 Hex* URG Page 89, optional
Lesson 6 **Focus on Word Problems** URG Pages 90–96 SG Pages 176–177 *Estimated Class Sessions* **1**	OPTIONAL LESSON **Optional Activity** Students solve problems that involve addition, subtraction, multiplication, or division. **Homework** Assign some or all of the problems for homework.	• 1 ruler per student	• 1 copy of *Centimeter Graph Paper* URG Page 94 per student

Unit 13: Parts and Wholes .... 6–8 Sessions

Unit Summary

Students investigate part-whole fractions by working with pattern blocks, solving word problems, playing games, and making and using paper models. Basic fraction concepts are emphasized; procedures are not. A fundamental idea in several activities is that the meaning of a fraction depends on what the whole is (e.g., half an inch is much less than half a mile). Other important ideas are that the whole must be divided into equal parts, that fractions can have more than one name, and that ordering fractions by size requires attention to both the numerator and denominator. The use of one-half as a benchmark for comparing fractions is emphasized. The utility of fractions in everyday life is highlighted in several activities and in the homework. The DPP for this unit provides practice with and assesses the multiplication facts for the square numbers.

Major Concept Focus

- fraction concepts
- multiple representations of fractions
- problem solving with fractions
- concept of whole
- part-whole fractions
- area model of fractions
- fractions of sets
- concept of addition of fractions
- comparing fractions
- equivalent fractions
- Game: finding a fraction of a number
- Game: comparing fractions
- practice and assessment of the multiplication facts for the square numbers

Pacing Suggestions

- Lesson 4 *Fraction Games* consists of two games that develop and practice fraction concepts. If the class plays both games, this lesson will take two class sessions.
- Lesson 5 *Fraction Problems,* an optional lesson, is a set of word problems involving fractions. These problems can be solved in class, or as homework throughout the unit. Since the lesson requires little teacher preparation, it is appropriate to leave for a substitute teacher.

Overview

Unit Planner

KEY: SG = Student Guide, DAB = Discovery Assignment Book, AB = Adventure Book, URG = Unit Resource Guide, DPP = Daily Practice and Problems, HP = Home Practice (found in Discovery Assignment Book), and TIG = Teacher Implementation Guide.

	Lesson Information	Supplies	Copies/Transparencies
Lesson 1 **Kid Fractions** URG Pages 18–27 SG Pages 180–181 DPP A–B HP Parts 4–5 *Estimated Class Sessions* **1**	**Activity** A group of students stands at the front of the class while the teacher presents a fraction based on some characteristic of the group. The rest of the class tries to determine what characteristic the teacher has in mind. **Math Facts** DPP Bit A reminds students to use the *Triangle Flash Cards: Square Numbers.* **Homework** 1. Assign the Homework section of the *Kid Fractions* Activity Pages. 2. Remind students to take home their flash cards to practice the square numbers at home. 3. Assign Parts 4 and 5 of the Home Practice.	• 1 envelope for storing flash cards per student	
Lesson 2 **What's 1?** URG Pages 28–39 SG Pages 182–184 DAB Page 199 DPP C–F *Estimated Class Sessions* **2**	**Activity** Students use pattern blocks to solve concept-of-unit problems. **Math Facts** DPP items D, E, and F provide practice with multiplication facts. **Homework** Assign the *Naming Wholes and Parts* Homework Page in the *Discovery Assignment Book.* Students do not need pattern blocks to complete this page. **Assessment** Assign the *Pattern Block Fractions* Assessment Blackline Master.	• pattern blocks (2 yellow hexagons, 10 green triangles, 5 blue rhombuses, and 4 red trapezoids) per student group • 1 resealable plastic bag per student group, optional • overhead pattern blocks	• 1 copy of *Pattern Block Fractions* URG Page 35 per student
Lesson 3 **Pizza Problems** URG Pages 40–51 SG Pages 185–187 DPP G–J HP Part 3 *Estimated Class Sessions* **2**	**Activity** Students solve word problems about sharing pizza fairly. These problems introduce basic fraction ideas. **Homework** 1. Assign the Homework section of the *Pizza Problems* Activity Pages. 2. Assign problems from the *Fraction Problems* Activity Pages (optional Lesson 5) as appropriate. 3. Assign Home Practice Part 3. **Assessment** Use the *Observational Assessment Record* to note students' abilities to represent fractions in pictures, words, and symbols.	• 1 pair of scissors per student	• 4 copies of *Ten Pizzas* URG Page 48 per student pair • 1 transparency of *Centimeter Grid Paper* URG Page 49, optional • 1 copy of *Observational Assessment Record* URG Pages 9–10 to be used throughout the unit

	Lesson Information	Supplies	Copies/Transparencies
Lesson 4 **Fraction Games** URG Pages 52–60 SG Pages 188–189 DAB Pages 201–213 DPP K–L HP Parts 1–2 *Estimated Class Sessions* **1-2**	**Games** *FractionLand:* Students advance tokens along a path and answer various questions along the way. Finding a fraction of a number is stressed. *Fraction Problem Game:* Students compare two fractions and say a number sentence to move their pieces. **Math Facts** DPP Bit K is the quiz on the square numbers. **Homework** 1. Students play the games at home. 2. Assign Parts 1 and 2 of the Home Practice. **Assessment** 1. Use DPP Bit K to assess students' fluency with multiplication facts for the square numbers. 2. Use the *Observational Assessment Record* to document students' abilities to find fractions of sets and to compare and order fractions. 3. Transfer appropriate documentation from the *Observational Assessment Record* to students' *Individual Assessment Record Sheets*.	• 1 envelope for storing flash cards per student • 1 pair of scissors per student • 50 counters (e.g., connecting cubes or beans) per student • 1 game token per student • 1 clear plastic spinner (or pencil with paper clip) per student group	• 1 copy of *Individual Assessment Record Sheet* TIG Assessment section per student, previously copied for use throughout the year
Lesson 5 **Fraction Problems** URG Pages 61–65 SG Pages 190–191 *Estimated Class Sessions* **1**	OPTIONAL LESSON **Optional Activity** Students solve a set of problems involving fractions. **Homework** Assign some or all of the problems for homework.	• counters • 1 calculator per student • 1 clock face per student, optional	

Overview

Unit 14: Collecting and Using Data . . . . 7–10 Sessions

Unit Summary

A major objective of this unit is to give students more autonomy as they work on a lab and solve problems. In the lab *Make Your Own Survey,* students work with a group to conduct a survey using the TIMS Laboratory Method. With as little assistance as possible, they choose a variable to study and then organize, collect, display, and analyze the data. The class also works cooperatively to plan and implement a "reading drive" by setting goals for the amount of reading they will do over a given period of time. They keep track of their reading by collecting and displaying the data. The data provides a context for problem solving using addition and subtraction of larger numbers, reading a clock to the nearest minute, and finding elapsed time. The DPP for this unit provides practice with and assesses the multiplication facts for the nines.

Major Concept Focus

- telling time to the nearest minute
- elapsed time
- Game: telling time on digital and analog clocks
- simple percentages as benchmarks
- TIMS Laboratory Method
- bar graphs
- importance of accurate data
- surveys
- multidigit addition
- multidigit subtraction
- addition algorithms
- subtraction algorithms
- variables and values
- practice and assessment of the multiplication facts for the 9s

Pacing Suggestions

- Lesson 3 *Tracking Our Reading* begins a long-term project that will take two to three weeks to complete. Setting up the investigation will take one day. Then students collect data over a two- or three-week period. The class will need another class session to analyze the collected data.
- In Lesson 5 *Reviewing Addition and Subtraction* students review using base-ten pieces, mental math strategies, and paper and pencil to add and subtract multidigit numbers. Students' abilities with these skills will determine the number of days students will need to solve the problems.

Unit Planner

	Lesson Information	Supplies	Copies/ Transparencies

Lesson 1

Time Again

URG Pages 19–33
SG Pages 194–200

DPP A–B
HP Part 1

Estimated Class Sessions

1

Activity
Students practice telling time to the nearest minute. They take part in various 5-minute activities, e.g., reading, practicing subtraction facts, listening to music. They note the time on an analog clock before and after each activity. They also practice finding elapsed time.

Math Facts
DPP Bit A reminds students to practice the multiplication facts using the *Triangle Flash Cards: 9s.*

Homework
1. Assign as homework any problems not used in class on the *Time Again* Activity Pages.
2. Assign Part 1 of the Home Practice.
3. Remind students to take home their *Triangle Flash Cards* to study with a family member.

Assessment
1. Students complete the *More Time* Assessment Blackline Master.
2. Use the *Observational Assessment Record* to document students' abilities to tell time to the nearest minute and to solve problems involving elapsed time.

Supplies:
- analog demonstration clock
- 1 pair of scissors per student
- 1 brad per student
- 1 envelope for storing flash cards per student
- things to do for 5 minutes such as read a book or *Triangle Flash Cards*, optional
- 1 clear jar with straight sides (e.g., small peanut butter jar) for each water clock (extension) per student, optional
- 1 large plastic jug with a cap (e.g., milk or soda bottle) for each water clock (extension) per student, optional
- masking tape (extension), optional
- food coloring (extension), optional
- small nail (extension), optional
- hammer (extension), optional

Copies/Transparencies:
- 1 copy of *Clock* URG Page 29 on card stock per student, optional
- 1 copy of *More Time* URG Page 30 per student
- 1 copy of *Observational Assessment Record* URG Pages 9–10 to be used throughout this unit

Lesson 2

Time and Time Again

URG Pages 34–40
SG Page 201
DAB Pages 221–227

DPP C–D
HP Part 2

Estimated Class Sessions

1

Game
Students play a variation of the card games *Concentration* and *Lotto,* in which players find pairs from memory. In this game, players turn over face-down cards, seeking to match the time on an analog clock to the corresponding digital time.

Math Facts
DPP Bit C provides practice with the multiplication facts for the 9s. Task D provides practice with the nines and multiples of ten.

Homework
1. Students take the cards home to play the game with a family member.
2. Assign Part 2 of the Home Practice.

Supplies:
- 1 pair of scissors per student

(Continued)

	Lesson Information	**Supplies**	**Copies/ Transparencies**
Lesson 3 **Tracking Our Reading** URG Pages 41–54 SG Page 202 DPP E–F HP Part 3 *Estimated Class Sessions* **1-2**	**Activity** This lesson is the beginning of a long-term class project that will continue for two or more weeks. During the first week, the class collects data on students' reading and uses the data to set a goal for the following week or two. The class continues to collect more data to see if they can meet their goal. **Math Facts** DPP Bit E provides practice with multiplication facts. **Homework** 1. Students will read at home and record their data. 2. Assign Part 3 of the Home Practice.	• large sheet of paper or a flip chart for recording class data	• 2 copies of *Eight-column Data Table* URG Page 53 per student, optional • 1 enlarged (and laminated) copy of *Reading Goal Scale* URG Page 52 for the class or 100 cc graduated cylinder and colored water
Lesson 4 **Make Your Own Survey** URG Pages 55–71 SG Pages 203–208 DPP G–J HP Part 4 *Estimated Class Sessions* **2-3**	**Lab** Students work in groups to gather survey data about the other students in the room. Students independently choose a variable to study. They investigate, collect and organize data, and present their findings to the class. The importance of reporting data accurately and honestly is discussed. **Math Facts** DPP Bit G is the Multiplication Quiz: 9s. Task J reviews square numbers. **Homework** 1. Students bring examples of survey data from newspapers or magazines. 2. Assign Part 4 of the Home Practice. **Assessment** 1. Assign scores to students' surveys and record comments on their performance using the *TIMS Laboratory Method Checklist* and the *TIMS Multidimensional Rubric*. 2. Use DPP Bit G to assess students' fluency with the multiplication facts for the nines.	• 1 class names list per student group	• 1–2 copies of *Centimeter Graph Paper* URG Page 65 per student • 1 *Three-column, Four-column, Five-column,* or *Eight-column Data Table* URG Pages 53 & 66–68 per student as selected • 1 *TIMS Laboratory Method Checklist* URG Page 64 per student pair for assessment, optional • 1 transparency of *Three-column Data Table* URG Page 66, optional • 1 transparency of *Centimeter Graph Paper* URG Page 65, optional • 1 copy of *TIMS Multidimensional Rubric* TIG, Assessment section
Lesson 5 **Reviewing Addition and Subtraction** URG Pages 72–85 SG Pages 209–215 DPP K–N *Estimated Class Sessions* **2-3**	**Activity** Students review adding and subtracting large numbers using base-ten pieces and pencil and paper. Using the data from *Tracking Our Reading* as a context, students solve problems involving addition and subtraction. **Homework** Assign the Homework section on the *Reviewing Addition and Subtraction* Activity Pages. **Assessment** 1. Students complete the *Addition and Subtraction* Assessment Blackline Master.	• 1 set of base-ten pieces (2 packs, 14 flats, 30 skinnies, and 50 bits) per student and 1 set for the teacher • magnetic base-ten pieces and a magnetic board or overhead base-ten pieces, optional	• 1 copy of *Addition and Subtraction* URG Pages 80–81 per student • 1 copy of *Individual Assessment Record Sheet* TIG Assessment section per student, previously copied for use throughout the year

Lesson Information	Supplies	Copies/Transparencies
2. Use the *Observational Assessment Record* to note students' abilities to represent multidigit addition and subtraction problems using base-ten pieces. 3. Transfer appropriate documentation from the Unit 14 *Observational Assessment Record* to the students' *Individual Assessment Record Sheets*.		

Overview

Unit 15: Decimal Investigations .... 8–9 Sessions

Unit Summary

This unit introduces decimals. Decimals for tenths and hundredths are presented as another way of writing certain common fractions. One important context for this initial work is measuring to the nearest tenth. To complete the lab *Number vs. Length,* students measure to the nearest tenth of a centimeter. Work with skip counting by tenths is included. Students also explore what happens when there are more than 10 tenths. Students use base-ten pieces to help them understand the relationship between decimals and common fractions (e.g., $0.1 = \frac{1}{10}$). Using this relationship, they tell whether a fraction is more than, less than, or equal to a given decimal. The DPP for this unit provides practice with and assesses the last six multiplication facts.

Major Concept Focus

- decimals concepts
- multiple representations of decimals
- concept of a whole
- decimal notation
- reading decimals
- comparing decimals
- length model for decimal fractions
- measuring length to nearest tenth of a centimeter
- estimating length
- Game: decimal and common fractions
- TIMS Laboratory Method
- point graphs
- best-fit line
- predicting
- checking predictions
- addition facts practice
- subtraction facts practice
- Game: addition and subtraction facts
- practice and assessment of the last six multiplication facts

Preparing for Upcoming Lessons

Place eyedroppers, graduated cylinders, and water in a learning center for students to begin exploring volume prior to Unit 16.

Begin collecting small objects (e.g., marbles, pens, pencil erasers) for Unit 16 Lesson 1.

Begin collecting jars for Unit 16 Lesson 2.

Begin collecting containers with volumes in pints, cups, quarts, or gallons for Unit 16 Lesson 3.

Unit Planner

	Lesson Information	Supplies	Copies/Transparencies
Lesson 1 **Decimal Fractions** URG Pages 21–37 SG Pages 218–221 DAB Pages 235–237 DPP A–D HP Part 1 *Estimated Class Sessions* **2**	**Activity** Students are formally introduced to decimal notation for tenths and hundredths. The primary emphasis of the activity is on connections between base-ten pieces, base-ten shorthand, and common and decimal fractions. A secondary emphasis is on counting with decimals. **Math Facts** DPP Bit A introduces the *Triangle Flash Cards: The Last Six Facts* and Task B develops facts strategies. **Homework** 1. Assign the *Decimal Hunt* Homework Page in the *Discovery Assignment Book*. 2. Assign Home Practice Part 1. 3. Remind students to take home their *Triangle Flash Cards* to study with a family member. **Assessment** 1. Observe students' abilities to skip count by tenths during the activity. Record your observations on the *Observational Assessment Record*. 2. The *Tenths Table* Activity Page can be adapted for use as an assessment. 3. Use a copy of the *Three-column Data Table* to create additional conversion problems between base-ten shorthand, common fractions, and decimal fractions.	• 1 set of base-ten pieces (2 packs, 14 flats, 30 skinnies, and 50 bits) per student pair or group of three • 1 calculator per student • 1 envelope for storing flash cards per student	• 1–2 copies of *Three-column Data Table* URG Page 34 per student pair, optional • 1 transparency of *One Whole, Ten Tenths* URG Page 32 • 1 transparency of *Ten Tenths, One Hundred Hundredths* URG Page 33 • 1 copy of *Observational Assessment Record* URG Pages 11–12 to be used throughout this unit
Lesson 2 **Measuring to the Nearest Tenth** URG Pages 38–50 SG Pages 222–226 DAB Pages 239–240 DPP E–H HP Parts 3–4 *Estimated Class Sessions* **2**	**Activity** Students measure the lengths of various objects to the nearest tenth of a centimeter. **Homework** 1. Send a copy of the *Measure Hunt* Activity Pages home for homework. Ask a family member to verify the measurements. 2. Assign Home Practice Parts 3 and 4. Students will need centimeter rulers. **Assessment** Students complete the *Measure My Desk* Assessment Blackline Master. Record students' abilities to measure to the nearest tenth of a centimeter on the *Observational Assessment Record*.	• 1 paper clip per student • 1 square-inch tile per student • 1 centimeter ruler per student • 1 meterstick per student group • overhead centimeter ruler	• 1 copy of *Measure My Desk* URG Page 46 per student

(Continued)

Overview

	Lesson Information	Supplies	Copies/Transparencies
Lesson 3 **Decimal Hex** URG Pages 51–56 DAB Pages 241–242 DPP I–J HP Part 2 *Estimated Class Sessions* **1**	**Game** Students use two tokens to travel across a game board by correctly comparing two decimal fractions or a decimal and a common fraction. **Math Facts** DPP Bit I and Task J provide practice with the last six multiplication facts. **Homework** 1. Encourage students to play *Decimal Hex* with a family member. 2. Assign Home Practice Part 2.	• 2 same color centimeter cubes as game markers per student • 1 set of base-ten pieces per student • 1 paper clip and pencil or clear plastic spinner per student group	
Lesson 4 **Length vs. Number** URG Pages 57–73 SG Pages 227–232 DPP K–P *Estimated Class Sessions* **3**	**Lab** Students apply decimal concepts by investigating the relationship between the number of identical objects in a row and the length of the row, measuring to the nearest tenth of a centimeter. They measure rows made with varying numbers of objects, record their data in a table, graph their results, and analyze them. **Math Facts** DPP item K practices the last six multiplication facts and item M is a quiz on those facts. **Homework** Assign homework *Questions 1–4* on the *Length vs. Number* Lab Pages. Students will need a copy of *Centimeter Graph Paper* for this assignment. **Assessment** 1. Use DPP Items L and O as an assessment. 2. DPP Bit M is a quiz on the last six multiplication facts. 3. The lab and the lab homework provide many opportunities to observe students' abilities to work with data and solve problems related to that data. Record your observations on the *Observational Assessment Record*. 4. Use *Question 9* of the Explore section of the lab to assess students' abilities to solve problems and communicate solutions. Use the *TIMS Multidimensional Rubric* to score student work. 5. Transfer appropriate Unit 15 observations to students' *Individual Assessment Record Sheets*.	• 1 centimeter ruler per student • 1 meterstick per student group • small identical objects for students to choose from, e.g., paper clips, pennies, square-inch tiles, etc. • 1 calculator per student group • 1 block of wood per student group, optional • 1 large piece of paper, per student group, for use as a pad for the experiment, optional • *Counting on Frank* by Rod Clement, optional	• 1 copy of *Centimeter Graph Paper* URG Page 69 per student • 1 copy of *Three-trial Data Table* URG Page 70 per student, optional • 1–2 copies of *Centimeter* or *Half-centimeter Graph Paper* URG Pages 69 & 71 per student • 1 copy of *TIMS Multidimensional Rubric* TIG Assessment section, optional • 1 copy of *Individual Assessment Record Sheet* TIG Assessment section per student, previously copied for use throughout the year

	Lesson Information	Supplies	Copies/Transparencies
Lesson 5 **Nothing to It!** URG Pages 74–78 SG Page 233 *Estimated Class Sessions* **1**	OPTIONAL LESSON **Optional Game** Students practice addition and subtraction facts while playing a simple card game. **Homework** Encourage students to play this game at home with a family member.		• 1 copy of *Number Deck 0–11* URG Pages 77–78 copied back to back per student

Overview

Unit 16: Volume . . . . 6–7 Sessions

Unit Summary

To begin the unit, students estimate the volume of small objects by building models with centimeter connecting cubes. They then check their estimates using a graduated cylinder and measuring the volume of the objects by displacement. In the lab *Fill 'er Up!,* students measure the volume of several containers, record the measurements in a data table, and graph the results. They use the data to predict how many of one container will be needed to fill another. This provides a context for investigating division with remainders and solving problems involving multiplication. In the Adventure Book, *Elixir of Youth,* two investigators use their volume skills when the liquid inside an ancient jar is stolen from a museum's collection. Students also discover the relationships between U.S. customary units of measuring volume—the cup, pint, quart, and gallon. The DPP for this unit practices and assesses the multiplication facts for the twos, fives, and tens.

Major Concept Focus

- estimating volume in cubic centimeters
- measuring volume with graduated cylinders
- TIMS Laboratory Method
- bar graphs
- number sentences
- multidigit addition and subtraction
- predicting
- checking predictions

- capacity
- measuring volume in metric and customary units
- *Adventure Book:* finding the volume of a container
- scales
- multiplication as repeated addition
- division as repeated subtraction
- practice and assessment of the multiplication facts for the 2s, 5s, and 10s

Pacing Suggestions

- Lesson 1 *Measuring Volume* and Lesson 2 *Fill 'er Up!* connect strongly to science. In Lesson 1 students measure volume by counting cubic centimeters and using graduated cylinders. Lesson 2 is a lab that uses science-process skills to investigate the volume of containers. Use science time to complete portions of these lessons.
- Lesson 4 *Elixir of Youth* connects to both social studies and language arts. Students can read the story during either of these classes.

Unit Planner

KEY: SG = Student Guide, DAB = Discovery Assignment Book, AB = Adventure Book, URG = Unit Resource Guide, DPP = Daily Practice and Problems, HP = Home Practice (found in Discovery Assignment Book), and TIG = Teacher Implementation Guide.

	Lesson Information	**Supplies**	**Copies/ Transparencies**

Lesson 1

Measuring Volume

URG Pages 19–37
SG Pages 236–243

DPP A–B
HP Part 1

Estimated Class Sessions
1

Activity
Students find the volume of various solid objects. First, they estimate the volume by making a model from centimeter connecting cubes. Then they measure the volume by placing the object inside a graduated cylinder and determining the amount of water that it displaces.

Homework
1. Assign the Homework section on the *Measuring Volume* Activity Pages.
2. Assign Part 1 of the Home Practice.

Assessment
Use the *Observational Assessment Record* to note students' abilities to measure volume by displacement.

Supplies:
- small solid objects that fit inside a graduated cylinder
- 1 graduated cylinder calibrated no more than 2 cc apart and large enough to hold small objects (250 cc preferred) per student group
- 1 eyedropper per student group
- 1 beaker or container of water per student group
- 2 handfuls of centimeter connecting cubes per student group
- several sheets of paper towels per student group
- 1 centimeter ruler per student

Copies/Transparencies:
- 1 copy of *Three-column Data Table* URG Page 34 per student
- 1 transparency of *Scale 1 with Blowup* URG Page 30
- 1 transparency of *Scale 2 with Blowup* URG Page 31
- 1 transparency of *Scale 3 with Blowup* URG Page 32
- 1 transparency of *Meniscus* URG Page 33
- 1 copy of *Observational Assessment Record* URG Pages 9–10 to be used throughout this unit

Lesson 2

Fill 'er Up!

URG Pages 38–59
SG Pages 244–248

DPP C–H
HP Parts 2–3

Estimated Class Sessions
3

Lab
Students find the volume of various containers by pouring graduated cylinders of water into each container (or vice versa) and using addition and subtraction to calculate the total volume. Students use the data to solve problems involving multiplication and division.

Math Facts
DPP Bits C, E, and G provide practice with multiplication facts for the 2s, 5s, and 10s.

Homework
1. For homework students finish questions not completed in class.
2. Assign Parts 2 and 3 of the Home Practice.
3. Students continue to practice the multiplication facts for the 2s, 5s, and 10s using their *Triangle Flash Cards*.
4. Assign *Questions 1–2* on the *Volume Hunt* Activity Pages for Lesson 3 in the *Discovery Assignment Book*.

Assessment
1. Use *Questions 10–11* on the *Fill 'er Up!* Lab Pages to assess students' understanding of how to measure volume.
2. Assign scores to one or more parts of the lab.
3. Use the *Observational Assessment Record* to note students' abilities to collect, organize, graph, and analyze data.
4. Use DPP Task F Volume as a quiz.

Supplies:
- 1 small, 1 medium, and 1 large container per student group
- 1 250 cc graduated cylinder per student group
- 1 eyedropper per student group
- paper towels
- 1 large irregular-shaped jar
- 1 cup or small container per student group
- 1 dishpan container per student group

Copies/Transparencies:
- 1 copy of *Centimeter Graph Paper* URG Page 51 per student
- 1 copy of *Three-trial Data Table* URG Page 52 per student, optional
- 1 copy of *Triangle Flash Cards 2s, 5s,* and *10s* URG Pages 53–55 per student, optional

(Continued)

	Lesson Information	Supplies	Copies/ Transparencies
Lesson 3 **Volume Hunt** URG Pages 60–67 DAB Pages 247–248 DPP I–J HP Part 4 *Estimated Class Sessions* **1**	**Activity** Students search at home for containers whose volume is measured in U.S. Customary Units: cup, pint, quart, and gallon. Activities at home and at school develop the relationships between these units of measurement. **Math Facts** Task J provides practice with multiplication facts and money. **Homework** 1. *Questions 1–2* of the *Volume Hunt* Activity Pages were assigned at the end of Lesson 2. 2. Assign Part 4 of the Home Practice. **Assessment** Use the *Observational Assessment Record* to document students' abilities to solve addition, subtraction, multiplication, and division problems involving volume.	• 1 dishpan or large container per student group • paper towels • 2 containers of different sizes at home: cup, pint, quart, or gallon per student and 1 each for the teacher	• 1 transparency of *Volume Hunt* data table DAB Page 248, optional
Lesson 4 **Elixir of Youth** URG Pages 68–76 AB Pages 95–114 DPP K–L *Estimated Class Sessions* **1**	**Adventure Book** Sam V. and Tess V. Shovel, ace volume investigators, are on a case at the Oriental Museum. Someone has stolen the liquid contents of an ancient jar in the museum's collection, and Tess and Sam must use their volume skills to solve the mystery. **Math Facts** DPP Bit K is a multiplication quiz on the 2s, 5s, and 10s. **Homework** Assign the word problems in Lesson 5. **Assessment** 1. Use DPP Bit K to assess students on the multiplication facts for the 2s, 5s, and 10s. 2. Use DPP Task L to assess students on measuring volume by displacement. 3. Use the *Observational Assessment Record* to note students' abilities to use addition, subtraction, multiplication, and division to solve volume problems. 4. Transfer appropriate documentation from the *Observational Assessment Record* to students' *Individual Assessment Record Sheets*.	• map of the Middle East, optional	• 1 copy of *Individual Assessment Record Sheet* TIG Assessment section per student, previously copied for use throughout the year

	Lesson Information	Supplies	Copies/Transparencies

Lesson 5

Paying Taxes Problems

URG Pages 77–79
SG Page 249

Estimated Class Sessions

1

OPTIONAL LESSON

Optional Activity

As a follow-up to Unit 15 *Decimal Investigations*, students solve problems involving money.

Homework

Assign some or all of the problems for homework.

Overview

Unit 17: Wholes and Parts .... 6 Sessions

Unit Summary

Students explore relationships between fractions, focusing on the idea that fractional parts of a whole must have equal areas and on the concept of equivalence. The activities include the use of geoboards and paper folding. They also find that different fractions can represent the same quantity. They may even begin to notice patterns in those fractions. They are encouraged to think about relationships between fractions other than equivalence, including greater than, less than, and comparisons with benchmarks such as 0, 1, and $\frac{1}{2}$. In the Adventure Book, *The Clever Tailor,* misunderstandings about fractions arise when the size of the unit whole is ignored. The DPP for this unit provides practice with and assesses the multiplication facts for the threes and nines.

Major Concept Focus

- multiple representations of fractions
- fraction concepts
- concept of a whole
- area model of fractions
- part-whole fractions
- congruence
- flips
- one-half as a benchmark
- equivalent fractions
- comparing fractions
- *Adventure Book:* concept of a whole
- Game: comparing fractions
- patterns
- practice and assessment of the multiplication facts for the 3s and 9s

Pacing Suggestions

Lesson 3 *The Clever Tailor* is a story based on a fairy tale by the Brothers Grimm. Students can read the story as part of language arts.

Unit Planner

KEY: SG = Student Guide, DAB = Discovery Assignment Book, AB = Adventure Book, URG = Unit Resource Guide, DPP = Daily Practice and Problems, HP = Home Practice (found in Discovery Assignment Book), and TIG = Teacher Implementation Guide.

	Lesson Information	Supplies	Copies/Transparencies
Lesson 1 **Geoboard Fractions** URG Pages 18–36 SG Pages 252–254 DPP A–D HP Parts 1–2 *Estimated Class Sessions* **2**	**Activity** Students make rectangles on geoboards and find different ways to divide them into halves, thirds, and fourths. **Math Facts** DPP Bit A provides practice with multiplication facts for the threes and nines. **Homework** 1. Students use *Triangle Flash Cards* to study for the quiz on the threes and nines in DPP Bit K. 2. Assign Parts 1 and 2 of the Home Practice for homework. **Assessment** 1. Students complete the *Halves of a Rectangle* Assessment Blackline Masters. 2. Use the *Observational Assessment Record* to record students' abilities to partition shapes into fractional parts.	• 1 geoboard per student • overhead geoboard • several rubber bands per student	• 1 copy of *Halves of a Rectangle* URG Pages 28–29 per student • 2 copies of *Large Geoboard Paper* URG Page 30 per student • 4 copies of *Geoboard Paper* URG Page 31 per student • 1 copy of *Triangle Flash Cards:3s* and *9s* URG Pages 32–33 per student, optional • 1 transparency of *Large Geoboard Paper* URG Page 30 or overhead geoboard • 1 transparency of *Geoboard Paper* URG Page 31 • several copies of *Large Geoboard Paper* URG Page 30 • 1 copy of *Observational Assessment Record* URG Pages 9–10 to be used throughout this unit
Lesson 2 **Folding Fractions** URG Pages 37–51 SG Pages 255–263 DAB Pages 253–254 DPP E–H *Estimated Class Sessions* **2**	**Activity** Students find equivalent forms for $\frac{1}{2}$, $\frac{1}{3}$, and other simple fractions by folding paper. **Homework** Have students complete the Folding One-fourth section in class or for homework. **Assessment** 1. Use *Questions 48–50* in the Folding One-fourth section as assessment. 2. Use the *Observational Assessment Record* to document students' abilities to find and name equivalent fractions using manipulatives.	• several sheets of scratch paper (large enough to be folded several times and preferably blank on one side) per student • markers or crayons • 1 ruler per student, optional	• 2 copies of *One-third Folding Sheet* URG Page 46 per student
Lesson 3 **The Clever Tailor** URG Pages 52–61 AB Pages 115–128 DPP I–J HP Part 3 *Estimated Class Sessions* **1**	**Adventure Book** This story complements the unit's fraction activities by helping students to see the misunderstandings about fractions that can arise when the size of the unit whole is ignored. **Math Facts** Bit I provides practice with the multiplication facts. Task J provides practice with multiplication facts for the 3s and 9s with multiples of 10 and 100. **Homework** 1. Have students find the prices of items in newspaper ads or catalogs. Then have them list things they would buy if they had $4050. Direct students to come as close to the figure as they can without going over.	• 1 meterstick per student, optional • play money: ten-, hundred-, and thousand-dollar bills, optional • pattern blocks, optional • counters, optional	

(Continued)

Overview

TIG • Grade 3 • Overview • Unit 17   **117**

	Lesson Information	**Supplies**	**Copies/ Transparencies**
	2. Suggest that students read the story to someone at home and discuss the story's fraction misunderstandings. 3. Assign Part 3 of the Home Practice. It reviews fractional parts using area models.		
Lesson 4 **Fraction Hex** URG Pages 62–67 DAB Pages 255–257 DPP K–L HP Part 4 *Estimated Class Sessions* **1**	**Game** Students compare fractions in the game *Fraction Hex.* **Math Facts** DPP Bit K is a short quiz that assesses multiplication facts for the threes and nines. **Homework** 1. Students take home *Fraction Hex* to play with their families. 2. Assign Part 4 of the Home Practice. **Assessment** 1. DPP Bit K Multiplication Quiz: 3s and 9s assesses the multiplication facts in these groups. 2. Transfer appropriate documentation from the Unit 17 *Observational Assessment Record* to students' *Individual Assessment Record Sheets.*	• 2 same color centimeter cubes or other game marker per student • pattern blocks • 1 clear plastic spinner or paper clip and pencil per student	• 1 copy of *Individual Assessment Record Sheet* TIG Assessment section per student, previously copied for use throughout the year.

Unit 18: Viewing and Drawing 3-D .... 6 Sessions

Unit Summary
In this unit students visualize and describe three-dimensional objects. They describe three-dimensional objects (e.g., rectangular prisms and objects made with connecting cubes) in words by talking about the faces, edges, and vertices (corners). They gather information about three-dimensional objects (cube models) by measuring and recording the height, volume, and area of the base. They also use three methods to represent three-dimensional shapes in two dimensions: sketching cubes and other boxes, making cube model plans, and recording three views of the cube models—the top, front, and right side views. The DPP for this unit provides practice and assesses the multiplication facts for the square numbers.

Major Concept Focus
- multiple representations of shapes
- three-dimensional objects
- cubes and rectangular prisms
- drawing cubes and rectangular prisms
- edges
- faces
- vertices
- cube models
- cube model plans
- area
- length
- volume
- multiple solution strategies
- practice and assessment of the multiplication facts for the square numbers

Unit Planner

	Lesson Information	Supplies	Copies/ Transparencies
Lesson 1 **Viewing 3-D Objects** URG Pages 21–32 SG Pages 266–269 DPP A–B HP Part 1 *Estimated Class Sessions* **1**	**Activity** Students view boxes from different perspectives and describe what they see. They compare 3-D objects to 2-D drawings of the objects. **Math Facts** DPP items A and B provide practice with the multiplication facts for the square numbers. **Homework** 1. For homework students collect drawings or pictures of boxes, paste the pictures on paper, trace the edges of each box, and record the number of faces and edges seen. 2. Assign Part 1 of the Home Practice. 3. Students study the multiplication facts for the square numbers using *Triangle Flash Cards*.	• 1 empty tissue box or box of similar size and shape per student pair and 1 for the teacher • Mr. Origin	• 1 copy of *Triangle Flash Cards: Square Numbers* URG Page 30 per student, optional
Lesson 2 **Drawing 3-D Objects** URG Pages 33–45 SG Pages 270–272 DAB Pages 263–265 DPP C–D HP Part 2 *Estimated Class Sessions* **1**	**Activity** Students compare a 2-D drawing of a cube to an actual 3-D cube. After comparing and describing faces, edges, parallel lines, and shapes, students draw cubes and other rectangular prisms (boxes). **Homework** 1. Students draw a box at home for homework. 2. Students complete the Journal Prompt at home. 3. Assign Part 2 of the Home Practice. **Assessment** As an assessment, students draw a rectangular prism using a box or other classroom object as a model.	• 1 cube (e.g. connecting cube or base-ten piece) per student • 1 large cube (e.g. large base-ten piece or cardboard box) • 1 empty cereal box per student pair • 3 different colored pens or pencils per student • 1 ruler per student • masking tape or self-adhesive notes, optional • 12 toothpicks per student and 12 for the teacher, optional • 8 miniature marshmallows per student and 8 for the teacher, optional • 3 blue pattern blocks per student, optional • 3 overhead blue pattern blocks, optional	

	Lesson Information	**Supplies**	**Copies/ Transparencies**
Lesson 3 **Building and Planning Cube Models** URG Pages 46–58 SG Pages 273–276 DPP E–F HP Part 3 *Estimated Class Sessions* **1**	**Activity** Students build and describe cube models using 2-D representations called cube model plans. Students use cube model plans to determine the area of a cube model's base, its volume, and its height. Given specifications, students build cube models and, in the process, solve problems with multiple solutions. **Math Facts** DPP Bit E provides practice with multiplication facts for the square numbers. **Homework** Assign Part 3 of the Home Practice. **Assessment** Use the *Observational Assessment Record* to record students' abilities to translate between a cube model, its cube model plan, and a drawing.	• 30 connecting cubes per student pair	• 3 copies of *3 × 3 Cube Model Plans* URG Page 55 per student • 1 transparency of *3 × 3 Cube Model Plans* URG Page 55, optional • 1 transparency of *Dee's Cube Model Plan* URG Page 56 • 1 copy of *Observational Assessment Record* URG Pages 11–12 to be used throughout this unit
Lesson 4 **Top, Front, and Right Side Views** URG Pages 59–72 SG Pages 277–281 DPP G–J HP Part 4 *Estimated Class Sessions* **2**	**Activity** Students view cube models from the top, front, and right side and then record these three views. Students also solve puzzles about cube models. **Math Facts** DPP item G provides computation and mental math practice. Bit I provides practice with the multiplication facts for the square numbers. **Homework** 1. Assign the *Three Ways to Show 3-D Models* Assessment Pages either for homework or in-class assessment. 2. Assign Home Practice Part 4. **Assessment** 1. Students complete the *Three Ways to Show 3-D Models* Assessment Blackline Masters. 2. Use the *Observational Assessment Record* to record students' abilities to identify the front, right, and top views of a cube model.	• 30 connecting cubes per student • masking tape, optional	• 2 copies of *3 × 3 Cube Model Plans* URG Page 55 per student • 2 copies of *Three-view Records* URG Page 69 per student • 1 copy of *Three Ways to Show 3-D Models* URG Pages 67–68 per student
Lesson 5 **Problems with Shapes** URG Pages 73–78 SG Pages 282–283 DPP K–L *Estimated Class Sessions* **1**	**Activity** Students solve a set of word problems involving geometric concepts. **Math Facts** DPP Bit K is the multiplication quiz on the square numbers. **Homework** Assign some or all of the problems for homework. **Assessment** 1. Students complete DPP item K Multiplication Quiz: Squares. 2. Use the *Observational Assessment Record* to document students' abilities to find the area of the base, height, and volume of a cube model.	• 20 connecting cubes per student • crayons or colored pencils	• 1 copy of *3 × 3 Cube Model Plans* URG Page 55 per student • 1 copy of *Individual Assessment Record Sheet* TIG Assessment section per student, previously copied for use throughout the year.

(Continued)

Overview

Lesson Information	Supplies	Copies/Transparencies
3. Transfer appropriate documentation from the Unit 18 *Observational Assessment Record* to students' *Individual Assessment Record Sheets*.		

Unit 19: Multiplication and Division Problems . . . . 9 Sessions

Unit Summary

Students solve multiplication problems by breaking products into the sum of simpler products using rectangular arrays drawn on grid paper. They begin with one-digit by one-digit problems and move to two-digit by one-digit problems. Students write and solve multiplication story problems giving particular attention given to partitioning numbers into tens and ones. These problems act as a catalyst for the conceptual development of an algorithm for multiplication involving two-digit by one-digit numbers. In this unit, students also solve division problems that deal with remainders and multistep problems that involve both multiplication and division. The DPP for this unit provides practice with and assesses the last six multiplication facts.

Major Concept Focus

- multiplication strategies
- multiplication stories
- one-digit by two-digit multiplication
- multiplication by multiples of ten
- division strategies
- division stories
- interpreting remainders
- multistep problems
- multiple solution strategies
- practice and assessment of the last six multiplication facts

Overview

Unit Planner

KEY: SG = Student Guide, DAB = Discovery Assignment Book, AB = Adventure Book, URG = Unit Resource Guide, DPP = Daily Practice and Problems, HP = Home Practice (found in Discovery Assignment Book), and TIG = Teacher Implementation Guide.

	Lesson Information	Supplies	Copies/ Transparencies

Lesson 1

Break-apart Products

URG Pages 23–38
SG Pages 286–289

DPP A–B
HP Part 1

Estimated Class Sessions
1

Activity
Students solve multiplication problems by breaking products into the sum of simpler products using rectangular arrays drawn on grid paper. They begin with multiplying one-digit numbers and move to multiplying a two-digit number by a one-digit number.

Math Facts
DPP Bit A provides practice with the last six multiplication facts.

Homework
1. Assign Home Practice Part 1.
2. Assign *Questions 1–20* in the Homework section of the *Student Guide*.
3. Remind students to practice the last six multiplication facts using the *Triangle Flash Cards*.

Supplies:
- crayons or colored pencils
- red and green overhead markers

Copies/Transparencies:
- 5–6 copies of *Centimeter Grid Paper* URG Page 31 per student
- 1 table from *Small Multiplication Tables* URG Page 32 per student
- 1 copy of *Triangle Flash Cards: The Last Six Facts* URG Page 33 per student, optional
- 1 transparency of *Rectangular Arrays* URG Page 30

Lesson 2

More Multiplication Stories

URG Pages 39–51
SG Pages 290–294

DPP C–J
HP Part 2

Estimated Class Sessions
4

Activity
Students solve problems that involve multiplying two-digit numbers by one-digit numbers, giving particular attention to partitioning numbers into tens and ones. They write stories to represent the multiplication problems and their partitions. This work leads to the conceptual development of a paper-and-pencil algorithm for multiplication.

Math Facts
DPP Bit E and Task H provide practice with the last six multiplication facts.

Homework
1. Assign Home Practice Part 2.
2. Assign the Homework section in the *Student Guide*.

Assessment
1. Ask students to solve the problem 4 × 34 representing their work Tyrone's Way. Record your observations using the *Observational Assessment Record*.
2. Use the homework problems in the *Student Guide* to assess students' understanding of the paper-and-pencil algorithm.

Copies/Transparencies:
- 1 table from *Small Multiplication Tables* URG Page 32 per student
- 1 copy of *Observational Assessment Record* URG Pages 11–12 to be used throughout this unit

	Lesson Information	**Supplies**	**Copies/ Transparencies**
Lesson 3 **Making Groups** URG Pages 52–59 DPP K–L HP Part 3 *Estimated Class Sessions* **1**	**Activity** Students consider the number of groups of equal size that they can make from various numbers of objects. The groupings involve dividing numbers between 25 and 50, including many that cannot be solved just by using fact families. Particular attention is given to remainders. **Math Facts** DPP Bit K provides practice with using doubles to solve multiplication problems. **Homework** 1. Assign Home Practice Part 3. 2. Ask students to complete a table for 56 like the one they completed in the lesson. **Assessment** 1. While students complete a table like the one in the lesson, observe their abilities to write number sentences for division situations and interpret remainders. Record observations on the *Observational Assessment Record*. 2. Use DPP Task L as an assessment.	• 50 connecting cubes per student	• 4–5 copies of *Four-column Data Table* URG Page 58 per student
Lesson 4 **Solving Problems with Division** URG Pages 60–70 SG Pages 295–298 DPP M–R HP Part 4 *Estimated Class Sessions* **3**	**Activity** Students solve multiplication and division word problems, including some division word problems that involve remainders. They also solve challenging multistep problems whose solutions use both multiplication and division. **Math Facts** DPP items P and Q provide practice with and assess multiplication facts. **Homework** 1. Assign Home Practice Part 4. 2. Assign the homework problems on the *Solving Problems with Division* Activity Pages. **Assessment** 1. DPP Bit Q is a quiz on the last six multiplication facts. 2. Assign the *Multiplication and Division* Assessment Blackline Master. Have multiplication tables available for students. 3. Note students' progress solving multiplication and division problems. Transfer appropriate Unit 19 *Observational Assessment Record* observations to students' *Individual Assessment Record Sheets*.	• base-ten pieces, optional • connecting cubes, optional • calculators, optional	• 1 table from *Small Multiplication Tables* URG Page 32 per student • 1 copy of *Multiplication and Division* URG Page 67 per student • 1 copy of *Individual Assessment Record Sheet* TIG Assessment section per student, previously copied for use throughout the year

Overview

Unit 20: Connections: An Assessment Unit .... 8–9 Sessions

Unit Summary

This unit provides summative evaluation information by engaging students in several tasks. As in the previous assessment units, Units 2 and 10, students complete both paper-and-pencil and hands-on activities. A class discussion of the labs completed during the year sets the stage for the final lab, *Tower Power.* Use the shorter activity, *Earning Money,* to assess students' abilities to solve an open-response problem and to communicate their problem-solving strategies. Two traditional paper-and-pencil tests and a review of student portfolios are also part of this assessment menu. Students are given many opportunities within this unit to demonstrate the many concepts and skills they have developed over the year. The DPP for this unit assesses all the multiplication facts.

Major Concept Focus

- TIMS Laboratory Method
- variables
- fixed variables
- point graphs
- interpreting graphs
- measuring length in centimeters
- measuring area in square centimeters
- measuring volume in cubic centimeters
- predicting
- money
- division concepts
- communicating problem-solving solutions
- assessing problem solving
- assessing the subtraction facts
- end-of-year test
- DPP assessment of all the multiplication facts

Unit Planner

KEY: SG = Student Guide, DAB = Discovery Assignment Book, AB = Adventure Book, URG = Unit Resource Guide, DPP = Daily Practice and Problems, HP = Home Practice (found in Discovery Assignment Book), and TIG = Teacher Implementation Guide.

	Lesson Information	Supplies	Copies/Transparencies
Lesson 1 **Experiment Review** URG Pages 19–27 SG Page 301 DPP A–B HP Part 1 *Estimated Class Sessions* **1**	**Activity** Students review the labs they completed during the year. **Homework** 1. Assign Home Practice Part 1. 2. Assign the multiplication facts as homework for students to review.	• poster board or large sheet of paper for class chart • student portfolios	• 1 transparency of *Stencilrama Graph* URG Page 26 • 1 transparency of a student's point graph from an experiment such as Unit 9 *Mass vs. Number,* optional
Lesson 2 **Tower Power** URG Pages 28–40 DAB Pages 279–287 DPP C–H *Estimated Class Sessions* **3**	**Assessment Lab** Students investigate the relationship between the height and volume of a tower made from centimeter connecting cubes. They graph data and use the graph to make predictions about the heights and volumes of larger towers. **Math Facts** DPP Bit E discusses multiplication facts strategies. **Homework** 1. Assign the Homework section in the *Discovery Assignment Book.* 2. Remind students to study the multiplication facts using the *Triangle Flash Cards.* **Assessment** Review and assess the lab based on the criteria outlined in the Lesson Guide.	• 40 centimeter connecting cubes per student group and 250 additional cubes available for checking predictions • 1 ruler per student • 1 calculator per student	• 1 copy of *Observational Assessment Record* URG Pages 9–10 to be used throughout this unit
Lesson 3 **Becca's Towers** URG Pages 41–48 DPP I–J HP Part 2 *Estimated Class Sessions* **1**	**Assessment Activity** Students solve word problems about cube towers. They graph and interpret information from a data table. **Math Facts** DPP Task J asks students to solve multiplication problems using skip counting. **Homework** Assign Home Practice Part 2. **Assessment** Use the *Observational Assessment Record* to record students' abilities to make and interpret a point graph. Transfer appropriate information from the Unit 20 *Observational Assessment Record* to students' *Individual Assessment Record Sheets.*	• 1 calculator per student • centimeter connecting cubes, optional	• 1 copy of *Becca's Towers* URG Page 45 per student • 1 copy of *Centimeter Graph Paper* URG Page 46 per student • 1 copy of *Individual Assessment Record Sheet* TIG Assessment section per student, previously copied for use throughout the year

(Continued)

Overview

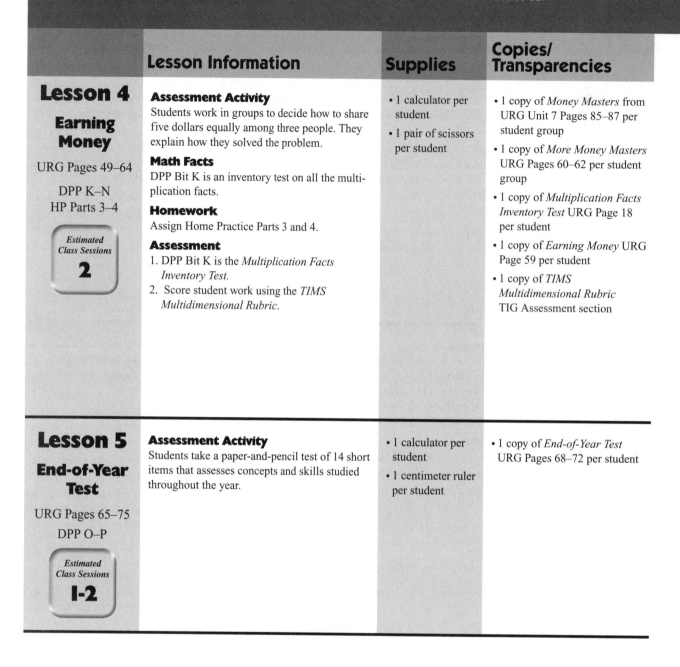

	Lesson Information	Supplies	Copies/ Transparencies
Lesson 4 **Earning Money** URG Pages 49–64 DPP K–N HP Parts 3–4 *Estimated Class Sessions* **2**	**Assessment Activity** Students work in groups to decide how to share five dollars equally among three people. They explain how they solved the problem. **Math Facts** DPP Bit K is an inventory test on all the multiplication facts. **Homework** Assign Home Practice Parts 3 and 4. **Assessment** 1. DPP Bit K is the *Multiplication Facts Inventory Test.* 2. Score student work using the *TIMS Multidimensional Rubric.*	• 1 calculator per student • 1 pair of scissors per student	• 1 copy of *Money Masters* from URG Unit 7 Pages 85–87 per student group • 1 copy of *More Money Masters* URG Pages 60–62 per student group • 1 copy of *Multiplication Facts Inventory Test* URG Page 18 per student • 1 copy of *Earning Money* URG Page 59 per student • 1 copy of *TIMS Multidimensional Rubric* TIG Assessment section
Lesson 5 **End-of-Year Test** URG Pages 65–75 DPP O–P *Estimated Class Sessions* **1-2**	**Assessment Activity** Students take a paper-and-pencil test of 14 short items that assesses concepts and skills studied throughout the year.	• 1 calculator per student • 1 centimeter ruler per student	• 1 copy of *End-of-Year Test* URG Pages 68–72 per student

Scope and Sequence
& the NCTM *Principles and Standards*

This section provides descriptions and tables that show how *Math Trailblazers* relates to the National Council of Teachers of Mathematics *Principles and Standards for School Mathematics*. A comprehensive scope and sequence for Grade 3 units and Daily Practice and Problems is included.

Students share their data by recording it on a class data table.

Math Trailblazers and the Principles and Standards

The National Council of Teachers of Mathematics (NCTM) *Principles and Standards for School Mathematics* and *Math Trailblazers* complement each other: The *Principles and Standards* is a vision of what school mathematics should be. *Math Trailblazers* is the curricular structure so teachers can turn that vision into reality. This section starts with an outline of how *Math Trailblazers* complements the five content and five process standards in the *Principles and Standards*. It concludes with a scope and sequence that specifies how the Grade 3 curriculum develops through the year. For information on the scope and sequence across the grades, see the *Math Trailblazers Scope and Sequence Chart* available from Kendall/Hunt Publishing Company.

Content Standards

Principles and Standards for School Mathematics outlines an articulated vision of how learning and teaching in each of five content areas should develop across the grades. These content areas are number and operations, algebra, geometry, measurement, and data analysis and probability. In *Math Trailblazers* the standards for all five content areas are addressed appropriately at every grade level, from Kindergarten through Grade 5. Five process standards prescribe a curriculum where problem solving, communication, reasoning, connections, and representation are integral, not ancillary, issues. By looking at the Scope and Sequence Chart in this section, one can see how mathematical ideas develop throughout the grade.

Many activities in *Math Trailblazers* address more than one of the content standards. Consider, for example, *Bouncing Ball,* a fourth-grade laboratory experiment in which students investigate the relationship between the drop height and the bounce height of a tennis ball. The investigation begins with a question: "What is the relationship between how far a tennis ball drops and how high it bounces?" Through class discussion, the variables are identified and named (D, the drop height and B, the bounce height) and experimental procedures are devised. A picture records this information. Next, the students drop the tennis balls repeatedly, measure drop height and bounce height each time, and record the data in a table. As students gather the data, they monitor the measurements for consistency and sense. Then when the data is complete, they examine the data table to see if they can discern a pattern. Next, students graph their data. As they work, they are asked how the data table and the graph relate to the physical system, what the relationship between drop height and bounce height is, and how that relationship is evident in the table and graph. Then students make and verify predictions. Finally, students generalize: "What would the graph look like for a Super ball?" "What would happen if the experiment were repeated on a carpeted floor?"

This single experiment involves measurement, data analysis, number sense, estimation, graphing, multiplication, patterns and functions (algebra), and mathematical reasoning. All these topics, moreover, relate to a single context that unites them. By weaving so many themes into one complex whole, that whole becomes more meaningful and the mathematics more powerful.

Lessons such as *Bouncing Ball* are embedded in a careful sequence of lessons and units that address all the standards. Other lessons develop single skills or concepts that students can then practice in the Daily Practice and Problems. These skills and concepts are extended and applied in more complex lessons and investigations. *Math Trailblazers* is therefore a comprehensive and balanced curriculum that includes geometry, statistics and probability, measurement, algebra, estimation, fractions, numeration, and computation—just what the *Principles and Standards* requires.

For more information on the *Math Trailblazers* approach to selected content areas, see the TIMS Tutors in Section 9 of this *Teacher Implementation Guide.*

Process Standards

The process standards highlight ways to acquire and use content knowledge. Each process standard is connected to the others. Moreover, the learning of mathematical processes is deeply embedded in the learning of content.

Problem Solving. A strong emphasis on problem solving is evident in the NCTM recommendations. Throughout *Math Trailblazers,* students are immersed in complex problem situations in which they both apply the mathematics they know and learn new mathematics. Students develop skills, procedures, and concepts as they work on the problems. For example, in the third-grade laboratory experiment, *The Better "Picker Upper,"* students explore the absorbency of various brands of paper towels by dropping water on each type of towel and comparing the areas of the spots. As students work through this complex problem, they learn about area (by tracing the spots on grid paper and counting square centimeters to find the areas), fractions (as they piece parts of square centimeters together to make whole square centimeters), averaging (as they aggregate the results of several trials), graphing (as they display and interpret their data in graphs), and computation (as they calculate the number of drops of water a whole paper towel absorbs). All this mathematics grows out of one problem: "Which is the more absorbent towel?"

Putting problems first is a different and difficult way to organize a mathematics curriculum. Having the focus on problems requires careful design, meticulous planning, and continual assessment to ensure the timely development of skills and concepts. Despite the difficulties, the benefits are clear: students not only master skills and concepts, they can apply them flexibly to solve problems.

Reasoning and Proof. This standard requires that reasoning permeate the curriculum. Students constantly explain their thinking and justify their solutions, first in small groups and then to the class as a whole. Sometimes they explain their thoughts orally and other times in writing or by using pictures and other tools. Students are always encouraged to find solutions in more than one way and to compare and contrast various solution methods. Thus, meaning and understanding are emphasized, and students find that mathematics makes sense.

"Mathematical reasoning develops in classrooms where students are encouraged to put forth their own ideas for examination. Teachers and students should be open to questions, reactions, and elaborations from others in the classroom. Students need to explain and justify their thinking and learn how to detect fallacies and critique others' thinking. They need to have ample opportunity to apply their reasoning skills and justify their thinking in mathematical discussion." (NCTM 2000, p. 188)

One example of an important area of mathematical reasoning that receives particular attention in *Math Trailblazers,* especially in Grades 3 through 5, is pre-proportional and proportional reasoning. This kind of reasoning is carefully developed over time through a sequence of real-life problems that students can solve with manipulatives, patterns, graphs, or symbols. Students choose the strategies and tools that make sense to them. Using these tools helps students create visual images of this important mathematical concept, which historically has largely been taught symbolically or procedurally and has been difficult for many students to grasp.

Communication. Students need frequent opportunities to communicate their mathematics. "Communication is an essential part of mathematics and mathematics education… Students gain insight into their thinking when they present their methods for solving problems, when they justify their reasoning to a classmate or teacher, or when they formulate a question about something that is puzzling to them." (NCTM 2000, p. 60) Communication is integral to *Math Trailblazers.* In many activities, students handle manipulatives, draw pictures, make graphs, and grapple with mathematical ideas. Many activities are collaborative exercises involving groups of students who work together to obtain, analyze, and generalize their results.

Just as people explain how they solve problems on the job, students who use the labs and activities talk about their mathematics. Students discuss, compare, contrast, and write about their problem-solving methods in both small-group and whole-class settings. This "publication" of students' mathematical thinking gives students access to a broader range of solution strategies and helps them become more reflective about mathematics.

Connections. This standard calls for connections within mathematics, between mathematics and other parts of the school curriculum, and between mathematics and their own interests. Integration of subject matter is a major focus of *Math Trailblazers.* Mathematics arises naturally in science, language, history, and daily life. *Math Trailblazers* does not artificially merge disparate ideas from distinct disciplines, but rather builds up the underlying unity between disciplines that we see in the real world. For example, the basic measurement variables that the curriculum covers extensively —length, area, volume, mass, and time—are fundamental not only to mathematics but also to science and daily life. The TIMS Laboratory Method effectively incorporates the method of science into the mathematics curriculum as a problem-solving tool.

The *Adventure Books* and Literature Connections integrate language arts and social studies with the mathematics curriculum. Some *Adventure Books* recount the history of science and mathematics; others show how the concepts and procedures students are learning apply to the work of real scientists or to everyday life. Students are continually required to communicate their mathematical thinking orally and in writing. *Math Trailblazers* is committed to the ideal of "writing across the curriculum."

Connections within mathematics are equally important. Like most real-world problems, activities in *Math Trailblazers* generally involve a combination of mathematical topics. A single laboratory experiment, for example, might involve arithmetic, data collection, estimation, geometry, probability, and algebraic concepts—each covered at an appropriate level for students.

Representation. "Representing ideas and connecting their representations to mathematics lies at the heart of understanding mathematics." (NCTM 2000, p. 136) *Math Trailblazers* is rich in the many opportunities it gives students to represent mathematical ideas. For example, whole numbers are represented as collections of objects (using manipulatives or drawings), as measurements, as points on a number line, or as items on a *100 Chart*. When children collect data they may organize it in a data table or represent it graphically. If there are patterns in the data, they can describe them numerically or graphically. Ultimately, they describe some relations symbolically.

Throughout *Math Trailblazers* students are encouraged to draw pictures and diagrams to illustrate their ideas and support their thinking. This communicates their reasoning, and as students create these representations, they clarify and build their thinking.

Developing a *Standards*-Based Classroom

The *Professional Standards for Teaching Mathematics* (NCTM, 1991) and the Teaching Principle in the *Principles and Standards* specify what classroom teachers, supervisors, teacher educators, and policy makers should do to improve mathematics instruction. Much of this discussion concerns four key areas: tasks, discourse, environment, and analysis. Teachers decide what tasks to set for students, foster discourse about mathematics, establish a classroom environment conducive to high achievement and positive attitudes, and engage in analysis of students' thinking and their own teaching. While accomplishing these things depends more on teachers' expertise than on curricula, materials that embody the *Principles and Standards* can make the work easier.

Tasks. *Math Trailblazers* provides a logical sequence of well-conceived tasks. Professional mathematicians and scientists helped develop the curriculum so lessons focus on significant concepts and skills. Teachers and mathematics educators also helped write the curriculum, so tasks are engaging, practical, and developmentally appropriate. Lessons develop both skills and concepts, so they make connections within mathematics and between mathematics and other subjects, portray mathematics as a human endeavor, and promote communication and problem solving.

Discourse. Many features of *Math Trailblazers* support discourse. Tasks in the curriculum have enough depth for significant discussion to be possible. An emphasis on multiple solutions to problems encourages students to talk about their own thinking. The *Student Guide* often displays and discusses multiple solutions to problems. Journal and discussion prompts in the teacher materials stimulate and focus classroom discussions. *Adventure Books* and children's literature help students understand that people really do talk about mathematics and science. The wide range of tools and technology in *Math Trailblazers*—manipulatives, calculators, pictures, tables, graphs, and symbols—enhance discourse by broadening the means of communication beyond what is traditional.

Environment. Creating a classroom environment conducive to the development of each student's mathematical power is necessary for the *Principles and Standards* to come alive. This involves arranging space, time, and materials in ways that maximize student learning. *Math Trailblazers'* diverse range of lessons—activities of varied length, activities for groups and individuals, hands-on and paper-and-pencil investigations, and activities that encourage multiple solution paths—all help teachers develop a classroom that builds mathematical understandings and skills for a wide range of students.

Analysis. The curriculum's activities and assessment program provide teachers with many opportunities to analyze students' learning. Teachers using the curriculum will know more about their students' mathematical abilities than they ever have before. The extensive background information in the unit guides and in the *Teacher Implementation Guide* provides accessible ways for teachers to gain additional insight into how students learn mathematics. This enhanced knowledge motivates the teaching of subsequent lessons. *Math Trailblazers* will help you become more attuned both to your students and to your teaching.

For additional discussion on these and related topics, see the following sections in the *Teacher Implemention Guide:*

- Building the *Math Trailblazers* Classroom
- Teaching the *Math Trailblazers* Student: Meeting Individual Needs
- Language in the *Math Trailblazers* Classroom
- Working with *Math Trailblazers* Parents and Families

Math Trailblazers: A Standards-Based Curriculum

In summary, NCTM calls for curricula to be coherent within and across the grades, to be conceptually oriented, to involve students actively, to emphasize development of students' mathematical thinking and reasoning abilities, to emphasize applications, to include a broad range of content, and to make appropriate use of calculators and computers.

These are admirable goals and high expectations. No curriculum can finally and fully attain such goals and fulfill such expectations—not only will there always be improvements to be made, but in the end much depends upon individual teachers and students. Yet a curriculum that has been developed specifically to be aligned with the *Principles and Standards* will provide the foundation. The goals and characteristics described above are all hallmarks of *Math Trailblazers.*

The best test of alignment with the *Principles and Standards,* however, is to observe students using the curriculum. Are they actively involved? Do they grapple with significant concepts while learning and applying basic skills? Are they thinking and reasoning? Do they use a broad range of tools to solve realistic problems? We think you will find that *Math Trailblazers* more than meets this test.

References

An Agenda for Action: Recommendations for School Mathematics of the 1980s. National Council of Teachers of Mathematics, Reston, VA, 1980.

Assessment Standards for School Mathematics. National Council of Teachers of Mathematics, Reston, VA, 1995.

Curriculum and Evaluation Standards for School Mathematics. National Council of Teachers of Mathematics, Reston, VA, 1989.

Essential Mathematics for the 21st Century: The Position of the National Council of Supervisors of Mathematics. National Council of Supervisors of Mathematics, Minneapolis, MN, 1988.

National Research Council. "Conclusions and Recommendations." In *Adding It Up: Helping Children Learn Mathematics.* J. Kilpatrick, J. Swafford, and B. Findell (Eds.). National Academy Press, Washington, DC, 2001.

Principles and Standards for School Mathematics. National Council of Teachers of Mathematics, Reston, VA, 2000.

Professional Standards for Teaching Mathematics. National Council of Teachers of Mathematics, Reston, VA, 1991.

Scope and Sequence

Scope and Sequence for Units

Math Trailblazers was developed to meet the NCTM *Principles and Standards for School Mathematics.* The scope and sequence on white on the following pages indicates how each unit aligns with the *Principles and Standards.* By reading the chart horizontally, you will see the integration of the various standards within a given unit. By reading the chart vertically, you can track the development of a specific standard throughout the third-grade curriculum.

Scope and Sequence for the Daily Practice and Problems and Home Practice

Every unit includes Daily Practice and Problems (DPP) and Home Practice. The scope and sequence in gray on the following pages indicates how the DPP and Home Practice align with the *Principles and Standards.* By reading the chart vertically, you will be able to track the development of a specific standard throughout the third-grade DPP and Home Practice. Each DPP item, which is denoted by a letter, has been correlated with one or more of the standards. Each part of the Home Practice, which is denoted by a number, has also been correlated with one or more of the standards. The appropriate letters and numbers are indicated in parentheses following each entry. Thus, the scope and sequence can also serve as a content map for the DPP and Home Practice.

For more information about the Daily Practice and Problems and the Home Practice, see the Daily Practice and Problems and Home Practice Guide.

	Number and Operations	Algebra	Geometry	Measurement	Data Analysis and Probability
Unit 1: Sampling and Classifying **Lessons**	• Developing mental math skills. • Practicing addition facts. • Solving problems involving addition and subtraction.	• Making and interpreting bar graphs. • Using data to make predictions and solve problems. • Identifying and using variables. • Naming values of variables.			• Collecting, organizing, graphing, and analyzing data. • Representing the elements of a laboratory investigation in a drawing. • Sorting and classifying objects. • Making and interpreting bar graphs. • Using data to make predictions and solve problems. • Identifying and using variables. • Naming values of variables. • Sampling a population. • Making predictions based on a sample.
Daily Practice and Problems (Lettered) **& Home Practice** (Numbered)	• Maintaining fluency with the addition and subtraction facts. (D, K, M, Q, S) (1, 2) • Adding with three addends. (1, 2) • Solving problems in more than one way. (3) • Developing strategies for the multiplication facts. (O) • Partitioning numbers. (A, C) (3) • Writing number sentences to show partitions of numbers. (C) (3) • Developing number sense. (A, B, D, K, M) (3) • Solving problems involving addition, subtraction, and multiplication. (F, J, L, T) (1) • Solving problems involving time. (E, F, G, H, I, J, O) (4) • Solving problems involving money. (2) • Choosing appropriate methods and tools to calculate (calculators, paper and pencil, mental math). (F) • Developing mental math skills. (K, M)	• Interpreting a data table. (R) • Making and interpreting a bar graph. (P)		• Converting between units of time. (F) • Solving problems involving time. (E, F, G, H, I, J, O) (4)	• Interpreting a data table. (R) • Making and interpreting a bar graph. (P)

Problem Solving	Reasoning	Communication	Connections	Representation
• Promoting these beliefs: that problems can be solved by more than one method and different methods should yield solutions that agree. • Solving multistep word problems. • Solving problems involving addition and subtraction. • Using data to make predictions and solve problems.	• Making predictions based on a sample. • Using data to make predictions and solve problems. • Developing mathematical reasoning.	• Representing the elements of a laboratory investigation in a drawing. • Communicating solutions verbally and in writing.	• Connecting mathematics and science to real-life events: making predictions based on a sample.	• Representing the elements of a laboratory investigation in a drawing. • Collecting, organizing, graphing, and analyzing data. • Making and interpreting bar graphs.
• Solving problems involving addition and subtraction. (F, J, L, T) (1) • Solving problems involving time. (E, F, G, H, I, J, O) (4) • Solving problems involving money. (2) • Solving problems in more than one way. (3) • Creating stories for number sentences. (L, N, T)	• Explaining the error in a math problem. (D)	• Creating stories for number sentences. (L, N, T) • Communicating solutions verbally and in writing. (K, M, R) (1, 2)		• Creating stories for number sentences. (L, N, T)

Scope and Sequence

	Number and Operations	Algebra	Geometry	Measurement	Data Analysis and Probability
Unit 2: Strategies: An Assessment Unit **Lessons**	• Using strategies to add and subtract. • Developing mental math skills. • Developing calculator skills. • Reviewing addition and subtraction facts. • Developing number sense. • Estimating prices. • Solving problems involving money. • Maintaining fluency with the subtraction facts for Groups 1 and 2.	• Using turn-around facts (commutativity) to add. • Using grouping strategies (associativity) to add. • Using patterns in data to make predictions and solve problems. • Making and interpreting bar graphs.			• Collecting, organizing, graphing, and analyzing data. • Using patterns in data to make predictions and solve problems. • Making and interpreting bar graphs.
Daily Practice and Problems (Lettered) **& Home Practice** (Numbered)	• Maintaining fluency with the addition and subtraction facts. (A, E, L, N, O, Q, R, T, U) • Developing number sense. (A, C, E, I, K, M, S, W, X) (4) • Using strategies to add and subtract. (A, E, L, M, N, O, Q, R, S, T, U, W, X) (1, 2, 4) • Adding numbers with ending zeros. (A) • Developing mental math skills. (A, E, O, U, W, X) (4) • Solving problems involving addition and subtraction. (B, G, L, M, N, P, R, S, T, W, X) (1, 2, 4) • Solving problems involving money. (B, F, G, H, V, W, X) (4) • Solving problems involving elapsed time. (D) • Writing number sentences. (O, P, U) • Counting by 1s, 2s, 5s, and 10s using a calculator. (C, I) • Estimating quantities. (K) • Creating stories for addition sentences. (P) • Estimating prices. (W, X) (4)	• Using data to make predictions. (C, I)	• Identifying square corners (right angles). (J) (3)	• Solving problems involving elapsed time. (D)	• Using data to make predictions. (C, I)

Problem Solving	Reasoning	Communication	Connections	Representation
• Using patterns in data to make predictions and solve problems. • Using the *Knowing* Rubric to self-assess problem-solving skills. • Solving problems involving money.	• Using turn-around facts (commutativity) to add. • Using grouping strategies (associativity) to add. • Using patterns in data to make predictions and solve problems.	• Communicating solutions verbally and in writing.	• Connecting mathematics with literature and social studies: the origin of magic squares.	• Collecting, organizing, graphing, and analyzing data. • Using patterns in data to make predictions and solve problems. • Making and interpreting bar graphs.
• Solving problems involving addition and subtraction. (B, G, L, M, N, P, R, S, T, W, X) (1, 2, 4) • Solving problems involving money. (B, F, G, H, V, W, X) (4) • Solving problems involving elapsed time. (D) • Creating stories for addition sentences. (P)	• Using data to make predictions. (C, I)	• Communicating strategies. (A. D, E, Q, W, X) • Creating stories for addition sentences. (P)		• Writing number sentences. (O, P, U) • Creating stories for addition sentences. (P)

	Number and Operations	Algebra	Geometry	Measurement	Data Analysis and Probability
Unit 3: Exploring Multiplication **Lessons**	• Representing multiplication and division using manipulatives, pictures, and words. • Connecting multiplication and repeated addition. • Connecting multiplication and addition of equal-sized groups. • Writing number sentences for multiplication situations. • Investigating multiples. • Using turn-around facts (commutativity) to multiply. • Multiplying by $\frac{1}{2}$ and $\frac{1}{4}$. • Dividing a set into equal-sized groups (with remainders). • Creating stories and drawings for multiplication sentences. • Solving problems involving multiplication and division.	• Interpreting bar graphs. • Using turn-around facts (commutativity) to multiply. • Using patterns in data to solve problems. • Identifying patterns.			• Interpreting bar graphs. • Using patterns in data to solve problems.
Daily Practice and Problems (Lettered) **& Home Practice** (Numbered)	• Maintaining fluency with the subtraction facts in Groups 3 and 4. (C, E, G, I, N) (1) • Developing strategies for the multiplication facts for the 5s and 10s. (A, K, M, O) (2, 4) • Developing number sense for whole numbers. (B, H) (1, 3) • Developing mental math skills. (F) (1, 3) • Skip counting forwards and backwards. (D, J) • Identifying number patterns. (D) • Adding and subtracting with ending zeros. (F, G) (1, 3) • Solving problems involving money. (J, L, O, P) (2) • Using addition, subtraction, multiplication, and division to solve problems. (J, K, L, O, P) (1, 2, 3) • Solving problems involving time. (J, L) • Dividing a set into equal groups (with remainders). (M) (4) • Writing number sentences. (M, O) (4)	• Describing number patterns. (D)		• Solving problems involving time. (J, L)	

Problem Solving	Reasoning	Communication	Connections	Representation
• Solving multistep word problems. • Solving problems involving multiplication and division. • Using patterns in data to solve problems. • Creating stories and drawings for multiplication sentences.	• Explaining mathematical reasoning.	• Creating stories for multiplication sentences. • Communicating solutions verbally and in writing. • Writing number sentences for multiplication situations.	• Connecting multiplication and repeated addition. • Connecting multiplication and addition of equal-sized groups.	• Representing multiplication using manipulatives, pictures, and words. • Interpreting bar graphs. • Writing number sentences for multiplication situations. • Creating stories and drawings for multiplication sentences.
• Solving mathematical puzzles. (F) • Solving problems involving money. (J, L, O, P) (2) • Using addition, subtraction, multiplication, and division to solve problems. (J, K, L, O, P) (1, 2, 3) • Solving problems involving time. (J, L) • Solving multistep word problems. (P) (2) • Creating stories and drawings for number sentences. (N)	• Solving mathematical puzzles. (F)	• Describing number patterns. (D) • Communicating solutions verbally and in writing. (2, 4) • Creating stories and drawings for number sentences. (N)		• Creating stories and drawings for number sentences. (N)

Scope and Sequence

	Number and Operations	Algebra	Geometry	Measurement	Data Analysis and Probability
Unit 4: Place Value Concepts **Lessons**	• Understanding place value. • Developing number sense for large numbers (to the thousands). • Partitioning 3- and 4-digit numbers and representing them with number sentences. • Representing 3- and 4-digit numbers with base-ten pieces. • Representing 3- and 4-digit addition problems with base-ten pieces. • Translating between different representations of numbers (base-ten pieces, pictorial, and symbolic). • Reading and writing large numbers (to the thousands). • Comparing and ordering large numbers (to the thousands). • Solving addition problems and explaining the reasoning. • Adding 2-digit numbers using paper and pencil. • Skip counting by 5s to tell time.			• Telling time to the nearest 5 minutes.	
Daily Practice and Problems (Lettered) **& Home Practice** (Numbered)	• Maintaining fluency with the subtraction facts for Groups 5 and 6. (E, G, K, M, S) (1, 2) • Developing strategies for the multiplication facts for the 2s and 3s. (B, C, D, F, T) • Adding and subtracting using counting and other strategies. (A, E, H, K) (1) • Adding and subtracting with ending zeros. (E, S) (2) • Developing mental math skills. (A, E, S) (1, 2) • Developing number sense. (C, D, J, U) (1) • Representing numbers using base-ten pieces. (U) (3) • Skip counting. (C) (1) • Partitioning numbers and writing number sentences. (I, L, U) (2) • Understanding place value. (I, U, V) (2) • Solving problems involving money. (L, N, Q, R) (4) • Using addition and subtraction to solve problems. (N, O, R, U, V) (3) • Adding multidigit numbers using paper and pencil. (P) • Solving problems involving time. (4) • Solving problems in more than one way. (P) (3)			• Solving problems involving time. (4)	

Problem Solving	Reasoning	Communication	Connections	Representation
• Solving addition problems and explaining the reasoning.	• Solving addition problems and explaining the reasoning.	• Solving addition problems and explaining the reasoning.		• Representing 4-digit numbers with base-ten pieces. • Representing addition problems with base-ten pieces. • Translating between different representations of numbers (base-ten pieces, pictorial, and symbolic). • Reading and writing large numbers (to the thousands). • Partitioning 4-digit numbers and representing them with number sentences.
• Solving mathematical puzzles. (D, H, U, V) • Solving problems involving money. (L, N, Q, R) (4) • Using addition and subtraction to solve problems. (N, O, R, U, V) (3) • Solving multistep word problems. (N, R) • Solving problems in more than one way. (P) (3) • Solving problems involving time. (4) • Creating stories and drawings for multiplication sentences. (B, F) (1)		• Communicating solutions verbally and in writing. (A, E, O, U) (3) • Creating stories and drawings for multiplication sentences. (B, F) (1)		• Creating stories and drawings for multiplication sentences. (B, F) (1) • Representing a number using base-ten pieces. (U)

	Number and Operations	Algebra	Geometry	Measurement	Data Analysis and Probability
Unit 5: Area of Different Shapes **Lessons**	• Developing mental math skills. • Developing number sense. • Solving problems involving money. • Solving addition, subtraction, and multiplication problems involving area.	• Identifying and using manipulated, responding, and fixed variables. • Making and interpreting bar graphs. • Using data to make predictions and solve problems. • Translating between graphs and real-world events.		• Measuring area in square centimeters. • Measuring area of shapes with straight or curved sides. • Estimating areas of irregular shapes. • Understanding that different shapes can have the same area. • Dealing with precision and accuracy. • Solving problems involving area.	• Representing the elements of a laboratory investigation in a drawing. • Collecting, organizing, graphing, and analyzing data. • Identifying and using manipulated, responding, and fixed variables. • Making and interpreting bar graphs. • Averaging: finding the median. • Using data to make predictions and solve problems. • Translating between graphs and real-world events.
Daily Practice and Problems (Lettered) **& Home Practice** (Numbered)	• Maintaining fluency with the subtraction facts in Groups 7 and 8. (A, C, I, K) (1) • Developing strategies for the multiplication facts for the square numbers. (H, J, P) • Adding and subtracting to solve problems. (B, L) (4) • Adding and subtracting using paper and pencil. (N) (2) • Developing number sense. (D, E, F, G) (1) • Representing numbers with base-ten pieces. (F) (2) • Translating between different representations of numbers (concrete, pictorial, words, and symbolic). (F) (2) • Understanding place value. (F) • Solving problems involving money. (H) (4) • Solving problems in more than one way. (N) • Writing number sentences. (1) • Maintaining fluency with the subtraction facts. (O)			• Finding area of irregular shapes by counting whole and partial square centimeters. (M) (3) • Estimating area of irregular shapes. (3)	• Interpreting a data table. (E, G) • Averaging: finding the median. (E, G)

Problem Solving	Reasoning	Communication	Connections	Representation
• Solving addition, subtraction, and multiplication problems involving area. • Using the Student Rubric: *Solving* to self-assess problem-solving skills. • Solving problems involving money. • Solving multistep word problems. • Solving open-response problems. • Using data to make predictions and solve problems.	• Using data to make predictions and solve problems.	• Representing the elements of a laboratory investigation in a drawing. • Communicating solutions verbally and in writing.	• Connecting mathematics and science and real-life situations: investigating absorbency of different paper towels. • Connecting mathematics and science and language arts: reading a story involving finding area. • Translating between graphs and real-world events.	• Representing the elements of a laboratory investigation in a drawing. • Collecting, organizing, graphing, and analyzing data. • Making and interpreting bar graphs. • Translating between graphs and real-world events.
• Solving mathematical puzzles: magic squares. (L) • Solving multistep word problems. (B, H) • Adding and subtracting to solve problems. (B, L) (4) • Solving problems involving money. (H) (4) • Solving problems in more than one way. (N) • Creating stories and drawings for multiplication sentences. (J, P) (4)	• Solving mathematical puzzles: magic squares. (L)	• Communicating solutions verbally and in writing. (A, I) (2) • Creating stories and drawings for multiplication sentences. (J, P) (4)		• Creating stories and drawings for multiplication sentences. (J, P) (4) • Representing numbers using base-ten pieces. (F) • Translating between different representations of numbers (concrete, pictorial, words, and symbolic). (F) (2)

	Number and Operations	Algebra	Geometry	Measurement	Data Analysis and Probability
Unit 6: More Adding and Subtracting **Lessons**	• Developing number sense for large numbers (to the thousands). • Understanding place value. • Representing 3- and 4-digit numbers with base-ten pieces. • Translating between different representations of numbers (base-ten pieces, pictorial, words, and symbolic). • Representing 3- and 4-digit addition and subtraction problems using base-ten pieces. • Adding and subtracting 3- and 4-digit numbers using paper and pencil. • Developing mental math skills. • Estimating sums and differences. • Determining the reasonableness of a solution. • Comparing and ordering large numbers (to the thousands). • Solving problems involving addition and subtraction. • Solving problems involving money. • Rounding numbers to nearest 10 and 100. • Identifying number patterns.	• Identifying number patterns.		• Measuring area in square centimeters. • Measuring area of shapes with curved sides.	
Daily Practice and Problems (Lettered) **& Home Practice** (Numbered)	• Maintaining fluency with the addition and subtraction facts. (C) (1) • Developing strategies for the multiplication facts for the 9s. (B, F, V, DD) • Solving problems involving time. (A, I, L, O, Q, R, T) • Solving problems involving money. (G, P, W, DD) (4) • Developing number sense. (B, C, D, H, M, P, S, X, Y, Z, AA, EE, FF) • Understanding place value. (S, X, EE, FF) • Adding and subtracting with ending zeros. (C) • Adding and subtracting using paper and pencil. (U, AA) • Developing mental math skills. (C, AA) • Adding, subtracting, multiplying, and dividing to solve problems. (D, E, G, H, J, L, R, T, W, X, Y, BB, CC, EE, FF) (2, 3, 4) • Solving problems with more than one solution. (G, P, X) • Skip counting forwards and backwards. (K, M) • Identifying number patterns. (M, N) • Estimating sums and differences. (R, Z) • Comparing and ordering large numbers. (S) (3) • Writing number sentences. (V)			• Converting between hours and minutes. (T) • Measuring length in centimeters. (BB) • Measuring area in square centimeters. (E, CC) • Solving problems involving time. (A, I, L, O, Q, R, T)	

Problem Solving	Reasoning	Communication	Connections	Representation
• Solving problems involving addition and subtraction. • Solving problems involving money. • Solving multistep word problems.	• Determining the reasonableness of a solution.	• Communicating solutions verbally and in writing.	• Connecting mathematics and social studies: history of the Hindu-Arabic number system. • Connecting mathematics and language arts: using a story to create addition and subtraction problems.	• Representing 3- and 4-digit numbers with base-ten pieces. • Translating between different representations of numbers (base-ten pieces, pictorial, words, and symbolic). • Representing 3- and 4-digit addition and subtraction problems using base-ten pieces.
• Solving problems involving time. (A, I, L, O, Q, R, T) • Solving problems involving money. (G, P, W, DD) (4) • Adding, subtracting, multiplying, and dividing to solve problems. (D, E, G, H, J, L, R, T, W, X, Y, BB, CC, EE, FF) (2, 3, 4) • Solving problems with more than one solution. (G, P, X) • Creating a story and a drawing for a multiplication sentence. (V) • Solving multistep word problems. (2, 3)	• Identifying and explaining the error in a math problem using base-ten pieces. (3)	• Communicating solutions verbally and in writing. (C, U, Z, AA) (1, 2, 3, 4) • Describing number patterns. (M) • Creating a story and a drawing for a multiplication sentence. (V)		• Creating a story and a drawing for a multiplication sentence. (V)

Scope and Sequence

	Number and Operations	Algebra	Geometry	Measurement	Data Analysis and Probability
Unit 7: Exploring Multiplication and Division **Lessons**	• Representing multiplication and division with manipulatives, number lines, data tables, graphs, pictures, and words. • Connecting multiplication and repeated addition. • Connecting division and repeated subtraction. • Interpreting remainders. • Developing number sense. • Writing number sentences for multiplication and division situations. • Choosing appropriate methods and tools to calculate (calculators, paper and pencil, mental math). • Solving problems involving multiplication and division. • Solving problems involving money.	• Making and interpreting bar graphs. • Making and interpreting point graphs. • Using patterns in tables and graphs to make predictions and solve problems. • Translating between graphs and real-world events. • Identifying and describing patterns.	• Identifying regular polygons. • Measuring perimeter. • Exploring the relationship between perimeter and length of sides of regular polygons.	• Measuring perimeter. • Measuring length in centimeters.	• Collecting, organizing, graphing, and analyzing data. • Making and interpreting bar graphs. • Making and interpreting point graphs. • Using patterns in tables and graphs to make predictions and solve problems. • Translating between graphs and real-world events. • Choosing an appropriate graph to display data.
Daily Practice and Problems (Lettered) **& Home Practice** (Numbered)	• Maintaining fluency with the subtraction facts for Groups 1 and 2. (A, C, G, I, U) (1, 2) • Developing strategies for the last six multiplication facts. (B, F, P, Q) • Adding and subtracting whole numbers with paper and pencil. (D, M, S, T, V) (1, 3) • Developing number sense. (E, H, J, S) • Comparing and ordering large numbers. (R) • Adding, subtracting, multiplying, and dividing with ending zeros. (F, J) (1, 2) • Representing numbers with base-ten pieces. (H, R) (3) • Understanding place value. (H, R, S) • Solving problems involving time. (E, K, L) (4) • Solving problems involving money. (F) (2, 4) • Solving problems involving addition, subtraction, multiplication, and division. (P, T, V) (2) • Interpreting remainders. (P) • Solving problems in more than one way. (4) • Estimating to determine the reasonableness of an answer. (4)		• Distinguishing regular from nonregular polygons. (N, O)	• Solving problems involving time. (E, K, L) (4)	

Problem Solving	Reasoning	Communication	Connections	Representation
• Solving problems involving multiplication and division. • Solving problems involving money. • Using patterns in tables and graphs to make predictions and solve problems. • Using the Student Rubrics: *Knowing* and *Telling* to self-assess problem-solving skills. • Choosing appropriate methods and tools to calculate (calculators, paper and pencil, mental math).	• Using patterns in tables and graphs to make predictions and solve problems. • Interpreting remainders.	• Communicating solutions verbally and in writing. • Using the Student Rubric: *Telling* to self-assess communication skills.	• Representing multiplication and division with number lines, data tables, and graphs. • Connecting multiplication and repeated addition. • Connecting division and repeated subtraction.	• Representing multiplication and division with manipulatives, number lines, data tables, graphs, pictures, and words. • Writing number sentences for multiplication and division situations. • Collecting, organizing, graphing, and analyzing data. • Making and interpreting bar graphs. • Making and interpreting point graphs. • Translating between graphs and real-world events. • Choosing an appropriate graph to display data.
• Solving problems involving time. (E, K, L) (4) • Solving problems involving money. (F) (2, 4) • Solving problems involving addition, subtraction, multiplication, and division. (P, T, V) (2) • Solving problems in more than one way. (4) • Creating a story and a drawing for a multiplication sentence. (B) • Solving multistep word problems. (2)	• Interpreting remainders. (P)	• Creating a story and a drawing for a multiplication sentence. (B) • Communicating solutions verbally and in writing. (H, M, R) (1, 2, 3, 4)	• Creating a story and a drawing for a multiplication sentence. (B)	• Creating a story and a drawing for a multiplication sentence. (B) • Representing numbers with base-ten pieces. (H, R) (3)

	Number and Operations	Algebra	Geometry	Measurement	Data Analysis and Probability
Unit 8: **Mapping and** **Coordinates** **Lessons**	• Practicing the addition facts. • Solving problems involving addition, subtraction, and multiplication. • Choosing appropriate methods and tools to calculate (calculators, paper and pencil, estimation, or mental math).	• Finding locations on maps and locating objects using positive coordinates. • Plotting points using positive coordinates. • Translating between a map on a coordinate grid and the real-world situation it represents.	• Finding locations on maps and locating objects using positive coordinates. • Plotting points using positive coordinates. • Translating between a map on a coordinate grid and the real-world situation it represents. • Choosing an appropriate scale for a coordinate grid. • Making and using a scale map.	• Measuring length in nonstandard units. • Measuring length in feet and centimeters. • Making and using a scale map. • Dealing with precision and accuracy.	• Interpreting a data table to solve problems.
Daily Practice **and Problems** (Lettered) **& Home** **Practice** (Numbered)	• Maintaining fluency with the subtraction facts for Groups 3 and 4. (A, C, G, I, M) • Developing strategies for the multiplication facts for the 2s, 5s, and 10s. (B, D, H, L) (2) • Representing addition and multiplication using a number line. (D) • Skip counting. (E) • Developing number sense. (E, J) (4) • Using addition, subtraction, multiplication, and division to solve problems. (F, H) (1, 2, 3) • Solving problems involving money. (E, F, H) (2, 3) • Finding number patterns. (E) • Estimating duration of time. (E) • Developing mental math skills. (K, L) • Adding and subtracting using paper and pencil. (K) (1, 3) • Representing numbers using base-ten pieces. (J) • Interpreting remainders. (H)	• Using positive coordinates to locate a point on a coordinate grid. (N)	• Using positive coordinates to locate a point on a coordinate grid. (N)	• Estimating duration of time. (E)	• Collecting and organizing data in a data table. (2, 4) • Making and interpreting a point graph. (4)

Problem Solving	Reasoning	Communication	Connections	Representation
• Solving problems involving addition, subtraction, and multiplication. • Choosing appropriate methods and tools to calculate (calculators, paper and pencil, estimation, or mental math). • Solving problems involving distance and direction using a map. • Interpreting a data table to solve problems.		• Communicating solutions verbally and in writing.	• Translating between a map on a coordinate grid and the real-world situation it represents. • Connecting mathematics and real-world situations: solving problems involving the height of tall buildings of the world. • Connecting mathematics and real-world events: drawing and reading maps. • Connecting mathematics and language arts: using a coordinate grid.	• Finding locations on maps and locating objects using positive coordinates. • Plotting points using positive coordinates. • Translating between a map on a coordinate grid and the real-world situation it represents. • Choosing an appropriate scale for a coordinate grid. • Making and using a scale map.
• Solving problems involving money. (E, F, H) (2, 3) • Using addition, subtraction, multiplication, and division to solve problems. (F, H) (1, 2, 3) • Creating a story and a drawing for a multiplication sentence. (B)		• Creating a story and a drawing for a multiplication sentence. (B) • Finding and describing number patterns. (E) • Communicating solutions verbally and in writing. (H, K) (1, 2, 3, 4)		• Representing addition and multiplication using a number line. (D) • Representing numbers using base-ten pieces. (J) • Creating a story and a drawing for a multiplication sentence. (B)

	Number and Operations	Algebra	Geometry	Measurement	Data Analysis and Probability
Unit 9: Using Patterns to Predict **Lessons**	• Solving problems involving multiplication and division. • Solving multiplication problems involving mass.	• Using patterns in data tables and graphs to make predictions and solve problems. • Identifying and using variables. • Making and interpreting point graphs. • Drawing and interpreting best-fit lines. • Translating between graphs and real-world situations. • Investigating how a change in one variable leads to a change in another variable.		• Measuring mass in grams. • Dealing with precision and accuracy. • Solving multiplication problems involving mass.	• Representing the elements of an investigation in a drawing. • Identifying and using variables. • Collecting, organizing, graphing, and analyzing data. • Using patterns in data tables and graphs to make predictions and solve problems. • Making and interpreting point graphs. • Drawing and interpreting best-fit lines. • Translating between graphs and real-world situations.
Daily Practice and Problems (Lettered) **& Home Practice** (Numbered)	• Maintaining fluency with the subtraction facts for Groups 5 and 6. (A, C, E, G, M) (1) • Developing strategies for the multiplication facts for the 3s, 9s, and squares. (B, I, J, K, L) • Developing number sense. (A, B, F, N) • Adding and subtracting using paper and pencil. (H) • Solving problems involving multiplication and division. (F, I, J, K, L) (2) • Solving problems involving time. (D) • Solving problems involving money. (L) (1) • Multiplying and dividing numbers with ending zeros. (F, L) (1, 2) • Developing mental math skills. (A, E, H) (1, 2) • Estimating to determine the reasonableness of an answer. (1)	• Using coordinates to locate items on a grid. (3)	• Finding perimeter in inches. (N) • Using coordinates to locate items on a grid. (3) • Finding area by counting square units. (4)	• Using multiplication and division to solve problems involving mass. (J, K, L) (2) • Dealing with precision and accuracy. (N) • Finding area by counting square units. (4) • Solving problems involving time. (D)	

Problem Solving	Reasoning	Communication	Connections	Representation
• Solving problems involving multiplication and division. • Solving multiplication problems involving mass. • Solving multistep word problems. • Using patterns in data tables and graphs to make predictions and solve problems.	• Using patterns in data tables and graphs to make predictions and solve problems. • Investigating how a change in one variable leads to a change in another variable.	• Representing the elements of an investigation in a drawing. • Communicating solutions verbally and in writing.	• Connecting mathematics and science and real-world situations: finding the mass of everyday objects.	• Representing the elements of an investigation in a drawing. • Identifying and using variables. • Collecting, organizing, graphing, and analyzing data. • Translating between graphs and real-world situations. • Making and interpreting point graphs. • Drawing and interpreting best-fit lines.
• Solving problems involving multiplication and division. (F, I, J, K, L) (2) • Solving problems involving time. (D) • Solving problems involving money. (L) (1)		• Communicating solutions verbally and in writing. (H, N)		• Using coordinates to locate items on a grid. (3)

	Number and Operations	Algebra	Geometry	Measurement	Data Analysis and Probability
Unit 10: Numbers and Patterns: An Assessment Unit **Lessons**	• Maintaining fluency with the subtraction facts. • Solving problems involving addition, subtraction, and multiplication. • Solving problems involving money. • Developing multiplication facts strategies. • Using data to solve problems involving multiplication.	• Using patterns in data to make predictions and solve problems. • Making and interpreting point graphs. • Identifying and using variables. • Using fixed variables. • Drawing and interpreting best-fit lines. • Translating between graphs and real-world situations.		• Measuring length in inches.	• Representing the elements of an investigation in a drawing. • Identifying and using variables. • Collecting, organizing, graphing, and analyzing data. • Translating between graphs and real-world situations. • Making and interpreting point graphs. • Drawing and interpreting best-fit lines. • Using patterns in data to make predictions and solve problems. • Using fixed variables.
Daily Practice and Problems (Lettered) **& Home Practice** (Numbered)	• Maintaining fluency with the subtraction facts in Groups 7 and 8. (A, C, E, G, I) (1) • Maintaining fluency with all the subtraction facts. (K) • Developing strategies for the multiplication facts for the last six facts. (F, J, L) • Adding and subtracting using paper and pencil. (B, D) (2) • Subtracting with ending zeros. (B) • Using addition, subtraction, and multiplication to solve problems. (F, N) • Solving problems involving time. (M) (4) • Solving problems with more than one answer. (F, N) • Estimating to check the reasonableness of an answer. (2) • Adding and subtracting with ending zeros. (1) • Developing number sense. (D) (2) • Understanding place value. (D) (2) • Developing mental math skills. (B, L) (1)			• Solving problems involving mass. (F) (3) • Finding area of an irregular shape by counting square centimeters. (H) • Solving problems involving time. (M) (4)	

Problem Solving	Reasoning	Communication	Connections	Representation
• Using patterns in data to make predictions and solve problems. • Solving a problem in more than one way. • Solving open-response problems. • Solving problems involving addition, subtraction, and multiplication. • Solving problems involving money. • Using the Student Rubrics: *Knowing, Solving,* and *Telling* to self-assess problem-solving skills.	• Using patterns in data to make predictions and solve problems.	• Representing the elements of a laboratory investigation in a drawing. • Communicating solutions verbally and in writing. • Using the Student Rubrics: *Knowing, Solving,* and *Telling* to self-assess communication skills.	• Connecting mathematics and social studies: using geometric art from different cultures.	• Representing the elements of an investigation in a drawing. • Identifying and using variables. • Collecting, organizing, graphing, and analyzing data. • Translating between graphs and real-world situations. • Making and interpreting point graphs. • Drawing and interpreting best-fit lines.
• Solving problems involving mass. (F) (3) • Using addition, subtraction, and multiplication to solve problems. (F, N) • Solving problems involving time. (M) (4) • Solving problems with more than one answer. (F, N) • Solving multistep word problems. (3)	• Identifying and explaining the error in a math problem. (J)	• Communicating solutions verbally and in writing. (B, N) • Communicating estimation strategies verbally and in writing. (2) • Identifying and explaining the error in a math problem. (J)		

	Number and Operations	Algebra	Geometry	Measurement	Data Analysis and Probability
Unit 11: Multiplication Patterns **Lessons**	• Developing fluency with the multiplication facts for the 5s and 10s. • Practicing the multiplication facts. • Identifying, describing, and using patterns in the multiplication table to develop multiplication strategies. • Representing multiplication and division problems with arrays. • Adding and subtracting with 0. • Multiplying with 0 and 1. • Solving division problems involving 0. • Multiplying numbers with ending zeros. • Identifying prime and square numbers. • Solving problems involving multiplication and division. • Using turn-around facts (commutativity) to multiply. • Understanding that commutativity does not apply to division. • Solving problems involving money. • Writing number sentences for multiplication and division situations.	• Using turn-around facts (commutativity) to multiply. • Understanding that commutativity does not apply to division. • Identifying, describing, and using patterns in the multiplication table to develop multiplication strategies.			
Daily Practice and Problems (Lettered) **& Home Practice** (Numbered)	• Developing fluency with the multiplication facts for the 5s and 10s. (B, C, F, J, K, L, O, P, Q, S) • Maintaining fluency with the multiplication facts. (D, E, N, O, R, T) (3, 4) • Developing mental math skills. (A) (1, 2) • Developing number sense. (C, D, F, H, I, L, Q, R, T) • Multiplying with 0 and 1. (E, S) • Multiplying fractions using pictures. (H) • Solving problems involving time. (G, M) • Solving problems involving money. (J, K, L, P) (1) • Solving problems involving addition, subtraction, multiplication and division. (I, O, T) (2) • Skip counting by 5s. (G, M) • Interpreting remainders. (I, T) • Writing number sentences. (B, H, N) (3, 4) • Representing multiplication using arrays. (N) (3) • Representing multiplication using a number line. (Q) (3)		• Representing multiplication using arrays. (N) (3) • Finding area by counting square centimeters. (3) • Identifying and describing a triangle by its properties. (4)	• Finding area by counting square centimeters. (3) • Solving problems involving time. (G, M)	

Problem Solving	Reasoning	Communication	Connections	Representation
• Solving problems involving money. • Solving problems involving multiplication and division.	• Using turn-around facts (commutativity) to multiply. • Identifying, describing, and using patterns in the multiplication table to develop multiplication strategies.	• Communicating solutions verbally and in writing. • Writing number sentences for multiplication and division situations.	• Connecting mathematics and science and language arts: reading a story about the properties of zero.	• Representing multiplication and division problems with arrays. • Writing number sentences for multiplication and division situations.
• Solving problems involving time. (G, M) • Solving problems involving money. (J, K, L, P) (1) • Solving problems involving addition, subtraction, multiplication and division. (I, O, T) (2) • Creating a story and a drawing for number sentences. (H, I) (4)		• Communicating solutions verbally and in writing. (I, N, O) • Describing a triangle in words. (4) • Creating a story and a drawing for number sentences. (H, I) (4)		• Creating a story and a drawing for number sentences. (H, I) (4) • Representing multiplication using a rectangular array. (N) • Representing multiplication using a number line. (Q) (3)

	Number and Operations	Algebra	Geometry	Measurement	Data Analysis and Probability
Unit 12: Dissections **Lessons**	• Solving problems involving addition, subtraction, and multiplication. • Solving multistep word problems. • Choosing to find an estimate or an exact answer.		• Identifying, describing, and classifying 2-dimensional shapes using their properties (number of sides, corners, right angles, and lines of symmetry). • Using geometric concepts and skills to solve problems. • Developing spatial visualization skills. • Representing shapes with tangrams, drawings, and words. • Using flips and turns to identify shapes that are congruent. • Identifying and using line symmetry.	• Measuring area in square inches. • Measuring perimeter in centimeters and inches.	• Collecting and organizing data.
Daily Practice and Problems (Lettered) **& Home Practice** (Numbered)	• Developing fluency with the multiplication facts for the 2s and 3s. (A, C, J, K, M) • Developing mental math skills. (C, E, G) • Developing number sense. (F, J) • Adding and subtracting multidigit numbers using paper and pencil. (G) (1, 2) • Multiplying numbers with ending zeros. (C) • Estimating to determine the reasonableness of an answer. (1) • Using addition, subtraction, multiplication, and division to solve problems. (E, H) (1, 2, 3) • Solving problems involving money. (F) • Solving problems involving time. (I) (2) • Grouping a set of items with leftovers. (3)	• Collecting and organizing data in a data table. (N)	• Identifying right angles. (B, D) (4) • Constructing 2-dimensional shapes using specific component shapes. (L, N) • Identifying and using line symmetry. (N) (4)	• Measuring area and perimeter. (N) • Solving problems involving time. (I) (2)	• Collecting and organizing data in a data table. (N)

Problem Solving	Reasoning	Communication	Connections	Representation
• Using geometric concepts and skills to solve problems. • Solving multistep word problems.	• Using geometric concepts and skills to solve problems and communicate reasoning. • Identifying when a problem has no solution or more than one solution and communicating reasoning. • Using logical and strategic thinking in a game situation.	• Communicating solutions verbally and in writing. • Using geometric concepts and skills to communicate reasoning.		• Representing shapes with tangrams, drawings, and words. • Collecting and organizing data.
• Solving problems involving addition, subtraction, multiplication, and division. (E, H) (1, 2, 3) • Solving problems involving money. (F) • Solving problems involving time. (I) (2) • Solving multistep word problems. (H) (3) • Creating a story and a drawing for number sentences. (J)		• Communicating solutions verbally and in writing. (B, G, K) (3) • Creating a story and a drawing for number sentences. (J) • Communicating estimation strategies verbally and in writing. (1)		• Creating a story and a drawing for number sentences. (J)

	Number and Operations	Algebra	Geometry	Measurement	Data Analysis and Probability
Unit 13: Parts and Wholes **Lessons**	• Comparing and ordering fractions using one-half as a benchmark. • Developing number sense for fractions. • Defining the numerator and the denominator. • Representing fractions using pattern blocks and drawings. • Finding fractional parts of sets using counters. • Finding fractional parts of an hour in minutes. • Identifying the unit whole when a fractional part is given. • Identifying the fraction for a given quantity when the unit whole is given. • Exploring equivalent fractions. • Exploring mixed numbers. • Recognizing that fractional parts of a whole must have equal areas. • Solving problems involving fractions. • Solving problems involving time.		• Describing fractions using an area model.	• Solving problems involving time.	
Daily Practice and Problems (Lettered) **& Home Practice** (Numbered)	• Developing fluency with the multiplication facts for the square numbers. (A, D, E, F, K) • Solving problems involving time. (C, L) (3) • Solving problems involving money. (4) • Using multiplication and division to solve problems. (F) • Solving problems involving fractions. (H) • Multiplying with ending zeros. (E) • Developing mental math skills. (E) • Developing number sense. (E) • Developing number sense for fractions. (I, J) (2, 4) • Understanding numerator and denominator. (G, H) • Finding fractions of sets. (G) (1) • Finding fractional parts of an hour in minutes. (L) (3) • Representing a fraction with a drawing. (H) • Skip counting fractions. (I) (2) • Comparing and ordering fractions. (J) (2) • Skip counting by fifteen minute intervals. (C) • Adding and subtracting fractions. (J) (2) • Adding and subtracting multidigit numbers using paper and pencil. (5) • Estimating to determine the reasonableness of an answer. (5)	• Interpreting a data table. (D)	• Finding the area of a shape by counting square units. (B)	• Finding the area of a shape by counting square units. (B) • Solving problems involving time. (C, L) (3) • Finding fractional parts of an hour in minutes. (L) (3) • Skip counting by fifteen minute intervals. (C)	

Problem Solving	Reasoning	Communication	Connections	Representation
• Solving problems involving fractions. • Solving problems involving time.		• Communicating solutions verbally and in writing.	• Connecting mathematics to real-world situations: finding fractional parts of sets using characteristics of classmates.	• Representing fractions using pattern blocks and drawings. • Translating between different representations of fractions (concrete, pictorial, and symbolic).
• Solving problems involving time. (C, L) (3) • Solving problems involving money. (4) • Using multiplication and division to solve problems. (F) • Solving problems involving fractions. (H)				• Representing a fraction with a drawing. (H)

	Number and Operations	Algebra	Geometry	Measurement	Data Analysis and Probability
Unit 14: Collecting and Using Data **Lessons**	• Solving problems involving elapsed time. • Solving problems involving addition and subtraction. • Using percentages (25%, 50%, 75%, and 100%) as benchmarks. • Translating between benchmark percentages and fractions. • Representing multidigit addition and subtraction problems with base-ten pieces. • Adding and subtracting multidigit numbers using paper and pencil.	• Using patterns in data to make predictions and solve problems. • Identifying and using categorical and numerical variables. • Choosing appropriate values for a variable. • Making and interpreting bar graphs.		• Telling time to the nearest minute. • Solving problems involving elapsed time.	• Representing the elements of a laboratory investigation in a drawing. • Collecting, organizing, graphing, and analyzing data. • Using patterns in data to make predictions and solve problems. • Identifying and using variables in a survey. • Using categorical and numerical variables. • Choosing appropriate values for a variable. • Making and interpreting bar graphs.
Daily Practice and Problems (Lettered) **& Home Practice** (Numbered)	• Developing fluency with the multiplication facts for the 9s. (A, C, D, E, G) • Finding a fractional part when the unit whole is given. (F) • Finding a percentage when the whole is given. (H) • Using the benchmark percentages 25%, 50%, 75%, and 100%. (H) • Representing a fraction with a drawing. (F) • Solving problems involving time. (B, I, K, M) (4) • Solving problems involving addition and subtraction. (1, 2) • Solving problems involving money. (4) • Multiplying numbers with ending zeros. (D) • Developing mental math skills. (D, N) (1, 2) • Developing number sense. (H, L) (1, 2, 4) • Skip counting backward by thirds. (L) • Adding and subtracting using paper and pencil. (N) (1, 2) • Representing multiplication using a number line. (3) • Estimating to determine the reasonableness of an answer. (N)		• Drawing shapes with determined measure. (F) • Representing square numbers using an array. (J) • Analyzing a geometric figure. (J) (3)	• Drawing shapes with determined measure. (F) • Measuring length in centimeters. (3) • Solving problems involving time. (B, I, K, M) (4)	• Collecting and organizing data in a data table. (I, K, M)

Problem Solving	Reasoning	Communication	Connections	Representation
• Solving problems involving elapsed time. • Solving multistep word problems. • Solving problems involving addition and subtraction.	• Using patterns in data to make predictions and solve problems.	• Representing the elements of a laboratory investigation in a drawing. • Communicating solutions verbally and in writing.	• Connecting mathematics and science with social studies: reading about early devices to measure time. • Connecting mathematics and science with real world-situations: surveying classmates.	• Translating between benchmark percentages (25%, 50%, 75%, 100%) and fractions. • Representing addition and subtraction problems using base-ten pieces. • Representing the elements of a laboratory investigation in a drawing. • Collecting, organizing, graphing, and analyzing data. • Identifying and using variables in a survey. • Using categorical and numerical variables. • Making and interpreting bar graphs.
		• Communicating solutions verbally and in writing. (N)		• Representing a fraction with a drawing. (F) • Representing multiplication using a number line. (3) • Representing square numbers using an array. (J)

Scope and Sequence

	Number and Operations	Algebra	Geometry	Measurement	Data Analysis and Probability
Unit 15: Decimal Investigations **Lessons**	• Representing decimals using number lines (rulers), base-ten pieces, and money. • Reading and writing decimals to hundredths. • Skip counting (forward and backward) by 0.1 and multiples of 0.1. • Developing number sense for decimals. • Comparing and ordering decimals and fractions. • Connecting common fractions and decimal fractions. • Translating between base-ten pieces, money, and decimal fractions. • Solving problems involving decimals. • Practicing addition and subtraction facts.	• Identifying and using variables. • Choosing appropriate values for a variable. • Making and interpreting point graphs. • Drawing and interpreting best-fit lines. • Using patterns in data to make predictions and solve problems.		• Measuring length to the nearest tenth of a centimeter. • Estimating length. • Choosing when it is appropriate to estimate length and when to find a more exact measurement. • Dealing with precision and accuracy.	• Identifying and using variables. • Choosing appropriate values for a variable. • Representing the elements of a laboratory investigation in a drawing. • Collecting, organizing, graphing, and analyzing data. • Making and interpreting point graphs. • Drawing and interpreting best-fit lines. • Using patterns in data to make predictions and solve problems. • Averaging: finding the median.
Daily Practice and Problems (Lettered) **& Home Practice** (Numbered)	• Developing fluency with the multiplication facts for the last six facts. (A, B, I, J, K, M) • Maintaining fluency with the addition facts. (N, H) • Developing number sense for whole numbers. (N) (2) • Developing number sense for fractions and decimals. (D, L, N, O, P) (4) • Translating between common fractions, equivalent fractions, and decimal fractions. (D, P) (4) • Comparing and ordering fractions and decimals. (D) • Developing mental math skills. (H) • Adding and subtracting using paper and pencil. (H) (1, 2) • Using addition and subtraction to solve problems. (1, 2) • Representing decimals using base-ten pieces. (L, O, P) (4) • Representing fractions using an area model. (3) • Solving problems involving time. (C, E, G)		• Drawing line segments to a specified length in centimeters and tenths of centimeters. (F) (3) • Using geometric concepts and skills to solve problems. (J) • Representing fractions using an area model. (3)	• Measuring length to the nearest centimeter and tenth of a centimeter. (F) (3) • Solving problems involving time. (C, E, G)	• Collecting and organizing data in a data table. (C, E, G)

Problem Solving	Reasoning	Communication	Connections	Representation
• Solving problems involving decimals. • Using patterns in data to make predictions and solve problems.	• Using logical and strategic reasoning in a game situation. • Using patterns in data to make predictions and solve problems.	• Communicating solutions verbally and in writing. • Representing the elements of a laboratory investigation in a drawing.	• Connecting common fractions and decimal fractions.	• Representing decimals using number lines (rulers), base-ten pieces, and money. • Reading and writing decimals to hundredths. • Connecting common fractions and decimal fractions. • Translating between base-ten pieces, money, and decimal fractions. • Representing the elements of a laboratory investigation in a drawing. • Identifying and using variables. • Collecting, organizing, graphing, and analyzing data. • Making and interpreting point graphs. • Drawing and interpreting best-fit lines.
• Using geometric concepts and skills to solve problems. (J) • Creating a story and a drawing for a number sentence. (K)	• Using geometric concepts and skills to solve problems. (J)	• Creating a story and a drawing for a number sentence. (K) • Communicating solutions verbally and in writing. (D, I) (4)		• Representing decimals using base-ten pieces. (L, O, P) (4) • Creating a story and a drawing for a number sentence. (K) • Representing fractions using an area model. (3)

	Number and Operations	Algebra	Geometry	Measurement	Data Analysis and Probability
Unit 16: Volume **Lessons**	• Solving problems involving addition, subtraction, multiplication, and division. • Solving problems involving volume. • Solving problems involving money. • Developing number sense. • Interpreting remainders.	• Using data to make predictions and solve problems. • Making and interpreting bar graphs. • Interpreting a point graph.		• Estimating volume using centimeter connecting cubes. • Reading a graduated cylinder. • Measuring volume by displacement. • Measuring volume in cubic centimeters. • Measuring the volume of containers. • Dealing with precision and accuracy. • Solving problems involving volume. • Investigating cups, pints, quarts, and gallons.	• Representing the elements of a laboratory investigation in a drawing. • Collecting, organizing, graphing, and analyzing data. • Making and interpreting bar graphs. • Interpreting a point graph. • Averaging: finding the median. • Using data to make predictions and solve problems.
Daily Practice and Problems (Lettered) **& Home Practice** (Numbered)	• Developing fluency with the multiplication facts for the 2s, 5s, and 10s. (C, E, G, J, K) • Developing number sense for decimals. (A, B, I) (2) • Developing number sense. (C, E, G) (4) • Developing mental math skills. (C, E, G) • Using addition, subtraction, multiplication, and division to solve problems. (D, H, I, L) (3, 4) • Adding, subtracting, multiplying, and dividing using paper and pencil. (D, H) (1) • Writing number sentences. (I, J) (2) • Solving problems involving money. (D, J) (3) • Choosing appropriate tools and methods to calculate (calculator, paper and pencil, or mental math). (D) • Solving problems in more than one way. (D, H) • Estimating half of a set. (1)	• Finding missing numbers in a pattern. (B)	• Finding the volume of a shape. (F) • Finding more than one shape with the same volume. (F)	• Finding volume by counting cubic centimeters. (F) • Reading a centimeter ruler to the nearest tenth. (I) (2) • Solving problems involving volume. (L) (3)	

Problem Solving	Reasoning	Communication	Connections	Representation
• Solving multistep word problems. • Solving problems involving addition, subtraction, multiplication, and division. • Solving problems involving volume. • Solving problems involving money. • Interpreting remainders. • Solving problems in more than one way. • Developing methods for measuring volume of irregular containers. • Using data to make predictions and solve problems.	• Developing methods for measuring volume of irregular containers. • Using data to make predictions and solve problems. • Interpreting remainders.	• Representing the elements of a laboratory investigation in a drawing. • Communicating solutions verbally and in writing.	• Connecting mathematics to social studies: reading about ancient civilizations of the Middle East.	• Representing the elements of a laboratory investigation in a drawing. • Collecting, organizing, graphing, and analyzing data. • Making and interpreting bar graphs. • Interpreting a point graph.
• Solving problems involving money. (D, J) (3) • Solving multistep word problems. (J, L) (3) • Choosing appropriate tools and methods to calculate (calculator, paper and pencil, or mental math). (D) (3, 4) • Solving problems in more than one way. (D, H)		• Representing a problem with a drawing. (L) • Communicating solutions verbally and in writing. (C, G) (3, 4) • Describing patterns. (C, E, G)		• Writing number sentences to represent a problem. (I) • Representing a problem with a drawing. (L) • Representing multiplication using a number line. (4)

Scope and Sequence

	Number and Operations	Algebra	Geometry	Measurement	Data Analysis and Probability
Unit 17: Wholes and Parts **Lessons**	• Developing number sense for fractions. • Partitioning shapes into fractional parts. • Finding a fractional part when the unit whole is given. • Identifying the unit whole when a fractional part is given. • Representing fractions using geoboards and paper folding. • Recognizing that fractional parts of a whole must have equal areas but can have different shapes. • Finding fractions equivalent to $\frac{1}{2}$, $\frac{1}{3}$, and $\frac{1}{4}$ using paper folding. • Identifying patterns in fractions to find equivalent fractions. • Comparing and ordering fractions.	• Identifying patterns in fractions to find equivalent fractions.	• Partitioning shapes into fractional parts. • Identifying congruent shapes.	• Measuring area by counting square units. • Understanding that different shapes can have the same area.	• Organizing data in a table.
Daily Practice and Problems (Lettered) **& Home Practice** (Numbered)	• Developing fluency with the multiplication facts for the 3s and 9s. (A, I, J, K) • Multiplying with ending zeros. (J) • Developing number sense for whole numbers. (G) (1, 2) • Developing number sense for decimals and common fractions. (B, D, F, H, L) • Ordering decimals and fractions. (D, L) • Representing decimals using base-ten pieces. (F) • Representing decimals, fractions, and percents using drawings and symbols. (H) • Representing fractions and percents using an area model. (3, 4) • Translating between decimals, fractions, and percents. (H, L) (3) • Skip counting by decimals. (B) • Adding, subtracting, and multiplying using paper and pencil. (G) (1, 2) • Estimating sums and differences. (G) (1) • Solving problems involving money. (C) (2) • Using addition, subtraction, multiplication, and division to solve problems. (C, E) (2) • Developing mental math skills. (K) (2)		• Representing decimals, fractions, and percents using drawings and symbols. (H) • Representing fractions and percents using an area model. (3, 4)	• Solving problems involving volume. (E) • Finding area by counting square units. (3) • Finding volume by counting cubic units. (4)	

Problem Solving	Reasoning	Communication	Connections	Representation
	• Identifying patterns in fractions to find equivalent fractions. • Using logical and strategic reasoning in a game situation.	• Communicating solutions verbally and in writing.	• Connecting mathematics and language arts: reading a "fairy tale" that uses fractions.	• Representing fractions using geoboards and paper folding. • Translating among different representations of fractions (concrete, pictorial, symbolic). • Organizing data in a table.
• Solving problems involving money. (C) (2) • Solving problems involving volume. (E) • Using addition, subtraction, and multiplication to solve problems. (C, E) (2) • Solving multistep word problems. (C) • Creating a story and a drawing for a number sentence. (J)		• Communicating solutions verbally and in writing. (A, I, L) • Creating a story and a drawing for a number sentence. (J)		• Representing decimals using base-ten pieces. (F) • Translating between decimals, fractions, and percents. (H) • Creating a story and a drawing for a number sentence. (J)

	Number and Operations	Algebra	Geometry	Measurement	Data Analysis and Probability
Unit 18: Viewing and Drawing 3-D **Lessons**			• Identifying faces, edges, and vertices of rectangular prisms. • Describing 3-dimensional objects from different perspectives. • Building a cube model using a cube model plan. • Finding the area of the base, height, and volume of cube models. • Translating between a cube model, its cube model plan, and a three-dimensional drawing. • Recording the top, front, and right side views of a cube model using a grid. • Drawing cubes and rectangular prisms.	• Solving problems involving volume. • Finding volume by counting cubic units. • Using appropriate units to measure. • Finding the area of the base, height, and volume of a cube model.	
Daily Practice and Problems (Lettered) **& Home Practice** (Numbered)	• Developing fluency with the multiplication facts for the square numbers. (A, B, E, I, K) • Skip counting backwards. (4) • Developing number sense for decimals and fractions. (D) • Developing number sense for whole numbers. (C, G, H, J) (4) • Developing mental math skills. (C, G, H, J) (1, 2, 4) • Adding and subtracting using paper and pencil. (C, L) (1, 2) • Adding, subtracting, and multiplying with ending zeros. (G, J) (1, 2, 4) • Converting between decimals and fractions. (D) • Solving problems involving money. (D) • Solving problems involving time. (L) • Using addition and subtraction to solve problems. (L) (1, 2) • Developing an alternative method for measuring volume. (F)		• Translating between a cube model and its cube model plan. (3) • Recognizing that differently shaped cube models can have the same volume. (3)	• Measuring volume using U.S. customary units. (F) • Converting between minutes and hours. (L) • Choosing appropriate units to measure. (3) • Recognizing that differently shaped cube models can have the same volume. (3)	

Problem Solving	Reasoning	Communication	Connections	Representation
• Solving problems that have multiple solutions. • Identifying problems that have no solution. • Solving problems involving volume. • Solving open-response problems. • Solving multistep word problems.	• Solving problems that have multiple solutions. • Identifying problems that have no solution.	• Describing 3-dimensional objects from different perspectives. • Communicating solutions verbally and in writing. • Recording the top, front, and right side views of a cube model using a grid. • Drawing cubes and rectangular prisms.		• Translating between a cube model, its cube model plan, and a three-dimensional drawing. • Recording the top, front, and right side views of a cube model using a grid. • Drawing cubes and rectangular prisms.
• Solving problems involving money. (D) • Solving multistep word problems. (L) • Solving problems involving time. (L) • Using addition and subtraction to solve problems. (L) (1, 2)	• Developing an alternative method for measuring volume. (F) • Finding the error in a problem and explaining the solution. (H)	• Finding the error in a problem and explaining the solution. (H) • Communicating solutions verbally and in writing. (D, H, L) (4) • Describing an alternative method for measuring volume. (F) • Creating a story and drawing for a multiplication sentence. (E)		• Translating between a cube model and its cube model plan. (3)

	Number and Operations	Algebra	Geometry	Measurement	Data Analysis and Probability
Unit 19: Multiplication and Division Problems **Lessons**	• Representing and solving 2-digit by 1-digit multiplication problems using manipulatives, arrays, and drawings. • Solving problems involving addition, subtraction, multiplication, and division. • Using the distributive property to multiply. • Multiplying numbers with ending zeros. • Multiplying 2-digit by 1-digit numbers using paper and pencil. • Dividing a set of objects into equal-size groups (with remainders). • Representing division problems using drawings and manipulatives. • Dividing 2-digit numbers. • Interpreting remainders. • Writing number sentences for multiplication and division situations. • Creating stories for multiplication and division sentences. • Solving problems involving money. • Choosing appropriate methods and tools to calculate (calculators, paper and pencil, or mental math).	• Using break-apart products (the distributive property) to multiply.			
Daily Practice and Problems (Lettered) **& Home Practice** (Numbered)	• Developing fluency with the multiplication facts for the last six facts. (A, E, H, K, P, Q) • Maintaining fluency with the addition facts. (B, G) • Adding numbers with ending zeros. (G) (1) • Developing mental math skills. (C, K) (1) • Developing number sense for whole numbers. (G, K, P) (1, 2) • Representing multiplication on a number line. (N) (4) • Estimating sums and products. (N) (1) • Adding, subtracting, and multiplying using paper and pencil. (C, O) (2) • Solving problems involving money. (C, F, I, R) • Solving problems involving time. (M) • Using addition, subtraction, multiplication, and division to solve problems. (H, I, N, R) • Solving multistep word problems. (H, R) • Multiplying by a fraction. (D) (4) • Skip counting. (H)		• Finding the area of the base, height, and volume of a cube model from its cube model plan. (B) • Identifying and describing 2-dimensional shapes. (J) • Comparing a square and a rectangle. (J) • Drawing a 2-dimensional shape according to specific instructions. (P) (3) • Using geometric concepts and skills to solve problems. (J, P) (3) • Understanding that different shapes can have the same area. (P)	• Using appropriate units to measure. (3) • Measuring perimeter. (3) • Solving problems involving time. (M)	

Problem Solving	Reasoning and Proof	Communication	Connections	Representation
• Solving problems involving addition, subtraction, multiplication, and division. • Solving problems in more than one way. • Solving multistep word problems. • Creating stories for multiplication and division sentences. • Solving problems involving money. • Choosing appropriate methods and tools to calculate (calculators, paper and pencil, or mental math). • Interpreting remainders.	• Solving multiplication and division problems and explaining reasoning. • Using the distributive property to multiply. • Interpreting remainders.	• Solving multiplication and division problems and explaining reasoning. • Writing number sentences for multiplication and division situations. • Creating stories for multiplication and division sentences.		• Representing and solving 2-digit by 1-digit multiplication problems using manipulatives, arrays, and drawings. • Representing division problems using drawings and manipulatives. • Creating stories for multiplication and division sentences. • Writing number sentences for multiplication and division situations.
• Using geometric concepts and skills to solve problems. (J, P) (3)		• Communicating solutions verbally and in writing. (C, F, G, J) • Creating a story and drawing for a multiplication sentence. (D, L) (4)		

	Number and Operations	Algebra	Geometry	Measurement	Data Analysis and Probability
Unit 20: Connections: An Assessment Unit **Lessons**	• Solving problems involving multiplication and division. • Interpreting remainders. • Solving problems involving money.	• Making and interpreting point graphs. • Using patterns in data tables and graphs to make predictions and solve problems. • Identifying and using variables. • Choosing appropriate values for a variable. • Comparing and contrasting elements of different laboratory investigations: problems solved, types of graphs, variables.	• Translating between a cube model, its cube-model plan, and a 3-dimensional drawing. • Investigating the relationships between height, area, and volume.	• Finding the area of the base, height, and volume of a cube model. • Investigating the relationships between height, area, and volume.	• Collecting, organizing, graphing, and analyzing data. • Making and interpreting point graphs. • Using patterns in data tables and graphs to make predictions and solve problems. • Identifying and using variables. • Choosing appropriate values for a variable. • Comparing and contrasting elements of different laboratory investigations: problems solved, types of graphs, variables.
Daily Practice and Problems (Lettered) **& Home Practice** (Numbered)	• Developing fluency with all the multiplication facts. (K) • Developing number sense for whole numbers, fractions, and decimals. (A, C, F, J, L, M, P) (4) • Choosing appropriate methods and tools to compute (calculator, paper and pencil, or mental math). (I, J, M, O) (1, 2) • Adding fractions. (F) • Finding the fraction of a set. (4) • Translating between equivalent fractions, decimals, and percents. (P) (4) • Comparing and ordering fractions and decimals. (4) • Developing mental math skills. (I, O) (1, 2) • Adding, subtracting, and multiplying using paper and pencil. (O) (1) • Representing multiplication using a number line. (J, M) • Using addition, subtraction, multiplication, and division to solve problems. (E, I) (1, 2, 3, 4) • Solving problems involving time. (1) • Solving problems involving money. (2)	• Interpreting a data table. (A, C) • Making and interpreting a point graph. (B, D)		• Solving problems involving volume and mass. (3) • Finding area by counting square centimeters. (G, N) • Measuring length to the nearest centimeter and nearest tenth of a centimeter. (H) • Drawing shapes with a specified area. (N) • Estimating length in centimeters. (3) • Solving problems involving time. (1)	• Interpreting a data table. (A, C) • Organizing data in a data table. (F, H) • Averaging: finding the median. (A, C) • Making and interpreting a point graph. (B, D)

Problem Solving	Reasoning and Proof	Communication	Connections	Representation
• Promoting these beliefs: Problems can be solved by more than one method and different methods should yield solutions that agree. • Solving a problem in more than one way. • Solving problems involving multiplication and division. • Interpreting remainders. • Solving problems involving money. • Solving open-response problems. • Using patterns in data tables and graphs to make predictions and solve problems. • Using the Student Rubrics: *Knowing, Solving,* and *Telling* to self-assess problem-solving skills.	• Comparing and contrasting elements of different laboratory investigations: problems solved, types of graphs, variables. • Using patterns in data tables and graphs to make predictions and solve problems. • Interpreting remainders.	• Communicating solutions verbally and in writing. • Using the Student Rubrics: *Knowing, Solving,* and *Telling* to self-assess communication skills.	• Connecting mathematics to real-life situations: dividing money fairly. • Comparing and contrasting elements of different laboratory investigations: problems solved, types of graphs, variables.	• Translating between a cube model, its cube-model plan, and a 3-dimensional drawing. • Collecting, organizing, graphing, and analyzing data. • Identifying and using variables. • Making and interpreting point graphs. • Comparing and contrasting elements of different laboratory investigations: problems solved, types of graphs, variables.
• Using addition, subtraction, multiplication, and division to solve problems. (E, I) (1, 2, 3, 4) • Solving problems involving time. (1) • Solving problems involving money. (2) • Solving multistep word problems. (E) (3) • Solving problems in more than one way. (L) • Solving problems involving volume and mass. (3)	• Finding and correcting the errors in a data table. (C)	• Communicating solutions verbally and in writing. (L, M, O) • Representing a fraction situation with a drawing. (4) • Creating a story and drawing for a multiplication sentence. (E)		• Interpreting a data table. (A, C) • Making and interpreting a point graph. (B, D) • Organizing data in a data table. (F, H) • Representing multiplication using a number line. (J, M) • Representing a fraction situation with a drawing. (4)

Math Facts and Whole-Number Operations

The Math Facts and Whole-Number Operations section outlines the *Math Trailblazers* approach to developing fluency with the math facts and whole-number operations.

Calculators are used as a tool for solving problems.

Math Facts and Whole-Number Operations

Work with whole numbers pervades the elementary mathematics curriculum. A major goal of *Math Trailblazers* is to prepare students to compute accurately, flexibly, and appropriately in all situations. Standard topics in arithmetic—acquisition of basic math facts and fluency with whole-number operations—are covered extensively.

In this section, we briefly describe our approach to developing fluency with the math facts and whole-number operations. Table 1 outlines the development of these two topics in Grades K–5. We also summarize below the fundamental characteristics of our work with whole numbers. You can obtain more detailed information from the following sources:

- Two TIMS Tutors *Arithmetic* and *Math Facts;* and
- Background sections and lesson guides from individual *Math Trailblazers* units.

Introduction to the Math Facts in *Math Trailblazers*

In developing our program for the math facts, we sought a careful balance between strategies and drill. This approach is based on a large body of research and is advocated by the NCTM *Principles and Standards for School Mathematics*. The research indicates that the methods used in the *Math Trailblazers* math facts program lead to more effective learning and better retention of the math facts and also helps develop essential math skills.

The *Math Trailblazers* program for teaching the math facts is characterized by these elements:

- *Early emphasis on problem solving.* Students first approach the basic facts as problems to solve rather than as facts to memorize. Students invent their own strategies to solve these problems or learn appropriate strategies from others through class discussion. Students' natural strategies, especially for counting, are explicitly encouraged. In this way, students learn that math is more than memorizing facts and rules that "you either get or you don't."
- *De-emphasis of rote work.* Fluency with the math facts is an important component of any student's mathematical learning. Research shows, however, that overemphasizing memorization and frequent timed tests are counterproductive. We encourage the use of strategies to find facts, so students become confident they can find answers to fact problems that they do not immediately recall.
- *Gradual and systematic introduction of facts.* Students study the facts in small groups of problems that can be solved using similar strategies. Students first work on simple strategies for easy facts and then progress to more sophisticated strategies and harder facts. By the end of the process, they gain fluency with all the required facts.

- *Ongoing practice.* Work on the math facts is distributed throughout the curriculum, especially in the Daily Practice and Problems (Grades 1–5), Home Practice (Grades 3–5), and games. This practice for fluency, however, takes place only after students have a conceptual understanding of the operations and have achieved proficiency with strategies for solving basic fact problems. Delaying practice in this way means that less practice is required to achieve fluency.

- *Appropriate assessment.* Teachers assess students' knowledge of the facts through observations as they work on activities, labs, and games as well as through the appropriate use of written tests and quizzes. Beginning in first grade, periodic, short quizzes in the Daily Practice and Problems naturally follow the study of small groups of facts organized around specific strategies. As self-assessment in Grades 3–5, each student records his or her progress on *Facts I Know* charts and determines which facts he or she needs to study. Inventory tests of all facts for each operation are used sparingly in Grades 2–5 (no more than twice per year) to assess students' progress with fact fluency. The goal of the math facts assessment program is to determine whether students can find answers to fact problems quickly and accurately and retain this skill over time.

- *Multiyear approach.* In Grades 1 and 2, *Math Trailblazers* emphasizes strategies that lead to fluency with the addition and subtraction facts. In Grade 3, students gain fluency with the multiplication facts while reviewing the addition and subtraction facts. In Grade 4, students achieve fluency with the division facts and verify fluency with the multiplication facts. In Grade 5, the multiplication and division facts are systematically reviewed and assessed. This is outlined in Table 1.

- *Facts are not gatekeepers.* Students are not prevented from learning more complex mathematics because they do not perform well on fact tests. Use of strategies, calculators, and other math tools (e.g., manipulatives, hundreds charts, printed multiplication tables) allows students to continue to work on interesting problems and important mathematical concepts while still learning the facts.

Whole-Number Operations in *Math Trailblazers*

Math Trailblazers helps students develop efficient and accurate methods for computation with the four basic operations. The treatment of whole-number computation proceeds in several stages. The grade levels for the stages vary with the operation—full development of division, for example, comes long after addition—but the general pattern is similar for all the operations. Roughly speaking, the stages are:

- developing meaning for the operation,
- inventing procedures for solving problems, and
- becoming more efficient at carrying out procedures, all leading to
- developing mathematical power.

Developing mathematical power with an operation means that students understand *when* to apply the operation and *how* to use varied computational methods to solve problems, even complex or nonroutine problems.

With each operation, we seek a balance between conceptual understanding and procedural skill. Standard methods for solving problems are not introduced until students develop good conceptual and procedural understandings. Research has shown that introducing such procedures too early may short-circuit students' common sense, encouraging mechanical and uncritical behavior. As a result, formal instruction in some standard procedures is delayed slightly beyond the traditional time, but problems that would normally be solved by standard procedures are often introduced sooner than is customary. This forces students to use their prior knowledge to devise their own methods to solve the problems.

Students practice using the operations in activities, games, and laboratory investigations. More practice is provided in the Daily Practice and Problems in Grades 1–5 and in the Home Practice in Grades 3–5. Even after analyzing and practicing standard methods, students are still encouraged to solve problems in more than one way. Flexible thinking and mathematical power are our goals, not rote fluency with a handful of standard algorithms.

The *Math Trailblazers* approach to all mathematics topics promotes the coordinated development of both procedural skill and conceptual understanding. This is particularly apparent in our approach to computation.

The following table describes the development of math facts and whole-number operations in *Math Trailblazers*. The shaded portions of the table highlight development of the math facts program in each grade. Expectations for fluency with math facts are indicated in bold. The white portions of the table highlight development of the whole-number operations.

Grade	Addition	Subtraction	Multiplication	Division
K	Introduce concepts through problem solving and use of manipulatives.			
1	Develop strategies for addition facts.	Develop strategies for subtraction facts.	Develop concepts through problem solving and use of manipulatives.	
	Solve addition problems in context.	Solve subtraction problems in context.		
2	Continue use of addition facts in problems. Continue use of strategies for addition facts. **Assess for fluency with addition facts.**	Continue use of subtraction facts in problems. Continue use of strategies for subtraction facts. **Assess for fluency with subtraction facts.**	Continue concept development through problem solving and use of manipulatives.	
	Continue solving addition problems in context. Introduce procedures for multidigit addition using manipulatives and paper and pencil.	Continue solving subtraction problems in context. Introduce procedures for multidigit subtraction using manipulatives and paper and pencil.		
3	Diagnose and remediate with addition facts as needed.	Maintain fluency with subtraction facts through review and assessment.	Continue use of multiplication facts in problems. Develop strategies for multiplication facts. **Assess for fluency with multiplication facts.**	Continue use of division facts in problems. Develop strategies for division facts.
	Develop procedures for multidigit addition using manipulatives and paper and pencil. Practice and apply multidigit addition in varied contexts.	Develop procedures for multidigit subtraction using manipulatives and paper and pencil. Practice and apply multidigit subtraction in varied contexts.	Solve multiplication problems in context. Introduce paper-and-pencil multiplication (1-digit $\times$ 2-digits).	Continue concept development. Solve division problems in context.
4	Diagnose and remediate with addition facts as needed.	Diagnose and remediate with subtraction facts as needed.	Maintain fluency with multiplication facts through review and assessment.	Continue use of division facts in problems. Continue development of strategies for division facts. **Assess for fluency with division facts.**
	Practice and apply multidigit addition in varied contexts. Review paper-and-pencil procedures for multidigit addition.	Practice and apply multidigit subtraction in varied contexts. Review paper-and-pencil procedures for multidigit subtraction.	Develop procedures for multiplication using manipulatives and paper and pencil (1-digit and 2-digit multipliers). Practice and apply multiplication in varied contexts.	Solve division problems in context. Develop procedures for division using manipulatives and paper and pencil (1-digit divisors).
5	Diagnose and remediate with addition facts as needed.	Diagnose and remediate with subtraction facts as needed.	Maintain fluency with multiplication facts through review and assessment.	Maintain fluency with division facts through review and assessment.
	Practice and apply multidigit addition in varied contexts.	Practice and apply multidigit subtraction in varied contexts.	Review paper-and-pencil procedures. Practice and apply multiplication in varied contexts.	Develop paper-and-pencil procedures (1-digit and 2-digit divisors). Practice and apply division in varied contexts.

Table 1: *Math Facts and Whole-Number Operations Overview*

Daily Practice and Problems and Home Practice Guide

The Daily Practice and Problems (DPP) and Home Practice (HP) Guide explains the purpose and use of the DPP and HP within the curriculum.

Students work cooperatively to solve a problem from the Daily Practice and Problems.

Daily Practice & Problems

Daily Practice and Problems and Home Practice Guide

Daily Practice and Problems

The Daily Practice and Problems (DPP) is a set of short exercises that provides ongoing review, practice, and study of math concepts and skills. These exercises are in each *Unit Resource Guide* immediately preceding the lesson guides and on the *Teacher Resource CD*. The DPP should become a routine part of daily instruction since the problems serve several important functions in the curriculum:

- They provide distributed practice in computation and a structure for systematic study of the basic math facts.
- They develop concepts and skills such as number sense, telling time, and working with money throughout the year; and
- They review topics from earlier units, presenting concepts in new contexts and linking ideas from unit to unit.

There are three types of items: Bits, Tasks, and Challenges. Bits are short and should take no more than 5 or 10 minutes to complete. They often provide practice with a skill or the basic math facts. Tasks take 10 or 15 minutes to complete. Challenges usually take longer than 15 minutes to complete and the problems are more thought-provoking. Use them to stretch students' problem-solving skills.

Two DPP items are included for each class session listed on the Unit Outline. The first item is always a Bit and the second is either a Task or a Challenge. Each item is composed of Student Questions and Teacher Notes as shown in Figure 1.

Figure 1: *DPP pages*

Unit 2 Daily Practice and Problems

Students may solve the items individually, in groups, or as a class. The items may also be assigned for homework. The DPPs are also available on the Teacher Resource CD.

Student Questions	Teacher Notes

A Quick Addition

Do these problems in your head. Write only the answers.

1. 4 + 9 =   2. 40 + 90 =
3. 20 + 90 =   4. 20 + 30 =
5. 30 + 50 =   6. 40 + 60 =
7. 10 + 90 =   8. 60 + 80 =
9. 80 + 70 =   10. Explain your strategy for Question 9.

TIMS Bit

These problems provide an opportunity for students to review a few addition facts and relate them to adding multiples of ten.

1. 13   2. 130
3. 110   4. 50
5. 80   6. 100
7. 100   8. 140
9. 150

10. Possible strategy: Students may break apart 70 into 20 and 50. Then by joining 20 and 80 to make 100, the remaining 50 is added to equal 150.

B Change

1. You go to the store with $1.00. You buy a pen that costs 73¢. The tax is 6¢. How much change will you get?

2. What coins could you get in change? How many different ways can you answer this question?

TIMS Task

Students may need to use coins to solve these problems.

1. 21¢

2. Possible solutions:

1¢	5¢	10¢
1	0	2
1	2	1
1	4	0
6	1	1
6	3	0
11	0	1
11	2	0
16	1	0
21	0	0

URG • Grade 3 • Unit 2 • Daily Practice and Problems   19

Student Questions	Teacher Notes

C Calculator Counting

Work with a partner to find how long it will take to count to 100. One partner will count. The other will time how long the counting takes. Take turns.

A. Use a calculator to count by ones to 100. How long did it take?

B. Predict how long it would take to count by twos to 100. Use a calculator to count by twos to 100. How long did it take?

TIMS Bit

Pressing 1 + = = = on a calculator with an addition constant will cause the calculator to count by ones. To count by twos, press: 2 + = = = =. Otherwise students can press 2 + 2 + 2 + 2 + ... or 2 + 2 = + 2 = + 2 = + 2 =. You do not necessarily need a calculator to do this activity. However, students will use skip counting on the calculator in later units on multiplication and decimals.

Discuss the results. Did students predict that it would take half as long to count by twos? Were their predictions close? Why or why not?

D Piano Practice

Abbey practices piano every day. Here are the songs she plays and the time it takes to play them:

"Evening Bells"   2 minutes
"Scottish Dance"   1 minute
"Air" by Mozart $\frac{1}{2}$ minute

A. Can she play all three songs ten times in half an hour?

B. How long will she play if she warms up for five minutes and then plays each song six times?

TIMS Challenge

There are many possible strategies for solving these problems. Make sure students explain their solutions.

A. No, since it will take 20 minutes (10 × 2 min) to play "Evening Bells" 10 times and 10 minutes to play the "Scottish Dance" 10 times, it will take her 30 minutes to play them both and she won't have time to play Mozart.

B. 26 minutes. Students may use repeated addition to solve this problem.

20   URG • Grade 3 • Unit 2 • Daily Practice and Problems

The Teacher Notes give the answers and often discuss possible problem-solving strategies. Eight icons designate the subject matter of the problems. See Figure 2.

The Scope and Sequence chart in Section 5 of the *Teacher Implementation Guide* lists the topics covered in the DPP in each unit. This chart correlates the items in the DPP to the standards from the National Council of Teachers of Mathematics *Principles and Standards for School Mathematics*. Teachers can use this chart to track the development of a particular standard throughout third grade and locate items on particular topics to use for review, extra practice, or enrichment. For example, by looking at the Number and Operations column, teachers can follow the sequence of items providing computation and facts practice. By looking at the Measurement column in the same way, teachers can find all the items that deal with measuring length and area. For a specific description of the study and assessment of the math facts as organized in the DPP, see the TIMS Tutor: *Math Facts*.

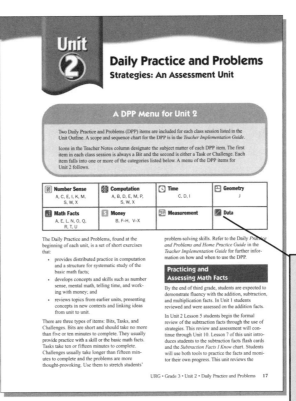

Grades 1–5 — Each set of DPP includes a Teacher's Guide which often provides specific information on the study and assessment of the math facts in the current unit.

Figure 2: *DPP icons and DPP menu on a DPP page*

Eight icons indicate the subject matter of each problem:

N **Number Sense** (estimating, partitioning numbers, skip counting, etc.);

Math Facts (practice with addition, subtraction, and multiplication facts);

Computation (solving problems using paper-and-pencil methods, estimation, mental math, or calculators);

$ **Money** (counting change, combining various coins, or estimating total cost);

Time (telling time, solving problems involving elapsed time);

Measurement (measuring length, area, mass, volume, and time);

Geometry (work with shapes, coordinates, or other geometric topics); and

Data (collecting, organizing, graphing, or analyzing data).

How to Use the Daily Practice and Problems

The Suggestions for Teaching the Lesson section and the At a Glance in most lessons provide suggestions on how and when to use each DPP item. These are only suggestions. The following provides further description on how to incorporate the DPP into your math instruction.

Assign a Bit each day to provide students with the review and fact practice they need. Bits are short, quick questions that need little instruction from the teacher. Students should be able to complete them independently. For many problems, it will be appropriate for students to work in pairs or groups. For other items such as facts quizzes, students should answer the questions individually. If students take more than 5 or 10 minutes to complete the problems, they are probably unfamiliar with a topic. For example, items intended to review second-grade topics may be new to students who are using *Math Trailblazers* for the first time in third grade. If students need more instruction on the material presented in the DPP, defer the problems and the instruction until a later date, possibly during an upcoming unit that covers similar subject matter.

Choose from the Tasks and Challenges as time permits according to the interests and needs of your students. Tasks can extend a topic or provide extra practice. Challenges can provide enrichment for those students who need less skill practice and are ready for more complex problems. Not all students will be able to complete all the Tasks and Challenges, but all should have the opportunity to try.

Teachers use the Daily Practice and Problems in many ways. Many problems can easily be written on the board or displayed using an overhead projector. Items can also be photocopied or printed (without the teacher portion) from the *Teacher Resource CD* and distributed to students daily, or several items can be stapled together in a packet and distributed weekly. For many items (such as facts practice or mental arithmetic), it is appropriate for students to just write answers on scrap paper. For others (such as skip counting), students can respond orally. One way to establish routines is to have students use their math journals for any written responses. This will also preserve a record of their work. Teacher notes sometimes recommend conducting a discussion of students' problem-solving strategies. These discussions are an important part of the problem-solving process, but they need not be extensive since topics are revisited many times.

When to Use the Daily Practice and Problems

At the Beginning of Math Class. Use Bits and other DPP items to begin class and focus students' attention on mathematics. Students immediately answer the questions and then the class can discuss the answers before they begin work on the current lesson. Alternatively, the teacher can assign the items at the beginning of a lesson and students can solve the problems as they have time during class. This is especially effective if students are collecting data for an experiment and have to take turns using equipment.

During Daily Routines. Bits can be used as part of morning (or afternoon) routines that also include taking the roll, calendar work, language arts practice, or geography questions. A "Problem of the Day" can also be part of the daily routine in which the teacher presents students with a Task or a Challenge that they can work on throughout the day or take home to complete for homework or as extra credit. For some Tasks and Challenges, it may be appropriate to ask students to describe their problem-solving process.

During Transition Times. You can use many items, especially practice with the math facts, during transition times throughout the day. Possible times include when students have completed an assignment, when money or permission slips are being collected, when an activity is delayed, or when an activity ends earlier than expected.

As Homework or Assessment. You can also assign problems for homework or use them for short assessments. See the TIMS Tutor: *Math Facts* for information on facts assessment in the DPP and the Assessment Overview in Part VI of the Assessment section for specific locations of Facts Quizzes.

Home Practice

The Home Practice (HP) is a series of problems that supplement the homework included in the lessons. The HP, like the DPP, distributes skill practice throughout the units and reviews concepts studied in previous units. For each unit, the *Discovery Assignment Book* begins with problems divided into different parts as shown in Figure 3.

How to Use the Home Practice

The At a Glance in many lessons provides guidance for how and when to use the Home Practice. Here are further suggestions.

One way to assign the HP is to send all parts home with students at some point during the unit. Students are responsible for completing the pages and returning them on a given day. This schedule allows flexibility for the teacher, students, and students' families. If some evenings are filled with athletic practices, meetings, family commitments, or the completion of other homework, students can choose their own times to work on the HP.

The HP is designed to be used in addition to (not as a replacement for) the unit homework. Since some parts may include content directly related to the current unit, often it is not appropriate to assign these parts during the first week of the unit. Rather, use such HP items after students solve similar problems in class.

Another way to occasionally use the HP is for the teacher (or parents) to complete one or more parts of the assignment. The adult makes some intentional mistakes and shows how he or she solved the problems. Then, students grade the adult's work, justifying the number of points awarded to each problem.

From time to time, teachers may ask students to reflect on how they completed the HP either in a short paragraph attached to the homework or in math journals. Did they need help? Who helped them? Did the helper give them new strategies for solving problems? How did they organize their time?

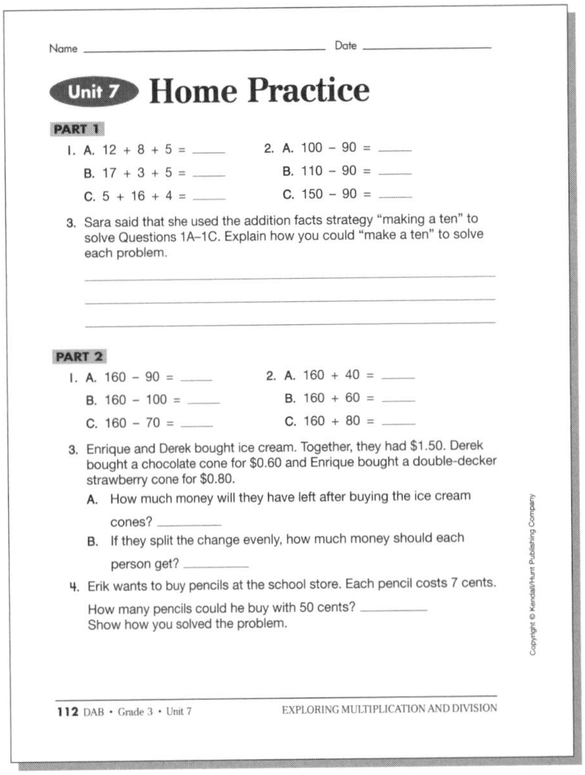

Name ______ Date ______

Unit 7 Home Practice

PART 1

1. A. 12 + 8 + 5 = ___
   B. 17 + 3 + 5 = ___
   C. 5 + 16 + 4 = ___
2. A. 100 − 90 = ___
   B. 110 − 90 = ___
   C. 150 − 90 = ___
3. Sara said that she used the addition facts strategy "making a ten" to solve Questions 1A–1C. Explain how you could "make a ten" to solve each problem.

PART 2

1. A. 160 − 90 = ___
   B. 160 − 100 = ___
   C. 160 − 70 = ___
2. A. 160 + 40 = ___
   B. 160 + 60 = ___
   C. 160 + 80 = ___
3. Enrique and Derek bought ice cream. Together, they had $1.50. Derek bought a chocolate cone for $0.60 and Enrique bought a double-decker strawberry cone for $0.80.
   A. How much money will they have left after buying the ice cream cones? ___
   B. If they split the change evenly, how much money should each person get? ___
4. Erik wants to buy pencils at the school store. Each pencil costs 7 cents. How many pencils could he buy with 50 cents? ___ Show how you solved the problem.

Copyright © Kendall/Hunt Publishing Company

112 DAB • Grade 3 • Unit 7 EXPLORING MULTIPLICATION AND DIVISION

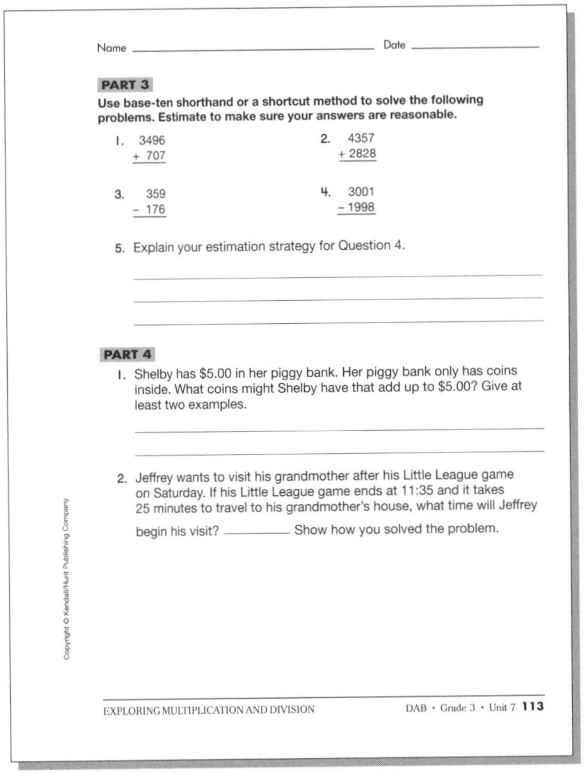

Name ______ Date ______

PART 3

Use base-ten shorthand or a shortcut method to solve the following problems. Estimate to make sure your answers are reasonable.

1. 3496 + 707
2. 4357 + 2828
3. 359 − 176
4. 3001 − 1998
5. Explain your estimation strategy for Question 4.

PART 4

1. Shelby has $5.00 in her piggy bank. Her piggy bank only has coins inside. What coins might Shelby have that add up to $5.00? Give at least two examples.
2. Jeffrey wants to visit his grandmother after his Little League game on Saturday. If his Little League game ends at 11:35 and it takes 25 minutes to travel to his grandmother's house, what time will Jeffrey begin his visit? ___ Show how you solved the problem.

Copyright © Kendall/Hunt Publishing Company

EXPLORING MULTIPLICATION AND DIVISION DAB • Grade 3 • Unit 7 113

Figure 3: *Home Practice pages*

Calculations: Paper-and-Pencil, Calculators, Mental Math, or Estimation?

The HP provides many opportunities for practice of computational skills. Practice of paper-and-pencil calculations is emphasized throughout the HP. However, besides developing skill with paper-and-pencil computations, students also need to be able to choose when it is appropriate to use paper-and-pencil procedures, calculators, mental math, or estimation.

The following problem serves as an example:

The Student Council is selling 1000 pencils to make money for a school project. They have already sold 450 pencils. How many more do they have to sell?

Students may use paper-and-pencil procedures, but subtracting across zeros is difficult and not particularly efficient. They may estimate that the student council needs to sell about 500 more, but a more exact answer is probably needed in this situation. Using a calculator is possible, but probably not necessary. Using a mental math strategy of counting up is effective and efficient. (Count up 50 from 450 to 500, then count up 500 more to 1000 to arrive at the answer of 550 pencils.) Before sending home the HP, you may discuss the possible strategies for particular problems and whether or not it is appropriate to use a calculator or another method of calculating. For more information on helping students choose appropriate strategies for computation, see the TIMS Tutor: *Arithmetic*.

Assessment

The Assessment section details the philosophy, goals, and components of assessment in the curriculum.

A teacher and her students assess their work on a problem.

Assessment

 **PART I** ## Philosophy of the Assessment Program in *Math Trailblazers*

Assessment in *Math Trailblazers* is ongoing and reflects the program's content and goals. Throughout the program, assessment serves several purposes:

- It helps teachers learn about students' thinking and knowledge. This information is then used to guide instruction.
- It communicates the instruction goals to students, parents, and others.
- It informs students, parents, and others about progress toward these goals.

The assessment program is built around two main principles: assessment should reflect the breadth and balance of the curriculum; and assessment activities should be valuable educational experiences.

Alignment with Goals

The National Council of Teachers of Mathematics (NCTM) *Principles and Standards for School Mathematics* describes the understanding, concepts, and skills students need to acquire. These principles and standards call for a mathematically rich curriculum for all students. The curriculum must teach a broad range of content and develop mathematical processes including problem solving, reasoning, and communication.

Math Trailblazers is designed to meet recommendations in the *Principles and Standards*. As such, the program requires significant shifts in emphases relative to a traditional program—changes in content, learning, teaching, evaluation, and expectations. The implications with regard to student assessment are also significant. We can no longer focus narrowly on the assessment of only isolated skills and procedures, using single sources of information at the end of a learning cycle. Instead, assessment needs to shift toward collecting information over the course of the year from a variety of sources, covering a wide range of mathematical content, and incorporating the rich problem-solving situations that are characteristic of the curriculum. The NCTM *Principles and Standards for School Mathematics* describes this as follows:

> *Many assessment techniques can be used by mathematics teachers, including open-ended questions, constructed-response tasks, selected-response items, performance tasks, observations, conversations, journals, and portfolios.* (NCTM, 2000, p. 23)

Integral with Instruction

Assessment is an integral part of instruction. All assessment activities are valuable educational experiences that have their own merit. By making assessment both integral to instruction and reflective of the overall mathematical content of the curriculum, we communicate what we value in mathematics. Again, the NCTM *Principles and Standards* addresses this idea:

> *To ensure deep, high-quality learning for all students, assessment and instruction must be integrated so that assessment becomes a routine part of ongoing classroom activity rather than an interruption.* (NCTM, 2000, p. 23)

Our assessment program gives teachers frequent opportunities to assess student progress. It assesses concepts and skills in many different ways but especially within the context of solving problems. Assessments are designed to elicit more than just an answer. In solving problems, students show their thinking and give a picture of their understanding of mathematical concepts, strategies, tools, and procedures.

Integrating assessment with instruction has significant implications for the structure of the assessment program. There is no separate assessment book; assessment activities and other components of the assessment program are fully integrated into units. Furthermore, because much of the curriculum's content is revisited many times in varying contexts, students are assessed many times on many concepts. This flavors both instruction and assessment. Teachers can focus on student progress since they know there will be other opportunities to review and assess and thus do not expect mastery at every juncture. At the same time, students' mathematical progress is not put on hold until they pass any particular assessment.

Balanced Assessment

The assessment program reflects the curriculum's instruction in another important way: it is varied and balanced. The *Math Trailblazers* curriculum is balanced across several dimensions:

- **Math Content.** The program incorporates a broad range of mathematical content and procedures, and connections between different topics abound.
- **Communication.** Students are expected to communicate their mathematical work and represent mathematical ideas in many different ways, such as written and oral explanations, number sentences, tables, graphs, pictures, and models.

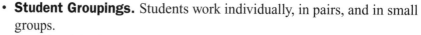

- **Student Groupings.** Students work individually, in pairs, and in small groups.
- **Length of Activities.** There are short activities (5–15 minutes), tasks that take a full class period, and longer investigations that take several days.
- **Amount of Teacher Direction.** Some activities involve considerable teacher direction; others are more student-directed.
- **Varied Contexts.** Mathematics is presented in a variety of contexts, such as laboratory experiments, real-life settings, word problems, and numerical problems.

Our assessment program is balanced in similar ways. A balanced assessment program gives each student an opportunity to demonstrate what he or she knows by allowing multiple approaches. It covers a wide range of content, allows access to tools when appropriate, varies the difficulty and pedagogy, and assesses within different kinds of contexts.

Using multiple sources of evidence improves the validity of judgments made about students' learning. With more than one source of information about students' progress, strengths in one source can compensate for weaknesses in others. It also helps teachers judge the consistency of students' mathematical work. (NCTM, 2000, p. 24)

Promoting Student Reflection

Assessment activities in *Math Trailblazers* do more than provide momentary snapshots of a student's progress. Students are often asked to revise work based on commonly understood criteria for excellence. In Grades K–2, these criteria are communicated largely by the teachers. Beginning in Grade 3, the Student Rubrics provide an additional source of information to students about what is expected of them. As students become more involved in the assessment process, they become more reflective and can make constructive, critical judgments about their work and the work of others.

Components in Grades 1–5

Watching students grow intellectually throughout the school year is one of the great satisfactions of teaching. The components of the assessment program provide teachers with the tools necessary to document students' progress over time as they acquire skills and concepts, develop their abilities to solve problems, and learn to communicate their thinking. While most components are included at all grade levels, the assessment program does vary from grade to grade based on the students' needs.

All materials provided to assess student learning are located in the units, either in the student materials or the *Unit Resource Guide.* Each unit contains assessment ideas and activities appropriate for the unit's content and goals. Many components are also available in electronic form on the *Teacher Resource CD.* This section describes the following components:

Observational Assessment
Assessment Indicators
Observational Assessment Record
Individual Assessment Record Sheet

Written Assessments
Assessment Pages
Math Journals
Assessment Section in
   the Lesson Guide
Assessment Lessons
   Assessment Labs
   Open-Response Problems
   Tests
Assessment Units
Portfolios
Facts Assessment

Observational Assessment

Teachers have always assessed student learning through informal classroom observations, thus integrating instruction and assessment. The NCTM *Principles and Standards* confirms the importance of these observations.

Observations and conversations in the classroom can provide insights into students' thinking, and teachers can monitor changes in students' thinking and reasoning over time with reflective journals and portfolios. (NCTM, 2000, p. 24)

Teachers use the information gathered from classroom observations to guide instruction. While watching, questioning, and listening to students, they make moment-to-moment instructional decisions that change the direction and emphasis of the lesson. Teacher evaluation of student responses during a lesson will also affect the content of succeeding lessons.

Teachers can also use classroom observations to evaluate student achievement and monitor student progress. Skills such as using a graduated cylinder to measure volume, habits such as estimating regularly to check results, and behaviors such as working effectively within a group are best assessed through observing students at work. Assessing students through observation is especially important in the primary grades, because students at this age can often communicate their thinking very well in a discussion, but not always in writing. Also, what we assess becomes what we value. If we only assess written work, we may neglect other important behaviors such as verbal communication. Finding a manageable way to organize and record these observations is critical to an effective assessment program.

Each unit includes two tools to help teachers organize and document informal assessments: Assessment Indicators and the *Observational Assessment Record*.

Assessment Indicators

The Background for each unit in Grades 1–5 lists several Assessment Indicators that orient teachers to important skills, behavior, and knowledge they should assess in the unit. See Figure 1.

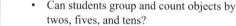

Assessment Indicators

- Can students group and count objects by twos, fives, and tens?
- Can students divide a collection of objects into groups of a given size and count the leftovers?
- Can students collect, organize, graph, and analyze data?
- Can students identify the relationships among pennies, nickels, and dimes?

Figure 1: *Assessment Indicators from Grade 1 Unit 5*

Observational Assessment Record

An *Observational Assessment Record* similar to the one shown for Grade 1 Unit 5 in Figure 2 follows the Background in each unit. The Assessment Indicators for that unit are listed at the top of each sheet. Each indicator is identified with an icon. An additional line is provided for teachers to include their own ideas. Each sheet has 32 rows for student names with columns for recording observations and extra space for comments. It is not necessary to record an observation about each child in each column. The grid provides a snapshot of the class's understanding of the unit's main concepts, procedures, and skills.

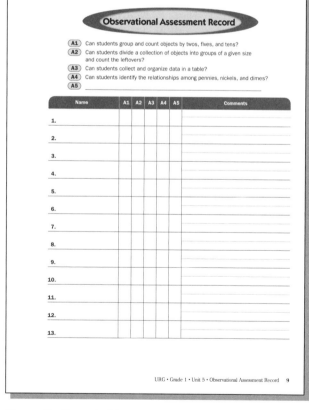

Figure 2: *Sample* Observational Assessment Record *from Grade 1 Unit 5*

In first and second grade, the icons are also placed in the At a Glance sections of the Lesson Guides. These indicate which skills and concepts described in the Assessment Indicators teachers might assess during that particular lesson. Figure 3 is a sample At a Glance section from Grade 1 Unit 5 Lesson 2. The use of the icon (A1) shows that during this lesson teachers can assess students on their abilities to count objects by twos, fives, and tens.

Individual Assessment Record Sheets

Information from the *Observational Assessment Record* can be transferred to *Individual Assessment Record Sheets*. The *Individual Assessment Record Sheet* is located at the end of Part VI of this section and provides an organizational tool for compiling a year-long, anecdotal record for each child. Assessment Indicators for the entire year are listed by unit along with a line for comments as shown in Figure 4.

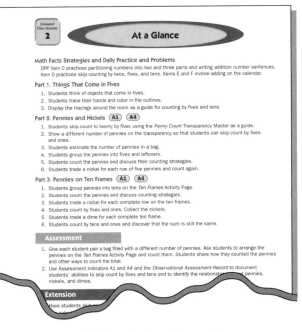

Figure 3: *Sample At a Glance from Grade 1 Unit 5 Lesson 2*

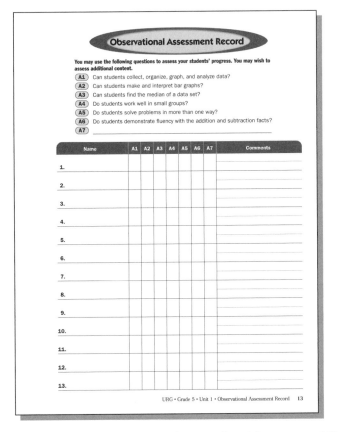

Figure 4: Observational Assessment Record *from Grade 5 Unit 1 and* Individual Assessment Record Sheet *from Grade 5*

Written Assessments

Assessment Pages

Many lessons in *Math Trailblazers* include short paper-and-pencil assessments that teachers can use to check skills or concepts developed in a unit. While teachers can use some assessment pages to assess students as they work in groups, they can often use these pages as quizzes to assess students individually. Checking student work gives both the teacher and the students feedback on their current abilities. The *What's the Volume?* Assessment Page from Grade 2 Unit 7 is shown in Figure 5. Students must combine their arithmetic skills with their measurement skills to complete the page correctly.

Math Journals

Students' entries in their math journals are a rich source of assessment information. Journal Prompts, a regular feature in the lesson guides, elicit information about students' understanding of specific concepts. Figure 6 shows an example of a Journal Prompt in Grade 5 Unit 1 Lesson 3.

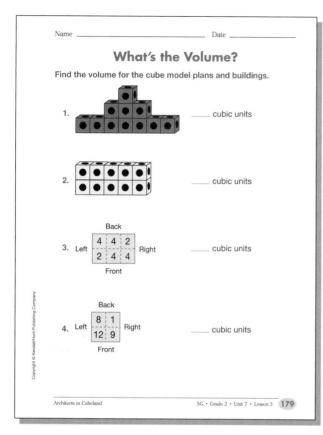

Figure 5: *Assessment Page from Grade 2 Unit 7*

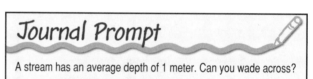

Figure 6: *A Journal Prompt from Grade 5 Unit 1 Lesson 3*

Figure 7: *A second-grade journal entry*

Regular journal writing provides teachers and parents with a means of documenting a student's growth in mathematical thinking, attitudes, and communication skills. (For information on math journals, see the TIMS Tutor: *Journals.*) Young children often begin by drawing pictures in their journals or combining pictures with a few words. The journal entry in Figure 7 is an early effort by Jayne, a second grader, at communicating her thoughts about a math lesson on doubling. Jayne used six circles and six squares to show two examples of doubling three. She also wrote a short paragraph about the class:

> *Today my class did some math. and we did some writ (write) some math too! I like it!*

Assessment Section

The Assessment section at the end of most lesson guides lists ideas for assessing the lesson's content. The following components are often recommended as assessment: Assessment Pages, Journal Prompts, classroom observations corresponding to the Assessment Indicators, and appropriate questions from the student pages and Homework sections. The teacher can also record the level of a student's response to these questions on the *Observational Assessment Record* or in a grade book. Figure 8 shows assessment for Grade 1 Unit 6 Lesson 2.

Assessment Lessons

Some units include specially designed assessment lessons. These lessons are generally one of three types: assessment labs, open-response problems, or written tests composed of short items. Each type provides different kinds of information to teachers so that they can develop and document a complete picture of their students' progress toward the curriculum's goals.

Assessment Labs

Two or three laboratory experiments in each grade are designated as assessment labs. Teachers can use them to assess students' abilities to work with a group on an investigation that takes several days. Teachers can also observe students to see if they are confident enough to tackle new ideas and to use previously learned mathematics in new contexts. Working on projects such as these—problems requiring integration and application of many concepts and skills over a period of time—more closely resembles the work of mathematicians and scientists (as well as working adults in many occupations) than any other kind of work students do in school. Suggestions for evaluating labs are included in Part III.

Open-Response Problems

In these lessons, students are given a task that requires them to demonstrate their problem-solving skills individually or while working in a group. Students are also assessed on their understanding of the mathematical content and their abilities to communicate their strategies. They must produce a product that allows teachers to examine their processes as well as their final answers. More than a few minutes are required to solve such a problem and students will often need a whole class period to find solutions and describe their strategies. To encourage students to give full explanations and improve their writing skills, teachers can comment on students' initial responses and ask them to make revisions. Part III includes rubrics for scoring student responses to these problems.

Math Facts Strategies

DPP item D provides practice with addition math facts.

Homework and Practice

- The *Two Car Roll-off* Homework Page shows a diagram of two cars that rolled down different ramps. Students count the links and compare the distances.

- DPP item C practices addition in a measurement context. For DPP item E, students estimate lengths of objects. Item F reviews even and odd numbers. Item G practices partitioning numbers. Students divide groups of cookies among 4 people and count leftovers. Item H asks students to solve problems using skip counting.

Assessment

- The *Brian's Class* Assessment Page asks students to examine the data for a fictional class. **Questions 1–4** are similar to questions found in the class discussion while **Question 5 is** a challenge.

- Use children's journal entries to assess whether students understand the connection between "fairness" and controlled variables.

- Use the *Observational Assessment Record* to record students' abilities to make and interpret bar graphs and also to solve problems using data involving length.

Extension

Provide additional measurement practice by leaving the ramp in an activity center for student use.

Figure 8: *Grade 1 Unit 6 Lesson 2—Math Facts Strategies, Homework and Practice, Assessment, and Extension*

Name _____ Date _____

Class Party

Suppose there are 25 students in your class and you have $10 for a class party. Use the prices in the table to plan a party.

Tell how you would spend the money, and explain why you would spend it that way. Use as much of the $10 as you can, but do not plan to spend more than $10. (There is no tax.) Be sure your plan works for a class of 25.

Write your plan on another piece of paper. Be sure to explain how you solved the problem and how you made your decisions.

Item	Cost
pitcher of lemonade (10 servings)	$2.50
paper cups (package of 24)	69¢
ice cream bars	30¢
oatmeal cookies (package of 16)	99¢
bag of popcorn (30 servings)	$1.09
napkins (package of 50)	49¢

Copyright © Kendall/Hunt Publishing Company

Assessment Blackline Master   URG • Grade 3 • Unit 10 • Lesson 3   73

Figure 9 shows Jayne's response to an open-response problem written at midyear of third grade. Jayne is the same student who wrote the journal entry shown in Figure 7. Compare her writing here with her paragraph from second grade and also with her work at the end of third grade on the Earning Money problem shown in Figure 19 in Part III. Comparing these three responses shows how she has developed her communication skills.

Tests

Tests that assess students' conceptual understanding and procedural skills are short items that teachers can easily grade. There is a test in the final unit of both first and second grade. In third grade, there is a midyear and an end-of-year test. In fourth and fifth grades, there is a midterm test in both the fall and spring semesters in addition to a midyear and end-of-year test.

Jayne

Steps
1. Lemonade $7.50
   2.50 × 3 = $7.50

2. Paper Cups $1.38
   69 × 2 = $1.38

3. Popcorn
   1.09
   1.09 × 1 = 1.09

4.
   1
   7.50 Lemonade
   1.38 Paper Cups
 + 1.09 Popcorn
   $ 9.97

4. 3 ¢ left over

I solved the problems the way I did because number sentences help you get the awnser

My way works because it helped me get the awnser.

The math is the same as other math because they both have driffrent ways of solving their problems and awnsering them.

Figure 9: *Jayne's work for an open-response problem*

Assessment Units

In each grade, specific units are designated as assessment units. They include lessons that emphasize assessment at the same time that content is reviewed and new material is introduced. Teachers can assess students' abilities to apply previously studied concepts in new contexts and their willingness to approach new mathematics.

Assessment units at the beginning of each grade provide opportunities to observe students and collect baseline data on students' mathematical knowledge. Teachers can use this information to plan instruction that meets students' needs and to begin documenting students' mathematical growth over the course of the year. See the Assessment Overview in Part VI for specific information on the assessment units.

Portfolios

Portfolios are important tools for documenting students' growth throughout the year. They are collections of students' written work and teachers' anecdotal records. To provide a complete picture of a student's learning, a portfolio should include assessments that demonstrate the range of the child's abilities. Samples of student work on labs, open-response problems, assessment activity pages, and tests can be included along with samples of students' daily work. Work from the year's beginning to end will show students' growth over time. Certain lessons in the assessment units are especially appropriate for inclusion in portfolios. Refer to the TIMS Tutor: *Portfolios* for more information.

Facts Assessment

In *Math Trailblazers,* teachers assess students' knowledge of the facts by observing them as they work on activities, labs, and games and through the appropriate use of quizzes and tests. Periodic, short quizzes in the Daily Practice and Problems naturally follow the study of small groups of facts organized around specific strategies. As self-assessment in third, fourth, and fifth grades, each student can record his or her progress on *Facts I Know* charts and determine which facts he or she needs to study. The goal of the math facts assessment program is to determine the degree to which students can find answers to fact problems quickly and accurately and whether they can retain this skill over time. For more information on teaching and assessing the math facts, see the TIMS Tutor: *Math Facts.*

PART III

Implementing the Assessment Program

Evaluating and reporting on a broad range of student achievement throughout the school year is a complex task. It is only practical if the assessment process is built into day-to-day instruction. Components of the assessment program are designed so teachers can gather information about students as they are learning. This section outlines a plan for gradually introducing the various components of the assessment program during the first weeks of instruction and provides information on evaluating and scoring written work.

Getting Started

An assessment program that emphasizes the documentation of students' growth over time establishes a climate in which each child is valued for the knowledge and skills he or she brings to the classroom and in which each student is expected to make significant gains in mathematics. These are high expectations that also reflect reality. Students begin and end the school year with varying abilities, backgrounds, and accomplishments. Therefore, it is important to record what each student can do initially, as well as during the learning process, so that the teacher, student, and parents can fully appreciate progress throughout the year.

Begin Observational Assessments

Activities in the first two or three units of each grade provide many opportunities to observe students as they use mathematics. These observations provide a rich source of baseline information about students. For example, in Units 1–3 of first grade, students count objects in many contexts. By routinely observing four or five students during appropriate lessons, the teacher can note those students who can count and those who may need additional help. At the same time, all students are working on their counting skills as well as on related concepts such as comparing numbers and organizing data.

Unit 2 of third grade is also designated as an assessment unit. In this unit, students review strategies to maintain fluency with the subtraction facts. Students discuss strategies, play games, work with flash cards, assess themselves using *Facts I Know* charts, and use subtraction facts as part of a data collection activity. Observing students participating in these activities gives teachers information about students' knowledge of the facts and, more importantly, about students' abilities to use the facts to solve problems. Since students will continually use the facts in many activities as well as in the Daily Practice and Problems, the teacher need only record observations for a small number of students at a time. (For more information on assessment of the math facts, see the TIMS Tutor: *Math Facts.*)

Using the *Observational Assessment Record.*
Before beginning assessment observations, teachers need a system for recording short, anecdotal records. Such a system should allow recording of a broad range of evidence of students' behavior, attitudes, and understanding of mathematics and should make recording and retrieving information easy and convenient. The *Observational Assessment Record* and the Assessment Indicators help organize data from observations. Teachers can develop their own shorthand to denote satisfactory progress toward a goal or proficiency with a skill or concept.

202 TIG • Grade 3 • Assessment • Implementing the Assessment Program

In Grades 1–5, information from the *Observational Assessment Record* can be transferred to *Individual Assessment Record Sheets* to create a year-long anecdotal record of growth for each child. The *Individual Assessment Record Sheet* is located at the end of Part VI of this section. Teachers can copy and place it in each student's portfolio. It is also available on the *Teacher Resource CD.* Teachers can use it to maintain records of each student's progress electronically.

As part of lesson planning, the teacher can choose one or two behaviors, concepts, or skills to check during class. The Assessment Indicators for each unit and the Assessment section in the lesson guides can facilitate this process. The teacher should choose no more than four or five students to observe in a day. Additional students can be observed in succeeding lessons or units to provide further information about individual students' progress and the improvement of the class as a whole.

Figure 10 is an example of an *Observational Assessment Record* for Grade 1 Unit 1 that shows one possible scheme for recording classroom observations. Note that the teacher chose to observe students' abilities to work together as well as counting skills.

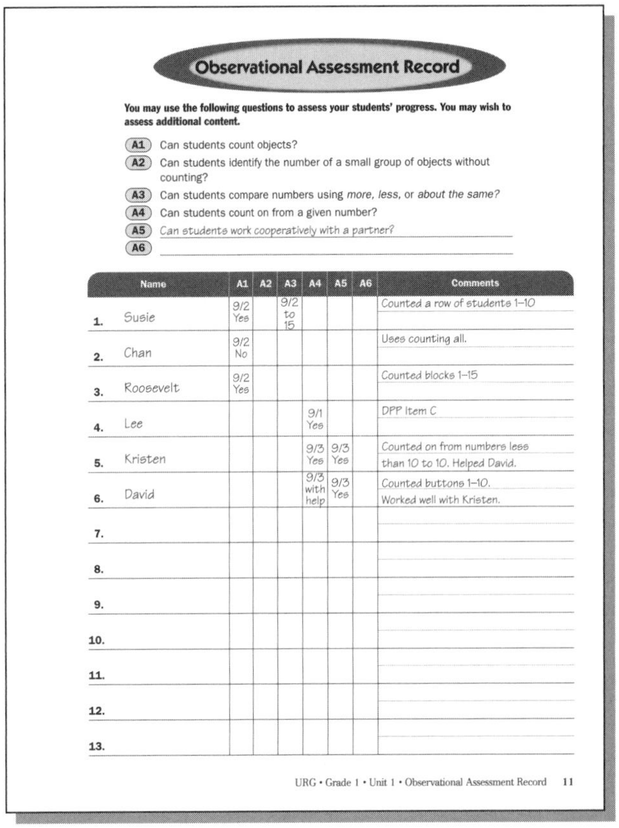

Observational Assessment Record

You may use the following questions to assess your students' progress. You may wish to assess additional content.

A1 Can students count objects?
A2 Can students identify the number of a small group of objects without counting?
A3 Can students compare numbers using *more, less,* or *about the same?*
A4 Can students count on from a given number?
A5 Can students work cooperatively with a partner?
A6

	Name	A1	A2	A3	A4	A5	A6	Comments
1.	Susie	9/2 Yes		9/2 to 15				Counted a row of students 1–10
2.	Chan	9/2 No						Uses counting all.
3.	Roosevelt	9/2 Yes						Counted blocks 1–15
4.	Lee				9/1 Yes			DPP Item C
5.	Kristen				9/3 Yes	9/3 Yes		Counted on from numbers less than 10 to 10. Helped David.
6.	David				9/3 with help	9/3 Yes		Counted buttons 1–10. Worked well with Kristen.
7.								
8.								
9.								
10.								
11.								
12.								
13.								

URG • Grade 1 • Unit 1 • Observational Assessment Record 11

Figure 10: *Sample* Observational Assessment Record *for Grade 1 Unit 1*

Other suggestions from teachers for organizing anecdotal records follow:

Student Grid. A teacher can make a grid that allows note-taking about all students on one piece of paper as shown in Figure 11. The grids include as many cells as there are students in the class, labeling each cell with a student's name. Observations are written in the cells. Like the *Observational Assessment Record,* this provides a view of the entire class's progress.

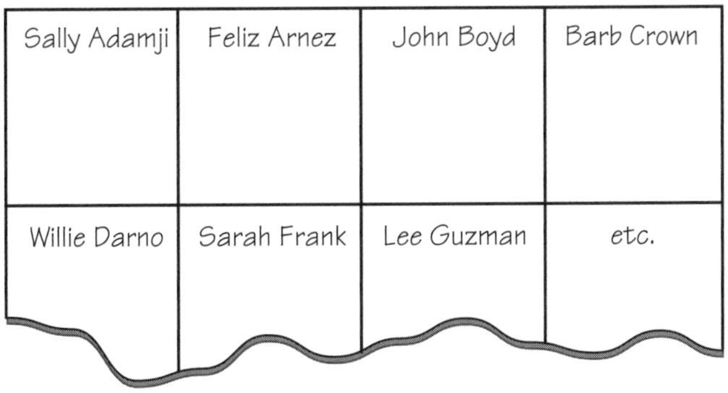

Figure 11: *Student grid*

Assessment

Flip Chart. A flip chart can be made by lining up index cards and taping them to a clipboard or a piece of heavy cardboard so they overlap by all but a strip of about $\frac{1}{2}$ inch as shown in Figure 12. Students' names are written on the uncovered area of each card, so the teacher can easily flip to a student's card and write a quick, dated note about the observation. As a card is filled, it can be removed to a card file or a student's portfolio and replaced with a new card.

Figure 12: *Flip chart*

Flip Cards. A variation of the flip chart can be made by fastening together a set of index cards—one card labeled for each student in the class. A binder ring is placed through a hole in a corner of each card.

Self-Adhesive Notes. Some teachers prefer to write their observations about individual students on self-adhesive notes, which are then attached to a sheet of paper in the student's portfolio. These notes have the advantage of being easily transferable, so they can be grouped and regrouped by student, subject, day, etc.

Begin Math Journals

At the beginning of the year, math journals provide a safe place for students to start communicating their insights. By writing regularly in their journals, they gain the experience necessary to write more and learn to express themselves clearly. Students can write in response to journal prompts or record answers to questions from the *Student Guide* or Daily Practice and Problems. See the TIMS Tutor: *Journals* for more information on using journals to assess students.

Begin Portfolios

The TIMS Tutor: *Portfolios* recommends establishing portfolios by starting small with modest goals. This implies using portfolios to document progress in one or two specific areas such as communicating mathematically or collecting and analyzing data. One way to begin is to assign each student a collection folder in which early examples of student work are saved. Later in the process, teachers can designate or students can select a smaller number of pieces that show growth in these areas.

It is important to choose examples of work from the beginning of the year so a student's first efforts can be compared to later work. The earliest entries in the portfolio will most likely show much less sophisticated results than those that are added toward the end of the year. For example, to compare students' use of the TIMS Laboratory Method at the beginning of the year to their abilities to conduct an experiment at the end of the year, include a data table and a graph from an early lab in each student's portfolio. Good choices of initial labs to collect in portfolios include the following: In Grade 1, save students' weather graphs from Unit 2; in Grade 2, use the Button Sizer Graph from Unit 3; and in Grade 3, choose student work from the lab *Kind of Bean* in Unit 1 or the graph and write-up from *Spinning Differences* in Unit 2. At the beginning of Grade 4, include *Arm Span vs. Height* from Unit 1 and *Perimeter vs. Length* from Unit 2. In Grade 5, begin portfolios with the labs *Searching the Forest* from Unit 1 and *Distance vs. Time* from Unit 3.

Scoring Open-Response Problems

In *Math Trailblazers,* most lessons involve multiple mathematical topics, skills, and processes. Assessing student progress requires tools that allow students to respond using multiple approaches and that let teachers evaluate student communication and problem-solving strategies as well as mathematical knowledge.

TIMS Multidimensional Rubric

To assist teachers in evaluating student performance and in communicating progress to students and parents, we have developed a rubric—a scoring guide—for evaluating student work on open-response problems. The *TIMS Multidimensional Rubric* addresses three dimensions of mathematical learning: (i) knowing, (ii) solving, and (iii) telling. Using these three dimensions broadens the assessment focus from the traditional emphasis on rote procedures to a more complete view of mathematics learning. The rubric outlines our criteria for excellence and provides an explicit indication of what we value in mathematics. Examples of using the rubric to score student work are included in lesson guides beginning in Grade 3. The ideas embodied in the rubric are generally applicable to younger children and can be modified for use in earlier grades. The rubric is displayed in Part V.

The three dimensions of mathematical understanding emphasized in the *TIMS Multidimensional Rubric* are described here briefly.

- *Solving.* This section focuses on students' understanding of a problem and their abilities to devise a plan for solving it, organize information, analyze results, and reflect on its mathematical implications.
- *Knowing.* This portion of the rubric examines students' comprehension of mathematical concepts and their abilities to apply procedures, rules, and facts to a given mathematical situation. This includes effective use of representations, such as written numbers, words, graphs, tables, or pictures, and the ability to make connections among different mathematical ideas.
- *Telling.* This part stresses students' abilities to explain their problem-solving strategies, justify their solutions, use symbols and terminology correctly, and discuss connections among mathematical topics.

The *TIMS Multidimensional Rubric* specifies criteria for assigning scores on each dimension to one piece of student work. Level 4 is the highest and is intended to represent excellence in that particular dimension. A paper might earn, for example, a 3 in *Solving*, a 4 in *Knowing*, and a 3 in *Telling*. It is not necessary to assign a score for all three dimensions for every task. For many tasks, it may be more appropriate to give scores for only one or two dimensions.

Student Rubrics

Corresponding Student Rubrics for each dimension make the expectations of student performance clear. These rubrics provide students with goals as they solve problems, communicate their solutions, and revise their work. Students also use these rubrics as guides when assessing their own work. The student rubrics are introduced gradually in the *Student Guide* throughout the first semester of third, fourth, and fifth grades. They are included in lessons with open-response problems.

The Student Rubrics are shown in Figure 13.

The Student Rubrics are located in Appendices A, B, and C and on the inside backcover of the *Student Guides* for Grades 3–5. Blackline Masters of the Student Rubrics are included in Part V so teachers can make transparencies or use a copier to enlarge the rubrics to make classroom posters.

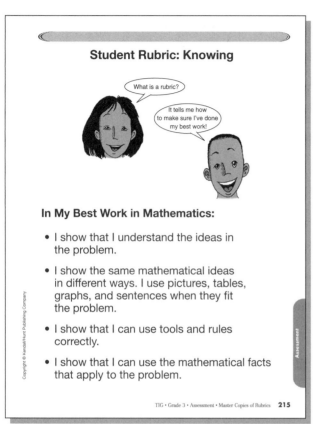

Student Rubric: Knowing

What is a rubric?

It tells me how to make sure I've done my best work!

In My Best Work in Mathematics:

- I show that I understand the ideas in the problem.

- I show the same mathematical ideas in different ways. I use pictures, tables, graphs, and sentences when they fit the problem.

- I show that I can use tools and rules correctly.

- I show that I can use the mathematical facts that apply to the problem.

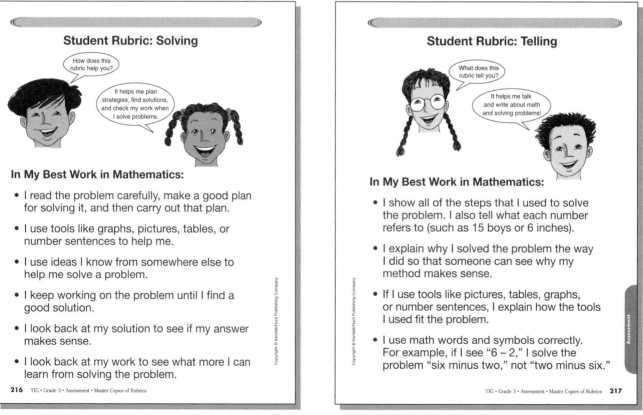

Student Rubric: Solving

How does this rubric help you?

It helps me plan strategies, find solutions, and check my work when I solve problems.

In My Best Work in Mathematics:

- I read the problem carefully, make a good plan for solving it, and then carry out that plan.

- I use tools like graphs, pictures, tables, or number sentences to help me.

- I use ideas I know from somewhere else to help me solve a problem.

- I keep working on the problem until I find a good solution.

- I look back at my solution to see if my answer makes sense.

- I look back at my work to see what more I can learn from solving the problem.

Student Rubric: Telling

What does this rubric tell you?

It helps me talk and write about math and solving problems!

In My Best Work in Mathematics:

- I show all of the steps that I used to solve the problem. I also tell what each number refers to (such as 15 boys or 6 inches).

- I explain why I solved the problem the way I did so that someone can see why my method makes sense.

- If I use tools like pictures, tables, graphs, or number sentences, I explain how the tools I used fit the problem.

- I use math words and symbols correctly. For example, if I see "6 − 2," I solve the problem "six minus two," not "two minus six."

Figure 13: *Student Rubrics:* Knowing, Solving, *and* Telling

Using the Rubrics: An Early Example

Using the student rubrics to inform students of your expectations as well as using the *TIMS Multidimensional Rubric* to score student work is a process that evolves throughout the year. For example, Grade 3 Unit 2 includes the first assessment lesson with an open-response problem. This is the students' first exposure to the student rubrics. The problem is shown in Figure 14.

To begin the lesson the class reads and discusses the problem. It is similar to the problem in an earlier lesson (Unit 2 Lesson 2 *Spinning Sums*), so students should be familiar with the procedures. They also read and discuss the Student Rubric: *Knowing*. The teacher may ask students what tools, rules, and mathematical facts apply to the problem. She explains that she will grade their work based on the rubric.

After students understand the problem, they work in groups to plan a strategy for solving the problem and to carry out their plans. Then students write paragraphs describing their problem-solving processes and their results. The teacher directs students either to write the paragraph with their groups or to write the paragraph individually. When students have completed their paragraphs, the teacher reviews their work and makes suggestions for improvement.

It is a good idea to make transparencies of exemplary work from previous years or the lesson guide. The teacher discusses the exemplary work with the class, comparing the work to the rubric's standards. Finally, students revise their work based on the teacher's comments. A student response with teacher comments is shown in Figure 15.

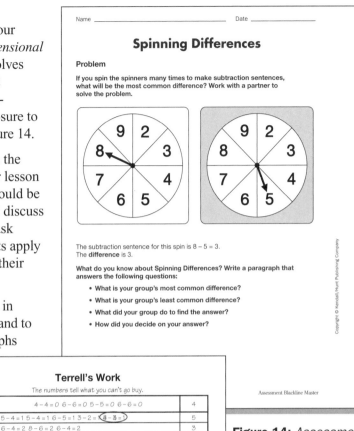

Figure 14: *Assessment lesson from Grade 3 Unit 2*

Figure 15: *A student response to a teacher's comments*

The teacher used the Knowing dimension of the *TIMS Multidimensional Rubric* to score students' work. The Lesson Guide provides questions specific to this problem to guide the teacher's scoring. The questions provided for this problem are given below:

- Were the data table and graph appropriately labeled?
- Was the graph scaled properly?
- Were the bars correctly drawn?
- Were the subtraction sentences correct?
- Were the most common differences identified?

Many of the criteria in the rubric overlap. In addition, the student's data table, graph, and written paragraphs tell us about more than one component of the problem. Consequently, the score for a dimension will result from the compilation of all the evidence, not necessarily from an arithmetic average of scores in each cell of the rubric. Figure 16 shows the Knowing dimension of the *TIMS Multidimensional Rubric* with the teacher's notations after she scored Terrell's paper.

How would you score Terrell's work? Terrell's teacher decided that he earned a 3. He worked with his group using tools to spin the spinners 30 times, record the results in a table, and display the data in a graph. The bars are drawn correctly on the graph and the axes are scaled correctly. However, the incorrect labels on both the data table ("The numbers that tell what you can't go buy") and graph ("Most Common Differences" and "N = of Letters") indicate that he was not clear on his goal for collecting data and therefore did not completely understand the problem's concepts and applications. The incorrect labels also show major errors translating between tables, graphs, and real situations, although he did correctly identify the most common and least common differences. The correct number sentences are evidence that he knows the subtraction facts. (See the Lesson Guide for *Spinning Differences* in Grade 3 Unit 2 for other examples of student work scored using the rubric.)

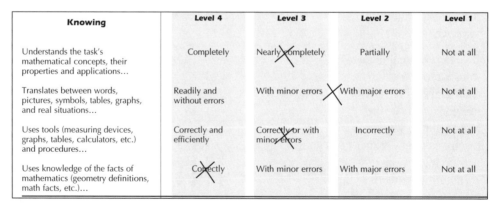

Knowing	Level 4	Level 3	Level 2	Level 1
Understands the task's mathematical concepts, their properties and applications…	Completely	Nearly completely	Partially	Not at all
Translates between words, pictures, symbols, tables, graphs, and real situations…	Readily and without errors	With minor errors	With major errors	Not at all
Uses tools (measuring devices, graphs, tables, calculators, etc.) and procedures…	Correctly and efficiently	Correctly or with minor errors	Incorrectly	Not at all
Uses knowledge of the facts of mathematics (geometry definitions, math facts, etc.)…	Correctly	With minor errors	With major errors	Not at all

Figure 16: *Scoring an open-response problem using one dimension of the* TIMS Multidimensional Rubric

Using the Rubrics: A Second Example

During the school year, students become familiar with all three student rubrics and use them as they solve problems. Depending on the problem, they may use one or more of the rubrics. The results of these assessments are often saved in portfolios to show students and parents progress over time. The problem in Figure 17 is posed to students in the final assessment unit of third grade.

Before students begin solving the problem, the class reads and discusses the problem. Students should understand that play money will be available to help solve the problem and that they will be asked how they can use calculators to solve the problem. The teacher also reviews all three student rubrics and advises students that their work for this problem will be scored using all three dimensions.

Students use the tools available to them to find solutions and write about their strategies. The teacher may use samples of students' work to provide good examples for students to emulate. The teacher also comments on students' first drafts and students revise their work accordingly.

Name ______________________ Date ______________

Earning Money

Daniel, Maria, and Cora earned five dollars baby-sitting for the Farleys. Mrs. Farley gave the three sitters one five-dollar bill.

1. If they share the money equally, how much should each baby-sitter get? Explain how you solved the problem.
2. What happens if you try to solve the problem on a calculator? Explain.

Write your solutions to Questions 1 and 2. Be sure to tell about all the ways you solved the problem.

Assessment Blackline Master   URG • Grade 3 • Unit 20 • Lesson 4 59

Figure 17: *An open-response problem from Grade 3 Unit 20*

Marco's Work

Marco's response the first day:

$3.65
× 3 kids

three dollars and sixey five cenes times three kids, and five dollers minus one doller and foty five cenes egels fore dollers.

$5.00
− $1. 45
$4.00 ← not good

Teacher comments:

I'm still not clear from your explanation what you tried. Maybe you should try to explain to me. Did you use the money or the calculator? Try to finish today.

Ms. Ho

Marco's response the second day:

I didn't use the money, But I used a calculator.

75¢
75
75
225

$4.50
× 3
$1.50

165
×3
4.95

$1.70
× 3
$5.10

1.67
× 3
5.01

3.13
× 3
3.39

1.69
× 3
5.07

3
$1.10
$1.10
+ $1.10
$3.30

1.66
× 3
4.98

Figure 18: *Marco's work*

Samples of two students' work are shown in Figures 18 and 19. Scores for both students for all three dimensions of the *TIMS Multidimensional Rubric* are discussed below. The teacher was guided by additional questions in the Lesson Guide that are specific to this problem and that point out elements to consider while scoring.

The teacher gave Marco a 2 on Solving. Marco chose a legitimate problem-solving strategy—guess and check—but did not use it systematically or efficiently, nor did he organize his work. His work does show evidence that he persisted in the problem-solving process, but does not show that he

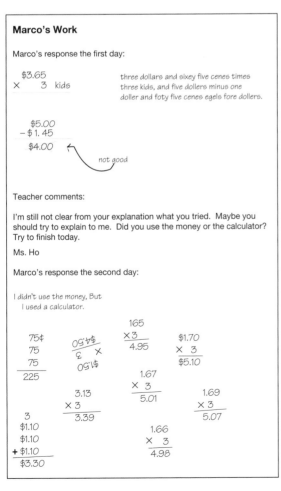

identified all the elements of the problem since he does not indicate that he knows that there will be money left over. He makes no connections to previously studied mathematics or previously solved problems.

On the Knowing dimension, the teacher gave Marco a 3 since he correctly used his knowledge of mathematics and he used appropriate tools (a calculator) and procedures (repeated addition and multiplication) to solve the problem. He did not demonstrate that he completely understood the nature of the task or show that he can translate between symbols and real situations since he did not calculate the amount of money that would be left over.

Marco received a 1 on the Telling dimension. His explanation was very short and totally unclear, with no supporting arguments. Since he did not identify which trial was successful, we are not even sure of his final answer. He used symbols to show his trials, but made no attempt to organize them. Appropriate terminology is not present.

A second sample of student work on the Earning Money problem is shown below:

Jayne's Work

Jayne's response the first day:

1.) Each person should get $1.66 and .2 left over. We got five dollars in change and we divided the money up between them. We got $1.66 for each person, and two cents left over.

2.) If you try on the calculator (5 ÷ 3) you would get 1.6666667. So I think it's much better to use play money or your head. The reason why you can't do it on the calculator is because the calculator will cut the coin up in half.

Teacher comments:

This is an excellent explanation! How can this problem help you solve other problems? Can you think of a way to find the remainder using your calculator?

Mrs. Vasquez

Jayne's response the second day:

1. You can check your answer by the calculator you can put $1.66 + $1.66 + $1.66 + $0.02 = $5.00.

2. This problem can help me solve other problems because it will help me divide money (if it involves money.)

3. A way to find how much is left $5.00 − $1.66 − $1.66 − $1.66 = $0.02.

Figure 19: *Jayne's work*

Jayne's teacher gave her a score of 4 for Solving. She fully met the criteria in the rubric. She clearly identified the elements of the problem when she described the problem first as dividing the play money "up between them." She then found the amount left over and used a calculator to divide (5 ÷ 3) resulting in a repeating decimal. With prompting from the teacher, she looked for other strategies and found she could use repeated addition and subtraction to find the remainder. All her strategies are effective and they are presented in an organized fashion. Jayne's first conclusion that "you can't do it (find the remainder) on the calculator is because the calculator will cut the coin up in half" is insightful, although not quite correct mathematically. Using both repeated addition and subtraction on the calculator to find the remainder shows that she made meaningful connections between the operations and that she was willing to persist in the problem-solving process.

Jayne also received a 4 in Knowing since she clearly understood the problem's mathematical concepts. She readily translated the real situation into words when she described the process of dividing up the money and then translated words into symbols using correct addition, subtraction, and division sentences. The use of play money and a calculator is evidence that she can use tools correctly and efficiently and her calculations show that she can use the facts of mathematics correctly as well.

The teacher gave Jayne a score of 3 for the Telling dimension. Her explanations and responses were fairly complete and clear. However, we are not entirely sure how the group shared the money. Did they trade the dollars for quarters and then the quarters for dimes, etc., or were they able to make the process more efficient in some way? Her supporting arguments are sound, but they contain a few minor gaps. Did she use repeated subtraction or repeated addition first to find the remainder? Why did she choose these operations? She used many symbols and terms correctly. However, she reported that two cents were left over and wrote it first as ".2."

Like any new tool, using the rubric efficiently will require practice. As you begin to work with the rubric, we suggest that you work closely with other teachers. For example, you might score a half-dozen papers and ask one or more colleagues to score the same set; then compare and discuss the results, negotiating any differences. Repeating this process over the course of the year will help establish school-wide norms for applying the rubrics.

Using Assessment Observations, Math Journals, and Portfolios

The rubrics can be combined with other components of the assessment program to provide a more complete picture of students' skills at solving open-response problems. For example, to assess students' willingness to tackle new problems or work cooperatively in a group, teachers can observe students as they work on the problem or ask them to write in their journals about the process. For example, the Journal Prompt for the Earning Money problem concerns students' feelings about working in groups in math class. (See Figure 20.)

Journal Prompt

How did your group share the work on this problem? How do you feel about working with a group in math class?

Figure 20: *Journal prompt for Earning Money (Grade 3 Unit 20)*

Considerable growth in mathematical power is often evident when several write-ups of open-response problems from different times of the year are included in a student's portfolio. We can see growth in Jayne's problem-solving and communication skills when we look at her work on both the Class Party and Earning Money problems. (See Figure 9 in Part II and Figure 19.)

Evaluating Labs

Teachers have used the following ideas to evaluate student performance on labs:

Group Work

Students work in their groups to polish a lab write-up and turn in one completed lab or to prepare an oral report to be presented to the class. Their reports may include how the work was distributed among the group members. Students can also write a paragraph in their journals describing how each member functioned in the group and how to improve the process.

Using the Multidimensional Rubric

Choose one or two important questions to score using one or more dimensions of the *TIMS Multidimensional Rubric.* Often suitable questions are suggested in the Assessment section of the Suggestions for Teaching the Lesson in the Lesson Guide. These are usually open-response questions that ask students to make predictions or solve a problem using the data collected during the experiment.

Self-Assessment

Students can grade their own labs in class. This provides a forum for discussing the most important aspects of the lab.

Using a Point System

To grade a lab, teachers can assign a given number of points to each part of the lab and grade each part based on the criteria below. Teachers can also choose to grade only a portion of the lab such as the picture or the graph.

1. Drawing the Picture
   - Are the procedures and the materials clearly illustrated?
   - Are the variables labeled?
2. Collecting and Recording the Data
   - Are the data organized in a table?
   - Are the columns in the data table labeled correctly?
   - Are the data reasonable?
   - Are the correct units of measure included in the data table?
   - If applicable, did students average the data (find the median or mean) correctly?
3. Graphing the Data
   - Does the graph have a title?
   - Are the axes scaled correctly and labeled clearly? Labeling should be consistent with the picture and the data table and should include appropriate units of measure.
   - If it is a bar graph, are the bars drawn correctly?
   - If it is a point graph, are the points plotted correctly?
   - If the points suggest a straight line or a curve, did the student draw a best-fit line or fit a curve to the points?
   - Did the students show any interpolation or extrapolation on the graph?

4. Solving the Problems
   - Are the answers correct based on the data?
   - Did students use appropriate tools (calculators, rulers, graphs, etc.) correctly?
   - Are the answers, including the explanations, clear and complete?

References

Elementary Grades Assessment. *Balanced Assessment for the Mathematics Curriculum.* University of California. Dale Seymour Publications, White Plains, NY, 1999.

Lane, Suzanne. "The Conceptual Framework for the Development of a Mathematics Performance Assessment Instrument" in *Educational Measurement: Issues and Practice.* Vol. 12, Number 2. National Council on Measurement in Education, Washington, DC, 1993.

Mathematics Resource Guide for Fourth- and Eighth-Grade Teachers. Vermont Department of Education, Montpelier, VT, 1996.

Middle Grades Assessment. *Balanced Assessment for the Mathematics Curriculum.* University of California. Dale Seymour Publications, White Plains, NY, 2000.

Pellegrino, J.W., N. Chadowsky, and R. Glaser (Eds.) *Knowing What Students Know: The Science and Design of Educational Assessment.* National Research Council. National Academy Press, Washington, DC, 2001.

Performance Assessment in Mathematics: Approaches to Open-Ended Problems. Illinois State Board of Education, Springfield, IL, 1994.

Principles and Standards for School Mathematics. National Council of Teachers of Mathematics, Reston, VA, 2000.

Stenmark, J.K. (Ed.) *Mathematics Assessment: Myths, Models, Good Questions, and Practical Suggestions.* National Council of Teachers of Mathematics, Reston, VA, 1991.

Master Copies of Rubrics

This section contains the blackline masters of the *TIMS Multidimensional Rubric* and the three Student Rubrics: *Knowing, Solving,* and *Telling.* The Scoring Open-Response Problems section in Part III describes the rubrics and provides examples of their use in the curriculum. The *TIMS Multidimensional Rubric* is provided here so that teachers can use it to score student work. The copies of the three student rubrics in this section can be used to make transparencies for the overhead projector or enlarged to make posters for the classroom.

TIMS Multidimensional Rubric

Solving	Level 4	Level 3	Level 2	Level 1
Identifies the elements of the problem and their relationships to one another.	All major elements identified	Most elements identified	Some, but shows little understanding of relationships	Few or none
Uses problem-solving strategies which are . . .	Systematic, complete, efficient, and possibly elegant	Systematic and nearly complete, but not efficient	Incomplete or unsystematic	Not evident or inappropriate
Organizes relevant information . . .	Systematically and efficiently	Systematically, with minor errors	Unsystematically	Not at all
Relates the problem and solution to previously encountered mathematics and makes connections that are . . .	At length, elegant, and meaningful	Evident	Brief or logically unsound	Not evident
Persists in the problem solving process . . .	At length	Until a solution is reached	Briefly	Not at all
Looks back to examine the reasonableness of the solution and draws conclusions that are . . .	Insightful and comprehensive	Correct	Incorrect or logically unsound	Not present

Knowing	Level 4	Level 3	Level 2	Level 1
Understands the task's mathematical concepts, their properties and applications . . .	Completely	Nearly completely	Partially	Not at all
Translates between words, pictures, symbols, tables, graphs, and real situations . . .	Readily and without errors	With minor errors	With major errors	Not at all
Uses tools (measuring devices, graphs, tables, calculators, etc.) and procedures . . .	Correctly and efficiently	Correctly or with minor errors	Incorrectly	Not at all
Uses knowledge of the facts of mathematics (geometry definitions, math facts, etc.) . . .	Correctly	With minor errors	With major errors	Not at all

Telling	Level 4	Level 3	Level 2	Level 1
Includes response with an explanation and/or description which is . . .	Complete and clear	Fairly complete and clear	Perhaps ambiguous or unclear	Totally unclear or irrelevant
Presents supporting arguments that are . . .	Strong and sound	Logically sound, but may contain minor gaps	Incomplete or logically unsound	Not present
Uses pictures, symbols, tables, and graphs that are . . .	Correct and clearly relevant	Present with minor errors or somewhat irrelevant	Present with errors and/or irrelevant	Not present or completely inappropriate
Uses terminology . . .	Clearly and precisely	With minor errors	With major errors	Not at all

Student Rubric: Knowing

What is a rubric?

It tells me how to make sure I've done my best work!

In My Best Work in Mathematics:

- I show that I understand the ideas in the problem.

- I show the same mathematical ideas in different ways. I use pictures, tables, graphs, and sentences when they fit the problem.

- I show that I can use tools and rules correctly.

- I show that I can use the mathematical facts that apply to the problem.

Assessment

Student Rubric: Solving

How does this rubric help you?

It helps me plan strategies, find solutions, and check my work when I solve problems.

In My Best Work in Mathematics:

- I read the problem carefully, make a good plan for solving it, and then carry out that plan.

- I use tools like graphs, pictures, tables, or number sentences to help me.

- I use ideas I know from somewhere else to help me solve a problem.

- I keep working on the problem until I find a good solution.

- I look back at my solution to see if my answer makes sense.

- I look back at my work to see what more I can learn from solving the problem.

Student Rubric: Telling

What does this rubric tell you?

It helps me talk and write about math and solving problems!

In My Best Work in Mathematics:

- I show all of the steps that I used to solve the problem. I also tell what each number refers to (such as 15 boys or 6 inches).

- I explain why I solved the problem the way I did so that someone can see why my method makes sense.

- If I use tools like pictures, tables, graphs, or number sentences, I explain how the tools I used fit the problem.

- I use math words and symbols correctly. For example, if I see "6 – 2," I solve the problem "six minus two," not "two minus six."

Assessment

PART VI | Assessment Overview for Third Grade

The assessment overview includes short descriptions of the components in the assessment program followed by a table that lists each assessment in third grade. The table names the assessments in each unit and gives the lesson name and number, the type of assessment, and the location of the assessment within the unit.

Component Summary

Assessment Indicators: A list of important topics covered in a given unit. The Assessment Indicators help the teacher focus on important skills and behaviors that should be assessed.

Observational Assessment Record Sheet: A tool that helps teachers organize student progress on the Assessment Indicators. Information about all students in the class can be recorded on the *Observational Assessment Record*. This provides a quick view of how both individual students and the class as a whole are progressing during the course of a unit. Student information can later be transferred to *Individual Assessment Record Sheets.*

Individual Assessment Record Sheet: A tool for tracking individual students' progress with the Assessment Indicators from all twenty units.

Assessment Section in the Lesson Guide: Suggested ways to assess student progress during a lesson are included as Assessment in the Suggestions for Teaching the Lesson section of the lesson guides. Assessments might highlight particular parts of an activity as appropriate for observations, direct teachers to an assessment page or activity, or suggest a journal prompt or homework questions for assessment.

Math Journals: As a part of the assessment for a lesson, students are sometimes asked to respond in their Math Journals to a specific question or prompt.

Assessment Pages: Short paper-and-pencil assessments that can be used to check skills or concepts developed in a unit. Some are designed for use in groups; others are for individual work.

Assessment Lessons: Specially designed lessons to gauge student progress. There are three basic types of assessment lessons: assessment labs, open-response problems, and written tests composed of short items.

Assessment Labs: 2–4 laboratory experiments each year are designated as Assessment Labs. They are used to assess students' abilities to work in a group on an investigation that takes several days.

Assessment Units: Specific units in each grade that are designed to help teachers monitor student progress as part of the learning process. Units 2, 10, and 20 are the Assessment Units in grade 3.

Fact Self-Assessment: As part of the Daily Practice and Problems (DPP), students regularly assess their knowledge of specific groups of math facts. Students categorize facts into three groups (facts I know quickly; facts I know using a strategy; facts I need to learn). They record this information on a special chart, which is updated regularly.

Facts Quiz: Periodic quizzes of small groups of math facts are given as part of the DPP. Facts are grouped to encourage the use of strategies in learning facts. Tests of the entire sets of facts are given at midyear and at the end of the year.

Portfolios: Collections of students' written work and teachers' anecdotal records. Portfolios are used to document students' growth over time.

Assessment Component	Component Description	Location
Unit 1—Sampling and Classifying		
Observational Assessment Record **Individual Assessment Record Sheet**	**Assessment Record** **Assessment Record**	**URG** **TIG**
Lesson 1—First Names Lisa's Class Graph Careless Professor Peabody	**Lab** Assessment Page Assessment Page	**URG** URG URG
Lesson 3—Kind of Bean Who's Right?	**Lab** Assessment Pages	**URG** URG
Lesson 4—Line Math Puzzles DPP Item P—Bar Graphs	**Lesson** Assessment Item	**URG** URG
Lesson 5—You Can't Do That DPP Item Q—Addition Facts Quiz: Doubles, 2s, and 3s	**Adventure Book** Addition Facts Assessment Item	**URG** URG
Lesson 6—A Sample of Problems DPP Item S—Addition Facts Quiz: More Addition Facts	**Lesson** Addition Facts Assessment Item	**URG** URG
Unit 2—Strategies: An Assessment Unit		
Observational Assessment Record **Individual Assessment Record Sheet**	**Assessment Record** **Assessment Record**	**URG** **TIG**
Lesson 1—Addition Facts Strategies Calculator Challenges	**Lesson** Assessment Page	**URG** URG
Lesson 5—Subtraction Facts Strategies DPP Item N—Magic Square: 4, 5, 6	**Lesson** Assessment Item	**URG** URG
Lesson 6—Spinning Differences Spinners 2–9 Spinning Differences Spinning Differences Data Table Student Rubric: *Knowing* TIMS Multidimensional Rubric	**Assessment Lesson** Assessment Page Assessment Page Assessment Page Student Rubric Scoring Guide	**URG, SG, DAB** DAB URG URG SG/TIG TIG
Lesson 7—Assessing the Subtraction Facts	**Assessment Lesson**	**URG, DAB**

Assessment

Assessment Component	Component Description	Location
Unit 3—Exploring Multiplication		
Observational Assessment Record **Individual Assessment Record Sheet**	**Assessment Record** **Assessment Record**	**URG** **TIG**
Lesson 2—In Twos, Threes, and More Home Practice Part 2	**Lesson** Assessment Page	**URG** DAB
Lesson 5—Multiples on the Calendar Home Practice Part 4	**Lesson** Assessment Page	**URG** DAB
Unit 4—Place Value Concepts		
Observational Assessment Record **Individual Assessment Record Sheet**	**Assessment Record** **Assessment Record**	**URG** **TIG**
Lesson 2—The TIMS Candy Company Are These the Fewest Possible? Are They the Same?	**Lesson** Assessment Page Assessment Page	**URG** URG URG
Lesson 3—Base-Ten Addition Student Rubric: *Knowing* Home Practice Part 3	**Lesson** Student Rubric Assessment Page	**URG** SG/TIG DAB
Lesson 5—It's Time Time	**Lesson** Assessment Page	**URG** URG
Lesson 6—Time for Problems DPP Item U—More Boxes	**Lesson** Assessment Item	**URG** URG
Unit 5—Area of Different Shapes		
Observational Assessment Record **Individual Assessment Record Sheet**	**Assessment Record** **Assessment Record**	**URG** **TIG**
Lesson 3—The Better "Picker Upper" DPP Item G—Averaging Home Practice Part 3	**Lab** Assessment Item Assessment Page	**URG** URG DAB
Lesson 5—Joe the Goldfish A Raincoat for Joe the Goldfish Student Rubric: *Knowing* Student Rubric: *Solving*	**Assessment Lesson** Assessment Page Student Rubric Student Rubric	**URG, SG** URG SG/TIG SG/TIG
Unit 6—More Adding and Subtracting		
Observational Assessment Record **Individual Assessment Record Sheet**	**Assessment Record** **Assessment Record**	**URG** **TIG**
Lesson 4—Subtracting with Base-Ten Pieces DPP Item R—Inventions Student Rubric: *Knowing* TIMS Multidimensional Rubric	**Lesson** Assessment Item Student Rubric Scoring Guide	**URG** URG SG/TIG TIG
Lesson 6—Leonardo the Blockhead DPP Item AA—Shortcut Subtraction	**Adventure Book** Assessment Item	**URG** URG

Assessment Component	Component Description	Location
Unit 7—Exploring Multiplication and Division		
Observational Assessment Record **Individual Assessment Record Sheet**	**Assessment Record** **Assessment Record**	**URG** **TIG**
Lesson 2—Katie's Job Katie's Job Student Rubric: *Telling* TIMS Multidimensional Rubric	**Assessment Lesson** Assessment Pages Student Rubric Scoring Guide	**URG, SG, DAB** URG SG/TIG TIG
Lesson 5—The Money Jar DPP Item P—Sharing Muffins	**Lesson** Assessment Item	**URG** URG
Lesson 6—Walking around Shapes DPP Item U—Subtraction Facts Quiz A Professor Peabody's Shapes Data Student Rubric: *Telling*	**Lesson** Subtraction Facts Assessment Item Assessment Page Student Rubric	**URG** URG URG SG/TIG
Unit 8—Mapping and Coordinates		
Observational Assessment Record **Individual Assessment Record Sheet**	**Assessment Record** **Assessment Record**	**URG** **TIG**
Lesson 3—Mapping a Tiny TIMS Town Maps	**Lesson** Assessment Pages	**URG** URG
Lesson 5—Tens Game DPP Item M—Subtraction Facts Quiz B DPP Item N—Maps	**Game** Subtraction Facts Assessment Item Assessment Item	**URG** URG URG
Unit 9—Using Patterns to Predict		
Observational Assessment Record **Individual Assessment Record Sheet**	**Assessment Record** **Assessment Record**	**URG** **TIG**
Lesson 1—Measuring Mass Balancing Masses	**Lesson** Assessment Pages	**URG** URG
Lesson 2—Mass vs. Number DPP Item J—Granola Robin's Marbles	**Lab** Assessment Item Assessment Page	**URG** URG URG
Lesson 3—More Mass Problems DPP Item M—Subtraction Facts: Quiz C	**Lesson** Subtraction Facts Assessment Item	**URG** URG

Assessment Component	Component Description	Location
Unit 10—Numbers and Patterns: An Assessment Unit		
Observational Assessment Record **Individual Assessment Record Sheet**	**Assessment Record** **Assessment Record**	**URG** **TIG**
Lesson 1—Stencilrama	**Assessment Lab**	**URG, SG, DAB**
Student Rubric: *Knowing*	Student Rubric	SG/TIG
Student Rubric: *Solving*	Student Rubric	SG/TIG
Student Rubric: *Telling*	Student Rubric	SG/TIG
TIMS Multidimensional Rubric	Scoring Guide	TIG
Lesson 3—Class Party	**Assessment Lesson**	**URG, SG**
DPP Item I—Subtraction Facts Quiz D	Subtraction Facts Assessment Item	URG
DPP Item K—Subtraction Facts Inventory	Subtraction Facts Assessment Item	URG
Class Party	Assessment Page	URG
Student Rubric: *Knowing*	Student Rubric	SG/TIG
Student Rubric: *Solving*	Student Rubric	SG/TIG
Student Rubric: *Telling*	Student Rubric	SG/TIG
TIMS Multidimensional Rubric	Scoring Guide	TIG
Lesson 5—Midyear Test	**Assessment Lesson**	**URG**
Midyear Test	Assessment Pages	URG
Unit 11—Multiplication Patterns		
Observational Assessment Record **Individual Assessment Record Sheet**	**Assessment Record** **Assessment Record**	**URG** **TIG**
Lesson 7—Cipher Force!	**Adventure Book**	**URG**
DPP Item R—A Product of 36	Assessment Item	URG
Lesson 8—Multiples of Tens and Hundreds	**Lesson**	**URG**
DPP Item S—Quiz on 5s and 10s	Multiplication Facts Assessment Item	URG
Unit 12—Dissections		
Observational Assessment Record **Individual Assessment Record Sheet**	**Assessment Record** **Assessment Record**	**URG** **TIG**
Lesson 3—Building with Four Triangles	**Lesson**	**URG**
Three Tans	Assessment Pages	URG
Lesson 5—Hex	**Game**	**URG**
DPP Item M—Quiz on 2s and 3s	Multiplication Facts Assessment Item	URG
Unit 13—Parts and Wholes		
Observational Assessment Record **Individual Assessment Record Sheet**	**Assessment Record** **Assessment Record**	**URG** **TIG**
Lesson 2—What's 1?	**Lesson**	**URG**
Pattern Block Fractions	Assessment Page	URG
Lesson 4—Fraction Games	**Games**	**URG**
DPP Item K—Quiz on the Square Numbers	Multiplication Facts Assessment Item	URG

Assessment Component	Component Description	Location
Unit 14—Collecting and Using Data		
Observational Assessment Record **Individual Assessment Record Sheet**	**Assessment Record** **Assessment Record**	**URG** **TIG**
Lesson 1—Time Again More Time	**Lesson** Assessment Page	**URG** URG
Lesson 4—Make Your Own Survey DPP Item G—Multiplication Quiz: 9s	**Lab** Multiplication Facts Assessment Item	**URG** URG
Lesson 5—Reviewing Addition and Subtraction Addition and Subtraction	**Lesson** Assessment Pages	**URG** URG
Unit 15—Decimal Investigations		
Observational Assessment Record **Individual Assessment Record Sheet**	**Assessment Record** **Assessment Record**	**URG** **TIG**
Lesson 2—Measuring to the Nearest Tenth Measure My Desk	**Lesson** Assessment Page	**URG** URG
Lesson 4—Length vs. Number DPP Item L—Decimal Base-Ten Shorthand DPP Item M—Multiplication Quiz: The Last Six Facts DPP Item O—Decimals for Base-Ten Shorthand Student Rubric: *Solving* Student Rubric: *Telling* TIMS Multidimensional Rubric	**Lab** Assessment Item Multiplication Facts Assessment Item Assessment Item Student Rubric Student Rubric Scoring Guide	**URG** URG URG URG SG/TIG SG/TIG TIG
Unit 16—Volume		
Observational Assessment Record **Individual Assessment Record Sheet**	**Assessment Record** **Assessment Record**	**URG** **TIG**
Lesson 2—Fill 'er Up! DPP Item F—Volume	**Lab** Assessment Item	**URG** URG
Lesson 4—Elixir of Youth DPP Item K—Multiplication Quiz: 2s, 5s, and 10s DPP Item L—Three Marbles	**Adventure Book** Multiplication Facts Assessment Item Assessment Item	**URG** URG URG
Unit 17—Wholes and Parts		
Observational Assessment Record **Individual Assessment Record Sheet**	**Assessment Record** **Assessment Record**	**URG** **TIG**
Lesson 1—Geoboard Fractions Halves of a Rectangle	**Lesson** Assessment Pages	**URG** URG
Lesson 4—Fraction Hex DPP Item K—Multiplication Quiz: 3s and 9s	**Game** Multiplication Facts Assessment Item	**URG** URG

Assessment

Assessment Component	Component Description	Location
Unit 18—Viewing and Drawing 3-D		
Observational Assessment Record **Individual Assessment Record Sheet**	**Assessment Record** **Assessment Record**	**URG** **TIG**
Lesson 4—Top, Front, and Right Side Views Three Ways to Show 3-D Models	**Lesson** Assessment Pages	**URG** URG
Lesson 5—Problems with Shapes DPP Item K—Multiplication Quiz: Squares	**Lesson** Multiplication Facts Assessment Item	**URG** URG
Unit 19—Multiplication and Division Problems		
Observational Assessment Record **Individual Assessment Record Sheet**	**Assessment Record** **Assessment Record**	**URG** **TIG**
Lesson 3—Making Groups DPP Item L—Multiplication Story 38 × 4	**Lesson** Assessment Item	**URG** URG
Lesson 4—Solving Problems with Division DPP Item Q—Multiplication Quiz: The Last Six Facts Multiplication and Division	**Lesson** Multiplication Facts Assessment Item Assessment Page	**URG** URG URG
Unit 20—Connections: An Assessment Unit		
Observational Assessment Record **Individual Assessment Record Sheet**	**Assessment Record** **Assessment Record**	**URG** **TIG**
Lesson 2—Tower Power	**Assessment Lab**	**URG, DAB**
Lesson 3—Becca's Towers Becca's Towers	**Assessment Lesson** Assessment Page	**URG, DAB** URG
Lesson 4—Earning Money DPP Item K—Multiplication Facts Inventory Test Earning Money Student Rubric: *Knowing* Student Rubric: *Solving* Student Rubric: *Telling* TIMS Multidimensional Rubric	**Assessment Lesson** Multiplication Facts Assessment Item Assessment Page Student Rubric Student Rubric Student Rubric Scoring Guide	**URG, SG,** **DAB** URG URG SG/TIG SG/TIG SG/TIG TIG
Lesson 5—End-of-Year Test End-of-Year Test	**Assessment Lesson** Assessment Pages	**URG** URG

Individual Assessment Record Sheet

Name _____

Unit 1: Sampling and Classifying   ✔   **Date and Comments:**

A1. Can students communicate solution strategies verbally and in writing?   _____   _____

A2. Can students identify and use variables?   _____   _____

A3. Can students make and interpret bar graphs?   _____   _____

A4. Can students collect, organize, graph, and analyze data?   _____   _____

A5. Can students use data in tables and graphs to make predictions and solve problems?   _____   _____

A6. Do students demonstrate fluency with the addition facts?   _____   _____

A7. _____   _____   _____

Unit 2: Strategies: An Assessment Unit   ✔   **Date and Comments:**

A1. Can students use strategies to add and subtract?   _____   _____

A2. Can students make and interpret bar graphs?   _____   _____

A3. Can students collect, organize, graph, and analyze data?   _____   _____

A4. Can students use patterns in data tables and graphs to make predictions and solve problems?   _____   _____

A5. Can students communicate mathematical reasoning verbally and in writing?   _____   _____

A6. _____   _____   _____

Unit 3: Exploring Multiplication   ✔   **Date and Comments:**

A1. Can students interpret bar graphs?   _____   _____

A2. Can students represent multiplication problems using manipulatives and pictures?   _____   _____

A3. Can students create stories for multiplication sentences?   _____   _____

A4. Can students write number sentences for multiplication situations?   _____   _____

A5. Can students solve multiplication and division problems and explain their reasoning?   _____   _____

A6. Can students divide a set of objects into equal-size groups (with remainders) and represent the situation with a number sentence?   _____   _____

A7. _____   _____   _____

Name _____

Unit 4: Place Value Concepts   ✔   **Date and Comments:**

A1.   Can students partition large numbers into two and three parts and represent them with number sentences?   _____   _____

A2.   Can students represent four-digit numbers using base-ten pieces, words, symbols, and place value charts?   _____   _____

A3.   Can students read and write large numbers (to the thousands)?   _____   _____

A4.   Can students compare and order large numbers (to the thousands)?   _____   _____

A5.   Can students represent addition problems using base-ten pieces?   _____   _____

A6.   Can students tell time to the nearest five minutes?   _____   _____

A7.   _____   _____   _____

Unit 5: Area of Different Shapes   ✔   **Date and Comments:**

A1.   Can students find the area of shapes with straight or curved sides by counting square units?   _____   _____

A2.   Do students recognize that different shapes can have the same area?   _____   _____

A3.   Can students find the median of a data set?   _____   _____

A4.   Can students identify and use variables?   _____   _____

A5.   Can students make and interpret bar graphs?   _____   _____

A6.   Can students collect, organize, graph, and analyze data?   _____   _____

A7.   Can students use data to make predictions and solve problems?   _____   _____

A8.   Can students solve open-response problems and communicate solution strategies?   _____   _____

A9.   _____   _____   _____

Unit 6: More Adding and Subtracting   ✔   **Date and Comments:**

A1.   Can students represent addition and subtraction using base-ten pieces?   _____   _____

A2.   Can students add using paper and pencil?   _____   _____

A3.   Can students subtract using paper and pencil?   _____   _____

A4.   Can students estimate sums and differences?   _____   _____

A5.   Can students determine the reasonableness of a solution?   _____   _____

A6.   Can students solve problems involving addition and subtraction?   _____   _____

A7.   _____   _____   _____

Name _____

Unit 7: Exploring Multiplication and Division   ✔   **Date and Comments:**

A1. Can students represent multiplication and division using manipulatives, number lines, data tables, graphs, pictures, and words?   _____   _____

A2. Can students write number sentences for multiplication and division situations?   _____   _____

A3. Can students solve multiplication and division problems and explain their reasoning?   _____   _____

A4. Can students make and interpret point graphs?   _____   _____

A5. Can students use patterns in data tables and graphs to make predictions and solve problems?   _____   _____

A6. Can students find the perimeter of regular shapes?   _____   _____

A7. Can students solve problems involving money?   _____   _____

A8. Do students demonstrate fluency with the subtraction facts in Groups 1 and 2?   _____   _____

A9. _____   _____   _____

Unit 8: Mapping and Coordinates   ✔   **Date and Comments:**

A1. Can students find locations on maps or locate objects using positive coordinates?   _____   _____

A2. Can students plot points using positive coordinates?   _____   _____

A3. Can students measure length in feet and centimeters?   _____   _____

A4. Can students use a scale map?   _____   _____

A5. Can students make a scale map?   _____   _____

A6. Do students demonstrate fluency with the subtraction facts in Groups 3 and 4?   _____   _____

A7. _____   _____   _____

Unit 9: Using Patterns to Predict   ✔   **Date and Comments:**

A1. Can students measure mass in grams?   _____   _____

A2. Can students collect, organize, graph, and analyze data?   _____   _____

A3. Can students make and interpret point graphs?   _____   _____

A4. Can students use patterns in data tables and graphs to make predictions and solve problems?   _____   _____

A5. Can students solve multiplication problems involving mass?   _____   _____

A6. Do students demonstrate fluency with the subtraction facts in Groups 5 and 6?   _____   _____

A7. _____   _____   _____

Assessment

Name _____

Unit 10: Numbers and Patterns: An Assessment Unit ✔ **Date and Comments:**

A1. Can students measure length in inches? _____ _____

A2. Can students identify and use variables? _____ _____

A3. Can students collect, organize, graph, and analyze data? _____ _____

A4. Can students use patterns in data tables and graphs to make predictions and solve problems? _____ _____

A5. Can students solve open-response problems and communicate solution strategies? _____ _____

A6. Do students demonstrate fluency with the subtraction facts in Groups 7 and 8? _____ _____

A7. Do students demonstrate fluency with all the subtraction facts? _____ _____

A8. _____ _____ _____

Unit 11: Multiplication Patterns ✔ **Date and Comments:**

A1. Can students represent multiplication and division problems using arrays? _____ _____

A2. Can students solve multiplication and division problems and explain their reasoning? _____ _____

A3. Can students multiply numbers with ending zeros? _____ _____

A4. Can students write number sentences for multiplication and division situations? _____ _____

A5. Can students use patterns in the multiplication table to develop multiplication strategies? _____ _____

A6. Can students use turn-around facts (commutativity) to multiply? _____ _____

A7. Can students solve problems involving money? _____ _____

A8. Do students demonstrate fluency with the multiplication facts for the 5s and 10s? _____ _____

A9. _____ _____ _____

Unit 12: Dissections ✔ **Date and Comments:**

A1. Can students analyze and describe 2-dimensional shapes using their properties (number of sides, corners, and right angles)? _____ _____

A2. Can students measure area and perimeter of 2-dimensional shapes? _____ _____

A3. Can students identify congruent shapes? _____ _____

A4. Can students identify line symmetry? _____ _____

A5. Can students use geometric concepts and skills to solve problems and communicate their reasoning? _____ _____

A6. Do students demonstrate fluency with the multiplication facts for the 2s and 3s? _____ _____

A7. _____ _____ _____

Name _____

Unit 13: Parts and Wholes   ✔   **Date and Comments:**

A1. Can students represent fractions using pattern blocks
and drawings?   _____   _____

A2. Can students identify fractional parts of a set?   _____   _____

A3. Can students partition shapes into given fractions?   _____   _____

A4. Can students identify the whole when given a fractional
part of the whole?   _____   _____

A5. Do students recognize that fractional parts of a whole
must have equal areas?   _____   _____

A6. Can students compare and order fractions using one-half
as a benchmark?   _____   _____

A7. Do students demonstrate fluency with the multiplication
facts for the square numbers?   _____   _____

A8. _____   _____   _____

Unit 14: Collecting and Using Data   ✔   **Date and Comments:**

A1. Can students tell time to the nearest minute?   _____   _____

A2. Can students solve problems involving elapsed time?   _____   _____

A3. Can students collect, organize, graph, and analyze data?   _____   _____

A4. Can students make and interpret bar graphs?   _____   _____

A5. Can students identify and use variables in a survey?   _____   _____

A6. Can students add and subtract multidigit numbers using
paper and pencil?   _____   _____

A7. Can students solve problems involving addition and
subtraction?   _____   _____

A8. Do students demonstrate fluency with the multiplication
facts for the 9s?   _____   _____

A9. _____   _____   _____

Unit 15: Decimal Investigations   ✔   **Date and Comments:**

A1. Can students represent decimals using number lines
(rulers) and base-ten pieces?   _____   _____

A2. Can students read and write decimals to hundredths?   _____   _____

A3. Can students skip count by tenths?   _____   _____

A4. Can students measure length to the nearest tenth of
a centimeter?   _____   _____

A5. Can students collect, organize, graph, and analyze data?   _____   _____

A6. Can students make and interpret point graphs?   _____   _____

A7. Can students use patterns in data tables and graphs to
make predictions and solve problems?   _____   _____

A8. Can students solve problems involving decimals?   _____   _____

A9. Do students demonstrate fluency with the multiplication
facts for the last six facts (4×6, 4×7, 4×8, 6×7,
6×8, 7×8)?   _____   _____

A10. _____   _____   _____

Assessment

Name _____

Unit 16: Volume   ✔   Date and Comments:

A1. Can students measure volume using a graduated cylinder?

A2. Can students collect, organize, graph, and analyze data?

A3. Can students make and interpret bar graphs?

A4. Can students solve addition, subtraction, multiplication, and division problems involving volume?

A5. Do students demonstrate fluency with the multiplication facts for the 2s, 5s, and 10s?

A6. _____

Unit 17: Wholes and Parts   ✔   Date and Comments:

A1. Can students represent fractions using geoboards and paper folding?

A2. Do students recognize that fractional parts of a whole must have equal areas but can have different shapes?

A3. Can students partition a shape into fractional parts?

A4. Can students find and name equivalent fractions using manipulatives?

A5. Do students demonstrate fluency with the multiplication facts for the 3s and 9s?

A6. _____

Unit 18: Viewing and Drawing 3-D   ✔   Date and Comments:

A1. Can students identify the faces, edges, and vertices of a box (rectangular prism)?

A2. Can students find the area of the base, height, and volume of cube models?

A3. Can students translate between a model, its cube model plan, and a three-dimensional drawing?

A4. Can students describe the top, front, and right side views of a cube model?

A5. Do students demonstrate fluency with the multiplication facts for the square numbers?

A6. _____

Name _____

Unit 19: Multiplication and Division Problems   ✔   Date and Comments:

A1. Can students represent 2-digit by 1-digit multiplication problems using manipulatives, arrays, and drawings?   _____   _____

A2. Can students solve 2-digit by 1-digit multiplication problems using manipulatives, arrays, and drawings?   _____   _____

A3. Can students multiply numbers with ending zeros?   _____   _____

A4. Can students write number sentences for multiplication and division situations?   _____   _____

A5. Can students create stories for multiplication and division sentences?   _____   _____

A6. Can students solve multiplication and division problems and explain their reasoning?   _____   _____

A7. Can students interpret remainders?   _____   _____

A8. Do students demonstrate fluency with the multiplication facts for the last six facts (4×6, 4×7, 4×8, 6×7, 6×8, 7×8)?   _____   _____

A9. _____   _____   _____

Unit 20: Connections: An Assessment Unit   ✔   Date and Comments:

A1. Can students find the area of the base, volume, and height of cube models?   _____   _____

A2. Can students collect, organize, graph, and analyze data?   _____   _____

A3. Can students make and interpret point graphs?   _____   _____

A4. Can students use patterns in data tables and graphs to make predictions and solve problems?   _____   _____

A5. Can students solve open-response problems and communicate solution strategies?   _____   _____

A6. Can students solve problems involving money?   _____   _____

A7. Do students demonstrate fluency with all the multiplication facts?   _____   _____

A8. _____   _____   _____

Additional Comments:

TIMS Tutors

The TIMS Tutors section provides an in-depth exploration of the mathematical concepts and ideas behind *Math Trailblazers*.

Students use a graduated cylinder to find the volume of small objects.

Introduction

TIMS Tutors

Arithmetic

Introduction

The last half-century has seen many changes in elementary school mathematics. For many people, "mathematics" is synonymous with "arithmetic." But today, while reasonable people can still debate the proper content of an elementary mathematics curriculum, nearly all agree that a curriculum focused largely on rote arithmetic will not meet the needs of students in the twenty-first century.

Much more than just arithmetic is now expected—geometry, probability, statistics, measurement, graphing, even algebra. Technology is dramatically changing the world, making it hard to imagine what our children will need to know in 20 or 40 more years, but also ensuring that many skills critical 50 years ago are less essential. Despite recent advances in psychology, educational research, and curriculum design, we are far from resolving all the uncertainties of the elementary school mathematics curriculum. A few things, however, do seem clear:

- The school mathematics curriculum can and must be more rigorous.
- Arithmetic is only one piece, albeit an important one, of a broad mathematics curriculum.
- We need to do better at helping children connect marks on paper to the real world. Too many children and adults fail to use common sense when dealing with mathematical symbolism. Discussing mathematics and integrating subject matter may help students make these connections.
- As we correct for the overemphasis on skills in the traditional mathematics curriculum, we should avoid over-correcting. Problem solving requires both procedural skill and conceptual understanding. As William Brownell (1956) noted during a previous period of reform, "In objecting to the emphasis on drill prevalent not so long ago, we may have failed to point out that practice for proficiency in skills has its place too." In *Math Trailblazers,* we consistently seek a balance between conceptual understanding and procedural skill.

The National Council of Teachers of Mathematics' (NCTM) *Principles and Standards for School Mathematics* advocates learning mathematics with understanding. "In recent decades, psychological and educational research on the learning of complex subjects such as mathematics has solidly established the important role of conceptual understanding in the knowledge and activity of persons who are proficient. Being proficient in a complex domain such as mathematics entails the ability to use knowledge flexibly, applying what is learned in one setting appropriately in another. One of the most robust findings of research is that conceptual understanding is an important component of proficiency, along with factual knowledge and procedural facility" (Bransford, Brown, and Cocking, 1999). The alliance of factual knowledge, procedural proficiency, and conceptual understanding makes all three components usable in powerful ways. Students who memorize facts or procedures without understanding often are not sure when or how to use what they know, and such learning is often quite fragile (Bransford, Brown, and Cocking, 1999; NCTM, 2000).

Several arguments support the NCTM position. One is that the computational proficiency of American students comes at too high a cost. The hundreds of hours devoted to arithmetic computation in elementary school leave too little time for other important topics. The traditional rote approach to computation undermines higher-level thinking: children learn that mathematics is blindly following rules, not thinking.

Another argument for shifting away from the traditional arithmetic curriculum is that technology has altered the role of paper-and-pencil calculation. As noted in the NCTM *Principles and Standards,* ". . . most of the arithmetic and algebraic procedures long viewed as the heart of the school mathematics curriculum can now be performed with handheld calculators. Thus more attention can now be given to understanding the number concepts and the modeling procedures used in solving problems." (NCTM, 2000) More practical topics—probability and statistics, geometry, measurement, mental computation and estimation—deserve more attention.

> A final and most important argument in favor of the changes NCTM recommends is that new approaches to arithmetic instruction are more effective in helping students learn both appropriate calculation skills and how to apply those skills in solving problems.

A final and most important argument in favor of the changes NCTM recommends is that new approaches to arithmetic instruction are more effective in helping students learn both appropriate calculation skills and how to apply those skills in solving problems. These new approaches build on students' own knowledge and intuitive methods and engage their common sense. This more meaningful approach helps students to be efficient and flexible in their computation and can reduce, though not eliminate, the amount of practice required. Thus a greater emphasis on conceptual understanding can lead to better procedural skills and problem-solving abilities (Brown & Burton, 1978; Skemp, 1978; Hiebert, 1984; Van Lehn, 1986; Carpenter, 1986; Baroody and Ginsburg, 1986; Good, Mulryan, and McCaslin, 1992; Hiebert, 1999; National Research Council, 2001).

Numeration and Place Value

Numeration in kindergarten emphasizes developing oral counting skills, making one-to-one correspondence between objects and numbers, developing the concept of cardinality, discovering patterns in our number system, and writing numbers. Students in Grade 3 continue to develop these skills and concepts. They take part in activities that help them become familiar with the structure of the number system.

In kindergarten and Grade 3, students practice their counting skills. They learn to count past 100 by ones, twos, fives, and tens. They count forward and backward from any given number. They group objects for counting.

Students use counting to solve addition and subtraction problems. They learn to write numbers up to and beyond 100. Beginning in kindergarten, a ten frame is frequently used as a visual organizer. See Figure 1. The *100 Chart* is introduced and used for a variety of purposes, including solving problems and studying patterns. Students partition, or break apart, numbers in several ways (25 = 20 + 5, 25 = 10 + 10 + 5, and so on). These activities help children develop number sense that allows them to use numbers flexibly.

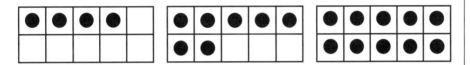

Figure 1: *Sample ten frame*

While formal study of place value is not a focus in kindergarten or Grade 3, the multiple grouping and counting experiences described above provide children with a foundation for building an intuitive sense for the meaning of place value.

Work with counting continues in Grade 2, especially skip counting and counting backwards. Place value is explored in the context of counting and grouping by tens. Children continue to count and group everyday objects such as buttons or beans. They use connecting cubes to represent these objects and often group the cubes by tens. Later, base-ten pieces represent these same objects, thus linking the base-ten representations with quantities of actual objects.

Students explore numbers well into the hundreds. Counting is still used for problem solving, but more elaborate procedures may be employed. For example, a student may solve 885 − 255 by counting up, first by hundreds (355, 455, 555, 655, 755, 855) and then by tens (865, 875, 885), yielding 630 as the answer.

More elaborate partitions of numbers are investigated in Grade 2. Particularly important are partitions in which every part is a single digit times 1, 10, 100, or 1000: 359 = 300 + 50 + 9 and so on. Attention is also given to partitioning numbers in more than one way:

$$359 = 300 + 50 + 9$$
$$= 200 + 150 + 9$$
$$= 100 + 250 + 9$$

This work with multiple partitioning is closely related to multidigit addition and subtraction. One way to think about addition and subtraction—indeed, one way to think about much of elementary mathematics—is as procedures for renaming numbers in more convenient forms. For example, 563 + 13 is a number we usually rename as 576. Another number, 875 ÷ 25, is renamable as 35 when it suits our purposes.

In Grade 3, more formal study of place value takes place. Students work in varied contexts involving numbers through the thousands. For example, students draw an outline of a coat and determine how many square centimeters of material are required to make the coat. Using contexts such as this encourages students to associate quantities of actual objects with representations of the quantities using base-ten pieces and with the numerals that represent them. Most of this work is closely connected with addition and subtraction of multidigit numbers. Indeed, a good reason for studying computational algorithms is that they provide a context for learning about place value.

In Grade 4, large numbers up to the millions are studied and used in various contexts. Continued efforts are made to connect the numbers with actual quantities. For example, the class creates its own base-ten pieces for large numbers—pieces we call super skinnies (10,000), super flats (100,000), and megabits (1,000,000). See Figure 2.

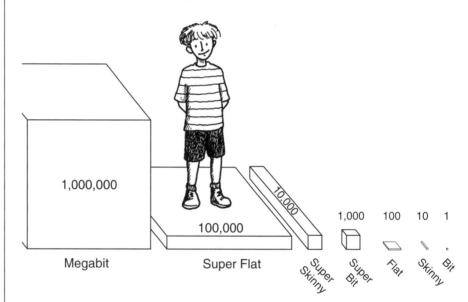

Figure 2: *Base-ten pieces for small and large numbers*

After reviewing and establishing the basics of the base-ten place value system for whole numbers, the system is extended to include decimals beginning in third grade. In Grade 4, the ten-for-one trading rules and other aspects of our number system are extended to the right of the decimal point for the first time.

In Grade 5, we extend the number system to even larger numbers. The story of Archimedes' attempt to calculate the number of grains of sand that would fill the observed universe introduces students to numbers far beyond what we encounter in everyday life. With the use of scientific calculators in Grade 5, scientific notation for large numbers is needed and introduced.

Basic Number Facts

In developing the math facts program, we sought a careful balance between strategies and drill. This approach is based on a large body of research and advocated by the NCTM *Principles and Standards for School Mathematics.* The research indicates that the methods used in the *Math Trailblazers* math facts program lead to more effective learning and better retention of the math facts and also helps develop essential math skills.

The *Math Trailblazers* program for teaching the math facts is characterized by these elements:

- *Early emphasis on problem solving.* Students first approach the basic facts as problems to solve rather than facts to memorize. Students invent their own strategies to solve these problems or learn appropriate strategies from others through class discussion. Students' natural strategies, especially counting strategies, are explicitly encouraged. In this way, students learn that math is more than memorizing facts and rules that "you either get or you don't."

- *De-emphasis of rote work.* Fluency with the math facts is an important component of any student's mathematical learning. Research has shown that an overemphasis on memorization and the frequent administration of timed tests are counterproductive. (National Research Council, 2001) We encourage the use of strategies to find facts, so students become confident they can find answers to fact problems they do not immediately recall.

- *Gradual and systematic introduction of facts.* Students study the facts in small groups that can be solved using similar strategies. Students first work on simple strategies for easy facts and then progress to more sophisticated strategies and harder facts. By the end of the process, they gain fluency with all the required facts.

- *Ongoing practice.* Work on the math facts is distributed throughout the curriculum, especially in the Daily Practice and Problems, Home Practice, and games. This practice for fluency, however, takes place only after students conceptually understand the operations and are proficient with strategies for solving basic fact problems. Delaying practice in this way means students need less practice to achieve fluency.

- *Appropriate assessment.* Teachers assess students' knowledge of the facts through observations as they work on activities, labs, and games as well as through the appropriate use of written tests and quizzes. Beginning in first grade, periodic, short quizzes in the Daily Practice and Problems naturally follow the study of small groups of facts organized around specific strategies. As self-assessment in Grades 2–5, students record their progress on *Facts I Know* charts and determine which facts they need to study. Inventory tests of all facts for each operation are used sparingly in Grades 2–5 (no more than twice per year) to assess students' progress with fact fluency. The goal of the math facts assessment program is to determine the degree to which students can find answers to fact problems quickly and accurately and whether they can retain this skill over time.

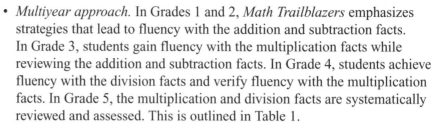

- *Multiyear approach.* In Grades 1 and 2, *Math Trailblazers* emphasizes strategies that lead to fluency with the addition and subtraction facts. In Grade 3, students gain fluency with the multiplication facts while reviewing the addition and subtraction facts. In Grade 4, students achieve fluency with the division facts and verify fluency with the multiplication facts. In Grade 5, the multiplication and division facts are systematically reviewed and assessed. This is outlined in Table 1.
- *Facts are not gatekeepers.* Students are not prevented from learning more complex mathematics because they do not perform well on fact tests. Use of strategies, calculators, and other math tools (e.g., manipulatives, hundreds charts, printed multiplication tables) allows students to continue to work on interesting problems and important mathematical concepts while they are still learning the facts.

The *Math Trailblazers* approach to the math facts is discussed more fully in the TIMS Tutor: *Math Facts.*

Concepts of Whole-Number Operations
Concepts and Skills

Throughout the past 150 years, there were numerous attempts to teach mathematics meaningfully rather than by rote. Unfortunately, as Lauren Resnick points out in *Syntax and Semantics in Learning to Subtract,* ". . . the conceptual teaching methods of the past were inadequate to the extent that they taught concepts instead of procedures and left it entirely to students to discover how computational procedures could be derived from the basic structure of the number and numeration system." (1987, p. 136)

Many educators have long recognized, however, that there is no real conflict between skills and concepts. (Whitehead, 1929; Dewey, 1938; Brownell, 1956; May, 1995; National Research Council, 2001) New conceptual understandings are built on existing skills and concepts; these new understandings in turn support the further development of skills and concepts. Thomas Carpenter describes the relationship in this way: ". . . It is an iterative process. Procedures are taught that can be supported by existing conceptual knowledge, and the conceptual knowledge base is extended to provide a basis for developing more advanced concepts. At every point during instruction, procedures are taught that can be connected to existing conceptual knowledge." (1986, p. 130) This integration of concepts and skills underlies our work with arithmetic in *Math Trailblazers.*

Subtraction in Grades K to 5
To illustrate how concepts and skills are balanced in *Math Trailblazers,* we outline in this section how one operation—subtraction—is developed with whole numbers in Grades K–4. Though the details may differ for the other operations, the same general approach described here with subtraction applies to all four arithmetic operations.

In kindergarten and Grade 3 of *Math Trailblazers,* students solve a variety of problems involving subtraction of numbers up to and even beyond 100. These problems are based on hands-on classroom activities and realistic situations from children's experiences. Different subtraction problem types are represented, including take-away, comparison, part-whole, and missing addend problems. (See the TIMS Tutor: *Word Problems* for a discussion of these and other problem types.)

Students in even the earliest grades are thus faced with problems for which they have no ready solution methods, problems that in the traditional view are beyond their ability. They do, however, have much prior knowledge that is relevant. They have their common sense—their conceptual knowledge of the problem situations. They know, for example, that if Grace begins with 50 marbles and loses 17, then she must end with fewer than 50 marbles. Young students also have considerable procedural knowledge, including various kinds of counting skills: ordinary counting, counting on, counting back, and skip counting by twos, fives, and tens. Students have tools to solve the problems. These include connecting cubes, links, *100 Charts,* ten frames, other manipulatives, paper and pencil, calculators, and number lines. Researchers note that initial work with any operation should involve classroom activities that use real-world or imaginary contexts, manipulatives, or drawings that highlight the attributes of the numbers and operations. (Carpenter et al., 1998; Fuson and Briars, 1990, Hiebert et al., 1997) This research further emphasizes the importance of long-term use of the manipulatives and of linking the manipulatives with written notation.

On one side, then, are hard problems involving many types of subtraction. On the other side are the kindergartners and first-graders, with their common sense, their counting skills, and tools. Traditionally, word problems and other applications involving subtraction (and other operations) were introduced only after students had extensive practice with a subtraction algorithm. Research on students' learning of addition and subtraction (Carpenter et al., 1998) strongly suggests that it is more effective to have students solve and pose word problems and other context-based problems (such as problems in the laboratory investigations in *Math Trailblazers*) before they learn formal, paper-and-pencil procedures for subtraction. As students apply their resources to solve the problems, they build their conceptual and procedural understanding of subtraction. They devise methods to solve the problems, make records of their work, and discuss their methods with their teacher and classmates. Their new knowledge about subtraction is closely linked to their prior knowledge, especially their out-of-school knowledge and their counting skills. (Baroody and Ginsburg, 1986)

You comment on students' methods and may show students how to use conventional symbols to describe their work, but you make no attempt to standardize students' methods. Any method that yields a correct result is acceptable—as long as it makes sense. The goal is to encourage students to apply their prior knowledge to problems they encounter and to let students know that their intuitive methods are valid.

> *As students apply their resources to solve the problems, they build their conceptual and procedural understanding of subtraction. They devise methods to solve the problems, make records of their work, and discuss their methods with their teacher and classmates.*

First grade focuses on various strategies students can use to solve single-digit subtraction problems. For example, they can solve a problem like $9 - 3$ by counting back 3 from 9: 8, 7, 6. This work aims not at achieving fluency with the subtraction facts, but rather at building conceptual understanding of subtraction and procedural skill with various strategies. (See the TIMS Tutor: *Math Facts.*)

At the beginning of Grade 2, the problem-solving approach to subtraction continues. Problems with numbers up to 1000 are introduced, but again no standard solution method is taught at this point. Students devise their own ways to solve the problems, drawing on their prior knowledge of the problem situations and the number system, and share their thinking with the class.

The strategies approach to the subtraction facts continues in Grade 2. As students' fluency with the addition facts and simple subtraction facts increases, more sophisticated strategies become feasible. For example, a child may solve $14 - 6$ by reasoning that "to take away 6 from 14, I first can take away 4, which leaves 10. Then I take away 2 more, which equals 8." These new strategies, sometimes called derived fact strategies or reasoning from known facts, illustrate how new knowledge builds on prior skills.

Later in Grade 2, systematic work begins on paper-and-pencil methods for subtracting two-digit numbers. Students solve two-digit subtraction problems using their own methods and record their solutions on paper. The class examines and discusses the various procedures that students devise. At this time, if no student introduces a standard subtraction algorithm, then the teacher does so, explaining that it is a subtraction method that many people use. The standard method is examined and discussed, just as the invented methods were. Students who do not have an effective method of their own are urged to adopt the standard method.

Problems that require borrowing are included from the beginning. Though this differs markedly from traditional approaches, we view it as important in developing a sound conception of subtraction algorithms. Giving children only multidigit problems that do not involve borrowing encourages the development of a rote and faulty algorithm that may not carry over into problems that require borrowing.

By the beginning of Grade 3, students have a strong conceptual understanding of subtraction and significant experience devising procedures to solve subtraction problems with numbers up to 1000. They also have some experience with standard and invented paper-and-pencil algorithms for solving two-digit subtraction problems. In Grade 3, this prior knowledge is extended in a systematic examination of paper-and-pencil methods for multidigit subtraction.

This work begins with a series of multidigit subtraction problems that students solve in various ways. Many of these problems are set in a whimsical context, the TIMS Candy Company, a business that uses base-ten pieces to keep track of its production and sales. Other problems are based on student-collected data, such as a reading survey.

> *Giving children only multidigit problems that do not involve borrowing encourages the development of a rote and faulty algorithm that may not carry over into problems that require borrowing.*

As in Grade 2, the class discusses and compares the several methods students use to solve these problems. Again, any method that yields correct results is acceptable, but now a greater emphasis is given to methods that are efficient and compact. This work leads to a close examination of one particular subtraction algorithm. See Figure 3. Students solve several problems with base-ten pieces and with this standard algorithm, making connections between actions with the manipulatives and steps in the algorithm. After a thorough analysis of the algorithm, including a comparison of the standard algorithm and other methods, students are given opportunities to practice the algorithm or other methods of their choice.

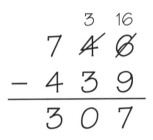

Figure 3: *A standard subtraction algorithm*

Practice in paper-and-pencil methods for multidigit subtraction is distributed throughout Grades 3 and 4. Students encounter sets of problems that encourage them to look at each problem and choose an efficient method to solve it. For many of these problems, a standard algorithm will be the most efficient choice. For others, students can use mental math or counting strategies. For example, students should identify the problem $4001 - 3998$ as a problem they can easily solve by counting up three from 3998 to 4001.

By the beginning of Grade 4, basic work with whole number subtraction is complete. Students have a firm conceptual understanding of subtraction and a diverse repertoire of methods they can use to solve subtraction problems. Work in Grade 4 is designed to maintain and extend these skills and understandings. Fluency with the subtraction facts is verified and remediation is provided for students who need it. In the laboratory experiments and other work, students solve a wide variety of subtraction problems using methods of their own choosing. The Daily Practice and Problems and Home Practice include distributed practice in paper-and-pencil subtraction so that those skills do not deteriorate.

In Grade 5 students continue to use subtraction in activities and labs. As in earlier grades, they are encouraged to decide when it is appropriate to use paper and pencil, calculators, or estimation. A review of subtraction modeled with base-ten pieces is included for students who have not used *Math Trailblazers* in previous grades. Distributed practice is provided in the Daily Practice and Problems and the Home Practice. Fluency with the subtraction facts is assessed in the first unit, and remediation is provided in the Addition and Subtraction Math Facts Review section in the *Facts Resource Guide.*

Whole-Number Computation in *Math Trailblazers*

Many other topics in *Math Trailblazers*—addition, multiplication, division, fractions, and decimals—are treated in ways similar to that sketched for subtraction above. In all these areas, we seek a balance between conceptual understanding and procedural skill. For all operations, standard methods for solving problems are not introduced until students have developed good conceptual and procedural understandings—the too-early introduction of such procedures may short-circuit students' common sense, encouraging mechanical and uncritical behavior. (Brownell & Chazall, 1935; Resnick & Omanson, 1987; Rathmell & Huinker, 1989; Perry, 1991; Hiebert, 1999)

> *We seek a balance between conceptual understanding and procedural skill. For all operations, standard methods for solving problems are not introduced until students have developed good conceptual and procedural understandings—the too-early introduction of such procedures may short-circuit students' common sense, encouraging mechanical and uncritical behavior.*

Grade	Addition	Subtraction	Multiplication	Division
K	• concepts of the operation	• concepts of the operation	• concepts of the operation	• concepts of the operation
1	• concepts of the operation • informal methods	• concepts of the operation • informal methods	• concepts of the operation	• concepts of the operation
2	• concepts of the operation • invented algorithms • standard methods for small numbers	• concepts of the operation • invented algorithms • standard methods for small numbers	• concepts of the operation • informal methods	• concepts of the operation • informal methods
3	• invented algorithms • standard methods for larger numbers	• invented algorithms • standard methods for larger numbers	• concepts of the operation • invented algorithms • standard methods for small numbers	• concepts of the operation
4	• review, practice, apply, and extend	• review, practice, apply, and extend	• invented algorithms • standard methods for larger numbers	• invented algorithms • standard methods for larger numbers
5	• review, practice, apply, and extend	• review, practice, apply, and extend	• review, practice, apply, and extend	• standard methods for larger numbers

Table 1: *Whole-number operations scope and sequence*

Even after analyzing and practicing standard methods students are still encouraged to solve problems in more than one way. Flexible thinking and mathematical power are our goals, not rote fluency with a handful of standard algorithms.

Varieties of Computation

There is much more to computation than the standard paper-and-pencil algorithms for adding, subtracting, multiplying, and dividing. These algorithms are good for obtaining exact answers with simple technology, but, depending on the resources available and the result desired, there are many other kinds of computation. For example, if you are in a supermarket check-out line with several items and you find only $10 in your wallet, then a quick judgment whether you have sufficient funds is desirable. In this case, a rough mental estimate of the total cost of your purchases is what you want. If you are planning an addition to your house, however, different computational demands must be met. The situation is more complex than the supermarket checkout, and the penalty for making a mistake is more severe, so greater care must be taken. You will want more resources—paper and pencil, a calculator, time to work, perhaps a computer spreadsheet—and you will probably want rather precise estimates for the cost of various alternative designs for the addition.

A well-rounded mathematics program should prepare students to compute accurately, flexibly, and appropriately in all situations. Figure 4 shows a classification of computational situations using two criteria, the result desired and the resources available. Although you may want to move some of the questions to other cells or insert your own examples, these six categories of computation indicate the scope required of a complete mathematics curriculum (Coburn, 1989).

Even after analyzing and practicing standard methods students are still encouraged to solve problems in more than one way.

Resources Available

	Paper & Pencil	Machine	Mental
Exact	How many students are in the three third grades at my school?	How much will my monthly payment be on my car loan?	How much baking soda do I need if I am tripling a recipe that calls for 2 teaspoons?
Approximate	What is my share of the national debt?	House remodeling: Which design(s) can I afford?	Supermarket checkout: Do I have enough money for these items?

(Result Desired)

Figure 4: *Six varieties of computation*

The TIMS Philosophy: Meaning, Invention, Efficiency, Power

The treatment of computation in *Math Trailblazers* proceeds in several stages. The grade levels for the stages vary with the operation—ideas of division, for example, develop long after addition—but the general pattern is similar for all the operations. Roughly speaking, the stages are

- developing meaning for the operation,
- inventing procedures for solving problems, and
- becoming more efficient at carrying out procedures, all leading to
- developing mathematical power.

Developing mathematical power with an operation means that students understand *when* to apply the operation and *how* to use varied computational methods to solve problems, even complex or nonroutine problems.

The goal of the first stage is to help students understand the meaning of the operation. Most of the work involves solving problems, writing or telling "stories" that involve operations, and sharing solution strategies. These methods typically involve a great deal of mental arithmetic and creative thinking. The use of manipulatives, pictures, and counting is encouraged at this stage. Discussing these informal methods helps develop students' understanding of the operation.

In the next stage, the focus shifts from developing the concept of the operation to devising and analyzing procedures to carry out the operation. At this stage, students "invent" methods for carrying out the operation, explaining, discussing, and comparing their procedures. Multiple solution strategies—mental, paper and pencil, manipulative, calculator—are encouraged, and parallels between various methods are explored. There is evidence that this "invented algorithms" approach enhances students' number and operation sense and problem-solving abilities (Madell, 1985; Sawada, 1985; Kamii, Lewis & Jones, 1991; Burns, 1992; Kamii, Lewis & Livingston, 1993; Porter & Carroll, 1995; Carroll & Porter, 1997). Inventing their own methods helps make mathematics meaningful for children by connecting school mathematics to their own ways of thinking. The expectation that mathematics should make sense is reinforced.

In the third stage, a standard algorithm for the operation is introduced. This algorithm is not presented as the one, true, and official way to solve problems, but rather as yet another procedure to examine. The algorithms used in *Math Trailblazers* are not all identical to the traditional ones taught in school. The addition and subtraction algorithms are only a little different, but the procedures for multiplication and division are considerably different. (See Figures 5 and 6.)

$$
\begin{array}{r}
5\ 8 \\
\times\ 3\ 6 \\
\hline
4\ 8 \\
3\ 0\ 0 \\
2\ 4\ 0 \\
1\ 5\ 0\ 0 \\
\hline
2\ 0\ 8\ 8
\end{array}
$$

Figure 5: *All-partials multiplication*

```
                1  9 R 31
        3 2 ) 6  3  9
          - 3  2  0      10
            3  1  9
          - 1  6  0       5
            1  5  9
          -    9  6       3
               6  3
          -    3  2       1
               3  1      19
```

Figure 6: *A division algorithm*

We chose these alternative algorithms for multiplication and division for several reasons. First, they are easier to learn than the traditional methods. Second, they are more transparent, revealing what is actually happening. Third, they provide practice in multiplying by numbers ending in zero, an important skill for estimation. Finally, even though they are less efficient than the traditional algorithms, they are good enough for most purposes—any problem that is awkward to solve by these methods should probably be done by machine anyway.

Students who have no reliable method of their own are urged to adopt the standard algorithm. However, even after introducing and analyzing a standard algorithm for an operation, alternative methods are still accepted, even encouraged, for students who are comfortable with them. In particular, the standard algorithm is very inefficient with some problems. For example, students using *Math Trailblazers* should be able to compute 40×30 mentally to get 1200. Using the standard algorithm here would be inefficient. Or consider $16,000 - 5$. Using a standard algorithm to solve this problem is tedious and often results in errors.

In the last stage, students achieve mathematical power through the mastery of procedures that solve entire classes of problems: efficient and reliable computational algorithms. This procedural fluency, moreover, is based on solid conceptual understandings so that it can be applied flexibly to solve problems. These procedures become part of the students' base of prior knowledge—on which they can build more advanced conceptual and procedural understandings.

Fractions and Decimals

The approach to fractions and decimals in *Math Trailblazers* parallels that for whole numbers. At first, the focus is on developing concepts and meanings for fractions and decimals. Next comes a period in which students invent procedures for solving problems, connecting school mathematics to their own informal methods and common sense. Finally, formal procedures are investigated, not as substitutes for common sense, but as more efficient methods for achieving desired results.

Fraction Meanings

One of the problems with fractions is that they are so useful. Consider some of the meanings for $\frac{1}{2}$:

- half of a cookie (a part-whole fraction)
- $1 \div 2$ (division)
- one cup water to two cups flour (a ratio, sometimes written 1:2)
- $\frac{1}{2}$ mile (a measurement)
- the point midway between 0 and 1 (the name of a point on a number line)
- the square root of $\frac{1}{4}$ (a pure number)
- the chance a fair coin will land heads up (a probability)

Because the same notation can mean so many different things, children and even adults sometimes become confused and may manipulate fraction symbols haphazardly, often with unfortunate results. A better approach develops sound meanings for the symbols before focusing on how to manipulate them.

Because the same notation can mean so many different things, children and even adults sometimes become confused and may manipulate fraction symbols haphazardly, often with unfortunate results. A better approach develops sound meanings for the symbols before focusing on how to manipulate them (Mack, 1990).

Part-Whole Fractions

Early fraction work focuses on part-whole fractions. Many fractions in daily life are part-whole fractions, so even young children are familiar with terms like one-half and three-fourths in part-whole contexts. Also, many key ideas about fractions are well illustrated in part-whole situations.

There are two concepts that are fundamental in understanding part-whole fractions: knowing what the whole is and understanding what a part is in relation to the whole. For example, to understand the statement, "Last night I ate three-fourths of a carton of ice cream," requires knowing what the whole is. Just how big a carton of ice cream was it? One must also understand that the parts into which the whole is divided must be equal—they should have the same area or mass or number, etc. A way to make this clear to children is to talk about "fair shares."

The whole in a part-whole fraction can be either a single thing (e.g., a pizza) or a collection (e.g., a class of students). When the whole is a collection, then counting is generally used to make fair shares; when the unit is a single thing, the fairness of the shares depends on some measurable quantity. Half of one pizza is different from half of three pizzas. Often, area is the variable that must be equally allocated among the parts; such a situation may be called an area model for fractions.

Symbols and Referents

A key idea in the *Math Trailblazers* approach to fractions is that fractions should be represented in several ways and that students should be able to make connections between those representations. The fraction two-thirds, for example, can be expressed in words, symbols, pictures, or real objects (Figure 7).

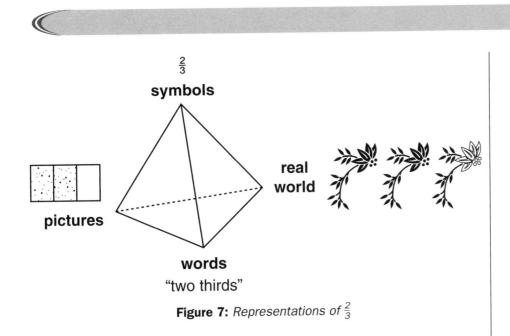

Figure 7: *Representations of $\frac{2}{3}$*

The ability to move freely between these several representations is an essential component of the mathematical understanding of fractions (Lesh, Post & Behr, 1987). Especially important are connections between fraction symbols and the real-world situations to which those fractions refer. Given symbols for a fraction, can students draw an illustrative picture or tell a story? Can students explain the relationship between a group of five girls and two boys and the fraction $\frac{5}{7}$?

Math Trailblazers makes extensive use of manipulatives in teaching fractions in all grades. Pictures, pattern blocks, geoboards, paper folding, and number lines are among many tools used to promote students' conceptual understanding of fractions. When paper-and-pencil procedures for adding, subtracting, multiplying, and dividing fractions are introduced in Grades 4 and 5, they are always linked closely with other representations of fractions, such as manipulatives or pictures.

Decimals

Decimals are treated in two ways in *Math Trailblazers:* first, as another way to write certain common fractions—those with denominators that are powers of ten—and second, as an extension of the whole number place value system. Similar to the coverage of other topics in *Math Trailblazers,* considerable attention is placed upon developing a solid conceptual foundation about decimals before formal, paper-and-pencil operations are introduced. Students with strong conceptual understandings of decimals learn procedures more easily and can apply those procedures to problem situations more effectively

> *The ability to move freely between these several representations is an essential component of the mathematical understanding of fractions. Especially important are connections between fraction symbols and the real-world situations to which these fractions refer.*

(Ball, 1993; Behr & Post, 1992; Hiebert, Wearne & Taber, 1991; Lesh, Post & Behr, 1987). Connections between fractions (common fractions) and decimals (decimal fractions) are stressed throughout.

As with work with whole numbers and fractions, work with decimal fractions includes extensive work with manipulatives. Often these models are used to make strong connections between fractions, decimals, and percents. Figures 8 and 9 show two examples of tools used in Grade 5 lessons on decimals. These representations create visual images of the decimal fractions and link those images with students' previous work with fractions and percent.

Figure 8: *Interlocking centiwheel disks model $\frac{1}{4}$, 0.25, and 25%.*

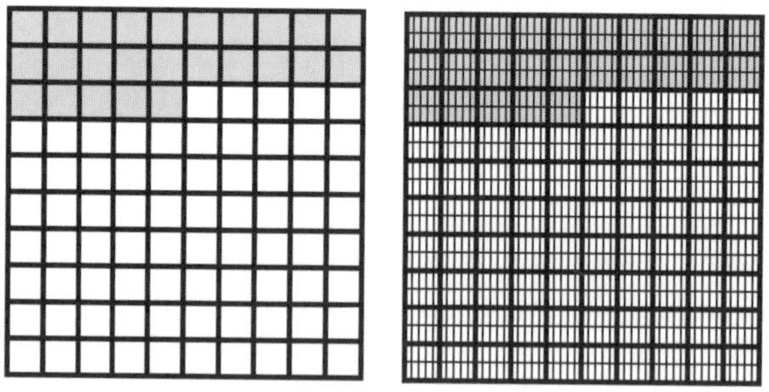

Figure 9: $\frac{25}{100} = 0.25$ and $\frac{250}{1000} = 0.250$

A Developmental Approach

Kindergarten fraction work emphasizes the idea that the fractional parts of a whole must be the same size. Work with symbols is not emphasized.

Fraction work in Grades 1–3 of *Math Trailblazers* focuses primarily on establishing links between symbols and referents for part-whole fractions. Children learn to make connections between marks on paper and the real world. Concepts of the unit—identifying the unit, knowing how the size of the unit affects the value of the fraction, appreciating the importance of fair shares—are also explored (Figure 10). Decimals are treated primarily as an alternative notation for certain fractions, and some attention is given to the interpretation of decimals that appear on calculators. Real-world situations, especially fair sharing, and area models predominate.

If [ ] is $\frac{1}{3}$,

then what is one whole?

Figure 10: *A concept-of-unit exercise*

In Grade 3, students continue to develop concepts of the unit, but they begin to use more varied models. Children explore the relative size of fractions, especially with respect to the benchmark numbers 0, $\frac{1}{2}$, and 1. They also study equivalent fractions in Grade 3. Fractions are represented with a variety of manipulatives—paper folding, pattern blocks, geoboards. Collections of objects are divided to represent fractions.

Decimals are investigated more extensively in Grade 3, again being treated as a kind of fraction. Decimals in metric length measurement and on number lines are investigated. Base-ten pieces are used to create concrete and visual representations of decimal fractions. Translating between common fractions and decimals is again stressed.

In Grade 4, work on operations with fractions and decimals begins, but standard procedures are not taught. As discussed above, modeling concepts and procedures with manipulatives is intended to establish a basis for more algorithmic work in Grade 5. In fourth grade, students solve problems involving addition and subtraction, largely with the aid of manipulatives and other fraction models.

Operations with fractions and decimals include more than simply the four arithmetic operations. Putting fractions and decimals in order by size, renaming the same number in several equivalent forms, and estimating sums, differences, and so on, are all operations that can be carried out with fractions and decimals. Again, manipulatives, such as pattern blocks and base-ten pieces, are used to develop conceptual understanding and provide a concrete representation of the symbols.

In Grade 5, paper-and-pencil procedures for addition, subtraction, and multiplication of fractions and decimals are explored, including use of common denominators and reducing. Repeating decimals are introduced. Students also use calculators to rename fractions as decimals for comparing and ordering common fractions.

Many contexts are used to reinforce students' understanding of fraction and decimal concepts. For example, in a Grade 5 laboratory investigation, *Comparing Lives of Animals and Soap Bubbles,* students collect data about the "life spans" of soap bubbles. As they analyze the data, they convert the data first to a fractional quantity, then to the equivalent decimal fraction. Making these connections between mathematical concepts and real-world situations helps students make sense of the mathematics they are learning.

Conclusion

Our goal in developing *Math Trailblazers* is to create a balanced program that promotes the coordinated development of both procedural skill and conceptual understanding. Students will connect school mathematics with intuitive knowledge and informal procedures. They will use a variety of techniques and manipulatives for modeling the mathematical ideas. In doing so, students will not only develop skills and concepts, but will be able to use those skills and concepts to solve problems.

References

Ball, D. "Halves, Pieces, and Twoths: Constructing and Using Representational Contexts in Teaching Fractions." In T.P. Carpenter, E. Fennema, and T.A. Romberg (Eds.), *Rational Numbers: An Integration of Research.* pp. 157–195. Lawrence Erlbaum Associates, Hillsdale, NJ, 1993.

Baroody, A.J., and H.P. Ginsburg. "The Relationship between Initial Meaning and Mechanical Knowledge of Arithmetic." In J. Hiebert (ed.), *Conceptual and Procedural Knowledge: The Case of Mathematics.* Lawrence Erlbaum Associates, Hillsdale, NJ, 1986.

Behr, M.J., and T.R. Post. "Teaching Rational Number and Decimal Concepts." In *Teaching Mathematics in Grades K–8: Research Based Methods.* Allyn and Bacon, Boston, MA, 1992.

Bransford, J.D., A.L. Brown, and R.R. Cocking, eds. *How People Learn: Brain, Mind, Experience, and School.* National Academy Press, Washington, DC, 1999.

Brown, J.S., and R.R. Burton. "Diagnostic Models for Procedural Bugs in Basic Mathematical Skills." *Cognitive Science,* 2, pp. 155–192, 1978.

Brownell, W.A., and C.B. Chazal. "The Effects of Premature Drill in Third-Grade Arithmetic." *Journal of Educational Research,* 29 (1), 1935.

Brownell, W.A. "Meaning and Skill—Maintaining the Balance." *Arithmetic Teacher,* 34 (8), pp. 18–25 (Original work published in 1956), 1987.

Carpenter, T.P. "Conceptual Knowledge as a Foundation for Procedural Knowledge." In J. Hiebert (ed.), *Conceptual and Procedural Knowledge: The Case of Mathematics.* Lawrence Erlbaum Associates, Hillsdale, NJ, 1986.

Carpenter, T.P., E. Fennema, and M.L. Franke. *Cognitively Guided Instruction: Building the Primary Mathematics Curriculum on Children's Informal Mathematical Knowledge.* A paper presented at the annual meeting of the American Educational Research Association, San Francisco, CA, April 1992.

Carpenter, T.P., M.L. Franke, V.R. Jacobs, E. Fennema, and S.B. Empson. "A Longitudinal Study of Invention and Understanding in Children's Multidigit Addition and Subtraction." *Journal for Research in Mathematics Education,* 29, pp. 3–20, 1998.

Carroll, W., and D. Porter. "Invented Algorithms: Helping Students to Develop and Use Meaningful Mathematical Procedures." *Teaching Children Mathematics,* pp. 370–374, March 1997.

Coburn, T.G. "The Role of Computation in the Changing Mathematics Curriculum." In P.R. Trafton (ed.), *New Directions for Elementary School Mathematics.* National Council of Teachers of Mathematics, Reston, VA, 1989.

Dewey, J. *Experience and Education.* Macmillan, New York, 1938.

Finn, C.E., Jr. "What If Those Math Standards Are Wrong?" *Education Week,* 20 January 1993.

Fuson, K.C., and D.J. Briars. "Using a Base-Ten Blocks Learning/Teaching Approach for First- and Second-Grade Place-Value and Multidigit Addition and Subtraction." *Journal for Research in Mathematics Education,* 21, pp. 180–206, 1990.

Good, T.L., C. Mulryan, and M. McCaslin. "Grouping for Instruction in Mathematics: A Call for Programmatic Research on Small-Group Processes." In D.A. Grouws (ed.), *Handbook of Research on Mathematics Teaching and Learning: A Project of the National Council of Teachers of Mathematics* (Chapter 9). Macmillan, New York, 1992.

Greenes, C., M. Cavanagh, L. Dacey, C. Findell, and M. Small. *Navigating through Algebra in Pre-kindergarten–Grade 2.* National Council of Teachers of Mathematics, Reston, VA, 2001.

Hiebert, J. "Children's Mathematical Learning: The Struggle to Link Form and Understanding." *Elementary School Journal,* 84 (5), pp. 497–513, 1984.

Hiebert, J. "A Theory of Developing Competence with Written Mathematical Symbols." *Educational Studies in Mathematics,* 19, pp. 333–355, 1988.

Hiebert, J. "Relationships between Research and the NCTM Standards." *Journal for Research in Mathematics Education,* 30 (1), pp. 3–19, 1999.

Hiebert, J. and D. Wearne. "Procedures over Concepts: The Acquisition of Decimal Number Knowledge." In J. Hiebert (Ed.), *Conceptual and Procedural Knowledge: The Case of Mathematics.* Lawrence Erlbaum Associates, Hillsdale, NJ, 1986.

Hiebert, J., D. Wearne, and S. Taber. "Fourth Graders' Gradual Construction of Decimal Fractions during Instruction Using Different Physical Representations." *Elementary School Journal,* 91 (4), pp. 321–341, 1991.

Hiebert, J., T. Carpenter, E. Fennema, K.C. Fuson, D. Wearne, H. Murray, A. Oliver, and H. Piet. *Making Sense: Teaching and Learning Mathematics with Understanding.* Heinemann, Portsmouth, NH, 1997.

Kamii, C., B.A. Lewis, and S. Jones. "Reform in Primary Mathematics Education: A Constructivist View." *Educational Horizons,* 70 (1), pp. 19–26, 1991.

Kamii, C., B.A. Lewis, and S.J. Livingston, "Primary Arithmetic: Children Inventing Their Own Procedures." *Arithmetic Teacher,* 41 (4), pp. 200–203, 1993.

Lesh, R., T. Post, and M. Behr. "Representations and Translations among Representations in Mathematics Learning and Problem Solving." C. Janvier, ed., *Problems of Representation in the Teaching and Learning of Mathematics.* Lawrence Erlbaum Associates, Hillsdale, NJ, 1987.

McKnight, C.C., F.J. Crosswhite, J.A. Dossey, E. Kifer, J.O. Swafford, K.J. Travers, and T.J. Cooney. *The Underachieving Curriculum: Assessing U.S. School Mathematics from an International Perspective.* Stipes, Champaign, IL, 1987.

Mack, N.K. "Learning Fractions with Understanding: Building on Informal Knowledge." *Journal for Research in Mathematics Education,* 21 (1), pp. 16–32, 1990.

Madell, R. "Children's Natural Processes." *Arithmetic Teacher,* 32 (7), pp. 20–22, 1985.

Mathews, J. "Psst, Kid, Wanna Buy a Used Math Book? They're Old-Fashioned and a Bit Tedious, but John Saxon's Books are Hot Stuff in the Education Underground." *Newsweek,* 121, pp. 62–63, 1993.

May, L. "Reflections on Teaching Mathematics Today." *Illinois Mathematics Teacher,* 46 (3), pp. 5–8, 1995.

National Council of Teachers of Mathematics. *Curriculum Focal Points for Pre-kindergarten through Grade 8 Mathematics: A Quest for Coherence.* Reston, VA, 2006.

National Research Council. *Adding It Up: Helping Children Learn Mathematics.* National Academy Press, Washington, DC, 2001.

National Research Council. "The Strands of Mathematical Proficiency." *Adding It Up: Helping Children Learn Mathematics.* pp. 115–156, J. Kilpatrick, J. Swafford, and B. Findell, eds. National Academy Press, Washington, DC, 2001.

Perry, M. "Learning and Transfer: Instructional Conditions and Conceptual Change." *Cognitive Development,* 6, pp. 449–468, 1991.

Porter, D., and W. Carroll. "Invented Algorithms: Some Examples from Primary Classrooms." *Illinois Mathematics Teacher,* pp. 6–12, April 1995.

Press, M. "Drill and Practice Add Up." *San Jose Mercury News,* 27 February 1995.

Principles and Standards for School Mathematics. National Council of Teachers of Mathematics, Reston, VA, 2000.

Rathmell, E.C., and D.M. Huinker. "Using 'Part-Whole' Language to Help Children Represent and Solve Word Problems." In P.R. Trafton (ed.), *New Directions for Elementary School Mathematics,* pp. 99–110. National Council of Teachers of Mathematics, Reston, VA, 1989.

Resnick, L.B. "Syntax and Semantics in Learning to Subtract." In R. Glaser (ed.), *Advances in Instructional Psychology* (Vol. 3). Lawrence Erlbaum Associates, Hillsdale, NJ, 1987.

Resnick, L.B., and S.F. Omanson. "Learning to Understand Arithmetic." In *Advances in Instructional Psychology* (Vol. 3). Lawrence Erlbaum Associates, Hillsdale, NJ, 1987.

Resnick, L.B., S. Lesgold, and V. Bill. *From Protoquantities to Number Sense.* A paper prepared for the Psychology of Mathematics Education Conference, Oaxtapec, Mexico, 1990.

Sawada, D. "Mathematical Symbols: Insight through Invention." *Arithmetic Teacher,* 32 (6), pp. 20–22, 1985.

Shuard, H. "CAN: Calculator Use in the Primary Grades in England and Wales." In J. T. Fey (ed.), *Calculators in Mathematics Education,* Reston, VA, 1992.

Skemp, R.R. "Relational Understanding and Instrumental Understanding." *Arithmetic Teacher,* 26 (3), pp. 9–15, 1978.

Swart, W.L. "Some Findings on Conceptual Development of Computational Skills." *Arithmetic Teacher* 32 (5), pp. 36–38, 1985.

Usiskin, Z. "Paper-and-Pencil Skills in a Calculator/Computer Age." *UCSMP Newsletter,* 16, pp. 7–14, 1994.

Van Lehn, K. "Arithmetic Procedures Are Induced from Examples." In J. Hiebert (ed.), *Conceptual and Procedural Knowledge: The Case of Mathematics.* Lawrence Erlbaum Associates, Hillsdale, NJ, 1986.

Whitehead, A.N. "The Rhythmic Claims of Freedom and Discipline." In *The Aims of Education and Other Essays.* Macmillan, New York, 1929.

Averages

Introduction

"Average" is one of those words that mean different things to different people. Baseball players talk about their batting averages. A teacher might confide to a colleague that "Jim is just an average student." At the university, students always want to know what the class average is on an exam. Sometimes you hear the statement that the temperature will be about average for this time of year. When someone asks you how you feel, you may reply, "Just average." In everyday usage, "average" is a word that can be anything from a synonym for "typical," "normal," or "usual," to a number derived according to some formula or rule. This TIMS Tutor lays out some of the different numerical meanings of "average" and explains some of the importance of averages in mathematics and science.

The Mean—A Wage Dispute

In his wonderful little book, *How to Lie with Statistics,* Darrell Huff gives the example of a factory owner and his workers who are arguing over wages. There are 25 workers including the owner. The owner pays himself $45,000. The others make $15,000, $10,000, $10,000, $5700, $5000, $5000, $5000, $3700, $3700, $3700, $3700, $3000, $2000, $2000, $2000, $2000, $2000, $2000, $2000, $2000, $2000, $2000, $2000, and $2000. The owner says the average wage is $5700 but the workers claim the average wage is only $3000. Even though prices have gone way up since Huff wrote his book 50 years ago, the discrepancy is clear: there is a big disagreement over what people are being paid, let alone what they should be paid.

So, what's going on here? Who's right, the owner or the workers? Both! The factory owner's average is the (arithmetic) mean; the workers' average is the median. There are other averages too, such as the **mode** (the number or value that occurs most often in a data set). However, in *Math Trailblazers,* we primarily use the mean and/or the median when finding average values. These two averages will be the focus of our discussion in this tutor.

Usually when people use the term "average," they are referring to the **mean.** This is the familiar add-up-all-the-numbers-and-divide average you learned in school. The mean has many useful properties that make it beloved by schoolteachers, statisticians, and scientists alike. Consider finding the average height of all the children in a class. Data for 23 children from a third-grade class is shown in Figure 1.

The mean height of these 23 children is

$$\langle H \rangle = \frac{\text{sum of heights}}{\text{number of children}}$$

$$= \frac{(133 + 136 + \ldots + 129 + 134) \text{ cm}}{23}$$

$$= \frac{3064 \text{ cm}}{23}$$

$$= 133.2 \text{ cm}$$

Name	H Height (in cm)
Karina	133
Federico	136
Ramon	135
Kiela	127
Aesha	126
Bravlia	128
Zuzia	133
Anthony	139
Iorta	146
Cordeli	135
Mary	137
Gennice	124

Name	H Height (in cm)
Curtis	139
Brian C	125
David	135
Anna	141
Brian M	131
Adriana	137
Boberto	134
Lucas	131
Gennifer	129
Amber	129
Nathan	134

Figure 1: *Data from a third-grade class*

Although no child may have this mean height, it gives everyone a point for making comparisons. For scientists, the mean is often the first number they calculate when looking at a data sample.

There is another way to interpret the mean height of this class. This may seem strange, but consider the following situation. Suppose you walk into another class and find 23 students all exactly the same height. The mean is clearly that height. If the mean height of this new class and the mean in our class are the same, then the sum of the heights of the children is the same. That is, imagine making two stacks of the children, one for our class and one

For scientists, the mean is often the first number they calculate when looking at a data sample.

for the new class. Stack the children one on top of another. Then the two stacks would be the same height. So, if two class means are the same and the number of children in each class is the same, then the sums of the heights in the classes are the same, even if the individual heights that make the sums are vastly different.

Statisticians like the mean because it is often the "best" estimate of an unknown quantity like a length, an area, or a mass. For example, suppose you are trying to measure the mass of a large steel sphere. You have an unbiased balance, and you know you need to take repeated readings to get an accurate measurement. So, suppose you make eleven measurements and find the sphere's mass to be 129 gm, 133 gm, 132 gm, 130 gm, 128 gm, 129 gm, 130 gm, 131 gm, 130 gm, 129 gm, and 131 gm. Then

$$\frac{(129 + 133 + \ldots + 130 + 129 + 131) \text{ gm}}{11}$$

$$= \frac{1432 \text{ gm}}{11}$$

$$= 130 \text{ gm}$$

This is the best estimate of the "true" mass of the sphere, given these measurements. (Notice that the quotient above is actually equal to 130.18181818 . . . gm. However, since our original measurements are to the nearest gram, it makes sense to give the average only to the nearest gram.)

Similar situations arise all the time in everyday life. Our factory owner is using the mean. He computes the average wage by adding up everyone's salary (including his big fat one) and dividing by the total number of workers:

$$\frac{\$142{,}500}{25} = \$5{,}700$$

As one final example, suppose Marty scores 85, 84, 86, 87, 84, 87, 85, 85, 83, and 85 on 10 rounds of golf and Ellen scores 83, 83, 95, 97, 81, 83, 82, 84, 96, and 84. Then Marty's mean score is

$$= \frac{85 + 84 + 86 + 87 + 84 + 87 + 85 + 85 + 83 + 85}{10}$$

$$= 85.1$$

and Ellen's mean score is

$$= \frac{83 + 83 + 95 + 97 + 81 + 83 + 82 + 84 + 96 + 84}{10}$$

$$= 86.8$$

So, it would appear that Marty is a better golfer than Ellen. (In golf, a lower score is a better score.)

But anyone who plays golf and bets will notice that if Marty and Ellen played 10 rounds against each other and scored as above, then Marty would win three times and Ellen would win seven times. And the factory workers still feel underpaid, despite that nice mean salary. So to get some perspective on what is happening here, let's look at another average, the median.

The Median

The **median** is the number in the middle. That is, roughly speaking, the median splits a set of numbers into two halves: one half is less than the median; the other half is more than the median. So to find the median, rank the numbers from smallest to largest and take the one in the middle.

Suppose you want to find the median selling price of homes in your town. At the town office you find that 15 homes sold in the last six months. The selling prices, in rank order, were $134,000, $156,000, $164,000, $170,000, $184,000, $194,000, $224,000, $236,000, $250,000, $264,000, $266,000, $278,000, $334,000, $350,000, and $372,000. The median price was $236,000: seven houses sold for less than $236,000 and seven houses sold for more than $236,000.

When there is an even number of values, then the median can be a little harder to find. Say only 14 of the homes above have sold. Suppose that the highest-priced house, the one costing $372,000, went unsold. What is the new median? Counting up seven from the $134,000 house, we end up at the $224,000. Counting down seven from the $350,000 house, we end up at $236,000. The seventh house from the bottom is not the seventh house from the top! What to do? Easy. Go halfway between the two numbers closest to the middle. Halfway between $224,000 and $236,000. That comes out to be $230,000. So the median price of the 14 homes that sold would be $230,000.

Going back to our factory workers' example, there were 25 employees including the owner. The thirteenth salary (from the top or from the bottom) is $3000: there are 12 employees who make less than $3000, and 12 who make more than $3000. So, the median salary is $3000.

Sometimes the median is a better average to use than the mean. One common situation where the median may be preferred is when there are extreme values. In such cases, the mean can give a distorted picture of the "average" because the extreme values tend to "pull" the mean away from the typical values. Statisticians say the median is more "robust" than the mean; that is, the median is less affected by extreme values than the mean. This is why the factory workers prefer the median: it gives a truer picture of what a typical worker earns than the mean, which is pulled up by the owner's big salary.

The median offers some insight into our golfing example, too. Marty's (ranked) golf scores were 83, 84, 84, 85, 85, 85, 85, 86, 87, and 87. The two numbers in the middle are 85 and 85, so Marty's median score is 85. Ellen's scores were 81, 82, 83, 83, 83, 84, 84, 95, 96, and 97. The two numbers in the middle are 83 and 84, so Ellen's median score is 83.5. Thus, using medians, Ellen is a slightly better golfer, on average. Every few rounds she has a high score, but her typical score is better than Marty's typical score, so she usually wins.

Obviously, the median has several advantages with respect to the mean: it is less affected by extreme values; it requires little computation; it can be a better indicator of what is typical. You will want to be flexible, sometimes using the mean, sometimes using the median.

The **median** is the number in the middle. That is, roughly speaking, the median splits a set of numbers into two halves: one half is less than the median; the other half is more than the median.

One common situation where the median may be preferred is when there are extreme values. In such cases, the mean can give a distorted picture of the "average" because the extreme values tend to "pull" the mean away from the typical values.

The Mode

The **mode** of a data set is the number that appears most often. For example, in Ellen's golf scores, the number that appears most often is 83. In our first example from *How to Lie with Statistics,* we considered the factory owner and his 25 workers who are arguing over wages. The owner pays himself $45,000. The others make $15,000, $10,000, $10,000, $5700, $5000, $5000, $5000, $3700, $3700, $3700, $3700, $3000, $2000, $2000, $2000, $2000, $2000, $2000, $2000, $2000, $2000, $2000, $2000, $2000, $2000, and $2000. To present their best argument, the workers could have argued that the modal salary was $2,000, since 12 workers had that salary.

*The **mode** of a data set is the number that appears most often.*

Making Sense of Measures of Central Tendency

The median, mean, and mode are all "measures of central tendency." They each tell us something about the way the information in the data set clusters. Of course, when we replace a whole data set with one number, we lose a lot of information. Depending on the nature of the data set, the mean, median, or mode may or may not provide us with useful information. These measures of central tendency are most useful when the data clusters around some value.

Averaging in the *Math Trailblazers* Classroom

So how are averages used in *Math Trailblazers?* Suppose your second-grade students collected the data shown in Figure 2 for the TIMS Laboratory Investigation, *Rolling Along in Centimeters.* There are three experimental values for each car, and students need some measure of the middle that fairly represents their data for each car. In this case, the median is a perfectly respectable average.

T Type of Car	*D* Distance (in cm/unit)			
	Trial 1	Trial 2	Trial 3	Median
Red	83	93	86	
Blue	44	44	43	
Orange	39	53	46	
Black	194	199	189	

Figure 2: *Data from* Rolling Along in Centimeters

One way to get a median from data like this is illustrated in Figure 3. The students cross out the largest and smallest numbers in each row and use the one that is left as their average value. Finding the median value of the three trials does not require young children to do any arithmetic and conceptually illustrates quite nicely the idea of an average representing a middle value.

T Type of Car	D Distance (in cm/unit)			
	Trial 1	Trial 2	Trial 3	Median
Red	~~88~~	~~85~~	86	86
Blue	~~44~~	44	~~43~~	44
Orange	~~39~~	~~55~~	46	46
Black	194	~~189~~	~~188~~	194

Figure 3: *Finding the median*

red truck

42
45
47

Figure 4: *Finding the median in* Rolling Along with Links

You can illustrate finding the median more concretely by using links (or string, adding machine tape, etc.) to create "lengths" that match the actual distance the cars roll each time. At the end of three rolls, students will have three lengths of links each representing the distance a car rolled in a trial.

This is illustrated in Figure 4. The median value can then be found by comparing the lengths and discarding the shortest and longest; the remaining length represents the median. A similar process is used in the first-grade experiment *Rolling Along with Links*.

In fourth grade, students begin finding the mean as well as the median. Again the concepts are introduced concretely. For example, students find the median value for several towers of cubes by lining them up from shortest to tallest and selecting the tower in the middle. This is illustrated in Figures 5a and 5b. Figure 6 illustrates an even number of trials. To find the median here, students have to find the halfway point between the two middle towers.

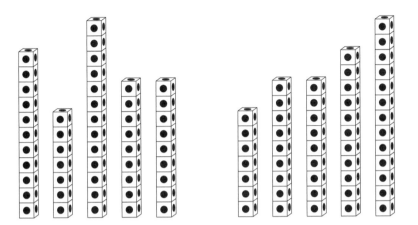

Figures 5a and 5b: *Finding the median with cubes*

Figure 6: *The median number of cubes is $7\frac{1}{2}$.*

You can also use cubes to introduce the mean. For example, suppose students begin with the same five towers illustrated in Figure 5a. They first estimate the mean by figuring out a way to "even out the towers," as illustrated in Figure 7. The mean, to the nearest whole cube, is ten cubes. In this manner, the concept of the mean as a representative measure is stressed rather than focusing purely on the arithmetic procedure. Students then learn to calculate the mean using numerical values.

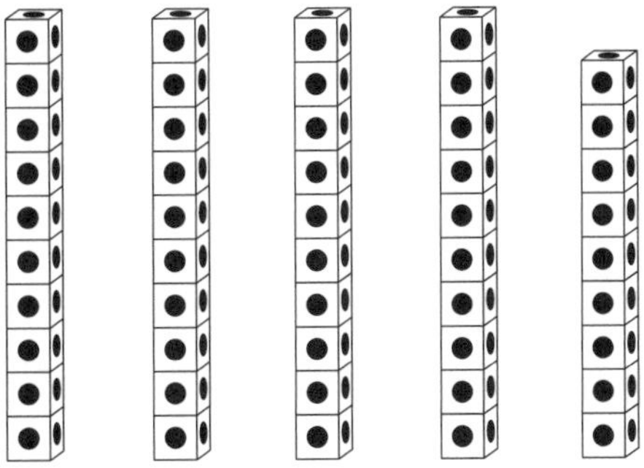

Figure 7: *Estimating the mean by "evening out" towers of cubes*

Students will often use calculators to calculate the mean of a data set. For example, the mean distance for the red car in Figure 2, when found by calculator, is:

$$\frac{(83 + 93 + 86) \text{ cm}}{3} = 87.333333 \text{ cm}$$

This is an example of too much of a good thing. In this case, the calculator gives many more digits than are meaningful. Students have to determine an appropriate level of significance. Keep in mind that our goal is to get a reasonable number to use as an average. Here, the original measurements were made to the nearest cm, so it makes sense to also report the mean value also to the nearest cm.

Why Average?

Finding the average is critical in a *Math Trailblazers* experiment. It is an important step from raw data to understanding. Errors are inevitable when making measurements, and averaging is one way to detect and control them. If a group of students makes the same measurement three times and gets 67 cm, 64 cm, and 84 cm, they should notice that the 84 cm is way off. They can detect their error and redo that measurement.

When we take a measurement, many factors prevent us from getting an exact answer. First is the precision of our measuring tools. A meterstick can measure only to the nearest tenth of a centimeter. When we measure the area of an irregular figure by counting square centimeters, we have to estimate the area of the fraction pieces of square centimeters, and so on. In addition, when we perform an experiment, we might get somewhat different measurements each time. If we drop a ball from a height of 100 centimeters and try to measure how high it bounces, we will get different answers each time. This is due to the difficulty in controlling variables (can we be sure we dropped the ball exactly the same way each time?) and the difficulty in measuring how high a moving object bounces. Nevertheless, if students are careful and practice measuring, they should get answers that are reasonably close. Even when all the measurements are close, the average minimizes error. If the measurements are 67 cm, 64 cm, and 67 cm, then the mean, 66 cm, is a more accurate prediction of future measurements than any of the actual measurements.

Another function of averaging is to aggregate raw data. Unlike computers, people cannot handle too many numbers at once. If I tell you the height of every child in a school, then you will be overwhelmed by numbers. If I tell you the median height of children in the school, you know less but probably understand more. The situation in a typical *Math Trailblazers* experiment is similar. From 12 actual measurements in *Rolling Along in Centimeters,* we cut down to four medians that are then used to display the data in a graph.

References

Huff, Darrell. *How to Lie with Statistics.* W.W. Norton & Co., New York, 1954.

Johnson, Robert. *Elementary Statistics,* 3rd ed., Wadsworth, Inc., Belmont, CA, 1980.

Estimation, Accuracy, and Error

For many people, one of the most attractive aspects of mathematics is that it is exact. The story problems that we worked on in our youth were reassuring (or terrifying) in the certainty of their answers. If one potato weighs 2 pounds, then 100 potatoes weigh 200 pounds. The only problem is that the real world is not so exact. One potato does not weigh exactly 2 pounds and 100 potatoes probably do not weigh 200 pounds. In this tutor, we discuss ways we deal mathematically with situations where exactness is not called for (when we estimate) or impossible (when we measure within a certain degree of accuracy).

Virtually all mathematics educators agree that estimation should be an important part of any elementary curriculum. Unlike content areas such as number and operation and geometry, there is very little traditional curriculum on estimation as well as some disagreement about exactly what is meant by estimation. Some mathematicians and educators make a distinction between estimation and approximation, but there is no generally agreed definition of these terms. This tutor provides a general overview of the concept of estimation and discusses some of the more common strategies and applications. For a more exhaustive treatment of estimation, we recommend the NCTM yearbook (1986).

What Is Estimation?

According to *Webster's Eleventh New Collegiate Dictionary,* **to estimate** means to judge tentatively or approximately the value, worth, or significance of something. Alternatively, it means to calculate approximately. **An estimate** is a general calculation of size, value, and so on, especially an *approximate* computation of the probable cost of a piece of work. This leads one to ask for the definition of **approximate.** The dictionary states that approximate means located close together, or nearly correct or exact. Moreover, **an approximation** is an *estimate,* guess, or mathematical result that is close in value but not the same as a desired quantity.

Although these definitions appear to be circular (an estimate is an approximation and an approximation is an estimate), the dictionary does give us a general idea of what these words mean. As with most words, these words have several meanings and their exact meaning is determined by the particular context in which they are used. In particular, these words are used in a variety of ways in mathematics. You should first note that unlike most mathematical concepts, estimate and approximate do not have precise definitions. What does it mean for two numbers to be "near in position, close together?" Is 5 close to 10? Is 1250 close to 1300? Is 1000 close to 3000? It's hard to say. In spite of our inability to precisely define closeness, we shall see that the varied uses of estimation are an important ingredient in mathematical problem solving.

Pedagogical Aspects of Estimation

In her survey article, "Estimation and Number Sense," Judith Threadgill-Sowder (1992) points out that

> *Good estimators are flexible in their thinking, and they use a variety of strategies. They demonstrate a deep understanding of number and operations, and they continually draw upon that understanding. Poor estimators seem to be bound, with only slight variations, to one strategy—that of applying algorithms more suitable for finding an exact answer. Poor estimators have only a vague notion of the nature and purpose of estimation; they believe it to be inferior to exact calculation (Morgan, 1988) and equate it with guessing.*

It follows from this view that teaching estimation is a complex task. Rather than being a simple skill that follows a few basic rules, estimation requires a variety of strategies. Rather than being a separate subject, estimation is a habit of mind that is carried out in many mathematical activities. Thus, there are few lessons in the *Math Trailblazers* curriculum devoted solely to estimation, while many lessons offer opportunities for estimation. While estimation is not a simple skill, a number of simple skills, such as rounding and mental multiplication, are extremely useful when doing estimation.

Students often have difficulty with estimation because they are uncomfortable about having more than one correct answer. They want to know "the right answer" and dislike being told "that's a good estimate." So it is your task to keep reminding students of the purpose of estimation and that different strategies can result in different correct answers. The laboratory experiments in *Math Trailblazers* help students develop an appreciation of the approximate nature of measurement and the fact that some problems can have more than one solution.

To help organize our thoughts about estimation, we will break the uses of estimation in the elementary mathematics curriculum into four major categories:

1. Estimating the result of a calculation (in particular, addition, subtraction, multiplication, and division) to see if the answer is reasonable.
2. Measurement error, experimental error, and predictions.
3. Estimating the magnitude of a measurement; for example, the height of a building, the area of a wall, the volume of a jar, or the weight of a person.
4. Estimating how many; for example, the number of peanuts in a jar, the number of students in a school, the number of people at a concert.

Good estimators are flexible in their thinking, and they use a variety of strategies. They demonstrate a deep understanding of number and operations, and they continually draw upon that understanding.

It is your task to keep reminding students of the purpose of estimation and that different strategies can result in different correct answers.

Estimating the Results of a Calculation

Two primary reasons for estimating calculation results are:

1. To check that the exact answer is (possibly) correct. The estimation can be done either before or after the calculation. Getting an answer that is far from your estimate indicates that the calculation is incorrect. On the other hand, an estimate close to the calculation does not guarantee that it is correct.

2. As a substitute for the exact answer. In many situations an exact answer is not needed and may not even make sense.

We will discuss a few of the more common strategies used to estimate the results of a calculation. Undoubtedly, you and your students will find other good strategies.

Addition and Subtraction

For estimation purposes, the most important digits in a number are the ones to the left, i.e., the leading digits. When estimating a sum or difference, one strategy you can usually carry out mentally is to look at the first one or two *place-value columns.* For example, here are some statistics on the New England states from a 1987 almanac:

	Population (1984)	Area (sq mi)
Maine	1,164,000	33,215
New Hampshire	998,000	9304
Vermont	535,000	9609
Massachusetts	5,822,000	8257
Rhode Island	968,000	1214
Connecticut	3,174,000	5009

When estimating a sum or difference, one strategy you can usually carry out mentally is to look at the first one or two place-value columns.

If we wanted to estimate the total population of New Hampshire and Vermont in 1984 using "front end estimation," we could look at the first column on the left. In this case, it is the hundred thousands column. Adding the 9 and the 5 we get 14, which tells us that the sum is approximately 14 hundred thousands; in other words, one million, four hundred thousand. In fact, the first two digits of the sum must be either 14 or 15 (depending on whether or not there is any carrying when we do the addition algorithm). Your estimate can be 1,400,000 or you can look at the next digits to see if there is likely to be any carrying. In this case, the digits in the ten thousands column are 9 and 3, so there will be carrying. Thus, 1,500,000 is an even better estimate. Of course, the whole point of estimation is to get a quick, approximate answer. If you start looking at too many digits, you might as well find the exact answer.

A second quick method for this estimate is to think that the population of New Hampshire was approximately 1 million and that of Vermont was about $\frac{1}{2}$ million, so the total is about 1.5 million. Since the "exact" answer is 1,533,000, an estimate of 1.5 million is only off by about 2 percent. A more rule-bound approach that says, "round off the nearest million" would give us 1 million plus 1 million which is 2 million. This is not a very close estimate (it's about 30 percent off). In fact, there is no simple rule that gives a good estimate in all situations. A rule that often gives good results is "round each number to one significant digit and then add." (A whole number has one significant digit if all digits after the first one equal zero.) That's what we did in this case, rounding 1,164,000 to 1,000,000 and 535,000 to 500,000.

You can apply the same strategies to estimate the results of subtraction calculations. For example, if we wanted to know how much larger the population of New Hampshire was than the population of Vermont, we could round each population to one significant digit, and subtract 500,000 from 1 million to get 500,000. Rounding to the nearest million definitely doesn't work in this problem, since both populations round to 1 million, and we would get the nonsensical estimate that there were no more people in New Hampshire than there were in Vermont! It should be noted that looking at the difference between two numbers is not always the best way of comparing them. If we wanted to compare the populations of New Hampshire and Vermont, it might be better to look at the ratio of their populations and say that New Hampshire had twice the population of Vermont.

The fact that the population figures are rounded off to the nearest thousand in the table is an acknowledgment that census figures themselves are estimates. In this case, there are two reasons that the data is not exact. Population data for the United States is based on census data. Since the U.S. population is so large and not everyone cooperates with the census takers, it is impossible to count everyone in the country. The population is also a moving target. Every day, tens of thousands of people are born or die. Finally, the figures for 1984 population are obtained by starting with the 1980 figures and extrapolating based on assumptions about the rate of population growth. Since many factors affecting population growth change, it is highly unlikely that predictions for population would be very accurate.

Rounding is also one effective strategy for mentally estimating the sum of a series of numbers. For example, to find the total population of New England from the individual state populations above, you might round the numbers in the population column to the nearest half million, namely 1, 1, $\frac{1}{2}$, 6, 1, and 3 million. Adding these mentally gives $12\frac{1}{2}$ million, which is pretty close to the actual total of 14,238,888 people. Try to estimate the total area of New England, mentally. The exact answer is 62,810 square miles.

Note that these are not the only strategies for estimating the sum or difference of several numbers. For example, if you want to purchase items that cost $3.79, $4.19, $2.23, and $6.49, you might add the dollars mentally ($3 + 4 + 2 + 6 = 15$) and then round the cents to the nearest quarter, i.e., 79 cents is about 75 cents, etc. This way, you see you need about $1.75 more (or 7 quarters). So, the total is pretty close to $16.75.

Multiplication: Rounding and Mental Math

The most basic technique for estimating the result of a multiplication problem is to replace (if necessary) the original numbers in the problem with other numbers that permit us to do the calculation mentally, or rapidly with paper and pencil. For example, if you want to know the number of minutes in a day, you would multiply 24 hours by 60 minutes per hour. Finding 24×60 is too hard for most people to do mentally, but 25×60 can be done by many fourth- and fifth-graders. Now, 25×60 is the same as $25 \times 6 \times 10$, and 25×6 is 150. (Think of 6 quarters as a dollar-fifty. Most of us are pretty good at calculating

The most basic technique for estimating the result of a multiplication problem is to replace (if necessary) the original numbers in the problem with other numbers that permit us to do the calculation mentally . . .

with multiples of 5, 10, and 25, since we have had a lot of practice doing mental arithmetic with money.) Finally, if 6×25 is 150, then $6 \times 25 \times 10$ is 1500. This is a pretty good estimate for 24×60. Note that we repeatedly used the commutative property of multiplication—i.e., the order in which we multiply several numbers does not affect the result. An alternative estimate for 24×60 can be obtained by rounding off 24 to 20 and multiplying 20 by 60 to get approximately 1200 minutes in a day. This estimate is not as close, but it may suffice for many purposes.

A basic skill fundamental to being able to estimate in multiplication and division situations is the ability to multiply and divide by ten and powers of ten (100, 1000, etc.). Thus, as early as third grade in *Math Trailblazers,* we observe the pattern that multiplying a whole number by 10 amounts to adding the digit 0 to the right of the number, i.e., $10 \times 57 = 570$, $10 \times 365 = 3650$, and so on. Similarly, multiplying by 100 amounts to adding two 0 digits to the right, and so on. When we start to work with decimals, we observe that multiplying a decimal by 10 amounts to moving the decimal point to the right one place. For example, $10 \times 45.76 = 457.6$. This is really the same pattern we see with whole numbers, since $10 \times 57.0 = 570$, etc.

Another fundamental process in the examples above was finding convenient numbers that were close to the numbers we started with. Here, convenient means numbers with which we can calculate mentally. For example, we rounded 24 to 25, since multiples of 25 are easy to figure out. Often, the convenient numbers are what we call round numbers. For example, when we used our second strategy to estimate 24×60, we rounded 24 to the nearest 10, which gave us 20. All this means is that 20 is the multiple of 10 that is nearest to 24 (since 24 is between 20 and 30 but is closer to 20).

Rounding

Traditionally, students were taught a lot of rules about rounding, but they often are not able to apply them successfully since they did not understand the purpose of rounding, nor did they have a good understanding of place value. When we are doing mental estimation, we frequently want to round a number in the hundreds to the nearest hundred, a number in the thousands to the nearest thousand, and so on. For example, 457 rounded to the nearest hundred is 500, while 447 rounded to the nearest hundred is 400. That's because both numbers are between 400 and 500, and 457 is closer to 500 and 447 is closer to 400. Now 450 is exactly halfway between 400 and 500, so it is not obvious how to round 450 to the nearest hundred. Strictly speaking, it does not make sense to talk about **the** nearest hundred in this situation, since 450 is 50 away from 400 and 50 away from 500. In the context of estimation, this means that you can use either 400 or 500 as an estimate for 450. For example, if we wanted to estimate 450×321, we could say $400 \times 300 = 120,000$ is an estimate for the answer. This estimate is certainly smaller than the actual answer, since 400 is less than 450 and 300 is less than 321. On the other hand, $500 \times 300 = 150,000$, which is probably bigger than the actual answer. So the answer is probably between 120,000 and 150,000 (it's actually 144,450).

It used to be taught that numbers halfway between should always be rounded up, but there is really no reason for doing so. In general, the choice is determined by the context in which the rounding takes place and the reason you are rounding. For example, if you want to make sure you have enough money to purchase the items in your grocery cart, it is probably best to make a conservative estimate and round items that cost $12.50 up to $13.

Division

It may be surprising to realize that the operation we need to estimate most frequently in daily life is division. This is because many decisions we have to make are based on proportional reasoning. How many miles per gallon is your car getting? Which brand of cereal is the least expensive? (One costs $2.65 for 14 oz and the other costs $3.55 for 24 oz.) A calculator can answer all these easily, but we often do not have a calculator handy. More significantly, students often perform the wrong calculations on the calculator. Letting students first solve their problem using convenient numbers allows them to focus on the essential parts of the problem, without being distracted by a lot of digits and a lot of mechanical manipulations. Once they have found a reasonable solution strategy, they can return to solve the original messy problem.

The easiest problems are ones that we can turn into a problem that requires dividing by a power of 10. Dividing by 10 is the inverse of multiplying by 10. Thus we can divide by 10 mentally by moving the decimal point one place to the left. For example, $\frac{279}{10} = 27.9$, $\frac{456.2}{10} = 45.62$, and so on. Similarly, we can divide by 100 by moving the decimal point two places to the left. When dividing a whole number by 10, we get a fairly good estimate for the result by just dropping the ones digit. For example, $\frac{279}{10}$ is approximately 27. Note that the estimate we get this way is always smaller than the exact answer.

One method for estimating the results of a division problem is to replace each number by a suitable nearby convenient number and then carry out the first step in the division algorithm. The rounding is chosen to make the division easy. For example, suppose we wanted to estimate the population density of Maine in 1984. The data in Table 1 tells us that the density is 1,164,000 people ÷ 33,215 square miles. We can round off the divisor to 30,000 square miles and round off the dividend to 1,000,000 people. To estimate 1,000,000 ÷ 30,000, we can ask what times 30,000 gives 1,000,000. Multiplying 30,000 by 10 gives 300,000 and multiplying this by 3.3 gets us near 1,000,000. So, our estimate is about 33. Another method is to replace the divisor and dividend with nearby convenient numbers. For example, 33,215 is near 30,000 and 1,164,000 is close to 1,200,000. We chose this pair of numbers because 12 is divisible by 3. So, our estimate now amounts to 1,200,000 people ÷ 30,000 square miles. Again, we see we need to multiply 30,000 by 40 to get 1,200,000. So 40 people per square mile is a reasonable estimate for the population density of Maine. Putting the numbers back into the context of the problem is important for checking any result.

A powerful technique for estimating the result of a division problem is to consider the division as a ratio. For example, suppose you traveled 637 miles and used 22 gallons of gas. To find miles per gallon, divide 22 into 637. Write the ratio 637 miles/22 gallons. Rounding 637 to 600 and 22 to 20 we get

$$\frac{637 \text{ mi}}{22 \text{ gal}} \approx \frac{600 \text{ mi}}{20 \text{ gal}}$$

Note that we used the symbol $\approx$ instead of the equal sign. This symbol means "approximately equal." Now, we can simplify the ratio $\frac{600}{20}$ by dividing both numerator and denominator by 10. So

$$\frac{600 \text{ mi}}{20 \text{ gal}} = \frac{60 \text{ mi}}{2 \text{ gal}}$$

and dividing numerator and denominator by 2 gives us

$$\frac{60 \text{ mi}}{2 \text{ gal}} = \frac{30 \text{ mi}}{1 \text{ gal}}$$

Putting this all together, we get 637 mi/22 gal $\approx$ 30 mi/1 gal; in other words, our estimate is 30 miles per gallon.

A note on canceling. Many people learned to simplify ratios by "canceling" the same thing in the numerator and the denominator. You might be tempted to say that when we wrote 600 mi/20 gal $\approx$ 60 mi/2 gal, we "canceled a 0" in the numerator and the denominator. Unfortunately, this can lead to some bad habits. For example, can you cancel the fives in $\frac{875}{25}$ to get $\frac{87}{2}$, or cancel the fives in $(X + 5)/(Y + 5)$ to get X/Y? You better not, since this amounts to subtracting the 5 from the numerator and denominator and results in a fraction that is not equal to the one we started with.

$$\frac{875}{25} \neq \frac{87}{2}$$

$$\frac{X + 5}{Y + 5} \neq \frac{X}{Y}$$

So canceling does not always result in an equal ratio. For this reason, we always say exactly what we are doing, dividing numerator and denominator by the same number, rather than using the word "cancel."

Here are some examples of estimation in a division context:

Example 1: Estimate the quotient $\frac{80,000}{30}$. This is approximately $\frac{8000}{3}$, which is between $\frac{7500}{3}$ and $\frac{9000}{3}$, i.e., between 2500 and 3000. Note that if we estimated $\frac{80,000}{30}$ by replacing 30 with 40 (since 40 goes into 80,000 evenly) we get $\frac{80,000}{40} = \frac{8000}{4} = 2000$, which is not as good as our previous estimate. This might be a little surprising, since we only made a change of 10 in replacing 30 by 40. But what is important here is not the size of the change (10), but the relative size of the change (10 out of 30 is 33%).

Here are some additional examples of estimation in a division context. See if you can follow the reasoning in these estimates. Can you make an estimate in a different way?

$$\frac{6206}{8271} \approx \frac{6000}{8000} = \frac{6}{8} = \frac{3}{4} = 0.75$$

$$\frac{78{,}221}{987} \approx \frac{80{,}000}{1000} = 80$$

$$\frac{77{,}921}{289} \approx \frac{75{,}000}{250} = \frac{7500}{25} = 300$$

$$\frac{828}{38{,}765} \approx \frac{800}{40{,}000} = \frac{8}{400} = \frac{2}{100} = .02$$

Measurement Error, Experimental Error, and Predictions

The theme of this tutor is the way to deal with "inexactness" in real-world mathematics. One class of situations that involve inexactness is measurement error or experimental error.

Measurement error is the unavoidable error that occurs due to the limitations inherent to any measurement instrument. Any measurement in the real world is an approximation. It is not really possible to guarantee that an object is exactly 1 meter long since any measuring instrument has a limit to its accuracy. For example, our centimeter ruler can only measure to the nearest tenth of a centimeter and the two-pan balance usually used in *Math Trailblazers* can only measure mass to the nearest gram.

Experimental error is the variation in measurement that results from the inability to control extraneous variables in an experiment.

These two types of error are closely related. Let's consider three examples of measurement in real-world contexts to get some idea of the meaning of measurement and experimental error:

Example 1: A volunteer is selected from the class and every student measures the circumference of her head to the nearest tenth of a centimeter. Most students get between 47 and 49 centimeters. One student gets 37.4 centimeters.

Example 2: Students drop a ball from a height of 80 centimeters three times to see how high it bounces. They get 41 centimeters, 45 centimeters, and 44 centimeters.

Example 3: Students measure the volume of a marble using a graduated cylinder. Most students get either 7 or 8 cubic centimeters. Two students get 67 cubic centimeters.

Example 4: A student finds that the mass of one blue pattern block is 11 grams. She predicts that 2 blue pattern blocks will have a mass of 22 grams and 4 blue pattern blocks will have a mass of 44 grams. When she checks her results, she finds that 2 pattern blocks do have a mass of 22 grams, but 4 pattern blocks have a mass of 42 grams.

> *Measurement error* is the unavoidable error that occurs due to the limitations inherent to any measurement instrument. . . .
> *Experimental error* is the variation in measurement that results from the inability to control extraneous variables in an experiment.

Errors vs. Mistakes

In Examples 1, 2, and 3, there were repeated measurements of the same thing that produced seemingly different answers. The fact that most students obtained slightly different answers in Example 1 is due to slight variations in how they performed the measurement—where they placed the tape measure, how tight they held it, etc. All these measurements are "close" to each other (see below for a discussion of "what's close?").

However, the student whose measurement was 37.4 centimeters probably made a *mistake* such as reading the tape measure incorrectly or placing the tape measure in the wrong position. In mathematics, we try to distinguish between the words "error" and "mistake." Of course, "mistake" is one of the common meanings of "error." *Webster's New World Dictionary of the American Language* gives as its first definition of the word "error," "the state of believing what is untrue, incorrect, or wrong."

In the current context, however, "error" has a different meaning. This is the fifth definition given for "error" in that dictionary, namely "the difference between a computed or estimated result and the actual value as in mathematics." The dictionary goes on to explain that "error implies deviation from truth, accuracy, correctness, right, [while] mistake suggests an error resulting from carelessness, inattention, misunderstanding, etc."

Most of the measurements in Example 1 involved some measurement error, but those measurements were correct. However, the student who measured 37.4 centimeters must have made a mistake. In this case, the teacher would help the student find the reason for the mistake and then repeat the measurement correctly.

In Example 2, it is not surprising that repeating the activity, that is, dropping the ball from 80 centimeters, results in a different measurement. It's pretty hard to measure how high the ball bounces, since the ball does not stop at the height of its bounce and wait for you to measure its distance from the floor. Also, there can be slight variations because different parts of the ball or different spots on the floor are "bouncier." This is a typical example of the experimental error that results from the inability to control all the fixed variables in an experiment. (See the TIMS Tutor: *The TIMS Laboratory Method,* Fixed Variables in Controlled Experiments.)

In Example 3, students used a graduated cylinder to measure the volume by displacement. Two students forgot to subtract the volume of the water in the cylinder, so they obtained measurements that were very different from the others. This is a clear example of a mistake. The actual volume of the marble was between 7 and 8 cubic centimeters.

Reducing Experimental Error

In Examples 1 through 3, we saw that repeating a measurement does not always give the same answer. To get more reliable and accurate results, scientists often repeat a measurement several times and then take the average of all the measurements. The "average" that we use in this situation can be

> *In mathematics, we try to distinguish between the words "error" and "mistake."*

> *To get more reliable and accurate results, scientists often repeat a measurement several times and then take the average of all the measurements.*

either the mean or the median. (See the TIMS Tutor: *Averages.*) In Example 2, we can take the median of the three measurements and say that dropping the ball from 80 centimeters results in a bounce height of 44 centimeters. We could also use the mean, in which case the bounce height would be nearly the same—approximately 43 centimeters.

In many experiments, we have another way of minimizing experimental error. If the data points plotted on a graph appear close to a straight line, we find a best-fit line that is close to all the data points. (See the TIMS Tutor: *The TIMS Laboratory Method.*) Using the best-fit line is a way of averaging out the experimental error. In *Math Trailblazers,* we draw a best-fit line "by eye," using a transparent ruler. In addition to averaging out the error, these lines help scientists and mathematicians make predictions based upon the patterns in the data. Scientists, mathematicians, and statisticians use a variety of sophisticated methods to find best-fit lines for data, but the "eyeball" method is pretty good for making approximate predictions.

One example of an activity that uses both averaging and best-fit lines to minimize experimental error is the *Math Trailblazers* fourth-grade lab, *The Bouncing Ball.* In this lab, students drop a ball from heights of 40, 80, and 120 cm and record their data in a data table. See Figure 1. Note that the ball was dropped three times from each height. When the data is graphed, we can see that the data points lie close to a straight line. In Figure 2, we see an estimated best-fit line drawn by a student. For further information, see the TIMS Tutor: *The TIMS Laboratory Method,* Point Graphs: Fitting Lines and Curves.

> *Scientists, mathematicians, and statisticians use a variety of sophisticated methods to find best-fit lines for data, but the "eyeball" method is pretty good for making approximate predictions.*

Tennis Ball

D Drop Height in cm	B Bounce Height in cm			
	Trial 1	Trial 2	Trial 3	Average
40	27	22	21	22
80	50	40	43	43
120	72	62	68	68

Figure 1: The Bouncing Ball *data table*

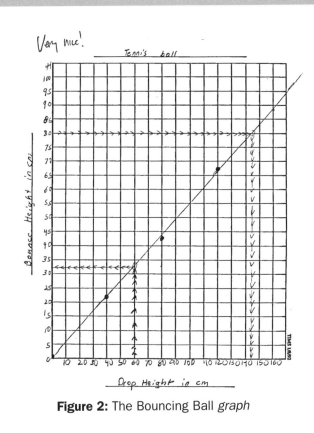

Figure 2: The Bouncing Ball *graph*

What's Close?

Recall that the notions of approximation and estimation involve the notion of finding a number that is close to a desired number. But how do we decide what is close? The most fundamental idea about closeness is that it is a **relative** idea. For example, suppose two merchants are selling the same item and the prices differ by $1. Are the prices close? If the merchants were selling cars that cost around $30,000, you would not make your decision based on a $1 difference in price. On the other hand, if you could buy a cup of coffee in one restaurant for $1 and it cost $2 at another restaurant, you might go out of your way for the $1 coffee (provided the quality was not vastly different). Why are these two choices for coffee significantly different? Because one brand costs twice as much as the other! This leads us to the fundamental idea for discussing closeness: when comparing closeness of numbers or measurements, we should look at the **ratio** of the two numbers, rather than the difference. The only problem with this approach is that the concept of ratio is difficult to understand fully. Developing this concept requires time and exposure to many experiences. We deal with this problem in two ways. First, instead of using ratios, we use a related concept—percent. Second, instead of calculating specific percentages (another difficult concept), we make comparisons to certain benchmark percentages, such as 10%. Using 10% as a benchmark for closeness, we see that $1 is not close to $2 since $2 is more than 10% bigger than $1 (in fact, it's 100% bigger). On the other hand, if we compare $30,000 and $30,001 we see that the difference, $1, is a lot less than 10% of $30,000.

> *The most fundamental idea about closeness is that it is a **relative** idea.*

In Example 1, the one in which many students measured the head circumference of one person, most measurements fell between 47 and 49 centimeters. A rough estimate for 10% of these numbers is 4 cm. Now the difference between 47 cm and 49 cm is 2 cm, so there is clearly less than 10% variation between the largest and smallest measurement. We can safely say these measurements are "close." On the other hand, the student who got 37.5 cm was almost 10 cm less than 47 cm. This is nowhere close to being within 10% of the other measurements, so we should suspect a mistake in that measurement. In Example 2, students took three measurements of the bounce height of a ball—41 cm, 45 cm, and 44 cm. Again, the variation is less than 10%. Finally, in Example 3, when students measured the volume of a marble, most obtained a value between 7 cc and 8 cc, while a few measured 67 cc. Now, 10% of 7 or 8 cc is less than 1 cc, so the students who measured 67 cc are nowhere close to the others. It should be pointed out that in situations such as Example 3, we do not decide who had the correct measurements by taking a majority vote. While the majority is usually right, it is not always right. The different results are a warning flag telling us to seek out the reasons for the discrepancies. Someone is making a mistake, but we can only find out who by looking more closely. Once we find the mistake, then we discard the incorrect information.

The 10 Percent Solution

It's natural to ask why we use 10% as a standard of closeness. We have a variety of reasons:

1. It's easy to find 10% of a number, or at least to estimate it. Just divide by 10. For whole numbers bigger than 10, the simplest estimate for 10% is obtained by dropping the last digit. Thus 10% of 187 is about 18 (it's between 18 and 19) and 10% of 5623 is about 562.
2. In many of the *Math Trailblazers* hands-on experiments, 10% is about the accuracy we can expect from students using the equipment they have, while 10% accuracy is still good enough for seeing the patterns in the data on graphs.
3. Psychologically, 10% is near the limit of our visual estimating ability. For example, if a person sees two drawings in sequence, one an enlargement of the other, in most cases that person will have difficulty distinguishing pictures that are less than 10% different in size, but will be able to distinguish figures that are much more than 10% different in size. Of course, this 10% borderline is not exact, and the point at which different people will be able to make distinctions is different.

Estimating the Magnitude of a Measurement

The basic measurement variables in the *Math Trailblazers* curriculum are length, area, volume, mass, and time. While much of the discussion that follows will apply to any type of measurement, it is a good idea to keep these few variables in mind. The examples given in this section will use these five variables.

There are two important types of knowledge used in many measurement estimation exercises. First, you need to know the measurements of some objects to use as a reference point. Second, you must know how to estimate unknown measurements by comparison with things you know. Very often this will involve some kind of proportional reasoning. The first type of knowledge is gained from experience. Therefore, students should have a wide variety of hands-on experiences as well as knowledge gained from external sources. For example, students should know the height of an average adult in English and metric systems ($5\frac{1}{2}$–6 feet, 160–185 cm), the length of their feet, and the width of their hands. We would hope that students have a general idea of the width of the continental United States from east to west (3000 miles) and from north to south (1000 miles). These facts can be used to make other estimates. For example, what is the area of the United States? The continental United States looks as though it would fit in a rectangle that is 3000 miles long and 1000 miles wide. This gives us an estimate of 3 million square miles. The actual area is close to 3.6 million square miles. To estimate the height of a three-story building (Figure 3), we could first estimate the height of one floor. Looking at an adult standing in the room, we might estimate that the distance from floor to ceiling is twice the height of the person. If the person is about 6 feet tall, then we get an estimate of 12 feet from floor to ceiling. If there are three floors, then the total height of the building is approximately $3 \times 12 = 36$ feet high.

Figure 3: *Estimating the height of a three-story building*

Accuracy and Precision

The accuracy required in a measurement depends on how we are going to use the measurement. By its very nature, any measurement we make in the real world is an estimation. What does it mean to say that a sheet of paper is 21.6 cm wide? How does one find this out? One way is to put the 0 cm mark on the ruler even with the left-hand edge of the paper and see that the right-hand edge of the paper is even with the 22.6 cm mark. If the paper is really 22.61 cm wide, we could not tell this with our ruler, which is only divided into tenths of a centimeter. So the measurements we make are really estimates that are accurate to the nearest tenth of a centimeter. Measuring the width of a piece of paper to an accuracy of more than a tenth of a centimeter would probably not make sense, since the sides cannot be perfectly even and measuring the width in different places would give different answers (like 22.613 cm and 22.615 cm). In any case, a measurement of 22.6 cm is probably more than sufficient for our purpose.

By its very nature, any measurement we make in the real world is an estimation.

One important fact to note is that in the course of solving a problem we can end up with a number that has many digits, most of which do not make sense in the real world (although they make mathematical sense). For example, suppose we wanted to share 16 ounces of orange juice among three students. When I divide 16 by 3 on my calculator, I get 5.3333333333. It makes no sense at all to say that we should give each student 5.3333333333 ounces of juice, since, with the tools we have, we cannot measure more accurately than to the nearest tenth of an ounce. In fact, when we say that we want to share 16 ounces of orange juice, we do not mean that we have exactly 16 ounces of juice. Unless we were using unusually sensitive measuring instruments, it would only make sense to say that we would give each student 5.3 ounces or $5\frac{1}{3}$ ounces of juice. Although 5.3 and $5\frac{1}{3}$ are not equal, they are approximately equal in this context.

Estimating "How Many"

In this type of estimation, we estimate the number of objects in some collection. It could be the number of trees in the United States, the number of students in a school district next year, or the number of beans in a jar. This class of problems has a lot in common with the estimation problems we have already discussed. Many problems that require estimating "how many" are similar to estimating a measurement in that they involve knowing how many objects there are in some known set and then comparing the unknown with the known. Here are some examples:

Example 1: Students are asked to estimate the number of peanuts in a jar. If students have no previous experience with peanuts or jars, this is not really an estimate, but rather a guess. Answers will vary widely because students do not have any idea of what the answer might be and no strategies to use to get a sensible answer. A more reasonable exercise is to give them a small jar and have them count how many peanuts can fit in the jar. If they are now given a larger jar, they should be able to make a sensible estimate by comparing the large jar to the small one. How many small jars would they think fit in the large jar? If the small jar holds 10 peanuts and it appears that 12 small jars fit in the large one, what is a reasonable estimate for the number of peanuts that fit in the large jar?

Example 2: How many students are in your school? The reference set here can be the number of students in a class. Students should know how many students are in their class. They should also be able to estimate the number of classes in the school. This gives an estimate for the number of students in the school (using multiplication).

Example 3: How many total hours of television were watched by all the children in the school? We can find the *exact* answer by asking every student how much they watched and then adding the number of hours. The answer can be *estimated* using a very important technique called sampling. Take a survey of some of the children in the school (say one class or two students in each class) and then scale up.

Example 4: We have a picture of the crowd at a basketball game. How can we determine the number of people at the game? It would be tedious to count the number of people in the picture. We could draw a square on the picture and count the number of people in that square. Then multiply that result by the number of such squares needed to cover the crowd. Figure 4 from the *Math Trailblazers* fourth-grade curriculum shows a picture used to pose a similar problem.

Figure 4: *Picture of a basketball game crowd*

Example 5: Will more people vote for Fred or Amy in the next election? This is another example of a kind of problem that frequently occurs in the real world. The common technique for estimating the answer is to take a sample of the voters and use the sample to predict the results for the whole population. For example, if 40% of the sample says they will vote for Fred and 60% says they will vote for Amy, we might predict that Amy will win. We might even predict that Fred will get 40% of the vote and Amy 60%. We know from real life that predictions like this are not always accurate. Some things that affect the accuracy of such estimates are the size of the sample (compared to the whole population) and the randomness of the sample (how well the sample represents the whole population).

Example 6: How many households are there in the United States? We can only make this estimate if we know enough facts about the population of the United States. We know that the population of the United States is about 250 million people and that the average family has 2.3 children. If we think that some households have only one person, while others have several generations living together, we might say that the average household size is about 4 or 5 people. Using a household size of 5 for our estimate (since 5 goes evenly into 25) we get a figure of 50 million households.

> *The best way to become a good estimator is to estimate.*

Conclusion

We hope that this tutor gives you an overview of the way estimation is treated in the *Math Trailblazers* curriculum. Naturally, it could not deal with all the types of estimation situations and all kinds of estimation strategies. The best way to become a good estimator is to estimate. The best way for children to learn to be good estimators is to be given meaningful situations that require estimation and to be given the opportunity to discuss their strategies with others. As with all mathematics instruction, the teacher plays a valuable role by moderating discourse and by adding new strategies when appropriate.

References

Schoen, Harold L., and Marilyn J. Zweng (eds.). *Estimation and Mental Computation—1986 Yearbook.* National Council of Teachers of Mathematics, Reston, VA, 1986.

Sowder, J., "Estimation and Number Sense," in *Handbook of Research on Mathematics Teaching and Learning.* Douglas A. Grouws (ed.). Macmillan Publishing Co., New York, 1992.

Threadgill-Sowder, J. "Computational Estimation Procedures of School Children." *Journal of Educational Research,* 77 (6), 1984.

Webster's Eleventh New Collegiate Dictionary. Merriam-Webster, Inc., Springfield, MA.

Functions

Introduction

Function is one of those words with a mathematical meaning that is not the same as its everyday meaning. In everyday life, a function can be an important celebration, a role someone or something has, or the purpose for something. In mathematics and science, a function is a special and very important kind of relationship between variables. Discovering functional relationships between variables is what science is all about.

Three Blind Men and an Elephant. There is a story about three blind men who encounter an elephant. The first comes up against one of the elephant's legs and says, "An elephant is like a tree." The second touches the side of the elephant and says, "No, no. An elephant is like a wall." The third blind man finds the elephant's trunk and claims, "You're both wrong. An elephant is like a big snake."

Each blind man has some notion of what an elephant is. The story doesn't tell whether they eventually resolve their differences and come to a proper understanding of elephants; we can only hope so. Our approach to functions will be similar: We will begin with three different views of functions. This, we hope, will lead to a fuller and more proper understanding of functions.

Tables

Many functions are displayed as tables. For example, consider this data table from the experiment *Mass vs. Number,* shown in Figure 1.

N Number of Erasers	M Mass (in gm)
1	39 gm
2	79 gm
4	158 gm

Figure 1: Mass vs. Number *data table*

This table displays a functional relationship between the variables N and M. For each value of N we have a value of M; we say that the mass is a function of the number of erasers. That is, if we know what N is, then we can find M. This is the essence of a function: knowing one variable's value enables us to find the corresponding value of the other variable. In this example, the data

> In mathematics and science, a function is a special and very important kind of relationship between variables. Discovering functional relationships between variables is what science is all about.

has a distinctive pattern: within experimental error, doubling one variable causes the other to double. *N* and *M* are said to be (directly) proportional.

Many functions we encounter in everyday life come to us as tables. You can think of stock tables, for example, as functions: one variable is the company, the other is the closing price. If you know the company, you can look up the price. Almanacs are filled with tables of information, most of which you can think of as functions: one variable is the name of the country, the other is the population, and so on. The sports pages are filled with tabular functions of team standings and individual statistics.

Many functions come to us first as tables, and some, like batting averages or almanac information, are normally given only as tables. Tables of numbers, however, can be very difficult to understand. Patterns in the data can go undetected—patterns that might help us better understand the function. One of the best ways to get a handle on patterns is to make a visual image of the data in the form of a graph.

Graphs

If a picture is worth a thousand words, a graph is worth a billion numbers. The graph of the *Mass vs. Number* data, seen in Figure 2, is a good example.

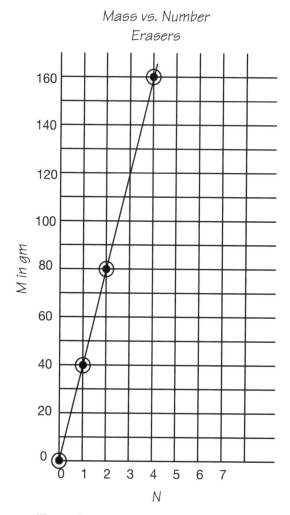

Figure 2: *Graph of* Mass vs. Number *data*

The key thing about this graph is that the data points lie on a straight line through (0,0). This confirms that N and M are proportional: we can fit a straight line through (0,0) if and only if the variables are proportional. Many other types of functions besides direct proportion are characterized by their graphs.

Often, experimental error obscures the nature of the relationship between the variables until the data is plotted. Like taking multiple measurements and averaging, graphing the data and fitting a curve can help control error. With error minimized, the true nature of the relationship between the variables may become clearer. Stock analysts graph their data to spot trends in order to make predictions (and money); such trends are unlikely to be noticed in the stock tables. Scientists graph their data almost as soon as they get it because the graph is so much more likely to be revealing than the raw data.

The graph is a crucial step on the road from the concrete apparatus to formal understanding. Sometimes, this formal understanding can be distilled in a few symbols, as in a formula.

The graph is a crucial step on the road from the concrete apparatus to formal understanding.

Formulas

A more abstract way to consider a function is as a formula. In our *Mass vs. Number* example, we can exploit the fact that when variables are proportional, their ratio is constant. The value of this constant ratio is the slope of the best-fit line. So,

$$\frac{M}{N} = \frac{39.5 \text{ gm}}{1 \text{ eraser}} .$$

This can be rewritten to give a formula for M as a function of N:

$$M = \frac{39.5 \text{ gm}}{1 \text{ eraser}} \times N$$

Such formulas are very useful when they can be found. When we do manage to obtain a formula, it allows us to solve problems quickly and accurately. We can also use formulas to ascend to higher levels of abstraction. This movement to ever greater abstraction and generality is the driving force behind much of science and mathematics.

G Number of Generations	A Number of Ancestors
1	2
2	4
3	8
4	16

Figure 3: *Ancestors data table*

Often students are not able to understand formulas, but they are, nevertheless, able to continue a pattern in a data table or devise a rule that works. For example, the pattern in the table shown in Figure 3 is easy to extend. Five generations back, you have 32 ancestors: each further generation doubles the number of ancestors (ignoring the inevitable overlap). Extending patterns like this is a first step towards formulas. Later, the students may be able to give a rule for a data table. For example, consider the table in Figure 4, the number of fence posts needed for a given length of fence.

L Length of Fence in _feet_	*N* Number of Fence Posts
10	2
20	3
30	4
40	5

Figure 4: *Fence posts data table*

The rule may be stated: the number of fence posts is just one more than $\frac{1}{10}$ the number of feet in the fence.

$$N = \frac{L}{10} + 1$$

It is not much harder for us to express this sentence as a formula, but this type of expression may be confusing to a third-grader. Often, a rule stated in ordinary language is more accessible.

Formulas are the most powerful way to look at functions but are often not appropriate for elementary school students. The great temptation is to move to formulas as quickly as possible. This sometimes leads to quick gains, but over the long run it is often problematic. Pushing formulas at children is like building a house of cards: students need to build a conceptual foundation by handling apparatus, gathering data, and graphing and analyzing it. Only after students develop an understanding of the relationship of the variables is it proper to distill that understanding into a formula. Extending patterns and figuring out rules are excellent alternatives for younger students moving towards higher levels of abstraction.

What Is a Function?

A **function** is a special kind of relationship between variables that can often be expressed as a data table, graph, or formula. One variable is the manipulated (or independent) variable; the other is the responding (or dependent) variable.

But not every relationship is a function. The main requirement for a relationship to be a function is that for each value of the manipulated variable, there is only one value of the responding variable. For example, suppose the manipulated variable is the edge length of a cube and the responding variable is the surface area. Then, for each given edge length there is exactly one surface area: if the edge is 3 cm, then the surface area is 54 sq cm, and so on. Or consider the manipulated variable to be the company and the responding variable to be the closing price: each stock has exactly one closing price each day. Notice that many stocks may have the same closing price; that's okay. The requirement says only that each value of the manipulated variable must have exactly one value of the responding variable. Values of the responding variable may repeat, and often do. One way to visualize this requirement is to think about functions as mappings. Figure 5 shows a map of a squaring function.

> *. . . not every relationship is a function. The main requirement for a relationship to be a function is that for each value of the manipulated variable, there is only one value of the responding variable.*

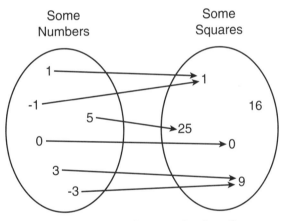

Figure 5: *Map of a squaring function*

Every number has exactly one square; this corresponds to the single arrow leaving each number on the left above. Notice that more than one arrow can end at a single number; the requirement is only that exactly one arrow leave each of the starting numbers. The mapping in Figure 6 is not a function because two arrows leave each number.

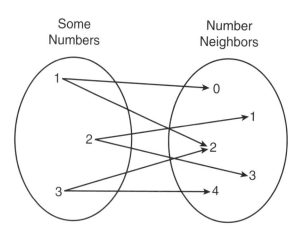

Figure 6: *Map of a relationship that is not a function*

But you may object, saying that when we do experiments we often have several different values of the responding variable for each value of the manipulated variable. Isn't there a functional relationship between variables like the drop height and the bounce height in *The Bouncing Ball?* In a word, yes. But with real data, things get more complicated. Experimental error creeps in; there are other uncontrolled variables; there is uncertainty inherent in all our measurements.

One useful way to think about the situation is to suppose there is some "true" value of the responding variable that we cannot measure exactly. So, instead we measure the responding variable several times and then take the average as our best estimate of the true value.[1] Then we have a function: for each value of the manipulated variable there is exactly one *true* value of the responding variable. The only trouble is, in most real-world situations, we usually don't know what that true value is.

Mathematicians have precise and abstract definitions of function. We could go on and on describing more precisely the requirements a relationship must have to be a function. We could spell out the meanings of technical terms having to do with functions—terms like *domain, range, one-to-one, many-to-one,* and so on. For most purposes, however, thinking about functions in the terms outlined above is enough.

Functions in the Classroom

The concept of a function is a powerful one for organizing and extending mathematical ideas. From time to time, we have activities that deal with functions, for example, *Function Machines* in second grade. The best approach to functions, however, is just doing the *Math Trailblazers* lessons. As your students do TIMS Laboratory Investigations and other activities, they will move naturally from the apparatus to the data table, graph, and questions. Much of the data analysis is designed to help children see how changes in one of these correspond to changes in the others. Thus, in each experiment the students will deal with specific functions in several guises and will gain facility in moving between different representations of functions. This is the best possible preparation for the explicit study of functions later in high school and beyond.

[1]See the TIMS Tutor: *Averages.*

As your students do TIMS Laboratory Investigations and other activities, they will move naturally from the apparatus to the data table, graph, and questions. Much of the data analysis is designed to help the children see how changes in one of these correspond to changes in the others. . . . This is the best possible preparation for the explicit study of functions later in high school and beyond.

Journals

We at TIMS embrace the idea of writing across the curriculum. We see helping students to write better as part of every teacher's job.

By writing in mathematics and science class, students improve their communication skills and develop their subject-matter understanding. Writing about mathematics and science helps students consolidate ideas, see connections between school and life, and think more abstractly.

> *Writing about mathematics and science helps students consolidate ideas, see connections between school and life, and think more abstractly.*

Another reason to have students write about mathematics and science lessons is so you can gain insight into how those lessons are being received and what the students are learning. Collecting and saving students' writing is also an excellent way to document long-term student progress.

We incorporate writing into *Math Trailblazers* in several ways. We often ask for students to write a short or extended answer to a question and we may also ask students to explain how they obtained their solutions. Students may be asked to write about problems they solved in cooperative groups.

Journals are another effective way to use writing in mathematics and science. Typically, a journal is a small, bound book in which students write regularly. The writing can be in response to various prompts, or it can be rather undirected. Because each student responds at his or her own level and rate, journal writing is accessible to all students.

The teacher reads students' journals regularly, possibly responding in writing to what students wrote. Usually journal writing is not corrected for grammar, spelling, and punctuation—the focus is on the content of the writing, not the form.

The physical form of the journal is not important. A cloth-covered bound book, a spiral notebook, or even several sheets of paper stapled together all work just fine.

Journal Prompts

We urge you to have your students write regularly, every day or at least every week. Start with short periods and gradually extend the amount of time. When a student fills up one journal, give him or her another. Students will also enjoy reading their writing aloud and discussing it.

Your students' journal writing should take a variety of forms. Here are some suggestions for assignments ranging from highly structured to rather open-ended.

We urge you to have your students write regularly, every day or at least every week. Start with short periods and gradually extend the amount of time.

Sentence Completion

Give part of a sentence and ask students to complete it (Azzolino, 1990). For example, you might ask students to complete sentences like these:

"A shape is symmetric when . . ."
"Today we learned . . ."
"Before you use an equal-arm balance it's important to . . ."

A variation of this activity is to give one or more complete sentences and then to ask students to continue.

Explanations of Procedures

Ask students to explain how to measure the area of a leaf, how to use an equal-arm balance, how to add two three-digit numbers, or how to make a graph of some data. This may require an explanation of an entire procedure or only of certain steps.

Answers to Specific Questions

Sometimes you may pose a specific question about a lesson. For example, ask students to describe the shape of the graph for a certain experiment and to explain why the graph has that shape. Many *Math Trailblazers* lessons include questions that require some writing; these questions can be answered in the journals.

A question to ask sometimes is, "How did working in your group turn out?" You may get valuable information that can help you improve the dynamics of your small groups.

Descriptions of Solutions

There are usually many ways to solve a mathematics problem; it is often worth exploring multiple solutions. To correct the common misconception that there is usually only one way to solve a problem, students need to learn that the process of problem solving is often as important as the answer. In *Math Trailblazers,* they see connections by comparing different solutions. They learn that mathematics makes sense because their own ideas are validated. They are exposed to advanced ideas through other students' solutions, but without undue stress if they fail to understand those advanced ideas.

One way to encourage multiple solutions is to ask students to write about how they solved a problem. Ask them to describe all the ways they solved a problem or to describe a single way in depth. Ask them to write about failed solutions or what they did when they got stuck. Such assignments will encourage students to see such efforts not as failures but as periodic by-products of the problem-solving process.

Definitions

Ask students to define a key concept like area or volume. You may be surprised at some of their answers.

Advice to Adventure Book Characters

Often the characters in the *Adventure Books* and other activities encounter problems that yield to the techniques the students have been learning in the labs and activities. You might stop part way through an *Adventure Book* story and ask your students to write some advice, perhaps in the form of a letter, to the hero. When you finish the book, compare what the hero actually did to the students' advice.

Reactions

Ask students what they liked or didn't like about a certain lab, activity, or adventure book. Or, ask what they learned or what confused them.

Word Banks

Supply a list of words or phrases and ask students to use those words in a piece of writing (Azzolino, 1990). For example, you might supply the following words, "ten, hundred, thousand, less than, seven, more than, nine."

Problems

Students enjoy writing their own problems. Ask them to write another problem like a given problem; to write an addition, subtraction, or sharing problem; to write a number riddle; or to make up any problem that classmates would find interesting to solve.

Free Writing

Other times, simply tell students to write whatever they want about a certain lesson.

Some Tips for Getting Started

- Start with brief periods of writing and gradually extend the amount of time.
- Encourage pictures, data tables, graphs, number sentences, and other mathematical and scientific forms of communication.
- Vary the prompt. Sometimes be very specific; other times make the assignment more open-ended.
- Do not worry about grammar, spelling, and punctuation. Focus on content.

One way to encourage multiple solutions is to ask students to write about how they solved a problem. Ask them to describe all the ways they solved a problem or to describe a single way in depth. Ask them to write about failed solutions or what they did when they got stuck.

Conclusion

The name of our project—TIMS (Teaching Integrated Mathematics and Science)—expresses our conviction that the teaching of mathematics and science should be integrated. But we also believe strongly that integration should not stop there; language arts and social studies can and should be integrated with mathematics and science. Journals are one way to use writing in mathematics and science. Reading and writing are too important to be confined to language arts lessons.

References

Azzolino, A. "Writing as a Tool for Teaching Mathematics: The Silent Revolution." In *Teaching and Learning Mathematics in the 1990s: 1990 Yearbook.* T.J. Cooney and C.R. Hirsch, Eds. National Council of Teachers of Mathematics, Reston, VA, 1990.

Burns, Marilyn, and Robyn Sibley. "Incorporating Writing into Math Class." *So You Have to Teach Math? Sound Advice for K–6 Teachers.* Math Solutions Publications, Sausalito, CA, 2000.

Countryman, Joan. *Writing to Learn Mathematics.* Heinemann, Portsmouth, NH, 1992.

Math Facts

Students need to learn the math facts. Estimation, mental arithmetic, checking the reasonableness of results, and paper-and-pencil calculations require the ability to give quick, accurate responses when using basic facts. The question is not if students should learn the math facts, but how. Which teaching methods are most efficient and effective? To answer this question, we as authors of *Math Trailblazers* drew upon educational research and our own classroom experiences to develop a comprehensive plan for teaching the math facts.

Philosophy

The goal of the *Math Trailblazers* math facts strand is for students to learn the basic facts efficiently, gain fluency with their use, and retain that fluency over time. A large body of research supports an approach that is built on a foundation of work with strategies and concepts. This not only leads to more effective learning and better retention, but also to development of mental math skills. Therefore, the teaching and assessment of the basic facts in *Math Trailblazers* is characterized by the following elements:

- *Early emphasis on problem solving.* Students first approach the basic facts as problems to solve rather than as facts to memorize. Students invent their own strategies to solve these problems or learn appropriate strategies from others through class discussion. Students' natural strategies, especially counting strategies, are explicitly encouraged. In this way, students learn that math is more than memorizing facts and rules that "you either get or you don't."

- *De-emphasis of rote work.* Fluency with the math facts is an important component of any student's mathematical learning. Research shows that overemphasizing memorization and frequent administration of timed tests are counterproductive. Both can produce undesirable results (Isaacs and Carroll, 1999; Van de Walle, 2001; National Research Council, 2001). We encourage the use of strategies to find facts, so students become confident they can find answers to fact problems they do not immediately recall.

- *Gradual and systematic introduction of facts.* Students study the facts in small groups they solve using similar strategies. Students first work on simple strategies for easy facts and then progress to more sophisticated strategies and harder facts. By the end of the process, they gain fluency with all required facts.

- *Ongoing practice.* Work on the math facts is distributed throughout the curriculum, especially in the Daily Practice and Problems (DPP), Home Practice, and games. This practice for fluency, however, takes place only after students have a conceptual understanding of the operations and have achieved proficiency with strategies for solving basic fact problems. Delaying practice in this way means that less practice is required to achieve fluency.

- *Appropriate assessment.* Teachers assess students' knowledge of the facts through observations as they work on activities, labs, and games as well as through the appropriate use of written tests and quizzes. Beginning in first grade, periodic, short quizzes in the DPP naturally follow the study of small groups of facts organized around specific strategies. As self-assessment in Grades 3–5, students record their progress on *Facts I Know* charts and determine which facts they need to study. Inventory tests of all facts for each operation are used sparingly in Grades 2–5 (no more than twice per year) to assess students' progress with fact fluency. The goal of the math facts assessment program is to determine the degree to which students can find answers to fact problems quickly and accurately and whether they can retain this skill over time.
- *Multiyear approach.* In Grades 1 and 2, *Math Trailblazers* emphasizes strategies that lead to fluency with the addition and subtraction facts. In Grade 3, students gain fluency with the multiplication facts while reviewing the addition and subtraction facts. In Grade 4, students achieve fluency with the division facts and verify fluency with the multiplication facts. In Grade 5, the multiplication and division facts are systematically reviewed and assessed.
- *Facts are not gatekeepers.* Students are not prevented from learning more complex mathematics because they do not perform well on fact tests. Use of strategies, calculators, and other math tools (e.g., manipulatives, hundred charts, printed multiplication tables) allows students to continue to work on interesting problems while still learning the facts.

Expectations by Grade Level

The following goals for the math facts are consistent with the recommendations in the National Council of Teachers of Mathematics *Principles and Standards for School Mathematics:*

- In kindergarten, students use manipulatives and invent their own strategies to solve addition and subtraction problems.
- By the end of first grade, all students can solve all basic addition and subtraction problems using some strategy. Fluency is not emphasized; strategies are. Some work with beginning concepts of multiplication takes place.
- In second grade, learning efficient strategies for addition and especially subtraction continues to be emphasized. Work with multiplication concepts continues. By the end of the year, students are expected to demonstrate fluency with all the addition and subtraction facts.
- In third grade, students review the subtraction facts. They develop efficient strategies for learning the multiplication facts and demonstrate fluency with the multiplication facts.
- In fourth grade, students review the multiplication facts and develop strategies for the division facts. By the end of year, we expect fluency with all the division facts.
- In fifth grade, students review the multiplication and division facts and are expected to maintain fluency with all the facts.

This is summarized in the following chart:

Grade	Addition	Subtraction	Multiplication	Division
K	• invented strategies	• invented strategies		
1	• strategies	• strategies		
2	• strategies • practice leading to fluency	• strategies • practice leading to fluency		
3	• review and practice	• review and practice	• strategies • practice leading to fluency	
4	• assessment and remediation as required	• assessment and remediation as required	• review and practice	• strategies • practice leading to fluency
5	• assessment and remediation as required	• assessment and remediation as required	• review and practice	• review and practice

Table 1: *Math Facts Scope and Sequence*

Strategies for Learning the Facts

Students are encouraged to learn the math facts by first employing a variety of strategies. Concepts and skills are learned more easily and are retained longer if they are meaningful. By first concentrating on concepts and strategies, we increase retention and reduce the amount of time necessary for rote memorization. Researchers note that over time, students develop techniques that are increasingly sophisticated and efficient. Experience with the strategies provides a basis for understanding the operation involved and for gaining fluency with the facts. In this section, we describe possible strategies for learning the addition, subtraction, multiplication, and division facts. The strategies for each operation are listed roughly in order of increasing sophistication.

Strategies for Addition Facts

Common strategies include counting all, counting on, doubles, making or using 10, and reasoning from known facts.

Counting All

This is a particularly straightforward strategy. For example, to solve 7 + 8, the student gets 7 of something and 8 of something and counts how many there are altogether. The "something" could be beans or chips or marks on paper. In any case, the student counts all the objects to find the sum. This is perhaps not a very efficient method, but it is effective, especially for small numbers, and is usually well understood by the student.

Counting On

This is a natural strategy, particularly for adding 1, 2, or 3. Counters such as beans or chips may or may not be used. As an example, consider 8 + 3. The student gets 8 beans, and then 3 more, but instead of counting the first 8 again, she simply counts the 3 added beans: "9, 10, 11."

Even if counters are not used, finger gestures can help keep track of how many more have been counted on. For example, to solve 8 + 3, the student counts "9, 10, 11," holding up a finger each time a number word is said; when three fingers are up, the last word said is the answer.

Doubles

Facts such as 4 + 4 = 8 are easier to remember than facts with two different addends. Some visual imagery can help, too: two hands for 5 + 5, a carton of eggs for 6 + 6, a calendar for 7 + 7, and so on.

Making a 10

Facts with a sum of 10, such as 7 + 3 and 6 + 4, are also easier to remember than other facts. Ten frames can create visual images of making a 10. For example, 8 is shown in a ten frame like the one in Figure 1:

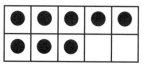

Figure 1: *A ten frame*

This visual imagery helps students remember, for example, that 8 + 2 = 10.

Using a 10

Students who are comfortable partitioning and combining small numbers can use that knowledge to find the sums of larger numbers. In particular, there are many strategies that involve using the number 10. For example, to find 9 + 7, we can decompose 7 into 1 + 6 and then 9 + 7 = 9 + 1 + 6 = 10 + 6 = 16. Similarly, 8 + 7 = 8 + 2 + 5 = 10 + 5 = 15.

Reasoning from Known Facts

If you know what 7 + 7 is, then 7 + 8 is not much harder: it's just 1 more. So, the "near doubles" can be derived from knowing the doubles.

Strategies for Subtraction Facts

Common strategies for subtraction include using counters, counting up, counting back, using 10, and reasoning from related addition and subtraction facts.

Using Counters

This method models the problem with counters like beans or chips. For example, to solve 8 − 3, the student gets 8 beans, removes 3 beans, and counts the remaining beans to find the difference. As with using the addition strategy "counting all," this relatively straightforward strategy may not be efficient but it has the great advantage that students usually understand it well.

Counting Up

The student starts at the lower number and counts on to the higher number, perhaps using fingers to keep track of how many numbers are counted. For example, to solve $8 - 5$, the student wants to know how to get from 5 to 8 and counts up 3 numbers: 6, 7, 8. So, $8 - 5 = 3$.

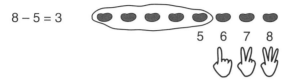

$8 - 5 = 3$

5   6   7   8

Figure 2: *Counting up*

Counting Back

Counting back works best for subtracting 1, 2, or 3. For larger numbers, it is probably best to count up. For example, to solve $9 - 2$, the student counts back 2 numbers: 8, 7. So, $9 - 2 = 7$.

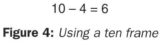

$9 - 2 = 7$ 9   8   7

Figure 3: *Counting back*

Using a 10

Students follow the pattern they find when subtracting 10, e.g., $17 - 10 = 7$ and $13 - 10 = 3$, to learn close facts, e.g., $17 - 9 = 8$ and $13 - 9 = 4$. Since $17 - 9$ will be 1 more than $17 - 10$, they can reason that the answer will be 8, or $7 + 1$.

Making a 10

Knowing the addition facts that have a sum of 10, e.g., $6 + 4 = 10$, can be helpful in finding differences from 10, e.g., $10 - 6 = 4$ and $10 - 4 = 6$. Students can use ten frames to visualize these problems as in Figure 4. These facts can then also be used to find close facts, such as $11 - 4 = 7$.

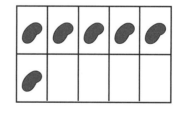

$10 - 4 = 6$

Figure 4: *Using a ten frame*

Using Doubles

Students can use the addition doubles, e.g., $8 + 8 = 16$ and $6 + 6 = 12$, to learn the subtraction "half-doubles" as well: $16 - 8 = 8$ and $12 - 6 = 6$. They can then use these facts to figure out close facts, such as $13 - 6 = 7$ and $15 - 8 = 7$.

Reasoning from Related Addition and Subtraction Facts

Knowing that $8 + 7 = 15$ would seem to be of some help in solving $15 - 7$. Unfortunately, however, knowing related addition facts may not be so helpful to younger or less mathematically mature students. Nevertheless, reasoning from known facts is a powerful strategy for those who can apply it and should be encouraged.

Strategies for Multiplication Facts

Common strategies for multiplication include skip counting, counting up or down from a known fact, doubling, breaking a product into the sum of known products, and using patterns.

Skip Counting
Students begin skip counting and solving problems informally that involve multiplicative situations in first grade. By the time they begin formal work with the multiplication facts in third grade, they should be fairly proficient with skip counting. This strategy is particularly useful for facts such as the 2s, 3s, 5s, and 10s, for which skip counting is easy.

Counting Up or Down from a Known Fact
This strategy involves skip counting forwards once or twice from a known fact. For example, if children know that 5×5 is 25, then they can use this to solve 6×5 (5 more) or 4×5 (5 less). Some children use this for harder facts. For 7×6, they can use the fact that $5 \times 6 = 30$ as a starting point and then count on by sixes to 42.

Doubling
Some children use doubling relationships to help them with multiplication facts involving 4, 6, and 8. For example, 4×7 is twice as much as 2×7. Since $2 \times 7 = 14$, it follows that 4×7 is 28. Since 3×8 is 24, it follows that 6×8 is 48.

Breaking a Product into the Sum of Known Products
A fact like 7×8 can be broken into the sum $5 \times 8 + 2 \times 8$ since $7 = 5 + 2$. See Figure 5. The previous two strategies are special cases of this more general strategy.

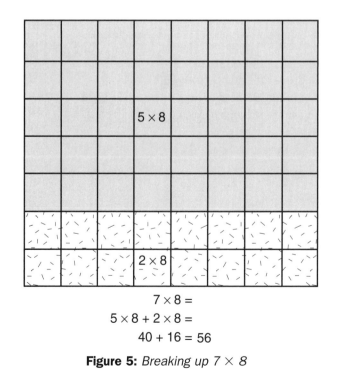

$7 \times 8 =$

$5 \times 8 + 2 \times 8 =$

$40 + 16 = 56$

Figure 5: *Breaking up 7×8*

Patterns

A. Perhaps the best-known examples of patterns are the nines patterns:

1. When the nines products are listed in a column, as shown below, it is easy to see that the digits in the tens place count up by one (0, 1, 2, 3, . . .) and that the digits in the ones place count down by one (9, 8, 7, . . .).

   9
   18
   27
   36
   45
   54
   63
   72
   81

2. The sums of the two digits in each of the nines products above are all equal to nine. For example, the sum of the digits in 36 is $3 + 6 = 9$; the sum of the digits in 72 is $7 + 2 = 9$. Adding the digits of a number to see whether they add up to nine can be a strategy in remembering a nines fact. For example, a student might think, "Let me see, does 9×6 equal 54 or 56? It must be 54 since $5 + 4$ is 9, but $5 + 6$ is not 9."

3. The digit in the tens place in a nines fact is one less than the number being multiplied. For example, $4 \times 9 = 36$, and 3 is one less than 4. This can be combined with the previous pattern to derive nines facts. For example, 3×9 is in the twenties. Since $2 + 7$ is 9, 3×9 must be 27.

4. Nines can easily be computed using the counting down strategy. Nine times a digit is the same as 10 times the digit, minus the digit. For example, 9×6 is $10 \times 6 - 6 = 54$.

B. Other patterns.

Other patterns that are useful in remembering other special facts:

1. 0 times a number equals 0.

2. 1 times a number equals the number.

3. 2 times a number is double the number.

4. 5 times a number ends in 0 or 5; even numbers times 5 end in 0 and odd numbers times five end in 5.

5. 10 times a number is the same number with a 0 on the end.

Sequencing the Study of Multiplication Facts

In kindergarten, children solve word problems involving multiplication situations. Beginning in first grade, the curriculum develops a conceptual foundation for multiplication through a variety of multiplication models, including repeated addition, the array model, and the number-line model. Fluency with the multiplication facts is expected by the end of third grade. Strategies are often introduced in specific, third-grade lessons. Practice is continued in subsequent lessons and especially in the Daily Practice and Problems and Home Practice. We do not introduce the multiplication facts in the order in which they are traditionally taught (first learning the 2s, then the

3s, then the 4s, etc.). Rather, we emphasize thinking strategies for the facts, introducing fact-groups in the following order:

2s, 3s, 5s, and 10s. The 2s, 3s, 5s, and 10s are easily solved using skip counting.

Square numbers such as $3 \times 3 = 9$, $4 \times 4 = 16$, and $5 \times 5 = 25$. These are introduced by arranging tiles into square arrays.

Nines. Students explore patterns for nines.

Last six facts. After students have learned the facts listed above and their turn-around facts ($9 \times 6 = 6 \times 9$), there are only six more facts to learn: 4×6, 4×7, 4×8, 6×7, 6×8, and 7×8.

Strategies for the Division Facts

The main strategy for learning the division facts is to think of the related multiplication fact. Therefore, students review the multiplication facts and develop fluency with the division facts by working with fact families. (Fact families are groups of related facts. An example of a fact family is $3 \times 4 = 12$, $4 \times 3 = 12$, $12 \div 3 = 4$, and $12 \div 4 = 3$.)

Using the Right Strategy

Different strategies appeal to different students. Students should not feel overburdened with the need to determine which is the "correct" strategy for a given fact. We do not intend to give them a new layer of things to learn. For example, when asked to explain a strategy for a fact, a student may say, "I've used it so much that now I just remember it." "Just remembering" is obviously an efficient strategy. The purpose of suggesting and discussing various strategies is to give students other, perhaps helpful, ways of learning the facts and to give them the confidence to think problems through when necessary. Students should have the opportunity to choose the strategies that work best for them or to invent their own.

Math Facts Lessons

The *Math Trailblazers* math facts program pervades most of the curriculum's components. Work with math facts are in different kinds of lessons. These are described in this section.

Figure 6: *Discussing fact strategies*

Everyday Work

As students work on problems in the labs and activities, encourage them to use and discuss various strategies for solving math facts problems. A number of important goals can best be reached through such discussions.

One goal is to legitimize all valid strategies, even those that may be less efficient. When students see their intuitive methods recognized and validated, they tend to perceive mathematical knowledge as continuous with everyday knowledge and common sense. We thus hope to avoid the unfortunate tendency of many students to separate their knowledge of mathematics from their knowledge of the real world.

By discussing strategies as they arise in context, students and teachers can explore how the strategies work and can verify that they are being used properly. Students should come to realize that a fact strategy that gives wrong answers is not very useful.

A second goal of our approach is to encourage students to communicate mathematical ideas. There are several reasons to stress communication: Students can learn from one another; communicating a method requires higher orders of thinking than simply applying that method; and skill at communicating is important in itself. We are social creatures. Mathematics and science are social endeavors in which communication is crucial.

A third goal of encouraging discussions of various methods is to give the teacher opportunities to learn about how students think. Knowing more about students' thinking helps the teacher ask better questions and plan more effective lessons.

Strategy Lessons

We feel that occasionally it is appropriate for lessons to focus on certain strategies that are developmentally appropriate for most students. Our plan is to begin with simple strategies that should be accessible to all students and to progress gradually to more complex forms of reasoning. For example, in the fall of first grade, we have several lessons that stress counting on to solve certain addition problems. Later, we explicitly introduce making a 10 and other, more sophisticated, strategies.

In general, you should expect your students to come up with effective strategies on their own. Our strategy lessons are intended to explore how and why various strategies work and also to codify and organize the strategies the students invent. They are not meant to dictate the only appropriate strategy for a given problem or to discourage students from using strategies they understand and like. They should be seen as opportunities to discuss strategies that may be appropriate for many students and to encourage their wider use.

Practice

Our ultimate goal is to produce students who can think mathematically, who can solve problems and deal easily with quantified information, and who enjoy mathematics and are not afraid of it. It is easier to do all of the above if one has fluency with the basic math facts. Practice strengthens students' abilities to use strategies and moves students towards fluency with the facts. Practice that follows instruction that stresses the use of strategies has been shown to improve

As students work on problems in the labs and activities, they should be encouraged to use and to discuss various strategies for solving math facts problems.

Our ultimate goal is to produce students who can think mathematically, who can solve problems and deal easily with quantified information, and who enjoy mathematics and are not afraid of it. It is easier to do all of the above if one has fluency with the basic math facts.

students' fluency with the math facts. We recommend, and have incorporated into the curriculum, the following practice to gain this fluency.

Practice in Context

The primary practice of math facts will arise naturally for the students as they participate in the labs and other activities in the curriculum. These labs and activities offer many opportunities to practice addition, subtraction, multiplication, and division in a meaningful way. The lessons involve the student visually with drawings and patterns, auditorily through discussion, and tactilely through the use of many tools such as manipulatives and calculators.

Pages of problems on the basic facts are not only unnecessary, they can be counterproductive. Students may come to regard mathematics as mostly memorization and may perceive it as meaningless and unconnected to their everyday lives.

Structured Practice

Student-friendly, structured practice is built into the curriculum, especially in the DPP, Home Practice, and games. One small group of related math facts is presented to the students at a time. The practice of groups of facts is carefully distributed throughout the year. A small set of facts grouped in a meaningful way leads students to develop strategies such as adding doubles, counting back, or using a 10 for dealing with a particular situation. Furthermore, a small set of facts is a manageable amount to learn and remember.

Beginning in the second half of first grade and continuing through fifth grade, a small group of facts to be studied in a unit is introduced in the DPP. Through DPP items, students practice the facts and take a short assessment. Beginning in second grade, students use flash cards for additional practice with specific groups of facts. Facts are also practiced in many word problems in the DPP, Home Practice, and individual lessons. These problems allow students to focus on other interesting mathematical ideas as they also gain more fact practice.

Games

A variety of games are included in the curriculum, both in the lessons and in the DPP items of many units. A summary of the games used in a particular grade can be found in the Games section. Once students learn the rules of the games, they should play them periodically in class and at home for homework. Games provide an opportunity to encourage family involvement in the math program. When a game is assigned for homework, a note can be sent home with a place for the family members to sign, affirming that they played the game with their student.

Figure 7: *Playing a game*

Use of Calculators

The relationship between knowing the math facts and the use of calculators is an interesting one. Using a multiplication table or a calculator when necessary to find a fact helps promote familiarity and reinforces the math facts. Students soon figure out that it is quicker and more efficient to know the basic facts than to have to use these tools. The use of calculators also requires excellent estimation skills so that one can easily check for errors in calculator computations. Rather than eliminating the need for fluency with the facts, successful calculator use for solving complex problems depends on fact knowledge.

When to Practice

Practicing small groups of facts often for short periods of time is more effective than practicing many facts less often for long periods of time. For example, practicing 8 to 10 subtraction facts for 5 minutes several times a week is better than practicing all the subtraction facts for half an hour once a week. Good times for practicing the facts for 5 or 10 minutes during the school day include the beginning of the day, the beginning of math class, when students have completed an assignment, when an impending activity is delayed, or when an activity ends earlier than expected. Practicing small groups of facts at home involves parents in the process and frees class time for more interesting mathematics.

Practicing small groups of facts often for short periods of time is more effective than practicing many facts less often for long periods of time.

Assessment

Throughout the curriculum, teachers assess students' knowledge of the facts through observations as they work on activities, labs, and games. In Grades 3–5, students can use their *Facts I Know* charts to record their own progress in learning the facts. This type of self-assessment is very important in helping each student to become responsible for his or her own learning. Students are able to personalize their study of facts and not waste valuable time studying facts they already know.

In the second half of first grade, a sequence of facts assessments is provided in the Daily Practice and Problems. A more comprehensive facts assessment program begins in second grade. This program assesses students' progress in learning the facts, as outlined in the Expectations by Grade Level section of this tutor. As students develop strategies for a given group of facts, short quizzes accompany the practice. Students know which facts will be tested, focus practice in class and at home on those facts, then take the quiz. As they take the quiz, they use one color pencil to write answers before a given time limit, then use another color to complete the problems they need more time to answer. Students then use their *Facts I Know* charts to make a record of those facts they answered quickly, those facts they answered correctly but with less efficient strategies, and those facts they did not know at all. Using this information, students can concentrate their efforts on gaining fluency with those facts they answered correctly, but not quickly. They also know to develop strategies for those facts they could not answer at all. In this way, the number of facts studied at any one time becomes more manageable, practice becomes more meaningful, and the process less intimidating.

Tests of all the facts for any operation have a very limited role. They are used no more than two times a year to show growth over time and should not be given daily or weekly. Since we rarely, if ever, need to recall 100 facts at one time in everyday life, overemphasizing tests of all the facts reinforces the notion that math is nothing more than rote memorization and has no connection to the real world. Quizzes of small numbers of facts are as effective and not as threatening. They give students, parents, and teachers the information needed to continue learning and practicing efficiently. With an assessment approach based on strategies and the use of small groups of facts, students can see mathematics as connected to their own thinking and gain confidence in their mathematical abilities.

Conclusion

Research provides clear indications for curriculum developers and teachers about the design of effective math facts instruction. These recommendations formed the foundation of the *Math Trailblazers* math facts program. Developing strategies for learning the facts (rather than relying on rote memorization), distributing practice of small groups of facts, applying math facts in interesting problems, and using an appropriate assessment program— all are consistent with recommendations from current research. It is an instructional approach that encourages students to make sense of the mathematics they are learning. The resulting program will add efficiency and effectiveness to your students' learning of the math facts.

References

Ashlock, R.B., and C.A. Washbon. "Games: Practice Activities for the Basic Facts." In M.N. Suydam and R.E. Reys (eds.), *Developing Computational Skills: 1978 Yearbook.* National Council of Teachers of Mathematics, Reston, VA, 1978.

Beattie, L.D. "Children's Strategies for Solving Subtraction-Fact Combinations." *Arithmetic Teacher,* 27 (1), pp. 14–15, 1979.

Brownell, W.A., and C.B. Chazal. "The Effects of Premature Drill in Third-Grade Arithmetic." *Journal of Educational Research,* 29 (1), 1935.

Carpenter, T.P., and J.M. Moser. "The Acquisition of Addition and Subtraction Concepts in Grades One through Three." *Journal for Research in Mathematics Education,* 15 (3), pp. 179–202, 1984.

Cook, C.J., and J.A. Dossey. "Basic Fact Thinking Strategies for Multiplication—Revisited." *Journal for Research in Mathematics Education,* 13 (3), pp. 163–171, 1982.

Davis, E.J. "Suggestions for Teaching the Basic Facts of Arithmetic." In M.N. Suydam and R.E. Reys (eds.), *Developing Computational Skills: 1978 Yearbook.* National Council of Teachers of Mathematics, Reston, VA, 1978.

Fuson, K.C. "Teaching Addition, Subtraction, and Place-Value Concepts." In L. Wirszup and R. Streit (eds.), *Proceedings of the UCSMP International Conference on Mathematics Education: Developments in School Mathematics Education Around the World: Applications-Oriented Curricula and Technology-Supported Learning for All Students.* National Council of Teachers of Mathematics, Reston, VA, 1987.

Fuson, K.C., and G.B. Willis. "Subtracting by Counting Up: More Evidence." *Journal for Research in Mathematics Education,* 19 (5), pp. 402–420, 1988.

Fuson, K.C., J.W. Stigler, and K. Bartsch. "Grade Placement of Addition and Subtraction Topics in Japan, Mainland China, the Soviet Union, Taiwan, and the United States." *Journal for Research in Mathematics Education,* 19 (5), pp. 449–456, 1988.

Greer, B. "Multiplication and Division as Models of Situations." In D.A. Grouws (ed.), *Handbook of Research on Mathematics Teaching and Learning: A Project of the National Council of Teachers of Mathematics* (Chapter 13). Macmillan, New York, 1992.

Hiebert, James. "Relationships between Research and the NCTM Standards." *Journal for Research in Mathematics Education,* 30 January, pp. 3–19, 1999.

Isaacs, A.C., and W.M. Carroll. "Strategies for Basic Facts Instruction." *Teaching Children Mathematics,* 5 May, pp. 508–515, 1999.

Kouba, V.L., C.A. Brown, T.P. Carpenter, M.M. Lindquist, E.A. Silver, and J.O. Swafford. "Results of the Fourth NAEP Assessment of Mathematics: Number, Operations, and Word Problems." *Arithmetic Teacher,* 35 (8), pp. 14–19, 1988.

Myers, A.C., and C.A. Thornton. "The Learning-Disabled Child—Learning the Basic Facts." *Arithmetic Teacher,* 25 (3), pp. 46–50, 1977.

National Research Council. *Adding It Up: Helping Children Learn Mathematics.* National Academy Press, Washington, DC, 2001.

Principles and Standards for School Mathematics. National Council of Teachers of Mathematics, Reston, VA, 2000.

Rathmell, E.C. "Using Thinking Strategies to Teach the Basic Facts." In M.N. Suydam and R.E. Reys (eds.), *Developing Computational Skills: 1978 Yearbook.* National Council of Teachers of Mathematics, Reston, VA, 1978.

Rathmell, E.C., and P.R. Trafton. "Whole Number Computation." In J.N. Payne (ed.), *Mathematics for the Young Child.* National Council of Teachers of Mathematics, Reston, VA, 1990.

Swart, W.L. "Some Findings on Conceptual Development of Computational Skills." *Arithmetic Teacher,* 32 (5), pp. 36–38, 1985.

Thornton, C.A. "Doubles Up—Easy!" *Arithmetic Teacher,* 29 (8), p. 20, 1982.

Thornton, C.A. "Emphasizing Thinking Strategies in Basic Fact Instruction." *Journal for Research in Mathematics Education,* 9 (3), pp. 214–227, 1978.

Thornton, C.A. "Solution Strategies: Subtraction Number Facts." *Educational Studies in Mathematics,* 21 (1), pp. 241–263, 1990.

Thornton, C.A. "Strategies for the Basic Facts." In J.N. Payne (ed.), *Mathematics for the Young Child.* National Council of Teachers of Mathematics, Reston, VA, 1990.

Thornton, C.A., and P.J. Smith. "Action Research: Strategies for Learning Subtraction Facts." *Arithmetic Teacher,* 35 (8), pp. 8–12, 1988.

Van de Walle, J. *Elementary and Middle School Mathematics: Teaching Developmentally.* Addison Wesley, New York, 2001.

Portfolios

A portfolio is a purposeful collection of a student's work that provides evidence of the student's skills, understandings, or attitudes. If the portfolio includes work collected over time, then it may also reflect the student's growth.

This tutor outlines reasons portfolios may be useful and provides some guidance for getting started and going further. A bibliography includes suggestions for additional reading.

Why Portfolios?

Portfolios can help teachers:

- better assess student learning;
- foster student autonomy;
- communicate the goals of instruction to students and parents; and
- improve their own teaching.

Student Assessment

Since a portfolio contains direct samples of student work, it may, for certain purposes, be superior to indirect indicators like grades. For example, an actual graph shows a student's skill at graphing better than a grade; and the juxtaposition of two graphs, one from September and the other from January, documents learning over time much more accurately than two grades could ever do.

Portfolios can assess many outcomes that are hard to assess by more conventional methods—communication, reasoning, problem solving, confidence, perseverance, flexibility, and so on. They also can help you learn more about how students think and track the development of that thinking.

Student Autonomy

Portfolios can encourage students to assess their own learning. Students become more self-directed and motivated by examining and reflecting on their own work and the work of their peers.

> *Portfolios can assess many outcomes that are hard to assess by more conventional methods . . . They also can help you learn about how students think and track the development of that thinking.*

Communication

Concrete examples of student work reveal much that is not easily conveyed in grades or comments. Parents and others can see progress and achievement for themselves.

The examples of student work in a portfolio also convey the content and goals of the curriculum in a specific way that complements the generalities of curriculum philosophies and scope and sequence charts. Portfolios focus on the work students actually do, not on ideology or wishful thinking. You can enhance communication between students and their parents, teachers, and peers by having particular examples to discuss.

Portfolios can help establish public norms for mathematics achievement. Focusing assessment on tests and grades communicates a narrow concept of what is valuable in mathematics. When assessment is more broadly based, it promotes a broader vision of mathematics.

Improvement of Instruction

Student portfolios are useful both for making instructional decisions and for evaluating and improving instruction.

Certainly, better understanding of how students think and feel can help you make better decisions about directions for future instruction. But portfolios can also help teachers improve their teaching more generally. Portfolios can facilitate discussions with professional colleagues about different approaches to the same topic; they can reflect the range of instructional opportunities offered; and they can indicate the use of manipulatives, group work, and technology in an implemented curriculum.

Student portfolios might be included in a Teaching Portfolio that a teacher can use for self-evaluation. You can refine your own teaching by collecting and examining several years of student portfolios. Some benefits that portfolios promise for students—collegiality, establishment of public norms, improvement of higher-level skills—may thus become available to teachers.

Getting Started

The beginnings of all things are small.

—Cicero

There is no single right way to do portfolios. The suggestions offered below have worked for others and may work for you, but you should expect to learn by trial and error and to rely on your own judgment. If you have used portfolios for writing or some other subject, then your experience will be invaluable. If you possibly can, work with a colleague as you implement portfolios for the first time.

Starting small, with modest goals, is a good idea. For example, you may organize your portfolio program around one well-defined area that is hard to assess by more traditional methods. For instance, choose one of the following areas as a theme for the portfolios:

- measurement,
- graphing,

There is no single right way to do portfolios.

- drawing pictures and diagrams, or
- communicating solution methods.

Besides starting small, start early so you have a baseline of student attitudes and achievement. Before and after comparisons are useful, but impossible without early samples. All materials in a portfolio must be dated.

A box with a file folder for each child's work is a simple way to start. If the box is easily accessible, then the portfolios are more likely to fit into classroom routines. Anticipate the need for more room as items are added to the portfolios.

What goes in the portfolios is a key decision. Figure 1 shows some kinds of materials you might include in a portfolio, although clearly no real portfolio will have such a wild collection. Figure 2 is a table of contents for a possible third-grade portfolio.

You might aim for balance in the selection of materials: group vs. individual assignments; short problems vs. longer projects; real life vs. purely mathematical problems; on-demand vs. no-deadline tasks; attitude vs. skill vs. concept-oriented work; and so on. The number of pieces should not be so few that there is not enough evidence about important outcomes, nor so many that there is no judgment about what is important or worthwhile. About eight to ten pieces might be enough for a semester.

You must also decide how to pick what to put in the portfolios. We suggest that students select items subject to constraints imposed by the teacher. Constraints might range from requiring particular items, to selecting items that meet certain criteria, to allowing complete freedom of choice by students. The amount of latitude you allow will depend on your class and goals. Younger children, for example, usually need more direction. Putting fewer constraints on what goes in the portfolios may foster student autonomy, but may result in portfolios with few overlapping items so comparisons between students are difficult, or may even yield useless collections of random scraps.

> *The number of pieces should not be so few that there is not enough evidence about important outcomes, nor so many that there is no judgment about what is important or worthwhile. About eight to ten pieces might be enough for a semester.*

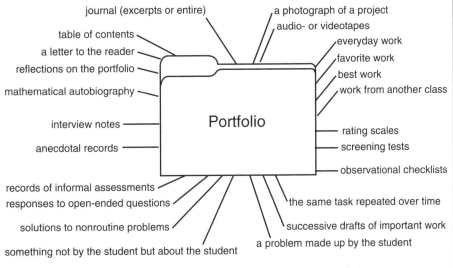

Figure 1: *Possible items for mathematics portfolios*

One way to organize the selection process is to have two folders for each child—a collection folder and the portfolio proper. Then, from time to time (once every several weeks or so), students can harvest the collection folder and add a few select items to the portfolio. At the same time, they can weed the portfolio so the total number of items does not become too large. Students can do this selection in small groups or pairs subject to teacher constraints as described above. Keep remaining items in the collection folder or send them home.

Eight to ten well-chosen and chronologically arranged pieces of work are most useful. You will have specific examples that communicate at parent conference time what your curriculum is and how your students are progressing; you will have a sampling of the products of your instruction so you can critically examine your teaching; and your students will see a cross section of their own work so they can attain greater self-awareness and autonomy. You have accomplished much even if your portfolios are no more than this.

Going Further

There are, however, other things you might want to try as you gain experience with portfolios, especially if you are working with older students. Periodic reviews of the portfolios, writing about the portfolios, and assessing the portfolios are worth considering.

Jarrett's Portfolio • Table of Contents		
Item	**Description**	**Date**
Letter to Reader	My letter tells what my portfolio shows about my math work this semester.	9/22
Journal	A few times a week we write about math in our journals. Mine has 35 pages so far!	
Spinning Differences	I used a spinner to make subtraction problems and then graphed how many times I got each difference.	9/27
The Better "Picker Upper"	I used water to make spots on different kinds of paper towels. Then I counted square cm to find the areas of the spots.	10/25
Joe the Goldfish	Joe needed a raincoat and I figured out how much cloth he would need to make it.	11/1
Palindromes	A palindrome is a number that is the same frontwards and backwards. I used addition to make numbers into palindromes.	11/10
Lemonade Stand	This was the first line graph I ever made.	11/15
Mass vs. Number	I measured the mass of different numbers of marbles. Then I made a line graph and used it to make some predictions.	12/5
Stencilrama	This was my favorite. We made stencils out of index cards and then used the stencils to make designs. We had to figure out how many times we would have to move the stencil to make a border around the bulletin board.	1/15

Figure 2: *Sample third-grade portfolio with an emphasis on graphing*

Portfolio Review

Most teachers will be hard-pressed to find time to meet with individual students to review portfolios. Whole-class discussion and peer consultations, however, can accomplish many of the same goals.

For example, ask students to look through their collection folders for their best graphs to add to their portfolios. First, through whole-class discussion, help students identify characteristics of a good graph. Then in small groups or pairs, students can examine their collections to pick out the best graphs. This opportunity for students to examine one another's work can help establish public norms for excellence.

Portfolio Writing

Asking students to write about the contents of their portfolios encourages reflection and self-assessment. This writing can take a variety of forms.

The most basic writing is a table of contents with the name of each piece, a brief description, and the date it was completed. Students can also include who chose the piece and why, who worked on the piece, and what was learned or liked or hard about the piece.

You might ask students to write a letter to the reader of the portfolio. The letter can identify favorite pieces and explain why they are favorites, or best work, or work that shows the most progress. The letter might show you what the portfolio reveals about the student as a learner of mathematics.

Assessing the Portfolios

You do not have to assess the portfolios. Most likely you already graded the work included in them, and the collection is itself a direct indicator of achievement and attitude. This indicator may be sufficient for your purposes.

Assessing the portfolios, however, can have advantages, especially if you are working with older students. For one, it shows that you care about the portfolios and so communicates to students that they should take them seriously. It can also model processes you want students to apply in peer- and self-assessment of the portfolios.

If you do intend to grade the portfolios, you should make your expectations known to the students in advance. The establishment of such public criteria for excellence, like the TIMS Student Rubrics, will help students know what they should aim for so their work can be better focused. You might concentrate on how well the portfolios are organized—table of contents, correct chronological order, completeness, etc.—or on the quality of the reflective writing about the portfolio. You may encourage a balanced selection of items, documentation of improvement over time, clarity of communication, accuracy of self-assessment, neatness, or something else. As long as your students know the criteria and you have the time to do it, such grading can be useful.

Conclusion

Portfolios will not solve all the problems of mathematics education. And there are some costs for using them. Using portfolios as part of an assessment program will certainly take extra time and can be difficult, especially at first. Getting students to reflect on their own learning is particularly hard. But despite such pitfalls, portfolios offer great promise for improving your teaching and your students' learning. The basic idea is simple: collect, select, reflect.

References

Crowley, Mary L. "Student Mathematics Portfolio: More Than a Display Case." *Mathematics Teacher,* 86 (7), pp. 544–547, 1993.

Kuhs, Therese. "Portfolio Assessment: Making It Work for the First Time." *Mathematics Teacher,* 87 (5), pp. 332–335, 1994.

Lambdin, Diana V., and Vicki L. Walker. "Planning for Classroom Portfolio Assessment." *Arithmetic Teacher,* 41 (6), pp. 318–324, 1994.

Mumme, Judith. *Portfolio Assessment in Mathematics.* (A publication of the California Mathematics Project.) University of California, Santa Barbara, CA, 1990.

Stenmark, Jean Kerr, ed. *Mathematics Assessment: Myths, Models, Good Questions, and Practical Suggestions.* National Council of Teachers of Mathematics, Reston, VA, 1991.

Word Problems

> In fact, word problems should not just be integrated into the mathematics curriculum; they should form the basis of the curriculum.
>
> —CARPENTER, FENNEMA, AND PETERSON, 1987

Although word problems are not the basis of the *Math Trailblazers* curriculum, we do agree that students should confront a wide variety of challenging word problems and exercises. Word problems can highlight applications of the mathematics students are learning. They can introduce, motivate, and develop new mathematics in meaningful contexts.

This tutor provides teachers with a summary of research and background information about word problems. It outlines the theoretical and practical frameworks that underlie the extensive use of word problems in *Math Trailblazers*.

Problem Representations

Problems are presented to us in different ways. Sometimes a problem arises from a real situation; other times we give problems in words, pictures, or symbols. These different ways are sometimes called modes of representation.

Real Situations

Consider this problem: "Jessica and Meri Joy baked 36 cookies. Then, Meri Joy dropped 12 cookies on the floor. How many were left?" Now this problem has a basis in reality: Jessica and Meri Joy are the daughters of two members of the *Math Trailblazers* development team; they really did bake cookies; some cookies really were dropped and spoiled. Note that Meri Joy and Jessica could answer the question simply by counting the cookies that were not dropped.

Such real-life situations are the most concrete level of problem representation. People rarely go wrong when they solve such problems. (Resnick, 1987)

Concrete Model

If, however, some time has passed and the cookies are no longer at hand, we can still ask and answer the question. One way is to get some beans and to pretend they are cookies. To solve the problem, we can count out 36 beans, separate 12, and count how many remain.

This use of beans to represent cookies is one step up the ladder of abstraction: a concrete model represents a real situation. Good evidence exists that even kindergarten students can handle complex problems that are represented by concrete models. (Carpenter, Ansell, Franke, Fennema, and Weisbeck, 1993)

Figure 1: *Twelve of 36 cookies dropped*

Pictures

Another way to approach the problem is via pictures. Each cookie can be represented by a circle. We can solve the problem by drawing 36 circles, crossing out 12, and counting those left.

This sort of pictorial representation is often useful in mathematics and science. Even when the picture does not lead immediately to a solution, it often helps us understand the problem situation and starts us on the road to a solution.

Verbal Representations

Most school problems are stated in words. This is often necessary (How else could we present our cookie problem in this essay?) and builds on a well-developed set of skills your students have—their language skills.

Language is the first and most powerful symbol system we learn. The recent emphasis on discourse and communication in learning is based at least in part on a recognition of the importance of language in human thought.

Symbols

We can also represent Jessica and Meri Joy's cookies in symbols:

$$36 - 12 = \square$$

Such symbolic representations are abstract and powerful. Much of the explosive growth of mathematics in the last 400 years is due to the invention of more efficient symbol systems.

Unfortunately, for too many students, mathematical symbolism is a code they never crack. Such students do not see the marks on paper as meaningful or related to the real world in any way. Instead, they see the marks as part of an arcane game.

When writing number sentences, it is important to use units. Of course, constantly writing the units can be tedious. One compromise is to omit the units in the middle of a sequence of symbolic representations, but be sure to include them at the beginning and again at the end.

> *Even when the picture does not lead immediately to a solution, it often helps us understand the problem situation and starts us on the road to a solution.*

We want students to learn to write, read, and understand mathematical symbolism, especially number sentences. Here, word problems can be particularly useful. The situations in many word problems are straightforward enough that the corresponding number sentences are simple.

Usually, several number sentences are appropriate for each problem. Consider, for example, the following problem: "Janice had 9 stickers. Then her mother gave her some more. Now Janice has 16 stickers. How many stickers did Janice's mother give her?"

An adult might see this as a subtraction problem and write

$$16 - 9 = 7 \tag{a}$$
or
$$16 - 9 = \square \tag{b}$$

These number sentences are in the normal or "canonical" form. That is, the known quantities are on the left-hand side of the equals sign and the unknown or the answer is on the right-hand side.

Many students, however, write something like

$$9 + \square = 16 \tag{c}$$
or
$$9 + 7 = 16 \tag{d}$$

These "non-canonical" forms reflect the students' way of thinking about the problem: Janice had 9 stickers, then she got some more, and now she has 16 stickers. Often a student who writes (c) or (d) will solve the problem by counting on from 9 to 16 rather than by subtracting 9 from 16. We consider these non-canonical number sentences to be as correct as the canonical forms. They can also be more understandable for the students.

Translations between Representations

So we have a hierarchy of levels of representation: real objects, physical models, pictures, words, symbols.

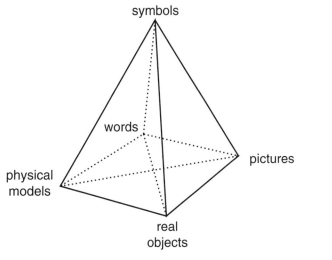

Figure 2: *Modes of representation*

But perhaps "hierarchy of levels" is not quite the right phrase; it may be better to consider that there are a number of different modes of representation, each of which has certain strengths and weaknesses. Recent cognitive theory indicates that the ability to translate from one representation to another is a crucial part of conceptual understanding and problem-solving skill. Connecting symbols with real referents, for example, permits one to understand symbolic manipulations and results in terms of real situations. Earlier, we saw how translating a problem from a real or verbal presentation to a concrete model could yield a solution by an elementary method.

Unfortunately, too much instruction in mathematics focuses exclusively on symbols. While symbolic representations are compact and powerful, they cannot stand alone. Our goal is to have students create mental "two-way streets" between symbols, words, concrete models, pictures, and real situations. Word problems are an excellent vehicle for reaching this goal.

Solving Problems

One view of problem solving is that the most critical step is developing the right representation: when we see the problem in the correct light, then the solution is obvious. Of course, the right representation for me might not be right for you. Accordingly, just as multiple representations should be part of the mathematics curriculum, so should multiple solutions. Estimation and attention to the reasonableness of results must also be part of instruction in problem solving.

Multiple Solutions

Many students think the main thing in mathematics is to get the right answer. Incorrect or partial answers are seen as failures, and re-solving a problem in a different way is considered futile.

On the contrary, students can learn much by solving problems in several ways. When different methods yield the same answer, students gain confidence both in the answer and in the various methods. This can be particularly useful for students learning more abstract and powerful methods: if a more powerful method gives the same answer as a more familiar method, then students are more likely to understand and trust the powerful method.

Students can also see connections within mathematics by comparing the points of view that generate different solutions to a problem. Making such connections is a key goal of the National Council of Teachers of Mathematics *Principles and Standards for School Mathematics* (NCTM, 2000). If students share their solution methods, then not only do they learn new methods from one another, but they also learn to communicate mathematically, another *Principles and Standards* goal.

Even incorrect or partial answers can be useful. Wrong answers are almost always the result of a student's honest attempt to get the problem right. Examining and discussing wrong answers and the procedures that generated them can make students' thinking explicit so that misconceptions can be identified and cleared up.

Sometimes a partial answer is the best we can reasonably hope for. In fact, many practical problems are impossible or prohibitively expensive to solve exactly. In some real situations, a partial answer may be all that is required.

A partial solution may be based on an idea that can be modified or extended to yield a complete solution. If a problem is hard, then making progress towards an answer is perfectly respectable, and certainly far better than giving up.

One way to get the most out of partial solutions is to encourage students to talk and write about the problem even if they cannot solve it. This will also help students stay with difficult problems longer.

Estimation

A common reason for estimating is that an exact answer is not necessary. If we have $5 and want to buy milk, bread, and eggs, a quick estimate will tell us if we have enough money. Sometimes an estimate must serve because an exact answer is impossible or impractical to obtain. The exact number of piano tuners who live in Chicago, for example, can only be estimated.

Another reason to estimate an answer is to verify the accuracy of a result obtained in some other way. This is especially important in our age of computing machines—if we do not have some idea what the answer should be, then we may be at a loss to know whether the answer the machine gives us is reasonable.

A less commonly recognized reason to make an estimate is as a step on the way to an exact answer. As one of our favorite teachers used to say, "Never solve a problem until you know the answer." We think he meant that finding an approximate answer can help in the search for the exact answer. By estimating an answer, we come to understand the problem better.

Learning to estimate builds number sense and encourages students to rely on their common sense rather than on rote procedures. Making a good estimate requires a flexible combination of common sense, experience, rules of thumb, and specific knowledge. Estimation is a high-level skill that takes a long time to develop. Estimation is, accordingly, built into *Math Trailblazers* from the beginning.

Reasonableness of Results

How often have you seen a student's paper with patently absurd answers? Such answers indicate that the student is not working at a meaningful level. Rather some procedures—half-understood, half-remembered—were carried out and something was produced, but the relationship of that product to the problem at hand is far from clear. No connection exists in the student's mind between the real situation and the symbolic manipulations.

Looking back when an answer is obtained, mapping the result of symbolic or other manipulations back onto the original problem statement, is a crucial part of the problem-solving process. George Polya, in his famous book *How to Solve It* (1957), included looking back as one of four basic steps in solving a problem. (Polya's other steps are to understand the problem; to make a plan to solve the problem; and to carry out the plan.)

When students look back at a solution, they should assess whether it is reasonable and correct. They can also look for ways to improve the solution, simplify it, or generalize it. By comparing their solution to other solutions, they can obtain further evidence of correctness and they have an opportunity to make connections between different approaches.

Addition and Subtraction Problem Types

Children typically use many varied methods to solve word problems. This, in part, relates to the fact that there is an underlying variety of problem types. Educational researchers in the last 20 years or so have explored the different problem types extensively. Several different examples are discussed here. Additional discussion about the methods children use to solve problems are in the TIMS Tutor: *Math Facts*.

Students should experience solving many different types of word problems. It is important to note, however, that in discussing the different problem types, we are not suggesting a new level of material for children to learn, i.e., we do not expect nor want children to have to learn about the different types of problems as a study in and of itself. Rather, we discuss the diversity in problem types so teachers recognize that this variety exists and subsequently are better prepared to present their students with a rich and varied collection of word problems.

Thomas Carpenter and his colleagues (Carpenter, Fennema, and Peterson, 1987; Carpenter, Carey, and Kouba, 1990; Carpenter, et al., 1999) have devised a classification scheme for problems that most adults would solve by simple addition or subtraction. They identify four general types of situations that give rise to 11 different kinds of addition or subtraction problems. (Other researchers have devised similar schemes. See, for example, Riley, Greeno, and Heller, 1983, and Rathmell and Huinker, 1989.)

Join Situations

Carpenter begins with "join" situations. Here, something is joined to a beginning quantity so a new quantity results. We think of these situations like this:

$$start + change = result$$

If the result is unknown, then we have an addition situation. Otherwise, we have a subtraction situation. Children often have more difficulty with problems in which the start is unknown than those in which the change is unknown.

Join/Result Unknown
Erick had 8 action figures. Then his father gave him 3 new ones. How many does he have now?

Join/Change Unknown
Janice had 9 stickers. Then her mother gave her some more. Now Janice has 16 stickers. How many stickers did Janice's mother give her?

Join/Start Unknown
Maria had some pennies. Then she found 3 more. Now she has 12 pennies. How many pennies did Maria have at first?

Separate Situations

Adults most often think of these situations as take-away problems:

$$\text{start} - \text{change} = \text{result}$$

If the result or change is unknown, then we have a subtraction (or take-away) situation. Otherwise, we have an addition situation.

Separate/Result Unknown
Thomas had 8 cookies. Then he ate 6. How many cookies does he have left?

Separate/Change Unknown
Leah had 12 dolls. She gave some of her dolls away. Then she had 7 dolls left. How many dolls did Leah give away?

Separate/Start Unknown
Michael had some marbles. He lost 5 of his marbles. Then he had 7 marbles. How many marbles did Michael have at first?

Part-Whole Situations

Carpenter's third category is part-whole. Here, a single whole is broken into two parts:

$$\text{part} + \text{part} = \text{whole}$$

This is similar to the join situation. The difference is that part-whole situations are static, the two parts coexisting from the beginning, whereas in join situations, two things are put together to form a new whole.

If the whole is unknown in a part-whole situation, then we have an addition situation. Otherwise, we have a subtraction situation.

Part-Whole/Whole Unknown
Ian has some action figures. He has 8 good guys and 3 bad guys. How many action figures does Ian have altogether?

Part-Whole/Part Unknown
There are 14 children who live in Clayton's building. Five of the children are boys. How many girls live in Clayton's building?

Compare Situations

Carpenter's last category is "compare." Here, two independent quantities are being compared:

$$q_1 - q_2 = \text{difference}$$

If the difference or q_2 is unknown, then we subtract. If q_1 is unknown, we add.

Compare/Difference Unknown
Samantha has $14. Kristin has $5. How much more money does Samantha have?

Compare/Q₂ Unknown
Jason has 13 crayons. Angela has 6 fewer than Jason. How many crayons does Angela have?

Compare/Q_1 Unknown

Lamar has some markers. Robin has 15 markers. Robin has 7 fewer markers than Lamar. How many markers does Lamar have?

Compare problems seem to be the hardest for children to solve. The other three types—join, separate, and part-whole—all involve a whole with parts in situations that are either static or dynamic. In compare problems, on the other hand, there is no whole. Rather, there are two independent quantities and a difference between them.

Need for Diversity in Problem Types

Traditionally, just two of these 11 kinds of problems have dominated American elementary mathematics textbooks, a dominance that contrasts sharply with customary practice abroad (Stigler, Fuson, Ham, & Kim, 1986; Fuson, Stigler, & Bartsch, 1988). These favored problem types, moreover, are the easiest to solve. Most of the subtraction problems are take-away situations (separate/result unknown). Most of the addition problems are join/result unknown. By presenting such a limited variety of problems, these texts give students a wrong impression about what addition and subtraction are. Carpenter's four situations—join, separate, part-whole, and compare—and the various types of problems reflect a much wider conception of addition and subtraction. In *Math Trailblazers,* we present this full range of addition and subtraction problems beginning in the earliest grades.

Diversity in Strategies

The description of the various problem types identified addition and subtraction situations. However, students may approach the problems in different ways. For example, while adults may immediately subtract when they encounter a take-away situation (8 cookies − 6 cookies = 2 cookies) some children may choose to use an addition strategy and count up. (Thomas ate 6 cookies and he has 2 left. Two more than 6 is 8 cookies.) Both are valid strategies.

Types of Multiplication and Division Problems

Researchers who have studied multiplication and division have identified different types of multiplication and division problems. While students do not need to be able to identify these different types of problems by name, it is important that they encounter and solve them. The different types of multiplication and division problems are outlined below.

Problems Involving a Number of Equivalent Sets

These sets can be groups of objects, arrays, or jumps on the number line. An example: Ask a class of 20 students to stand in a group. Instruct them to break into teams of four.

Using this situation, three different questions emerge. One question is interpreted as a multiplication problem, the other two as division problems.

The Unknown Is the Total Number in All the Groups

If there are 5 teams with 4 members on each team, how many players are there in all? There are two known factors and a missing product. Using established knowledge, students often interpret this correctly as a repeated addition problem (4 + 4 + 4 + 4 + 4 = 20). Through classroom experiences with many such problems, they can connect the repeated addition sentence to a multiplication sentence (5 × 4 = 20).

The Unknown Is the Number of Groups

Twenty members of a class are divided into teams of four members each. How many teams are there? The problem gives the total number in all the groups and the measure or size of each group. This aspect of division is called *measurement division.*

The Unknown Is the Number in Each Group

Twenty members of a class are divided equally into five teams. How many students are on each team? The problem gives the total number of students and the number of partitions or groups. This aspect of division is known as *partitive division.*

Jumps on a number line and arrays provide additional experience with the multiplication and division of equivalent sets. Successive jumps of equal size on a number line provide a model for multiplication as repeated addition and division as repeated subtraction. In *Math Trailblazers,* we model this situation using mythical creatures called "mathhoppers." For example, a +2 mathhopper starts at 0 and hops 4 times. On what number will it land? (8)

An array is a group of objects arranged in rows and columns. For example, a candy box that contains 5 rows with 6 pieces in each row is a 5 × 6 array. One virtue of the array model is that it makes it very clear that 5 × 6 = 6 × 5. You can rotate the box 90 degrees to form a 6 × 5 array. Another advantage is that it creates a visual image for both multiplication and division problems.

Problems Involving Scale Factors

This type of problem is often found in TIMS Laboratory Investigations. For example, after students have rolled different cars down a ramp, they might be asked if one car rolled three times as far as another. Similarly, when finding the mass of objects, they may be asked if the mass of one object is one-half the mass of another object.

A Cartesian Product

This problem involves two sets of objects (such as shirts and pants) that must be joined into pairs (shirt-and-pant sets). The answer for this type of problem then becomes the number of unique pairs that students can form from these two sets. While this type of problem is difficult for young children, they are able to solve it using manipulatives and diagrams.

Experiences with many types of problems should provide a strong conceptual foundation not only for multiplication and division, but for fractions, ratios, and proportional reasoning as well.

Problem Contexts

Most word problems in *Math Trailblazers* are embedded in a larger context; this is often an advantage since situational problems are more meaningful to students than abstract problems. Sometimes, however, providing a context is constraining or distracting. Also, problems may come to us without context; often, we have to provide extra information to make sense of a problem. Accordingly, in an attempt to provide a balance between problems embedded in situations and problems that are self-contained, we often provide free-standing word problems.

Teaching Word Problems

A variety of approaches to teaching word problems can be useful and stimulating. Here are several:

Whole Class, Then Small Groups

First, present a sample problem to your whole class. Discuss the problem and ask students to estimate the answer. Also ask students to explain how they made their estimates. Neither the estimates nor the explanations are likely to be very good, but this is only the beginning.

Next, ask students to solve the problem in groups of two or three students. Tell them you want (1) an answer for the problem, (2) an explanation of how they obtained the answer, and (3) a number sentence for the problem.

Require students who need help to seek it first from other students in their groups. Clearly, this is beneficial for the students who need the help, but those who give the help also benefit since they must make explicit what they may understand only implicitly. You will also be freed up since your students will be helping one another instead of depending so much on you.

As students work, move among the groups, listening to the various strategies. Use your judgment about what questions to ask and how much help to give, but try to restrain yourself. It is often better if students struggle on their own and find a solution themselves.

When the groups have answers, reconvene the whole class and ask students to explain their solutions and number sentences for the problem. Be sure they assess the reasonableness and correctness of their results. During these discussions, emphasize that every student is responsible for understanding his or her group's solution. One way to accomplish this is to call on random students to explain each group's work.

Encourage students to solve problems in more than one way by accepting only novel solutions during class discussions. This will motivate students to search for multiple solutions so they can contribute to the class discussion.

Small Groups, Then Whole Class

As your students gain experience, you can abbreviate or eliminate the whole-class introduction to the problem. Again, a whole-class discussion of solutions is appropriate.

Individual Work, Then Small Groups

Another approach is for students to work individually first and then to come together in pairs or small groups to compare solutions. Then, the small-group solutions can be shared with other groups during a class discussion.

Other Suggestions

Find some word problems appropriate for homework or for individual seatwork. Other problems may be so hard that no student is able to solve them; use such problems for whole-class investigations. You may use certain problems to introduce new mathematics like multiplication and division. Use an interesting problem as an "opener" when students arrive or when math class begins.

TIMS Tips

- If students cannot solve a problem, ask them to describe the problem and to restate it in their own words or ask them to draw a picture. This may lead to a better understanding of the problem and then to a solution.
- Do only a few problems at a time. Distributed practice will be more effective than bunched practice.
- Vary the format: individual, small group, whole class, homework.
- Be sure to discuss multiple solution strategies. Compare and contrast strategies, and point out advantages of each, but accept all correct strategies.
- Discuss several number sentences for each problem. Ask students to explain how a given number sentence fits the problem situation.
- Ask students to explain why their answers are reasonable.
- Provide manipulatives and calculators to each group. Just having them available in the room may not be enough—these resources should be immediately at hand.

Conclusion

As your students work word problems and share solutions, they will be applying mathematics they already know and learning new mathematics. Word problems deserve a prominent place in your mathematics lessons.

References

Carpenter, T.P., E. Fennema, M.L. Franke, L. Levi, and S.E. Empson. *Children's Mathematics: Cognitively Guided Instruction.* Heinemann, Westport, CT, 1999.

Carpenter, T.P., E. Fennema, and P. Peterson. "Cognitively Guided Instruction: The Application of Cognitive and Instructional Science to Mathematics Curriculum Development." In *Developments in School Mathematics Education Around the World,* I. Wirszup and R. Streit, eds. National Council of Teachers of Mathematics, Reston, VA, 1987.

Carpenter, T.P., D. Carey, and V. Kouba. "A Problem-Solving Approach to the Operations." In *Mathematics for the Young Child,* J.N. Payne, ed. National Council of Teachers of Mathematics, Reston, VA, 1990.

Carpenter, T.P., E. Ansell, M.L. Franke, E. Fennema, and L. Weisbeck. "Models of Problem Solving: A Study of Fourth Grade Children's Problem-Solving Processes." *Journal for Research in Mathematics Education,* 24 (5), pp. 428–441, 1993.

Fuson, K.C., J.W. Stigler, and K. Bartsch. "Grade Placement of Addition and Subtraction Topics in Japan, Mainland China, the Soviet Union, Taiwan, and the United States." *Journal for Research in Mathematics Education,* 19 (5), pp. 449–456, 1988.

National Council of Teachers of Mathematics. *Principles and Standards for School Mathematics.* National Council of Teachers of Mathematics, Reston, VA, 2000.

Polya, G. *How to Solve It.* Princeton University Press, Princeton, NJ, 1957.

Rathmell, E.C., and D.M. Huinker. "Using Part-Whole Language to Help Children Represent and Solve Word Problems." In *New Directions for Elementary School Mathematics,* P.R. Trafton, ed. National Council of Teachers of Mathematics, Reston, VA, 1989.

Resnick, L.B. "Presidential Address: Learning In School and Out." *Educational Researcher,* 16 (9), pp. 13–20, 1987.

Riley, M.S., J.G. Greeno, and J.I. Heller. "Development of Children's Problem-Solving Ability in Arithmetic." In *The Development of Mathematical Thinking,* H.P. Ginsburg, ed. Academic Press, New York, 1983.

Stigler, J.W., K.C. Fuson, M. Ham, and M.S. Kim. "An Analysis of Addition and Subtraction Word Problems in American and Soviet Elementary Mathematics Textbooks." *Cognition and Instruction,* 3 (3), pp. 153–171, 1986.

The TIMS Laboratory Method

Math Trailblazers is a comprehensive mathematics program that incorporates many important scientific ideas. Scientific concepts often provide contexts for developing and practicing math concepts and skills. The tools and processes of science are integral to mathematical problem solving throughout the curriculum.

This tutor expands upon the *Math Trailblazers* connection with science. It outlines the Teaching Integrated Math and Science (TIMS) Project's view of science and describes the TIMS Laboratory Method, a version of the scientific method. This method forms a framework throughout the curriculum for students to explore science in much the way scientists work.

The TIMS View of Science

Traditionally, school science has focused on the results of science. Students learn about parts of the body, types of rocks, the solar system, evolution, and so on. Knowing basic facts of science is seen as part of being educated, today more than ever. However, the facts of science, important and interesting as they are, do not alone comprise a comprehensive and balanced science curriculum.

The great educator and philosopher John Dewey expressed this idea some 100 years ago. In 1910, he wrote:

> *At times, it seems as if the educational availability of science were breaking down because of its sheer mass. There is at once so much of science and so many sciences that educators oscillate, helpless, between arbitrary selection and teaching a little of everything.*
>
> *Visit schools where they have taken nature study conscientiously. This school moves with zealous bustle from leaves to flowers, from flowers to minerals, from minerals to stars, from stars to the raw materials of industry, thence back to leaves and stones.*
>
> *Thus, . . . science teaching has suffered because science has been so frequently presented just as so much ready-made knowledge, so much subject-matter of fact and law, rather than as the effective method of inquiry into any subject-matter.*

Surely if there is any knowledge which is of most worth it is knowledge of the ways by which anything is entitled to be called knowledge instead of being mere opinion or guess-work or dogma.

Such knowledge ... is not information, but a mode of intelligent practise, an habitual disposition of mind.

In 1996, the National Research Council (NRC) published the *National Science Education Standards* for K–12 science education. Among the many recommendations of the NRC document is a direction for decreased emphasis on teaching scientific facts and information, and increased emphasis on teaching for understanding of scientific concepts and developing abilities of inquiry. The NRC *Standards* state:

Emphasizing active science learning means shifting away from teachers presenting information and covering science topics. The perceived need to include all the topics, vocabulary, and information in textbooks is in direct conflict with the central goal of having students learn scientific knowledge with understanding.

These points of view underlie the TIMS approach to science. If we were to describe the TIMS approach in the most concise way possible, we would choose two words, *variable* and *experiment*. The essence of modern science, as it is practiced by scientists, is to understand the relationships among variables. Out of the great sea of variables we have selected those that we feel are fundamental to the understanding of all areas of science, namely: length, area, volume, mass, and time. These variables might be considered the fundamental vocabulary of science. They are integral to the everyday work of biologists, chemists, physicists, astronomers, and earth scientists. The more a child explores these variables, the greater will be his or her command of scientific language and the more complete will be his or her ability to take up the adventure of science.

> *If we were to describe the TIMS approach in the most concise way possible, we would choose two words, variable and experiment.*

We have therefore made these variables the focus of experiments and activities in Grades K through 5 of *Math Trailblazers*. Explorations in kindergarten are conceptual in nature. As the curriculum progresses through the grades, students revisit the variables many times in increasingly more sophisticated ways. In Grade 5, students are able to move on to compound variables such as density and velocity, which involve two of the basic variables. For example, density involves both mass and volume while velocity involves both length and time. To understand these compound variables, it is important that students are first familiar with the more basic variables. Through repeated investigation of the variables in different contexts, fundamental science concepts and skills become generalized.

Variables in Scientific Experiments

A **variable** is a quantity that may assume any one of a set of values. The variable is the heart and soul of science because the variable is to scientific investigation what the word is to language—its foundation and the basis of its structure. All experiments center around at least two variables, and the ability to measure these variables satisfactorily will determine the success or failure of the experiment.

Variables and Values

Variables fall into two broad categories: categorical and numerical. Would you say that a person's hair color is a categorical or a numerical variable? Would you say that a person's height is a categorical or numerical variable? A **numerical variable** is one that may assume a numerical set of values. In contrast, a **categorical variable** is one that does not assume numerical values.

Color, then, which can take on values such as red, blue, or yellow, is a categorical variable. Other categorical variables are shape, kind of object, and type of material the object is made of. In each case, you have the broad classification, the variable, and then the values the variable can assume.

The simplest kind of numerical variable is the number of objects in a set. For example, if we were studying the number of students who came to class each day, the variable would be "Number of Students," and the possible values of the variable would be 0 students, 1 student, 2 students, etc. A second category of numerical variable involves measurement. The basic measurement variables stressed in *Math Trailblazers* are length, area, volume, mass, and time. The values for these variables are what we measure during the course of an experiment. For example, if we are investigating the variable length, the values might be the number of meters, centimeters, millimeters, or other appropriate unit of length. When the variable is area, the values might be the number of square centimeters. Or if volume is the variable, the value might be the number of cubic centimeters, and so on. The variable is the broad classification; the **values** for the variable describe what we are counting or measuring for that variable.

One point in studying variables that will take repeated practice for your students to master is the regular use of units of measure. In science, we never deal with numbers without understanding what their units are. For example, say that we tell you that Mary dropped a ball from a height of 30. A question your students will learn to ask is, "Thirty what?" Was it 30 centimeters, 30 feet, or 30 miles? The name after the number 30 is what we call the unit of measure, and every variable has a set of them. $5 + 4 = 9$ can be meaningless unless we know 5 of what. 5 apples + 4 apples = 9 apples, but 5 apples + 4 pears does not equal either 9 apples or 9 pears. The sum is equal to 9 pieces of fruit. Invariably, children will give you the numerical value of the variable and leave off its unit. Learning to use units is merely a matter of discipline; that is, using them correctly so often that you feel uncomfortable when you either forget them or use them incorrectly. Developing this discipline in your students will help them later in their schooling as they examine more complicated scientific concepts.

Manipulated and Responding Variables in Controlled Experiments

In an experiment, a scientist tries to find a relationship between two variables. Where possible, the experimenter chooses ahead of time the values of one of the variables. This variable is called the **manipulated variable.** The values of the second variable are determined by the results of the experiment—something that the experimenter does not know ahead of time. We shall call the variable whose values result from the experiment, the **responding variable.**

For example, consider the following situation from a fourth-grade experiment, *The Bouncing Ball.* In this experiment, children study how high a ball bounces. They drop a ball from various heights and measure how high it bounces. As the experimenters, they decide what drop heights they want to use in the experiment, say 40 cm, 80 cm, and 120 cm. The drop height is the manipulated variable. But the height to which the ball bounces can only be determined after you drop the ball. It is not known ahead of time. So, the bounce height is the responding variable.

Or, say you fill a plastic jar with different-colored blocks and choose red, yellow, and blue as the colors of your blocks. You then ask a child to reach in and pull out as many pieces as he or she can in one grab, sort the blocks by color, and count them. Color is the manipulated variable in this experiment. The number of each color that he or she pulls out is the responding variable. You choose the values of the colors that go in but you have no choice over the number of each color that comes out.

Beginning in the first grade of *Math Trailblazers,* the experimental variables are identified in all laboratory experiments. This is an essential part of conducting any scientific experiment. It is not until fourth grade, however, that we introduce the formal terms "manipulated" and "responding."

Note that in *Math Trailblazers,* we have elected to use the terms "manipulated" and "responding" to describe experimental variables. We have found manipulated and responding to be less abstract for children (and adults) and easier to understand than the more commonly used terms for variables, "independent" and "dependent."

Fixed Variables in Controlled Experiments

Experiments often have more than two variables. In an ideal experiment, more easily realized in the laboratory than in the real world, a scientist focuses on only two variables—the ones we have called manipulated and responding—and strives to hold all others constant. If too many variables change simultaneously in an experiment, obtaining meaningful results can be difficult or impossible.

Consider a laboratory experiment done in second grade, *Rolling Along in Centimeters.* Students roll different kinds of cars down a ramp and use metersticks to measure the distance each car rolls. Here, the "type of car" is the manipulated variable and the distance each car rolls is the responding variable. The height of the ramp, the starting line, the floor onto which the cars roll, and the method for releasing the car are all held constant each time a car is rolled down the ramp. We refer to these as the **fixed variables** (or controlled variables) in the experiment. Children intuitively understand this as "keeping things fair" while the data are collected during the course of the experiment.

In many situations, some variables in an experiment are hidden; that is, they are not immediately obvious, although changing them will greatly alter the results of your experiment. Consider an experiment in which you collect data on the kinds of pets owned by each child in the classroom. The kind of pet is the manipulated variable and the number of each kind of pet is the

In an ideal experiment, more easily realized in the laboratory than in the real world, a scientist focuses on only two variables—the ones we have called manipulated and responding—and strives to hold all others constant. If too many variables change simultaneously in an experiment, obtaining meaningful results can be difficult or impossible.

responding variable. If you think about it, you can see that your results depend on where the pet owners live—in a high rise or a single-family house, in the city or a farm community, and even in which country. Thus the variable, "location," can drastically change the results.

One of the reasons cancer research is so difficult is because there are so many variables which are either difficult or impossible to control (such as environmental factors, personality traits, multitudinous viruses) that it is hard to pinpoint the variables that might be the cause of cancer. It is the complexity of biological and sociological systems that makes doing repeatable experiments in these areas very difficult.

Nonetheless, children can learn how to deal with simple physical systems where three or four variables are present. They should learn how to recognize the different variables involved and understand the importance of controlling all but two—the manipulated and the responding variable.

The TIMS Laboratory Method

Throughout *Math Trailblazers,* children carry out quantitative investigations in which they explore the relationships between variables. Each investigation is carried out with the same general format, which we call the TIMS Laboratory Method. One may call this our version of the scientific method. There are four phases: beginning the investigation and drawing the picture, collecting and organizing the data, graphing the data, and analyzing the experimental results. We discuss these four phases below, illustrating our discussion with references to *The Bouncing Ball* experiment described above and to *Marshmallows and Containers,* a second-grade experiment in which children study the number of marshmallows that fit into different-sized jars.

Phase 1: Beginning the Investigation and Drawing the Picture

Most investigations begin with a question. The question does not have to be momentous, but it must be meaningful to children. If the question connects in some authentic way with their experience, children will need no flashy inducements to want to find the answer. This is illustrated in the following classroom anecdote involving *Marshmallows and Containers.*

> *As class begins, students sit together in groups of three. Each group has three different containers: a margarine tub, a 100 cc graduated cylinder, and a small paper cup. The teacher shows the class a bag of miniature marshmallows and asks, "Which container will hold the most marshmallows? Why do you think so?"*

> *The teacher encourages the groups to discuss their predictions and explanations and to record their ideas in their journals. When the groups report to the class, many groups think that the graduated cylinder will hold the most because it is the tallest. One boy explains that he thinks the cylinder holds the most because even if he could stretch the plastic in the bowl so it was tall like the cylinder, it still would not be as tall and would not hold as much. Other groups choose the tub because it is fatter than the other containers.*

The teacher then asks, "How could you find out which container holds the most marshmallows?" This question leads naturally to an experiment: The students will fill each of the containers with marshmallows, count them, and record the numbers in a data table.

Once a suitable question has been posed—and posing such questions is far from trivial—then you must identify variables related to the question. *Marshmallows and Containers* examines the kind of container and the number of marshmallows. The size of the marshmallows and the method for packing the marshmallows into the jars is held fixed. In *The Bouncing Ball,* students measure the drop heights and bounce heights of a ball, while holding fixed the type of ball, the floor on which the ball is dropped, and the method for dropping the ball.

Through class discussion, the original question has been refined into a precise query about the relationship between two variables. These variables become defined well enough so children know how to gather information about them. Drawing a picture is an excellent way to summarize and communicate this beginning phase, and also to plan what is to come.

Figure 1: *Picture for* Marshmallows and Containers

Scientists often make sketches in experimental situations. In the TIMS Laboratory Method, drawing pictures helps children understand and organize what they are to do. A sketch gives the child time to think, to see relationships between variables, to place diverse relationships in a compact form, and to "explain" the experiment or problem to someone at a glance. Pictures also help teachers assess whether students are ready to proceed. Figure 1 shows one student's picture for

Figure 2: *Picture for* The Bouncing Ball

Marshmallows and Containers. The picture indicates the student's understanding of the experimental variables and the procedure. Note that the student is using an egg carton to make groups of 10 when counting marshmallows. Figure 2 shows a picture from *Bouncing Ball,* indicating the manipulated and responding variables (the drop height and the bounce height) and the procedure for the experiment. The students who drew these pictures are ready to go on to the next step, gathering data.

> *Scientists often make sketches in experimental situations. In the TIMS Laboratory Method, drawing pictures helps children understand and organize what they are to do. A sketch gives the child time to think, to see relationships between variables, to place diverse relationships in a compact form, and to "explain" the experiment or problem to someone at a glance.*

Phase 2: Collecting and Organizing the Data

In Phase 2 of the TIMS Laboratory Method, children gather the data and organize it in a table. To illustrate, we return to our classroom anecdote involving *Marshmallows and Containers:*

> On the next day, the children use their pictures to review the experiment before beginning the data collection. Each group receives a two-column data table, fills in the column headings, and writes the names (or draws pictures) of the containers in the first column. The teacher emphasizes the need for accuracy in counting, and the children discuss various methods for grouping and counting the marshmallows. As students begin to collect the data, the teacher circulates among the groups, coaching and assessing.

> After the children complete their data tables (Figure 3), the teacher leads a discussion in which the groups compare their results. This discussion centers on whether the groups' results are reasonable or not. Most groups report about 130 marshmallows in the graduated cylinder. Students agree that numbers close to 130, but not exactly 130, are acceptable. Based on this discussion, a group that had recorded only 110 marshmallows for the cylinder decides to refill the cylinder and count again.

Container	**N** Number of _Marshmellow_ ᵒⁿᵈˢ
Graduated cylinder	133
Cup	121
bowl	181

Figure 3: *Data table from* Marshmallows and Containers

Tennis Ball

D Drop Height in cm	**B** Bounce Height in cm			
	Trial 1	Trial 2	Trial 3	Average
40	27	22	21	22
80	50	40	43	43
120	72	62	68	68

Figure 4: *Data table from* The Bouncing Ball

Figure 3 shows a student's data table for *Marshmallows and Containers.* Figure 4 is a student's data table from *The Bouncing Ball.* The name of a variable, including units if appropriate, heads each column.

When creating data tables, scientists and mathematicians generally place the manipulated variable in the left column and the responding variable in the right column. Since the experimenter chooses values for the manipulated variable before the experiment begins, the first column of the data table can be filled out prior to the experiment. Values of the responding variable can only be filled in as the experiment is conducted.

Data tables are tools for organizing data. In a real laboratory experiment, scientists have to record the data clearly and correctly the first time, during the experiment. It has to be recorded in such a way that not only you can read it, but also your colleagues and even a stranger. A story is told about the Nobel Prize-winner James Watson, who helped discover DNA. His teacher at Indiana University was asked if he suspected that Watson might go on to great things when he graduated. Yes, he answered. Watson would go far. Why? The teacher replied that although Watson did not take great care of his personal appearance, and his desk was a mess, he kept a neat notebook. That is a lesson that even young children can understand.

The data table is also useful in controlling error and identifying patterns. Children can detect blunders when a measurement deviates too much from established patterns (as in the *Marshmallows and Containers* anecdote above), and they can control inevitable measurement error by averaging several trials.

Note that in *The Bouncing Ball* lab, the students performed three trials for each measurement. In other words, to answer the question of how high does the ball bounce when dropped from 40 centimeters, they dropped the ball three times from 40 centimeters and recorded the bounce height, in this case (Figure 4), 27, 22, and 21 centimeters. The students then take the average (they used the median for the average) bounce height for their value of the bounce height. This is done to minimize the effect of measurement and experimental error on the experiment. (See the TIMS Tutors: *Averages* and *Estimation, Accuracy, and Error.*)

Phase 3: Graphing the Data

Graphing is the heart of scientific analysis. Graphs are powerful communication tools that create a picture of the data and "tell its story." They allow you to compare, predict, and infer. If there is a pattern in the relationship between the variables, you are more likely to see it clearly in a graph. Being able to read a graph and produce a graph from data should be a major goal of school science. Graphing cuts across many disciplines: biology, chemistry, sociology, and economics. Students using *Math Trailblazers* work extensively with graphs from kindergarten on.

Bar Graphs vs. Point Graphs

In *Math Trailblazers,* data are mostly graphed as either a bar graph or a point graph; these two types of graphs will thus be the focus of our discussion in this section. Since a graph is a visual representation of the relationship between variables, the type of graph used depends upon the types of variables studied in the experiment.

When both variables are numerical, a point graph is often (though not always) appropriate. In *The Bouncing Ball,* for example, both variables—the drop height and the bounce height—are numerical. Since the values for these variables are numbers and are not discrete—that is, there are values between the data points that make sense, such as 52.5 cm—it is possible to use points and lines on the graph instead of bars to represent the data. Drawing a line or a curve makes sense only when the variables are numerical and there is a pattern in the data. Figure 5 shows a student's graph from *The Bouncing Ball.*

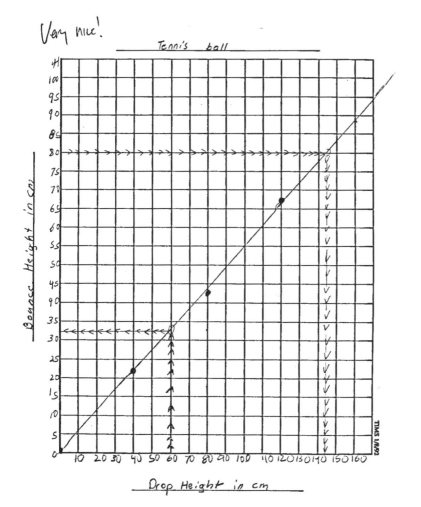

Figure 5: *Point graph from* The Bouncing Ball *showing best-fit lines, interpolation, and extrapolation*

Point graphs are introduced in *Math Trailblazers* in third grade and are used to represent a variety of different mathematical situations as well as to display data from laboratory experiments.

A bar graph is usually best when one of the variables is categorical (qualitative). In *Marshmallows and Containers,* for example, the type of container is a categorical variable and the number of marshmallows is numerical. Figure 6 shows the graph for *Marshmallows and Containers.* There are no values that make sense between the types of containers. Thus it does not make sense to connect them on the graph with a line. A bar graph, therefore, is appropriate for these kinds of situations.

A bar graph is usually best when one of the variables is categorical (qualitative).

Although point graphs are most often used when both experimental variables are numerical, that is not always the case. For example, in the experiment *First Names* from third grade, students collect data about the number of letters in the first names of classmates. The two primary variables in this experiment are the number of letters (the manipulated variable) and the number of names (the responding variable). A graph for the experiment is shown in Figure 7. While both variables in this experiment are numerical, they are also discrete—that is, it is not meaningful to speak of $6\frac{1}{2}$ letters in a name or $3\frac{1}{4}$ people who have that number of letters in their names. Thus, we can see why a point graph, in which values between the data points are represented, would not be appropriate in this case. Instead, the data is best represented on a bar graph.

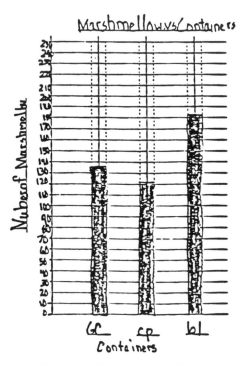

Figure 6: *Bar graph from* Marshmallows and Containers

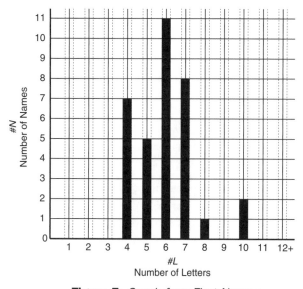

Figure 7: *Graph from* First Names

Labeling the Axes

With most types of data, it is conventional in science to place the manipulated variable along the horizontal axis and the responding variable along the vertical axis. The horizontal axis is labeled with a word or letter describing the manipulated variable and the vertical axis with a word or letter describing the responding variable. In Figure 7, for example, the horizontal axis—the manipulated variable—is labeled "#*L,* Number of Letters" and the vertical axis—the responding variable—is labeled "#*N,* Number of Names."

Once the axes are in place, the children can label the axes with the values for each variable. In the case of the *Marshmallows and Containers* in Figure 6, the student wrote in labels to represent the different kinds of containers.

With most types of data, it is conventional in science to place the manipulated variable along the horizontal axis and the responding variable along the vertical axis.

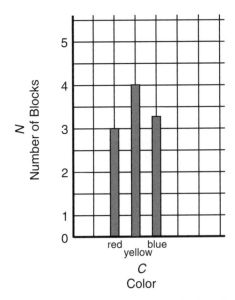

Figure 8: *Common errors in labeling the axes*

A common error in labeling axes is illustrated in Figure 8. This graph shows irregular spacing on both axes. The vertical axis in Figure 8 is incorrect with one space between 0 and 1 and two spaces between the other numbers. Technically, the categorical variables displayed on the horizontal axis do not have to be equally spaced, but it is a good idea to get your students into the habit of spacing their bars across the axis in regularly spaced intervals. This is because when dealing with numerical data, the values *must* be equally spaced.

Scaling the axes for numerical data requires an analysis of the range of the data and comparing it with the number of available intervals on your particular graph paper. Scaling by ones, two, fives, tens, or other numbers might be appropriate depending on the data for a particular experiment. What is essential, however, is that the intervals are all equal along a given axis. Students will learn that it is best to determine the appropriate interval ahead of time. Otherwise they will end up plotting their initial data points and later discovering that other points will not fit on the graph.

In most cases, the scale on the horizontal axis is independent of the scale on the vertical axis. Students should number the axes in ways that make sense for the data. For example, the horizontal axis in *The Bouncing Ball* graph

(Figure 5) is scaled by tens but the vertical axis is scaled by fives. One exception to this is when making scale maps. Here, using different scales for the different axes would create a distorted image and make it difficult to find distances on the map.

As scientists do, students using the TIMS Laboratory Investigations often use their graphs to make predictions about physical phenomena. When making point graphs, therefore, we often encourage students to scale their axes to allow room for extrapolation. (See the section below entitled *Predictions from Point Graphs: Interpolation and Extrapolation* for information about extrapolation.)

Bar Graphs in *Math Trailblazers*

As early as kindergarten, students using *Math Trailblazers* work on graphing concepts, including making and interpreting simple graphs. A quick way to make bar graphs of classroom data is to place self-adhesive notes on a labeled graph. An example of this with *First Names* is illustrated in Figure 9. In this graph, each student placed a self-adhesive note with the data for his or her name on the graph. The data are clearly represented. The one-to-one correspondence between data points and the number of students in the class is particularly apparent in this type of graph, which we use primarily in kindergarten, first, and second grades.

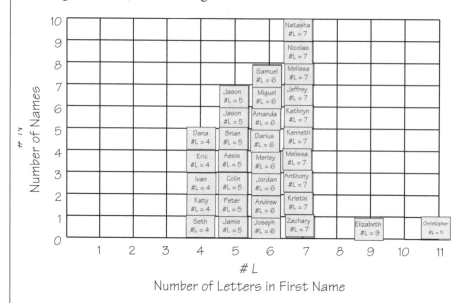

Figure 9: First Names *graph using self-adhesive notes*

In first grade, we introduce a graphing protocol that is different in *Math Trailblazers* than in some other programs. When making bar graphs, we encourage students to create their bars along the vertical lines in the graph rather than in the spaces between the lines. (See Figures 6, 7, and 9.) This does not affect the data or the reading of the graph. Rather it prepares students for making point graphs, where data points are plotted at the intersection of lines extending from the horizontal and vertical axes.

To assist students with this, we have created a special graph paper for making bar graphs. A version of this graph paper is shown in Figure 10. The dark vertical grid lines across the page are where the data for the manipulated variable is plotted. These lines are surrounded on both sides by a pair of dashed guide lines. Students make bars by coloring in the space on either side of the dark vertical lines. The result is a straight bar that is centered along a vertical line. The values for the manipulated variable are indicated on the horizontal axis directly below each bar.

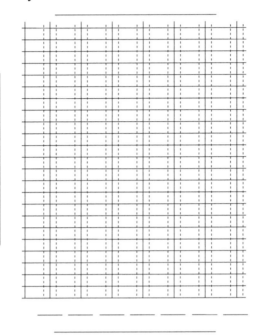

Figure 10: *TIMS bar graph paper*

The benefit of making bar graphs in this manner is most apparent in third grade as students make the transition to creating point graphs. To simplify students' initial attempt at creating a point graph, they first graph a data set as a bar graph and then convert the bar graph to a point graph. This is shown in Figure 11.

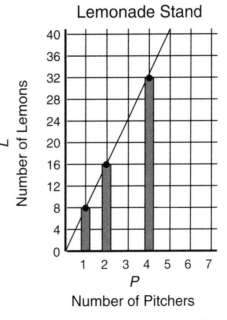

Figure 11: *Transition from bar graphs to point graphs in third grade*

Point Graphs: Fitting Lines and Curves

With point graphs, the data are plotted at the junction of the values of each variable. Once the data are plotted, we look for patterns. If the data points form a line or close to a line, we try to fit a line through the points. If the data form a curve, we try to fit a smooth curve through the points.

Figure 11 shows a graph in which the data points lie exactly on a straight line. Fitting a line to these data points is simply a matter of laying down a ruler and connecting the points.

For most experiments, we cannot expect the data to be so precise. In these experiments, the data may lie close to, but not exactly on a straight line. The "zigzags" in the data are due to experimental error. (See the TIMS Tutor: *Estimation, Accuracy, and Error.*) To average the error, one fits a line that comes as close to the data points as possible even though the line may not pass through any of these points. To assure a good fit, you would like as many points above the curve as below. You do not want to force the line through two points while missing the third by a mile. It is better to miss them all but come close to all than be too far from any one point.

As shown on *The Bouncing Ball* graph in Figure 5, you can fit a line to the data points, not by using some complicated statistical procedure, but simply "by eye." The student uses a clear ruler or a thread and moves it around until it fits the data points as closely as possible. This best-fit line is useful for minimizing error and making predictions.

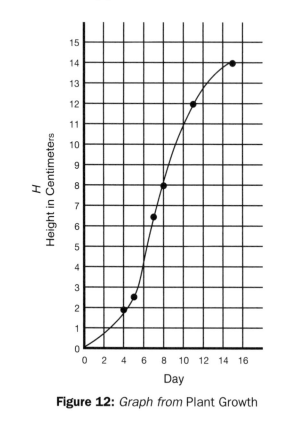

Figure 12: *Graph from* Plant Growth

Of course, not all experimental relationships result in data that yields straight lines on graphs. In *Math Trailblazers,* we also explore data that exhibits other kinds of patterns. Figure 12 shows the graph from a fourth-grade experiment, *Plant Growth,* where the data shows a pattern, but not a straight line.

When you can fit a smooth curve through the data points, you have uncovered one of nature's secrets—that the variables are related, that there is a predictable pattern to the data. We are then not restricted only to our specific data points, but can now use the pattern to predict what the value of the responding variable will be for any value of the manipulated variable.

Predictions from Point Graphs: Interpolation and Extrapolation

A major goal of mathematics and science is to find patterns in data and to use the patterns to make predictions. Interpolating and extrapolating on a point graph are two ways to do this.

Using the graph to find data points that lie between those in your data table is called **interpolation.** *Inter* means between or among. The simplest situation is when the pattern of data points produces a straight line. In the graph in Figure 5, the student interpolated to predict that a ball dropped from 60 cm would bounce about 32 cm. Note that in Figure 5 the student showed how she made her interpolation by starting at 60 cm on the horizontal axis, drawing a line (with arrows) up to the best-fit line, and then drawing a horizontal line to find the corresponding value of the bounce height—about 32 cm.

Extrapolation is an attempt to predict information beyond the last data point. *Extra* means outside or beyond. To extrapolate, we must extend the line into a region where there is no data. You can do this easily by laying a ruler on the straight line, extending the line, and reading off your prediction. In Figure 5, the student extrapolated to predict that a ball that bounced 80 cm was dropped from a height of about 144 cm. Here, the student began with values on the vertical axis (the bounce height) and predicted a value on the horizontal axis (the drop height). It is possible to interpolate and extrapolate in either of two directions: from values on the horizontal axis to values on the vertical axis or vice versa.

Having used these techniques to make predictions, it is important to have the children check their predictions experimentally and see how close their new data comes to the curve. This is one of the joys of science—to see that nature is often regular and predictable and that you can make predictions that come true! Checking predictions, though time-consuming, is worthwhile because it reinforces connections between mathematical abstractions and the real world.

Phase 4: Analyzing the Data

After making the graph, students explored the relationship between the variables in four ways: with the physical materials, in the picture, in the data table, and in the graph. The last phase of the TIMS Laboratory Method is the analysis of the entire situation, where students explore the relationship quantitatively and represent it symbolically (i.e., with numbers).

> *A major goal of mathematics and science is to find patterns in data and to use the patterns to make predictions. Interpolating and extrapolating on a point graph are two ways to do this.*

One way to structure this analysis is to ask a series of questions. The questions usually begin on the literal level: *Did the tallest container hold the most marshmallows? How high did the tennis ball bounce when dropped from 60 cm?* More demanding questions require prediction: *How many marshmallows would two bowls hold? If a ball bounced to 45 cm, what height was it dropped from?* Asking what would happen if one of the fixed variables is changed can build a broader understanding of the situation: *What would happen if we used large instead of miniature marshmallows? What would happen if we used a Super ball instead of a tennis ball?* This quantitative analysis of the data is one place in *Math Trailblazers* where students regularly practice and reinforce arithmetic and other math skills.

The end of the investigation may be a completely satisfying answer to the original question, but, more often than not, the end is another question that can lead to further investigations. *Marshmallows and Containers,* for example, might lead to an investigation of the liquid capacities of other short and tall containers. After an initial experiment with tennis balls in *The Bouncing Ball,* children carry out an investigation using another type of ball and compare the results from the two experiments.

Picture, Table, Graph, and Questions: Putting It Together

Each of the four phases previously described may require one or more class periods. In addition, you may spend time becoming familiar with the equipment at the beginning and on further experiments at the end. Thus, a lab is an extended activity that may last a week or even longer. This is much longer than a typical mathematics or science lesson, but there are significant benefits.

First, the four phases simplify the scientific method enough for children to use, but not so much that it fails to resemble what scientists do. Identifying variables, drawing pictures, measuring, organizing data in tables, graphing data, and looking for patterns are part of many scientists' work. Students are thus inducted via this method into the authentic practice of science.

The method fosters children's sense-making. Children handle numbers they have generated themselves by counting or measuring, numbers that are thus meaningful to them. As they deal with experimental error, they develop number sense and estimation skills. As they look for patterns in their tables and graphs, they make sense of the numbers before them. Arithmetic in context is more understandable.

The approach is multimodal, which has benefits for both individual students and heterogeneous groups of students. The multiple representations of relationships between the variables permit problems to be solved in more than one way, allowing different students to approach the same content in ways they understand. The container that holds the most marshmallows, for example, can be found from the graph, from the data table, or from the marshmallows themselves. A prediction about a bounce height might be obtained by extrapolating on the graph or by extending patterns in the data table, and can then be verified using the apparatus. Students can compare these various approaches, thus helping them make connections within mathematics as well as between the informal mathematics of their everyday experience and more formal mathematics.

Identifying variables, drawing pictures, measuring, organizing data in tables, graphing data, and looking for patterns are part of many scientists' work. Students are thus inducted via this method into the authentic practice of science.

Mathematics in Context

Two principles underlie the TIMS Laboratory Method. First, an investigation should begin within the children's own experiences. Children use objects from their everyday lives to investigate a familiar situation. Children's everyday knowledge, like a scientist's theory, provides a framework for interpreting the results of the investigation. Without that framework, the investigation would remain hollow and meaningless.

The second principle is that an investigation should also transcend children's everyday experiences. The exploration must go somewhere; it must lead the children both to a better understanding of the immediate situation and to improved skills, understandings, habits, and attitudes. The concepts can then be extended and transferred to new contexts.

Balancing these principles requires teacher judgment. The key is to enable students to follow their own ideas, but with the intention that those ideas will lead somewhere. How much scaffolding to provide, how much to guide students in directions that are fruitful rather than sterile, must be decided by the teacher in context. The goal is that students should advance not only in skill and understanding, but also in autonomy and perseverance. Just how much structure to provide along the way is perhaps a teacher's most important and difficult job.

The TIMS Laboratory Method helps children connect their everyday experiences with formal mathematics. As they investigate everyday situations quantitatively, children handle variables, explore relationships between variables, master a few powerful techniques for representing these relationships, and use these multiple representations to generate a wide variety of problem solutions. By beginning and ending in familiar situations, the abstractions of mathematics are linked to children's everyday knowledge. As students master this method, they become increasingly autonomous and flexible in its application. Then we can truly say they understand the fundamentals of *doing* science.

References

Archambault, Reginald D. (ed.), *John Dewey on Education: Selected Writings*. Modern Library, 1964.

Bruner, Jerome S. "The Course of Cognitive Growth." *American Psychologist* 19 (1), pp. 1–15, 1964.

Dewey, John. "Science as Subject-Matter and as Method." *Science* 31 (787), pp. 121–7, January 28, 1910.

Goldberg, Howard, and F. David Boulanger. "Science for Elementary School Teachers: A Quantitative Approach." *American Journal of Physics* 49 (2), pp. 120–124, 1981.

Goldberg, Howard, and Philip Wagreich. "Focus on Integrating Science and Math." *Science and Children* 2 (5), pp. 22–24, 1989.

Goldberg, Howard, and Philip Wagreich. "A Model Integrated Mathematics and Science Program for the Elementary School." *International Journal of Educational Research* 14 (2), pp. 193–214, 1990.

Hiebert, James. "A Theory of Developing Competence with Written Mathematical Symbols." *Educational Studies in Mathematics* 19, pp. 333–355, 1988.

Isaacs, Andrew C., and Catherine Randall Kelso. "Pictures, Tables, Graphs, and Questions: Statistical Processes." *Teaching Children Mathematics* 2 (6), pp. 340–345, 1996.

Isaacs, Andrew C., Philip Wagreich, and Martin Gartzman. "The Quest for Integration: School Mathematics and Science." *American Journal of Education* 106 (1), pp. 179–206, 1997.

Lesh, Richard, Thomas Post, and Merlyn Behr. "Representations and Translations among Representation in Mathematics Learning and Problem Solving." In C. Janvier (ed.), *Problems of Representation in the Teaching and Learning of Mathematics.* Lawrence Erlbaum Associates, Hillsdale, NJ, 1987.

National Research Council. *National Science Education Standards.* National Academy Press, Washington, DC, 1996.

Silver, Edward. "Using Conceptual and Procedural Knowledge: A Focus on Relationships." In J. Hiebert (ed.), *Conceptual and Procedural Knowledge: The Case of Mathematics.* Lawrence Erlbaum Associates, Hillsdale, NJ, 1986.

The Concept of Length

Units

In dealing with scientific problems, we must often know such things as the location of an object, the distance between objects, how tall or wide an object is, or how fast it is moving. Central to all these ideas is the concept of length. In this tutor, we shall examine the various disguises in which length can appear.

First, however, we must note the messy problem of units. The kinds of units chosen for length were for a long time quite arbitrary. The cubit, used by several ancient civilizations, was the length of a forearm between the tip of the middle finger and the elbow. The fathom was the width of a Viking sailor's embrace. (Fathom that!)

The foot was a convenient length defined as the length of a person's foot. Of course, everyone has a different-sized foot, so if we want to use, say, the king's foot as a standard, we will have to mark it permanently; we cannot very well lug the king around! Since the king is the ruler of the land, it was both rational and proper to call this marker a ruler as well. To show students the chaos caused by not having a standard length, have them measure the length of their desks in cubits or the width of the room in feet with each child using his or her own body measurements. You will have as many different values as measurers.

The foot was a convenient length defined as the length of a person's foot. Of course, everyone has a different-sized foot, so if we want to use, say, the king's foot as a standard, we will have to mark it permanently; we cannot very well lug the king around! Since the king is the ruler of the land, it was both rational and proper to call this marker a ruler as well.

Nonstandard Units

At first, we have the children measure length using nonstandard units, often links. A link is shown in Figure 1 along with a chain of links. The measurement of the object shown is $4\frac{1}{2}$ links. The reasons we go to links are: (1) to make counting the unit length easy and (2) to keep the numbers manageable. Rather than dealing with hundreds of cm, we can count 50 links. And to count a link is easy since they are so large.

By alternating link colors (2 reds, 2 whites, 2 reds, etc.), one can make the counting even easier by skip counting by 2s. If you want to have the children skip count by 5s, then have a chain with 5 blues, 5 yellows, 5 blues, etc.

With links, it is also easy to round off to $\frac{1}{2}$ link as shown in Figure 1. If the edge we are measuring is near the middle, then the length is $4\frac{1}{2}$ links. If shorter, then the length is 4 links; if longer, the length is 5 links.

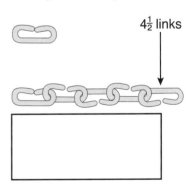

$4\frac{1}{2}$ links

Figure 1: *Links*

The Metric System

Of course, links are not a commonly used standard of measure. In the United States, it is feet. Unfortunately, many objects are smaller than a foot. This means one must subdivide the standard unit. For some miserable reason, the smaller unit, the inch, is $\frac{1}{12}$ of a foot. Who likes to divide by 12? So, the French scientific community at the time of the French Revolution (c. 1790) chose as the standard unit of length a distance that they called a meter.
It was chosen so that 10^7 (10 million) metersticks laid end to end would just fit between the North Pole and the equator, as shown in Figure 2. A platinum-iridium rod was constructed with two marks a meter apart and stored in a vault near Paris. Every meterstick, albeit indirectly, comes from this standard. Having defined the meter, the French were smart enough to define all subsequent subdivisions of the meter as integral powers of ten. The foot is divided into $\frac{1}{12}$s and $\frac{1}{48}$s, and other equally horrible numbers; for the meter, the divisions are $\frac{1}{10}$s, $\frac{1}{100}$s, and $\frac{1}{1000}$s. We shall now explore this point further.

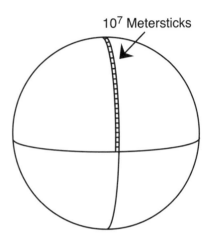

Figure 2: *Metersticks from the North Pole to the equator*

For measuring ordinary objects in the classroom, the meter is divided into three other units; the millimeter, the centimeter, and the decimeter (although the latter is rarely used). Without being specific as to the size of each unit, we can order them using the greater than (>) or less than (<) sign. Starting with the smallest, we have:

$$1 \text{ millimeter} < 1 \text{ centimeter} < 1 \text{ decimeter} < 1 \text{ meter}.$$

Reversing the order and starting with the largest, we have:

$$1 \text{ meter} > 1 \text{ decimeter} > 1 \text{ centimeter} > 1 \text{ millimeter}.$$

It is important that students know at least this much before going on to more exact relations.

The key to the subdivision of the meter is the prefix *milli*. Milli is related to the word mile. Mile was the distance it took a Roman soldier to step off 1000 paces, a pace being two steps. Since an average pace is approximately 5 feet (try it and see), a mile would be approximately 5000 feet. The crucial point is the number 1000 as related to the word mile. Milli is the prefix for "$\frac{1}{1000}$ of." Thus, a millimeter is one-thousandth of a meter. There are 1000 millimeters in a meter just as there are 1000 paces in a mile. In each case, we have a subunit that is one-thousandth of the main unit. The word mile is to remind us that there are 1000 paces in a mile. The word millimeter is to remind us that there are 1000 millimeters in a meter. One should try to picture this in one's mind. Millimeters are tiny; it takes a lot of them to make up any macroscopic length. (By macroscopic, we are referring to something one can see unaided versus microscopic where one would need a magnifying glass or microscope to see it.) On the other hand, because a meter is large, a millimeter is usually a fraction of most lengths one would measure in the lab. Thus, it is reasonable that a third-grader knows how to measure the length of his thumb as 3 cm or 30 mm, but not as 0.03 m.

How are mm, cm, dm, and m related? Let's start with the smallest and see how many mm are in a cm, a dm, and a meter.

1 centimeter contains 10 mm;
1 decimeter contains 100 mm;
1 meter contains 1000 mm.

Based on these relationships, we should be able to figure out how many centimeters are in a decimeter or in a meter. Here, however, the French have made it easy for us; the prefix for each word gives the answer away. *Centi* stands for 100th and *deci* stands for one-tenth. Thus one centimeter is one-hundredth of a meter; there are 100 cm in a meter. A decimeter is one-tenth of a meter; there are 10 dm in a meter. What this boils down to then is the following:

1 decimeter contains 10 cm;
1 meter contains 100 cm;
1 meter contains 10 dm.

Everything depends upon the size of the meter. Once that is fixed (by our rod in Paris), the sizes of all other metric units are determined.

Measuring Length

The simplest way to get started in the metric system is to count, using a meterstick, the number of mm or cm (and if they do not equal fractions, dm or meters) in a given length. Say we measure the width of the sheet of paper in cm. Then depending upon the accuracy of the meterstick (a cheap one could be off a bit) and the judgment of the student, one can see that there are between 21 and 22 cm across the page. If you stick to cm, then for students who are not yet comfortable with fractions or decimals, this is all you can say. As they begin to learn decimals, the children can determine the width as 21.6 cm. However, you can get still better accuracy even without decimals by going to mm instead of cm. Here, all one has to be able to do is count beyond 100. Thus, the width is 216 mm. In fact, one of the neat things about the metric system is that you can always choose a set of units to obtain almost any accuracy you want without going to fractions or decimals. On the other hand, you can purposely choose units that will give decimal or fractional answers. As we just saw, in cm units, the width of the page is a decimal, 21.6 cm. We could have asked for the width in meters. Since the width is less than a meter, we are dealing with fractions. In this case, the width is 0.216 meters or roughly $\frac{1}{5}$ of a meter. Clearly, there is great potential in the metric system for teaching math and linking this to scientific measurement.

With regard to addition, when adding numbers they must always have the same units. For example:

(a) 5 cm + 6 m = ? This is a "no-no"; the units are mixed.

(b) 5 cm + 600 cm = 605 cm. This is okay—we are adding the same units.

(c) 8 mm + 50 cm = ? We should convert the cm to mm and get:

8 mm + 500 mm = 508 mm.

Thus, if we ask a student to measure the length of his arm by separately measuring his hand (say in mm), his lower arm (say in cm), his upper arm (say in decimeters), and then adding them, he will first have to convert to a set of consistent units that he or she can handle. If you do not choose to have the students work with fractions, the students can change the units to millimeters as shown above. If you want to give the students a chance to work on decimal fractions, they can change the units to centimeters.

$$.8 + 50 \text{ cm} = 50.8 \text{ cm}$$

This brings us to another point—how to use a ruler. At first it seems quite apparent: just place the end of the ruler at the end of the object and read the length directly (Figure 3). However, a better test of whether students really understand how to use a ruler as well as a test of their ability to subtract is to place the object in the center of the ruler. Clearly, the length of the object should not depend upon its position vis-a-vis the ruler, but we have found that many young people (and even a few at our university) have trouble understanding how to find the length in the latter case.

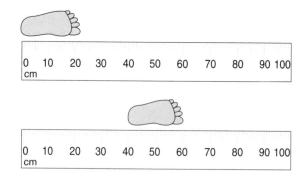

Figure 3: *How to use a ruler*

Since we do not always have a ruler handy, a few "natural" rulers might be fun to discuss and use. For example, say the length of a person's upper thumb from knuckle to tip is generally about 3 cm while his spread-out fingers span about 20 cm, as shown in Figure 4. Either can now be used to measure the length of an object. Of course, as shown in Figure 3, there is the foot, a convenient measure for stepping off distances. This person's foot, without his shoes, is 23 cm or about 9 inches. Anyway, you should have the children measure a few objects using natural rulers and have them compare their results with that of a meterstick.

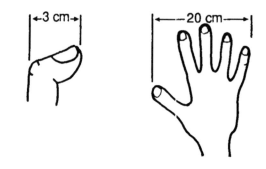

Figure 4: *Natural rulers*

The Concept of Area

Defining Area

The area of a shape or object can be defined in everyday words as the "amount of stuff" needed to cover the shape. Common uses of the concept of area are finding the amount of tile needed to cover a floor, the amount of wallpaper needed to cover a wall, and the amount of paint needed to cover a ceiling. You can often directly compare areas of different objects without measurement. For example, if one piece of carpet completely covers another, we know the top piece has more area.

Just as with length, to measure area we need a unit of measure. Many different units have been used throughout history. The acre is still used as a measure of land area, along with square miles. The square inch, square foot, and square yard are area units in the English system. For example, square yards is the unit of area measure for carpeting in the United States. Most of the world and all scientists use the metric system. For the classroom, the most frequent metric unit of area is the square centimeter. It is defined as the amount of flat surface within a square that is 1 cm on a side. This is illustrated in Figure 1.

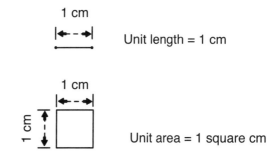

Figure 1: *Units of length and area*

A note on terminology: Scientists often use the term "centimeters squared" in place of "square centimeters." This may be due to the fact that one way of writing the symbol for square centimeters is cm^2. We prefer to use sq cm for square centimeters. On occasion, the use of cm^2 can confuse students. Since 7 squared is 49, they may reason that 7 centimeters squared is 49 square centimeters. Unfortunately, the symbols $7\ cm^2$ and $(7\ cm)^2$ sound the same when spoken, if you say cm^2 as "centimeters squared." For that reason, we stick to "square centimeters" and sq cm.

Measuring Area by Counting Square Centimeters–Part I

One way to find an area is to count the number of sq cm needed to cover a surface. To count the number of sq cm, you can construct unit squares within the desired area. For example, the rectangle in Figure 2 is 3 cm wide and 4 cm high. You can find its area by completing the following steps.

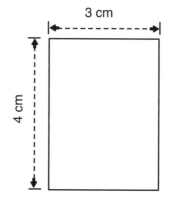

Figure 2: *A rectangle*

1. Draw a grid of lines so that each square in the grid is 1 cm on a side. (Figure 3.)

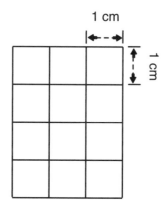

Figure 3: *A rectangle tiled with centimeter squares*

2. Count the number of sq cm enclosed in the rectangle. (Figure 4.)

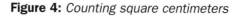

Figure 4: *Counting square centimeters*

There are 12 sq cm in a rectangle that is 3 cm wide and 4 cm high. So the area of the rectangle is 12 sq cm.

Why Not Use Length × Width?

You may be wondering why we did not use the formula *length × width* to find the area of the rectangle. After all, 4 × 3 = 12. The formula works. Indeed, the reason the formula works is precisely because the rectangle can be represented by an ordered array of squares, 3 squares in each row and 4 rows of 3 squares each.

In any ordered array, you can count the total number of elements by multiplying the number of rows by the number of columns. Figure 5 shows 24 apples arrayed in 6 rows. Instead of counting each apple, we take advantage of the array and multiply 4 × 6 to obtain 24 apples. Using the length times width formula does give the area of a rectangle, but we delay teaching the formula for two reasons. First, we want students to build a mental image of the concept of area. Premature use of the formula for area of rectangles leads to rote use of the formula without understanding. In particular, many students are led to believe that the definition of area is length times width and that this formula works for any shape. While there are formulas for the areas of rectangles, circles, and other geometric shapes, there is no formula for the area of a leaf!

> *Premature use of the formula for area of rectangles leads to rote use of the formula without understanding. In particular, many students are led to believe that the definition of area is length times width and that this formula works for any shape.*

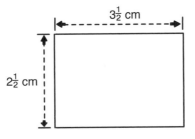

Figure 5: *An array of apples*

Furthermore, using the formula can be harder than counting square centimeters when the sides of the rectangle are not whole numbers.

For example, what is the area of the rectangle, $3\frac{1}{2}$ cm wide and $2\frac{1}{2}$ cm high, shown in Figure 6? We asked a group of sixth-graders to find the area of this rectangle. Even though the students knew the length × width formula, 80 percent could not find the area. They were not able to multiply fractions. It is likely that these students would have been able to find the area by counting sq cm, as we shall see in the next section.

$3\frac{1}{2}$ cm

$2\frac{1}{2}$ cm

Figure 6: *Another rectangle*

Counting Square Centimeters–Part II

In Figure 7, we set up the square cm grid. To keep track of the sq cm, we first number the whole square centimeters. There are six whole sq cm in the rectangle. Next, we turn to the fractions of sq cm. Students can manipulate sq cm pieces of paper to complete the task. The two half sq cm on the right make up the seventh sq cm and so both are numbered 7. The two half sq cm along the bottom make up the eighth sq cm and are numbered 8. One half sq cm and one fourth square cm make up the remaining areas. The area is $8\frac{3}{4}$ sq cm.

1	2	3	7
4	5	6	7
8	8	$\frac{1}{2}$	$\frac{1}{4}$

Figure 7: *Whole and part centimeter squares*

Most students can count squares to find area—no multiplication is necessary. But what if there is no "order" to the figure? The shape in Figure 8 has no unique length or width; the formula *length* × *width* does not apply. The only way to find the area is to count the number of sq cm contained within the boundary of the figure.

Figure 8: *A blob*

First, construct a sq cm grid to fit over the shape of Figure 8. It's often easier if the horizontal and vertical boundary of the grid each touch the figure at one point. The grid should extend beyond the figure. The completed grid would look similar to the grid in Figure 9.

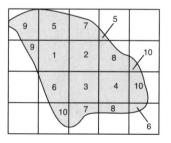

Figure 9: *Finding area by counting centimeter squares*

Next, count and number the whole sq cm. There are four. Now estimate which fractions of grid squares add together to form one square centimeter. For example, square centimeter number 5 is a big piece upper left and a little piece farther to the right. Number 6 is two pieces, a big piece on the left and a smaller piece in the lower right corner. Square centimeter number 7 is two pieces, each around a half square cm. Square centimeter 8 is made up of a $\frac{3}{4}$ and $\frac{1}{4}$ square cm piece. So is square centimeter 9. Three pieces make up square centimeter 10, two half square cm pieces and a smaller piece to the right.

Now all the shape is covered and counted in square centimeters. The shape has an area of about 10 square cm. While the method does not give an exact area, the result is usually close. And the primary benefit of this method is that students will have the opportunity to "see" area, aiding their understanding of this important mathematical concept.

Surface Area

Often, students who understand area quite well seem to have difficulty with the notion of surface area. One problem may be that they were led to believe that area and surface area are two different things. This is not surprising, since we use two different words. However, area and surface area are identical; a measure of the number of sq cm (or square units) needed to cover an object. Customarily, the term "surface area" is usually used for three-dimensional shapes and "area" for two-dimensional shapes.

To measure the surface area of a three-dimensional object, we count the number of square centimeters needed to cover it, just as with flat shapes. In some cases, this is easy as in the case of a rectangular box (since it is made up of flat pieces). Another easy example can be made by taking a sheet of flat paper and rolling it to make a cylinder (Figure 10). As long as the edges do not overlap, the surface area of the outside of the cylinder will be the same as the flat piece of paper. Another way to find the area of a cylinder is to cover it with one square centimeter "stamps." As with flat shapes, you may need some fractional pieces. With more complex shapes, like a sphere, it is hard to get an exact measurement of the surface area, but we can approximate the surface area by covering the object with square centimeters or smaller squares.

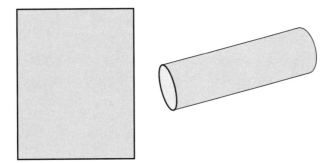

Figure 10: *Paper flat and rolled*

The Concept of Volume

Defining Volume

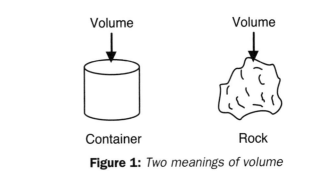

Figure 1: *Two meanings of volume*

Figure 1 shows a container and a rock. The space that the container surrounds (and is occupied by air) and the space that the rock takes up (and is occupied by elements such as oxygen, silicon, and aluminum) are both called **volume.**[1] The concept of volume is tricky. Two objects (like our container and rock) might occupy the same volume but contain totally different amounts of matter. Children often confuse the amount of matter, which we call mass, with the space occupied, which we now know is volume. Thus children tell us that a "heavy" object has more volume than a "light" object even though the latter may actually occupy more space. Indeed, volume is so oversimplified in the elementary schools that many eighth-graders we asked thought of volume as length × width × height, no matter what the shape of the object. Others told us that volume was length squared. Misconceptions such as these are a result of a curriculum that emphasizes memorization of formulas without attention to the conceptual foundations of volume.

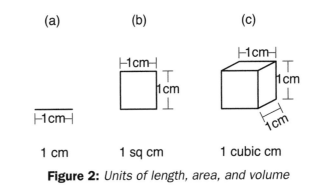

Figure 2: *Units of length, area, and volume*

---

[1]Sometimes, the space inside a container is called the capacity of the container. For simplicity, we prefer to use one term, volume, to denote both "space inside" and "space occupied."

Units

As with length and area, if we wish to measure volume, we need to decide on a unit of measure. In the metric system, the metric unit of length is the centimeter (Figure 2a), and the unit of area is the square centimeter (the extent of the plane surface that is bounded by a square 1 cm on a side) (Figure 2b), so it is not unreasonable that we take as our unit of volume the space occupied within a cube that is 1 cm on a side (Figure 2c). The volume occupied by such a cube is defined as 1 cubic centimeter whether that volume is occupied by a solid object (Figure 3a) or by empty space (Figure 3b).

(a)   (b)

Figure 3: *Full and empty cubic centimeter*

Unlike area, it is very hard to divide an object up and count cubic cm. We can't trace the volume the way we trace areas on square cm paper. In theory we could slice it up into 1 cubic cm pieces, but this process will destroy the object. Therefore, learning to understand and measure volume can be more difficult than understanding and measuring area.

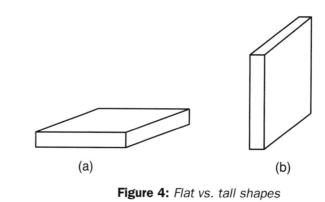

(a)   (b)

Figure 4: *Flat vs. tall shapes*

In everyday life, we are accustomed to a variety of other units of volume measure. Gallons, quarts, pints, and fluid ounces are one set of units, usually used to measure the capacity of a container. Cubic feet and cubic inches are also frequently used. For example, in the United States, air conditioners are often rated on the volume of space they can cool, measured in cubic feet. The remainder of this tutor uses metric units of measure, but many of the same underlying ideas apply to any system of measure.

Problem of Dimensionality

Another great difficulty in understanding volume is that the concept deals with three dimensions. As Piaget pointed out, it is much easier, and therefore usual, for a child to focus on one dimension. They will decide that a tall object has lots of volume because they only focus on the height and fail to take into account the other two dimensions to make a proper estimate. In Figure 4, the two objects have the same volume, but because (a) is flat and (b) is upright, young children will tell you that (b) has the greater volume.

Volume is an extremely important scientific variable. The way it is related to area and to mass and the manner in which it may change with time are all intrinsic to every area of scientific investigation. It is well worth our time to do a good job on volume.

Measuring Volume–Early Activities

Kindergarten students explore volume by filling containers with rice, water, pasta, sand, or beans. Another way to deal with volume in the primary grades is to have the children make figures out of a set of cubes. In first and second grade, we usually use connecting cubes that are about $\frac{3}{4}$-inch on a side. At the end of second grade, we start using standard centimeter linking cubes. For example, you can give each child 10 cubes and ask him or her to make a figure whose volume is 10 cubic units. You will get a variety of shapes, all of which have the same volume. This will begin to impress upon the children the idea that many different shapes can have the same volume.

Another centimeter cube activity to build the children's understanding at this level involves building shapes with different volumes. Give each child a few (3–10) centimeter cubes. Have each child make a shape with his or her centimeter cubes. Then have the children sort themselves into groups according to the volume of their shapes.

You can bring in some simple solid shapes, like a piece of chalk, a match box, a pile of washers, etc., and have the children make figures out of cubic units that approximate the volume (size and shape) of these objects. In this way, they can estimate the volume of the original object by keeping track of the number of cubic cm they used. An example is given in Figure 5 of a marking pen and cubic cms linked together to make a shape of approximately the same volume.

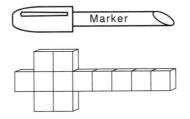

Figure 5: *A marker and a cm cube model*

> Another great difficulty in understanding volume is that the concept deals with three dimensions. As Piaget pointed out, it is much easier, and therefore usual, for a child to focus on one dimension. They will decide that a tall object has lots of volume because they only focus on the height and fail to take into account the other two dimensions to make a proper estimate.

The next step would be for you to make several cube models and have children count the number of unit cubes in each. Pictures of three typical models, each a bit more complex than the previous, are given in Figures 6a, b, and c. There are two potential problems here. The children may confuse surface area and volume and count the faces of the cubes calling each face a cubic cm. A subtle problem, exemplified by Figure 6c, is when there are one or more "hidden" cubic centimeters buried inside the figure.

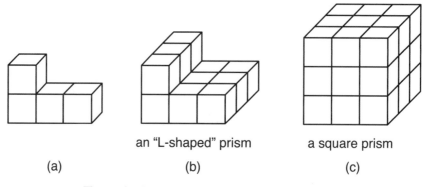

an "L-shaped" prism   a square prism

(a)   (b)   (c)

Figure 6: *Shapes made from centimeter cubes*

We want the children to learn to be systematic, look for patterns, and use simple addition and multiplication to count the cubic cm.

A very basic problem is learning to count the cubic centimeters properly. It is relatively easy to pick up 12 cubic centimeters, make a figure, and say the volume is 12 cc. It is quite another to hold a centimeter cube figure like that in Figure 6b, turn it over, and keep track of all the centimeters. We want the children to learn to be systematic, look for patterns, and use simple addition and multiplication to count the cubes. For example, Figure 6a is easy since it is only 4 cc. Figure 6b is made up of three layers, each of which is exactly like Figure 6a. Your students can then use addition to see that the volume is 4 cc + 4 cc + 4 cc, or use multiplication, 3 × 4 cc. Likewise in Figure 6c, it would be difficult to find and keep track of each cubic cm. A systematic approach allows the children to solve the problem easily. There are 9 cc in the top layer, and there are three layers; therefore the volume is

$$9 \text{ cc} + 9 \text{ cc} + 9 \text{ cc} = 27 \text{ cc}.$$

Note that Figures 6b and 6c are labeled as prisms. This means they are made of a number of identical layers. Figure 6b has three "L-shaped" layers and 6c has three "square-shaped" layers. It is important to know that these are prisms. Otherwise, there might be some hidden cubes behind the object that we cannot see, or there might be missing cubes "inside" the object.

A more difficult skill is finding the volume of an object directly from a perspective drawing, without actually building the object. You can develop this kind of spatial visualization skill by first having students build cube models from pictures. Students as early as first grade can build simple models from pictures. As the models get more complex, this task can become quite difficult. One important subtlety is that pictures such as 6b and 6c do not give enough information to reconstruct the model. For example, there might be some unexpected cubes hidden behind the model in Figure 6c (see Figure 7).

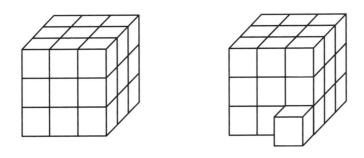

Front View   Rear View

Figure 7: *Front and rear views of Figure 6c*

For example, in Figure 7 we see what appears to be a 3 × 3 × 3 cm cube from the front, but when we view the model from the rear, we see there is an "extra" cube stuck on.

Finally, and hardest of all, you can ask the children to try to draw a figure with a given number of cubic centimeters. It is very hard for anyone to draw a cube, and a figure with several cubic centimeters is harder still. Nevertheless, it is worth a try since doing so will help them improve their spatial perception and will force them to think in three dimensions.

Let's review the four steps we just described:

1. Make figures out of a given number of centimeter cubes.
2. Count cubic centimeters in a cube model.
3. Count cubic centimeters in the drawing of a cube model—usually prisms.
4. Draw a figure with a given number of cubic centimeters.

This discussion covers volumes of objects made from cubes. The most important tool, however, for determining volume will be the graduated cylinder which we will discuss in the section after next. But first we want to talk about how to calculate the volume of prisms.

Calculating Volume—An Upper Grade Exercise

The volume of a rectangular prism made of cubic centimeters can be found using multiplication. The number of cubic centimeters in the top layer is just the product of 3 × 6 since there are 3 rows of 6 cubic cm (see Figure 8). Thus, in each layer there are 18 cc. Because there are 5 layers, the total number of cubic centimeters is 5 × 18 cc = 90 cc. As often written in math books, this type of counting is expressed as

$$V = l \times w \times h.$$

You should interpret this as the number of cubic cm in the top layer (given by the value of $l \times w$) times the number of layers (given by the value of h).

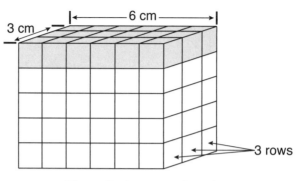

Figure 8: *A rectangular prism*

If the top layer is not rectangular but the figure is a right solid (sides perpendicular to top and bottom), then we can still find the volume by the above technique. The formula *length $\times$ width $\times$ height* will no longer work since the layers are not rectangular. However, since each horizontal slice has the same shape (see Figure 9), all we have to do is find the number of cubic cm in the top layer and multiply this by the number of layers. To find the number of cubic centimeters in the top layer, we have to find the number of square centimeters in the top surface, since each square centimeter of the surface is attached to a cubic centimeter in the top layer. Thus, if in Figure 9 by counting square cm we find that there are 22 sq cm on the top surface, then there must be 22 cubic cm in the top layer and in each subsequent layer. The total volume, then, is:

$$\frac{22 \text{ cubic cm}}{1 \text{ layer}} \times 5 \text{ layers} = 110 \text{ cubic cm}$$

for the object shown in Figure 9. As a general formula we have:

$$V = A \times h,$$

where the area A of the top tells us the number of cc in the top layer, and the value of h tells us the number of layers. Children should not just memorize each formula; they should understand what is behind the formulas.

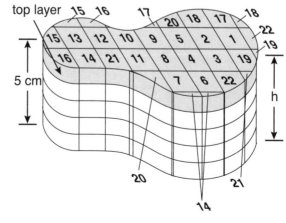

Figure 9: *A right solid*

When using a formula like $l \times w \times h$, the old bugaboo of units reappears. Since l, w, and h are all measured in centimeters, it is tempting to say that the units of volume are centimeters cubed written as $(cm)^3$. And indeed this is what is often done in scientific texts. Yes, it's technically correct to write $(cm)^3$ or cm^3, but again it can be misleading for children just as "centimeter squared" can be misleading for area. If we say a volume is 7 centimeters cubed, is that $(7 \text{ cm})^3 = 343$ cc? We can avoid this confusion by writing what we mean; that the volume is 7 cubic centimeters or 7 cc.

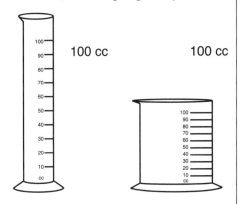

Figure 10: *Graduated cylinders*

Clearly, the ability to calculate volume is rather limited to certain special shapes. An irregularly shaped container or object will require a different approach.

A Volume Measurer: The Graduated Cylinder

We have seen that a ruler which is calibrated in cm can be used to measure length. There is no comparably simple device for measuring area, but there is one for measuring volume. It is the graduated cylinder calibrated in cubic centimeters. Two graduated cylinders are shown in Figure 10. They can be made of glass or Pyrex, both of which are breakable, or plastic, which is not. The cylinder most suitable for classroom use would be calibrated in 1 cc, 5 cc, or 10 cc divisions and have a capacity of 100 to 150 cc. When filled with a liquid (usually water) or a fluid substance like sand or salt, one can read the volume of the material off the side of the graduated cylinder. One cannot use this device to directly measure the volume of a number of marbles since the marbles piled in the cylinder will leave an unknown volume of air spaces between them. This is illustrated in Figure 11b. As we shall see in the next section, we can find the volume of solid objects like marbles by the method of displacement. The rest of this section will discuss using the graduated cylinder for finding the volume of liquid, particularly water.

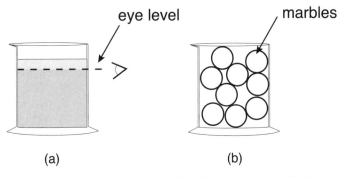

Figure 11: *Liquid and marbles in graduated cylinder*

To read the volume of water in a graduated cylinder, your eyes must be level with the liquid, as shown in Figure 11a. Since water is pulled up at the sides of the cylinder into a curved surface called a meniscus, one must measure the water level at the center of the cylinder. This is done by using the lower of the two lines that one sees (Figure 12) when looking at the water from the side. The top line is due to the pulled up water and should be ignored. (This phenomenon tends to be more pronounced when using glass rather than plastic graduated cylinders.)

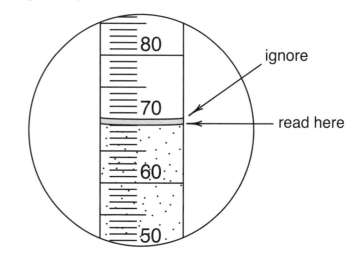

Figure 12: *The meniscus*

One must be careful about what one puts into a graduated cylinder. A tall, narrow one will generally have 1 cc divisions and thus can be used for accurate measurements. The trouble is, that because it is narrow, you can use only small objects. Many a time a student has misjudged the size of an object and found it stuck in the narrow cylinder never to come out again.

Chalk off one cylinder. A good general size that we like is one about 4 cm in diameter with a 150 cc capacity and made of plastic. The divisions are usually 5 or 10 cc. We shall discuss in the next section how to use a "big" graduated cylinder to measure the volume of small objects.

Many graduated cylinders that you purchase will have several different scales along the sides. This is due to the diversity of units for liquid measurements. Many cylinders will have a scale for fluid ounces and another for milliliters. The metric unit of volume is the milliliter, which is defined to be 1 cubic cm:

$$1 \text{ ml} = 1 \text{ cc.}$$

The liter is often encountered in daily life (for example, soda bottles are often 1 or 2 liters). It is exactly 1000 ml.

One of the first exercises the children can do with a graduated cylinder is simply to fill the cylinder to a specified level—10 cc, for example. An eyedropper is handy for getting the volume exactly right, since by pouring one usually overshoots or undershoots the mark. Whatever the divisions of the cylinder are, choose some volumes that fall right on a major division and some that fall between divisions, where the children will have to interpolate. An example is shown in Figure 13 for a cylinder with 10 cc divisions.

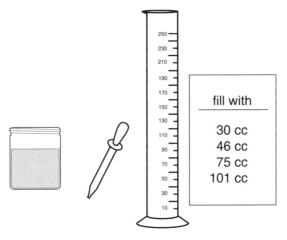

Figure 13: *A graduated cylinder exercise*

Once the second- or third-graders are good at reading the scale, they can use the graduated cylinder to find the capacity or volume of a set of three jars (Figure 14). You should build up a collection of jars of all shapes and volumes, from small baby food jars, through peanut butter containers, to large coffee jars. Exotic shapes are nice. To find the volume of a jar, one can either fill the jar to the brim and then keep pouring the water into the graduated cylinder, or one can keep filling the graduated cylinder and pour the water into the jar until it is filled. Either way, the children have to keep track of the number of times the graduated cylinder is filled and the total volume of water accumulated this way. This activity appears as a lesson called *Fill 'er Up* in third grade.

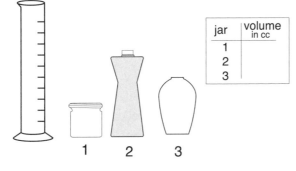

Figure 14: *A capacity exercise*

Volume Measurement by Displacement

How would you measure the volume of a small rock? This problem is dealt with in lessons on volume beginning in Grade 2. The technique is illustrated in Figure 15. First, you fill the graduated cylinder with a convenient amount of water, for example, 40 cc rather than 43 cc. Then you place the rock in the graduated cylinder without losing any water (there must be enough water in the cylinder initially to cover the object). You then read the new volume V. Since the volume of water V_{water} stays constant, the volume V is due to the water plus the rock. The rock displaces, or pushes aside, its volume in water and the water level rises. Thus, we have:

$$V_{rock} = V - V_{water}.$$

For example, in Figure 15 the volume of the rock is 22 cc. Note that subtraction is easier if you start with a multiple of ten for the volume of water. The technique works for any solid object no matter what its shape. To start with, then, ask children to find the volume of a wide variety of objects, some spheres, cubes, rocks, coins, washers, etc.

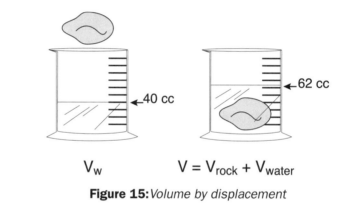

$$V_w \qquad\qquad V = V_{rock} + V_{water}$$

Figure 15: *Volume by displacement*

But what if the object is too big to fit into the graduated cylinder? If a bigger graduated cylinder isn't handy, then use your graduated cylinder to calibrate a large jar, and then away you go. One word of warning: When you place a large object in a graduated cylinder or jar, a considerable amount of water may splash out, even though you are very careful. You can get around this by placing the object in the graduated cylinder first and then pouring in a known amount of water V_w, and then read $V = V_{rock} + V_{water}$ off the scale. An alternative method is to find a large container and fill it with water to the brim. When the object is carefully placed in the container, it overflows, and the volume of the overflow liquid is equal to the volume of the object. If you catch all the overflow liquid in a second container, you can then use a graduated cylinder to find the volume of that liquid.

Finding the volume of small objects is also a problem, since the object may be so small you can't see the water level rise. Of course, you can always use a smaller graduated cylinder, one with 1 cc divisions instead of 5 or 10 cc divisions. The trouble is that sometimes even 1 cc per division is too large. The only way out is to measure the volume of several of the small objects at once (Figure 16b). (The volume of the several objects are identical.) For example, suppose you have 10 identical objects. To find the volume of one object, subtract the volume of the water and divide by 10. In this fashion, children can find the volume of small washers, paper clips, pins, and so on. Using 10 objects is a good idea since it is easy to divide by 10.

Too big   Too small

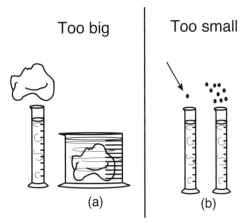

(a)   (b)

Figure 16: *Finding volumes of large or small objects*

Obtaining Accurate Results

A few words about accuracy are appropriate here. Most of the time you have to interpolate between divisions in order to read the volume. This usually leads to a reading error of about 20% of the value between the scale marks. Thus, if your graduated cylinder has 10 cc divisions, you might expect an error (i.e., children will get readings that differ) by up to 2 cc. This is illustrated in Figure 17a. If the object has raised the water level several divisions, then this 20% per division uncertainty is not a serious problem. For example, our rock changed the water level from 40 cc to 62 cc. If a reading error is up to 2 cc, then three children who read the same graduated cylinder might read 62 cc, but possibly 61 cc or 63 cc (if they are careful; maybe even more if they are not). But the volume of the rock is 62 cc − 40 cc = 22 cc for one child, but 23 cc for another, and 21 cc for the third. Thus we have a spread in reading of about 2 parts in 22 or 10%. A bigger rock, with a volume of, say, 46 cc would still have the same reading error of 2 cc, but its volume error would only be 2 parts in 46 or about 5%.

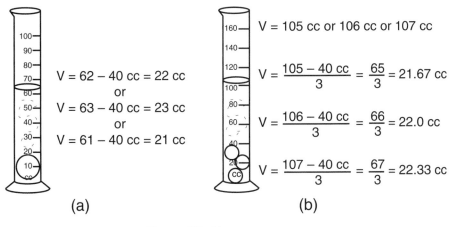

(a)   (b)

Figure 17: *Measurement error*

A good rule of thumb is that your reading will not be accurate unless the object raises the water level by more than one division. There are two ways to achieve this. One, use a narrow graduated cylinder, or two, use several identical objects if they are available. In the case of the latter, you find the volume of one object by dividing by the number of identical objects, as we did above for very small objects. For example, three objects would still produce a reading error of 2 cc but a volume error of only 2 cc/3 = 0.67 cc. This is illustrated in Figure 17b where three marbles give a volume spread of only 0.67 cc in 22 cc or 3%, compared to 10% for one marble. Of course, this would not work for finding the volume of a rock, since it would be difficult to find three identical rocks.

If the object floats, you have to push it under in order to measure its volume. In this situation, what is important is how you push it under. If you use your finger, then what you measure is the volume of the object plus the volume of your submerged finger. Since the volume of your finger may be comparable to the volume of the object, this is clearly not a good idea. What you need is a pusher whose volume is much less than the volume of the object. A straightened paper clip or a pin will do (Figure 18).

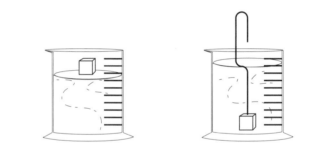

Figure 18: *Finding the volume of something that floats*

Two Misconceptions

Early on, the children should come to grips with two important ideas concerning volume:

1. The volume of an object is independent of the material it is made of.
2. The volume of an object does not change when its shape changes.[2]

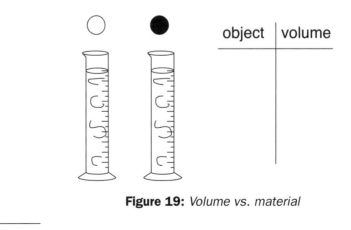

Figure 19: *Volume vs. material*

---

[2]Usually. See later discussion.

As to the first point, you can study spheres of the same volume but made of a wide variety of materials (steel, lucite, glass, even wood). The children should discover that their volumes are the same. As illustrated in Figure 19, students can fill two identical cylinders to the same level with water, carefully place both objects in, and see that the volume displaced is the same. Initially, many children will say that the heavier object has more volume and that the water will go up higher in its graduated cylinder. They are confusing mass and volume. If you take a clay cube and mash it into a thin disk, many children will say that the disk has less volume than the cube. Here they confuse one dimension, thinness, with volume: they mistakenly assume all thin objects have a small volume. Again, using the graduated cylinder the child can see that the volumes are the same. Figure 20. They can make all kinds of shapes out of a single piece of clay and determine that they all have the same volume. Indeed, the only way they can change its volume is to tear off a piece.

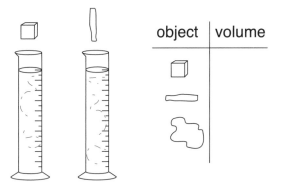

Figure 20: *Volume vs. shape*

The Concept of Mass

Defining Mass

Mass is one of the most difficult variables to understand. It is also one of the most important. Length, area, and volume have straightforward definitions. The volume of an object, for example, is defined as a measure of the space it occupies. Does mass have a similar straightforward definition? In a sense it does and in a sense it does not. Basically, **mass** is a measure of the quantity of matter in an object. That is its simple definition. Unfortunately, that begs the question. One can ask, what is matter, and we are back to where we started. So we have to look more closely at mass. And that is where things get difficult. Mass is defined through what it *does,* and this sets it apart from length, area, and volume. Moreover, mass does two things which means, in a sense, it has two definitions.

> *Basically, **mass** is a measure of the quantity of matter in an object.*

One of the things that mass does is absolutely crucial for the existence of our universe. Mass is the cause of the force of gravity. Without mass, there would be no gravity, and without gravity, matter would not have clumped into galaxies and stars and us. Since mass causes gravity, we can define mass through the pull of gravity—the greater the pull, the greater the mass an object has.

The other thing that mass does has to do with the motion of an object. All other variables being equal, the mass of an object determines how much the velocity of an object will *change* when subject to a given force. In layman's terms, the larger the mass of an object, the harder you have to push to change its speed. Since we are not ready to study motion, we will not discuss the details of this aspect of mass. Nevertheless, we might note that it was Einstein's contemplation of both properties of mass (gravity and motion) that led him to his general theory of relativity.

One way, then, to determine which of two objects has more mass is to determine which one is pulled on more strongly by the Earth's gravitational force. One possible way to do this is to drop two objects, as shown in Figure 1, and see which reaches the ground first. You might suppose, since the more mass an object has, the bigger the force of gravity, that the more massive object would fall faster and reach the ground first. If you do this exercise, however (as Galileo did), you will find that

Figure 1: *Dropping two objects*

both objects reach the ground at the same time! What went wrong? Well, we are breaking one of our cardinal rules, which is keeping variables fixed. When the objects fall, we not only have gravity pulling on them, but their velocity is changing as well. Therefore, both definitions of mass are involved and the overall effect is no longer obvious. It appears that in some way the effects cancel!

So we need a way of measuring the pull of gravity (i.e., using definition 1) without having the object move (i.e., eliminating definition 2). As we shall see in the next section, we can do this with a two-pan balance.

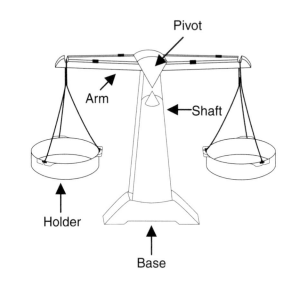

Figure 2: *A balance*

Equal Arm Balance

The equal arm, or two-pan, balance is the key to our operational definition of mass for children. If two objects balance, they have the same mass. If the arm tilts to one side, the object in the lower of the two pans has more mass than the object in the other pan.

Basically, the balance is a stick that is pivoted at its center and has two holders that are mounted on at points which are equidistant from the pivot (hence the name equal arm balance). Figure 2 pictures a balance that we often use in *Math Trailblazers*. It is quite sturdy and accurate enough for use in the elementary classroom. The tall shaft and long arms of the balance make it very useful in a variety of balancing experiments. If you would like to make your own, you can use a block of wood (Figure 3a) or a book to hold the pivot rod (Figure 3b). A ruler can act as the arm and the bottom of paper cups as pans. These latter pieces can be attached to the arm with string and paper clips.

The equal arm, or two-pan, balance is the key to our operational definition of mass for children. If two objects balance, they have the same mass. If the arm tilts to one side, the object in the lower of the two pans has more mass than the object in the other pan.

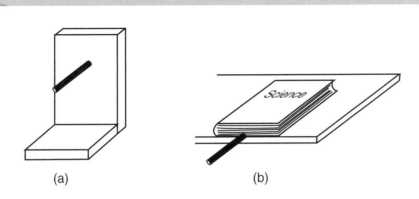

(a)   (b)

Figure 3: *Making a balance*

Once you have put your two-pan balance together, it must be zeroed. That is, the arm must be level before any masses are added. We suggest that you zero each balance and then have the children check to see that it is level before and during each experiment.

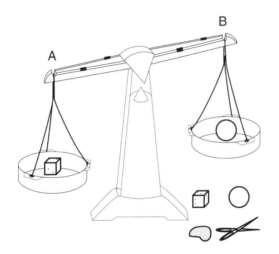

A	B	More Mass
Cube	Ball	Cube
Scissors	Ball	Scissors

Figure 4: *Comparing masses*

We are now ready to find out which of two objects, A or B, has greater mass. One is placed in each pan. Since the object with more mass will experience the bigger gravitational pull, the balance will tilt either one way or the other. If A has more mass it will tilt to the left, as shown in Figure 4, while if B has more mass it will tilt to the right. If the masses in the pans are equal, the pull of gravity on both is the same and the balance will remain level. One word of caution, though: If the masses are the same and the arm is tilted when the masses are placed on the balance, then the ruler will often remain tilted. Thus, to be sure, bring the arm back to level and see if it remains there.

One of the first exercises you can do with children in kindergarten through second grade is to have them compare, two at a time, the masses of a wide variety of objects. Then they should order the objects from the most massive to the least massive (see *Putting Masses in Order* in Grade 2 Unit 10). You can use a washer, connecting cube, small scissors, steel ball, and so on. Notice that the two-pan balance does away with the motion definition of mass since the balance is at rest when the measurement is made. Thus, the balance allows us to relate the object's mass directly to the pull of gravity.

Measuring Mass: The Mass Standard

The above is fine for comparing masses, but how do we measure *the* mass of an object? In other words, how do we assign a number to the mass of our object? Just as when we measure length, area, and volume, we need to decide on a unit. Say that we take as our standard masses a set of identical washers (paper clips would do as well). Let's call the mass of each washer 1 *ugh*. Then, if our object is balanced by 4 washers, its mass is 4 ughs, as shown in Figure 5. If the mass of the object is between 4 and 5 ughs, then the balance will not level out but tilt one way for 4 washers and the other way for 5. In this way, the child can assign unique masses to a wide range of objects. Clearly, the smaller the washer, the more accurately one can determine the mass of an object.

But washers are not a very satisfactory standard. The washers in your class may not have the same mass as those used in another school in your district, much less in another city or another country. What we need is a universal standard that is accepted by the entire scientific community. This problem was recognized by scientists a long time ago and was resolved when the Paris Academy of Sciences submitted a report to the French National Assembly in which 1 cc of

*The Paris Academy of Sciences submitted a report to the French National Assembly in which 1 cc of water was defined to have a mass of 1 gm, the **gram** being the name chosen for the unit of mass.*

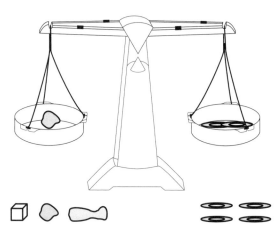

Object	Number of Washers	Mass in ughs
Ball	4	4
Cube	2	2

Figure 5: *Measuring masses*

water was defined to have a mass of 1 gm, the **gram** being the name chosen for the unit of mass. Then, using this definition, a platinum cylinder was made and declared to be the standard for 1000 grams. In 1875, an international treaty was signed by most "civilized" nations which established an International Bureau of Weights and Measures in Sevres, France, near Paris. The international prototype kilogram, made of platinum iridium alloy, is kept there. If you want your own kilogram, you have to go to Paris with an equal arm balance and some material and hack away at the material until it balances the platinum iridium standard. The National Bureau of Standards in Washington, DC, has an accurately constructed copy as do other governments throughout the world.

For small measurements, one needs a mass that is smaller than a kilogram, just as one needs a length that is smaller than a meter. The gram, like the centimeter, is perfect for this. Most objects you will deal with in the elementary school science program will have masses between 1 and 100 grams. Masses are commercially available, usually in 1-, 5-, 10-, 20-, 50-, 100-, 200-, 500-, and 1000-gram pieces. It might be a good idea to have one good set of very accurate standard masses for your school (locked in a closet marked "Paris," of course), but they are expensive. For general classroom use, there are less expensive sets of plastic masses available. However, since the plastic masses may not be as accurate, you may wish to compare them to a good set of standard masses or find their mass using a triple beam balance or other accurate scales.

The cheapest standard mass is a nickel. It has a mass very close to 5 grams! But alas, a dime does not have a mass of 10 grams. There are two ways to get around having to buy sets of expensive standard masses. To determine the mass of a small object, measure the mass of several of the objects and then divide the total mass by the number of objects. For example, if it turns out that 10 small objects balance a 5-gram piece, then each object will have a mass of 0.5 grams. (5 grams ÷ 10 objects = 0.5 grams per object.)

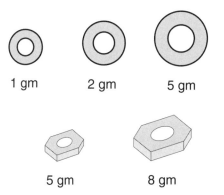

If you go to a hardware store and make a pest of yourself—bring your two-pan balance—you can usually find washers that have "nice" masses, like 1, 2, 5, 8 grams, etc. Figure 6 shows such a collection that can be used as standard masses. Once you have the washers, give each child several of each and a lot of objects whose mass you want them to determine. A good data table is a big help since you want to keep track of the number of different washers it takes to balance the object.

Figure 6: *Using washers as standard masses*

Then, as shown in Figure 7, a little multiplication and addition is necessary to obtain the final mass in grams. In the example above, the total mass is:

$$m_{\text{total}} = 3 \times 1 \text{ gm} + 1 \times 2 \text{ gm} + 2 \times 5 \text{ gm} + 2 \times 8 \text{ gm} = 31 \text{ gm}.$$

Finding masses in grams is a great way to practice multiplication, addition, and mental math.

Object	Number of Standard Masses				Mass in gm
	1 gm	2 gm	5 gm	8 gm	
Plastic Cylinder	3	1	2	2	31

Figure 7: *Finding mass using washers*

A second way to get around using expensive standards is again to use washers but place them in packages of sets of 1, 5, 10, 20 grams, etc. The package can be composed of several washers wrapped in masking tape with enough tape or small washers to make an even 5 gm, 10 gm, and so on. Either way, the cost of a washer is small enough that children can have a set of masses for a few dollars.

Mass vs. Weight

In everyday language, we talk about the weight of an object rather than its mass. Are these two words for the same thing? Technically, weight and mass are distinct concepts. In scientific terms, the **mass** of an object is the amount of matter in the object. Mass is measured in kilograms and grams in the metric system and in pounds and ounces in the English system. The **weight** of an object is the measure of the pull of gravity on that object. Sir Isaac Newton first explained the importance of gravity for the motions of the planets and for the fall of an object more than 300 years ago.

Because of the awareness of space travel, most children know that the pull of gravity is different on different planets and that there is essentially no gravity in outer space. Many museums and planetariums have exhibits that show your weight on the moon and various planets. For example, since the moon's gravity is weaker than the Earth's, the pull on an individual object would be less. Thus, a human being would weigh less on the moon than on Earth.

How is the mass of an object affected by gravity? The mass of an object remains constant regardless of space travel since gravity does not influence mass. Since we use a two-pan balance to measure mass, both sides of the balance are equally affected by gravity. If an 11-gram pencil balances one 1-gram and two 5-gram standard masses on Earth, it will balance those same masses on the moon.

However, since most of us are likely to spend our lives on Earth, the distinction between mass and weight may be lost on many students.

We suggest two pedagogical alternatives with regard to the distinction between mass and weight:

1. Ignore it. This point is fairly subtle and eludes many adults.
2. Provide a simple explanation, but don't worry about it too much.

Building the *Math Trailblazers* Classroom

This section focuses on establishing a flexible and challenging learning environment for all students. Strategies include addressing classroom culture, effectively grouping students, managing manipulatives, and pacing instruction.

Students work effectively in groups assisted by easy access to math manipulatives.

Building the MTB Classroom

Building the *Math Trailblazers* Classroom

Using strategies like those described here enables students to develop confidence and expertise in problem solving.

Two factors essential to student learning are the curriculum and a classroom environment that supports and challenges students (NCTM, 2000; Reys & Bay-Williams, 2003). Data on classroom implementation of the *Math Trailblazers* curriculum came from pilot test results, classroom observations, videos of lessons, and teacher feedback. From these sources, effective classroom management and teaching strategies emerged. These strategies enable students to develop confidence and expertise in problem solving. This section summarizes the following teaching and classroom management strategies: addressing classroom culture, student grouping, organization and management of manipulatives, and curriculum pacing.

 PART 1

Classroom Culture

Creating a classroom culture that promotes thinking and learning requires an explicit focus on high student expectations and cooperation. The following strategies result in high performance among students (Kersaint, 2007) and should become part of *Math Trailblazers* classrooms:

- *Allow time for students to reason mathematically.* While many teachers may think they have high expectations, their well-intentioned actions can lower the difficulty level of students' work (Smith, Stein, Henningson, & Silver, 2000). For example, a teacher may model a detailed solution path for a challenging problem. However, when students mimic the teacher's solution path, they lose the opportunity to think about the problem and attempt their own strategies. This reduces the challenge of the problem. Instead, develop a challenging classroom culture that encourages mathematical reasoning by allowing students to discuss their strategies and ideas with classmates prior to starting the problem.

- *Provide opportunities for students to freely discuss mathematical understandings.* One noticeable characteristic of an effective *Math Trailblazers* classroom is the nature of the discussion that takes place consistently. When discourse is part of the classroom culture of learning, students are confident in sharing their ideas and questioning other students' contributions. Good classroom discourse is vital to the implementation of *Math Trailblazers.* "Academically Productive Talk" (Chapin & O'Connor, 2007) is the vehicle through which students make sense of new concepts. The Language in the *Math Trailblazers* Classroom section explores the connection between classroom discourse and learning.

- *Have students explain how they solve problems.* Teachers can encourage students to persevere in the problem-solving process by having them try different approaches or seek help from their classmates. Support students' thinking and classroom discourse by asking them to reflect on earlier completed tasks. References to previously completed tasks helps students make connections in their learning and in their problem-solving processes. Once students have drawn parallels in their learning, have them communicate their understandings in writing or share their ideas in class discussions.

- *Let students be responsible for their own learning.* One indicator of a classroom culture that supports and challenges students is that students realize they alone are responsible for solving problems. The teacher only provides the tools that assist students in solving problems. Students further understand that the teacher is not the owner of answers. Students should solve problems and offer explanations, not the teacher. The following two anecdotes are examples of students taking responsibility for their learning:

Jeremy, a fifth grader, whispered to a math coach who came regularly to his classroom, "I think you've known the answers all year! But you want us to figure them out!"

Hannah, a second grader, raised her hand to answer a question the teacher had posed. She paused and before responding, asked, "Will I have to explain my answer?" When the teacher assured her she would have to explain, she said, "Then let me think about it a little longer."

Use of the above strategies results in students who value mathematics, increase their persistence in solving a problem, become confident in their ability to do mathematics, become mathematical problem solvers, and believe that mathematics makes sense.

Establishing Classroom Norms

PART II

Establishing a classroom culture that promotes high expectations and inquiry means establishing classroom norms for participation. When you enter a classroom that "works" it seems effortless. The students and teacher respect each other's ideas. There is a true sense of collaboration and exploration. To create such an environment requires intentional and ongoing effort on the part of the teacher. The following recommendations represent ideas from numerous effective *Math Trailblazers* teachers.

> *To create an environment of true collaboration and exploration requires intentional and ongoing effort on the part of the teacher.*

- *Set clear expectations and remind students of them daily.* Some teachers use a "Rights and Responsibilities" approach to classroom rules. These rights and responsibilities can be framed in a positive way and encourage student ownership. Some examples include:

  1. I have the right to be heard when speaking.
  2. I will speak clearly.
  3. I will not interrupt others.
  4. I will listen carefully when others speak.
  5. I have the right to learn.
  6. I will ask questions when I do not understand.
  7. I will not distract others from learning.

Chapin and O'Connor (2007) use the concept of "obligations" when considering students' participation in classroom discourse. Regardless of the rules you select, or whether you negotiate those rules with students or set them yourself, it is essential that you teach and model those expectations for students. In the beginning of the year, dedicate time each day to teaching and practicing students' rights and responsibilities. Take easy tasks and use them to teach desired behaviors. Be explicit and let students know which outcomes are being practiced. Some teachers discuss the expectations and post them in the front of the room. The investment in the beginning of the year and daily reminders are powerful in creating a risk-taking learning environment. For video examples of how some teachers prepare for and begin the year with *Math Trailblazers* go to www.Trailblazers.com.

- *Teach children to be mathematicians.* Provide opportunities for students to work in groups, struggle to find a solution path, argue their mathematics solution, and settle differences. These opportunities mirror the work of mathematicians.

- *Create a flexible and dynamic classroom environment.* Allow opportunities for further exploration or extensions of a topic. Often as students explore new problems, they make connections to other mathematical teaching opportunities.

PART III — Grouping Students for Effective Instruction

Working with a partner or in small groups enhances students' opportunities to communicate about mathematics in a nonthreatening environment. Students learn from and help each other. However, selecting and managing effective groups requires important considerations. They include:

- Do I group heterogeneously?
- What size groups should I use?
- Do I just choose names randomly?
- Do I plan groups that mix students by ability, temperament, or both?
- Do I give students in a group "jobs" to ensure that everybody works?
- What individual accountability measures can I use?
- Will each student prepare a product, or will the group produce one shared product?

There are many ways to group students to ensure success. Some important considerations in grouping and facilitating group work follow.

Grouping needs to be flexible. Flexibility in grouping means that the number of people in the group changes based on the task. Also, sometimes pairing students with like abilities makes more sense then pairing a struggling learner with a very strong student. It may be effective to establish cooperative groups of three to four students that remain constant for a period of time, such as one month or one unit. Some days students may work in their cooperative group and other days they may be in a new partnership, based on your decision of what size group will best support student thinking and engagement.

The following are appropriate ways to group students for instruction:

- Small groups of two, three, or four students seem to be the most successful. In primary classrooms, pairs are the most effective groupings with the occasional exception of bringing two strong pairs together to form a group of four. Sometimes groups of three work best depending on the task. For example, in third grade, the *The Better Picker Upper* lab compares the absorbency of three types of paper towels. In this case it is best to assign each member of the group the responsibility of examining one type of paper towel. When it comes to grouping in your classroom, the important idea is to keep groupings flexible and to stress the importance of cooperation and respect no matter the group size.

Flexibility in grouping means that the number of people in the group changes based on the task.

- Teach pair-sharing where students turn quickly to a partner and discuss new concepts, strategies, or new vocabulary with a classmate. This breaks up teacher talk time and allows students to scaffold ideas for one another.
- Pick names randomly from a hat or jar when you want to increase the flexibility of students' working relationships.
- Have children choose partners.
- Place children in groups that match how they best work—the quiet ones all in one group and the boisterous all together.
- Assign groups by ability, heterogeneous or homogeneous when targeting specific skills with specific students.
- Keep the whole class together in one group.

While whole-class instruction and working individually are not often considered grouping strategies, both are appropriate and essential in learning mathematics. Whole-class instruction is especially useful when explaining the day's problem, introducing a new manipulative, correcting a common mistake, or summarizing the lesson. Whole-group instruction is most effective when it is brief, focused, and the information applies to all students. Clarity is enhanced when teachers provide a few minutes for pairs to discuss new ideas.

Working alone is powerful and effective as well. Giving students time to reflect and record their strategies before joining the group increases participation and helps students assess their own needs. When students do begin group time, they are able to focus on the lesson's goals and contribute thoughtfully to the discussion. In concluding the lessons, individual reflection in the form of journal writing can be a powerful assessment tool. Teachers can keep close tabs on student thinking as they develop from each day's lesson and also help catch any misinformation before big gaps in learning take place (DeBellis & Rosenstein, 2007).

Giving students time to reflect and record their strategies before joining the group increases participation and helps students assess their own needs.

Room Arrangement Matters. Seating students at tables or with desks pulled together does not necessarily guarantee that students will work well together, but sitting in rows and columns makes cooperation much more difficult. Have students sit around a group of desks that may be pulled together as a work surface to facilitate discussion and focus.

Build in Individual Accountability. Individual accountability is also important when students work in groups. To balance individual responsibility with cooperation, some teachers adopt a procedure that numbers students in each group 1, 2, 3, 4. The teacher prompts the class by saying, "3s may start the conversation at each table" or "odds talk to each other" or "1s and 3s talk and 2s and 4s listen." The important things to remember are that all students are held accountable and that the questions for groups are rich enough to push understanding.

Group members also need to be accountable to each other. They need to use one another as a resource before consulting the teacher. Be disciplined and not answer questions from group members unless they have carefully consulted each member. It is especially when working together on laboratory investigations that it is the group's responsibility to make sure all members have appropriate and accurate data tables and graphs. Students need to learn to rely on and trust one another for group work to be successful.

Here is a summary of how a *Math Trailblazers* classroom might use different student groupings:

- Students work independently giving each child a chance to think through a question and come up with a way to problem solve.

- Students turn to a partner to rehearse their answers or to make their answers more complete.

- Students work in groups to complete a task. They share ideas, responsibilities, and materials. These tasks would be difficult to complete independently. There are many ways to choose groups so that all students benefit from working with others.

- Students work as a whole class evaluating peer problem-solving strategies or receiving direction from the teacher.

PART IV Managing Math Manipulatives

Most *Math Trailblazers* lessons suggest or require the use of manipulatives. Manipulatives facilitate student learning, but effective manipulative use requires attention to their management. The following suggest ways to manage manipulatives within the classroom:

Manipulatives need to be prepared and organized ahead of time.

- When appropriate, the "Preparing for Upcoming Units" section of the Unit Planner identifies a manipulative to be used in the next unit. Gather manipulatives in advance and place them in a center for exploration.

- At the appropriate grade, have laminated copies of full-size or desk-size ten frames, *100* or *200 Charts,* and multiplication tables available for students.

- Store commonly used materials such as laminated flash cards and base-ten boards in accessible locations such as pocket charts. Make copies of these for students and allow them to take home their originals for practice.

- Allow students to explore manipulatives during indoor recess or center time. This casual experience helps them to be more focused when the lesson begins.

- Try all the manipulatives yourself before using them with students. Some grade levels use common planning time to try the lab activities together.

- Prepare and store copies of frequently-used items such as data tables and graphs. These can be copied in bulk before the school year saving both time and money.

Store manipulatives with easy access for students in mind.

- Have the most frequently used manipulatives, such as connecting cubes, links, coins, and base-ten pieces, available all year at student desks, on counters, or stored in nearby tubs for quick availability.

- If sharing a manipulative kit between teachers, develop a system to catalog manipulatives for easier accessibility.

- Store manipulatives in clear plastic bags, boxes, or cartons. Organize them so there are enough pieces in each bag or box for partners or whole tables. Have students who needs practice counting arrange links and connecting cubes in sets of ten by color.

- When working in groups with manipulatives, assign one person in each group the responsibility of collecting and returning items to their original location.

- Create a personal Daily Practice and Problem (DPP) manipulative kit for students to use when solving their DPPs each day. These kits include manipulatives frequently used to solve DPP problems. They may include things like links, coins, and connecting cubes at the primary grades, and base-ten pieces and pattern blocks at the middle grades.

- Label manipulative kits with quantities of materials to help prevent their loss. A label such as "This kit should contain 4 rulers, 4 calculators, and 4 sets of base-ten pieces" will help students (and teachers) track all materials before they are stored.

- Easy accessibility and visibility are key to efficient use of storage devices. Organizers, such as those with clear plastic shoe pockets designed to be hung on a door are a good resource for storing calculators or other manipulatives. By adding students' names to the outside of each pocket, you can tell quickly who has or has not returned their manipulatives.

Use manipulatives in instruction to promote understanding.

- Introduce each manipulative and discuss its use. For example, when students first use graduated cylinders, say, "What do you see when you look at a graduated cylinder?" Or for a balance ask, "What do you notice about this balance?" The conversations that groups have first and then share with the whole class are rich and exciting. Students often see interesting things that teachers may not.

- Include calculators as an option for students. As with most tools, the more they use them, the more commonplace they become. Be open about discussing when calculators are an appropriate choice.

- Post a list of the day's manipulatives to be used for each lesson. Make older students responsible for retrieving and returning their own supplies according to that list.

- Designate a "hands off" area on the desk or table for manipulatives to be kept while listening to a student or teacher.

Above all, remember that the more experience students have with manipulatives, the more equipped they will be for solving problems.

Ideas on the Pacing of *Math Trailblazers* Lessons

Teach math 60 minutes per day, every day. The National Council of Teachers of Mathematics established a standard of 60 minutes per day of mathematics instruction for children beginning in grade 1. *Math Trailblazers* is designed to be used for 60 minutes per day, every day. Sequence activities that follow the day's schedule and the children's ability to focus. For example, you can begin the day with a Daily Practice and Problem item, do a math activity that keeps the children working in groups at tables, and do an activity that has the children walking around to gather data later in the day. Not all 60 minutes of instruction need to be offered continuously.

Use manipulatives in instruction to promote understanding.

The National Council of Teachers of Mathematics established a standard of 60 minutes per day of mathematics instruction for children beginning in grade 1.

The early units in each grade contain many opportunities for teachers to get to know the children and to assess their math abilities from the first day. Encourage your colleagues to join you in reaching the goal of a full hour of math, every day.

Use the Pacing Suggestions in the *Unit Resource Guide*. Suggestions for pacing are given within each *Unit Resource Guide* at the beginning of the lessons and Unit Outlines. They are also in the Overview section of the *Teacher Implementation Guide*. Often the suggestions will recommend omitting or adding certain lessons if this is your first year with *Math Trailblazers*. For example, pacing suggestions for fifth grade will sometimes direct you to add a lesson from fourth grade or skip sections of the unit if your students are new to *Math Trailblazers*.

Use the multidisciplinary structure of *Math Trailblazers* to your advantage. Teach the lessons involving *Adventure Books* during literature blocks or read aloud times. Pull the science-heavy lessons or units into your science time. The lessons involving "Mr. Origin" can be completed during Social Studies lessons to address map skills. There are many creative ways to incorporate more mathematics into each day.

If this is your first year teaching *Math Trailblazers*, work towards teaching as much of the material as possible. This is especially true for teachers at grades 3–5. Teachers in the primary grades often complete all the lessons as outlined in the *Unit Resource Guide* with little trouble. To do this, teachers must start on the first day of school and dedicate an hour to math instruction each day through the last day of school. Completing all the lessons in the primary grades greatly impacts students at grades 3–5.

Teachers in the upper grades should strive to complete more and more of the curriculum each year. However, there is more content in grades 4–5 than can be taught in one school year. *Math Trailblazers* is aimed at a national audience. Because content expectations vary from state to state, some content included in grade 4 may be taught in grade 5 in your district. Thus, you and your colleagues need to carefully choose what content to teach at what time.

Upper-grade teachers in their first year with *Math Trailblazers* should teach the lessons as described and try not to stay too long on any one concept. Although this may be the first time your students see concepts presented in this way, they will have several opportunities to explore the ideas. Each lesson is not designed to be taught for mastery. The concepts will spiral back throughout the year in the Daily Practice and Problems and later units. Each time a concept is presented, the approach is slightly different. If students struggled the first time, they will have more opportunities as the year progresses to acquire the concept or skill.

Respecting differences in classrooms. Some schools or districts establish a pacing chart for each grade so classrooms stay together and all students will receive the same mathematics instruction. Asking teachers to move through a curriculum at exactly the same rate is very difficult to implement. Sometimes individual teachers find that students need more time with one concept and less time with another. We find that schools and districts with the best implementations recommend the lessons and units that need to be completed within a quarter and allow teachers some flexibility in the weekly pacing of the materials.

Rearranging lesson order. If changes must be made to the order of the lessons, make decisions as a grade level in a school or district. These decisions should be made with the advice of a math specialist or coordinator who understands the development of the mathematics content within and across grades. It is very important to the integrity of the curriculum that individual teachers not make pacing decisions on their own. Sometimes the timing of state tests determines when a particular unit should be covered. In these cases, teachers benefit from cross-grade level discussions.

Whole-group decisions can consider timing of the math facts program and Daily Practice and Problems. Teachers can use the *Facts Resource Guide* at grades 2–5 to keep on track with the math facts while making adjustments to other content. When making decisions as a school, teachers from one grade to the next can adjust for gaps in learning when items are missed or altered. It is very helpful to have at least one person with access to the entire curriculum to help guide these types of discussions for your school or district. If you do not have a qualified person in your district contact Kendall/Hunt for additional resources.

This section is just the beginning of what the *Math Trailblazers* classroom can be. The conversation continues with other sections of the *Teacher Implementation Guide*. Sections on classroom discourse, working with parents, and meeting the needs of individual students add to the information presented here. Also the online communities at Mathtrailblazers.com and the listserv give you direct access to teachers in the field. To join the *Math Trailblazers* Listserv, send a note to TIMS@uic.edu.

References

Chapin, Suzanne H., and Catherine O'Connor. "Academically Productive Talk: Supporting Students' Learning in Mathematics." *The Learning of Mathematics*. Portia C. Elliot, W. Gary Martin, and Marilyn E. Strutchens, eds., pp. 113–128. National Council of Teachers of Mathematics, Reston, VA, 2007.

Curriculum and Evaluation Standards for School Mathematics, National Council of Teachers of Mathematics, Reston, VA, 1989.

DeBellis, Valerie A., and Joseph G. Rosenstein. "Creating an Equitable Learning Environment for Teachers of Grades K–8 Mathematics." *The Learning of Mathematics*. Portia C. Elliot, W. Gary Martin, and Marilyn E. Strutchens, eds., pp. 271–288. National Council of Teachers of Mathematics, Reston, VA, 2007.

Kersaint, Gladis. "The Learning Environment: Its Influence on What is Learned." *The Learning of Mathematics*. Portia C. Elliot, W. Gary Martin, and Marilyn E. Strutchens, eds., pp. 83–96. National Council of Teachers of Mathematics, Reston, VA, 2007.

Principles and Standards for School Mathematics, National Council of Teachers of Mathematics, Reston, VA, 2000.

Reys, B.J., and J.M. Bay-Williams. "The Role of Curriculum Materials In Implementing the Curriculum and Learning Principles." *Mathematics Teaching in the Middle School.* 9(2), pp. 120–124, 2003.

Stein, M.K., M.S. Smith, M.A. Henningson, & E.A. Silver. *Implementing Standards-based Mathematics Instruction: A Casebook for Professional Development.* Teacher's College Press, New York, 2000.

Teaching the *Math Trailblazers* Student: Meeting Individual Needs

This section concentrates on meeting the needs of individual students, specifically focusing on the needs of English Language Learners, special education students, and talented or gifted students as they access the rigorous mathematics in *Math Trailblazers*.

Student and teacher working together to access the rigorous mathematics in Math Trailblazers.

Teaching the MTB Student

Teaching the *Math Trailblazers* Student: Meeting Individual Needs

Today's world is increasingly more diverse, and educators frequently need to attend to this diversity. New issues, ideologies, and calls for accountability surface almost daily, highlighting the need for teachers to address all forms of diversity within their classrooms. It may be surprising to some, but every classroom is diverse in some ways. Students vary in their prior knowledge, interests, and learning styles, among other things. Many classrooms have students from different cultures or ethnic groups. Within a student group, some may have special learning needs while others are gifted or talented in mathematics. All have the right to access the rigorous mathematics in *Math Trailblazers*.

The importance of making rigorous mathematics available to all students is articulated in the Equity Principle in the *Principles and Standards for School Mathematics* (NCTM, 2000). The Equity Principle states:

> Excellence in mathematics education requires equity—high expectations and strong support for all students. . . . All students, regardless of their personal characteristics, backgrounds, or physical challenges must have opportunities to study and support to learn mathematics. Equity does not mean that every student should receive identical instruction. . . . All students need access each year to a coherent, challenging mathematical curriculum taught by competent and well-supported mathematics teachers. (p. 12)

From its inception, the *Math Trailblazers* writers intended to design a curriculum that would support all learners. According to Robert Marzano (2003), the school-level factor that has the most impact on student achievement for all students is a "guaranteed and viable curriculum." Marzano defines a guaranteed and viable curriculum as one in which students are provided with both the opportunity to learn and the time in which to learn. This means that the sequence and organization of the curriculum must support students as they learn.

Math Trailblazers materials (lessons, labs, games, and assessments) include a variety of strategies that address the needs of students of differing learning styles, cultural and linguistic differences, and mathematical abilities. To assist teachers in creating a flexible learning environment, these strategies as well as some of the opportunities for meeting the needs of a wide variety of learners are identified in the Unit Outline in grades 1–5.

While the design of *Math Trailblazers* makes great strides in supporting a wide range of learners, it is still important to consider the unique needs of learners and adapt lessons appropriately. English Language Learners, for example, benefit from the use of the language that is part of the *Math Trailblazers* design, but these learners will be more successful when teachers implement additional language support. Gifted learners certainly benefit from the challenging open-ended tasks that are found throughout the curriculum, but can learn more when these tasks include extensions or

> *All students, regardless of their personal characteristics, backgrounds, or physical challenges must have opportunities to study and support to learn mathematics.*

adaptations. Special education students are supported with the language, models, and strategies used throughout the curriculum, but additional scaffolding and reading and writing support can enhance their experience.

This section was created for teachers to understand how the curriculum design supports specific groups of learners *and* to provide ideas for additional strategies that can further support each learner. The populations addressed in this section are:

Part 1. English Language Learners

Part 2. Special Education Students

Part 3. Talented and Gifted Students

These sections are not a review of all research in the field nor are they intended to be exhaustive lists of appropriate strategies. Instead they are an overview of some math-specific issues that are likely to be true in many classrooms. They also include some tried and true strategies that *Math Trailblazers* teachers have found to support their efforts to provide a challenging and supportive learning environment for their students.

Resources

Marzano, Robert. *What Works in Schools: Translating Research into Action.* Association for Supervision and Curriculum Development, Alexandria, VA, 2003.

Principles and Standards for School Mathematics. National Council of Teachers of Mathematics, Reston, VA, 2000.

Using *Math Trailblazers* with English Language Learners

A. Introduction

Mathematics classrooms no longer operate within a universal environment of "just numbers." Students are now expected to reason, explore, justify, and record their strategies for solving complex problems. This shift in practice, while excellent in rigor, presents a different challenge for students who are learning English. Their needs are unique and, therefore, warrant special attention.

Whether your district has adopted a small group instruction model or a mainstream classroom model for English Language Learners (ELLs), they deserve access to the rich mathematics presented throughout *Math Trailblazers.* If you teach in a district that has adopted or is considering adopting *Math Trailblazers,* be prepared to instruct all students with this curriculum. You can be confident that students with special needs, whether linguistic or academic, will benefit immensely from the hands-on, concept-based instruction provided in *Math Trailblazers.*

Whether your district has adopted a small group instruction model or a mainstream classroom model for English Language Learners (ELLs), they deserve access to the rich mathematics presented throughout Math Trailblazers.

With the move away from isolated computation as the primary focus of mathematics instruction, it is important to ask, "How can I help English Language Learners succeed in a language-rich math class?" Rather than seeing the amount of listening, reading, writing, and speaking in *Math Trailblazers* as an obstacle, consider it as an opportunity for ELLs to learn and use their new language in a meaningful way. In fact, the only way they will learn English and mathematics is if they have the opportunity to use language in their math class.

The section in the *Teacher Implementation Guide,* titled Language in the *Math Trailblazers* Classroom, provides many ideas for supporting language use in general. In this section, the focus is on the unique needs of ELLs. While certainly not exhaustive, the ideas presented in this section offer a starting point for further thought, discussion, and collaboration. The section begins with a brief overview of research and theory related to language learning. It identifies and discusses tools already in the structure of *Math Trailblazers* and shares additional strategies that will increase access to the content.

B. Second Language Learning: Theory in Review

Early theories of second language learning were rooted in behaviorist theories of education. Behaviorists believed that language was learned through exposure to controlled grammar and language structure with minimal thought to social or cultural impact. (Ricard-Amato and Snow, 2005) In a time when much of education was decontextualized and rote, language instruction was no different.

From research in the field of second language learning starting in the late 1970s, we now know that second languages are not "learned" through rules and structures. Rather, they are acquired through context-embedded interactions much as children learn their first language. The work of Stephen Krashen, James Cummins, and others greatly shape our current views of how children acquire a language (*Schooling and Language Minority Students: A Theoretical Framework* Pp. 3–79, 1991).

Krashen (ibid, 1991) proposes that children acquire a second language naturally as they are exposed to comprehensible input through a low affective filter. In other words, as students interact in a safe, concrete environment they are able to understand and take risks in language. Through high motivation and purposeful use of the new language over time, students move towards proficiency in that language.

Cummins (ibid, 1991) adds further insight into second language learning by documenting the amount of time it takes most students to become proficient in the target language as described above. According to his research, it takes approximately two years for a student to master face-to-face, context-embedded communicative fluency. This level of competency is necessary to succeed in day-to-day social conversations such as those on the playground for example.

Ease at simple exchanges by ELLs, however, is often mistaken for advanced fluency in the new language. Therefore, Cummins (1984) identified an important distinction between the ease of social language and the unique demands required to succeed in the classroom's academic environment. To become proficient in the cognitively demanding language of the classroom, students need five to seven years to reach the level of their native English-speaking peers. That means even though students seem proficient in everyday conversations, they have years of academic language to master. The distinction between the two language proficiencies is crucial in ensuring the success of English Language Learners in our schools. The distinction allows teachers and researchers to identify and address the unique demands of academic language instruction.

Donaldson (1978) predated Cummins in her identification of "embedded and disembedded thought and language." By expanding on Donaldson's ideas, Cummins developed a framework for defining language use in the classroom. Cummins (1984) cites her framework when explaining why students acquire conversational language more rapidly due to the embedded contextual clues and high motivation of face-to-face communication. In addition, the framework reiterates the difficulty experienced by students in completing the cognitive demands of abstract tasks within the classroom. Cummins articulates the major aim of schooling as developing students' abilities to manipulate and interpret abstract texts. Therefore, the more we can do as educators to relate the abstract, academic world to the concrete, familiar world of students, the more accessible that knowledge becomes.

C. Tools in *Math Trailblazers* to Support English Language Learners

By using *Math Trailblazers* you are already well on your way to providing ELLs access to rigorous mathematics. This curriculum has numerous effective tools for making the abstract come to life. As you plan your lessons using the *Unit Resource Guide* consider the following features:

- Abundance of visuals
- Extensive use of manipulatives
- Graphic organizers
- Labs
- Problem solving from everyday life
- Connections to literature
- Group and partner work
- Opportunities to write and read in English

Math Trailblazers uses many of these features daily. Simply implementing all aspects of the curriculum will increase the support of your English Language Learners.

> *By using* Math Trailblazers *you are already well on your way to providing English Language Learners access to rigorous mathematics.*

D. Language-rich Approach to Instruction

We now know that English Language Learners develop skills in listening, speaking, reading, and writing at the same time, although we once believed they progressed in a linear fashion (Richard-Amato and Snow, 2005). Therefore, every lesson should provide meaningful opportunities for English Language Learners to experience and use language. *Math Trailblazers* provides excellent opportunities for students to use and learn language in a safe environment. Language is two-way communication: receptive (listening and reading) and productive (speaking and writing). This section takes each of these four domains and explains what is built into *Math Trailblazers* along with a discussion of the related needs and strategies of English Language Learners.

> *Every math lesson should provide meaningful opportunities for English Language Learners to experience and use language.*

Listening. *Math Trailblazers* provides problem solving in motivating scenarios. In these tasks, students listen to others in their groups as they work on solutions. For example, students sell lemonade and plan class parties in third grade. They track the weather and investigate healthy eating habits in first grade. They take trips to famous places to study mathematical concepts. They consider the height of the Sears Tower and the circumference of the large Ferris wheel at Navy Pier in Chicago. They even predict the number of pennies in a stack from Earth to the moon!

Students listen to original or adapted literature in the *Adventure Book* and trade books recommended in the curriculum. The *Unit Resource Guides* and the *Teacher Implementation Guides* list literature selections that are either suggested or essential to completing each unit. Research is overwhelming as to the benefits of daily read alouds for all students, especially English Language Learners (Krashen, 1993; Trelease, 2001). If you are unable to read each selection to the students, add math-related titles to your listening center, or for high motivation, your podcasting center.

For English Language Learners it is essential that you monitor their abilities to listen and comprehend what they hear, whether it is listening to you or their peers. Use strategies like "numbered heads together" where each group member is assigned a number for the teacher to use in monitoring participation or drawing names from a cup to ensure that all students share. Be careful, of course, to allow generous wait time for ELLs to form their thoughts, and even allow them to share in alternative ways like drawings or motions. Allow students to be the teacher as they share their strategies for solving problems. By limiting the sharing of duplicate strategies, you also encourage students to listen carefully and evaluate each other's ideas.

There are teacher actions that can improve the listening and comprehension skills of English Language Learners. These include:

- As you speak to your English Language Learners, use clear language with lots of expression and movement.
- Be your own dictionary, always explaining difficult words as you use them.

- Use Art Costa's 10/2 principle. Do not speak for more than 10 minutes without giving students at least 2 minutes to process and make connections with the new information (Brechtel, 1998).

- Familiarize students with the process of turning quickly to their neighbor and interacting with what they are hearing.

- Allow students time to draw a picture or do a quick write.

However you manage it, just give students time to connect the new learning to a familiar idea.

Reading. Math class is a great opportunity for students to apply all their reading skills in a different context. English Language Learners benefit from paired reading especially when paired with strong English readers. (Diaz-Rico and Weed, 2002) They also benefit when expository texts, such as the *Student Guide,* are reworded into summary statements. (Echevarria and Graves, 2003) These strategies encourage groups of students to rewrite each paragraph or section using one sentence. Summarizing helps English Language Learners focus on the important information and not get lost in the details.

Again, use all the reading resources in the curriculum:

- Use the literature in the Literature Connections and the *Adventure Book* in addition to the *Student Guide.*

- Transfer key sentences from the *Student Guide* to sentence strips for English syntax examination.

- Omit key words for vocabulary development or "cloze" activities where students use the context of the sentence to find the missing key term or terms.

- Consider using math-related words in your spelling or vocabulary program.

- Do NOT focus on teaching key words like "in all" or "how many left" as indicators of certain operations. These terms can mislead and distract students from thinking about the whole problem. Instead teach students to read the problem carefully by focusing on its action or by considering the picture it creates.

Speaking. Use cooperative groups to put English Language Learners into situations where they can use their language and hear other native speakers. The Lesson Guides suggest ways for students to work in groups. Keep the groups flexible while varying their size and purpose. Students may work in groups to complete labs or in pairs to share strategies for problem solving. Because students need constant guidance and encouragement when working with others, spend the time needed to create a classroom environment of constructive student-to-student relationships. Give children the language needed to help each other or clarify ideas. Be sensitive to cultural and dominance issues that hinder equity among students. Do not be discouraged if it takes longer than you expect for students to work well together. Suggestions include:

- Provide sentence frames and sentence starters for discussion.

- Teach new vocabulary. (For more information and teaching ideas refer to the end of this section.)

- In primary classes use a key term as the "word of the day." Each time you transition within the lesson use the new term as a signal to move or begin work. You may even want to associate a physical movement or sound with the term to further involve the children with the new concept. (Brechtel, 1998)

- Encourage students to share their thinking by refusing to be the only expert in the room.

- Foster a safe environment where students are not ridiculed for making mistakes in English (or in math). For more information on establishing classroom norms, see the Building the *Math Trailblazers* Classroom section.

- Try numbering the participants in each group to encourage each student to speak. Use numbers or other identifiers as triggers to begin conversations. For example, "Twos, begin the conversation on prime numbers." Or "Fours, be ready to report back to the class at the end of your discussion." Using numbers or other identifiers in this way provides gentle accountability for all students.

- Keep in mind that the less time you talk, the more time students will have to talk.

- Set time for students to 1) work alone, 2) work in small groups before coming together in a whole-group discussion. This gives students a chance to think about the problem and test their ideas with a few others, before sharing with the whole class.

Writing. Take advantage of the many opportunities for children to write that exist in *Math Trailblazers*. English Language Learners need to see good writing modeled for them everyday, especially in math class. Even native speaking English students struggle to express their thinking and strategies for problem solving. All students need the language of thought. They need words for what is happening in their head. Therefore, encourage the use of terms such as counting on, skip counting, and regrouping. Use this vocabulary in class, not as words to be tested, but rather as language that gives meaning to the solution paths that students present. In the beginning you do the drawing and the writing; students give the ideas. Little by little as students become more confident, encourage them to draw, and later write, about their solutions. Save student work and show problem-solving examples to your students. You can score those just as you would score formal writing pieces in other subjects.

In addition, consider the following suggestions for improving writing for English Language Learners:

- Use the journal prompts. Make the journal prompts interactive by responding to the students in writing whenever possible.

- Model mathematical language by using shared writing strategies in which you and your students write together (McCarrier, Pinnell, and Fountas, 2000).

- Use the writing required in *Math Trailblazers* to support good writing in general. For example, reinforce transition words in strategy explanations as you would in expository writing.

- Use sentence frames or sentence starters to help English Language Learners model correct structure.

- Develop a respectful safe environment for students to share their strategies, so that English Language Learners will have more opportunities to develop that inner sense of what "sounds right" in English.

E. Issues Frequently Raised in Discussions with Teachers of English Language Learners

Planning Lessons When Some or All of the Students are ELLs

Use the *Unit Resource Guide* in planning your lessons. This component remains the center of each daily activity. The *Unit Resource Guide* outlines the content goals for each lesson. For the English Language Learners in your room, it is extremely important that the grade-level content goals are as close to the goals of their peers as possible. Not only do they need access to the same rich mathematics, for English Language Learners each new lesson is another opportunity for language growth as well. Therefore every lesson now needs to accomplish two goals: learning rigorous mathematics content and improving English skills (Echevarria, Vogt, and Short, 2000).

The following lesson from Grade 2 Unit 3 is an example of one way you might adapt a *Math Trailblazers* lesson to accommodate English Language Learners. This level of detail is NOT necessary for each lesson, but might be useful in getting started. Once you become more familiar with these strategies, the lesson planning will become second nature. You will be more confident making the adaptations right from the *Unit Resource Guide*.

> *English Language Learners need access to the same rich mathematics as their classmates, and each new lesson is another opportunity for language growth as well.*

Teacher:	Grade 2 Unit 3 Lesson 3	Date:

Envision Outcomes:

Content Goals:
- Sorting objects by size.
- Collecting and recording data in a table.
- Making and interpreting bar graphs.

Posted goal for students:

"Students will sort buttons into groups by size, record the numbers in each group in a data table, and study them in a graph"

Language Goals:
- "There are ___ (small, medium, large) buttons in our handful."
- _____ buttons are the most common in our handful.
- _____ buttons are the least common in our handful.
- See Journal Prompt.
- Student pairs discuss how to sort their piles of buttons.
- Students review their graph at the end of class focusing on trends in the data.

Vocabulary:

sort	size*
button	small
medium	large
data table	graph
label	handful
most/least	common
tally	

*Word of the day

Enlist Help:

Consult the TIMS Tutor: *The TIMS Laboratory Method.* Ask adult helpers, if available, to monitor partner discussions.

Equip the Learners:
- Ask partners to identify a small, medium, and large object in the room and share with their table. Report a few examples to the class.
- Break down the word "handful." Ask students to predict its meaning from its construction.
- Bring in a soup can to show an example of a label. Discuss the function of a label.
- Review the pictures from *The Button Box* by M. Reid read in Unit 3 Lesson 1.

Engage Motivation:
- Give student pairs a handful of buttons and ask them to sort them into three groups: small, medium, and large. Show the transparency and model with a small group of buttons.
- Remind students of the sentence starters listed in the "Language Goals" they can use for discussion.
- Walk around and observe students as they work together. Praise appropriate use of mathematical language and cooperative behavior.

Execute the Lesson:
- Using the data table as a visual, remind students how to fill out the bottom of page 57 in their *Student Guide.* Ask pairs how they can record "Number of Buttons."
- If no groups suggest it, remind them how to draw tallies to keep track of the buttons.
- On a transparency or chart paper, review the parts of a graph. Pay close attention to the "labels" on each axis. Remind them of the soup can.
- Ask students to graph their data.
- Refer to the sentence frames to help students discuss their graphs with the class. Encourage student pairs to share.

Evaluate the Progress:
- Use the addition and subtraction problems suggested on page 34 of the *Unit Resource Guide* to continue problem solving in pairs.
- Have groups compare and contrast their graphs using sentence starters like, "Our group had ___ more/less buttons than…" or "Our graph looks like a _____, while their graph looks like a _____."
- Place graphs in portfolios to use as a baseline for future activities.
- Interact with the students' entries in their math journals.
- Record observations as groups work together. (See the Assessment section.)

Teacher:	Grade __ Unit __ Lesson __	Date:

Envision Outcomes:

Content Goals:	Language Goals:	Vocabulary:

Enlist Help:

Equip the Learners:

Engage Motivation:

Execute the Lesson:

Evaluate the Progress:

Effective Lesson Planning for English Language Learners using the *Unit Resource Guide:*

ENVISION OUTCOMES:

Content Goals: These should be clear and posted for students at the beginning of the lesson. They may be in the form of a question that students will answer or a task they can complete. The Key Content section of the Lesson Guide is a good place to start formulating your goals. Regardless of their form, review them before the lesson begins and as you progress to help the students (and you) keep focus.

Language Goals: Here is the major adjustment needed for English Language Learners. As you review the lesson in the *Unit Resource Guide,* consider what language needs will arise for your students. Identify the English structure or vocabulary you must address as you proceed through the lesson. Be direct and explicit as you teach the language lessons. See below for more ideas on teaching new vocabulary.

ENLIST HELP:

Connect with other teachers in your building if you need help making your goals accessible to English Language Learners. If you have staff trained specifically in providing instruction to English Language Learners, ask them to team teach with you on occasion. If they work with some of your students in a small group either outside or inside the classroom, have them build background knowledge for your upcoming lessons. Be careful, however, to keep them from giving direct instruction before students have a chance to develop the concepts for themselves. Consult the *Teacher Implementation Guide* for any content-related questions involving the curriculum. You can also use the Background and Content Notes in the *Unit Resource Guides* to review the mathematics for yourself.

EQUIP THE LEARNERS:

Take a few minutes at the beginning of the lesson to awaken the background knowledge of your students. This is a great time to use picture or literature books recommended in the *Unit Resource Guide.* Also, as you review the *Unit Resource Guide* record any new vocabulary words that might pose a challenge to English Language Learners. This includes at least the Key Vocabulary section, but most likely additional terms as well. Remember to highlight new definitions of familiar terms or homophones relating to math. Take time to introduce new vocabulary before you begin the lesson as long as it does not take away from student exploration and discovery. (See the vocabulary section for more ideas.)

ENGAGE MOTIVATION:

Motivate students by providing manipulatives or engaging them in a real-life problem-solving scenario. Again the *Unit Resource Guide* is your best source for ideas regarding appropriate manipulatives for each lesson. Remind students of previous work they have done related to this topic. The *Student Guide* includes many opportunities for problem solving that relate to students.

EXECUTE THE LESSON:

Teach the lesson once the students are engaged. Use lots of visuals and graphic organizers to increase comprehension. For every ten minutes of instruction, give two minutes of process time. Remember to keep focused on the goals, language, and content that were introduced at the beginning of the lesson. Help the students remember the important, not just the interesting.

EVALUATE THE PROGRESS:

Finish the lesson by checking for understanding. Review the goals and check students' progress. Use response journals or pictures. Ask students to monitor their own learning as to how well they met the lesson's goals. Consult the lesson's Assessment section in the *Unit Resource Guide* for suggestions on assessment activities.

Strategies to Help English Language Learners Remember all the New Academic Language

The amount of new academic vocabulary can be overwhelming. As teachers we want to make every effort to familiarize the students with new vocabulary within the context of the lesson (Coggins, et al. 2007). This is not a directive for isolated vocabulary instruction.

- Help students to see new words all over the classroom.
- Include them in spelling lists and on word walls.
- Use a "word of the day" to signal transition times between activities.
- Create personal dictionaries that students update daily with pictures and descriptions of new terms.
- Remember that many terms specific to mathematics have multiple meanings from common words. For example, mean, average, foot, product, and difference are a few of the words that have new meanings related to math content. Other words are homophones like sum, whole, plane, or weight that have common definitions when spelled differently. It is important to acknowledge these nuances in meaning when it comes to content-specific vocabulary.

Help English Language Learners explore new words on a deeper level:

- Look for patterns between words and how words relate to each other.
- Uncover root words and prefixes to predict meanings.
- Map words according to their relationship to other words.
- Compare and contrast words.
- Consider non-examples as a way to define unfamiliar terms.
- Take words out of their original sentences or paragraphs to help students focus on context clues. This familiar technique is referred to as a "cloze" exercise, and it has been effective for years at helping students uncover meanings of new words from their surroundings.

Teaching the MTB Student

Ultimately, students will leave your classroom and have to take responsibility for their own learning:

- Move students toward independence by teaching them to use available tools.

- Teach them to use the glossary or index section at the back of their *Student Guides.*

- Remind them that when they look up an unknown term in a standard dictionary, the definition relating to math may not be the first one mentioned.

- Help students assess their knowledge when they come across familiar or unfamiliar words. Teach them to ask themselves questions like, "Where have I heard that term before?" or "How is this familiar word being used in a new way?" Then, they can evaluate where they need to go for more information.

Strategies to Increase Use of Nonverbal Communication in the Classroom

Math Trailblazers includes many opportunities for students to discover knowledge and content through experience. Capitalize and extend those daily opportunities. For example, in the first-grade activity called *Sharing Cookies,* bring in a box of cookie-shaped cereal for the students to use instead of cubes. Use cardboard pizzas in third grade for the *Pizza Problems.* Have kids make a paper T-shirt to decorate for *T-shirt Factory Problems,* also in third grade. Collect actual coins for money problems. Whenever possible, use real or close to real objects in presenting lessons.

If the objects are too hard to gather, bring in pictures, videos, or online images to show new concepts. Save old magazines and laminate pictures to use for vocabulary development. Make your own Shape Book using digital photography during the first-grade *Shape Walk* activity. Enlist the help of older classes to make resources for the younger grades. Video and internet services like UnitedStreaming.com can also be useful for collecting visuals. Save your work in an organized file from year to year to make the task more manageable.

Help build background knowledge by setting up an exploratory center of the coming unit. Use the Preparing for Upcoming Lessons section of the *Unit Resource Guide* to give you ideas of what is coming. Have your English Language Learners explore some of the new vocabulary with a native speaking peer. Just try not to give direct instruction robbing the learner of the joy of future discovery.

In this growing field of education stay connected to current research through national organizations such as the National Council of Teachers of Mathematics, TODOS: Mathematics for All, and National Association of Bilingual Education.

> Math Trailblazers *includes many opportunities for students to discover knowledge and content through experience.*

References

Blachowicz, Camille, and Peter J. Fisher. *Teaching Vocabulary in All Classrooms.* Pearson Education, Upper Saddle River, NJ, 2002.

Brechtel, Marcia. *Bringing the Whole Together: An Integrated Whole Language Approach for the Multilingual Classroom.* Dominie Press, Carlsbad, CA, 1998.

Coggins, Debra, et al. *English Language Learners in the Mathematics Classroom.* Corwin Press, Thousand Oaks, CA, 2007.

Cummins, James. "Language Proficiency, Bilingualism, and Academic Achievement." *Academic Success for English Language Learners: Strategies for K–12 Mainstream Teachers.* Patricia A. Richard-Amato, and Marguerite Ann Snow, eds., pp. 76–86. Pearson Education, White Plains, NY, 2005.

Donaldson, Margaret. *Children's Minds.* Collins, Glasgow, 1978.

Diaz-Rico, L., and K. Weed. *The Crosscultural, Language, and Academic Development Handbook.* Allyn & Bacon, Needham Heights, MA, 2002.

Echevarria, Jana, and Anne Graves. *Sheltered Content Instruction: Teaching English-Language Learners with Diverse Abilities.* Allyn & Bacon, Boston, MA, 2003.

Echevarria, Jana, MaryEllen Vogt, and Deborah J. Short. *Making Content Comprehensible for English Language Learners: The SIOP Model.* Allyn and Bacon, Boston, MA, 2000.

Herrell, Adrienne, and Michael Jordan. *Fifty Strategies for English Language Learners.* Pearson Education, Upper Saddle River, NJ, 2004.

Hill, Jane D., and Kathleen M. Flynn. *Classroom Instruction That Works with English Language Learners.* Association for Supervision and Curriculum Development, Alexandria, VA, 2006.

Krashen, Stephen. "Bilingual Education and Second Language Acquisition Theory." *Schooling and Language Minority Students: A Theoretical Framework.* Charles F. Leyba, ed., pp. 51–79. Evaluation, Dissemination and Assessment Center, Los Angeles, CA, 1991.

Krashen, Stephen. *The Power of Reading.* Libraries Unlimited, Englewood, CO, 1993.

Leyba, Charles F, ed. *Schooling and Language Minority Students: A Theoretical Framework.* Evaluation, Dissemination and Assessment Center, Los Angeles, CA, 1991.

McCarrier, Andrea, Gay Su Pinnell, and Irene C. Fountas. *Interactive Writing: How Language and Literacy Come Together, K–2.* Heinemann, Portsmouth, NH, 2000.

Ortiz-Franco, Luis., et al., eds. *Changing the Faces of Mathematics: Perspectives on Latinos.* National Council of Teachers of Mathematics, Reston, VA, 1999.

Richard-Amato, Patricia A., and Marguerite Ann Snow, eds. *Academic Success For English Language Learners: Strategies for K–12 Mainstream Teachers.* Pearson Education, White Plains, NY, 2005.

Trelease, Jim. *The Read Aloud Handbook.* Penguin Books, New York, NY, 2001.

PART II | Using *Math Trailblazers* with Special Education Students

A. Introduction

Finding appropriate strategies for working effectively with students who receive special education services is a challenge in any classroom. Depending on a student's disability, he or she may struggle with some or many aspects of mathematics instruction. This section highlights strategies designed to help all students, including those who experience difficulties with mathematical concepts, access the mathematics concepts and skills as presented in the *Math Trailblazers* curriculum.

In particular, this section focuses on issues related to using *Math Trailblazers* with students who have mathematics learning disabilities. You may find the information useful for other students who do not have a diagnosed disability but are experiencing learning difficulties in mathematics.

The 2004 reauthorization of the *Individuals with Disabilities Education Act* (IDEA) and associated regulations on implementing the law outline the parameters that schools must follow in providing specially designed instruction for students with disabilities. This includes the provision that students with disabilities must receive education in the least restrictive environment possible, where they have access to the general education curriculum and role models of typically developing classmates. This often means that students with disabilities have opportunities to learn challenging curricula alongside their peers without disabilities.

As part of the *No Child Left Behind Act* (NCLB) of 2001, school districts are held accountable for ensuring that all students, including those with special needs, make adequate yearly progress in reading and mathematics. The combination of IDEA and NCLB regulations has created new challenges for teachers and schools. With special-needs students being assessed on the full mathematics curriculum and schools being held accountable for the progress in mathematics of most students with disabilities, schools and districts are exploring new ways to ensure that all students including those with disabilities have access to the district's general mathematics curriculum.

Math Trailblazers was developed with a strong commitment to providing high-quality mathematics instruction for all students, including those with special needs. As such, the authors of *Math Trailblazers* incorporated approaches and tools into the curriculum to address the diverse learning needs of a wide range of students and to assist teachers with the task of differentiating their instruction. The authors of *Math Trailblazers* have designed this section to provide greater detail about strategies to support teachers to effectively plan their *Math Trailblazers* lessons for use by students in need of additional support in mathematics.

> *This section highlights strategies designed to help all students, including those who experience difficulties with mathematical concepts, access the mathematics concepts and skills as presented in the* Math Trailblazers *curriculum.*

The following section (Part B) highlights how the approaches used in *Math Trailblazers* align with the best practice research on differentiating mathematics instruction for students with disabilities. Part C includes additional resources developed by the Addressing Accessibility in Mathematics Project at Education Development Center (EDC) that can help teachers develop appropriate accommodations for students who have special learning needs in mathematics. References are included at the end of Part II.

B. *Math Trailblazers* Instruction and Special Education Research

The study of mathematics learning disabilities is relatively new when compared with research into reading disabilities (Geary, 2005; Gersten et al., 2004). Much of the work with mathematics learning disabilities has focused on simple arithmetic competencies, with little research on more complex arithmetic and other mathematical domains (Geary, 2004). While more research is needed, there is a research base of modifications and accommodations that can support (or inhibit) a student with learning disabilities. Some of the most promising strategies are shared here.

There is no single method or approach you can adopt for all students with disabilities or even all those with a specific disability. By definition, appropriate services for students with disabilities must be individualized. An essential element of working effectively with a student struggling with mathematics is identifying the source(s) of the student's difficulties. Accurately diagnosing mathematics learning disabilities is tricky (Ginsburg, 1997; Geary, 2005; Gersten et al., 2005). Different cognitive competencies are required for counting, recalling basic facts quickly; developing effective arithmetic procedures with whole numbers, fractions, and decimals; and learning mathematics that requires visual or spatial understandings, such as geometry or data representation. Students may have disabilities in one domain but function well in another.

It is also true that a student with significant language-based disabilities may appear to have a mathematical-based disability. It is therefore important that the full range of available assessment data be utilized to determine appropriate accommodations for each child.

However, there are general research-based teaching practices that seem to enhance learning for children with some mathematics learning disabilities. This section discusses those practices in relation to *Math Trailblazers*.

Strategies used within *Math Trailblazers* for all students are consistent with approaches researchers recommend for students who either are struggling with mathematics or those receiving special education services. As a result, accommodations for many special needs students will not likely require the development of drastically different approaches or lessons. Rather, teachers will need to examine lessons in relation to the learning preferences and needs of individual students, and highlight the specific approaches and strategies from within *Math Trailblazers* that make good instructional sense for the individual child. Good instruction for children with special needs ultimately depends upon reflective, knowledgeable, and flexible teachers who plan lessons carefully (Kilpatrick et. al., 2001).

Good instruction for children with special needs ultimately depends upon reflective, knowledgeable, and flexible teachers who plan lessons carefully.

Math Facts and Computation

Many students who are diagnosed with mathematics learning disabilities also have memory-related difficulties. Memory deficits can impact students' abilities to quickly recall math facts or routinely follow multiple steps in arithmetic procedures, but memory demands differ with the task. For example, the memory demands required for retrieval of math facts differ from those required for the recall of steps in a multistep procedure or to learn geometric shapes and properties.

Students with memory difficulties must use effective strategies to work around rote memorization of facts, procedures, or definitions. Following are examples that show how the design of the curriculum supports students with special needs.

1. Instruction on the math facts focuses on patterns and connections among and between facts. *Math Trailblazers* approach for teaching and learning math facts is an example of how a strategies-based approach can assist some students who are not able to memorize the math facts. For those children, explicitly teaching strategies for figuring out the answers to math facts can be helpful. Such instruction connects the learning of one fact with knowledge of another. Research has consistently affirmed that carefully constructed, explicit instruction on problem-solving strategies provides students with learning disabilities more opportunities to figure out the correct answer and can dramatically improve their computation skills (Bottge, 2001; Gersten and Chard, 2001). See the TIMS Tutor: *Math Facts* for more information on this strategies-based approach.

Math Trailblazers interweaves conceptual understanding with development of procedural competency.

2. *Math Trailblazers* interweaves conceptual understanding with development of procedural competency. This aligns with best-practice recommendations for instructing students with learning disabilities (Bottge et al., 2001; Thorton & Jones, 1996; Rittle-Johnson et al., 2001; Ginsburg, 1997). The *Math Trailblazers* approach to teaching arithmetic operations draws attention to tools within the curriculum that can assist special-needs learners to develop the needed conceptual understanding of the operations in order to gain fluency with the procedures.

3. Students use a variety of strategies for doing computation. The introduction of more than one valid procedure for each arithmetic operation offers students alternative options that might align better with their learning strengths. The regular use of calculators may be of great assistance and is a common accommodation for students who can effectively set up problems but have difficulty developing facility with paper-and-pencil procedures.

4. Extensive and ongoing use of multiple representations of arithmetic operations, such as manipulatives (e.g., connecting cubes and base-ten pieces), pictures (e.g., tallies, base-ten shorthand), and other visual representations (e.g., mathhoppers, rulers and number lines, part-part-whole mats) support students with special needs by providing different "entry points" for understanding the operations.

Use of multiple representations or alternative procedures are not panaceas in and of themselves. Most learners, but especially those with learning disabilities, will require instruction that explicitly helps them connect the various models and visual representations with the symbolic (numerical) representations of the concept (Fuson, 1992; Ginsberg, 1997). Students with learning disabilities often have difficulty making choices when multiple options are presented, and they often need more practice than other students. Introducing too many representations or alternative procedures may make it difficult for some students to make effective use of the information (Gersten & Chard, 2001). A lesson adaptation may include more explicit guidance identifying which procedures and representations are best suited to individual students at different times.

5. Daily Practice and Problems (DPPs) provide additional opportunities to practice. Once an appropriate method is identified as best suited for an individual student, additional practice is important. Most times, the practice opportunities are within the DPP or simple extensions of problem-solving contexts in daily lessons. Occasionally, the teacher may need to seek other resources for the extra practice.

> **Facts about Practice**
>
> - Arithmetic worksheets with many practice problems may not be helpful to many students with learning disabilities.
> - Shorter, carefully constructed problem sets may be more effective in helping students with special needs develop fluency with facts and procedures (Diezman et al., 2003).
> - In their meta-analysis of research on learning disabilities, Swanson and Deshler (2003) stated, "Although intensive practice of newly learned information in the early stages of learning is necessary, the cognitive intervention literature suggests that distributed practice is better for retention. Several studies have also suggested that the long-term retention of all kinds of information and skills is greatly enhanced by distributed practice" (p. 129).

Problem Solving

A fundamental assumption in *Math Trailblazers* is that students learn mathematics more effectively if they are using mathematics in meaningful contexts to solve problems. Engagement in mathematical problem solving is particularly important for students with special needs. Rich problems add context that may help such students make sense of the mathematics, build upon their previous knowledge, and judge the reasonableness of results. The problems also provide a source for the extra practice that students may require. As such, researchers caution against holding off problem solving because some basic skills are not yet in place (Bottge et al., 2001; Ginsburg, 1997; Gersten & Chard, 2001). The games and puzzles included in every grade of *Math Trailblazers* provide another source of motivation and practice that can be used effectively with special needs students.

Engagement in mathematical problem solving is particularly important for students with special needs.

Problem-solving situations in *Math Trailblazers* require students to transfer their mathematical knowledge to new situations. While these situations may be challenging for some students with learning disabilities, researchers emphasize that these students not be excluded from this important part of the mathematics curriculum. The kinds of mathematics problems they will encounter in *Math Trailblazers* can be successfully solved by the great majority. Some recommendations for supporting students are offered here:

1. Explicitly teach strategies for solving different kinds of problems (Fuchs and Fuchs, 2002; Fuchs and Fuchs, 2003; Baker et al., 2002; Swanson and Deschler, 2003). Such instruction often offers a series of steps that help students navigate through a problem, find the relevant information, and connect the problem with previous learning.

2. Consistently use tools such as advance organizers, picture-based models, or other explicit learning strategies that help students successfully work through complicated problems (Swanson and Deschler, 2003).

3. Help students make connections between varied aspects of instruction. Students with learning disabilities may need extra assistance making the connection between problem-solving experiences, concrete representations, and formal procedures (Gersten and Baker, 1998; Gersten and Chard, 1999; Ginsburg, 1997). They also will likely require additional, specific assistance with decision making, information use, vocabulary, sequencing, and patterning (Bley and Thorton, 1995).

4. Explicitly connect current or upcoming lessons with previous learning in the form of advance organizers. This may also be helpful, particularly with older students (Swanson and Deshler, 2003; Gersten and Baker, 1998).

Communication about Mathematics

Regular communication of mathematical ideas using different representations is a hallmark of instruction with *Math Trailblazers*. Classrooms that encourage students to discuss their solution strategies and justify their answers enable students with learning disabilities to communicate their mathematical understandings in ways that align with their strengths—using actions, symbols, words, or manipulatives. Students with learning disabilities are more likely to understand and retain concepts when they:

- rephrase problems in their own words;

- describe solution approaches and results; and

- summarize what others have reported. (Diezman et al., 2003).

Multiple modes of classroom communication also provide teachers with richer data to assess student progress and offer regular feedback to students. Evidence suggests that students with learning disabilities tend to overestimate their academic performance and therefore depend even more than

> *Classrooms that encourage students to discuss their solution strategies and justify their answers enable students with learning disabilities to communicate their mathematical understandings in ways that align with their strengths—using actions, symbols, words, or manipulatives.*

Communication Strategies

Deizmann et al. (2003) suggest the following communication strategies, among others, to assist students with learning difficulties:

- Allow students to communicate their thinking and solution strategies in ways that align with their preferred learning styles and strengths, using actions, symbols, words, or manipulatives.
- Use a buddy system or other means to highlight the links between what is said, manipulated, and written during a task.
- Ask students to rephrase a task or problem in their own words because virtually all these students need to hear themselves so they can understand and retain ideas; ask them to repeat the solution strategies shared by other students in the class.
- Break tasks into smaller parts and require students to report in as each part is finished.
- Ask students to write on a slate or the board as opposed to paper.

other students on consistent feedback from teachers about their progress (Heath and Glenn, 2005; Bottge, 1999).

The balance in *Math Trailblazers* of whole class instruction, small group interactions, and individual work is well-suited to promoting the communication and learning needs of students with learning disabilities. Many special needs educators recommend varying group sizes to provide students with a range of opportunities for participation. Smaller groups also allow students with learning difficulties to experiment with ideas prior to sharing with a larger group.

Homework

Homework in *Math Trailblazers* presents special challenges because it often is atypical of parents' own experiences with mathematics homework. Parents may feel ill-equipped to assist with math homework and will likely need additional, explicit discussions about expectations for mathematics learning, homework policies, and ways to assist their children. Students with learning disabilities will benefit from strong, at-home homework support structures (parents, siblings, other relatives or adults, peers). The following suggestions may be helpful as teachers plan their homework assignments for students with learning disabilities. (ERIC/OSEP, 2001).

- Be sure the homework is meaningful and focuses on the essential mathematics that students must learn.
- The assignment should be clear and doable.
- Communicate clearly, taking extra time to explain assignments and use various means to remind students about the homework and due dates.
- Adjust the length of the assignment; assign the homework in small units.
- Adapt the assignment to address the individual needs and strengths of students; allow alternative methods for students to turn in their work, e.g., audio taping rather than writing assignments.
- Provide learning tools, such as calculators or manipulatives; don't assume those tools will be available at home.
- Identify a peer tutor or assign the student to a study group.
- Use various methods to communicate with parents about homework assignments; try to develop at-home homework support structures (e.g., parents, siblings, peers, other adults).

C. Lesson Planning Tools

The preceding section underscored two major points:

- The instructional approaches used regularly in *Math Trailblazers* align with the prevailing research on teaching students with learning disabilities.
- The curriculum already has many embedded tools and structures that can help students with mathematics learning disabilities succeed in mathematics.

Homework that prepares students for an upcoming lesson may be particularly useful for those with learning disabilities. Such homework may review previously taught concepts and skills needed in the upcoming lesson or preview some individual pieces of the upcoming lesson giving students some extra time prior to class to think about and process parts of problems they will see in class.

Careful lesson planning is the cornerstone of effective work with students who have mathematics learning disabilities. The Addressing Accessibility in Mathematics Project, based at the Education Development Center, has developed a lesson planning process and a set of tools that can assist teachers using *Math Trailblazers.* The project's goals are to make mathematics curricula and instruction more accessible to students with disabilities and to promote collaboration between mathematics teachers and special needs educators.

The Project's lesson planning process provides a framework for thinking proactively about the kinds of barriers that students may encounter in a lesson. Like many suggested planning routines for working with special needs students, the concept behind the Addressing Accessibility in Mathematics Project lesson planning process is that once barriers are identified, they can be addressed by providing the scaffolding and support that students need to reach the mathematics goals.

As part of the lesson planning, the Project suggests that teachers begin by considering instructional practices, such as pairing students or using large visuals, before deciding to alter the curriculum materials. They caution that some strategies can go too far and lose the integrity of the mathematics content and pedagogy or set expectations too low for students (Brodesky et al., 2004).

The steps in the Addressing Accessibility in Mathematics Project lesson planning process are summarized in the following table. Keep the guiding questions in mind as you plan. Making lessons accessible is a combination of proactive planning and on-the-spot decision-making. The expectation is not to make an individual lesson plan for each student; the goal is for teachers to create one lesson plan with accessibility strategies built in, recognizing that additional accommodations will be needed for some individuals. By examining the lesson through an accessibility lens, teachers can anticipate potential barriers for their students, plan strategies, and "keep them in their back pockets" to use as needed.

Addressing Accessibility in Mathematics Project Lesson Planning Process[1]	
Step	**Guiding Questions**
1. Focus on the mathematics of the lesson.	• What are the mathematics goals? What are the tasks? • What is most important for *all* students to learn?
2. Focus on the students.	• What are the student's strengths and weaknesses?
3. Identify potential barriers.	• What is the match or mismatch between the lesson's mathematics content and tasks and the student's strengths and weaknesses?
4. Consider accessibility strategies.	• What strategies might meet the student's needs and enable them to reach the mathematics goals?
5. Plan and implement the lesson.	• How do I integrate the accessibility strategies into my lesson plan? • How do I collect evidence to see if the strategies were effective?
6. Plan follow-up actions.	• Did the student achieve the mathematics goal for the lesson? Did the accessibility strategies help? How do you know? • How do the results of this lesson impact planning for future lessons?

[1] Adapted from Brodesky et al., 2004.

Tools for Planning Lessons

To assist *Math Trailblazers* teachers, we include several tools here that were developed by the Addressing Accessibility in Mathematics Project. These documents are reprinted here with permission from the Education Development Center for use by *Math Trailblazers* teachers. Teachers and school and district-based staff developers may make up to 10 copies. ***For all other uses, please contact Fred Gross (fgross@edc.org) for permission.*** These and other documents can also be accessed in electronic format from the Addressing Accessibility in Mathematics web site (http://edc.org/accessmath/).

• *Instructional Strategies to Increase Accessibility*
  This one-page document lists strategies to consider for planning and teaching accessible lessons. It is a good introduction to a more detailed resource developed by the Addressing Accessibility in Mathematics Project: the *Accessibility Strategies Toolkit for Mathematics,* which is available from the project web site
  (http://edc.org/accessmath/resources/strategies.asp).

The goal of the *Accessibility Strategies Toolkit for Mathematics* is to provide an organized list of strategies for making mathematics more accessible to students with disabilities. Students' strengths and needs in six areas—conceptual processing, language, visual-spatial processing, organization, memory, and attention—are examined. For each of these six areas, the authors identified common types of tasks in *Standards*-based mathematics curricula, student needs and challenges, and corresponding teaching strategies for promoting accessibility.

- *Accessibility Planners*
  The Accessibility Planners are templates that provide guiding questions for identifying mathematical goals, potential barriers, and strategies to enable students to reach the goals. The planners are typically used in professional development workshops and with groups where teachers work together to analyze lessons and brainstorm accessibility strategies. They can, however, be used by individual teachers. Two different Planners are included here. Additional Planners are available from the Addressing Accessibility in Mathematics web site (http://edc.org/accessmath/resources/planners.asp).

  - *Individual Focal Student Planner*
    This planner is designed for recording observations on the strengths and weaknesses of an individual student. There is a space for listing accessibility strategies that are helpful for the student.

  - *Lesson Planner*
    This template can be used to plan accessibility strategies for individual lessons.

Instructional Strategies to Increase Accessibility

Helping Students Understand Tasks

- Reword directions or questions
- Have students paraphrase directions and questions
- Provide visual *and* auditory directions
- Preview vocabulary
- Have students highlight key information
- Change context to make it more familiar or appealing to students
- Show examples of the finished product

Helping Students Access Math in Varied Ways

- Build on students' prior math knowledge
- Make connections across math topics
- Move from concrete to representational to abstract
- Use multiple representations
- Provide additional examples
- Offer manipulatives
- Use technology strategies
- Use visuals like charts or projected images
- Offer alternative ways for students to show what they know
- Provide kinesthetic learning opportunities

Building Student Independence

- Offer timers to help students with pacing
- Teach highlighting and color-coding
- Use "think alouds" and other metacognitive strategies
- Teach *and* model strategies for:
  - Organization
  - Self-questioning and self-monitoring
  - Problem-solving
  - Memory (such as mnemonics)
- Clarify expectations (use rubrics)

Providing Tools and Handouts

- Provide study guides with key information to reduce copying and note-taking
- Offer calculators and multiplication charts
- Provide resource sheets
- Provide templates for tables, graphs, writing, and other tasks
- Use graphic organizers
- Provide practice problems
- Provide a word bank with key vocabulary words and visuals

Promoting Understanding through Discourse

- Have students work in pairs or small groups
- Use cooperative learning
- Keep class discussions short and focused
- Provide timely and constructive feedback
- Check in frequently with students
- Use questions, prompts, and hints

Helping Students Manage Tasks and Organization

- Reformat handouts to provide more workspace
- Reduce amount of copying
- Provide a checklist
- Provide time management cues
- Set up a notebook organizational system
- Provide project organizers to help the students keep track of tasks
- Offer tools such as highlighters and post-its to help students focus

Adjusting Tasks to Student Needs

- Adjust level of difficulty
- Use friendlier numbers
- Break complex tasks into smaller parts
- Adjust amount of time for tasks
- Adjust amount of work
- Create multiple versions of a problem, in order to offer alternatives to a range of learners
- Adjust pacing to optimize attention

Creating a Supportive Environment

- Post and reinforce classroom expectations
- Post homework assignments in a consistent location
- Seat students strategically, based on needs like vision or hearing. Seat distractible students away from windows or doors.
- Use nonverbal signals to cue attention or behavior
- Use consistent and familiar routines
- Provide easy access to manipulatives, templates, and other tools in the classroom

Teaching the MTB Student

Observations and Strategies for Focal Student: _____

	Student's Strengths	Student's Difficulties
Conceptual		
Language		
Visual-Spatial		
Organization		
Memory		
Attention		
Other		
Helpful Strategies for this Student		

Lesson Planner for _____

Math Goals: *What are the priorities?*		
Lesson Demands *What's involved for students?* *Consider tasks and content.*	**Potential Barriers** **& Student Difficulties** *What difficulties do you anticipate?*	**Accessibility Strategies** *What strategies would you* *use to meet students' needs?*

References

Baker, S., R. Gersten, and D. Lee. "A Synthesis of Empirical Research on Teaching Mathematics to Low-achieving Students." *The Elementary School Journal,* 103(1), pp. 51–74, 2002.

Bley, N.S., and C.A. Thornton. *Teaching Mathematics to Students with Learning Disabilities.* Pro-Ed, Austin, TX, 1995.

Bottge, B.A. Reconceptualizing Mathematics Problem Solving for Low-achieving Students. *Remedial and Special Education,* 22(2), pp. 102–112, 2001.

Bottge, B.A., M. Heinrichs, S.Y. Chan, and R.C. Serlin. "Anchoring Adolescents' Understanding of Math Concepts in Rich Problem-solving Environments." *Remedial and Special Education,* 22(5), pp. 299–326, 2001.

Brodesky, A.R., C. Parker, M. Murray, and L. Katzman. *Accessibility Strategies Toolkit for Mathematics.* Education Development Center, Newton, MA, 2002.

Brodesky, A.R., F.E. Gross, A.E. McTigue, and C.C. Tierney. "Planning Strategies for Students with Special Needs: A Professional Development Activity." *Teaching Children Mathematics,* 11(3), pp. 146–154, 2004.

Diezmann, C.M., C.A. Thornton, and J.J. Watters. "Addressing the Needs of Exceptional Students Through Problem Solving." F.K. Lester & R.I. Charles, eds. *Teaching Mathematics Through Problem Solving: Prekindergarten–Grade Six*, pp. 169–182. National Council of Teachers of Mathematics, Reston, VA, 2003.

ERIC/OSEP Special Project. "Homework Practices That Support Students with Disabilities." *Research Connections in Special Education No. 8.* (EC 308348), Spring 2001.

Fuchs, L.S., and D. Fuchs. "Enhancing the Mathematical Problem Solving of Students with Mathematics Disabilities." H.L. Swanson, K.R. Harris, and S.E. Graham, eds. *Handbook on Learning Disabilities,* pp. 306–322. Guilford, New York, 2003.

Fuchs, L.S, and D. Fuchs. "Mathematical Problem-solving Profiles of Students with Mathematics Disabilities with and without Comorbid Reading Disabilities." *Journal of Learning Disabilities,* 35(6), pp. 563–573, 2002.

Fuson, K.C. "Research on Learning and Teaching Addition and Subtraction of Whole Numbers." G. Lenihardt, R. Putnam, and R. Hattrup, eds. *Analysis of Arithmetic for Mathematics Teaching.* Lawrence Erlbaum Associates, Hillsdale, NJ, 1992.

Geary, D.C. "Mathematics and Learning Disabilities." *Journal of Learning Disabilities,* 37(1), pp. 4–15, 2004.

Geary, D.C. "Role of Cognitive Theory in the Study of Learning Disability in Mathematics." *Journal of Learning Disabilities,* 38(4), pp. 305–307, 2005.

Geary, D.C., M.K. Hoard, J. Byrd-Craven, and M.C. DeSoto. "Strategy Choices in Simple and Complex Addition: Contributions of Working Memory and Counting Knowledge for Children with Mathematical Disability." *Journal of Experimental Child Psychology,* 88, pp. 121–151, 2004.

Gersten, R., and D. Chard. "Number Sense: Rethinking Arithmetic Instruction for Students with Mathematical Disabilities." *The Journal of Special Education,* 33(1), pp. 18–28, 1999.

Gersten, R., N.C. Jordan, and J.R. Flojo. "Early Identification and Interventions for Students with Mathematics Difficulties." *Journal of Learning Disabilities,* 38(4), pp. 293–304, 2005.

Gersten, R., and S. Baker. "Real World Use of Scientific Concepts Integrating Situated Cognition with Explicit Instruction." *Exceptional Children,* 65(1), pp. 23–25, 1998.

Ginsburg, H.P. "Mathematics Learning Disabilities: A View from Developmental Psychology." *Journal of Learning Disabilities,* 30, pp. 20–33, 1997.

Heath, N., and T. Glen. "Positive Illusory Bias and the Self-protective Hypothesis in Children with Learning Disabilities." *Journal of Clinical Child and Adolescent Psychology.* 34 (2), pp. 272–281, 2005.

Kilpatrick, J., J. Swafford, and B. Findell, eds. *Adding It Up: Helping Children Learn Mathematics.* National Academy Press, Washington, DC, 2001.

Lovin, L., M. Kyger, and D. Allsopp. "Differentiation for Special Needs Learners." *Teaching Children Mathematics,* pp. 158–167, 2004.

Marolda, M.R., and P.S. Davidson, eds. "Assessing Mathematical Abilities and Learning Approaches" C.A. Thornton and N.S. Bley, eds. *Windows of Opportunity: Mathematics for Students with Special Needs,* pp. 41–60. National Council of Teachers of Mathematics, Reston, VA, 1994.

McGilly, K., ed. *Classroom Lessons.* Bradford, Cambridge, MA, 1994.

Rittle-Johnson, B., R.S. Siegler, and M.W. Alibali. "Developing Conceptual Understanding and Procedural Skill in Mathematics: An Iterative Process." *Journal of Educational Psychology,* 93(2), pp. 346–362, 2001.

Smith, D.D., ed. *Introduction to Special Education: Teaching in an Age of Opportunity* (5th ed.). Pearson Education, Inc., Boston, MA, 2004.

Swanson, H.L., and D. Deshler. "Instructing Adolescents with Learning Disabilities: Converting a Meta-analysis to Practice." *Journal of Learning Disabilities,* 36(2), pp. 124–35, 2003.

Thornton, C.A., and N.S. Bley, eds. *Windows of Opportunity: Mathematics for Students with Special Needs.* National Council of Teachers of Mathematics, Reston, VA, 1994.

Thornton, C.A., and G.A. Jones. "Adapting Instruction for Students with Special Learning Needs, K–8." *Journal of Education,* 178(2), pp. 59–69, 1996.

Womack, D. *Special Needs in Ordinary Schools: Developing Mathematical and Scientific Thinking in Young Children.* Cassell Educational Limited, London, 1988.

Teaching the MTB Student

PART III

Meeting the Needs of the Mathematically Gifted or Talented Student in the *Math Trailblazers* Classroom

A. Introduction

The design of Math Trailblazers *is well aligned with the needs of talented or gifted students, and the curriculum provides many opportunities for extending and differentiating instruction.*

Talented or gifted students are quite different from other students in the classroom. For example, they remember things easily, needing very little review. They like to be engaged in problem solving, can work with abstract concepts beyond the scope of their peers, and approach problems in novel ways (Wilkens, Wilkens, & Oliver, 2006). A teacher's challenge with talented or gifted students is unique; rather than finding ways to make the content comprehensible to students, the teacher must move beyond the curriculum to provide additional challenge. Given this fact and that high stakes assessments focus on bringing low achieving students up to proficient levels, attention has shifted away from the talented or gifted student. Fortunately, the design of *Math Trailblazers* is well aligned with the needs of talented or gifted students, and the curriculum provides many opportunities for extending and differentiating instruction.

According to Zaccaro (2006), mathematically gifted children need to be given material that truly and appropriately challenges them. Assouline and Lupkowski-Shoplik (2005) list key elements of a curriculum that supports mathematically talented or gifted students. These elements include a broad scope of content studied in depth and at a high level with problem solving at the core of the instruction. Students solve problems, communicate solution strategies, represent problem situations in a variety of ways, and reflect on the efficiency of their problem-solving methods. Students should discover mathematical content that connects to real life as well as to other subjects.

The *Math Trailblazers* curriculum was developed with a commitment to both equity and excellence for all students, including the talented or gifted student. The following are some *Math Trailblazers* features that align with the needs of talented or gifted students:

- Students construct new knowledge as well as practice mathematical concepts through rigorous and authentic problem-solving situations.

- Students are frequently asked to communicate their solution strategies orally and in writing.

- Students solve problems using multiple problem-solving processes and provide multiple representations for their solutions.

- Students are encouraged to reflect and evaluate the efficiency of both their problem-solving strategies and the strategies of others.

B. Talented or Gifted Students in Mathematics

The following topics explore issues related to teaching talented or gifted children. Information includes insights from research, work with teachers, and how the structure of *Math Trailblazers* addresses these issues.

Identifying Talented or Gifted Students

One prevailing myth about mathematically talented students is that only students identified for a gifted program can be mathematically talented. There are a range of ways to identify students as gifted, some based on IQ scores (above 130) or on standardized test scores (above 95%). These types of criteria, however, can eliminate a student who has a special talent in one area and average or above average abilities in other areas. As a result a mathematically talented student may not meet the criteria for his or her school's gifted program (Assouline and Lupkowski-Shoplik, 2005).

The National Association for Gifted Children (NAGC) calls for a more comprehensive definition of a gifted student. They describe a gifted person as:

. . . someone who shows, or has the potential for showing, an exceptional level of performance in one or more areas of expression.

Some of these abilities are very general and can affect a broad spectrum of the person's life, such as leadership skills or the ability to think creatively. Some are very specific talents and are only evident in particular circumstances, such as a special aptitude in mathematics, science, or music. The term giftedness provides a general reference to this spectrum of abilities without being specific or dependent on a single measure or index. It is generally recognized that approximately five percent of the student population, or three million children, in the United States are considered gifted.

A person's giftedness should not be confused with the means by which giftedness is observed or assessed. Parent, teacher, or student recommendations, a high mark on an examination, or a high IQ score are not giftedness; they may be a signal that giftedness exists. Some of these indices of giftedness are more sensitive than others to differences in the person's environment.

(http://www.nagc.org/index.aspx?id=574)

In this discussion, we consider the talented or gifted student as those formally identified as gifted in the area of mathematics through assessment procedures and those students not formally identified as talented, but whom a teacher determines, through assessments, observations, and classroom assessments to be talented in mathematics.

Content Note

Although students are referred to as being either talented or gifted, programs developed for such students use the title Talented and Gifted.

While every student is different, talented or gifted students in mathematics commonly exhibit particular traits in a mathematics classroom. They begin to grasp mathematical concepts at an early age. Many of these students enter school having established their own theories of number sense, computational strategies, problem solving, and patterns. Teachers describe these children as being able to see connections among topics and ideas without formal instruction. They are often able to discern answers with unusual speed and accuracy. Also, due to their intuitive understanding, they may skip steps and be unable to explain how they arrived at their answer (Rotigel & Fello, 2005). According to Sheffield (1999), students who demonstrate giftedness in mathematics may demonstrate uneven understanding of mathematical concepts. These students are frequently less interested in the computational "how to," preferring to engage in problem solving that is both challenging and interesting (Zaccaro, 2006).

Though these students are usually able to understand difficult mathematical concepts more readily than their same age peers, these same students may also appear to be disinterested or unmotivated in a one-size-fits-all classroom. Diezmann and Watters (2005) identify boredom as a major concern for gifted students, which results from a lack of challenging academic tasks and from a perception that the learning experience has limited value to them. This lack of challenge may be furthered when teachers try to address the needs of these students by: simply increasing the amount of work the students are to complete without addressing the complexity of the task; assigning these students to help others who are still working; or asking them to work on something else quietly while they wait for others to finish (Tomlinson, 1999; Diezmann and Watters, 2005). Both the *Principles and Standards* (NCTM, 2000) and Zaccaro (2006) caution educators that the practice of simply pushing students through the curriculum at a faster pace is not the answer.

The NCTM *Principles and Standards* states:

> One traditional way for students to learn additional mathematics in which they have a particular interest is differential pacing—allowing some students to move rapidly through the mathematical content expected of all so that they can go on to additional areas. However, some alternatives to differential pacing may prove advantageous. For example, curricula can be offered in which students can explore mathematics more deeply rather than more rapidly. This model allows them to develop deep insights into important concepts that prepare them well for later experiences instead of experiencing a more cursory treatment of a broader range of topics. (p. 369)

Zaccaro (2006) explains that expecting more work from students increases the likelihood that gifted students will develop a lack of interest. More work does not nurture the student's passion for mathematics. He compares this to "teaching all scales and no music." (p. 3)

This model (differential pacing) allows them [students] to develop deep insights into important concepts that prepare them well for later experiences instead of experiencing a more cursory treatment of a broader range of topics.

Teaching Talented or Gifted Students: Classroom Learning Community

Providing the best classroom support for talented or gifted students begins with a classroom learning community that focuses on deep understanding of important mathematics for all learners. Hiebert et al. (1997) explain that effective learning means providing rich environments for developing deep understanding of mathematics through collaboration, communication, and the creation of cognitive conflict. Having these foundations in place allows the teacher to facilitate the most effective work with talented or gifted students.

The literature suggests that there are some common foundations present in a healthy classroom learning community. They include:

- Ideas and methods expressed by all students deserve and are given respect.

- Students are encouraged to work out their own methods and communicate them with understanding to others.

- Teachers help students make their own sense of ideas and methods.

- Teachers provide high expectations and the necessary scaffolding to move each child to his or her next learning benchmark.

- Mistakes are seen as sites for learning. Challenge and frustration are a part of learning and life and should be viewed as part of the learning process.

- The authority for determining whether something is correct and sensible lies with the logic of the subject rather than with the status of the teacher. The teacher strives for student independence. (Hiebert, et al., 1997; Tomlinson, 1999; Zaccaro, 2006; Kilpatrick, Swafford, & Findell, 2001)

For additional information on establishing and maintaining effective classrooms, see the Building the *Math Trailblazers* Classroom section.

Teaching Talented or Gifted Students: Homogeneous and Heterogeneous Grouping

Appropriate grouping of students in math class is often a concern of both new and experienced teachers. In an attempt to meet the needs of all learners, educators have often separated students by achievement, grouping them with students who have similar achievement levels. Many educators believed that these homogeneous classrooms would allow students to learn at their own pace and would allow teachers to meet the needs of the students more consistently. According to the National Research Council, however, data from international comparisons (especially Asia) support the assumption that all students can achieve important mathematical learning goals within heterogeneously grouped classrooms. Tomlinson (1999) further argues that students learn best in a heterogeneous classroom only when teachers create "effective communities of learning in which all learners are specifically and systematically addressed." (p. 22) She further states that classroom learning communities grounded in best-practice and that are responsive to the diverse needs of the learners benefit all students through differentiation of instruction.

Providing the best classroom support for talented or gifted students begins with a classroom learning community that focuses on deep understanding of important mathematics for all learners.

Teaching the MTB Student

The tasks within Math Trailblazers *lessons are challenging and involve problem solving and reasoning—curriculum qualities appropriate for the talented or gifted child.*

Math Trailblazers is designed for heterogeneous grouping and contains the strategies described above to support and challenge talented or gifted students. The tasks within lessons are challenging and involve problem solving and reasoning—curriculum qualities appropriate for the talented or gifted child. In addition, tasks are solved using a range of strategies, which allows those more advanced to implement more sophisticated strategies. *Math Trailblazers* lessons provide the support for discussion about math concepts. These supports help students learn to be effective communicators and to work collaboratively. Many of the lessons involve working in pairs or small groups. This sets the stage for providing the differentiation and individualization that may not occur in classrooms that are more teacher directed or designed exclusively for whole class instruction.

Tasks That Support the Learning of Mathematically Talented or Gifted Students

According to Doyle (1983, 1988) students learn from the kind of work they do. The tasks students are asked to complete determine the nature of that work. When designing mathematical tasks for talented or gifted students, Diezmann and Watters (2005) identify four defining characteristics, each of them at the heart of the *Math Trailblazers* curriculum.

Defining Characteristics of Curriculum that Challenges and Supports Talented or Gifted Students (Diezmann and Watters 2005)

1. The tasks are authentic. Students are able to emulate the practices of mathematicians at an appropriate level.

2. The tasks develop mathematical abstract reasoning. These allow the student who is gifted mathematically to explore patterns and relationships, produce holistic and lateral solutions, and work abstractly.

3. The tasks develop meta-cognitive skills. Hiebert et al. (1997) describes this as knowing how to use information as a result of understanding how it is connected or related to new knowledge or skills. Additionally, meta-cognition is being able to decide when to use a strategy by judging whether or not it is efficient.

4. The tasks increase motivation and passion for mathematics. Tasks that are challenging and meaningful allow mathematically talented students to construct meaning and develop autonomy as a learner.

One of the unique strengths of the *Math Trailblazers* curriculum is its integration with science and language arts. This interdisciplinary approach to problem solving allows students to emulate the real-world work of mathematicians and scientists. Throughout the curriculum, students are involved in scientific investigations of everyday phenomena that develop and apply mathematical skills and concepts to generate meaningful situations.

The laboratory experiments in *Math Trailblazers* are examples of authentic tasks, crucial to the success of talented or gifted students. In each experiment, students identify variables, draw pictures of their methodology, collect and organize data in tables and graphs, and look for and use patterns to analyze their data. For example, in second grade, students compare the distance different vehicles can roll. Students are introduced to the concept of "multiple trials" in an investigation and to the use of the median as a way to average their data.

Students in fifth grade first explore the geometry of circles informally and then formally. Students use collected data to find an accurate approximation for the ratio of the circumference to diameter of a circle. Discussion ensues to cement the connection between this investigation and the constant pi (π). Students then use the constant to find a formula for the circumference of a circle. In each activity, the context of authentic tasks helps the talented or gifted students make connections between previous learning and new information. Students are able to apply what they have learned in a new or different context. According to the *Principles and Standards* (NCTM, 2000), students develop deeper and more lasting understanding when they can identify the rich connection among mathematical topics in contexts they can relate to other subjects, their own interests, and their experience. For a more in-depth discussion about *Math Trailblazers* integration with science and language arts, refer to the Foundations of *Math Trailblazers* section.

Communication is also an integral part of the *Math Trailblazers* curriculum. Students increase their understanding of mathematics by discussing the mathematics they are doing. Students are expected to share their strategies for problem solving during classroom discourse and through written explanations. Journal and discussion prompts are standard features in the lesson guide for many lessons. You can use these prompts to focus classroom discussions. Asking talented or gifted students to communicate the results of their thinking to others provides them an opportunity to clarify and deepen their understanding. Students become better able to justify their solution paths to others, especially when there are divergent solution paths. For a more in-depth discussion about communication in the *Math Trailblazers* classroom refer to the Language in the *Math Trailblazers* Classroom section.

The *Math Trailblazers* curriculum also emphasizes problems that have multiple solution paths. These problems give students opportunities to talk about their own thinking in both small group and whole-class discussions. As students share their problem-solving strategies with their classmates and teacher, and as they listen to the strategies of others, they become more reflective about mathematics. The consistent inclusion of opportunities for reflection helps the talented or gifted student think about his or her own learning and leads to more efficient strategies for problem solving.

Problems with multiple solutions give students opportunities to talk about their own thinking in both small group and whole-class discussions.

A Sample Task from *Math Trailblazers*

This sample task from *Math Trailblazers* includes the components discussed above, especially the importance of communication between student and teacher. Sharing such a task with parents, teachers of talented or gifted students, or administrators can illustrate the opportunities and challenge in this curriculum that make it appropriate for the talented or gifted student.

To develop an understanding of the base-ten number system, the students in first grade are asked to fill in numbers on an empty 50's chart, consisting of

5 rows of 10 squares per row, as shown in Figure 1. The students begin by choosing a number from a deck of digit cards. They then use a variety of strategies to determine where to record the selected number. Students continue this way until all the cards are used.

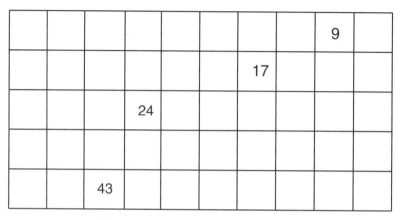

Figure 1: *A partially completed 50's chart*

> *Lessons are designed to encourage students to develop efficient strategies for problem solving as they build deep conceptual understandings of the mathematics.*

This activity provides a launching point for developing important concepts in mathematics. The classroom described at left demonstrates that, when students are given the opportunity to construct meaning through open-ended problem solving and when they are provided the opportunity to reflect on and share their thinking with others, they are able to discover patterns and relationships, and deepen their understanding of mathematics.

C. Planning for Instruction

The *Math Trailblazers* curriculum was developed to provide high quality, rigorous mathematics for all students. Lessons are designed to encourage students to develop efficient strategies for problem solving as they build deep conceptual understandings of the mathematics. The teacher's role is integral to this process as he or she designs complex instruction with the needs of each learner in mind. Complex instruction is defined by Cohen (1994) as, "a rich strategy developed to deal with the sorts of academic ranges that frequently exist in classrooms that are academically, culturally, and linguistically heterogeneous." (p. 68)

Cohen's definition creates the underlying foundation for differentiated classrooms. In education, differentiation is defined as a teacher's responsive reaction to the needs of the learners in the classroom. In other words, differentiation is responding to individual or small group needs as opposed to teaching as if the class were a singular unit in which all students are alike.

50's Chart: From the Classroom

First graders were observed completing the task described above. They used a variety of problem-solving strategies to determine where to place the number represented on the selected card. Some students made a representation of that number using trains (or groups) of connecting cubes. The cubes were made into groups of tens and leftovers. The students placed the cubes directly onto the 50's chart to help them identify the correct box in which to record the number. Other students counted the squares, placing the number in the correct box. Still other students used the strategy of counting by tens and then by ones to identify where to place the number.

As the students continued to work, one child began to see a pattern emerging on the chart and was able to use this pattern to place the numbers. For example, he recognized that the number 47 would go in the same column as 17 only down 3 rows because 4 is 3 more than 1. This student may have been beginning to develop an abstract understanding of the value of 10 and using this to understand the relationship between the various numbers on his chart. He then asked the teacher, "Does this always work?" He was trying to make sense of the situation, make connections to what he knew, and devise a rule that explained how this system worked. The teacher continued to stretch this child's understanding by encouraging him to try to think about numbers greater than 50 asking, "Where would the number 93 fit on your chart?" He pointed to 43 and said, "Under this number, just more tens."

The goal of differentiation is maximum student growth and individual success (Tomlinson & Allen, 2000).

In the differentiated classroom, effective instruction begins with teacher planning. Tomlinson (1999) identifies the following three critical elements of the curriculum that must be linked for effective instruction:

- Content—The content is what we want students to know, understand, or do as a result of instruction. The content is the "input" for instruction.
- Process—The process includes the activities or tasks that allow a student to make sense of the content.
- Product—The product is the "output." The product represents the way in which a student demonstrates what he or she understands and can do as a result of learning.

The lessons in the *Math Trailblazers* curriculum are designed and organized to clearly focus on the content, the process, and the products so students develop understandings of the key concepts, guiding principles, essential skills, and necessary facts of mathematics. For the talented or gifted student, the teacher must consider if the content, processes, and products are appropriately challenging, and when necessary, to adapt the lesson.

Instructional Strategies for Differentiation in the *Math Trailblazers* Classroom

In any lesson plan, a teacher needs to consider three important questions: What should be differentiated? For what purpose? And, how will this be accomplished? (Tomlinson, 1999)

When considering what to differentiate, a teacher needs to remember the three critical elements of the curriculum: content, process, and product. Additionally the teacher needs to consider the learning profile of each student, student interest, and student readiness. Another aspect that can be differentiated is the physical learning environment. Differentiating the physical learning environment might include the classroom configuration, use of specific grouping strategies, use of manipulatives both real and virtual, and student choice of product.

There are many effective instructional strategies for working with talented or gifted students in a heterogeneous setting. Centers, stations, and using tiered lessons provide the greatest flexibility since the teacher can use these instructional strategies to differentiate instruction for all students in the classroom.

There are many effective instructional strategies for working with talented or gifted students in a heterogeneous setting. Centers, stations, and using tiered lessons provide the greatest flexibility since the teacher can use these instructional strategies to differentiate instruction for all students in the classroom.

Key Principles of a Differentiated Classroom

- The teacher is clear about the key concepts of the unit.
- The teacher is clear about which skills are fundamental to supporting conceptual learning.
- The teacher understands, appreciates, and builds upon student differences.
- Assessment and instruction are inseparable.
- The teacher adjusts content, process, and product in response to student readiness, interests, and learning profile.
- All students participate in respectful work.
- Students and teachers are collaborators in learning.
- Goals of a differentiated classroom are maximum growth and individual success.
- Flexibility is the hallmark of a differentiated classroom. (Tomlinson, 1999)

Centers. There are two types of centers that a teacher may use in a classroom to provide differentiation of instruction. The first, a learning center, is an area of the classroom that contains activities designed to teach, reinforce, or extend a skill or concept. Teachers can design classroom centers to focus on current instruction, review past instruction, or preview and explore an upcoming concept or skill set. The second type is the interest center. This center is designed to increase a student's motivation by providing opportunity to explore topics of interest to the student. In general a center provides students with materials and activities that address a wide range of instructional levels and learning styles. Center activities can vary from structured to open-ended, and promote individual learning toward a defined goal.

In the *Math Trailblazers* classroom, teachers can use centers effectively with talented or gifted students. A teacher may set up learning or interest centers with activities or materials that focus on practice or extension of a core concept or skill. Configuring a center for talented or gifted students is more than just giving them more work. The skillful use of centers permits the teacher to challenge talented or gifted students with content appropriate to their levels of understanding.

Stations. While similar to a center, stations provide a structure in which teachers can assign students to specific areas of the room to complete different tasks. The tasks can be varied according to the ability level of students assigned to that station. Stations invite flexibility in the classroom in that not all students need to go to every station. Stations may also be used sequentially to build desired skills or conceptual understandings.

Teachers in a *Math Trailblazers* classroom may develop stations in which all students are working on the same content but where each station represents a different entry point into the content. For example, at one station, students may work with manipulatives to construct concrete models for problem solving while at another station students might be asked to solve problems using more abstract representations for their solutions. The essential consideration in doing such lesson design is that each station is still focused on the goals of the lesson and of the unit. It is inappropriate to have stations that are limited to more trivial expectations—this interpretation of differentiated lessons has resulted in the propagation of inequities in the classroom.

In grades 3–5, the task and challenge items in the Daily Practice and Problems can be a rich resource for both centers and stations. The items identified as a task are designed to take about 15 minutes to complete, and often expand a concept or provide extra practice on a skill. Challenge items are designed to be more thought provoking and to stretch a student's problem-solving skills.

Tiered Lessons. Using tiered lessons is a differentiation strategy that allows teachers to develop multiple pathways for students to take as they address the same concept or skill. Although much of the content in *Math Trailblazers* is intentionally structured as tiered lessons, understanding how a tiered lesson is structured helps teachers more efficiently and effectively reach the talented or gifted student. Teachers can identify the challenge of each of the defined tiers in a lesson to determine which best meets the learning needs of the students in the classroom (Kingore, 2006; Pierce & Adams, 2005; Kettler & Curliss, 2005; Tomlinson, 1999).

Factors that Influence the Complexity of Tiered Learning Experiences

Degree of Assistance and Support

- Teacher directs instruction
- Teacher as facilitator
- Small group support
- Individual autonomy

Degree of Structure

- Clearly defined parameters
- Open ended

Complexity of Activity or Task

- Process and product are concrete
- Process and product involve abstract thinking

Complexity of Process

- Pacing
- Number and complexity of steps
- Simple to high levels of thinking
- Sophisticated research skills are required

Complexity of Product

- Simple, correct answers
- Varied and complex responses
- Integration of advanced skills and concepts is required

Adapted from Kingore (2006)

While there are several different models for developing a tiered lesson, some general characteristics span them all. The following list, which describes the tiered structure found in *Math Trailblazers* is adapted from Tomlinson (1999); Kingore (2006); and Pierce & Adams (2005).

1. Identify the key concepts, skills, or generalizations that are the focus of the lesson. Ask yourself the following: What do I want students to know and be able to do as a result of this lesson?

2. Think about the students in your classroom. Keep in mind that tiered lessons assume that all children are able to learn the same essential concepts, skills, or generalizations in different ways. The groups of students working at each tier should be flexible depending on the

content, process, and products assigned at each tier. As you define your groups consider the range of readiness in your classroom, as well as the interests, talents, and learning styles of each student.

3. Determine the complexity of the activity along a continuum from least complex to greatest complexity. In other words, will the task challenge your most talented or gifted students, your students working at grade level, or your less advanced students. Once you determine where this activity falls on the continuum you can determine if the task meets the needs of all in your classroom. One example of a lesson's tiered structure is that in the laboratory experiments, the questions are successively more difficult.

4. If you find that this activity does not meet the level of your most talented or gifted student, identify who needs another version of the learning experience.

5. Only when necessary, create a different version of the task to address the learners in your classroom. You will find that different *Math Trailblazers* lessons have different quantities of tiers depending on the concepts and skills.

6. Use appropriate assessment for the lesson. Assessments will vary depending on the tier.

Math Trailblazers was designed with many of its lessons structured according to the characteristics of tiered lessons. Lessons begin by clearly identifying the key content that is the focus for all students. Throughout the lesson students are presented with tasks and questions that allow for multiple solution paths that vary in complexity. The following is an example of a tiered lesson from *Math Trailblazers*.

In the fourth-grade lesson *Perimeter vs. Length,* students explore the relationship between the area and perimeter of a rectangle as the area is increased in a specified way. Students first create the rectangles with square inch tiles. They then record the rectangle on grid paper. This lesson is tiered because students are asked increasingly more complex questions about the area and perimeter of the rectangle. Students are provided multiple entry points to the problems presented. Some students will use the square-inch tiles to build concrete models to represent each figure and count the number of tiles to determine either the area or the perimeter. Other students will create representations of the figures using grid paper and rely on the figures they draw to solve the problem. Still others will begin to use mathematical formulas to find the area or perimeter of the figures as they build them.

Because this lesson is already "tiered," it allows children to access the mathematics in ways that make sense to them and to push their understanding as far as possible. The talented or gifted students engaged in this lesson are likely to apply mathematical formulas to find the area or perimeter of geometric figures. These learners are more likely to see that they can decompose more complex figures into simpler geometric shapes. For example they may decompose a trapezoid into a rectangle and two triangles. These students may also see the relationship between shapes, for example two triangles might make a square. These learners benefit from lessons such as this one that contain challenges that are an integral part of the curriculum.

D. Resources for Teachers

Meeting the needs of all learners in the classroom can be challenging but also very exciting. The *Math Trailblazers* curriculum provides many resources for teachers in the *Teacher Implementation Guide* (TIG). This resource includes information for teachers that explores mathematical concepts and ideas addressed in the curriculum.

To learn more about working with students identified as talented or gifted in the classroom the following websites may be helpful:

National Association for Gifted Children (NAGC) The NAGC has been in existence for more than 50 years. This organization is dedicated to serving professionals who work on behalf of gifted children. NAGC publishes a journal for professionals entitled, Gifted Child Quarterly.
http://www.nagc.org

The Association for the Gifted (TAG) TAG is a special interest group of the Council for Exceptional Children (CEC).
http://www.cec.sped.org

American Association for Gifted Children (AAGC) The AAGC is the oldest organization dedicated to advocacy for gifted children.
http://www.aagc.org

Hoagies Gifted Education Page An extensive listing of conferences, resources, articles, and support for teachers.
http://www.hoagiesgifted.com

References

Assouline, S., and A. Lupkowski-Shoplik. *Developing Mathematical Talent: A Guide for Challenging and Educating Gifted and Advanced Learners in Math.* Prufrock Press, Waco, TX, 2005.

Diezmann, C., and J. Watters. "Catering for Mathematically Gifted Elementary Students." *Math Education for Gifted Students.* S. Jensen and J. Kendrick, eds., pp. 33–46. Prufrock Press, Waco, TX, 2005.

Hiebert, J., T. Carpenter, E. Fennema, K. Fuson, D. Wearne, H. Murray, A. Olivier, and P. Human. *Making Sense Teaching and Learning Mathematics with Understanding.* Heinemann, Portsmouth, NH, 1997.

Kettler, T., and M. Curliss. "Mathematical Acceleration in a Mixed-Ability Classroom." *Math Education for Gifted Students.* S. Jensen and J. Kendrick eds., pp. 83–92. Prufrock Press, Waco, TX, 2005.

Kilpatrick, J, J. Swafford, and B. Findell, eds. *Adding it Up: Helping Children Learn Mathematics.* National Research Council (NRC), Washington, DC, 2001.

Kingore, B. "Tiered Instruction: Beginning the Process." *Teaching for High Potential.* NAGC, winter 2006.

Pierce, R., and C. Adams. "Tiered Lessons." *Math Education for Gifted Students.* S. Jensen and J. Kendrick, eds., pp. 49–60. Prufrock Press, Waco, TX, 2005.

Principles and Standards for School Mathematics. National Council of Teachers of Mathematics, Reston, VA, 2000.

Reed, C. "Mathematically Gifted in the Heterogeneously Grouped Mathematics Classroom." *Math Education for Gifted Students.* S. Jensen and J. Kendrick, eds., pp. 17–31. Prufrock Press, Waco, TX, 2005.

Rotigel, J., and S. Fello. "Mathematically Gifted Students How Can We Meet Their Needs?" *Math Education for Gifted Students.* S. Jensen & J. Kendrick, eds., pp. 3–16. Prufrock Press, Waco, TX, 2005.

Sheffield, L.J., ed. *Developing Mathematically Promising Students.* National Council of Teachers of Mathematics, Reston, VA, 1999.

Shore, B.M., and M.A.B. Delcourt. "Effective Curricular and Program Practices in Gifted Education and the Interface with General Education." *Journal for the Education of the Gifted* 20(2), pp. 138–154, 1996.

Tomlinson, C. *The Differentiated Classroom Responding to the Needs of all Learners.* Association for Supervision and Curriculum Development, Alexandra, VA, 1999.

Wilkins, M.M., J.L. Wilkins, and T. Oliver. "Differentiating the Curriculum for Elementary Gifted Mathematics Students." *Teaching Children Mathematics,* 13(1), pp. 6–13, 2006.

Zaccaro, E. "The Seven Components of Successful Programs for Mathematically Gifted Children." *Teaching for High Potential,* NAGC, winter 2006.

Language in the
Math Trailblazers Classroom

This section focuses on the use of language while students read, write, speak, and listen in the *Math Trailblazers* classroom. Students' language abilities increase while using a curriculum rich in opportunities to communicate mathematically.

A teacher helps students solidify their understanding of mathematical concepts by listening to their explanations, helping them read the problems, and write their solutions.

Language in the Classroom

Language in the Math Trailblazers Classroom

The use of language—listening, reading, speaking, and writing—is emphasized throughout the *Math Trailblazers* curriculum. This enables students to consider and communicate ideas and solidify their understanding of mathematical concepts. In the past, many mathematics textbooks and lessons limited students' use of language. Parents, administrators, and other teachers may not understand the need for so much reading and writing in a mathematics class. Moreover, getting students to read, write, speak, and listen, while crucial to the learning process, is sometimes a challenge.

This section offers support for developing language use in your classroom. Part I provides a brief rationale of why language is important and how it is used in *Math Trailblazers*. This information is useful in working with colleagues and parents who may not understand the need for reading and writing in mathematics class. Part II provides additional background and support for incorporating language into your daily lessons. Specifically, support is provided on three overlapping areas of language use: reading, writing, and discourse strategies.

PART I

> *Listening, reading, speaking, and writing enable students to consider and communicate ideas and solidify their understanding of mathematical concepts.*

Incorporating Language into Mathematics Lessons

Using language to learn mathematics is grounded in learning theory and research. While there are many reasons to incorporate reading, writing, listening, and speaking into mathematics instruction, we discuss issues that may arise when discussing language with parents, administrators, and other teachers.

Reasons to Focus on Language in Mathematics Lessons

Language can help students understand mathematics. The value of studying mathematics is to learn both processes and skills necessary for solving real-life problems. In *Math Trailblazers,* students investigate and solve mathematical problems in real-world contexts. They design accurate and efficient strategies. Discussing possible approaches during the problem-solving process and presenting various solution strategies broadens and deepens students' understanding. It also solidifies their ideas as they learn to use mathematics language.

The context of many mathematics lessons are language-dependent. *Math Trailblazers* uses real-life contexts to develop mathematical concepts in a concrete, visual manner. The contexts actually help students understand math concepts and promote student interest in the math lessons. The contexts provide meaning and concrete examples for thinking about abstract concepts.

Incorporating problem-solving contexts into the lessons, however, requires increased use of language in the text and in implementing of the lesson (through speaking, listening, and writing). For example, second-grade students use the context of a car moving through a neighborhood to develop initial concepts of geometry known as slides, flips, and turns. Without this context, which requires students to both read and listen as they solve the problems, the lesson would not be accessible to all learners. In later grades, these language-dependent contexts provide an opportunity for students to make sense of symbolic representations; e.g., 9×4 becomes 9 groups of 4 boxes, and so on. While tempting to remove the contexts to reduce the language demands, such adaptations interfere with a student's ability to make sense of what they are doing. The contexts also connect ideas within mathematics and between mathematics and their world.

Using language in mathematics results in improved literacy. Some teachers, parents, or principals may believe that the increased use of language interferes with the learning of mathematics. This is most often suggested for English-language learners and students with language-related learning disabilities. While such students may need additional support in interpreting the language in the problem, having a familiar context to ground thinking is more often a support to students, not a hurdle. In addition, English-language learners will only learn the language of mathematics if there is significant use of productive (speaking and writing) and receptive (listening and reading) forms of language. Language use in a mathematics classroom has the benefit of not just improving students' abilities to communicate mathematically, but to communicate in general. Everyday language is improved while using it within the context of math class.

Proficiency in mathematics language is essential for success in mathematics. There are three types of language involved in mathematical discourse. The first is conversational language used for giving instruction, explaining a process, and so on. The second is discrete language used for understanding symbols such as $+$, $-$, $\times$, $\div$, and the words and meaning attached to symbols. The third is mathematical language, which includes terms such as *range, product,* and *sample.* These have definitions specific to mathematics that are different from everyday usage. All three types of mathematical language are important to effectively communicate. Since mathematical language is not often a part of students' experiences outside the mathematics classroom, it is particularly important to make them a regular part of their mathematics learning.

Where Students Encounter Language in the *Math Trailblazers* Curriculum

In *Math Trailblazers,* students engage in all facets of language use including:
- reading introductory vignettes at the start of many lessons,
- explaining the process they used to solve a problem,
- listening to and comparing solution strategies,
- working collaboratively with classmates,
- writing responses to open-ended problems,
- reporting observations either orally or in writing, and
- reading and discussing the trade books and *Adventure Books.*

Assisting Students with Reading, Writing, and Discourse

Reading

Only if students comprehend the text can they begin to understand the problem and engage in doing mathematics.

Reading Comprehension: Background

George Polya (1973) outlined a 4-step problem-solving process. "Understand the problem" is the first step, followed by devising a plan, carrying out the plan, and looking back. Understanding first involves comprehending the text and then understanding what the mathematics is within the text. If students do not comprehend the text, they can't begin to understand the problem, therefore they cannot engage in doing mathematics. This is true even for reading symbolic expressions as simple as $8 \div 2 = 4$. At the beginning of the problem-solving process, it is important to realize the complexity of reading in mathematics. Mathematics text is different from other text; it is very dense, containing more ideas per sentence than any other type of text (Kenney, 2005). In addition, it can contain words as well as numeric and nonnumeric symbols. Students may have to comprehend illustrations that relate to the text, including tables, graphs, charts, pictures, and coordinate axes. Finally, the syntax of mathematics story problems is different from everyday language. Making these distinctions explicit supports reading comprehension for all students and is absolutely essential for those struggling with language or learning English.

Reading Comprehension: Strategies

The following strategies can increase students' reading comprehension:

1. Help students understand the goal of the lesson. Understanding the lesson's goal helps them with reading comprehension.
2. Find out whether the context is familiar to students. Bring meaning to that context. For example, students may not know the meaning of sampling a population. Ask, "Can you share how you have heard the word 'sampling' used?" Students may report on sampling food, samples of wallpaper or paint, or other experiences. If not, share a personal experience such as when you participated in a survey.
3. Model the process of interpretation through "think aloud." This includes articulating what dilemmas or questions arise as you read and what words and phrases help you figure out what to do.
4. Ask students what difficulties they have understanding the problem. As students try to find words to describe what they don't understand, they often solve the problem themselves. Sometimes, other students offer helpful input.
5. Restate the problem in an interactive manner. Ask students to use the pair-share strategy: one partner tells what the problem is about (e.g., finding volunteers to work at the science fair) and the other partner tells the question they will need to answer (e.g., how many people will be needed).

6. Help students with phrases and their meanings. For example, consider the question: "Which group has twice as many small lids as large lids?" Ask students to think about what that phrase "twice as many . . . as" means and then describe how they know. Add these phrases to a journal or math word wall. Note that this helps students see how the meaning of words are influenced by other words around them. This is very different from a key-word approach, which can result in limited comprehension (see the section on using key words later in this document).

7. Allow students time to read aloud and time to listen to others read aloud. Follow with "What is this question asking you to do?" and "How did you know?" Asking "how" makes explicit the connection between words and mathematical concepts and procedures.

To support students as they read (or listen to) children's books connected to *Math Trailblazers* lessons, we recommend the following strategies:

- Preview or review vocabulary that may be problematic.
- Ask students to predict or summarize story contents.
- Ask questions related to the story, but beyond the discussion prompts.

Grades 1–5 in *Math Trailblazers* each has a series of *Adventure Books,* short stories written like graphic novels (comic book style) or illustrated, connected text. The stories are used to illustrate a math or science concept with children as the problem solvers.

You can share these stories in a variety of ways:

1. Read the story as students follow along.
2. Read the story, then have students read it with a partner.
3. Students read the story with a partner.
4. Assign the story for homework the night before for students to pre-read with family members.
5. Students read the story in a reader's theater format.
6. Record the story and place it in a listening center with accompanying questions for students to answer.

Reading Levels

In any classroom there is a range of reading abilities. While the curriculum is written to be accessible to all students, struggling readers or nonreaders may need additional support. One way is to read the text first as a whole class. Another is to group the nonreaders with the teacher at the start to be sure they understand the text. Heterogeneous grouping can support nonreaders or reluctant readers, especially if you insist that when you visit the group every student can explain the task. The following story demonstrates how one second-grade teacher organized her classroom with reluctant and nonreaders to provide access to all students.

A Classroom Example of Accommodating Different Reading Levels

(This second-grade lesson deals with making a map on the x- and y-axis with Mr. Origin (a referent object) at the origin of the coordinate plane.)

The room is full of second graders with varying degrees of reading abilities. I had planned the Mr. Origin lab for one class period, but didn't think we would get to the questions about the map. But these kids were wonderful and finished making their maps and measuring with ease. So, since they were in groups, I said to each group as they finished, "Go ahead and start answering the questions about your map."

There were groans, but each group began to read the questions and respond to them. One group put their heads together and answered all the questions. A second group got started but one child asked to be excused for a moment (a nonreader). A third group immediately split into two pairs and began answering questions (but didn't finish). When group 4 was stuck, I asked one boy to read the questions to the group. There was a nonreader in that group and he wouldn't listen to the questions being read. So, I asked him to read. He read the words but obviously couldn't read for meaning (yet). The first boy read it one more time and then the group answered the questions. Before they were finished they had read the question a total of 6 times and then answered the question.

Afterwards, I reflected on the lesson, in particular how the students were able to answer the questions. I thought that pairs might be better than larger groups for tasks involving reading.

I also thought about which child needed to be paired with which child during a reading part of a math lesson. One idea I had was to pull my nonreaders together and read to them before having them work in pairs on the questions.

When I looked at the papers, I found that only two children had not answered all or most of the questions successfully, both nonreaders. I made a mental note that I need to ask each nonreader to respond to me orally to check for understanding.

Working together, the students had helped each other understand the questions and respond to them successfully.

Caution: Key-Word Approach Can Limit Comprehension

Some reading strategies can inhibit learning. In mathematics, the most common is searching the story problem for key words that indicate a specific operation. Research shows that while teachers help identify what are sometimes called "key words" to support student thinking, students use these words to abandon reasoning about the problem (Kenney, Hancewicz, Heuer, Metsisto, Tuttle, 2005; Sowder, 1988). The reasons why a "key-word approach" can be detrimental to comprehension include:

1. Key words often have multiple meanings.
2. The list of key words continues to grow over the years making it difficult to remember.
3. The key words might indicate an operation, but the question may be asking for more than the response to a computation.
4. Key-word search doesn't help students understand the meaning of the problem.
5. For problems involving multiple steps, it doesn't work and students are then ill-prepared to read for understanding. Instead, students need opportunities to find meaning in the reading.
6. Phrases can shift the meaning of words in the phrase. For example "how," "many," and "how many" signify different things in mathematics.
7. Addition of (or removal of) a single letter changes meaning (e.g. "percent of" versus "percent off," "ten" versus "tens").

Appropriate Attention to Key Words

It is important to develop vocabulary that is specific to mathematics. Although, this point may seem to contradict the previous section, there is an important distinction. In the "keyword" approach, students memorize that a word (e.g., difference) means to "subtract" regardless of the content of the sentence; in a precision-of-vocabulary approach, students become familiar with the common phrases (e.g., more than) and relationships among words (e.g., if-then) and how they interact with the rest of the sentence. As a teacher, one way to support student-reading skills is to make explicit some of these vocabulary considerations specific to mathematics. Some common examples of the subtleties in mathematics language follow:

1. Here are two problems using the term *more than,* one requiring subtraction (or counting down) and one requiring addition (or counting up):
   - Jenny has 9 apples. She has 3 *more than* Linda. How many apples does Linda have?
   - Jenny has 9 apples. Linda has 3 *more than* Jenny. How many does Linda now have?
2. Here are two problems in which "by" indicates two different operations:
   - Linda had four cats in her stuffed animal collection. After her birthday, the number of cats *increased by* three. How many cats does Linda have?
   - Linda had four cats in her stuffed animal collection. After her birthday, the number of cats was *multiplied by* three. How many cats does Linda now have?

3. In this example, the operation is the same, but a different response is required for each:
   - The third grade went on a field trip. There are 50 students in the third grade. Twenty students fit on each bus. How many buses were needed?
   - The third grade went on a field trip. There are 50 students in the third grade. Twenty students fit on each bus. How many buses were full?
4. In these statements the key word *of* is used in different ways:
   - What is the area *of* a triangle? (indicating find the space inside)
   - What is one-half *of* 24? (indicating $\frac{1}{2} \times 24$ or $24 \div 2$)
     Find the perimeter *of* the rectangle. (indicating where the perimeter is).

Writing

Writing: Background

The value of having students write in math is quite simply that writing improves learning. Pugalee (2005) explains:

As students write, they manipulate, integrate, and restructure knowledge through using and reflecting on what they know and believe. This process facilitates the development of meaningful understanding: the more a student works with ideas and concepts, the more likely those ideas and concepts will be understood and remembered. (p. xii)

Writing can allow more flexibility in how much time a student has to describe a solution and provides the opportunity for reflection and correction. If students struggle with the words to explain, they can supplement or replace with illustrations. While writing has clear benefits, it is also very challenging. Students are learning to write as they are learning mathematics, so the thought processes are demanding, the precision required in communicating mathematically increases the difficulty of this task, and even students willing to share orally, may be reluctant to share their ideas in writing. Because writing does improve learning, but is difficult, it is essential that students have ample opportunity and support for writing.

Math Trailblazers offers many opportunities for students to write. Just as in a writing lesson, students benefit when they submit a written explanation, receive input from the teacher, and then revise the explanation based on feedback. In the early grades, writing might include a simple process of asking students to tell in words or sentences how many objects they found altogether. Teachers can help primary students learn to write by having them dictate their thinking to an adult or by drawing pictures. Teachers at all grade levels, including kindergarten, should expect students to submit written work, even if the thoughts are incomplete or inaccurate. Students become better writers by writing. As noted earlier, as students improve their writing in mathematics, they improve their writing skills in general. Math class is just one of many situations in which students need to learn effective written communication.

Writing: Strategies

Because writing may be the most difficult literacy skill, it is important to explicitly teach students to write (or illustrate) their work. Here are some ways teachers support student writing:

1. Use and display the *Math Trailblazers* Student Rubrics in grades 3–5. If students have the rubrics in front of them as they work, they will produce better products. If you use a sample, have students collectively respond to whether the sample meets the expectations in the *Telling* or other rubrics. Students will learn how to be more clear and thorough in their writing. For more information on rubrics, see the Assessment section.

TIMS Tip

Post enlargements of the rubrics in the classroom where they are easy to point to and read.

2. Prior to writing, ask students to verbally summarize the important concepts of the lesson. You can even list key points on the board so students can synthesize the information into complete sentences in their own way. Sharing key points can serve as a good review and an opportunity for speaking and reading that further solidifies the concept for students.

3. For students having trouble beginning, sentence starters are a good tool. Another related tool is a graphic organizer with sections where students are prompted to write the question, process, and solution. Some teachers use Polya's (1973) 4-step problem-solving process as a guide, asking students to (1) state the problem, (2) tell what approach they used, (3) explain what solution they got, and (4) tell how their solution answers the original problem.

4. Incorporate creative writing prompts that engage your students. For example, use a genre introduced in language arts, like poetry, fables, or persuasive narratives.

5. Ask students to draw pictures, diagrams or, for older students, concept maps of what they later explain in words. Using pictures can support writing and help you to see what they are trying to explain.

6. Have students keep a math journal of the written summaries of lessons or problems. In this way students can see their improvement in explaining mathematics and have a resource for looking up information they might have forgotten. See the TIMS Tutor: *Journals* for a range of prompts and tips on keeping a math journal.

7. Make a transparency of a well-written response to share with students. To preserve anonymity, use a sample from another class or save samples from year to year.

8. Ask students to fold a paper in half, solve the problem on the first half, and then open the paper and write the steps on the second half.

Regardless of the strategies you use, it is important to remember that the goal is to capture students' ideas and thinking. Creativity and novel solutions are important, and writing opportunities should not impose ways for students to begin or solve a problem.

Because Math Trailblazers *engages students in problem solving and inquiry, there are opportunities for students to approach a problem differently and share different solution strategies.*

Discourse

Discourse: Background

Those who start teaching with a *Standards*-based curriculum like *Math Trailblazers* often see a change in their classroom discourse. Because *Math Trailblazers* engages students in problem solving and inquiry, there are opportunities for students to approach a problem differently and share different solution strategies. Students learn from hearing others' approaches, and such conversations allow teachers to help students focus on key mathematical ideas. This is different from asking questions to get students to a particular teacher-determined endpoint, a model of questioning often referred to as funneling, where the teacher uses questions to funnel students to a particular formula, approach, or term (Herbel-Eisenmann and Breyfogle, 2005).

Post-exploration discussions are essential to the learning process. As Chapin, O'Conner, and Anderson (2003) write, "When a teacher succeeds in setting up a classroom in which students feel obligated to listen to one another, to make their own contributions clear and comprehensible, and to provide evidence for their claims; that teacher has set in place a powerful context for student learning." (p. 9)

Discourse is not only a concluding activity in a lesson, however, but is important as student work is in progress. This can help stimulate new ideas across working groups. Whitin & Whitin (2000) call this "rough draft thinking" and argue that it allows classmates and the teacher to get a glimpse into other students' thought processes and to revise one's own thinking (p. 220).

Having classroom discourse means establishing norms for how students interact with each other. Hiebert, et al. (1996) describe four critical features of establishing a social culture for learning mathematics, shared in brief here:

Ideas are the currency of the classroom. Ideas, expressed by any participant, have the potential to contribute to everyone's learning and consequently warrant respect and response.

Students have autonomy with respect to the methods used to solve problems. Students must respect the need for everyone to understand their own methods and must recognize that there are often a variety of methods that will do the job.

The classroom culture exhibits an appreciation for mistakes as learning sites. Mistakes afford opportunities to examine errors in reasoning and thereby raise everyone's level of analysis. Do not cover up mistakes; use them constructively.

The authority for reasonability and correctness lies in the logic and structure of the subject, rather than in the social status of participants. The persuasiveness of an explanation or the correctness of a solution depends on the mathematical sense it makes, not on the popularity of the presenter. (pp. 9–10)

Discourse: Strategies

Facilitating discourse improves with practice. As students become more accustomed to explaining their thinking, listening to others, and asking their own questions, knowing what questions you should ask and when to ask them is an important skill. Discourse that "focuses" rather than "funnels" is less predictable and requires skills on your part. Some strategies to support effective discourse include the following:

1. Allot time for students to share and compare strategies and solutions at the end of the lesson, even if it is not the end of the period. It takes time for students to articulate their ideas. If you are running out of time, build it into the next day. Reflecting about the lesson helps children develop an understanding of math concepts and helps you to understand what it is they learned.

2. Shift classroom procedures from general ones like "listen to one another" to specific ones, such as "We need to listen and understand what the speaker is saying. We all have an obligation to ask questions when we don't understand."

3. Focus on the important mathematical concepts in the lesson. If these objectives are written on the board it helps both you and students keep the dialogue focused.

4. Ask good questions. Interesting questions that have answers not already known support good classroom discussions. Use questions that prompt students to listen to each other. For example, "Can you repeat in your own words what you just heard?" "How is this strategy similar to or different from your strategy?" and "What can you add to what was just said?" "Do you agree or disagree with it? Why or why not?" In all cases, the response is neither punitive nor evaluative. If the student who is asked these questions cannot answer, he or she can always ask, "I didn't understand, could you please repeat what was said?" These questions communicate to students that you expect them to listen and learn from each other. Good questions for facilitating discourse are offered in *Professional Standards for Teaching Mathematics* (NCTM, 1991) or can be accessed through Public Broadcasting Service Teacherline.

5. Engage all students in discussion. Participation is not optional. If students are sharing with the whole group, stop at times and ask them to share their thoughts with a partner. Ask students to write an idea on paper or in their journals so they are ready to share.

6. Focus on student understanding. Kenney, et al. (2005) characterize three types of discourse. First, the traditional, in which the teacher and several students talk. Second is a "probing" discussion, where the teacher is still generating the questions, but the questions are more open-ended. Third, is "discourse-rich," where students are working together toward mathematical understanding. An important distinction in the third type is the student-to-student and student-to-class interactions.

7. Decide when to guide students and when to wait, when to ask a student for further elaboration and when to elicit input from others. Quiet pauses should not be uncomfortable dead time, but "think time" for all students to think about what was just said, process it, and then respond.

In addition to these strategies, Easley (1990) offers guidelines for establishing an environment that fosters discourse (see below).

Ten Suggestions for Practice in Communication

From *Dialogue and Conceptual Splatter in Mathematics Classes* by Jack Easley

1. Try to maintain an atmosphere of freedom in the classroom, that is, an atmosphere that encourages students* to feel free to express themselves.
2. When in doubt, remain silent! Give students a chance to work through their mathematical difficulties.
3. Don't paraphrase because paraphrasing is usually a technique for pushing the students too quickly towards the teacher's point of view. Let the students' words stand by themselves. Ask students to clarify the expression of their own thoughts rather than comply with your thoughts.
4. Encourage constructive arguments. For example, ask, "Do you believe that?" "Do you agree or disagree?" "How do you know?" or say, "Tell me what you mean."
5. Play dumb, but avoid condescension. Let the students teach you as well as each other.
6. Don't focus on "right" answers. Alternative answers can create a tension that leads to lively and fruitful interaction. In addition, many good problems have more than one right answer, or at least more than one possible solution technique.
7. Let students have time to work on a problem as individuals before you ask them to share their thoughts in a small or large group, thereby encouraging each student to get involved in the problem.
8. No best way exists to form small groups. For example, you can group students at random or on the basis of ability levels or of their conflicting opinions.
9. Dialogue groups, whether small or large, can be called "meetings." Take time to model expected etiquette for the meetings.
10. Save the written work of the students to evaluate and substantiate their learning. Record the classroom dialogues on videotapes, audiotapes, and in your own journal of the activities; share these recordings with the students. And finally, bring continuity to the dialogues by basing future sessions on your evaluation of the conceptual splatter that has been expressed. (p. 36)

*Students is used here to replace "pupils," which was used in the original publication.

Arithmetic Teacher by Jack Easley. Copyright 1990 by National Council of Teachers of Mathematics. Reproduced with permission of National Council of Teachers of Mathematics in the format Textbook via Copyright Clearance Center.

For further information on developing a language-rich classroom for English Language Learners, see the Teaching the *Math Trailblazers* Student: Meeting Individual Needs section.

References

Assessment Standards for School Mathematics. National Council of Teachers of Mathematics, Reston, VA, 1995.

Burrill, G. "Changes in your Classrooms: From the Past to the Present to the Future." *Mathematics Teaching in the Middle School,* 4(3), pp. 184–190, 1998.

Chapin, S.H., C. O'Conner, and N.C. Anderson. *Classroom Discussions: Using Math Talk to Help Students Learn.* Math Solutions Publications, Sausalito, CA, 2003.

Cummins, J. "Supporting ESL Students in Learning the Language of Mathematics." *Research Says: Issues and Trends in Mathematics.* Pearson Education, New York, 2007.

Cuoco, A., E.P. Goldenberg, and J. Mark. "Habits of Mind: An Organizing Principle for Mathematics Curricula." *Journal of Mathematical Behavior,* 15, pp. 375–402, 1996.

Curriculum and Evaluation Standards for School Mathematics (1st ed.). National Council of Teachers of Mathematics, Reston, VA, 1989.

Easley, Jack. "Research into Practice. Dialogue and Conceptual Splatter in Mathematics Classes." *Arithmetic Teacher,* 37(7), pp. 34–37, 1990.

Galima, L., and T. Hirsch. "Making Mathematics Accessible to English Learners." Paper presented at the National Council of Teachers of Mathematics (NCTM) annual meeting, Atlanta, GA, March 2007.

Herbel-Eisenmann, B.A., and M.L. Breyfogle. "Questioning our Patterns of Questioning." *Mathematics Teaching in the Middle School,* 10(9), pp. 484–489, 2005.

Hiebert, J., et al. *Making Sense: Teaching and Learning Mathematics with Understanding.* Heinemann, Portsmouth, NH, 1997.

Kenney, J.M., E. Hancewicz, L. Heuer, D. Metsisto, and C.L. Tuttle. *Literacy Strategies for Improving Mathematics Instruction.* Association for Supervision and Curriculum Development, Alexandria, VA, 2005.

McIntosh, M.E. "500 Writing Formats." *Mathematics Teaching in the Middle School,* 2(5), pp. 354–358, 1997.

Polya, G. *How to Solve It: A New Aspect of Mathematical Method.* Princeton University Press, Princeton, NJ, 1973.

Principles and Standards for School Mathematics. National Council of Teachers of Mathematics, Reston, VA, 2000.

Professional Standards for Teaching Mathematics. National Council of Teachers of Mathematics, Reston, VA, 1991.

Pugalee, D.K. *Writing for Mathematical Understanding.* Christopher Gordon Publishers Norwood, MA, 2005.

Sowder, L. "Children's Solutions of Story Problems." *Journal of Mathematical Behavior* 7, pp. 227–238, 1988.

Van de Walle, J.A. *Elementary and Middle School Mathematics: Teaching Developmentally.* Pearson Education, New York, 2007.

Whitin, D.J., and P. Whitin. "Exploring Mathematics Through Talking and Writing." M.J. Burke, and F.R. Curcio, eds. *Learning Mathematics for a New Century: 2000 Yearbook,* pp. 213–222. NCTM, Reston, VA, 2000.

Wood, T. "Alternative Patterns of Communication in Mathematics Classes: Funneling or Focusing?" H. Steinbring, M.B. Bussi, and A. Sierpinska, eds. *Language and Communication in the Mathematics Classroom,* pp. 167–178. NCTM, Reston, VA, 1998.

Working with *Math Trailblazers* Parents and Families

The Parents and *Math Trailblazers* section provides suggestions and tips to help parents participate in their child's understanding of *Math Trailblazers* and to enhance its benefits for their children.

A teacher, student, and parent work together to solve a problem.

Working with *Math Trailblazers* Parents and Families

 PART I   *Math Trailblazers* **Features**

Parents' understanding and support of your mathematics curriculum plays an important role in its successful implementation and can be a key factor in children's success with mathematics. This section provides suggestions and tips to help parents understand the *Math Trailblazers* curriculum. It is arranged in three parts. The first part describes several built-in features to help you communicate with parents. The second part gives advice on preparing two types of special programs: math nights for families and parent presentations at school or district meetings. The third part provides blackline masters to copy and distribute to parents.

Parents need to understand the careful balance that Math Trailblazers *maintains between developing skills, underlying mathematical concepts, and problem solving.*

Parents want assurances that the content and approaches of the school's mathematics program will not only educate and interest their children now, but also benefit them later when test scores and school admissions become serious realities. Most adults experienced a mathematics curriculum that focused almost exclusively on teaching facts and standard procedures for computing. In contrast, *Math Trailblazers* maintains a careful balance between developing skills, underlying mathematical concepts, and problem solving. Parents need to understand this balance. Moreover, parents must understand the importance of teaching the other mathematics strands (algebra, geometry, measurement, and data analysis and probability). As you work with parents throughout the year, communicate the following:

- Varied contexts for solving problems in *Math Trailblazers* help children learn to use mathematics in meaningful ways;

- The activities in *Math Trailblazers* are designed to provide children with the skills they will need in the workplace of the 21st century.

- Current research supports the approaches used in *Math Trailblazers* for teaching mathematics. In regard to computation and facts, the approaches in *Math Trailblazers* allow students to gain fluency with less drill and memorization than former methods and with better retention;

- Practice with skills and procedures is distributed between homework, Daily Practice and Problems, and within most problem-solving activities in the program;

- *Math Trailblazers* encourages students to develop varied ways to solve problems—not just the solutions that adults might select; and

- Mathematical ideas are represented with manipulatives, pictures, tables, graphs, and numbers—and how these representations allow children to access the mathematics in varied ways.

Communicating with Parents

Gaining parent support early will save effort in the long term. Anticipate potential parental concerns about a new math program and address them proactively through an ongoing parent education effort.

Math Trailblazers includes a parent brochure, letters home, homework notes, and parent information blackline masters to help you communicate about the curriculum.

Parent Brochure

The parent brochure provides an introduction to the curriculum. Blackline masters of this brochure (in English and Spanish) are at the end of this section. They are designed for you to send home at the beginning of the year or use as a handout at a fall parent meeting.

Letters Home

Parent letters are included at the beginning of each unit to give specific information about what children will study. These letters describe the concepts presented in each unit and how parents or family members can provide follow-up and encouragement at home. A sample Letter Home is shown in Figure 1.

Letter Home

Grouping and Counting

Date: ____________

Dear Family Member:

In this unit, students group and count objects. They count by twos, fives, and tens.

Ask your child to tell you about the book *The Doorbell Rang* by Pat Hutchins. The book describes the problem of how to share twelve cookies with unexpected guests. Your child will explore similar problems involving cookies and discuss fair shares and leftovers.

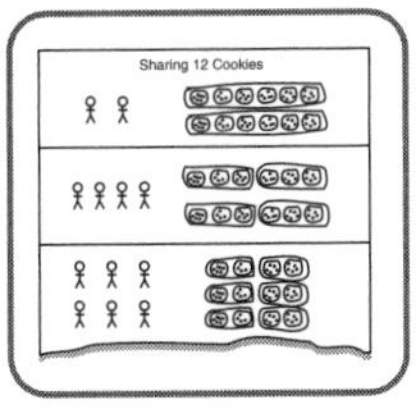

Ways to group 12 cookies

The unit ends with a laboratory investigation. *Colors* is an experiment about sorting and sampling. The lab provides a real-life context for children to use grouping and counting skills.

You can extend your child's classroom activities by doing the following at home:

- **Coin Jar.** Stock a small jar with several dimes and nickels and about 20–30 pennies. Ask your child to take some coins from the jar, name the coins, and count the total value. Be sure there are enough nickels and dimes to practice counting by 5s and 10s.
- **Play *Care to Share?*** Give your child a small container of cereal or other small objects. Ask him or her to make a pile of 17 objects. Tell him or her to share this pile fairly with three people. Allow time for your child to solve the problem. Ask how many objects each person should get and how many objects will be left over. Repeat sharing objects with two, four, or five people.

Thank you for your continued efforts to help your child with math ideas through discussion and games.

Sincerely,

____

URG • Grade 1 • Unit 5 iii

Figure 1: *Sample letter home from Grade 1*

Homework Notes

Many homework assignments, especially in grades K–3, include a separate explanation for family members, outlining the activity's purpose and providing hints for assisting with the assignment. An example of such a note is shown in Figure 2. These explanations are to help parents feel comfortable with the curriculum's content and goals. We encourage you to supplement the parent instructions with your own notes and to provide a way for parents to get their homework questions answered (e.g., via emails, phone, or after school).

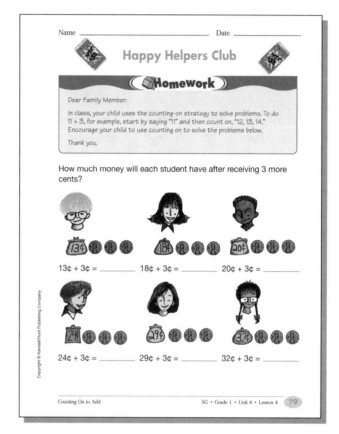

Figure 2: *Sample Grade 1 homework note for parents*

Parent Information Blackline Masters

Additional information on selected topics is available to be copied for parents at the end of this section. Topics include:

- Math Facts Philosophy
- Multiplication Methods in *Math Trailblazers*
- Long Division in *Math Trailblazers*
- Internet Resources for Families of *Math Trailblazers* Students

Roles for Parent Volunteers

Parent volunteers can support the implementation of *Math Trailblazers* in a variety of capacities.

Parent volunteers can be an important support to the implementation of Math Trailblazers in a variety of capacities.

Math Trailblazers incorporates many hands-on activities. In addition to the commercially purchased manipulatives such as base-ten pieces, many activities call for materials such as jars, container lids, paper towel cores, and so on. Parent volunteers can ease the job of gathering and managing these materials.

Parent volunteers also can assist with classroom activities. They can work on special projects or lesson extensions with small groups. Some teachers periodically invite several parents to assist with station activities, where student groups rotate from station to station. Often it is helpful to have an extra set of hands and eyes in the classroom to assist as needed.

Parents can assist students during a lesson. Assign parents to work with particular groups of students or with individual students who need extra assistance. With guidance on appropriate ways to support student thinking, this can be a great support for students, as well as educate parents in the instructional approaches used in *Math Trailblazers*.

You can obviously tailor the roles parents play in providing support to your needs and the interests and capabilities of individual parents. There is little doubt, however, that parent volunteers are a valuable asset as you work with *Math Trailblazers*.

Special Programs for Families and Parents

One way to help parents understand and support the goals and philosophy of *Math Trailblazers* is to organize special math-related programs for parents and families. One type of program is a math night, during which parents participate in math activities with their children. Another is a more formal presentation given by a teacher or other curriculum leader at a school parent night or special informational meeting. Many schools combine both types of programs by giving a short presentation as part of a math night. The following are suggestions to help you plan parent and family programs for your school.

Family Math Nights

A typical math night involves families coming to school to participate together in math activities. A variety of successful math night formats include:

- **Math Night Carnival**
  Families move from one math activity to another at their own pace. This format is typically held in a large space such as a gymnasium or lunchroom.

- **Teacher-Led Math Night**
  Families visit their child's math classroom and work together through grade-level specific activities and games.

- **Math Night Classroom Rotation**
  Families rotate through a series of classrooms. Each classroom presents a specific math activity or game. Families may encounter activities from a variety of grade levels.

> *One way to help parents understand and support the goals and philosophy of* Math Trailblazers *is to organize special math-related programs for parents and families.*

The best format of any math night differs from school to school and even from year to year within the same school. The following is what happened at one school.

The school invited parents and students to a math night designed as a carnival, held in the gym. Students and parents played a game at each booth and got a prize when they finished. As the evening progressed though, parents congregated in the middle of the gym while their children played the games alone. This event did not meet the goal of getting parents involved with and learning about Math Trailblazers.

The next year, the staff decided to reorganize the math night to keep parents involved in Math Trailblazers *activities with their children. In preparation for the math night, teachers chose primary and intermediate activities and planned them to be held in classrooms. They made a display about the activity that included information on how the activity aligned with the state and NCTM* Standards. *Teachers also hung estimation activities in the hallways to keep families busy as they moved through the school. As families worked their way from the primary to the middle grades, they saw how the mathematics develops across the grades. Parental involvement on this math night was a big improvement over previous years.*

Suggested Activities

When planning a math night, choose activities that illustrate key ideas from the *Math Trailblazers* curriculum and engage parents. For example, choose activities that focus on problem solving, address a range of mathematical content, or have connections to science.

Doing parts of one of the labs is an effective way for parents to experience how mathematics in the curriculum is embedded in meaningful contexts. Consider using labs you have already done in class. That way, students can lead their parents. Students won't mind repeating the lab, since in many cases, the data will be new to them.

Following is a list of activities that worked well in math night programs. We chose these activities because the concepts underlying them are easily understood, and require minimum preparation. They also show the impact of *Math Trailblazers* work with the scientific method and ways for children to practice computation in a context.

Kindergarten:
- sorting apples from *Data Collection* in the *Ongoing Content* section
- *A Garden's Area,* Month 7 Lesson 4

Grade 1:
- *Pockets* activities in Unit 3 (selected pieces)
- *More or Less Than 100,* Unit 9 Lesson 2

Grade 2:
- *High, Wide, and Handsome,* Unit 4 Lesson 1 (selected pieces)
- *Tile Designs,* Unit 2 Lesson 1
- *Marshmallows and Containers,* Unit 6, Lesson 5 (selected pieces)

Grade 3:
- *First Names,* Unit 1 Lesson 10
- *The Better "Picker Upper,"* Unit 5 Lesson 3
- *Floor Tiler,* Unit 11 Lesson 5

Grade 4:
- *Arm Span vs. Height,* Unit 1 Lesson 5 (selected pieces)
- *Investigating Area and Perimeter,* Unit 2 Lesson 1

Grade 5:
- *Three in a Row,* Unit 8 Lesson 2
- *Factor 40,* Unit 11 Lesson 1
- *Fraction Cover All,* Unit 5 Lesson 3

Tips for Math Nights

The following list of recommendations reflects the experiences of teachers in many different settings. The list is intended to help you make decisions for your own Math Night, but not all may be appropriate in your setting.

- Hold more than one math night, with different grade levels (e.g., K, 1–2, 3–5) grouped together. If you target multiple grades, families with children in different grades can participate together. On the other hand, if you offer grade-level classes, parents can learn more about their child's particular grade.

- Require that students come with an adult. Explain that this is not just a program for children, but a chance for families to enjoy mathematics together.

- If using the teacher-led classroom format, make sure there is enough room for everyone. Some schools divide participants into groups of eight to ten families, so there are about 25 people per class.

- Consider offering babysitting for younger siblings, so parents can devote their attention to their school-age children.

- Ask families to register in advance so you will know how many people to plan for. This also lets you know whether you need further recruitment efforts. However, some schools believe that asking families to register discourages some from attending.

- Involve as many people as you can. Include groups such as the parent-teacher organization. Ask high school students to help as volunteers—some schools offer credit for volunteer service.

- Involve parent volunteers in planning the event and leading the activities. This gives parents a first-hand look at the curriculum and makes the planning more manageable. Parents who are not comfortable leading activities can help with registration, shop for supplies, arrange for food, and babysit.

- Advertise. Send home fliers, have students make invitations for their parents, feature articles in school newsletters, put up posters.

- Offer rewards for coming, such as packages of manipulatives or math games that can be played at home. Offer a reward to the class that has the highest attendance.

- Provide food. Find local sponsors or ask the parent organization for donations of food or beverages.

- Have a raffle. Items can be donated by local businesses. Include information about the raffle in the flyer. Math trade books and gift certificates make great prizes.

- Be sure to try the activities yourself before leading them.

- Use manipulatives in the activities so parents can see how their children use them for meaningful math activities.

- Use one or more of the math facts games to illustrate one way to engage students in practicing math facts.

- Send home a packet of games so families can continue to play at home.

- Hand out an evaluation form to help plan for future programs.

- Have a math day, instead of math night. Parents can visit their children's math classes and stay for lunch. Or set up math stations around the school and have students as tour guides.

Content Note

Getting the most from your work with parents
Just as teachers ask students to reflect on their learning, be sure to ask parents what they learned from any *Math Trailblazers*-related parent activities. Invite parents to think about a question as the final activity. This can help provide insights into what parents have learned, but also provide feedback for the next parent session.

Here are some additional tips for programs that use a carnival or classroom rotation format:

- Hand out "passports." Ask families to get "stamped" at each station and enter their completed passports in a prize drawing.

- If you want participants to spend equal amounts of time at each station, then plan a second activity or open-ended task at short stations.

- Include stations that feature brief sessions on various aspects of *Math Trailblazers,* for example, how to use strategies to learn math facts, the TIMS Laboratory Method, and so on.

Other Resources for Planning Math Nights

- *Family Math* is an excellent resource for planning a math program for families. It describes stimulating math games and activities for a series of classes in which parents and children participate together. Included are an early childhood book and a K–8 book, and translations into Spanish. The goals of *Family Math* complement the goals of *Math Trailblazers* and as a result, parents who participate in *Family Math* are likely to have a good understanding of the approach used in *Math Trailblazers.* Whether you plan a one-night event to introduce *Math Trailblazers* or a longer series of classes, *Family Math* gives practical advice to help you plan. It also has useful handouts on topics such as math and careers that are interesting to families. For more information about the program, including training for Family Math workshop leaders, or to order a book, contact:

Family Math
Lawrence Hall of Science
University of California at Berkeley
Berkeley, CA 94720-5200
www.lhs.berkeley.edu/equals

- As part of their continued professional development and support for *Math Trailblazers* users, Kendall/Hunt Publishing Company offers assistance in planning math nights tailored to the needs of your school. You may contact them at 1-800-542-6657.

Presentations to Parents

Since the *Math Trailblazers* program is different from what is familiar to most parents and grandparents, curriculum presentations and the reasons your school selected it can help build support. These range from formal presentations at district-wide or school-wide meetings to less formal discussions at classroom parent nights. Some schools hold monthly meetings that focus on different grade levels or different topics. Others schedule one district-wide or school-wide presentation that gives an overview of the program. Suggestions of topics to include in a presentation are discussed below. Additional resources for preparing your presentation are at the end of this section.

> **Suggested Topics for a Parent Presentation**
> - Description of *Math Trailblazers*
> - Your District's Implementation
> - A Closer Look
> - Computation and Math Facts in *Math Trailblazers*

Description of *Math Trailblazers*

The following are ways to describe *Math Trailblazers*. For further elaboration, see the Foundations section.

- *Math Trailblazers* is a *Standards*-based curriculum. It follows the recommendations of the *Principles and Standards for School Mathematics,* developed by the National Council of Teachers of Mathematics (NCTM, 2000) to improve the teaching and learning of mathematics. These recommendations outline a vision for school mathematics that includes:
  - a mathematically challenging curriculum that covers a broad range of mathematical content;
  - a strong focus on engaging students in mathematical problem solving;
  - instruction that is conceptually oriented and stresses thinking, reasoning, and the application of appropriate uses of calculators and computers; and
  - a strong commitment to promoting success in mathematics among all students—not only those who traditionally do well.

- *Math Trailblazers* is a research-based curriculum. The first edition was the result of more than six years of work by the Teaching Integrated Math and Science Project (TIMS) at the University of Illinois at Chicago, including extensive pilot- and field-testing of the materials. In developing *Math Trailblazers,* the authors drew upon research findings from a wide variety of sources, as well as from the broad experiences of the authoring group, which included mathematicians, scientists, and former teachers. The National Science Foundation funded development of *Math Trailblazers* and has continued to support research on the impact of *Math Trailblazers* on student achievement and research-based development of revised editions.

- *Math Trailblazers* is a problem-solving curriculum. A fundamental principle is that mathematics is best learned through active involvement in solving real problems. Problem solving in *Math Trailblazers* is not a distinct topic, but one that permeates the entire program, providing a context for students to apply the mathematics they know and learn new

> *Since the Math Trailblazers program is different from what parents and grandparents are familiar with, presentations about the curriculum and the reasons your school selected it can help build support.*

mathematics. For example, in a third grade laboratory experiment, *The Better "Picker Upper,"* students investigate which paper towel is more absorbent. They explore the absorbency of various brands of paper towels by dropping water onto each and comparing the areas of the resulting spots. In the process, they learn about area, fractions, averaging, and computation. As students work on problems such as these, they develop skills, procedures, and concepts.

- *Math Trailblazers* is a full mathematics curriculum, with a focus on science and language arts. It uses science as a context for much of the problem solving built into the program. In Kindergarten students collect and analyze data at least once every week, and in each of grades 1–5, students engage in eight to ten laboratory investigations that serve as a rich source of real-world mathematics problems. In these investigations, students identify variables, draw pictures, take measurements, organize data in tables, graph data, and look for and use patterns—all important mathematics skills that are used by scientists. *Math Trailblazers* also focuses on language arts, with lessons that emphasize reading, writing, and oral communication. Collections of original math-related stories are found in the *Math Trailblazers Adventure Book*. Math trade books are recommended to accompany many lessons.

Your District's Implementation of *Math Trailblazers*

Include some of the following as you discuss your district's implementation:

- **Selection process.** Assure parents that a careful and thoughtful process was used to select the curriculum. Consider inviting a representative from the selection committee to describe the process.

- **Reasons for choosing *Math Trailblazers* over other curricula.** Describe the features of the program that appeal to the selection committee. How does *Math Trailblazers* help meet the goals of your school? If your district pilot-tested the curriculum before adoption, discuss feedback from teachers who have piloted the program. Invite one or more of those teachers to share their experiences.

- **Professional development.** Explain the program your district has in place to assure that teachers are trained to use the curriculum effectively. Describe the professional development opportunities teachers have had or will have to support their implementation.

- **Evidence of success.** If your district has used the program for a few years, describe teacher and student experiences with it. If you are new to the program, report on some of the experiences of other districts. Information on the success of *Math Trailblazers* around the country is available on the Kendall/Hunt web site, http://www.kendallhunt.com/mtb3.

- **Examples of what students are doing.** A good way to communicate to families that their children are learning more than just computational skills is to show examples of student work. Pick samples that illustrate how students solve complex multistep problems.

A Closer Look at *Math Trailblazers*

To help parents understand some of the strengths of *Math Trailblazers*, show them examples of specific lessons. If possible, ask them to solve a problem or play a game so they can experience firsthand the problem-solving approach to *Math Trailblazers*. Debrief from the activity in the way that you would with students. Ask parents to reflect on the lesson's content, how it compares to their experience, and what this means in terms of opportunities for students to learn. Consider using student work to show the kinds of problems *Math Trailblazers* students solve. Use work collected from your own students or samples available in the *Math Trailblazers* support material.

One source of student work examples is a component of *Math Trailblazers* called the Teacher Enhancement Resource Modules (TERMs). The TERMs were designed to help staff developers assemble workshops for teachers, but portions can also be presented to parents. They contain a guide for presenters with blackline masters, explanatory text, and discussion questions and answers. A set of TERMs is usually available in each district. Check with your principal or district office or call Kendall/Hunt at 1-800-KH-Books.

Most TERMs also include videos showing *Math Trailblazers* teachers and students engaged in activities from the curriculum. These streaming videos are available through the Kendall/Hunt website, mymathtrailblazers.com. Check with your principal or district office for information on how to access these resources.

Another source of appropriate sample student work, video, and explanatory text are from a grade 2 activity, *Measuring Volume*. This source contains a selection of relevant text, blackline masters, and the video you can use to develop a presentation for parents. These materials are available on the web, www.mymathtrailblazers.com.

The following are modules that can be adapted for use with parents (found in TERMS Set #1):

- **Why Reform?**
  This TERM presents information to introduce *Standards*-based mathematics. It includes a video *How Many in the Bag?* that shows students talking with their partners about their solutions to subtraction problems that arise from pulling handfuls of cubes from a bag. The interaction of the students talking about the problems shows how communication helps students clarify their thinking, correct mistakes, and hear different strategies from fellow students.

  A selection of text, blackline masters, and the video of one TERM, *Why Reform?* is available for download at www.mymathtrailblazers.com

- **Operations: Meaning, Invention, Efficiency, Power**
  Use this TERM to help guide the discussion of how the concept of division develops across grades K–5 and to describe the *Math Trailblazers* philosophy of computation. This TERM also shows how this philosophy applies to the development of other operations and to teaching the math facts.

- **Area: A Look Across the Grades**

  Use the *Area* TERM to help parents see how science is a rich context for applying and learning mathematics. This TERM includes representative area activities from each grade to show growth in mathematics and development of the concept of area through the grades.

- **Computation and Math Facts in *Math Trailblazers***

  Many parents think of computation when they think of mathematics, so it is natural for them to be curious about the way *Math Trailblazers* teaches computation. Explain that a balanced approach fosters the development of both mathematical concepts and skills. The following points might be useful in talking with parents about computation and basic math facts.

  1. Computation. In today's world, students compute using paper-and-pencil algorithms, calculators, and mental arithmetic. They need to get exact answers to problems as well as make and recognize reasonable estimates. *Math Trailblazers* helps students develop efficient and accurate methods for computation with the four basic operations. The treatment of each operation proceeds in the following stages:

     - Developing meaning for the operation

     - Inventing procedures for solving problems

     - Becoming more efficient at carrying out procedures

     - Developing mathematical power

  2. "Mathematical power" means that students understand when to apply the operation and how to use varied computational methods to solve problems. Students practice using the operations in activities, games, and laboratory investigations. More practice is provided in the Daily Practice and Problems in Grades 1–5 and in the Home Practice in Grades 3–5. Flexible thinking and mathematical power are our goals. The above computation stages are discussed more thoroughly in the Math Facts and Whole-Number Operations section.

  3. The paper-and-pencil algorithms for multiplication and long division taught in *Math Trailblazers* are probably somewhat different from those that parents learned in school. We introduce the "all-partials method" for multiplication first since many children find it easier to learn. Then we introduce the more efficient "compact method," the algorithm traditionally taught. (See Figure 3.)

All-Partials Method	Compact Method
15	15
× 22	× 22
10 (2 × 5)	30 (2 × 15)
20 (2 × 10)	+ 300 (20 × 15)
100 (20 × 5)	330
+ 200 (20 × 10)	
330	

Figure 3: *Paper and pencil algorithms for multiplication*

For division, we teach the "forgiving method" because many students find it easier to learn than the traditional method. While this method involves making estimates about the quotient, as does the traditional method, the forgiving method encourages the use of "easy" numbers, such as division by 10 or 100 in the estimates. The forgiving method also allows underestimates so it doesn't involve as much erasing and re-calculating as done by some children when using the traditional method. In the case where the highest possible estimate is made, the two methods are essentially the same. (See Figure 4.) Parent information sheets that describe the multiplication and division algorithms used in *Math Trailblazers* are at the end of this section.

Forgiving Method	Traditional Method
$$\begin{array}{r} 335 \\ 5\overline{)1675} \\ -1500 \\ \hline 175 \\ -150 \\ \hline 25 \\ -25 \\ \hline 0 \end{array}$$ $\quad$ 300 (estimate quotient 1675 ÷ 5) $\quad$ 30 (estimate quotient 175 ÷ 5) $\quad$ 5 (25 ÷ 5) $\quad$ 335	$$\begin{array}{r} 335 \\ 5\overline{)1675} \\ -15 \\ \hline 17 \\ -15 \\ \hline 25 \\ -25 \\ \hline 0 \end{array}$$

Figure 4: *Paper and pencil algorithms for division*

4. Math Facts. The goal of the *Math Trailblazers* math facts program is for students to learn the basic facts efficiently, gain fluency with their use, and retain that fluency over time. A large body of research supports an approach that is built on a foundation of work with strategies and concepts. This leads not only to more effective learning and better retention, but also to the development of mental math skills.

The *Math Trailblazers* math facts program is characterized by the elements below. These are summarized in the *Math Facts Philosophy* Blackline master at the end of this section.
• Early emphasis on problem solving
• Use of strategies to find facts and the de-emphasis of rote work
• Gradual and systematic introduction of the facts
• Ongoing practice
• Appropriate assessment
• Facts are not gatekeepers
• Multiyear approach

As you discuss the math facts program, give parents a few examples of math fact strategies such as the subtraction strategies of "counting up" and "using a ten." Other strategies are discussed in the *Math Facts* Tutor. This tutor is available to parents on the Kendall/Hunt website, as are several other TIMS Tutors.

Other Resources for Planning Your Presentation

The *Family* section of the Kendall/Hunt Website http://www.mymath trailblazers.com has several links to documents that can help you plan your presentation. Here are a few:

- *An Introduction for Families* includes answers to the following questions:

  What is in the *Math Trailblazers* curriculum?

  What is a *Math Trailblazers* classroom like?

  What connections does *Math Trailblazers* make with other school subjects?

  Why is my child using calculators with *Math Trailblazers?*

  How can parents talk with their children about math?

- *Frequently Asked Questions* includes answers to the following questions:

  How is *Math Trailblazers* different from other mathematics curricula?

  What is the opinion of the scientific community regarding the standards set by the National Council of Teachers of Mathematics?

  What science does *Math Trailblazers* include?

  How does *Math Trailblazers* integrate mathematics with other content areas?

  What kind of assessment does *Math Trailblazers* use?

  Does *Math Trailblazers* make use of collaborative learning?

  Can *Math Trailblazers* facilitate teaching children with learning styles and ability levels in a heterogeneous classroom?

Additional resources for working with parents include:

Stenmark, Jean Kerr, Virginia Thompson, and Ruth Cossey. *Family Math.* University of California, Lawrence Hall of Science, Berkeley, CA, 1986.

Funkhouser, J.E., and M.R. Gonzales. *Family Involvement in Children's Education: Successful Local Approaches: An Idea Book.* U.S. Department of Education, Washington, DC, 1997. http://www.ed.gov/pubs/FamInvolve/

Shartrand, A.M., H.B. Weiss, H.M. Kreider, and M. Lopez, *New Skills for New Schools: Preparing Teachers in Family Involvement.* Harvard Graduate School of Education, Harvard Family Research Project, Cambridge, 1997. (Available from the U. S. Department of Education http://www.ed.gov/pubs/NewSkills/index.html.)

Mira, A. *A Family's Guide: Fostering your Child's Success in School Mathematics.* National Council of Teachers of Mathematics, Reston, VA, 2005.

National Council of Teachers of Mathematics Families Web page, http://nctm.org/resources/families.aspx

Parent Information Blackline Masters

- Parent Brochure (English and Spanish versions)
- Math Facts Philosophy
- Multiplication Methods in *Math Trailblazers*
- Long Division in *Math Trailblazers*
- Internet Resources for Families of *Math Trailblazers* Students

Math Trailblazers™

A Mathematical Journey Using Science and Language Arts

An Introduction for Families

A TIMS® Curriculum from the University of Illinois at Chicago

Published by Kendall/Hunt Publishing Company

How can parents talk with their children about math?

Your child will have a lot to share with you about mathematics. Here are some conversation starters to help your child communicate what he or she is doing in mathematics:

☞ What problems did you solve in math today? How did you solve the problems? Are there other ways to solve that same problem?

☞ Did you use any special materials in math today? What were they? How did you use them?

☞ Did you measure anything in school today? What did you measure?

☞ Did you collect data in math today? How did you record the data?

☞ Did you hear a math story today? Please tell me the story.

> **"One of the things I've noticed … is that when he [my child] brings home an activity and he brings a measuring tape or something kind of special, he's excited about doing it. The fact that we're involved in the games—he loves that—and he's proud of what he's doing."**
>
> **Parent**

You can contact the developers of *Math Trailblazers* at the following address:

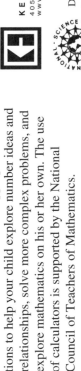

UIC The University of Illinois at Chicago

TIMS Project
Institute for Mathematics and Science Education (M/C 250)
950 South Halsted Street, Room 2075 SEL
Chicago, IL 60607-7019
www.math.uic.edu/IMSE

KENDALL/HUNT PUBLISHING COMPANY
4050 Westmark Drive Dubuque, Iowa 52002
www.mathtrailblazers.com

Development of *Math Trailblazers* was supported in part by the National Science Foundation.

What connections does *Math Trailblazers* make with other school subjects?

> **"It seems a lot of this carries over to different subject areas. It's not just isolated to math."**
>
> **Teacher**

In *Math Trailblazers*, children learn mathematics, in part, by applying it in many different contexts. This makes mathematics meaningful for students and models the way mathematics is used outside of school.

Science investigations are used often in *Math Trailblazers* to provide a context for learning and applying mathematics. Children design experiments; collect, organize, and graph data; and analyze experimental results in much the same way scientists do. Measurement of length, area, volume, mass, and time is done repeatedly within the context of scientific experiments. This strong connection with science engages students in rich problem-solving activities and introduces students to the tools and methods scientists use.

Math Trailblazers also has many connections with language arts—communication of math ideas in writing and orally is an integral part of every lesson. Children write journal entries, record data, and share ideas. They also read children's books and *Math Trailblazers* Adventure Books that connect with many class lessons. As children communicate their methods for solving problems and justify their answers, they better understand important math concepts. Their writing and other communication skills also improve.

Why is my child using calculators with *Math Trailblazers*?

The calculator is a tool used in appropriate situations to help your child explore number ideas and relationships, solve more complex problems, and explore mathematics on his or her own. The use of calculators is supported by the National Council of Teachers of Mathematics.

A curriculum for your children

The mathematics curriculum being taught in many schools today is very similar to the curriculum that was taught when the parents, grandparents, and even great-grandparents of today's school children attended school. Many of the math skills in that curriculum remain important today. But the world has changed considerably since the time of our grandparents. Advances in technology have created many other essential math skills that your children will need when they complete their formal schooling and enter tomorrow's work force. The National Council of Teachers of Mathematics recognized these needs when, in 1989 and 2000, it made a series of recommendations for updating math instruction in U.S. schools. *Math Trailblazers* was developed to reflect these national recommendations.

Math Trailblazers will prepare students to:

★ know and apply basic math skills;

★ solve problems using many different strategies;

★ be independent thinkers;

★ reason skillfully in diverse situations;

★ effectively communicate solutions to problems and methods for solving them;

★ work alone and in groups to solve problems.

Math Trailblazers was developed and tested over a seven-year period by a team from the Teaching Integrated Mathematics and Science (TIMS) Project at the University of Illinois at Chicago. Using the results of educational research and over 15 years of previous experience in curriculum development, the TIMS Project has written an innovative program that will prepare your children with math skills needed for the 21st century.

What is in the *Math Trailblazers* curriculum?

Math Trailblazers is a comprehensive curriculum that maintains a balance between the development of math concepts and basic skills. Students apply basic math skills while working on meaningful and challenging tasks. The math content of the traditional math curriculum is studied; but other topics—estimation, geometry, measurement, patterns and relationships, algebra concepts, and statistics and probability—are investigated at an appropriate level in each grade.

The curriculum includes different types of lessons:

Activities—explorations of math concepts and skills that use a variety of tools and methods.

Labs—extended investigations that use a simplified version of the method scientists use.

Daily Practice and Problems—items that provide practice in math skills and concepts.

Games—math games that build familiarity with math skills and concepts.

Adventure Books—illustrated stories that deal with math and science ideas.

Assessments—activities that allow the teacher and student to assess progress.

> "When my older daughter started out, she didn't feel confident with math. And now that she's had *Math Trailblazers*, she says that she's good at math. I feel good about that."
>
> **Parent**

What is a *Math Trailblazers* classroom like?

When you walk into a classroom when you see your child's *Math Trailblazers* class, you will probably notice that it does not look like the mathematics classroom you experienced when you were your child's age. Children might be working in groups, rolling cars down ramps, dropping water onto paper towels, or pulling jellybean samples from bags. As they work, children discuss different ways to solve problems. The room is filled with a feeling of excitement and discovery.

In a *Math Trailblazers* classroom, children are:

☆ learning mathematics by using it to solve many different kinds of problems;

☆ drawing on their own experiences and working with real-world problems;

☆ using concrete objects to understand abstract mathematical concepts;

☆ communicating mathematical ideas to their peers and teacher;

☆ gaining confidence in mathematics and developing an "I can do it" feeling.

> "I just love walking into a classroom when you see kids all over the room doing their data gathering. Some of them are on the floor measuring this or working with that or asking questions. It is so exciting to see children engaged in this kind of math discovery."
>
> **Elementary School Principal**

Math Trailblazers™*

Una Aventura en Matemáticas usando Ciencias y el Arte de Lenguaje

Una Introducción para Familias

Desarrollando por el Proyecto de TIMS—Teaching Integrated Mathematics and Science— (Integrando la Enseñanza de las Matemáticas y de las Ciencias) de la Universidad de Illinois en Chicago

Publicado por Kendall/Hunt Publishing Company

*Abriendo un camino de matemáticas

¿Qué es lo que los padres de familia pueden hacer?

Su hijo/a tendrá mucho que compartir con usted acerca de matemáticas. Aquí hay algunos temas para iniciar conversaciones que ayudarán a su hijo/a a que él o ella comunique lo que esté haciendo en matemáticas.

☞ ¿Qué problema resolviste el día de hoy en tu clase de matemáticas? ¿Cómo lo resolviste? ¿Hay alguna otra forma de resolver ese mismo problema?

☞ ¿Utilizaste algúnos materiales especiales en tu clase de matemáticas? ¿Qué eran? ¿Cómo los usaste?

☞ ¿Mediste hoy algo en la escuela? ¿Qué fue lo que mediste?

☞ ¿Acumulaste algunos datos en matemáticas? ¿Cómo registraste esos datos?

☞ ¿Escuchaste alguna historia en matemáticas? Por favor cuéntame la historia.

> "Una de las cosas que he notado… es que cuando él [mi hijo] trae una actividad a la casa y trae una cinta métrica o algo especial, está emocionado para hacerlo. El hecho que nosotros estamos enredados en los juegos—le encanta—y está orgulloso de lo que está haciendo."
>
> **Un padre de familia**

Se puede comunicar con los diseñadores de *Math Trailblazers* a la siguiente dirección:

 **UIC** The University of Illinois at Chicago

TIMS Project
Institute for Mathematics and Science Education (M/C 250)
950 South Halsted Street, Room 2075 SEL
Chicago, IL 60607-7019
www.math.uic.edu/IMSE

 KENDALL/HUNT PUBLISHING COMPANY
4050 Westmark Drive   Dubuque,   Iowa   52002
www.mathtrailblazers.com

 El desarrollo de *Math Trailblazers* fue ayudado en parte por la National Science Foundation.

¿Qué conexiones hace *Math Trailblazers* con otras materias escolares?

En *Math Trailblazers*, los estudiantes aprenden matemáticas, en parte, aplicandolo a diversas situaciones. De esta manera las matemáticas se hacen interesantes y adquieren sentido.

Investigaciones científicas en *Math Trailblazers* proveen la oportunidad frecuente de la aplicación de las matemáticas. Los estudiantes diseñan experimentos; acumulan y organizan datos; hacen gráficas de datos; y analizan los resultados de los experimentos en una manera semejante a lo que hacen los científicos. Se hacen mediciónes de longitud, area, volumen, masa, y tiempo como parte de experimentos científicos. Esta fuerte conexión con la ciencia hace que los estudiantes resuelvan problemas como "científicos," usando métodos y herramientas de la ciencias.

Math Trailblazers también tiene muchas conexiones con el arte de lenguaje. La comunicación de ideas en matemáticas—a través de escribir, hablar, y dibujar—es una parte integral de cada lección. Los estudiantes escriben en sus diarios, registran datos, y comparten ideas. Ellos también leen libros infantiles y "libros de aventuras" que se conectan con muchas lecciónes. Los estudiantes mejoran en su entendimiento de conceptos matemáticos al comunicar sus métodos de resolver problemas y explicar sus respuestas. Sus habilidades en escribir y comunicar también mejoran.

¿Por qué mi hijo/a está usando calculadoras en *Math Trailblazers*?

Las calculadoras son instrumentos usados para ayudar a su hijo/a a investigar ideas con números y sus relaciones, resolver problemas complejos, y explorar la matemática. El uso de estas herramientas es recomendado por el Concejo Nacional de Maestros de Matemáticas.

Un programa para sus hijos

Los programas de matemáticas que se encuentran hoy día en muchas escuelas son muy semejantes a las classes que tenían los padres, abuelos, y aún bisabuelos de los estudiantes de hoy. Mucha del material de esos programas todavía se necesita hoy. Pero el mundo ha cambiado desde el tiempo de nuestros abuelos. Avances en tecnología han creado la necesidad de desarrollar otras técnicas especiales que sus hijos necesitarán en el mundo de trabajo del futuro. El Concejo Nacional de Maestros de Matemáticas reconoció estas necesidades cuando hizo una serie de recomendaciones para mejorar la enseñanza de matemáticas en las escuelas de los Estados Unidos. Hemos desarrollado el programa *Math Trailblazers* para incorporar esas recomendaciones nacionales.

Math Trailblazers preparará estudiantes para:

★ aprender y usar técnicas básicas en matemáticas;

★ resolver problemas usando varias estrategias diferentes;

★ pensar independientemente;

★ razonar con habilidad en diversas situaciones;

★ comunicar efectivamente tanto las soluciones como los métodos;

★ resolver problemas trabajando solos y en grupos.

El programa *Math Trailblazers* fue desarrollado y ensayado por un equipo del Proyecto de TIMS—Teaching Integrated Mathematics and Science— (Integrando la Enseñanza de las Matemáticas y de las Ciencias) de la Universidad de Illinois en Chicago. Han creado un programa innovativo que proveerá a sus hijos con las bases matemáticas necesarios para poder competir en el campo del trabajo en el Siglo XXI.

> **"Cuando mi hija mayor comenzó, no tenía confianza con las matemáticas. Y ahora que ha tenido *Math Trailblazers*, dice que es buena en las matemáticas. Eso me hace sentir bien."**
>
> **Un padre de familia**

¿Qué hay en el programa Math Trailblazers?

El programa *Math Trailblazers* es un programa integral que mantiene un balance entre el desarrollo de los conceptos y las técnicas básicas de matemáticas. Los estudiantes usan las técnicas básicas mientras están trabajando con problemas interesantes y estimulantes. Se estudian los tópicos matemáticos de un programa tradicional; pero también se investigan otras materias—estimación, geometría, medición, patrones y relaciones, conceptos de álgebra, estadística y probabilidad—en un nivel apropriado para los niños.

El programa contiene varios tipos de lecciones:

Actividades—exploraciones de conceptos matemáticos y técnicas usando diferentes herramientas y métodos.

Laboratorios—investigaciones que usan una versión simplificada del método que los científicos usan.

Prácticas y Problemas Diarios—problemas breves que proveen práctica con técnicas y conceptos matemáticos.

Juegos—juegos matemáticos que estimulan familiaridad con técnicas y conceptos matemáticos.

Libros de Aventuras—historietas ilustradas que tratan con conceptos de las ciencias y matemáticas.

Evaluaciones—actividades que permiten al maestro y a los estudiantes evaluar el progreso.

¿Cómo es una clase de Math Trailblazers?

Si usted entra a un salón de clases *Math Trailblazers*, probablemente notará que no se parece al que usted asistía cuando tenía esa edad. En ese salón, los niños puedan estar trabajando en grupos, poniendo gotas de agua a toallas de papel, o analizando muestras de confites. Mientras los estudiantes trabajan, ellos discuten diferentes formas para resolver los problemas matemáticos. Se percieve en clases *Math Trailblazers* los sentimientos y la emoción de descubrimiento matemático.

> **"Me encanta llegar a una clase donde los estudiantes están recolectando datos. Algunos están en el piso midiendo esto o trabajando con aquello o haciendo preguntas. Es tan emocionante ver los niños enredados en este tipo de descubrimiento de matimáticas."**
>
> **Director de escuela primaria**

En un salón de estas clases los alumnos están:

☆ aprendiendo matemáticas en la resolución de problemas;

☆ usando experiencias propias y trabajando con problemas verdaderas;

☆ usando objetos concretos para entender conceptos matemáticos abstractos;

☆ comunicando sus ideas de matemáticas a sus compañeros y maestros;

☆ adquiriendo confianza en las matemáticas y desarrollando un sentimiento de, "Yo sí lo puedo hacer."

Math Facts Philosophy

The goal of the math facts strand in *Math Trailblazers* is for students to learn basic facts efficiently, gain fluency with their use, and retain that fluency over time. A large body of research supports an approach in which students develop strategies for figuring out the facts rather than relying solely on rote memorization. This not only leads to more effective learning and better retention, but also to the development of mental math skills. Therefore, the teaching of the basic facts in *Math Trailblazers* is characterized by the following elements:

Use of Strategies. Students first approach the basic facts as problems to solve rather than as facts to memorize. We encourage the use of strategies to find facts, so students become confident that they can find answers to fact problems they do not immediately recall. In this way, students learn that math is more than memorizing facts and rules that "you either get or you don't." (For information on common math fact strategies, see the *Math Facts* Tutor on the *Just for Math Trailblazers Families* page of the Kendall Hunt website http://kendallhunt.com. Click on "K–12," then "Just For Families," then "Math Trailblazers Families." Then scroll down to the list of TIMS Tutors.)

Distributed Facts Practice. Students study small groups of facts they found using similar strategies. They review the facts as they use them to solve problems in labs, activities, and games. In Grades 2–5, students are given flash cards to study each group of facts at home.

Appropriate Assessment. Teachers assess students' knowledge of the facts through observations as they work on activities, labs, and games as well as through the appropriate use of written tests and quizzes. Quizzes follow the study of small groups of facts organized around specific strategies. In Grades 2–5, students take inventory tests of facts at the end of each semester. In grades 3–5, each student records his or her progress on *Facts I Know* charts and determines which facts he or she needs to study.

A Multiyear Approach. In Grades 1 and 2, the curriculum emphasizes strategies that enable students to develop fluency with the addition and subtraction facts. In Grade 3, students gain fluency with the multiplication facts while reviewing the addition and subtraction facts. In Grade 4, the addition and subtraction facts are checked, the multiplication facts are reviewed, and students develop fluency with the division facts. In Grade 5, the multiplication and division facts are systematically reviewed and assessed.

Facts Will Not Act as Gatekeepers. Use of strategies and calculators allows students to continue to work on interesting problems and experiments while learning the facts. Thus students are not prevented from learning more complex mathematics because they do not have quick recall of the facts.

Multiplication Methods in *Math Trailblazers*

As your child learns paper-and-pencil multiplication in *Math Trailblazers,* he or she is introduced to more than one method. The **all-partials method** is introduced first since many children find it easier to learn. Then the more efficient **compact method**—the method traditionally taught in schools in the United States—is introduced. After children work with both methods, they choose which is most comfortable for them. We present both methods below so you will be familiar with them.

Both methods are based on the same idea, but the recording is different. In the all-partials method, every step is written down. In the compact method, some steps are not recorded.

Example 1. Compute 6×73.

In both methods, we break 73 into two parts: $73 = 3 + 70$. Then we multiply each part by 6 and add:

$$6 \times 73 = 6 \times 3 + 6 \times 70.$$

All-Partials Method	Compact Method
In this method, every step is written down on separate lines.	In this method, some steps are combined and the answer is recorded on one line.
$$\begin{array}{r} 73 \\ \times\ 6 \\ \hline 18 \\ 420 \\ \hline 438 \end{array}$$ (This is 6×3) (This is 6×70)	$$\begin{array}{r} {\scriptstyle 1} \\ 73 \\ \times\ 6 \\ \hline 438 \end{array}$$ (This is $6 \times 3 + 6 \times 70$)
The partial products are recorded in the lines under the multiplication sign, then the lines are added.	The partial products are added as they are recorded: First compute $6 \times 3 = 18$; then write the 8 in the ones' column and carry the 1 into the tens' column (some people write down the carry, others just remember it). Next, compute 6×7 tens $= 42$ tens. Add the 1 that was carried to get 43 tens. Write the 3 in the tens' column and the 4 in the hundreds' column.

Multiplication Methods in *Math Trailblazers (continued)*

Example 2: Compute 73×46.

Again, both methods involve breaking the numbers into two parts and multiplying. Since $46 = 6 + 40$, the product is

$$73 \times 46 = 73 \times (6 + 40)$$
$$= 73 \times 6 + 73 \times 40$$
$$= (6 \times 3 + 6 \times 70) + (40 \times 3 + 40 \times 70)$$

All-Partials Method	Compact Method
In this method, every step is written down on separate lines.	In this method, some steps are combined and recorded on one line.

All-Partials Method

In this method, every step is written down on separate lines.

```
    73
  × 46
    18   (6 × 3)
   420   (6 × 70)
   120   (40 × 3)
  2800   (40 × 70)
  3358
```

The partial products are recorded in the rows under the multiplication sign, then the rows are added.

Compact Method

In this method, some steps are combined and recorded on one line.

```
    73
  × 46
   438   (This is 6 × 73)
  2920   (This is 40 × 73 or 4 tens × 73)
  3358
```

For the first line, compute $6 \times 73 = 438$ as in Example 1.

For the second line, compute $40 \times 73 = 2920$. (Some people omit the 0 in the ones' column because 2920 is 292 tens and no ones. In this case, be sure nothing is written in the ones' column.)

Here are the details for the second line:

$40 \times 73 = 40 \times 3 + 40 \times 70$. First compute $40 \times 3 = 120$; record the 20 tens by writing 2 in the tens' column and 0 in the ones' column, then carry the 1 into the hundreds' column (you can write the carry or just remember it). Next, compute $40 \times 70 = 2800$. That is 28 hundreds. Add the one 1 hundred that was carried to get 29 hundreds. Write the 9 in the hundreds' column and the 2 in the thousands' column.

Finally, add both lines.

Long Division in *Math Trailblazers*

In *Math Trailblazers,* your child will learn a long division method that may be different from the method you learned. We teach the **forgiving method** because many students find it easier to learn than the traditional method. Both methods make estimates about the quotient (the answer to the division problem), but the forgiving method allows underestimates, so it doesn't involve as much erasing and recalculating as the traditional method sometimes does.

As an example, let's divide 95 by 3. Think of dividing 95 objects such as marbles into groups of 3. How many groups will there be? (Or, think of putting the objects into 3 groups. How many will be in each group?)

First, estimate the answer. A good estimate would be 30, but lower numbers would work too. Suppose we choose 20. Then, since $3 \times 20 = 60$, we have taken care of 60 marbles. Subtract 60 from 95 and record the estimate to the right of the problem.

$$
\begin{array}{r}
3\overline{)95} \\
-60 \quad\quad 20 \\
\hline
35
\end{array}
$$

Now divide the remaining 35 marbles by 3. Let's estimate that $35 \div 3$ is about 10. Since $3 \times 10 = 30$, write

$$
\begin{array}{r}
3\overline{)95} \\
-60 \quad\quad 20 \\
\hline
35 \\
-30 \quad\quad 10 \\
\hline
5
\end{array}
$$

Since 3 "goes into" 5 one time, write

$$
\begin{array}{r}
3\overline{)95} \\
-60 \quad\quad 20 \\
\hline
35 \\
-30 \quad\quad 10 \\
\hline
5 \\
-3 \quad\quad\; 1 \\
\hline
2
\end{array}
$$

Since 3 does not divide 2, there are 2 marbles left over. This is the remainder. Add up the number of 3s we took away: $20 + 10 + 1 = 31$. Thus, 95 divided by 3 is 31 with remainder 2. We write this on top of the problem, as in the traditional division method.

$$
\begin{array}{r}
31\text{R}2 \\
3\overline{)95} \\
-60 \quad\quad 20 \\
\hline
35 \\
-30 \quad\quad 10 \\
\hline
5 \\
-3 \quad\quad\; 1 \\
\hline
2 \quad\quad\; 31
\end{array}
$$

As students become familiar with the forgiving method, they make better estimates to keep the number of steps at a minimum. Below is another way to do this problem using the forgiving method. Note that this time, making the highest possible estimates (without overestimating) results in the same number of steps as the traditional method. If the highest estimate is made each time, the two methods are essentially the same.

$$
\begin{array}{r}
31\text{R}2 \\
3\overline{)95} \\
-90 \quad\quad 30 \\
\hline
5 \\
-3 \quad\quad\; 1 \\
\hline
2 \quad\quad\; 31
\end{array}
$$

The forgiving method allows students to underestimate as they develop their estimation skills. But, although this method forgives underestimates, overestimates are not forgiven. When students overestimate, they have to erase, just as with the traditional method.

This method can be extended to solve problems with multidigit divisors. However, *Math Trailblazers* students usually use calculators for such problems.

Internet Resources for Families of *Math Trailblazers* Students

Here are several websites that can help families support their children's learning of Mathematics:

Mymathtrailblazers.com Family section

The publisher of *Math Trailblazers,* Kendall/Hunt, maintains a website at http://www.mymathtrailblazers.com to help the families of children using *Math Trailblazers* understand the curriculum. It contains an introduction to the program and a discussion of its research basis, answers to frequently asked questions, glossaries, TIMS Tutors (which provide an in-depth exploration of the mathematical concepts and ideas behind *Math Trailblazers*), homework help, and recommended software and literature lists. Contact Kendall/Hunt regarding granting families access to this site.

NCTM Families Web page

http://nctm.org/resources/families.aspx

The National Council of Teachers of Mathematics (NCTM) Families Web page includes lessons and activities, resources, links to other family sites, as well as brochures that answer questions such as

> Why does my child's math look different from the math I remember?
>
> What can I do to make sure my child succeeds in math?
>
> Math homework is due tomorrow—how can I help?

NCTM Illuminations

http://illuminations.nctm.org

This site contains a library of online math activities and interactive tools for students to use to explore, learn, and apply mathematics in the classroom and at home. It also has links to hundreds of online resources that an editorial panel has reviewed and rated as exemplary.

The Math Forum

http://mathforum.org

The Math Forum is a very broad-based website maintained by Drexel University. It has such features as Ask Dr. Math, where students can ask mathematical questions, and an extensive mathematics resource library for students in elementary school through graduate school. Other features include discussion groups, a collection of good problems, teacher resources, and information on issues in mathematics education.

National Library of Virtual Manipulatives for Interactive Mathematics

http://nlvm.usu.edu

Utah State University developed and maintains this web site. It includes an extensive collection of virtual manipulatives and accompanying activities. Students can work interactively with geoboards, pattern blocks, tangrams, base-ten pieces, balance scales, and other materials. This provides the opportunity to work with materials that are perhaps not otherwise available.

Helping Your Child Learn Mathematics http://www.ed.gov/parents/academic/help/math/index.html

This is a downloadable booklet available at the website of the Department of Education that contains "fun activities that parents can use with their children from preschool age through grade 5 to strengthen their math skills and build strong positive attitudes toward math."

Figure This!

http://www.figurethis.org

The Family Corner of the Figure This! website provides math challenges for families. It has downloadable brochures on topics such as Families and School, Families and Math, Families and Homework, and Math and Literature, as well as recommended books. The focus is on families of middle-school students, but much of the advice is appropriate for families of elementary-school students as well.

Copyright © Kendall/Hunt Publishing Company

TIG • Grade 3 • Working with Math Trailblazers Parents and Families • Parent Information Blackline Masters **461**

SECTION 14

Manipulatives List

The Manipulatives List outlines all manufactured manipulatives and other materials needed to implement *Math Trailblazers* successfully.

Students explore shapes using geoboards.

Manipulatives List

TIG • Grade 3 • Manipulatives List 463

Manipulatives List

Following are the manipulatives for Grade Three. There are several categories of manipulatives listed here:

Manufactured Manipulatives: a list of each of the manipulatives needed to implement fully the *Math Trailblazers* curriculum. Many of these manipulatives may be available already in your classroom or school.

Manipulatives which you need can be purchased:

- in grade level complete kits from Kendall/Hunt Publishing Company;
- as a customized kit from Kendall/Hunt;
- or individually for your specific needs.

Please contact Kendall/Hunt directly for additional information.

Other materials are needed for the successful implementation of the *Math Trailblazers* curriculum for the entire year. These materials are listed in three categories to aid in planning for the year:

- **Consumables** (one-use items such as beans, paper towels, etc.)
- **Collectibles** (throwaway items such as magazines, egg cartons, jars, etc.)
- **School Supplies** (items usually available in classrooms such as tape, glue, markers, etc.)

Manipulatives for *Math Trailblazers* Grade 3

Manufactured Manipulative	Number per Group	TOTAL per Classroom of 30 Students

base-ten pieces, set consists of:
    2 packs (10 cm × 10 cm × 10 cm),
    14 flats (10 cm × 10 cm × 1 cm),
    30 skinnies (10 cm × 1 cm × 1 cm),
    50 bits (1 cm × 1 cm × 1 cm)
	1 set per student	30 sets

*calculator	1 per student	30
cm connecting cubes	60 per group of 3	600
connecting cubes	50 per student	1500
eyedropper, plastic	1 per group of 3	10 + 5 extra
geoboard	1 per student	30
graduated cylinder, 100 cc	1 per classroom	1
graduated cylinder, 250 cc	1 per group of 3	10

gram masses
 	
  10   5-gram masses
   5 10-gram masses
   2 20-gram masses
  10   1-gram masses
	1 set per group of 3	10 sets

meterstick	10 per classroom	10
Mr. Origin	1 per group of 3	10
overhead base-ten pieces	1 per classroom	1 set
overhead coins	1 set per classroom	1 set

*Students need a calculator with addition, subtraction, multiplication, and division with a constant operation function.

Manipulatives for *Math Trailblazers* Grade 3 (*Continued*)

Manufactured Manipulative	Number per Group	TOTAL per Classroom of 30 Students
overhead geoboard	1 per classroom	1
overhead pattern blocks	2 sets per classroom	2
pattern blocks	3 sets per classroom	3 sets
rubber bands	5–8 per student	1 pack of 300
ruler, cm/inch, transparent	1 per student	30
spinner	1 per student pair	15
square-inch tiles, colored	25 per student	2 sets of 400
standard masses (See gram masses.)		
tangram set (need to make 4-inch square)	2 sets per group of 3	20 sets
two-pan balance	1 per group of 3	10
*wall chart, laminated: data tables & graph	1 set per classroom	1 set

Additional Materials or Equipment Needed for *Math Trailblazers* Grade 3

Collectible Materials	Number Required
cereal boxes, empty	1 per student pair
container or bucket, large	1 per student group
containers, empty: cup	1 per class
pint	1 per class
quart	1 per class
gallon	1 per class
containers, medium	1 per group of 3
containers, small (margarine tubs)	1 per student pair
dish pans, plastic	1 per group of 3
playing cards	1 deck per student pair
play money	1 set per student pair
teaspoons	1 per student pair
tissue boxes, empty	1 per student pair

Consumable Materials	Number Required
beans: red,	1 lb per class
navy	2 lbs per class
pinto	4 lbs per class
paper towels	3 or 4 different brands, 1 roll of each

*The wall chart is available through Kendall/Hunt Publishing Company 1-800-228-0810.

Additional Materials or Equipment Needed
for *Math Trailblazers* Grade 3 (*Continued*)

School Supplies	Number Required
analog clock with second hand	1 per classroom
brass fasteners (brad)	2 per student
classroom calendar, large	1 per classroom
clay	1 small piece per two-pan balance
easel paper	1 pad per class
envelopes	15 per student
index cards, 3- by 5-inch	10 per student

The following supplies are used throughout the year:

crayons

glue

markers

paper clips

pencil erasers, flat

rubber bands

scissors

self-adhesive notes, 2- by 1.5-inch

tape

Literature List

The Literature List provides suggested titles and recommended reading of commercially available trade books, which are used in many *Math Trailblazers* lessons.

Students connect math and literature by reading a trade book.

Literature List

Many lesson guides in *Math Trailblazers* suggest the use of commercially available trade books. A listing of these trade books is provided here. These books can be used to extend or enhance a particular lesson.

Unit 1—Sampling and Classifying
Suggested Titles

- Aber, Linda Williams. *Who's Got Spots?* The Kane Press, New York, 2000.
- Jenkins, Emily. *Five Creatures.* Douglas & McIntyre Publishing Group, Canada, 2001.
- Mosel, Arlene. *Tikki Tikki Tembo.* Henry Holt & Company, New York, 1989.
- Tang, Greg. *The Grapes of Math: Mind Stretching Math Riddles.* Scholastic Press, Inc., New York, 2003.

Unit 2—Strategies: An Assessment Unit
Suggested Titles

- Murphy, Frank. *Ben Franklin and the Magic Squares.* Random House, Inc., New York, 2000.
- Newschwander, Cindy. *Sir Cumference and the Isles of Immeter.* Charlesbridge Publishing, Watertown, MA, 2006.
- "The Straw, the Coal, and the Bean" from *The Complete Grimm's Fairy Tales.* Random House, Inc., New York, 1992. (Lesson 3)

Unit 3—Exploring Multiplication
Suggested Titles

- Aker, Suzanne. *What Comes in 2s, 3s, and 4s?* Simon and Schuster, New York, 1992.
- Brenner, Martha. *Stacks of Trouble.* The Kane Press, New York, 2000.
- Calvert, Pam. *Multiplying Menace: The Revenge of Rumplestiltskin (A Math Adventure)* Charlesbridge Publishing, Watertown, MA, 2006.
- Clemson, Wendy and David. *Math Magic: Multiplying and Dividing.* Two-Can Publishing, Princeton, NJ, 2002.
- Giganti, Paul Jr. *Each Orange Had Eight Slices: A Counting Book.* Mulberry Books, New York, 1999.
- Long, Lynette. *Marvelous Multiplication: Games and Activities That Make Math Easy and Fun.* John Wiley & Sons, Inc., New York, 2000.
- Slobodkina, Esphyr. *Caps for Sale: A Tale of a Peddler, Some Monkeys and Their Monkey Business.* HarperTrophy, New York, 1997. (Lesson 4)
- Thompson, Lauren. *One Riddle, One Answer.* Scholastic Press, New York, 2001.

Unit 4—Place Value Concepts
Suggested Titles

- Hutchins, Pat. *Clocks and More Clocks.* Aladdin Library. Hong Kong, 1994.
- Murphy, Stuart J. *Earth Day—Hooray.* HarperCollins Publishers, New York, 2004.
- Owen, Claire. *Magic Squares and More.* ETA/Cuisenaire, Vernon Hills, IL, 2005.

- Pinczes, Elinor. *One Hundred Hungry Ants.* Houghton Mifflin Company, Boston, MA, 1993.
- Tang, Greg. *Math Appeal.* Scholastic Press, New York, 2003.
- Wells, Robert E. *How Do You Know What Time It Is?* Albert Whitman and Company, Morton Grove, IL, 2002.

Unit 5—Area of Different Shapes

Suggested Titles

- Gabriel, Nat. *Sam's Sneaker Squares.* The Kane Press, New York, 2002.
- Murphy, Stuart J. *Room for Ripley.* HarperCollins Publishing, New York, 1999.

Unit 6—More Adding and Subtracting

Essential Titles

- Seuss, Dr. *The 500 Hats of Bartholomew Cubbins.* Random House, New York, 1989. (Lesson 1)

Suggested Titles

- Agee, Jon. *Go Hang a Salami! I'm a Lasagna Hog!* Douglas & McIntyre Ltd., Canada, 1991.
- Bergerson, Howard W. *Palindromes and Anagrams.* Dover Publications, New York, 1973. (Lesson 7)
- Cleary, Beverly. *Henry Huggins* (50th Anniversary Edition). HarperTrophy, New York, 2000. (Lesson 1)
- Hulme, Joy N. *Wild Fibonacci.* Tricycle Press, Berkeley, CA, 2005.
- LoPresti Sparagna, Angelina. *A Place for Zero.* Charlesbridge Publishing, Watertown, MA, 2003.
- McKissack, Patricia C. *A Million Fish . . . More or Less.* Alfred A. Knopf, New York, 1996. (Lesson 1)
- Murphy, Stuart J. *The Shark Swimathon.* HarperCollins Publishing, New York, 2001.
- Schwartz, David M. *If You Made a Million.* HarperCollins Publishing, New York, 1989.
- Tang, Greg. *Math Appeal.* Scholastic Press, New York, 2003.
- Terban, Marvin. *Too Hot to Hoot.* Clarion Books, New York, 1985. (Lesson 7)

Unit 7—Exploring Multiplication and Division

Suggested Titles

- Billin-Frye, Paige. *Everybody Wins!* The Kane Press, New York, 2001.
- Burns, Marilyn. *Spaghetti and Meatballs for All!* Scholastic Press, New York, 1997.
- Murphy, Stuart J. *Divide and Ride.* HarperCollins Publishers, New York, 1997.
- Pinczes, Elinor. *A Remainder of One.* Houghton Mifflin Company, Boston, MA, 1995.
- Schwartz, David. *If You Hopped Like a Frog.* Scholastic Press, New York, 1999.
- Silverstein, Shel. "Smart" from *Where the Sidewalk Ends,* p. 35. HarperCollins Children's Books, New York, 1974. (Lesson 5)
- Stamper, Judith Bauer. *Breakfast at Danny's Diner.* Grosset and Dunlap, New York, 2003.

Unit 8—Mapping and Coordinates
Suggested Titles

- Glass, Dr. Julie. *Fly on the Ceiling.* Random House Books for Young Readers, New York, 1998.
- Hartman, Gail. *As the Crow Flies: A First Book of Maps.* Simon & Schuster, Hong Kong, 1993.
- Leedy, Loreen. *Mapping Penny's World.* Henry Holt and Company, LLC, New York, 2000.
- Penner, Lucille Recht. *X Marks the Spot.* The Kane Press, New York, 2002.

Unit 9—Using Patterns to Predict
Suggested Titles

- Adler, David. *How Tall, How Short, How Far Away.* Holiday House, New York, 2000.
- Schwartz, David M. *Millions to Measure.* Harper Trophy, New York, 2006.

Unit 10—Numbers and Patterns: An Assessment Unit
Suggested Titles

- Bartok, Mira. *West Africa: Nigeria.* Good Year Books, Parsipanny, NJ, 1994.
- *West Africa: Ghana, Ancient Japan, and Ancient Mexico* from the Ancient and Living Cultures series. Good Year Books, Scott Foresman, Glenview, IL, 1993. (Lesson 1)
- Xiong, Blia. *Nine-In-One, Grr! Grr!* Children's Book Press, San Francisco, CA, 1993. (Lesson 1)

Unit 11—Multiplication Patterns
Suggested Titles

- Calvert, Pam. *Multiplying Menace: The Revenge of Rumpelstiltskin (A Math Adventure).* Charlesbridge Publishing, Watertown, MA, 2006.
- Carroll, Lewis. *Alice's Adventures in Wonderland.* Illustrated by Helen Oxenbury. 1st Candlewick Press Edition. Candlewick Press, Cambridge, MA, 1999. (Lesson 6)
- Hulme, Joy N. *Sea Squares.* Hyperion Books for Children, New York, 1993. (Lesson 3)
- Mills, Claudia. *7 X 9 = Trouble!* Farrar Straus Giroux, New York, 2004.
- Neuschwander, Cindy. *Amanda Beans Amazing Dream.* Scholastic Press, Inc., New York, 1998.
- Tang, Greg. *The Best of Times: Math Strategies That Multiply.* Scholastic Press, Inc., New York, 2002.

Unit 12—Dissections
Suggested Titles

- Burns, Marilyn. *The Greedy Triangle.* Scholastic Press, Inc., New York, 1995.
- Maccarone, Grace. *Three Pigs, One Wolf, & Seven Magic Shapes.* Scholastic Press, Inc., New York, 1998.
- Pilegard, Virginia Walton. *The Warlord's Puzzle.* Pelican Publishing Company, Gretna, LA, 2000.
- Tompert, Ann. *Grandfather Tang's Story.* Crown Publishers, Inc., New York, 1990. (Lesson 1)

Unit 13—Parts and Wholes

Suggested Titles

- Adler, David. *Fraction Fun.* Holiday House, New York, 1997.
- Mathews, Louise. *Gator Pie.* Sundance Publishing, Littleton, MA, 1995. (Lesson 3)
- Pallotta, Jerry. *Apple Fractions.* Scholastic, Inc., New York, 2002.
- Stamper, Judith Bauer. *Go, Fractions.* Penguin Putnam Books for Young Readers, New York, 2003.

Unit 14—Collecting and Using Data

Suggested Titles

- Hutchins, Pat. *Clocks and More Clocks.* Aladdin Paperbacks, Hong Kong, 1994. (Lesson 1)
- Murphy, Stuart J. *Get Up and Go!* HarperCollins Publishers, New York, 1996.
- Nagda, Ann Whitehead and Cindy Bickel. *Tiger Math: Learning to Graph From a Baby Tiger.* Henry Holt and Company, New York, 2000.

Unit 15—Decimal Investigations

Suggested Titles

- Adler, David. *How Tall, How Short, How Far Away.* Holiday House, New York, 2000.
- Clement, Rod. *Counting on Frank.* Gareth Stevens Children's Books, Milwaukee, WI, 1991. (Lesson 4)
- Mathews, Louise. *Gator Pie.* Sundance Publishing, Littleton, MA, 1995.
- Schwartz, David M. *Millions to Measure.* Harper Trophy, New York, 2006.

Unit 16—Volume

Suggested Titles

- Adler, David. *How Tall, How Short, How Far Away.* Holiday House, New York, 2000.
- Brown, Stephanie Gwyn. *Aesop's The Crow and the Pitcher.* Tricycle Press, Berkeley, CA, 2003.
- Schwartz, David M. *Millions to Measure.* Harper Trophy, New York, 2006.

Unit 17—Wholes and Parts

Suggested Titles

The Adventure Book in this unit, *The Clever Tailor,* is based on "The Valiant Little Tailor," a fairy tale by the Brothers Grimm. Two collections that include this story are:

- *The Complete Grimm's Fairy Tales.* Pantheon Books, New York, 1980.
- Lang, Andrew. *Blue Fairy Book.* Dover Publications, New York, 1975.
- Silverstein, Shel. "Smart" from *Where the Sidewalk Ends.* HarperCollins, New York, 1994. (Lesson 3)

Unit 18—Viewing and Drawing 3-D

Suggested Titles

- Adkins, Jan. *How a House Happens.* Walker and Company, Inc., New York, 1972. (Lesson 4)

Unit 19—Multiplication and Division Problems

None

Unit 20—Connections: An Assessment Unit

None

Games List

The Games List includes descriptions of games used in *Math Trailblazers.*

A student uses counting strategies while playing a math game.

Games List

Games are often used in *Math Trailblazers* to engage students in practicing basic arithmetic and other math concepts. A complete listing of the games for your grade and a description of the games are provided below.

Once introduced, these games can be used throughout the year for ongoing practice. We suggest that after the games have been introduced and played in class, they be placed in a math center somewhere in the classroom so that students can replay the games during indoor recess, when they have completed other assignments, and at other times during the day.

Unit 1—Sampling and Classifying
Turn Over in *Unit Resource Guide* Unit 1 Lesson 2 Pages 40–47 and *Student Guide* Page 7

Students place digit cards 0–9 face up on a table. They select a target number, turn over cards, and keep a running sum. The goal is to make a sum equal to the target number. The student who makes a sum equal to or greater than the target number first wins.

Unit 2—Strategies: An Assessment Unit
Nine, Ten in *Unit Resource Guide* Unit 2 Lesson 5 Pages 73–80, *Student Guide* Pages 24–27, and *Discovery Assignment Book* Page 35

Students spin two spinners and write a subtraction sentence based on the numbers spun. One spinner tells the players to subtract nine or ten. If players write a sentence correctly, they record it on a data table. The first player to fill his or her data table is the winner.

Unit 3—Exploring Multiplication
None

Unit 4—Place Value Concepts
None

Unit 5—Area of Different Shapes
None

Unit 6— More Adding and Subtracting
Digits Game in *Unit Resource Guide* Unit 6 Lesson 8 Pages 109–116 and *Discovery Assignment Book* Page 109

Cards are drawn one at a time from a deck of digit cards 0–9. Students attempt to make both largest or smallest answers to multidigit addition or subtraction problems accordingly. The player with the smallest or largest answer as specified wins.

Unit 7—Exploring Multiplication and Division
None

Unit 8—Mapping and Coordinates

Find the Panda in *Unit Resource Guide* Unit 8 Lesson 2 Pages 33–43 and *Student Guide* Pages 101–102

Players try to locate a panda on a grid by guessing coordinates and using clues.

Tens Game in *Unit Resource Guide* Unit 8 Lesson 5 Pages 76–84 and *Student Guide* Pages 109–110

Students make sums of ten with digit cards using cards in their hands, those played by players, or cards drawn from the pile. The player with the most cards at the end of the game wins.

Unit 9—Using Patterns to Predict

None

Unit 10—Numbers and Patterns: An Assessment Unit

Problem Game in *Unit Resource Guide* Unit 10 Lesson 2 Pages 45–63, *Student Guide* Page 135, and *Discovery Assignment Book* Pages 151–153

Students draw a card and solve a subtraction problem. If a player answers the problem correctly, he or she spins a spinner and advances his or her token on a game board. The first player to reach the finish is the winner.

Unit 11—Multiplication Patterns

Floor Tiler in *Unit Resource Guide* Unit 11 Lesson 5 Pages 70–75 and *Discovery Assignment Book* Pages 171–173

After spinning two numbers, players use the products of the two numbers to color in grid squares in the shape of a rectangle on their grid paper. Players take turns spinning and filling in their grids.

Unit 12—Dissections

Hex in *Unit Resource Guide* Unit 12 Lesson 5 Pages 84–89 and *Discovery Assignment Book* Page 191

Players place markers in adjacent hexagons and move their markers across the game board to connect X's and O's on opposite sides.

Unit 13—Parts and Wholes

FractionLand in *Unit Resource Guide* Unit 13 Lesson 4 Pages 52–60, *Student Guide* Page 188, and *Discovery Assignment Book* Pages 201–205

A player picks a fraction card and a whole number card. The player then finds the number that is that fraction of the whole number and moves that many spaces on the game board. The first player to reach the finish space wins.

Fraction Problem Game in *Unit Resource Guide* Unit 13 Lesson 4 Pages 52–60, *Student Guide* Page 189, and *Discovery Assignment Book* Pages 207–213

Players pull cards from a deck and say a sentence comparing the fractions pulled. If they say a correct sentence, they spin the spinner and move that many spaces. If they say an incorrect sentence, their turn ends. The first player to reach the finish rectangle wins.

Unit 14—Collecting and Using Data

Time and Time Again in *Unit Resource Guide* Unit 14 Lesson 2 Pages 34–40, *Student Guide* Page 201, and *Discovery Assignment Book* Pages 221–227

Players turn over time cards to match times shown in analog and digital formats. The player with the most cards at the end of the game wins.

Unit 15—Decimal Investigations

Tenths, Tenths, Tenths in *Unit Resource Guide* Unit 15 Lesson 1 Pages 21–37 and *Student Guide* Pages 220–221

A player shows a number with skinnies and flats. An opposing player writes the common and decimal fraction for the number and says it aloud. If the opposing player is correct, he or she gets one point. The player with the most points at the end wins.

Decimal Hex in *Unit Resource Guide* Unit 15 Lesson 3 Pages 51–56 and *Discovery Assignment Book* Pages 241–242

Players place game markers on a game board and spin to see if they can move to adjacent game spaces with decimals greater than, less than, or equivalent to their current game space. The winner of the game is the player who has moved his or her game piece across the board to a position opposite to the starting position.

Nothing to It! in *Unit Resource Guide* Unit 15 Lesson 5 Pages 71–78 and *Student Guide* Page 233

Students draw four number cards and use those cards to create an addition or subtraction number sentence that has the smallest possible result. Sentences cannot have results less than zero. The player whose number sentence has the smallest result wins.

Unit 16—Volume
None

Unit 17—Wholes and Parts

Fraction Hex in *Unit Resource Guide* Unit 17 Lesson 4 Pages 62–67 and *Discovery Assignment Book* Pages 255–257

Players place game markers on a game board and spin to see if they can move to adjacent game spaces with fractions greater than, less than, or equivalent to their current game space. The winner of the game is the player who has moved his or her game piece across the board to a position opposite to the starting position.

Unit 18—Viewing and Drawing 3-D
None

Unit 19—Multiplication and Division Problems
None

Unit 20—Connections: An Assessment Unit
None

Software List

The Software List outlines recommended computer software used to enhance *Math Trailblazers* lessons.

Students use software to practice math facts and solve problems.

Software List

Software Titles by Topic

*Data Collection/Reading and Interpreting
Graphs/Probability*
Graph Master
Graphers
Ice Cream Truck
Math Concepts One . . . Two . . . Three!
Tabletop Jr.

Fractions/Decimals/Percents
Fraction Attraction
Math Arena
Math Munchers Deluxe
Tenth Planet: Representing Fractions

Geometry
Building Perspective Deluxe
The Factory Deluxe
Make a Map 3D
Math Arena
Math Concepts One . . . Two . . . Three!
MicroWorlds Ex
Mighty Math Calculating Crew
Shape Up!

Logical Thinking/Problem Solving/Patterns
Building Perspective Deluxe
Carmen Sandiego's Math Detective
The Factory Deluxe
Ice Cream Truck
Math Arena
Math Concepts One . . . Two . . . Three!
Tabletop Jr.
Ten Tricky Tiles
Thinkin' Things Collection I: Toony the Loon's
    Lagoon
Zoombinis Logical Journey

Measurement
The Factory Deluxe
Math Concepts One . . . Two . . . Three!
Shape Up!

Number Theory (Factors and Primes)
Math Munchers Deluxe
Mighty Math Calculating Crew

Practice with Basic Operations
Carmen Sandiego's Math Detective
Math Arena
Math Concepts One . . . Two . . . Three!
Math Munchers Deluxe
Mighty Math Calculating Crew
Number Facts Fire Zapper
Numbers Recovered
Ten Tricky Tiles

Programs for Illustrating
Kid Pix

Time and Money
Discover Time
Ice Cream Truck
Math Arena
Math Concepts One . . . Two . . . Three!
Money Challenge
Penny Pot

Understanding of Basic Operations
Fraction Attraction
Math Concepts One . . . Two . . . Three!
Mighty Math Calculating Crew
Numbers Recovered
Ten Tricky Tiles
Tenth Network: Grouping and Place Value

Websites
The Math Forum: www.mathforum.org
National Library of Virtual Manipulatives for
    Interactive Mathematics: www.matti.usu.edu
One resource for additional mathematics links and
    sites: http://illuminations.nctm.org/swr/index.asp

Recommended Software for
Third-Grade Units

Unit 1—Sampling and Classifying

Discover Time provides practice telling time to the nearest hour, half hour, quarter hour, and in five-minute intervals.

Graph Master allows students to organize data and create graphs.

Graphers is a graphing tool appropriate for young students.

Kid Pix allows students to create their own illustrations.

Math Concepts One . . . Two . . . Three! provides practice estimating and measuring time, money, length, and mass.

Number Facts Fire Zapper provides practice with number facts in an arcade-like game.

Numbers Recovered provides practice with bar graphs.

Tabletop Jr. provides work with data and develops logical thinking.

Thinkin' Things Collection 1: Toony the Loon's Lagoon develops attribute discrimination, spatial sense, and logical thinking.

Zoombinis Logical Journey develops thinking skills as students find patterns to solve puzzles.

Unit 2—Strategies: An Assessment Unit

Graphers is a data graphing tool appropriate for young students.

Ice Cream Truck develops problem solving, money skills, and arithmetic operations.

Math Concepts One . . . Two . . . Three! provides exploration and practice with the four operations including work with magic squares.

Mighty Math Calculating Crew poses short-answer questions about number operations, 3-dimensional shapes, and money skills.

Money Challenge provides practice with money.

Number Facts Fire Zapper provides practice with number facts in an arcade-like game.

Numbers Recovered provides practice with bar graphs.

Penny Pot provides practice with counting coins.

Unit 3—Exploring Multiplication

Kid Pix allows students to create their own illustrations of objects in groups. (Lesson 3)

Math Concepts One . . . Two . . . Three! provides exploration and practice with the four operations including work with magic squares.

Math Munchers Deluxe includes practice with basic facts and factors and multiples in an arcade-like game.

Mighty Math Calculating Crew poses short-answer questions about number operations and money skills.

National Library of Virtual Manipulatives website (http://matti.usu.edu) allows students to work with manipulatives including geoboards, base-ten pieces, the abacus, and many others.

Number Facts Fire Zapper provides practice with math facts.

Tenth Network: Grouping and Place Value provides opportunities for students to group objects by 2s, 5s, and 10s.

Unit 4—Place Value Concepts

Math Concepts One . . . Two . . . Three! develops number sense through practice with estimation, rounding, ordering, comparing, and writing numbers.

Mighty Math Calculating Crew poses short-answer questions about number operations and money skills.

Money Challenge provides practice with money.

National Library of Virtual Manipulatives website (http://matti.usu.edu) allows students to work with manipulatives including base-ten pieces, the abacus, and many others.

Numbers Recovered provides practice working with place value.

Penny Pot provides practice with counting coins.

Ten Tricky Tiles provides practice with number facts through engaging puzzles.

Tenth Network: Grouping and Place Value provides practice grouping objects by 2s, 5s, and 10s.

Unit 5—Area of Different Shapes

The Factory Deluxe promotes spatial reasoning and practices finding area.

Graphers is a data graphing tool appropriate for young students.

Kid Pix allows students to create their own illustrations.

National Library of Virtual Manipulatives website (http://matti.usu.edu) allows students to work with manipulatives including geoboards, base-ten pieces, the abacus, and many others.

Unit 6—More Adding and Subtracting

Carmen Sandiego's Math Detective provides practice with math facts, estimation, ordering numbers, and word problems.

Discover Time provides practice in telling time to the nearest hour, half-hour, quarter-hour, and five-minute intervals.

Math Arena is a collection of math activities that reinforces many math concepts.

Math Concepts One . . . Two . . . Three! provides practice estimating, rounding, ordering, comparing, and writing numbers.

Math Munchers Deluxe provides practice in basic facts in an arcade-like game.

Mighty Math Calculating Crew poses short-answer questions about number operations, three-dimensional shapes, and money skills.

Money Challenge provides practice with money.

National Library of Virtual Manipulatives website (http://matti.usu.edu) allows students to work with manipulatives including base-ten pieces, the abacus, and many others.

Numbers Recovered provides practice comparing numeric expressions and working with place value.

Penny Pot provides practice with counting coins.

Ten Tricky Tiles provides practice with number facts through engaging puzzles.

Tenth Network: Grouping and Place Value provides opportunities for students to group objects by twos, fives, and tens.

Unit 7—Exploring Multiplication and Division

Graphers is a data graphing tool appropriate for young students.

Ice Cream Truck develops problem solving, money skills, and arithmetic operations.

Mighty Math Calculating Crew poses short-answer questions about number operations and money.

Money Challenge provides practice with money.

National Library of Virtual Manipulatives website (http://matti.usu.edu) allows students to work with manipulatives including rectangular arrays, number lines, and bar graphs.

Penny Pot provides practice with counting coins.

Unit 8—Mapping and Coordinates

Make a Map 3D practices map reading and direction skills.

Math Arena is a collection of math activities that reinforces many math concepts.

MicroWorlds Ex is a drawing program that helps students develop spatial reasoning and an understanding of coordinates while making shapes.

Unit 9—Using Patterns to Predict

Graphers is a data graphing tool appropriate for young students.

Kid Pix allows students to create their own illustrations.

Math Concepts One . . . Two . . . Three! provides students the opportunity to estimate and measure length, area, temperature, and mass.

Tabletop Jr. provides students the opportunity to work with data and develops logical thinking.

Thinkin' Things Collection 1: Toony the Loon's Lagoon develops logical thinking.

Zoombinis Logical Journey develops thinking skills as students find patterns to solve puzzles.

Unit 10—Numbers and Patterns: An Assessment Unit

Graphers is a data graphing tool appropriate for young students.

Ice Cream Truck develops problem solving, money skills, and arithmetic operations.

Kid Pix allows students to create their own illustrations.

Math Arena is a collection of math activities that reinforces many math concepts.

Money Challenge provides practice with money.

Number Facts Fire Zapper provides practice with number facts in an arcade-like game.

Penny Pot provides practice with counting coins.

Unit 11—Multiplication Patterns

Math Arena is a collection of math activities that reinforces many math concepts.

Math Munchers Deluxe provides practice with basic facts in an arcade-like game.

Mighty Math Calculating Crew poses short-answer questions about number operations and money skills.

National Library of Virtual Manipulatives website (http://matti.usu.edu) allows students to work with manipulatives including base-ten pieces, the abacus, and many others.

Unit 12—Dissections

Math Munchers Deluxe provides practice with basic facts, angles, and identifying geometric shapes in an arcade-like game.

National Library of Virtual Manipulatives website (http://matti.usu.edu) allows students to work with manipulatives including geoboards and tangrams.

Shape Up! is a geometry program that contains five sets of shapes that students can manipulate and explore.

Unit 13—Parts and Wholes

Math Arena is a collection of math activities that reinforces many math concepts.

Math Munchers Deluxe provides practice finding equivalent fractions in an arcade-like game.

Mighty Math Calculating Crew poses short-answer questions about number operations and money skills.

National Library of Virtual Manipulatives website (http://matti.usu.edu) allows students to work with fractions using electronic versions of manipulatives including fraction circles, rectangles, bars, and number lines.

Unit 14—Collecting and Using Data

Discover Time provides practice in telling time to the nearest hour, half-hour, quarter-hour, and five-minute intervals.

Graphers is a data graphing tool appropriate for young students.

Kid Pix allows students to create their own illustrations.

Math Arena is a collection of math activities that reinforces many math concepts.

Mighty Math Calculating Crew poses short-answer questions about number operations and money skills.

National Library of Virtual Manipulatives website (http://matti.usu.edu) allows students to work with manipulatives including base-ten pieces, the abacus, and many others.

Tabletop Jr. provides students the opportunity to work with data and develops logical thinking.

Unit 15—Decimal Investigations

Fraction Attraction develops understanding of fractions using fraction bars, pie charts, hundreds blocks, and other materials.

Graphers is a data graphing tool appropriate for young students.

Kid Pix allows students to create their own illustrations.

Math Arena is a collection of math activities that reinforces many math concepts.

Math Concepts One . . . Two . . . Three! provides practice measuring length.

National Library of Virtual Manipulatives website (http://matti.usu.edu) allows students to work with manipulatives including base-ten pieces.

Penny Pot provides practice with counting coins.

Tenth Planet: Representing Fractions provides a conceptual introduction to fractions.

Unit 16—Volume

Building Perspective Deluxe develops spatial reasoning and visual thinking in three dimensions.

Graphers is a data graphing tool appropriate for young students.

Kid Pix allows students to create their own illustrations.

Unit 17—Wholes and Parts

Fraction Attraction develops understanding of fractions using fraction bars, pie charts, hundreds blocks, and other materials.

National Library of Virtual Manipulatives website (http://matti.usu.edu) allows students to work with manipulatives including geoboards and fraction pieces.

Shape Up! is a geometry program that contains five sets of shapes that students can manipulate and explore.

Tenth Planet: Representing Fractions provides a conceptual introduction to fractions.

Unit 18—Viewing and Drawing 3-D

Make a Map 3D develops map reading and direction skills.

Math Arena is a collection of math activities that reinforces many math concepts.

Building Perspective Deluxe develops spatial reasoning and visual thinking in three dimensions.

MicroWorlds Ex is a drawing program that helps students develop spatial reasoning and an understanding of coordinates while making shapes.

Mighty Math Calculating Crew poses short-answer questions about three-dimensional shapes.

Unit 19—Multiplication and Division Problems

Carmen Sandiego's Math Detective provides practice with math facts, estimation, ordering numbers, and word problems.

Ice Cream Truck develops problem solving, money skills, and arithmetic operations.

Kid Pix or other drawing software allows students to illustrate stories using computers. (Lesson 2)

Math Arena is a collection of math activities that reinforces many math concepts.

Mighty Math Calculating Crew poses short-answer questions about number operations and money skills.

National Library of Virtual Manipulatives website (http://matti.usu.edu) allows students to work with manipulatives including rectangle multiplication that models the all-partials algorithm. (Lesson 2)

Unit 20—Connections: An Assessment Unit

Building Perspective Deluxe develops spatial reasoning and visual thinking in three dimensions.

Graphers is a data graphing tool appropriate for young students.

Kid Pix allows students to create their own illustrations.

MicroWorlds Ex is a drawing program that helps students develop spatial reasoning and an understanding of coordinates while making shapes.

Mighty Math Calculating Crew poses short-answer questions about number operations, three-dimensional shapes, and money.

Recommended Software List–
Brief Descriptions of the Programs

Building Perspective Deluxe by Sunburst
This program develops students' problem-solving skills, spatial perception, and visual thinking skills. Students are presented with ground-level views of an array of buildings. The task is to predict how the buildings will look when viewed from above. This program is recommended for grades 4–adult.

Carmen Sandiego's Math Detective by Riverdeep—The Learning Company
In this program students work as detectives to foil the evil Carmen Sandiego's plot to crystallize famous world landmarks. In order to do so they must collect clues from five different math activities. The activities can be accessed in a practice mode. The activity Atom Smasher works on developing accuracy and speed with math facts. Teachers can customize the problems in this part of the program. Crime Wave Sensor develops estimation. Students are presented with a math equation with a missing number. Students then click on a number chart to begin guessing the missing number. The program calculates the equation with the student's guess so that the student can refine the guess. This provides a powerful tool to develop mental imagery of numbers and their proximity to one another. Light Spectrometer requires students to place numbers in one pile from smallest to largest, much like the Tower of Hanoi puzzle. Microchip Decoder asks students to draw shapes and asks multiple-choice questions focusing on vocabulary. In Molecular Scope students write equations from word problems. The teacher's manual is well organized and there are many support materials provided as well. The program is recommended for grades 3 to 7.

Discover Time by Gamco
This program provides practice with identifying time in a game setting. Treasure is hidden in a cave. Students move pirates along a path trying to reach the treasure first. The pirates move when questions are answered correctly. Times are given on analog and digital clocks and written in clock symbols, e.g., 9:00 and as words, e.g., 9 o'clock. The preferences can be changed so that questions are about hour, half-hour, quarter-hour, and five-minute intervals. The program allows the teacher to keep track of individual student progress on specific types of problems. For example the program shows the percent correct of all problems involving translating digital to analog clocks. Some reading is involved. The program is recommended for grades K to 3.

The Factory Deluxe by Sunburst
Students are asked to produce or duplicate products in a simulated assembly line. Students direct the machines to punch, rotate, and stripe a variety of geometric shapes. Students explore sequences, patterns, and spatial relationships. There are also two games in the program. Ship It! is a game that develops logical thinking. Several shapes with a variety of attributes are presented. The student must place the shapes in the best containers. The containers are labeled with some sort of attributes. At the advanced levels, it is possible that more than one shape fits an attribute, i.e., goes into a container. In the second game, Deliver It!, students control trucks that compete on a racecourse. The trucks move as correct answers to area problems are given. This game develops estimation of area using a grid as well as measuring and using formulas. The program is recommended for grades 4 to 8.

Fraction Attraction by Sunburst
Fraction Attraction provides conceptual development of fractions in four games. Students develop understanding of equivalent fractions by turning a Ferris wheel. Other games address ordering fractions and positioning fractions on the number line. The concept of fraction as a distance is included also. In every game students can get an explanation of the mathematics in the diagnostic help section, not just correct answers. The explanations use fraction bars, pie charts, and hundreds blocks to show alternate representations. There are different levels of difficulty and students can choose to work with decimal and percent equivalents as well. The teacher's guide offers other off-computer activities and teaching suggestions to build understanding. The program is recommended for grades 3 to 8.

Graph Master by Tom Snyder Productions
Graph Master allows students to collect data into the program or import data from outside. There are 9 different types of graphs available, depending on the type of data: bar graph, pictograph, circle graph, line graph, scatterplot, frequency chart, histogram, line plot, and box plots. The user decides on graph type, scale, variables, and labels. The program allows two graphs to be open side by side so that students can compare the same data in different formats or different data. Students can also sort and tally data, get statistics (mean, median, mode, and range), and filter data. The program provides help in interpreting the types of graphs and there are ten sample data sets available.

Graphers by Sunburst
This program provides a data graphing tool for young students. The program allows even very young students to create pictographs, bar graphs, circle graphs, and data tables from data they have collected. It can also be used to provide practice in reading and interpreting different types of graphs. Students can write their interpretation of the graphs directly into an on-screen notebook to be printed out with the graph. The program is recommended for grades K–4.

Ice Cream Truck by Sunburst
Ice Cream Truck simulates a real life business. Students own an ice cream truck and their goal is to make as big a profit as possible. Students buy ice cream from a warehouse. They decide how much to buy, what to charge, and where to sell. The program provides information about the temperature outside and the time of day they will be selling. The program then simulates the customers and determines how much ice cream was sold that day. Students must make informed decisions. They have a spreadsheet available and must keep track of their profits and expenses, including gas. This program promotes multistep problem solving and decision making. The program is recommended for grades 3 to 6.

Kid Pix by Riverdeep—The Learning Company
This program allows students to create their own illustrations for many different applications throughout the curriculum. In mathematics, students can use this program to illustrate problems they have been given to solve or they can create and illustrate their own patterns and problems. The program is recommended for grades K–4.

Make a Map 3D by Sunburst
Make a Map 3D teaches the elements of a map and allows students to create their own maps. In You Lead the Way, students write directions and then

travel the route. In Which Way Up students learn about compass directions and then practice their skills following and writing directions. The program also includes a section on building geographic knowledge of the United States. The program includes many activities about maps and directions and is recommended for grades 2–5.

Math Arena by Sunburst
Math Arena is a collection of 20 well-thought-out problem-solving and skill-reinforcing games. Each activity begins with a short tutorial, which can be skipped. The games include practice in estimating angles, using symmetry to finish a quilt, finding a person lost in a coordinate grid, using transformations to form triangular designs, and forming arrays consisting of a given number of squares. Students practice making change and estimating if the total bill at a store is over an allotted amount of money and finding the sale price of an item, given the discount percent. Other games practice arithmetic skills. Students must recognize equivalent amounts and catch arithmetic errors. In other activities students must find equivalent fractions and find the next number in a pattern. In another game students practice forming Venn diagrams. The level of play can be changed and there are teacher options. The manual comes with worksheets to complement the computer work. This program is recommended for grades 4 to 7.

Math Concepts One . . . Two . . . Three! by Gamco
This program is a collection of activities covering numeration, number sense, geometry, measurement, data management and probability, and patterning and algebra. Grade levels further divide each of the sections and there are numerous activities within each grade level. Many of the activities focus on developing conceptual understanding and connecting symbols with actions with the manipulatives. Teachers can keep track of student progress and choose grade levels for individual students. There are also supplemental non-computer activities available. The program is recommended for grades K to 3.

The Math Forum (www.mathforum.org)
The Math Forum is a very broad-based website maintained by Drexel University. The site has such features as Ask Dr. Math, where students can ask mathematical questions. There is an extensive mathematics resource library for students in elementary school through graduate school. Other features include discussion groups, an extensive collection of good problems, teacher resources, and issues in mathematics education.

Math Munchers Deluxe by Riverdeep—The Learning Company
Math Munchers Deluxe allows students to practice operations and identify primes, multiples, and factors. The student moves a Muncher around the screen as it devours expressions that fit given criteria. For example, one task is to devour all expressions that are equivalent to .5. The Muncher tries to avoid being eaten by Troggles, but this feature can be turned off, allowing the student to focus on the mathematics. The program allows the user to choose a grade level, and choose between whole numbers, fractions, decimals, and geometry. Within the topics students choose evaluating expressions, finding equivalent expressions, and comparing expressions. The program is recommended for students in grades 3–6.

MicroWorlds Ex by LCSI
MicroWorlds is an interactive program that allows users to create geometric shapes by issuing commands. As students construct figures, they learn about the geometric properties of shapes. There are several commercially available programs. Recent versions include MicroWorlds Jr. and MicroWorlds Ex by LCSI. In these versions, students can add text, animation, and sound. This program is recommended for grades 2 to adult.

Mighty Math Calculating Crew by Riverdeep—The Learning Company
This very versatile skills program has four sections with about 20 specific goals in each section. The Nautical Number Line presents lost treasures under a number line. Students must move a ship to the correct number to acquire a treasure. The skills here focus on locating numbers on the line, rounding, adding and subtracting whole numbers, fractions, and decimals, and working with negative numbers. The Superhero Superstore focuses on money skills and operations involving numbers with ending zeros. Dr. Gee's 3D Lab acquaints students with nets of solids. Students must match nets with solids and identify attributes of the nets and solids. Nick Knack, Supertrader, develops conceptual understanding of multiplication as repeated addition and division as partitioning equally. There are long-division practice problems too. The program is recommended for 3rd to 6th grade.

Money Challenge by Gamco
Students practice working with money in a game-like setting. There are four activities to choose from. First, students can count money displayed on the screen. Another activity asks students to make a certain amount using the fewest coins. Third, students are asked if they can buy a certain item with the money they have been given. In the last activity, students are asked how much money they will have left after purchasing a given item. For each activity, the student can choose the set of money. The smallest set contains pennies, nickels, and dimes while the full set contains all the coins and dollar bills. The program allows the teacher to keep track of individual student progress on specific types of problems. Some reading is involved. The program is recommended for grades K to 2.

National Library of Virtual Manipulatives for Interactive Mathematics (www.matti.usu.edu)
This website was developed and is maintained at Utah State University. It includes an extensive collection of virtual manipulatives and accompanying activities. Students can work with geoboards, pattern blocks, tangrams, base-ten pieces, balance scales, and other materials interactively. This provides the opportunity to work with materials that are perhaps otherwise not available. For students who have access to the concrete materials, using the interactive manipulatives provides opportunity to move from concrete to pictorial representations.

Number Facts Fire Zapper by Gamco
Number Facts Fire Zapper's goal is to develop proficiency and speed at basic math facts in a fun arcade-type game. Students must move firefighters around a screen and spray math facts with the correct answer in order to extinguish the flames. Students choose what operation they want to practice. The length of the game and the speed at which the number facts appear can

be changed. The program allows the teacher to keep track of individual student progress. The teacher can also see an analysis of how a student did on particular fact groups. For example the program shows the percent correct of all problems involving the multiples of seven. The program is recommended for grades 1 to 8.

Numbers Recovered by Sunburst

Students help the number detective recover stolen numbers by completing four activities. The activities can be accessed independently. In Puzzling Place Values students match the correct amount of 1s, 10s, and 100s to meet the packing goal of a gumball factory. The first level deals with 1s and 10s. In Comparison Capers and Sorting Sleuth students compare numbers to tally marks and numerical expressions. Practice with money is included. Graphing Gumshoes allows students to practice reading and interpreting bar graphs. There are three levels for each activity. The program also includes base-ten pieces that students manipulate to solve problems. The program is recommended for grades K to 3.

Penny Pot by Sunburst

Penny Pot includes four activities that promote facility with coins. Poppers asks students to pop balloons labeled with coin values to add up to a given amount. In Hook a Fish students catch fish with various values. At the end of the game the coin values are displayed and students must give the total. Coincentration is a concentration game, which matches coins with their values. Speed Cents involves estimating money amounts as students choose from three coin collections to match a target value. The program is recommended for grades 2 and 3.

Shape Up! by Sunburst

Shape Up! is a very versatile geometry program consisting of five sets of shapes. The user can choose to work with pattern blocks or tangrams designed to correspond to the manipulatives. Another set of shapes involves regular triangles, pentagons, hexagons, octagons, squares, and circles. These shapes can be dissected and put back together in any desired fashion. In addition, the user can choose from two sets of three-dimensional shapes. One set is the platonic solids and the other a variety of shapes. Students can explore area, symmetry, tessellations, similarity, and congruence. It allows users to view inside 3-dimensional shapes using the Transparent function. Any of the shapes can be moved and rotated. The teacher's guide includes an extensive implementation guide to use the program to its fullest capacity and an in-depth reference section. This program develops student van Hiele levels with opportunities to explore shapes more easily than working with concrete materials. The program is recommended for grades K to 8.

Tabletop Jr. by Sunburst

This program focuses on developing logical thinking and working with data as an age-appropriate introduction to statistics. Students make objects from thirteen different possible kits. The objects have a variety of attributes. Students can then use these objects as data to manipulate. The data can be arranged, for example, on axes, as pictographs, and as Venn diagrams. Students sharpen their discrimination skills as they look for like and unlike objects and patterns in the data. There are many excellent classroom activities in the teacher's manual. The program is recommended for grades K to 5.

Ten Tricky Tiles by Sunburst

Ten Tricky Tiles develops understanding of number relations, addition and subtraction fact practice, and logical thinking. Students must fit number tiles 0–9 into the correct places to make number sentences true. The number tiles must be arranged so that all the sentences are correct in order to get points. The program also reinforces the concept of equality with operations on both sides of the equals sign. There are three activities with increasing difficulty to choose from. The most challenging activity is a number crossword puzzle where the number sentences are all interrelated. The ten number tiles must be placed so horizontal and vertical number sentences are true. There are accompanying worksheets and suggestions for helping students develop efficient strategies. The program is recommended for grades 2 to 6.

Tenth Network: Grouping and Place Value by Sunburst

This program develops the concept of groups by allowing students to use the computer mouse to move muffin pans and other containers and group objects on the screen into 2s, 5s, and 10s easily. The program helps students count a large number of objects by skip counting. In one activity students find a target number by grouping, in another they package table tennis balls. In still another activity, students are given coins in denominations of 1s, 10s, and 100s and they must buy items with exact change. Students exchange larger denominations for the next smaller by breaking up a 10. The program has many extension activities and is recommended for grades 1 to 3.

Tenth Planet: Representing Fractions by Sunburst

The program contains video clips and activities that promote conceptual understanding of what a fraction is. The focus is on fractions naming equal parts of a whole and that there are different ways to cut a whole into equal pieces. Through real-life examples students see that a fraction of one object may be very different in size from the same fractional part of another object. The notion that as the denominator gets bigger, the fractional piece that it represents gets smaller is also addressed. There are several activities where students cut fractions, identify fractions, and construct the whole. Fractions are used in linear, area, and volume models. The program is recommended for grades 2 to 4.

Thinkin' Things Collection 1: Toony the Loon's Lagoon by Riverdeep— The Learning Company

This program is not meant to develop numerical skills but rather general thinking skills. The program is divided into six activities. Three of these have very strong mathematical connections. In Fripple Shop, students must find the characters with specified attributes. At the more advanced levels, students must match up to four attributes using "and," "or," and "not." Similarly, in the activity Feathered Friends, students must build a bird with specified attributes that increase in difficulty and require pattern discrimination. Problems can be heard (by clicking the telephone), seen (by clicking the fax machine), or both by clicking on the door. The activity Blox-Flying Shapes develops spatial sense as students move shapes and change color, motion, and sound. The program is recommended for grades K to 3.

Zoombinis Logical Journey by Riverdeep—The Learning Company
This program builds thinking skills. The student must guide the Zoombinis to a new land by solving logic puzzles. The Zoombinis are little creatures that have different attributes (feet, hair, noses, etc.). In many of the challenges, students must discover how the attributes are grouped in order to proceed. Patterning, collecting evidence, graphing, sorting, and hypothesis testing are developed as the game progresses. There are twelve different puzzles with four levels of difficulty that change each time the program is played. The program is recommended for grades 3 to 8.

Software Companies Addresses and Telephone Numbers

Gamco
The Siboney Learning Group
325 N. Kirkwood Road, Suite 200
Saint Louis, MO 63122
1-888-726-8100
www.gamco.com
www.siboneylearninggroup.com

LCSI
P.O. Box 162
Highgate Springs, VT 05460
1-800-321-5646
www.microworlds.com

Riverdeep—The Learning Company
100 Pine Street, Suite 1900
San Francisco, CA 94111
1-888-242-6747
www.riverdeep.net

Sunburst Technology
1550 Executive Drive
Elgin, IL 60123
1-888-492-8817
www.sunburst.com

Tom Snyder Productions
80 Coolidge Hill Road
Watertown, MA 02472
1-800-342-0236
www.tomsnyder.com

Glossary

This glossary provides definitions of key vocabulary terms in the Grade 3 lessons. Locations of key vocabulary terms in the curriculum are included with each definition. Components Key: URG = *Unit Resource Guide,* SG = *Student Guide,* DAB = *Discovery Assignment Book,* and TIG = *Teacher Implementation Guide.*

A

Area (URG Unit 5 pp. 8, 24; SG p. 58; TIG p. 345)
The area of a shape is the amount of space it covers, measured in square units.

Array (URG Unit 7 p. 9 & Unit 11 p. 9)
An array is an arrangement of elements into a rectangular pattern of (horizontal) rows and (vertical) columns. (*See* column and row.)

Associative Property of Addition (URG Unit 2 p. 31)
For any three numbers $a, b,$ and c we have $a + (b + c) = (a + b) + c.$ For example in finding the sum of 4, 8, and 2, one can compute $4 + 8$ first and then add 2: $(4 + 8) + 2 = 14.$ Alternatively, we can compute $8 + 2$ and then add the result to 4: $4 + (8 + 2) = 4 + 10 = 14.$

Average (URG Unit 5 pp. 34, 35; TIG p. 257)
A number that can be used to represent a typical value in a set of data. (*See also* mean and median.)

Axes (URG Unit 8 p. 9; SG pp. 96, 97)
Reference lines on a graph. In the Cartesian coordinate system, the axes are two perpendicular lines that meet at the origin. The singular of axes is axis.

B

Base (of a cube model) (URG Unit 18 p. 51; SG p. 274)
The part of a cube model that sits on the "ground."

Base-Ten Board (URG Unit 4 p. 27)
A tool to help children organize base-ten pieces when they are representing numbers.

Base-Ten Pieces (URG Unit 4 pp. 43, 44; SG p. 44)
A set of manipulatives used to model our number system as shown in the figure at the right. Note that a skinny is made of 10 bits, a flat is made of 100 bits, and a pack is made of 1000 bits.

Base-Ten Shorthand (SG p. 46)
A pictorial representation of the base-ten pieces as shown.

Nickname	Picture	Shorthand
bit		·
skinny		/
flat		
pack		

Best-Fit Line (URG Unit 9 pp. 8, 46; SG p. 120; DAB p. 141)
The line that comes closest to the most number of points on a point graph.

Bit (URG Unit 4 pp. 27, 43; SG p. 44)
A cube that measures 1 cm on each edge. It is the smallest of the base-ten pieces that is often used to represent 1. (*See also* base-ten pieces.)

C

Capacity (URG Unit 16 p. 8; TIG p. 351)
1. The volume of the inside of a container.
2. The largest volume a container can hold.

Cartesian Coordinate System (URG Unit 8 p. 9)
A method of locating points on a flat surface by means of numbers. This method is named after its originator, René Descartes. (*See also* coordinates.)

Centimeter (cm)
A unit of measure in the metric system equal to one-hundredth of a meter. (1 inch = 2.54 cm)

Column (URG Unit 11 pp. 9, 47)
In an array, the objects lined up vertically.

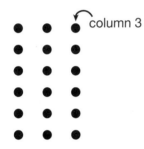
column 3

Common Fraction (URG Unit 15 p. 26; SG p. 218)
Any fraction that is written with a numerator and denominator that are whole numbers. For example, $\frac{3}{4}$ and $\frac{9}{4}$ are both common fractions. (*See also* decimal fraction.)

Commutative Property of Addition (URG Unit 2 p. 31 & Unit 11 p. 48)
This is also known as the Order Property of Addition. Changing the order of the addends does not change the sum. For example, $3 + 5 = 5 + 3 = 8$. Using variables, $n + m = m + n$.

Commutative Property of Multiplication (URG Unit 11 p. 48)
Changing the order of the factors in a multiplication problem does not change the result, e.g., $7 \times 3 = 3 \times 7 = 21$. (*See also* turn-around facts.)

Congruent (URG Unit 12 pp. 45, 46 & Unit 17 pp. 22, 24, 28; SG pp. 168, 253)
Figures with the same shape and size.

Convenient Number (URG Unit 6 p. 84)
A number used in computation that is close enough to give a good estimate, but is also easy to compute mentally, e.g., 25 and 30 are convenient numbers for 27.

Coordinates (URG Unit 8 pp. 8, 9, 25; SG p. 97)
An ordered pair of numbers that locates points on a flat surface by giving distances from a pair of coordinate axes. For example, if a point has coordinates (4, 5) it is 4 units from the vertical axis and 5 units from the horizontal axis.

Counting Back (URG Unit 2 p. 10; TIG p. 295)
A strategy for subtracting in which students start from a larger number and then count down until the number is reached. For example, to solve $8 - 3$, begin with 8 and count down three, 7, 6, 5.

Counting Down (*See* counting back.)

Counting Up (URG Unit 2 p. 10; TIG p. 295)
A strategy for subtraction in which the student starts at the lower number and counts on to the higher number. For example, to solve $8 - 5$, the student starts at 5 and counts up three numbers (6, 7, 8). So $8 - 5 = 3$.

Cube (SG p. 270)
A three-dimensional shape with six congruent square faces.

Cubic Centimeter (cc) (URG Unit 16 pp. 8, 23; SG p. 236; TIG p. 319)
The volume of a cube that is one centimeter long on each edge.

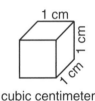
cubic centimeter

Cup (URG Unit 16 p. 62)
A unit of volume equal to 8 fluid ounces, one-half pint.

D

Decimal Fraction (URG Unit 15 p. 26; SG p. 218)
A fraction written as a decimal. For example, 0.75 and 0.4 are decimal fractions and $\frac{75}{100}$ and $\frac{4}{10}$ are called common fractions. (*See also* fraction.)

Denominator (URG Unit 13 p. 22)
The number below the line in a fraction. The denominator indicates the number of equal parts in which the unit whole is divided. For example, the 5 is the denominator in the fraction $\frac{2}{5}$. In this case the unit whole is divided into five equal parts.

Density (URG Unit 16 p. 23)
The ratio of an object's mass to its volume.

Difference (URG Unit 2 pp. 84, 89, 90)
The answer to a subtraction problem.

Dissection (URG Unit 12 p. 8 & Unit 17 p. 24)
Cutting or decomposing a geometric shape into smaller shapes that cover it exactly.

Distributive Property of Multiplication over Addition (URG Unit 19 p. 8)
For any three numbers a, b, and c, $a \times (b + c) = a \times b + a \times c$. The distributive property is the foundation for most methods of multidigit multiplication. For example, $9 \times (17) = 9 \times (10 + 7) = 9 \times 10 + 9 \times 7 = 90 + 63 = 153$.

E

Equilateral Triangle (URG Unit 7 p. 92)
A triangle with all sides of equal length and all angles of equal measure.

Equivalent Fractions (SG p. 255)
Fractions that have the same value, e.g., $\frac{2}{4} = \frac{1}{2}$.

Estimate (URG Unit 5 p. 25 & Unit 6 p. 85; TIG p. 265)
1. (verb) To find *about* how many.
2. (noun) An approximate number.

Extrapolation (URG Unit 7 p. 33; TIG p. 337)
Using patterns in data to make predictions or to estimate values that lie beyond the range of values in the set of data.

F

Fact Family (URG Unit 11 p. 79; SG p. 153; TIG p. 298)
Related math facts, e.g., $3 \times 4 = 12$, $4 \times 3 = 12$, $12 \div 3 = 4$, $12 \div 4 = 3$.

Factor (URG Unit 11 pp. 37, 63; SG p. 150)
1. In a multiplication problem, the numbers that are multiplied together. In the problem $3 \times 4 = 12$, 3 and 4 are the factors.
2. Whole numbers that can be multiplied together to get a number. That is, numbers that divide a number evenly, e.g., 1, 2, 3, 4, 6, and 12 are all the factors of 12.

Fewest Pieces Rule (URG Unit 4 pp. 29, 48 & Unit 6 p. 46; SG p. 47)
Using the least number of base-ten pieces to represent a number. (*See also* base-ten pieces.)

Flat (URG Unit 4 p. 44; SG p. 44)
A block that measures 1 cm × 10 cm × 10 cm. It is one of the base-ten pieces that is often used to represent 100. (*See also* base-ten pieces.)

Flip (URG Unit 12 p. 46)
A motion of the plane in which a figure is reflected over a line so that any point and its image are the same distance from the line.

Fraction (URG Unit 15 p. 26)
A number that can be written as $\frac{a}{b}$ where a and b are whole numbers and b is not zero. For example, $\frac{1}{2}$, 0.5, and 2 are all fractions since 0.5 can be written as $\frac{5}{10}$ and 2 can be written as $\frac{2}{1}$.

Front-End Estimation (URG Unit 6 p. 85)
Estimation by looking at the left-most digit.

G

Gallon (gal) (URG Unit 16 p. 62)
A unit of volume equal to four quarts.

Gram (SG p. 115; TIG pp. 368–369)
The basic unit used to measure mass.

H

Hexagon (SG p. 170)
A six-sided polygon.

Horizontal Axis (SG p. 4)
In a coordinate grid, the *x*-axis. The axis that extends from left to right.

I

Interpolation (URG Unit 7 p. 33; TIG p. 337)
Making predictions or estimating values that lie between data points in a set of data.

J

K

Kilogram (SG p. 115; TIG p. 369)
1000 grams.

L

Likely Event (SG p. 6)
An event that has a high probability of occurring.

Line of Symmetry (URG Unit 12 p. 43)
A line is a line of symmetry for a plane figure if, when the figure is folded along this line, the two parts match exactly.

Line Symmetry (URG Unit 12 p. 43; SG p. 169)
A figure has line symmetry if it has at least one line of symmetry.

Liter (l) (URG Unit 16 p. 8; SG p. 237)
Metric unit used to measure volume. A liter is a little more than a quart.

M

Magic Square (URG Unit 2 p. 67)
A square array of digits in which the sums of the rows, columns, and main diagonals are the same.

Making a Ten (URG Unit 2 p. 10)
Strategies for addition and subtraction that make use of knowing the sums to ten. For example, knowing $6 + 4 = 10$ can be helpful in finding $10 - 6 = 4$ and $11 - 6 = 5$.

Mass (URG Unit 9 pp. 7, 32 & Unit 16 p. 23; SG p. 114; TIG pp. 365, 370)
The amount of matter in an object.

Mean (URG Unit 5 p. 35; TIG p. 257)
An average of a set of numbers that is found by adding the values of the data and dividing by the number of values.

Measurement Division (URG Unit 7 p. 8; TIG p. 319)
Division as equal grouping. The total number of objects and the number of objects in each group are known. The number of groups is the unknown. For example, tulip bulbs come in packages of 8. If 216 bulbs are sold, how many packages are sold?

Measurement Error (URG Unit 9 pp. 8, 26; TIG p. 272)
The unavoidable error that occurs due to the limitations inherent to any measurement instrument.

Median (URG Unit 5 pp. 34, 35; DAB p. 91; TIG p. 260)
For a set with an odd number of data arranged in order, it is the middle number. For an even number of data arranged in order, it is the number halfway between the two middle numbers.

Meniscus (URG Unit 16 p. 24; SG p. 239; TIG p. 358)
The curved surface formed when a liquid creeps up the side of a container (for example, a graduated cylinder).

Meter (m) (TIG p. 342)
The standard unit of length measure in the metric system. One meter is approximately 39 inches.

Milliliter (ml) (URG Unit 16 p. 8; SG p. 237; TIG p. 358)
A measure of capacity in the metric system that is the volume of a cube that is one centimeter long on each edge.

Multiple (URG Unit 3 p. 61 & Unit 11 p. 37)
A number is a multiple of another number if it is evenly divisible by that number. For example, 12 is a multiple of 2 since 2 divides 12 evenly.

N

Numerator (URG Unit 13 p. 22)
The number written above the line in a fraction. For example, the 2 is the numerator in the fraction $\frac{2}{5}$. (*See also* denominator.)

O

One-Dimensional Object (URG Unit 18 p. 25; SG p. 266)
An object is one-dimensional if it is made up of pieces of lines and curves.

Ordered Pairs (URG Unit 8 p. 49)
A pair of numbers that gives the coordinates of a point on a grid in relation to the origin. The horizontal coordinate is given first; the vertical coordinate is given second. For example, the ordered pair (5, 3) tells us to move five units to the right of the origin and 3 units up.

Origin (URG Unit 8 pp. 8, 26)
The point at which the *x*- and *y*-axes (horizontal and vertical axes) intersect on a coordinate plane. The origin is described by the ordered pair (0, 0) and serves as a reference point so that all the points on the plane can be located by ordered pairs.

P

Pack (URG Unit 4 p. 46; SG p. 44)
A cube that measures 10 cm on each edge. It is one of the base-ten pieces that is often used to represent 1000. (*See also* base-ten pieces.)

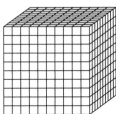

Palindrome (URG Unit 6 p. 103)
A number, word, or phrase that reads the same forward and backward, e.g., 12321.

Parallel Lines (URG Unit 18 p. 38)
Lines that are in the same direction. In the plane, parallel lines are lines that do not intersect.

Parallelogram (URG Unit 18 p. 38)
A quadrilateral with two pairs of parallel sides.

Partitive Division (URG Unit 7 p. 8; TIG p. 319)
Division as equal sharing. The total number of objects and the number of groups are known. The number of objects in each group is the unknown. For example, Frank has 144 marbles that he divides equally into 6 groups. How many marbles are in each group?

Pentagon (SG p. 170)
A five-sided, five-angled polygon.

Perimeter (URG Unit 7 p. 92; DAB p. 123)
The distance around a two-dimensional shape.

Pint (URG Unit 16 p. 62)
A unit of volume measure equal to 16 fluid ounces, i.e., two cups.

Polygon
A two-dimensional connected figure made of line segments in which each endpoint of every side meets with an endpoint of exactly one other side.

Population (URG Unit 1 p. 10; SG p. 8)
A collection of persons or things whose properties will be analyzed in a survey or experiment.

Prediction (SG p. 6)
Using data to declare or foretell what is likely to occur.

Prime Number (URG Unit 11 p. 48)
A number that has exactly two factors. For example, 7 has exactly two distinct factors, 1 and 7.

Prism
A three-dimensional figure that has two congruent faces, called bases, that are parallel to each other, and all other faces are parallelograms.

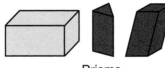

Prisms   Not a prism

Product (URG Unit 11 pp. 37, 63; SG p. 150; DAB p. 172)
The answer to a multiplication problem. In the problem $3 \times 4 = 12$, 12 is the product.

Q

Quadrilateral (URG Unit 18 p. 38; SG p. 170)
A polygon with four sides.

Quart (URG Unit 16 p. 62)
A unit of volume equal to 32 fluid ounces; one quarter of a gallon.

R

Recording Sheet (URG Unit 4 p. 43)
A place value chart used for addition and subtraction problems.

Rectangular Prism (URG Unit 18 p. 26; SG p. 268)
A prism whose bases are rectangles. A right rectangular prism is a prism having all faces rectangles.

Regular (URG Unit 7 p. 92; DAB p. 123)
A polygon is regular if all sides are of equal length and all angles are equal.

Remainder (URG Unit 7 p. 73)
Something that remains or is left after a division problem. The portion of the dividend that is not evenly divisible by the divisor, e.g., $16 \div 5 = 3$ with 1 as a remainder.

Right Angle (SG p. 166)
An angle that measures 90°.

Rotation (turn) (URG Unit 12 p. 46)
A transformation (motion) in which a figure is turned a specified angle and direction around a point.

Row (URG Unit 11 pp. 9, 47)
In an array, the objects lined up horizontally.

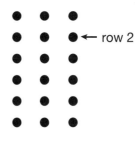

Rubric (URG Unit 2 p. 9)
A written guideline for assigning scores to student work, for the purpose of assessment.

S

Sample (URG Unit 1 p. 10; SG p. 8)
A part or subset of a population.

Skinny (URG Unit 4 pp. 27, 43; SG p. 44)
A block that measures 1 cm $\times$ 1 cm $\times$ 10 cm. It is one of the base-ten pieces that is often used to represent 10. (*See also* base-ten pieces.)

Square Centimeter (sq cm) (SG p. 59; TIG p. 345)
The area of a square that is 1 cm long on each side.

Square Number (SG p. 147)
A number that is the product of a whole number multiplied by itself. For example, 25 is a square number since $5 \times 5 = 25$. A square number can be represented by a square array with the same number of rows as columns. A square array for 25 has 5 rows of 5 objects in each row or 25 total objects.

Standard Masses
A set of objects with convenient masses, usually 1 g, 10 g, 100 g, etc.

Sum (URG Unit 2 p. 42; SG p. 16)
The answer to an addition problem.

Survey (URG Unit 14 p. 58; SG p. 203)
An investigation conducted by collecting data from a sample of a population and then analyzing it. Usually surveys are used to make predictions about the entire population.

T

Tangrams (SG p. 158)
A type of geometric puzzle. A shape is given and it must be covered exactly with seven standard shapes called tans.

Thinking Addition (URG Unit 2 p. 10)
A strategy for subtraction that uses a related addition problem. For example, $15 - 7 = 8$ because $8 + 7 = 15$.

Three-Dimensional (URG Unit 18 p. 25; SG p. 267)
Existing in three-dimensional space; having length, width, and depth.

TIMS Laboratory Method (URG Unit 1 p. 9; SG p. 9; TIG p. 323)
A method that students use to organize experiments and investigations. It involves four components: draw, collect, graph, and explore. It is a way to help students learn about the scientific method.

Turn (URG Unit 12 p. 46)
(*See* rotation.)

Turn-Around Facts (URG Unit 2 p. 42 & Unit 11 p. 48; SG p. 146)
Addition facts that have the same addends but in a different order, e.g., $3 + 4 = 7$ and $4 + 3 = 7$. (*See also* commutative property of addition and commutative property of multiplication.)

Two-Dimensional (URG Unit 18 p. 25; SG p. 266)
Existing in the plane; having length and width.

Two-Pan Balance
A device for measuring the mass of an object by balancing the object against a number of standard masses (usually multiples of 1 unit, 10 units, and 100 units, etc.).

U

Unit (of measurement) (URG Unit 18 pp. 50, 51)
A precisely fixed quantity used to measure. For example, centimeter, foot, kilogram, and quart are units of measurement.

Using a Ten (URG Unit 2 p. 10; TIG p. 295)
1. A strategy for addition that uses partitions of the number 10. For example, one can find $8 + 6$ by thinking $8 + 6 = 8 + 2 + 4 = 10 + 4 = 14$.
2. A strategy for subtraction that uses facts that involve subtracting 10. For example, students can use $17 - 10 = 7$ to learn the "close fact" $17 - 9 = 8$.

Using Doubles (URG Unit 2 p. 10; TIG p. 295)
Strategies for addition and subtraction that use knowing doubles. For example, one can find $7 + 8$ by thinking $7 + 8 = 7 + 7 + 1 = 14 + 1 = 15$. Knowing $7 + 7 = 14$ can be helpful in finding $14 - 7 = 7$ and $14 - 8 = 6$.

V

Value (URG Unit 1 p. 27; SG p. 10; TIG p. 325)
The possible outcomes of a variable. For example, red, green, and blue are possible values for the variable *color*. Two meters and 1.65 meters are possible values for the variable *length*.

Variable (URG Unit 1 pp. 9, 27; SG p. 9; TIG p. 325)
1. An attribute or quantity that changes or varies.
2. A symbol that can stand for a variable.

Vertex (URG Unit 12 p. 44; SG pp. 166, 268)
1. A point where the sides of a polygon meet.
2. A point where the edges of a three-dimensional object meet.

Vertical Axis (SG p. 4)
In a coordinate grid, the *y*-axis. It is perpendicular to the horizontal axis.

Volume (URG Unit 16 pp. 8, 23; SG p. 236; TIG p. 351)
The measure of the amount of space occupied by an object.

Volume by Displacement (URG Unit 16 p. 8; TIG p. 360)
A way of measuring volume of an object by measuring the amount of water (or some other fluid) it displaces.

W

Weight (URG Unit 9 pp. 7, 32; TIG p. 370)
A measure of the pull of gravity on an object. One unit for measuring weight is the pound.

X

Y

Z

Grade 3 Index

This index provides the unit number in parentheses followed by the page number for the multivolume URG (*Unit Resource Guide*). It provides page references for the SG (*Student Guide*), the DAB (*Discovery Assignment Book*), the AB (*Adventure Book*), and the TIG (*Teacher Implementation Guide*). Definitions or explanations of key terms can be found on the pages listed in bold type.

URG (14) 7, URG (15) 7, URG (16) 7, URG (17) 6, URG (18) 7, URG (20) 6

laboratory experiments, URG (1) 7, URG (5) 7, URG (9) 6, URG (10) 7, URG (14) 7, URG (15) 7, URG (16) 7, URG (18) 7, URG (20) 6

Digital clocks, DAB 225–227, SG 201, URG (4) 9, 90, URG (14) 37

Digit cards, SG 7

Digits, DAB 33, TIG 264, 278

Digits Game, DAB 109, TIG 79, 473, URG (6) iii, 26, 109–116, URG (7) 23, URG (20) 17

Dimensions, URG (18) 8–9. *See also* Three-Dimensional objects

Discourse, TIG 134, 374, 434–436. *See also* Communication

Discovery Assignment Book (DAB), TIG 24, 48

Discrete variables, URG (7) 10–11

Displacement, volume measurement by, SG 241, TIG 360–361, 367, URG (16) **8**, 18, 25–27, URG (17) 14

Dissections, DAB 189, SG 158–175, TIG 98–100, 160–161, URG (12) iii, **8**–9, 19, 20, 48, 74–80, URG (17) 24

Distances, URG (8) 51, 57–58, URG (16) 74

Distortion, TIG 260

Distributive property of multiplication, URG (19) **8**, 27

District implementation of *Math Trailblazers,* TIG 448–449

Diversity, in problem types, TIG 318

Dividends, URG (11) 10, 89, URG (19) 63

Divisibility, URG (3) 61

Division, AB 113, DAB 47, 216, SG 148, 152–154, TIG 80–83, 123–125, 150–151, URG (4) 21, URG (6) 20, URG (7) iii, **8**–11, 22–23, 61, URG (9) 17–18, URG (12) 16, URG (19) iii, 56, 60–67, URG (20) 32

estimation in, TIG 270–272

Fact families in, SG **153**

by five, TIG 64

into 2 digit numbers, URG (19) 52, 55–57

into equal parts, URG (19) 52, 55–57

Math Facts on, SG 153, TIG 298

Mathhoppers for, SG 88–94

for miles per gallon, AB 110

of money, DAB 217, URG (3) 19–21, URG (4) 19, URG (5) 16, URG (7) 78–87, URG (8) 17, URG (10) 64–73, URG (20) 37–50

multiplication and, SG 153–154, TIG 96–97, URG (11) 76–82

point graphs and, URG (7) 32

problem solving, SG 295–297

problem types in, TIG 318–320

remainders and, URG (19) 8

as repeated subtraction, AB 81

represent using manipulatives, URG (7) 79–84, URG (19) 52, 55

symbols for, SG 153

by ten, TIG 64

in volume measurements, URG (16) 45

word problems on, DAB 179, SG 152, 295–297, TIG 174–175, URG (3) 66–69, URG (7) 70–75, URG (11) 76–82

by zero, SG 153, URG (11) 10, 79–80, 87, 89

Divisors, URG (11) 10, 89

Dollars. *See* Money

Doubling, DAB 80, TIG 294–296, URG (1) 20, URG (2) 10, 21, 108, URG (5) 12, 16, URG (6) 17, 29, URG (7) iii, 30, URG (10) 18, URG (13) iii, URG (16) 13, 15, URG (19) 17, 19

Drawing three-dimensional objects, URG (18) 33–42

cubes, URG (18) 33, 37–42

rectangular prisms, URG (18) 23, 33, 40

edge, URG (12) 22–33, 44, URG (18) 21, 26, 28, 37–40

edge-to-edge rule, URG (12) 44

Duration, URG (14) 25

E

Edges, DAB 191, SG 268, URG (18) iii, 9, 26, 37–38, 75

Edge-to-edge rule, URG (12) 9, 44

Education Development Center (EDC), TIG 399, 404–409

Eight, grouping by, DAB 53, URG (3) 34–35

Eight-Column data tables, URG (14) 45, 53

Eighths, AB 127, URG (17) 58–59

Either-or **rhetoric,** TIG 15

Elapsed time, URG (4) 98, URG (14) 25

Elements of experiments, URG (20) 19–26

measurement procedures, URG (20) 19

number of trials, URG (20) 19, 22–23

problems solved, URG (20) 19, 22–25

types of graphs, URG (20) 19, 23, 26

variables, URG (20) 19, 22–23

Eleven, grouping by, DAB 53, URG (3) 34–35

Elixir of Youth, AB 95–114, TIG 114, URG (16) 68–76

Empty set, URG (11) 88

End of the Year Test, URG (20) 65–72

English language learners, TIG 3, 385–397

improving skills of, TIG 427

introduction to, TIG 385–386

language-rich approach to, TIG 388–391

lesson plan examples for, TIG 392–393

nonverbal communication and, TIG 396

outcomes, TIG 392

strategies for, TIG 395–396

support, TIG 387

teachers issues with, TIG 391

theory on, TIG 386–387

tools supporting, TIG 387

introduction to, TIG 412

lesson planning for, TIG 418–423

resources on, TIG 423

supporting learning of, TIG 416–418

teaching, TIG 415–417

Glossary, TIG 4, 493–498

Goal setting, URG (14) 47–49, 52

Graduated cylinders, AB 113, DAB 245, SG 239, TIG 357–359, URG (14) 44, URG (16) iii, 18, 23, 25, 30–33, 43, URG (17) 14

Grams (g), DAB 142, 145, 245, SG **115,** TIG 368–369, URG (9) 7, 62

Graphic organizers, TIG 387, 433

Graphing Data, SG 120

Graphs, AB 36, 76, DAB 4, 8, URG (1) iii, 34–35, 58, URG (7) 9–11, URG (20) 22. *See also* Bar graphs, Best-Fit lines, Labs, Point graphs

of area measurements, DAB 95–97

assessment activity on, URG (7) 46–54

bar graph, URG (16) 45, URG (20) 19, 26

data on, SG 120

functions in, TIG 282–283

of hexagon measurements, DAB 126

interpreting, SG 33, 249

patterns on, SG 83

point graph, URG (20) 19, 23

predictions from, SG 84, URG (9) 8

in TIMS Laboratory Method, TIG 330–337

of triangle measurements, DAB 124

Gravity, TIG 365–371, URG (9) 7, 32

Greater than **(>) symbol,** URG (13) 56, URG (17) 17

Grids, AB 66–67, 73, URG (8) 36, 38, 57

for area measurement, DAB 87, 137, TIG 346–347

student, TIG 203

Grouping, DAB 53, TIG 125, URG (3) iii, URG (19) 52–58. *See also* Partitioning numbers, Regrouping

equal, URG (7) 8

by fifteen, DAB 57

by five, DAB 53, URG (3) 34–35

multiplication and, URG (3) 30–37

in teams, URG (3) 51–56

by ten, DAB 57

Groups, estimation of, TIG 278–279

Guess-and-check approach, URG (1) 67

Half-Centimeter Graph Paper, URG (15) 61

Halves, AB 119, 122–123, 127, DAB 80, 131, 231, 251, 253, URG (13) iii, 31, 43, URG (14) 47, URG (17) 22–24, 28–29, 43, 55–57

of circles, DAB 199

counting by, URG (17) 13

lines of symmetry and, DAB 179

measuring to, DAB 217

of rectangles, DAB 199

Haunted House, The, AB 26–42, TIG 75, URG (5) 59–65

Height, DAB 239–240, URG (2) 60, URG (6) 25, URG (18) 27, 75, URG (20) iii, 28–36

volume and, URG (20) iii

word problems on, URG (8) 85–88

Helping Your Child Learn Mathematics **(ed.gov/parents/academic/help/math/index/html),** TIG 462

Heterogeneous grouping of students, TIG 364

Hexagons, DAB 125–126, SG **170,** URG (7) 21, 93–94, URG (12) 9, 60, 86–89, URG (13) 32, URG (15) 42, URG (17) 64. *See also* Decimal Hex Game, Fraction Hex Game, Hex Game

Hex Game, DAB 191, TIG 100, 475, URG (12) 84–89

Hindu-Arabic numerals, URG (6) 91–100

Hoagies Gifted Education Page, TIG 423

Home Practice, TIG 54, 137

guide, TIG 189–190

scope and sequence for, TIG 137–177

Homogeneous grouping of students, TIG 415–416

Horizontal axis, AB 69, DAB 140, SG **4,** 10, 83, URG (1) 30

labeling, DAB 116, 126, 128, TIG 333–334, URG (3) 26, URG (9) 8

on point graphs, URG (7) 32

quantitative, URG (7) 9–11

scaling, URG (7) 93, URG (20) 32

variables on, URG (9) 45

Hours, URG (14) 23, 29–30

Hundred

on abacus, AB 46–47

multiples of, TIG 97, URG (11) 94–99, URG (14) 14, URG (17) 16

multiplication by, SG 155

skip counting by, DAB 60

Hundreds Template, URG (6) 84, 88

Hundredths, URG (15) 25–26, 33

Hypotenuse, of triangles, URG (12) 43

I

Icons, in daily practice and problems, TIG 31–32

Improper fractions, URG (15) 27

Inches, TIG 342, URG (16) iii

Independent variables, URG (9) 8

Individual assessment record sheets, TIG 197, 218, 225–231

Individual student needs, TIG 383–424, URG (1) 7, URG (2) 8, URG (3) 7, URG (4) 7, URG (5) 7, URG (6) 8, URG (7) 7, URG (8) 7, URG (9) 6, URG

Index

Index

from data tables, SG 137
of distances, URG (8) 51
from graphs, SG 84, 130, TIG 337, URG (1) 31, URG
(20) 32–33
from labs, DAB 11–12, 141–142, URG (20) 23
in 100 Chart, URG (6) 103–104, 107
patterns and, TIG 154–155, URG (9) iii, 7–9
from point graphs, URG (7) 9, 31
in relationships, URG (15) 62
from survey data, URG (14) 44, 50, 61
of volume measurements, URG (16) 46
Prices, DAB 115–117, URG (10) 73. *See also* Money
Prime factors, TIG 67
Prime numbers, SG 146, URG (11) **48, 50**
Principles and Standards for School Mathematics
(National Council of Teachers of Mathematics),
TIG 2–3, 8–10, 129–135, 192–193, 235–236, 292,
315, URG (1) 82, URG (2) 9, URG (10) 8
Prisms, TIG 355–357, URG (18) 38
rectangular, SG **268,** URG (18) 8, **26,** 40, 75
Probability, TIG 130, 132, 138, 140, 142, 144, 146, 148,
150, 152, 154, 156, 158, 160, 162, 164, 166, 168,
170, 172, 174, 176, URG (6) 112
Problems, open-response, TIG 199–200, 205–206, URG
(7) 32
Problem solving, TIG 10, 16, 314–315, URG (7) 49. *See
also* Word problems
as process standard, TIG 119–122
in scope and sequence, TIG 131, 133, 139, 141, 143,
145, 147, 149, 151, 153, 155, 157, 159, 161, 163,
165, 167, 169, 171, 173, 175, 177
Process standards, TIG 131–133
Products, DAB **172,** SG **150,** URG (11) 24, **37,** 62–**63,**
URG (19) 21. *See also* Multiplication
break-apart, SG 286–294, TIG 124, 296, URG (19) 8,
23–33, 44
Cartesian, TIG 319, URG (7) 8–9
of fractions, URG (3) 43
zero and, URG (11) 10
Professional development, TIG 448
Professional Standards for Teaching Mathematics,
National Council of Teachers of Mathematics,
(NCTM), TIG 133, 435
Profit, AB 101
Proof, TIG 123, URG (12) **48**
Proportional reasoning, SG 137, TIG 11
Proportions, TIG 283
Puzzles. *See also* Dissections
line math, DAB 15–19, URG (1) 64–69, URG (2) 23, 68
number, URG (4) 15, URG (6) 16
tangram, DAB 185, TIG 99, URG (12) iii, 8–9, 57–68

Q

Quadrilaterals, SG **170,** 175, URG (12) 9, 60, URG (18)
8, 37–**38**
Quarters
as coins, DAB 195. *See also* Money
of hours, URG (4) 89
Quarts, DAB 247–248, URG (16) iii, **63,** URG (18) 17
Quick Reference Guide, TIG 50–52
Quizzes, TIG 219, 301–302, URG (2) 99
addition, URG (1) 20, 22
multiplication, URG (11) 24, URG (14) 15, URG (15)
19, URG (16) 17, URG (17) 17, URG (19) 21
square numbers, URG (18) 19
on square numbers, URG (13) 17
subtraction, URG (7) 24–25, URG (8) 19–20, URG (9)
19, URG (10) 17, 20

R

Radius, AB 111, URG (16) 75
Randomness, TIG 279
Rates, URG (11) 9–10
Ratios, TIG 275, 283–284, URG (13) 7
Reading, TIG 12, 106, URG (14) 8, 16–17, 41–53, 77,
URG (15) 15–17, URG (18) 20
accommodating different levels of, TIG 430
assisting students, TIG 428
caution of key-word approach, TIG 431
levels, TIG 429
strategies, TIG 428
Reasonable answers, DAB 113, 144, 195, TIG 315, URG
(9) 26. *See also* Estimation
Reasoning
from known facts, TIG 294–295
in open-response problems, URG (7) 32–33
as process standard, TIG 119, 123
proportional, SG 137, TIG 11
from related facts, URG (2) 10
in scope and sequence, TIG 132, 133, 139, 141, 143,
145, 147, 149, 151, 153, 155, 157, 159, 161, 163,
165, 167, 169, 171, 173, 175, 177
Recording Sheet, URG (4) 43
Rectangles, AB 124, DAB 157, 172, SG 58, URG (7) 22,
URG (11) 73, URG (12) 60, URG (14) 15, URG
(15) 18, URG (18) 38, URG (19) 19, 21
fractions of, DAB 251
half of, DAB 199, URG (17) 23–24, 28–29
multiplication and, SG 145–148, TIG 66–67, URG (11)
22, 34–41

Student Rubric: *Solving,* SG 304, TIG 216, URG (5) 70–72, URG (7) 50, URG (10) 30–32, 67–70, URG (15) 66, URG (20) 52–56

Student Rubric: *Telling,* SG 305, TIG 217, URG (7) 49–51, URG (10) 30–32, 67–70, URG (15) 66, URG (20) 52–56

Subtraction, DAB 2, 22, 46, 49–53, 63–66, 83–86, 100, 112, 130–131, 136, 144, 156, 195, 230, 244, 250, SG 209–215, TIG 63–64, 76–79, 148–149, 240–243, URG (1) 16, 18, URG (2) 24, URG (3) 20, URG (4) 18, 21, URG (5) 12, 16, 19, URG (6) iii, 17, 22, URG (12) 17, URG (14) 18, URG (15) 17, URG (16) 16, URG (17) 15, URG (18) 16, URG (20) 15. *See also* Differences

algorithms for, URG (6) 9–10, 68–70

on Base-Ten Board, DAB 105–108

with base-ten pieces, SG 71–73, 211–212, URG (6) 61–72

counting strategies for, URG (4) 14, 16

estimation in, TIG 267–268

Facts I Know chart for, DAB 43, URG (2) 98–99, URG (10) 47

facts strategies for, SG 22–24, 135, URG (2) 73–79, URG (4) 13

inventory test on, URG (10) 18, 21

of large numbers, TIG 106–107

making a ten for, URG (3) 16, 18

Math Facts on, DAB 37–40, SG 136, TIG 62–64, 183, 294–295, URG (2) 10, 73–79, 93–100, URG (3) 13, URG (5) iii, 11, URG (6) iii, 15, URG (7) iii, 15–16, 18–19, URG (8) 13–14, 16, URG (9) iii, 13–14, 18, URG (10) 11, 22

of money, URG (19) 15

multi-digit, URG (6) 27–31

Nine, Ten Game on, URG (2) 77–78

number sentences on, DAB 80, URG (2) 90

paper-and-pencil, SG 73–76, 213

place value and, AB 53–56

problem solving, URG (14) 72, 75–81

problem types in, TIG 316–318

quiz on, URG (7) 24–25, URG (8) 19–20, URG (9) 19, URG (10) 17, 20

regrouping in, URG (4) 49–50

repeated, AB 81, URG (7) 61, URG (11) 10

representation, URG (14) 72

review of, URG (14) 72–81

shortcut, URG (6) 25, 68, URG (7) 21, URG (8) 18

Triangle Flash Cards for, URG (3) 17, 19, URG (4) 16, 19, URG (5) 13, 17, URG (7) 17, URG (8) 14, 17, URG (9) 15–16, URG (10) 14, 16

using paper and pencil, URG (6) 33–39, 61–72

word problems on, SG 74–75, 79–80, 213–215, URG (6) 29

of zero, AB 85–86, 91, URG (11) 90

Summarizing stories, TIG 428

Sums, AB 13, DAB 19, 27, 244, SG **16,** TIG 62, URG (1) 29, 67, URG (2) 24, **42**–45, URG (4) 22, URG (6) iii, URG (10) 14, URG (19) 8, 21

Digits Game and, URG (6) 26, URG (20) 17

estimation of, URG (6) 10

in magic squares, URG (2) 67

spinning, DAB 31, SG 16, URG (2) 39–50

Surface area, TIG 349

Surveys, SG 2–6, **203,** TIG 106, URG (14) 41–53, 55–68, **58,** URG (15) 15–17, URG (18) 20

Symbols, TIG 248–249, 312–313

for *about equal* (≈), URG (6) 85

base-ten shorthand as, URG (4) 9

division, AB 113, SG 153

for fractions, URG (13) 7, URG (15) 26–28, URG (17) 7

for *greater than* (>), URG (13) 56, URG (17) 17

for *less than* (<) URG (13) 56, URG (17) 17

manipulatives' connection to, URG (4) 27–28

on maps, URG (2) 59

multiplication, URG (3) 8, URG (19) 45

Symmetry, DAB 179, SG 172, URG (2) 54, 60, URG (6) 37, URG (12) 20, **43,** 51

Talented Students. *See* Mathematically Gifted Students

Tallies, URG (12) 87

Tangrams, DAB 185, SG **158**–165, TIG 99, URG (12) iii, 8–9, 21–33, 57–68

Teacher Enhancement Resource Modules (TERMs), TIG 449–450

Teacher Implementation Guide (TIG) features, TIG 24, 42

Teacher Resource CD, TIG 24, 44

Teachers, use of *Math Trailblazers* **by,** TIG 4–6

Teaching, TIG 234, 266, 320–321

grouping students, TIG 376–378

incorporating language in lessons, TIG 426–428

planning lessons, TIG 405–406

Teaching Integrated Mathematics and Science Project **(TIMS),** TIG 15

Teams, DAB 55, URG (3) 51–56

Telling **rubric,** SG 305, TIG 217. *See also* Rubrics, Student rubrics

Temperature, DAB 216

Ten, DAB 27. *See also* Base-Ten, Base-Ten pieces, Base-Ten shorthand

on abacus, AB 46–47

in estimation, TIG 270

as factor, URG (19) 44–45

grouping by, DAB 53, 57, URG (3) 34–36

making, URG (2) 10, URG (3) 16, 18
metric system and, URG (9) 7
multiples of, TIG 97, URG (4) 8, URG (11) 94–99, URG (14) 14, URG (17) 16
multiplication by, SG 155, URG (11) 18–19
powers of, URG (6) 94
skip counting by, DAB 60
Triangle Flash Cards for, DAB 167
using a ten strategy, DAB 25, TIG 294–295, URG (2) 31, 76

Ten percent benchmark, TIG 276
Tens Game, SG 109–110, TIG 475, URG (8) 76–80
Tenth, AB 121, DAB 235–236, TIG 109, URG (14) 15, URG (15) 25–27, 32–33, URG (17) 56
counting by, URG (16) 12
measurement to nearest, DAB 239–240, 244, URG (15) 38–46

Testing, TIG 92, 128, 200, 301–302, URG (2) 99, URG (10) 80–90, URG (20) 55–57
on multiplication, URG (20) 15, 18
on subtraction, URG (10) 18, 21

Tests
end of year, URG (20) 68–72
mid-term, URG (10) 80–90
subtraction facts inventory, URG (10) 21

The Association for the Gifted (TAG), TIG 423
Thinking Addition, URG (2) 10
Thirds, AB 123, DAB 194, 231, 251, 253, URG (14) 17, URG (17) 24, 41–43, 46, 56–57
Thousand, AB 46–47, URG (4) 47
Thousandths, URG (16) 8
Three
grouping by, DAB 53, URG (3) 34–36
multiplication math facts, URG (12) 18–19, URG (17) 12, 16
Triangle Flash Cards for, DAB 183, URG (12) 14

Three-Column data tables, URG (8) 26–27, 31, URG (11) 49, URG (14) 59
Three-Dimensional objects, SG 266–272, **267,** TIG 119–123, 172–173, 349, URG (18) iii, 8–9, 21, 77. *See also* Cubes, Measurement of volume, Rectangular prisms
drawing, SG 268–271, URG (18) 33–42
views of, URG (18) 59–69, 73–77
word problems on, URG (18) 73–77

Three-Trial data tables, URG (15) 63, URG (16) 44
Tiered lessons, TIG 420–423
Time, AB 65, DAB 3, 61, 77, 113, 145, 178, 217, SG 194–201, TIG 71, 105, URG (1) 16–18, URG (2) 20, URG (4) iii, 84–93, URG (6) 16, 19, 21–22, URG (8) 70, URG (9) 15, URG (10) 18, URG (11) 21, URG (12) 18, URG (13) 13, 15, URG (14) iii, 13, 19–30, URG (19) 20, URG (20) 70
on analog clocks, DAB 221–223, SG 196–198, 201, URG (4) 9, 90, URG (14) 37

counting by, URG (7) 20
on digital clocks, DAB 225–227, SG 201, URG (4) 9, 90, URG (14) 37
elapsed, SG 197–200, URG (14) 25–26
fractions of, SG 191, URG (13) 17
historical, URG (16) 71
for math study, TIG 13–14
telling, SG 54–55, 196–198, 201, URG (4) 88–90, URG (14) 23–24, 30
word problems on, SG 56, 197–198, URG (4) 96–99

Time and Time Again Game, DAB 221–228, SG 201, TIG 105, 476, URG (14) 34–39
TIMS Laboratory Method, DAB 9–12, SG 9, 61, TIG 11, 324–340, URG (1) **9,** 51, 53, URG (5) 50, URG (9) 43, URG (14) 8, URG (16) 43
analyzing data (phase 4) in, TIG 337–338
beginning investigation (phase 1) in, TIG 327–328
checklist for, URG (14) 64
collecting data (phase 2) in, TIG 329–330
graphing data (phase 3) in, TIG 330–337
TIMS Tutor on, TIG 323–340
variables and values in, TIG 324–327

TIMS Multidimensional Rubric, TIG 205–206, 212, 213–217, URG (2) 9, 84–88, URG (7) 50, URG (10) 31–32, URG (20) 52. *See also* Rubrics, Student rubrics

TIMS philosophy, TIG 246–247
TIMS Tutors, TIG 3, 233–371
Area, TIG 345–349
Arithmetic, TIG 235–254
Averages, TIG 257–264
Estimation, Accuracy, and Error, TIG 265–280
Functions, TIG 281–286
Journals, TIG 287–290
Length, TIG 341–344
Mass, TIG 365–371
Math Facts, TIG 291–303
Portfolios, TIG 305–310
TIMS Laboratory Method, TIG 323–340
Volume, TIG 351–363
Word Problems, TIG 311–322

TODOS: Mathematics for all, TIG 396
Top view, URG (18) 59–69
Tower Power Lab, TIG 127, URG (20) 28–36
Tracing shapes, AB 32, URG (5) iii, 46, URG (6) 36, URG (12) 28
Tracking reading, URG (14) 16–17, 41–53, 77, URG (15) 15–17, URG (18) 20
Trading, in place value, AB 47, 52, URG (4) 48, 74, URG (6) 49, 65, 96, URG (15) 28
Translations, TIG 313–314, URG (18) 64
Trapezoids, URG (12) 8–9, URG (18) 38
Trends, TIG 283
Trial-and-error problem solving, URG (7) 49

Index

in labs, DAB 9, 93–98, 96, 139, 147, URG (1) 26–28, **27,** 51–54, URG (15) 63, URG (16) 43–44

main, DAB 9, URG (10) 26–27, URG (20) 22

manipulated, TIG 287, **325**–327, 330, 333, URG (9) 8

mass as, TIG 365

numerical, TIG **325,** 331, URG (1) 27

qualitative, URG (7) 9–11

quantitative, URG (7) 9–11

responding, TIG 285, 325–326, 330, 333, URG (9) 8

in surveys, URG (14) **45,** 58

in TIMS Laboratory Method, TIG **324**–327

volume as, TIG 353

Variation, URG (9) 26

Velocity, TIG 324, 365

Vertex, SG **166,** 169, **268,** URG (18) iii, 9, 26–27, 37, 75, URG (20) 69

of angles, URG (12) **44**

of shapes, URG (12) 65–68

of triangles, DAB 187–188

Vertical axis, AB 69, DAB 140, SG **4,** 10, 83, URG (1) 30. *See also* Graphs, Labs

labeling, DAB 116, 126, 128, TIG 333–334, URG (3) 26, URG (9) 8

on point graphs, URG (7) 32

scale of, URG (7) 93, URG (14) 60, URG (20) 32

variables on, URG (9) 45

Views, top, right, side, SG 277–281

Vocabulary words, mathematical, URG (12) 9

Vocabulary

English language learners and, TIG 389

special education students and, TIG 402

Volume. *See* Measurement of volume

actual volume, URG (16) 19–33, 43–44

estimated volume, URG (16) 24, 26–29, 42–43, 46

measuring, URG (16) 19–23, 42–44

by displacement, URG (16) 27–28, 68 URG (20) 72, 75

irregular containers, URG (16) 42–43

liquids, URG (16) 24–25, 72–73

problem solving, URG (16) 38–39, 41–43, 60–63, 72–76

solids, URG (16) 25–32

units of measure, URG (16) 23–27, 30–33, 60–65

Weight, TIG 370–371, URG (9) iii, **7**–8, 24, **32**

West African Anansi, URG (2) 60

Whole, unit, URG (13) **31**

Whole numbers, TIG 3, 17, 244–251, URG (3) 43

FractionLand Game and, DAB 201–205

operations on, TIG 179–183

rounding to the nearest, URG (5) 63

Wholes and parts, AB 34, DAB 3, 60, 199, SG 180–182, TIG 116–118, 170–171, URG (17) iii, 7, 52–60. *See also* Parts and wholes

Width, DAB 239–240, URG (5) 62, URG (15) 42, URG (18) 27

Word problems, SG 11, 62–64, 90–92, 136–137, 142–144, 148, 176–177, 185–186, 190–191, 197–198, 249, 297, TIG 59, 100, URG (1) 79–83, URG (12) 90–94. *See also* Labs

on addition, SG 74–75, 79–80, 111, 213–215, URG (6) 29, URG (14) 75, 80–81

for assessment, TIG 92, URG (10) 75–78

on cubes, SG 276, 281

on division, DAB 179, SG 152, 295–297, TIG 123–125, 174–175, URG (3) 66–69, URG (7) 8–9, 70–75, URG (11) 76–82

on fractions, SG 190–191, TIG 102, URG (13) 40–49, 61–64

on grouping, URG (3) 34–36

on height, URG (8) 85–87

on mass, URG (9) 61–64

on Mathhoppers, URG (7) 60–62

on money, TIG 82, 115, URG (5) 77–80, URG (7) 78–87

on multiplication, SG 33–36, 41, 290–294, 297, TIG 68, 123–125, 174–175, URG (3) 40–46, 66–69, URG (7) 8–9, URG (11) 26–31, 76–82

on multiple step, URG (12) 90–93

open-response, TIG 199–200, 205–206, URG (7) 32

on point graphs, URG (7) 32–33

on shapes, TIG 121–122, URG (18) 73–77

in Stencilrama Lab, DAB 148–150

on subtraction, SG 74–74, 79–80, 213–215, URG (6) 29, URG (14) 75, 80–81

on taxes, URG (16) 77–79

on time, SG 56, 197–198, TIG 71, URG (4) 96–99

TIMS Tutor on, TIG 311–322

Writing

background, TIG 432

English language learners and, TIG 387, 390

for language skills, TIG 432–433

multiplication stories, URG (19) 43

numbers, URG (4) 47

strategies, TIG 433

Written assessment, TIG 198–199

X–axis, SG **96,** URG (8) **9.** *See also* Horizontal axis

Y–axis, SG **97,** URG (8) **9.** *See also* Vertical axis
You Can't Do That, AB 1–11, TIG 59,
        URG (1) 72–78
Yü the Great: A Chinese Legend, AB 12–25,
        TIG 62, URG (2) 54–62

in division, SG 153, URG (11) 10, 79–80, 87, 89
on graph axes, DAB 140
multiplication by, DAB 161, URG (11) iii, 89, URG
        (13) 14
numbers less than, URG (7) 62, URG (15) 76
in place value, AB 48–49
subtraction of, URG (10) 13, URG (11) 90

Z

Zero, AB 77–94, URG (11) 88, URG (15) 64
    addition of, URG (11) 90